Social Psychology

The Revised Edition

ALFRED R. LINDESMITH

INDIANA UNIVERSITY

ANSELM L. STRAUSS

UNIVERSITY OF CHICAGO

THE DRYDEN PRESS

NEW YORK

SOCIAL PSYCHOLOGY

THE REVISED EDITION

TO

Gertrude and Frances

Preface

ALTHOUGH THIS EDITION represents a considerable enlargement of the original, there has been no fundamental change in the authors' position or purpose. A number of years' experience with teaching from the original edition have made us conscious of many of its shortcomings. In general, we have tried to take the opinions of our severest critics into most careful account, but since they disagreed among themselves we have surely not satisfied them all.

Among the principal changes which we have made are the following: (1) More attention has been given to introducing the reader to other theoretical positions, notably those of behavioristic psychology and Freudian psychoanalysis. (2) Our ideas of language behavior have changed, and in the present edition this change is indicated by a stress on conversation as the prototype of linguistic behavior. (3) Our discussion of personality has been greatly enlarged and, we hope, enriched. (4) Much more attention has been paid to the relationships between social structure and personality. (5) We have illustrated and documented our points by more extensive use of materials from the local American cultural setting. (6) We have omitted two chapters on "collective behavior," although we have incorporated some of the material elsewhere. (7) We have added discussions of a number of topics that were either not discussed or hardly touched upon in the earlier edition; among these are childhood personality development, personality change, motivation, and social structure and personal organization.

A minor change in organization has been the addition of suggestions for discussion and special reports at the end of each chapter. These, in addition to suggesting discussions or reports, as stated, may also suggest additional topics to the lecturer who may wish to supplement the materials presented in the text. The statement of position in the first chapter, although intended primarily for the teacher, should also interest the student, either at the beginning of the course or at a later stage.

As is usual with the authors of textbooks, we are indebted to our wives, students, colleagues, and friends for their suggestions and assistance. We should like to acknowledge our especial indebtedness to Professors William Form, of Michigan State University, and Manford Kuhn, of the State University of Iowa, who read the revised manuscript and criticized it in detail. Others of our colleagues who contributed very directly to the revision, but who are in no way responsible for the final product, are: Professor Annabelle Motz, of the University of Maryland; Professor Leonard Schatzman, of Coe College; Professor Tomatsu Shibutani, of the University of California; Professor Charles Bolton, of Colorado College; and Professor Orrin Klapp, of San Diego State College. Also, of course, we have received considerable informal criticism and counsel from our colleagues at Indiana University and the University of Chicago, and we are appreciative of this effective if pleasant educational process.

ALFRED R. LINDESMITH
ANSELM L. STRAUSS

Indiana University
University of Chicago
March 1956

Contents: An Overview

(For a complete table of contents, see pages x-xiv)

Contents

1 · Introduction

2 · Levels of Symbolic Behavior

5 · Motivation and Learning

4 · Socialization

5 · Personality Structure and Change

6 · Deviation

Illustrations and Tables

PART 1

INTRODUCTION

CHAPTER 1 · · ·

A
Statement
of
Position

SOCIAL PSYCHOLOGY, as the term suggests, is concerned with societies, institutions, and groups and with the behavior of individuals as well. It is focused, however, upon explaining the behavior of individuals as it is controlled, influenced, or limited by the social environment. Human beings are first of all biological organisms, and as such they engage in behavior which is characteristic of living beings. The social psychologist is not primarily concerned with activity on this level, but deals instead with the distinctive aspects of human activity which set it apart from the behavior of lower forms of life. He is, in short, concerned with "social" behavior, or those aspects of human behavior which depend upon the existence of cultural phenomena such as institutions, customs, and beliefs. His problem is to explain how man has come to be an inherently social animal of whom it can be said that he has "society" within him.

3

Social psychology is sometimes conceived of as an independent discipline or is thought of as a part of psychology or sociology. It is also sometimes described as a meeting place where the interests of various social sciences merge. It has even been maintained that social psychology is, or ought to be, identical with psychology as such, except for that part of the latter which is biological in nature. Some writers have also leaned toward the position that social psychology is really the heart of sociology. It is not necessary or desirable to commit oneself finally to any of these views.

The idea that social psychology should be thought of as a relatively separate and independent field dates from about the turn of the century and reflects developments within the fields of psychology and sociology. Courses in social psychology are taught in both of these fields and, indeed, social psychology is sometimes thought of as a part of psychology or sociology. In psychology they reflect a growing appreciation of the importance of the social environment and the realization that the concept of "the isolated individual" is an abstraction of little significance or applicability. In sociology, the growing popularity of social psychology probably stems from dissatisfaction with the vague and abstract nature of generalizations which affirm the importance of institutional or cultural influences without relating them to the actions of individuals.

An illustration may serve to clarify the relationship of social psychology to these traditional older conceptions. When it was customary to say that psychologists studied individuals whereas sociologists studied groups, a phenomenon such as crime was regarded by typical representatives of these two disciplines in characteristic ways. The psychologist looked at crime, like other behavior, from the standpoint of the individual. Explanations for it were sought within the psychological make-up of the person in terms of the establishment of reaction patterns, habits, traits, or other individual attributes. In contrast, the sociologist of the older school took a broad view of crime as a kind of social disease or symptom of social disorganization. He noted at the outset that crime is an institutionalized phenomenon involving the violation of socially prescribed norms, that it is adopted by some as a way of life and a means of livelihood, and that crime rates fluctuate in characteristic ways from group to group. In explaining this he made little or no reference to psychological processes or individual traits but had recourse, instead, to differences in social and economic organization, to the structure of the family, class differences, poverty, and other broad societal conditions.

The contemporary social psychologist argues that both of these views are correct to a certain extent but that neither is complete in itself. He rejects the sharp separation of individual and society upon which the distinction between sociology and psychology was once believed to rest. Instead, he holds that the psychological processes and traits which are found in individuals can be understood only in relationship to the institutional framework within which they arise. He also says that although broad societal conditions may be assigned as explanations for variations in crime rates, for example, if one wishes to give specific, concrete form to these broad generalizations it is necessary to consider how these conditions actually impinge on particular individuals. Whereas the older psychology stressed the individual and slighted the situation, sociology stressed the situation and slighted the individual. Social psychology seeks to bring these two rationales together in what may be called a situational approach. In this approach, psychological processes and the social environment are thought of as parts of an inseparable whole.

Many textbooks in social psychology are eclectic; they do not take a definite or consistent position on the nature of social behavior, but pick and choose among the many different and opposing doctrines in the field. In justification of this it is argued that too little is known of human behavior to warrant dogmatism. The eclectic scholar therefore chooses what he regards as the strong points of various theories, or simply presents diverse theories and lets the reader take his choice. There are obvious disadvantages in such a method. It has not been followed in this book.

Theories of Human Behavior

SYMBOLIC INTERACTIONISM

The present volume is designed to present in a reasonably consistent and systematic manner a point of view about human social behavior which has gained considerable favor among sociologists in the last several decades. In setting forth this point of view, other rival positions have frequently been mentioned and criticized; but the reader who wishes to understand them fully must consult the literature. There are disadvantages, of course, in this procedure; but it is believed that they are outweighed by the advantages. Presenting a systematic position contributes to clarity of thought and is likely to be more challenging than the mere description of differences of opinion. It is also more likely to promote an evolution of ideas. The reader, however, should be aware of the fact that there are very many views of the proper ways of studying human behavior and many theories which purport to explain that behavior. A brief consideration of the rationale of this book will call attention to some of the current conflicts of theory.

The basic ideas developed in the chapters that follow are that the distinctive attributes of human behavior, which grow from man's immersion in a cultural environment, depend upon the existence of language behavior, or the creation and manipulation of high-order signs (symbols). Society means communication. Language is both the vehicle by means of which culture is transmitted from generation to generation and also an integral part of all aspects of culture. The features of human behavior which distinguish it from the behavior of other animals are derived from the fact that man is a symbol manipulator—the only symbol-manipulating animal. Complex forms of social organization, institutions, codes, beliefs, and customs—indeed all cultural phenomena—depend upon and are made possible by the prior evolution of language. Language behavior, epitomized in conversation, is a learned form of interaction which has its biological basis in the nature of the human brain. This book is designed to survey the rational grounds for these ideas and to trace some of their most important implications.

BIOLOGICAL DETERMINISM

A contrasting theory of human behavior which has found various expressions is known as "biological determinism." According to this theory, social behavior is derived from the nature of the human body; and since the latter is determined largely by inheritance, the influence of heredity upon behavior is stressed. The old "instinct" doctrine may be taken as an example. In this view, large ranges of human behavior were regarded as the expressions of instinctual drives, and the latter were thought of as inherited forces common to the species. War, for example, was attributed to man's innate instinct of pugnacity; and all the behavior relating to courtship and marriage was attributed to the sex, maternal, and paternal instincts. Some small part in modifying the expression of instincts was assigned to cultural influences and learning processes; but instincts were thought of as the basic determinants of behavior.

Another typical belief of biological determinists has been that the behavior of individuals is largely a consequence or expression of physical or constitutional make-up. Thus, a contemporary psychologist has classified males as endomorphs, mesomorphs, and ectomorphs, according to physical types, and found that each type has a characteristic mode of reaction. (A fuller discussion of this typology will be found in Chapter 15.) Another contemporary writer has sought to demonstrate that criminals constitute a physical type and suggests that criminality is a direct consequence of physical inferiority. Other theorists have speculated that behavior may be determined largely by glandular activity. The idea that human behavior is a matter of fulfilling biological needs or other needs built upon them has a strong tinge of biological determinism.

Since the theory presented in this book stresses language, or symbolic communication, as a basic process in the determination of behavior, it is clearly opposed to biological determinism. Language behavior is obviously learned behavior; even in the heyday of instinct theory no one suggested that the people in the English-speaking parts of the world were born with an instinct to speak that language.

The stress on language behavior and the cultural accumulation that it makes possible with the passing of generations also makes much more historical sense than does biological determinism. Human remains from the last ten thousand years give no evidence of any startling biological progress in the human species; but in the meantime, civilization has progressed from the Stone Age to the Atomic Age.

BEHAVIORISM AND MENTALISM

It is assumed in this book that human behavior provides the primary data with which social psychology deals, and that the explanation of any particular form of behavior requires that its relations to other types be traced and demonstrated. Thus a given kind of behavior is explained in terms of its interrelationships with other kinds of behavior and not in terms of "forces," "drives," or anything else which lies outside the behavioral field or which is inferred from behavior. In accordance with this principle we reject the idea that behavior is "caused" by psychological states, desires, motives, states of consciousness, or unconscious motives when these are taken to refer to forces which "make" things happen. From our point of view, terms such as these are only ways of naming various kinds of activity and have no special explanatory value. We believe that it is entirely fallacious to explain the existence of science in terms of a "rational faculty" or innate "reason." It is much more plausible to look at reason, not as a force or faculty, but as a complex and highly evolved form of symbolic activity which has emerged gradually as an historical product from other, simpler types of behavior. Similarly, "conscience" should not be thought of as a psychic force mysteriously implanted in man, but as a special form of regulatory behavior by means of which other activities are inhibited or facilitated.

Psychologists who belong to the "behaviorist" school have emphasized ideas similar to those just stated, and on the basis of them have either rejected or redefined many of the old terms of the "psychology of consciousness." Practically all of the terms used by the layman to refer to what he calls "mental" phenomena, such as "mind," "idea," "insight," "imagination," "reason," "consciousness," "understanding," and many others, have been conceived as activities rather than as entities or faculties or have been dropped entirely as useful concepts. When we say this we mean that the words listed are, in effect, treated by behaviorists as though they were verbs rather than nouns; and the behavior is then usually described in as precise and unambiguous a way as possible. As we shall see later, behaviorists have tended to define these "mentalistic" terms by means of behavior which can be elicited from lower animals in the experimental setting and have tended to reject them entirely when this cannot be done.

It is not our purpose to launch into a critique of behaviorism at this point, but only to indicate that we start out with some of the same assumptions but reach different conclusions. We believe that the psychological behaviorist has unduly restricted his perspective by not taking a sufficiently broad view of behavior. He has paid too much attention to gross bodily movement and to lower animals, and has thus come to ignore language behavior or to treat it as a minor matter. It is our contention that mentalistic terms like "consciousness," "conception," "reason," and the like need to be related to language behavior and conceived of as forms or aspects of symbolic behavior.

The implication of this for social psychology is that in order to explain why people do what they do we must know how they think. The chief source of information about how people think is what they say. These conclusions, however, are not of the type which behaviorist psychologists endorse. In addition to the usual tendency of behaviorists to ignore language, to treat it as a minor factor in behavior, or even to refuse to regard it as genuine behavior, they also try to avoid dealing with behavior which cannot be directly observed. The internal symbolic processes which constitute mental activity are admittedly not accessible to direct observation, and for this reason, among others, they are neglected by the behaviorists. Evidence of mental activity in human beings is usually secured through introspection or from verbal testimony; but the lower animals most often utilized in experimental work do not give verbal reports or engage in introspection. Moreover, evidence so obtained is difficult to interpret. Nevertheless, if it is agreed that human thought is a vital feature of human behavior, no evidence of any kind concerning it should be passed over.

REDUCTIONISM

Sometimes the behaviorist becomes a biological determinist by seeking explanations of behavior in the biological mechanisms involved. A common expression of this tendency is to refer to the nervous system or to neural mechanisms to explain certain acts or kinds of behavior. The layman may, for example, say that his "nerves are on edge," or "frayed," or that he is "nervously exhausted." Neurologists and physiologists sometimes account for behavior which they observe by reference to some supposed neural or physiological process. Explanations of this type are called "reductionistic" because they tend to reduce behavioral problems to the biological level.

The view adopted in this text is opposed to reductionism. It is based instead upon the assumption that complex social behavior should be analyzed on its own level. It is admitted that physical, biochemical, physiological, and neurological processes and structures are involved in all behavior and that these can and should be studied. Such study, however, can only contribute to the understanding of phenomena that *accompany* behavior; they do not *account* for it. A football game, for example, could be described within the framework of mechanics as a number of bodies moving in certain paths with certain velocities and colliding frequently. Needless to say, the fans would not enjoy reading such an account; nor would anyone feel that it dealt with the essentials of the game.

Freudian theory is in many respects at the opposite pole from behaviorism and biological determinism. It makes no mention of the nervous system or of neural mechanisms as explanations of behavior. Neither is there any reliance in Freudian theory upon concepts derived from study or observation of lower animals. The explanatory scheme of Freudian psychology relies primarily upon motives or desires as the forces that determine behavior. The criticism we have made—that reference to inner psychic forces does not yield causal explanations of behavior—is therefore especially applicable to their type of psychologizing.

The Plan of the Book

The presentation of our theory begins in Part II (Chaps. 2 through 8), with Chapter 2 considering man's place in the evolutionary scheme and comparing the behavior of lower animals with that of human beings. It is argued that although man has evolved from lower forms, the study of lower animals cannot contribute much to the understanding of man's uniquely human behavior. Sociology and most of the other social sciences are concerned almost entirely with human activities which have no counterparts in the behavior of lower animals. The tendency of some scholars to emphasize likenesses between man and lower forms, to minimize differences and maintain that they are solely matters of degree, is examined and criticized. It is proposed that the main behavioral differences between man and other animals can be accounted for by the absence of language in the latter.

In Chapters 3 and 4 a more detailed examination of the nature of sign behavior is made, and it is shown that adult human beings live and act largely within a symbolic environment of their own creation. Sign behavior is equated with psychological behavior, and various levels of complexity in psychological activity are indicated. Complex human psychological activity is described as symbolic activity arising from the incorporation of language in the individual personality. Language is discussed as the basic social bond, the essential aspect of what is called "culture," and as the mechanism which has opened up the world of ideas to man.

In Chapter 5 the negative aspect of this argument is explored by asking what happens to human beings who for one reason or another fail to acquire language or who lose it. Chapters 6, 7, and 8 resume the positive development of the basic theme by considering the manner in which language is acquired by children and how, at the same time, the ability to reason makes its appearance and grows. The inherent connection between human thought and the social environment is indicated and illustrated.

In Part III (Chaps. 9 through 11), various current theories bearing on the vexing problem of the nature of motivation are considered and a sociological explanation of the matter is outlined and applied to sexual behavior. Psychological learning theory is briefly considered in this connection; its shortcomings with respect to human behavior are indicated by a discussion of the nature of addiction and habit.

In Part IV, embracing Chapters 12 through 14, further consequences of the individual's assimilation of language from his environment are examined in a discussion of the concepts of "role" and "self." The phenomenon of self-control is discussed, and the manner in which the basic theory of this book relates self-control to social control is developed.

Chapters 15 through 19 (Part V) deal with personality organization and development and seek to trace the implications of our theories of human behavior in this field as they are related to social structure and personality change. Two other developmental theories are presented for comparative purposes. The section ends with discussions of personality change and of the nature of disorganization and conflict.

Part VI, including the last two chapters, examines the problem of accounting for that behavior of individuals and subsocieties which is at odds with accepted social standards.

PART 2
LEVELS OF SYMBOLIC
BEHAVIOR

CHAPTER 2 · · ·

The Evolutionary Setting of Human Behavior

WE BEGIN OUR BOOK with a consideration of social behavior of the lower animals in an effort to show what differentiates it from human behavior. The behavior of all animals, human beings included, is social in some degree; even among the lowest species, organisms stimulate one another and may live in some sort of group. Social groups as we know them among men require organization, psychological unity, and a division of labor, however simple, whereby group members cooperate toward group goals. Another type of group, exemplified by a mass of people waiting for a train, is known as an "aggregate": members of the aggregate, whether it is composed of human beings or animals, do not act concertedly toward group goals or like members of social groups but do affect one another's behavior, thereby making the behavior "social" to a limited degree. An aggregate is thus not a genuine social group because it involves only the most rudimentary social relations and lacks most of the features of social groups noted above.

15

The Evolution of Social Behavior

SOCIAL INTERACTION IN LOWER SPECIES

Just where to draw the line between the social and nonsocial in the interorganismal contact of the very lowest animals is an indeterminate matter.

H. S. Jennings,[1] the well-known student of protozoa, has confessed that in his younger days he concluded that aggregates of infusoria exhibited no social characteristics, only to be reprimanded later by a critic who noted that the reactions he had described actually were social relations of the protozoan kind. Although the one-celled animal requires no other to aid it to perform its vital functions, it does, nevertheless, on occasion gather together with others of its kind. Dense aggregates may be produced by convergence toward a source of light or by movement against a current. These are aggregates in the literal sense of the term: there is no division of labor, no cooperative activity.

In the lower species, W. Allee[2] has pointed out the mere crowding of organisms of the same species produces beneficial results: the animals multiply faster, eat more, enjoy better chances of survival under adverse conditions. Some animals learn more rapidly in the presence of others. Allee hesitates to call the simpler aggregates "cooperative," and he refers to them as showing "automatic mutual interdependence." He and others have remarked that various "integrative levels" are reached by different species aggregations. The existence of a simple form of group organization is shown by the synchronous behavior engendered in densely clustered insects by the transmission of tactile stimuli from one individual insect to another. Touch one individual and all react almost immediately.

TWO ASPECTS OF EVOLUTION: CONTINUITY AND EMERGENCE

Although it is certain that various forms of group organization exist among the lower species, biologists find it no easy matter to classify one as more complex, or social, than another if the forms are not very similar. Allee, for example, speaks of small but real differences of group organization:

> We are confronted with a gradual development of real differences without being able to put a finger with surety on any one clearly defined break in the continuity. The slow accumulation of more and more social tendencies leads finally by small steps to something that is apparently different. If we disregard the intermediate stages, the differences may appear pronounced, but if we focus on these intermediates, it will be only for the sake of convenience that we interrupt the connecting chain of events at some comparatively conspicuous link and arbitrarily make this the dividing point, when one is needed, between the more and the less social.[3]

This statement brings out two aspects of evolution: one is the continuity of species and the other is the notion of distinct "levels" or the emergence of new properties. The latter has been stated in this way:

> The principle of levels has come into current usage through a recognition of important differences in the complexity, the degree of development, and the interdependent organization of behavior functions through the animal series. The evidently superior properties that appear on a new level of organization are not to be explained as due to a new kind of energy or new vital properties, but as functional properties arising from a new system of organization which differs in given ways from "lower" and "higher" systems.[4]

The "levels" concept thus assumes the existence of continuity and of similarity among species but stresses also the emergence of new properties of organization.[5] The differences in levels have to do with *"what kinds of processes and capacities are available* to an animal and its species mates in adapting to their environments."[6] Ants and bees, which live in organized colonies, operate at higher levels of capacity than do sponges or protozoa, which live as individuals or in aggregates. Different animal aggregations reach the same general ends—such as providing food and shelter—but the organization of the aggregate, and the processes through which ends are attained, may be very dissimilar.

Interestingly enough, extreme complexity in group organization may exist together with relatively low level of capacity and operation. Some species of army ants engage in highly complex and successful expeditions in search of food. As many as 30,000 ants may move in a column more than 15 yards wide. The swarm continues to move as a body for some hours after it starts, but eventually divides into two or more subswarms. Despite the seeming complexity of these maneuvers, it turns out that the capacities of the individual ants are very limited and that the collective action is based on fairly simple responses to chemical and tactile stimulation. It is the "heterogeneous forest environment" which leads to the building up of the complicated swarm, for under simpler laboratory conditions no such organized behavior occurs and the "ants will run for days in an endless circular column . . ."[7]

ANTHROPOMORPHISM AND MORGAN'S CANON

The concept of behavioral levels leads us to be on our guard against anthropomorphizing. Anthropomorphism (from the Greek *anthropos*, man, and *morphe*, form) means the projection of human traits upon things not human, and it is a fallacy to be guarded against in studying the lower animals. We are especially given to making the anthropomorphic mistake when the behavior of an animal or species seems to resemble human behavior: for example, when a pet dog does something for which he is usually punished and is then spoken of as feeling guilty or looking ashamed.

In a certain sense, however, the human vocabulary must always be anthropomorphic. Suppose one makes a statement as simple as "The chimpanzee placed the box so that by standing on it, he could reach the banana." Surely this sentence does not mean that the chimpanzee has verbally formulated his purpose within the framework of English or any other language, as might be assumed by a too-literal reader. We should remember that, although we apply human words to the actions of animals, the animals themselves do not.

It is not only in common speech that animal behavior is described and accounted for in human terms. Many years ago a comparative psychologist, Lloyd Morgan, attacked the then general propensity of both laymen and scholars to find resemblances between the mental processes of human beings and those of lower animals. He enunciated a canon which has been quoted with general approval ever since by comparative psychologists:

> In no case may we interpret an action as the outcome of the exercise of a higher psychical faculty, if it can be interpreted as the outcome of the exercise of one which stands lower in the psychological scale.[8]

At the time that Morgan was writing, it was customary to prove similarities between animals and human beings by narrating anecdotes. The anecdotal method has long since disappeared from scholarly writing, but there are numerous references to animal reasoning, generalization, hypothesis, concepts, dominance, leadership, purpose, goals, neuroses, communication, and cooperation. The terms are often used within quotation marks to indicate that the reader is not supposed to take the analogy to human behavior too seriously. But that many writers and readers take the analogies seriously there is little doubt. Schneirla, who has attacked this kind of anthropomorphic writing, suggests that a distinction be drawn between the *description* of behavior and its causal *explanation*. We may, perhaps, speak loosely of protective behavior, food-getting, and courtship in various species, but a genuine causal description of the behavior will make clear that several processes are involved. Whereas, for example, intent and exchange of information and sentiment are involved in human courtship, none need be imputed to various of the lower species when they engage in sexual activity.

The concept of levels of behavior, we believe, is a particularly fruitful one because it forces attention both on the continuity of species and upon the differences among them. It makes mandatory that concepts and hypotheses concerning the behavior of any species be inductively derived from the study of that particular species— rather than, as is common, by extrapolation to lower species of the principles derived from mammalian investigation, or by the explanation of human behavior in terms of principles derived from lower mammalian types ("zoomorphism"). Morgan, advocating this same view at the turn of the century, said cogently:

When the doctrine of evolution was winning its way to acceptance, it was natural that its advocates should employ every means at their command to strengthen their position and to emphasize the continuity underlying diversity of aspect. But now that the position is secure, and continuity is generally admitted, it seems desirable to mark off, by restriction of the range of the use of terms we employ, the stages of differentiation.[9]

A comparative psychology based upon this principle would be of great significance to social psychologists.

The sections which are to follow will describe the behavior of species far removed from each other: insects and great apes. The apes are just below humans in the phylogenetic series. The "social insects" have one of the most conspicuously organized group lives known below the level of man. Since the symbolic life, and especially language, is of such import in the human, communication among insects and apes will be of especial interest to us.

Insect Societies

ORGANIZED INSECT GROUPS

Entomologists have studied certain "social insects," including bees, wasps, termites, and ants. Members of these species, unlike most others, are born, live, and die as members of "societies" or communities. That is why they have been called the "social insects."

These insect groupings are often complex and highly organized, involving the cooperative and systematic efforts of great numbers of individual insects. Ant communities, for example, may consist of thousands of members, each of whom carries on specialized activities: breeding, nursing, child-rearing, providing communal rations, feeding other members, engaging in group warfare, cultivating fungi as food, bequeathing "real estate" to the young, working on "engineering" projects, and "training" other insects to be docile slaves.

Such communal activities are possible only because members of the insect society are able to cooperate with one another. The care of eggs and larvae by "nurses" illustrates the cooperative and coordinated nature of activity among ants:

> The eggs soon develop into minute larvae, fragile and helpless things that need close and constant care to preserve them. . . . From the beginning and throughout their growth . . . they must be fed and cared for. Their care is always a first consideration. . . . The nurses continually hover over them. They lick them as a cat does her kittens. The larvae learn to perk up their weak black heads and open their mouths, into which the nurses place food and drink. . . . For the most part, nurse ants take up and go through their duties in a business-like way. It is done thoroughly, and does not cease until the larvae have spun up around them their silken cocoons. Nor then; for these cocoons are constantly watched, cleaned and cared for, and when the time comes for the young imago to escape, it is aided by the scissors-like jaws of the nurses, whose obstetrical services are aided by the efforts of the out-coming nymph.[10]

DIVISION OF LABOR AND BIOLOGICAL DIFFERENTIATION

In any insect community there exist physical differences among the individual members. Indeed, although ant communities consist mainly of the same sex (female), physical differentiation among ants is often very striking. This differentiation involves differential functions, each physical type being suited by nature for certain communal activities and absolutely or relatively unsuited for others. The anatomical structure of a queen ant is very dissimilar to that of a worker, and her activities and social functions are correspondingly different; soldier ants, who are physically unlike queens and workers, engage in still different activities. All three ant types are genuine specialists. Bee and termite communities are similarly organized along biological lines.

Members of ant and other insect communities acquire their physiological structure through hereditary transmission. Wheeler, a recognized American authority on the species, believes that ants have undergone no important structural modification for approximately fifty-five to sixty-five million years and that ant activities today are virtually identical with those carried on millions of years ago.

The physiological structure of the insect not only determines its behavior but results in activity that is largely automatic. Entomologists have described ant behavior as composed of: (1) reflexes, (2) instincts (chains or series of reflexes), and (3) modifiable behavior. Modifiable, or learned, behavior is not automatic or stereotyped but varies according to the demands of the environment.[11] The point is that the behavior of each insect is largely determined by its biological structure and by its individual experiences. Learned behavior, however, is of limited importance in the organization of the insect group, *because it is not transmitted from one generation to the next.* The learning dies with the insect whose possession it is. And each insect must learn for himself anew.

By contrast to human beings (whose societies are organized largely in terms of codes, laws, customs, folkways, and symbolic understandings, and whose children must learn these in order to participate properly in the community), the capacity to learn "seems to be secondary in the early adjustment of new [insect] individuals. Its function may be largely held to a generalized approach to the colony chemical, established through early feeding."[12] By the latter point, Schneirla has reference to the fact that insects recognize other insects of the same species because of learning. This learning takes place so early that it appears to be automatic or instinctive, although it is not. A mixed colony of ants can be formed if ants of different species are put together immediately after they emerge from their cocoons.

The preponderance of biological factors in the insect social pattern may be emphasized by terming such a pattern *biosocial;* that of the psychological (or learning) factors in the human pattern, by terming it *psychosocial.*[13]

NATURE OF INSECT COMMUNICATION

Although insects possess neither speaking nor hearing organs comparable to those of human beings, communication of a sort does take place among them by means of certain sensory organs. Sounds are produced by several methods: by wing vibrations, through breathing tubes, by the friction of one part of the body against another. Gestures are made by body movements. The antennae of insects are also used as sensitive instruments by which excitement, discovery, and similar "emotions" are transmitted. Ants are said to congregate swiftly around a bit of food found by one of their number because the finder produces sound through the friction of one part of his body against another. The sounds are produced involuntarily in response to the smell of the food.

Such communication is necessary to all insect life, even among the most solitary, since some sort of sign behavior is required if individual insects are to mate. Where there are familial relationships, as between the female and her offspring, sensitivity to signs is more apparent. A biologist, C. D. Michener,[14] has suggested the important connection between elaborate insect communication and nest-building. Since food must be brought back, colony members must follow one another's trails, danger signals must be responded to, and many other cooperative actions must be engaged in.

Such communication among ants—and among other social insects —should not be confused with articulate and symbol-using human communication. The language of man consists of articulated systems of sounds—codified, conventionalized sets of symbols. Careful studies of bees, ants, termites, and other insects have not revealed the slightest shred of evidence suggesting the existence of symbolic communication among them. Moreover, although techniques of communication among young insects apparently require a simple initial process of learning, that process is in no way comparable to the complex one by which human infants acquire the use of language. The basic character of insect communication is so different from the symbolic communication of men that Schneirla[15] suggests that we "use a term such as 'social transmission' for inter-individual arousal in insects, reserving the term 'communication' for higher levels on which a conceptual process of social transmission is demonstrable."

An example of modes of communication between insects is furnished by an investigation of mosquitoes. In 1878, Hiram Maxim noted that the whine of a hotel dynamo attracted large numbers of male mosquitoes but few females. No one paid attention to this observation until relatively recently, when it was discovered that mosquitoes communicate by sound and that when two cages, one containing male and the other female mosquitoes, are placed within several feet of each other, the males all congregate on the side nearest the females, even when sheets are draped over the cages and the transmission of all scent is prevented.[16] The two Cornell scientists who discovered this have used the knowledge by setting up electrified cages in which loudspeakers amplify the mosquitoes' buzz 500,000 times. Mosquitoes fly to the cages from miles around, only to be electrocuted there.

It was found that each variety of mosquito has a characteristic pair of sounds, both emitted by the female. One of these is the "love call," which attracts males of the same variety within hearing distance of the call; the other is a "lust call," which signalizes to other females the discovery of a source of blood. (The female mosquito is the disease carrier and biter, because she must have blood to complete the process of fertilizing her eggs. The male is strictly vegetarian, living on nectar and fruit juices.) The use of both lust and love calls on the amplifiers thus attracts both male and female mosquitoes. It was found that more than 90 percent of the mosquitoes in a vicinity respond to the sounds, unless they are made too loud, in which case they repel. It is believed that the mosquitoes' antennae act as receivers for sound. The mosquitoes of Florida and those of West Africa are attuned to different frequencies and hence do not "understand" each other.

A more complicated form of communication exists among bees and relates to the manner in which a bee signalizes to the rest of the hive the discovery of a source of honey. Knowledge of this derives mainly from the remarkable studies of K. von Frisch, a German investigator who specialized in the study of bees.[17] Von Frisch found that when a bee discovers a rich source of food about 50 to 100 yards from the hive, she at once becomes excited and liberates there a characteristic odor. When the bee returns to the hive she gives some of the nectar or syrup that she has collected to other bees and then starts a "round dance," circling alternately to the right and to the left. Other bees are excited by the dance and move in close and touch the dancer with their antennae. During pauses in the dance they are given droplets of nectar regurgitated by the dancer. One by one these bees then leave the dance to fly about at random near the hive until they find the food source, which they identify from the clues furnished them by the dancer. This interesting communicative process is more complex than similar behavior of the ant, which simply leaves an odor trail to the food source to be followed by others.

Because bees collect nectar and pollen from sources as much as two miles or more from the hive, the round dance and the taste and odor cues described above are not always adequate, because the area of a circle of two-mile radius is too great. Hence, when the distance from the food source is in excess of about a hundred yards, the dance of the returning bee is a different one. It becomes a short straight run on the honeycomb during which the abdomen is waggled from side to side. The speed of the dance indicates "estimated flying time" to the source of food and is slower (indicating more time required) if there is a strong head wind on the way to the feeding place. The direction of the source is indicated in relation to the position of the sun by the direction of the bee's straight run on the comb (which is vertical in the hive)—a downward run means away from the sun. Other bees that follow the dancer's movement with their feelers are so well guided by it that, when they emerge from the dark hive and fly in search of the indicated source of food, they rarely make an error of more than fifteen degrees in direction.

It is unnecessary to indicate here the arguments for denying that honeybees possess language in the human sense. It is sufficient to note that this is not claimed even by those who study insect communication. They note that the transmission of the behavior from generation to generation is a purely biological process and that the system of communication used is determined by membership in a species, not by membership in a language community or culture. Michener[18] refers to the dance of the bees as "a sort of stereotyped, automatic symbolism," and Schneirla says, after a careful observation of various kinds of insect communication,

There is no evidence . . . that it is symbolic in the sense that human words are symbolic. Rather, the insect forms are derived from biological processes characteristic of the species and are fixed in nature rather than culturally changeable.[19]

The Behavior of Chimpanzees

The great apes, who of all the animals stand closest to us on the evolutionary ladder, offer perhaps the most interesting comparison with human beings, for they are unquestionably more intelligent than our usual house pets or farm animals. The great ape that has been most thoroughly studied is the chimpanzee. We shall attempt to show, first, what a sociable animal he is. In describing his behavior we shall use language which will bring out his seemingly human qualities. We shall then point to his limitations, which emerge when we compare him to the more complex human being.

SOCIAL BEHAVIOR OF CHIMPANZEES

Group Solidarity · "It is hardly an exaggeration to say that a chimpanzee kept in solitude is not a real chimpanzee at all."[20] This statement indicates the extraordinary extent to which chimpanzees are influenced by the presence of other chimpanzees. When forcibly removed from his companions or his group, this great ape "cries, screams, rages, struggles desperately to escape and return to his fellows. Such behavior may last for hours. All the bodily functions may be more or less upset. Food may be persistently refused, and depression may follow the emotional orgy."[21] The chimpanzee will, in these circumstances, even risk his life in an effort to return to his group. When he rejoins it, there is great rejoicing and the one who had been isolated displays the deepest excitement.

A chimpanzee locked alone in a cage will stretch his hands out through the bars toward his companions, wave and call to them, or push various objects through the bars in their direction. If the isolated animal's cries are audible and his gestures visible to the others, they may embrace him through the bars of the cage and otherwise give evidence of what seems to be human sympathy for their unhappy fellow. But if they cannot hear him or see him, they show no awareness of his absence. If one of their number is taken away because of illness or death, there is usually no evidence that the others grieve for their missing companion or even know that he is no longer in their midst.

Chimpanzees have a characteristic cry of distress. When this cry is emitted in connection with some action taken by the human investigator, other chimpanzees tend to rally to the support of their companion and threaten or actually attack the offender. Sometimes it is difficult to train the animals when they are in a group because of this danger of attack, particularly when the chimpanzees are adults.

Cooperative Behavior · Investigators have noted numerous instances of cooperative activity among chimpanzees in the solution of problems. Each of two apes was individually trained to pull on a rope. Then a box of food was placed a short distance from a cage containing the two animals. Two ropes were attached to the box, and the rope-ends were left inside the cage. One of the chimpanzees, when he found himself unable to move the box by pulling on one of the ropes, solicited help from the other animal. He did this by such activities as pulling him toward the bars and placing his companion's hands on the second rope. Pulling in unison, the two chimpanzees succeeded in bringing the box close enough to reach for, grasp, and eat the food it contained.

Köhler has amusingly described what may be called a cooperative joke. A group of chimpanzees eating bread in a cage one day grew fond of teasing some chickens. The fowl would approach the cage, and the chimpanzees would offer them a piece of bread. The moment the chickens were about to peck at it, the bread would be withdrawn. One of Köhler's animals on his own initiative shared his piece with the chickens, watching them with an air of genial detachment. Sometimes while this was going on, another chimpanzee would poke a stick or a piece of wire at the chickens. Having hit upon this scheme, the two animals would then continue the game: one of them luring the chickens to the bars of the cage by holding out bread toward them, the other manipulating the stick or wire.

Fads and Ornamentation · Köhler also describes behavior among captive chimpanzees which bears a striking resemblance to human interest in fads and ornamentation. Thus, some chimpanzees inside a cage pushed straws through the bars, holding them among some ants just outside. When a straw was covered with ants, it was withdrawn, the ants were eaten, and the performance then repeated. Other chimpanzees adopted this activity as a kind of sport. Several of the animals might be seen seated like fishermen in the yard alongside a path used by ants. Each of the chimpanzees held a straw which he lowered into the path and pulled up when it was covered with ants. After a time they evidently wearied of this game: they gave it up and turned to something else—for example, digging in the ground with a stick or jumping with a pole.

The chimpanzees' use of ornaments involved walking about with a rag, a bit of rope, some grass, or a bundle of twigs on them, or with strings dangling over their ears and around their faces. Köhler describes this as an almost daily occurrence and notes that the chimpanzees derived some kind of satisfaction from it. He also describes how the animals became interested in what we may perhaps call chimpanzee art. They smeared a white paint-like substance over objects in their cages and sometimes over themselves. Like some young children, they did this deliberately and rather methodically, and apparently with some obscure kind of enjoyment.

Response to Mirrors · When Köhler first allowed Sultan to look at himself in a mirror, that gifted chimpanzee extended his hand with the palm turned inward: the typical chimpanzee gesture of greeting to a comrade. When the mirror was given to the animals, they all appeared eager to obtain it, snatching it from one another and peering curiously into the glass surface. One female chimpanzee finally captured it, took it away from the others, and proceeded to examine it carefully, making repeated efforts to grasp or touch the chimpanzee that seemed to be peering at her from the mirror.

In this way another curious fad was initiated in Köhler's ape community. The animals began to pay attention to their reflections in pools of water, in shiny objects, in pieces of metal, and the like.

The chimpanzees could sometimes be observed standing for relatively long periods of time over a pool, watching their reflections, grimacing, and swaying back and forth.

Economic Behavior · In an ingenious experiment[22] chimpanzees were trained to insert poker chips of various colors into a slot machine. A blue chip yielded two grapes, a white chip one, and a brass chip none. The animals were also shown how to obtain chips by performing work on a different machine. They learned to operate both machines, developed a preference for blue as against white chips, and preferred both over the brass ones. When denied access to the "chimp-o-mat," they learned to hold on to their "money" for a time. When shown a chip they often responded to it by extending their lips and smacking them as they did when they were offered grapes.

Behavior Toward Human Beings · Apes, like domestic animals, act in quasi-human fashion toward human beings. On one occasion Köhler inadvertently ran a splinter into his finger. He called it to the attention of a chimpanzee. The animal immediately assumed the mien and expression characteristically assumed in mutual skin-grooming among apes: he examined the wound, placed two fingernails on each side of the splinter, and skillfully squeezed it out. Then he examined the finger very closely and allowed his hand to drop as though he were satisfied with a job well done.

Other interesting instances of quasi-human behavior toward people have been reported. Investigators have noted repeatedly that apes in captivity make sexual advances toward human beings, as well as toward other animals, such as dogs. Some visitors have been greeted with something suspiciously like a "Bronx cheer." Sultan, Köhler's chimpanzee "genius," tried to enforce disciplinary action in Köhler's absence. Frequently apes that have been scolded or punished seem to ask their human master for forgiveness by whimpering and throwing their arms around his neck.

Chimpanzees often display what may be characterized as a willingness to accept a human being as one of them. Köhler, for example, describes his participation in a chimpanzee dance around a pole. The apes seemed to relish his part in their sport and showed obvious disappointment when he withdrew. It is also notable that chimpanzees—particularly, it would seem, the adult females—show a kind of special and "benevolent" interest in human children.

A common form of play among apes is what may be called bluffing. One animal approaches another, making threatening gestures or waving a stick. The second apparently recognizes the situation and responds in kind. That this is a form of play is indicated by their behavior: if the animals become really angry, they drop their sticks and their posturing and attack each other with hands, feet, and teeth. The "bluffing" ape may approach human beings also and perhaps frighten them. The animals scarcely ever misunderstand one another's gestures and cries.

Other Quasi-human Behavior · On the other hand, some kinds of typically human response have not been observed among the apes. They do not weep. Although they have various ways of indicating pleasure, they do not really laugh. Nor do they seem to have the slightest appreciation of human laughter; they tend to respond to it with bewilderment or rage.

LIMITATIONS OF CHIMPANZEES

When we consider the collective achievements of civilized man, we are overwhelmingly impressed by the vast gulf between him and the apes. One could go on almost indefinitely enumerating specific kinds of human behavior which are "beyond" the ape. It is not so easy, however, to determine the exact sources of the chimpanzee's limitations or to define the precise limits of his accomplishments. This is a problem whose solution depends upon further experimental and observational investigation of animals. Here we can indicate only some of the main types of differences between human and subhuman behavior, which are to a degree substantiated by the work of comparative psychologists.

Animals Are Limited to the "Here" and "Now" · All subhuman behavior is sharply, although not absolutely, limited to the immediate, concrete situation. This limitation is one of (1) time and (2) space. Thus, Köhler states as a major difference between man and chimpanzee that the time in which the chimpanzee lives stretches back and forward only a little way. The chimpanzee's ability to solve problems appears to be determined principally, Köhler says, by his "optical apprehension of the situation." Sticks and other instruments are most readily used as tools when they are in the immediate proximity of the problem situation. If they are moved away from it —as, for example, to the rear of the cage or into an adjoining room or corridor—the ape virtually ceases to perceive them as potential tools, even though he may be perfectly familiar with them and see them daily. Similarly, as we have noted, a group of chimpanzees may react violently when one of their number is removed, particularly if he cries out or struggles. But once the animal has been taken out of sight and hearing, the group appears to forget about him almost at once, although the solitary animal continues for some time to seek the company of his fellows.

The assertion that animals are limited to the "here" and "now" requires some qualification: the limitation is not absolute, nor does it warrant overemphasis. Thus, if chimpanzees in a cage see bananas buried in the sand outside and are not allowed out of the cage until the next day, when they are released they run quickly to the approximate spot to search for the buried fruit. Other experiments clearly indicate that delayed responses of this type are well within the range of the chimpanzee's abilities. Moreover, a chimpanzee separated from a human being to whom he has become accustomed will give unmistakable signs of recognition when he sees him again after months of separation. But, by and large, one may regard chimpanzees as limited to the here and now.

Working Together but Not in Common · That there are very distinct limits to cooperation among chimpanzees is evident from a highly significant experiment. Several animals were trained individually to build structures consisting of three boxes placed upon one another in order to obtain bananas hung up out of reach. Later, when the animals were given the same problem to solve collectively, each one proceeded to build as though he were alone. Thus, a chimpanzee in search of a second box would appropriate one already being used by another animal and become involved in a fight for its possession. When only two of the boxes were placed upon each other, a few of the animals usually attempted to climb the uncompleted structure simultaneously, thus upsetting it and necessitating a fresh start. Constant fighting and repeated failures to complete the three-box structure eventually exhausted all the animals but one. This chimpanzee then completed the structure and obtained the prize—without permitting the others to share it. Repetition of this experiment always produced the same results, with the same animal outlasting the others and winning the reward.

The vain attempts of four chimpanzees to build a three-box structure are described by Köhler as "building together but not in common." We may understand what he means if we compare the building activities of the chimpanzees with those of men. Obviously, if each workman on the job sought to build for himself without regard to the activities of his fellow-workers, the results would hardly be satisfactory. The activities of workmen are organized and co-ordinated according to a plan, a blueprint, which is passed around from one to the other, discussed by them, and at least generally understood by all of them. In other words, each man subordinates his individual activity to the purpose or plan which they all have in common. By virtue of possessing this common plan, each man can—and often must—engage in an activity different from that of his fellows but each man will—and must—contribute to the final result.

Keeping the foregoing illustration in mind, we may say by way of contrast that the cooperative behavior of lower animals is determined by inherited mechanisms rather than by goals and plans collectively comprehended. The sex act may be taken as an illustration of this type of unlearned cooperative behavior. Apart from such an instinctive response, however, it is exceedingly difficult to train a number of animals to work cooperatively on any but the simplest project. If the task requires each animal to do only what he would do if he were working alone, an apparently cooperative solution may be reached. Two chimpanzees may, for example, team up to lift or pull an object which is too heavy for either to manage alone. But when the project requires that the animals learn to perform dissimilar but coordinated tasks—as in building a tower with boxes in order to obtain suspended fruit—they fail because success would

Each of the animals could build a three-box structure by himself, but the four could not do so collectively. (From W. Köhler, *The Mentality of Apes*, Harcourt, Brace, 1926. Reproduced by permission of the author and the publisher.)

require some degree of verbal formulation of purposes and plans—
and apes cannot make verbal formulations. We shall soon see the
further consequences of this inability.

THE USE OF TOOLS

Although chimpanzees can use various kinds of objects as tools
and can even construct certain types of tools, they show almost no
tendency to store the tools for future use or to transport them systematically from place to place. Moreover, chimpanzees show practically no disposition to store or hoard food against future contingencies. At this point one may note that other animals, especially
certain insects, do store and transport food in very complex and
systematic ways. Such behavior, however, does not have to be
learned: it is biologically determined.

Chimpanzees have what seems to be an "innate destructive impulse," Yerkes states, which expresses itself in their tendency to
break down into its constituent elements any complex object made
up of various movable or removable parts. Chimpanzees explore,
pull, poke, and otherwise manipulate the object; they do not rest
until it has been taken apart and the pieces strewn about. In this
respect they are like small boys. When a chimpanzee does actually
construct a tool—for example, by fitting two sticks together to make
one long one—his action seems remarkable because it contrasts so
sharply with his usual mode of behavior.

Moreover, unless he is continuously trained, there is a strong
tendency for the animal soon to slough off most of the new behavior
he has learned in the experimental training situation. As Köhler says:

> If one is able to produce a—very temporary—type of behavior
> which is not congenial to the chimpanzee's instincts, it will soon
> be necessary to use compulsion if he is to keep it. And the
> slightest relaxation of that compulsion will be followed by a
> "reversion to type."[23]

Yerkes exclaimed over the remarkable manner in which the
chimpanzees of his laboratory colony learned certain human activi-

ties. Thus, when push-button drinking fountains were installed in their cages, only some animals were shown how to use them. The others learned from watching their fellows. Yerkes also observed that each generation became more tractable as experimental animals, certain of the activities required by the experiments being passed on from ape to ape "by imitative process" and from one generation to the next "by social tradition." These effects which Yerkes mentions are the result of constant contact with human beings and with an environment arranged by human beings. If the entire colony were returned to its native habitat, in a very short time probably few if any traces of human influence would remain; a new generation would not profit from the older generation's contact with civilization. This is particularly so since drinking fountains, hammers, keys, and the like are not usually found in the ape's native environment. It is clear, too, that such transmission as may occur among trained chimpanzees is not the result of language communication as humans know it.

Absence of Language Among Lower Animals

Apes never learn to speak like human beings. Little success has been achieved in training them to imitate the sounds of human speech, although many investigators have tried. Relevant to this point are the reports of two experiments in which young chimpanzees were reared for a time in the homes of psychologists.[24] The Kelloggs report that they were entirely unable to train their chimpanzee, Gua, to utter any words or to imitate human speech. The Hayeses, on the other hand, report that their animal, Vicki, acquired a vocabulary of three words—"mama," "papa," and "cup." From a demonstration witnessed by the authors, it was clear that the imitation was so crude that the sounds could hardly be identified and could be called words only by a stretch of the imagination. It was also clear that Vicki used them in a mechanical and uncomprehending manner.

Apes, of course, emit characteristic sounds of their own, but these do not constitute language in a genuine sense. This may easily be shown by considering three features of so-called "ape language." (1) The sounds are unlearned. This point has been proved conclusively by Boutan,[25] who raised an ape, wholly isolated from other apes, from birth until its fifth year. It uttered the same cries as those made by other apes. (2) The sounds emitted by apes, as various investigators have noted, are "subjective": that is, they merely express emotions; they do not designate or describe objects. In the words of one writer:[26] "Chimpanzees can exclaim 'Kha' or 'Nga' over their food just as humans delightedly cry 'yum-yum,' but they cannot say 'banana, today.'" Their cries of enthusiasm are responses to an immediate situation: such cries "cannot be used between meals to talk over the merits of the feast." (3) Ape sounds do not constitute a system of symbols. Yerkes has summarized this lack of system:

> Certainly chimpanzees communicate effectively with one another by sounds, gestures, facial and bodily expression, postures, and visible attitudes which function as meaningful signs. Symbols probably are rare and play a subordinate, if significant, role in their linguistic expression. Therefore, the composite language of the chimpanzee differs greatly from our own. They, for example, have no system, or even assemblage, of sounds which may properly be termed speech, and nothing remotely like a written language.[27]

The sounds emitted by apes, or by any other animal, clearly do not constitute systematized animal languages similar to the languages of men. Neither may one refer to animal sounds as words, for if one does, one is forced to recognize that human children also communicate their needs to one another and to their elders by means of cries, cries as natural for them as are chimpanzee cries to the chimpanzee. One would thus be led to say that children have language before they learn a language, and that they speak words immediately after birth. It is more in accord with accepted usage to restrict the term "language" to such conventionalized systems of sounds or words as those designated as the English, French, German, Spanish, and other languages. All such systems have to be learned, and they vary by communities rather than by species.

The biologist J. Bierens de Haan, in a paper entitled "Animal Language in Its Relation to That of Man,"[28] has clearly and conclusively summarized the arguments against the possible existence of unknown animal languages. He notes, first of all, that human language has six characteristics:

> . . . the sounds used in it are *vocal, articulate*, and have some *conventional meaning*, they *indicate* something, are uttered with the *intention* of communicating something to somebody else, and are *joined* together to form new combinations, so that phrases of various and different content are formed.[29]

Animals, Bierens de Haan reasons, possess, at best, "pseudo-languages," since man's language is of a decisively different order. We may summarize the evidence he offers for this judgment as follows:

1. "Vocal": the great majority of animals—including most of the vertebrates—are mute.

2. "Articulate": syllables are joined together. This is impossible when sounds are produced by organs other than the mouth. Among the higher animals that possess voices, there is generally no joining together of syllables. Humans combine syllables into words.

3. "Conventional meaning": there is, with few exceptions, no direct relation between meaning and the nature of the sound. Even among the higher animals, sounds are innate and typical of the whole species.

4. "Indication": with the aid of conventional meaning it becomes possible to indicate something—an object, situation, etc. Among the animals, sounds do not name objects or situations, but express "sentiments" and "emotions."

5. "Intention": animal sounds are generally uttered without reference to other beings. Although not made with intent to influence others, these sounds may be responded to by other animals.

6. "Joined together to form new combinations": combining

words into phrases does not occur among animals. Only man does this.

Just as there is no doubt of the existence of communication in the lower animals, there is also no doubt that man is the only language animal. We shall be concerned with the nature of language behavior in the next chapter, but we may anticipate our discussion of it here by noting briefly that conversation is the fundamental form of linguistic intercommunication. Any intelligent person, given the proper training, can learn to converse with any other person on earth. However, one cannot converse with lower animals. Despite this fact, it should also be constantly kept in mind that, as one ascends the evolutionary scale, sign behavior and communication become increasingly subtle.

Some Consequences of the Lack of Language

The fundamental difference, then, between human and animal behavior, basic to and in a sense determining all other differences, is that men can talk and animals cannot. The human being's possession of language symbols and his ability to produce them voluntarily enables him to overcome the time-and-space limits in which, as we have noted, subhuman organisms may be said to be enclosed. Indeed, it may be more accurate to say that the possession of language has enabled human beings to "invent" space and time: past, present, and future. Man has the capacity to respond to events which took place hundreds or even thousands of years ago, to predict or conceive future events, and to imagine objects and events which are remote in space or entirely nonexistent. This capacity involves nothing more mysterious than the ability to formulate propositions and to make statements about such objects and events, and in turn to be influenced by those propositions and statements.

As Köhler significantly remarks,[30] the chimpanzee's reaction to a situation is determined by his "optical apprehension" of that situation. Similarly, one may also say that the crucial difference is not that animals lack purposes but that they do not make or formulate propositions about their purposes. It is this fact, coupled with the ape's inability to make verbal responses to his physical environment, which probably accounts for the animal's failure to store food and tools or to transport them systematically for future use. The same may perhaps be said of what we described above as the chimpanzee's tendency to destroy complex objects rather than to preserve them, since he may react impulsively to features of them that momentarily attract his attention.

We shall be concerned, more or less throughout this book, with human behavior which is not duplicated, although it is sometimes foreshadowed, in the behavior of lower animals. The extent and significance of the range of behavior opened up by language can be suggested by referring to religion, morality, science, philosophy, and art; by noting the immense volume of printed matter in the world; or by calling attention to the existence in human beings of reflective self-consciousness, of conscience, reason, imagination, and conceptual thought.

The differences between man and the lower animals may be summarized by saying that the lower animals do not have a culture. The term "culture" is generally used to refer to behavior patterns, including beliefs, values, and ideas, which are the shared possession of groups and which are symbolically transmitted. A culture also includes artifacts or products which are handed down in a physical sense but whose significance resides in their relationships with human behavior. Since language is both an integral part of culture and the indispensable vehicle for its transmission, the assertion that animals do not possess it is a far-reaching one for comparative psychology.

Although one may say that the lower animals are able to communicate with one another and that they exhibit a surprising range of social behavior, in the sense that they form aggregates at many levels, they do not reach the level of sociality which is embodied in conventional symbols and the shared or common purposes of man. Even among the anthropoids, the significance of the behavior which the young learn from adults is limited, and the animal reared in isolation from his own kind is not much handicapped or changed thereby. As the term "social" has been used in this context, it is clearly a broader term than "cultural," since it refers to interstimulation of acting organisms in general. It should be remarked that "social" is sometimes used in a more restricted sense to apply only to interpersonal relations. In this latter sense, too, it is not identical with "cultural," since there are many aspects of interpersonal relationships which are learned but which are not transmitted from generation to generation as part of the cultural heritage.

Significance of Subhuman Behavior

The study of subhuman behavior has two general purposes for the social psychologist. First, it provides a picture of response mechanisms and adaptive devices which gradually increase in complexity, sensitivity, and variability as one ascends the evolutionary scale to man. The social insects live in societies based on principles altogether different from those which form the foundations of human groups; and these principles are instructive chiefly in a negative way, showing us what human behavior is not, rather than what it is. The second main purpose in studying subhuman behavior is to bring into sharper focus the differences among organisms of various degrees of complexity. As the organisms develop to more complex and more specialized levels, new behavioral possibilities and properties emerge. These new behavioral possibilities and properties, if they are to be investigated as such, must be conceived of as related to the previous possibilities and properties from which they have evolved. This does not mean, however, that they are to be identified with what they have evolved from.

With reference to understanding human social behavior, the study of subhuman organisms enables us to form tentative conceptions of (1) similarities (common features) of human and subhuman behavior, and (2) differences (unique elements) which distinguish man's behavior from that of all other living forms. We must not neglect to give adequate attention to both of these two aspects. Experimental and comparative psychologists frequently stress the similarities and underplay or altogether disregard the differences between man and other animals; theologians and philosophers, on the other hand, often stress the differences to the point of failing to recognize that man is, after all, an animal.

Social scientists are concerned largely with political, economic, legal, moral, religious, and other specific forms of behavior which are found almost exclusively in human beings living in groups. They are concerned, in other words, with analyzing the unique phases of human behavior; therefore it is inevitable that they should seek explanations of this behavior in terms of something which human beings have and which other organisms lack. Such expressions as "culture," "cultural heritage," "mores," "institutions," "traditions," "law," "politics," "economics," "philosophy," "religion," "science," "art," "literature," and "mathematics" all point to unique attributes of human behavior. These differences between men and apes cannot be logically explained by referring to things which human beings and animals have in common.

Social psychology as the study of the influence of groups on the behavior of individuals is, in a sense, merely a part of the broader comparative study of species, each of which presents its own particular problems but all of which share certain attributes in the sense that they are all living forms. It is unnecessary to insist either that only the differences be investigated and emphasized or that exclusive attention be focused on the similarities. It is understandable that such disciplines as economics and political science and sociology, dealing as they do with behavior which is for the most part not found except in human society, should directly concern themselves little, or not at all, with subhuman behavior. Since social psychology is, in a way, a part of comparative psychology, it must concern itself to some degree with the behavior of lower animals in order to understand the evolutionary emergence of civilization, culture, reason, and intelligence.

Summary

Among the major differences between lower animals and man, differences in communication are of central interest to social psychology, for language behavior is a uniquely human achievement and a basic fact in human society. Hence, understanding of the nature of groups and of social behavior among the lower animals lays a groundwork for the study of social relations and behavior in man.

Observation of the cooperative behavior of certain species of insects and of chimpanzees, among other animals, has made it clear that the idea that evolution leads only to changes in degree and not in kind of behavior should be rejected. Instead, the evolutionary process leads both to quantitative change and to the gradual emergence of genuinely new forms and properties of behavior. We turn now to one of these emergents: human language.

SUGGESTIONS FOR DISCUSSION AND SPECIAL REPORTS

1. Analyze and criticize the following statement by J. Corbett, a famous hunter: "Tigers do not know that human beings have no sense of smell, and when a tiger becomes a man-eater it treats human beings exactly as it treats wild animals, that is, it approaches its intended victims up-wind, or lies in wait for them down-wind."

2. Consider what would be likely to happen if a lower animal species should suddenly become capable of genuine speech.

3. What psychological mechanisms are involved in anthropomorphism? May adults be anthropomorphic with respect to young children?

4. If, as is often maintained, differences between or among species are matters of degree, why not study the behavior of the amoeba to discover the basic laws of human learning?

5. Discuss the following statement by a psychologist, T. Ryan: "It is not true that man alone among the animals has a language. Every animal with a conditioned response is reacting to a symbol, for the conditioned stimulus is a symbol of the unconditioned stimulus. The dog who salivates when he hears the dinner bell understands the meaning of the bell, which has become for him a symbol for food."

6. Does "economic" behavior occur in the lower animals?

NOTES

[1] In R. Redfield, *Levels of Integration in Biological and Social Science* (rev. ed.), in *Biological Symposia*, Vol. 8, Lancaster, Pa.: J. Cattell Press, 1942, p. 111.

[2] W. Allee, *Animal Aggregations: A Study in General Sociology*, University of Chicago Press, 1931, pp. 147 ff.

[3] W. Allee, *Cooperation Among Animals* (rev. ed.), Henry Schuman, 1951, p. 158.

[4] T. Schneirla, "Levels in the Psychological Capacities of Animals," in R. Sellars (ed.), *Philosophy for the Future*, Macmillan, 1949, p. 245.

[5] This part of the chapter is largely quoted from A. L. Strauss, "Concepts, Communication, Groups," in M. Sherif and M. Wilson, *Social Relations at the Crossroads*, Harper, 1953, pp. 99-105.

[6] T. Schneirla, "The Concept of Levels in the Study of Social Phenomena," in M. Sherif and C. Sherif, *Groups in Harmony and Tension*, Harper, 1953, p. 57.

[7] *Ibid.*, p. 59.

[8] L. Morgan, *Introduction to Comparative Psychology*, London: W. Scott, 1894, p. 53.

[9] Morgan, *op. cit.* (1906 ed.), pp. 282-283.

[10] H. C. McCook, *Ant Communities*, Harper, 1909, pp. 154-155, 167.

[11] W. M. Wheeler, *Ants*, Columbia University Press, 1910, p. 507.

[12] T. Schneirla, in Sherif and Wilson, *op. cit.*, p. 69.

[13] *Ibid.*, p. 69.

[14] C. D. Michener, "Problems in the Development of Communication Among Insects," in L. Bryson *et al.* (eds.), *Symbols and Values: An Initial Study*, Harper, 1954, p. 499.

[15] T. Schneirla, "Problems in the Biopsychology of Social Organization," *J. Ab. and Soc. Psych.*, 41(1946): 391.

[16] New York *Times*, Sunday, July 11, 1954, p. E9.

[17] K. von Frisch, *Bees: Their Vision, Chemical Sense, and Language*, Ithaca, N. Y.: Cornell University Press, 1950.

[18] Michener, *op. cit.*, p. 506.

[19] T. Schneirla, "Animal Behavior

and Human Relations," in Sherif and Sherif, *op. cit.*, p. 64.

[20] W. Köhler, *The Mentality of Apes*, Harcourt, Brace, 1926, p. 293.

[21] R. M. Yerkes, *Chimpanzees: A Laboratory Colony*, Yale University Press, 1943, p. 45.

[22] J. B. Wolfe, "Effectiveness of Token-Reward for Chimpanzees," *Com. Psych. Monograph*, Vol. 12, No. 5, 1936.

[23] Köhler, *op. cit.*, p. 70.

[24] W. N. Kellogg and L. A. Kellogg, *The Ape and the Child*, Whittle-sey House, 1933; C. Hayes, *The Ape in Our House*, Harper, 1951.

[25] L. Boutan, "Le Pseudo-langage: Observations effectuées sur un anthropoide: Le Gibbon," *Actes Soc. Linn. de Bordeaux*, 16, 1913.

[26] S. K. Langer, *Philosophy in a New Key*, Harvard University Press, 1942, p. 85.

[27] Yerkes, *op. cit.*, pp. 189-190.

[28] In *Biological Reviews*, 4(1929): 249-268.

[29] *Ibid.*, p. 249.

[30] Köhler, *op. cit.*, p. 277.

SELECTED BIBLIOGRAPHY

Allee, W., *Cooperation Among Animals* (rev. ed.), Henry Schuman, 1951. Reviews the available literature.

Bierens de Haan, J., "Animal Language in Its Relation to That of Man," *Biological Reviews*, 4(1929): 249-268. Shows in interesting detail why animal sounds do not constitute language.

Cattell, J. (ed.), *Biological Symposia*, Vol. 8, Lancaster, Pa.: J. Cattell Press, 1942. A series of articles which, taken together, provides an illuminating general comparison of various animal species including man. Some of the articles are rather difficult reading.

Emerson, A., "Communication Among Termites," *Fourth International Congress of Entomology*, 2(1929): 722-727. Useful for its description of sublinguistic mechanisms of communication.

Hebb, D. O., and W. R. Thompson, in G. Lindzey (ed.), *Handbook of Social Psychology*, Cambridge, Mass.: Addison-Wesley, 1954, Vol. 1, Chap. 15, "The Social Significance of Animal Studies," pp. 532-561. A competent review of literature.

Huxley, J., "The Uniqueness of Man," in *Man in the Modern World*, New York: New American Library of World Literature, 1948, pp. 7-28. Emphasizes the biological prerequisites for man's unique capacity for conceptual thought.

Katz, D., *Animals and Men*, Longmans, Green, 1937. A very readable survey of complex behavior among animals and a comparison of human and animal behavior.

Kellogg, W. N., and L. A. Kellogg, *The Ape and the Child,* Whittlesey House, 1933. A comparison of the behavior and development of a human infant and a chimpanzee infant brought up in the same household.

Köhler, W., *The Mentality of Apes,* Harcourt, Brace, 1926. A delightfully written and classic account of the behavior of chimpanzees under observational and experimental conditions.

Lindesmith, A. R., "Can Chimpanzees Become Morphine Addicts?" *J. Comp. Psych.,* 39(1946): 109-117. Refutes the widespread belief that chimpanzees become morphine addicts in the same sense that humans do, since language behavior is requisite for addiction.

Révész, G., "The Language of Animals," *J. Gen. Psych.,* 30(1944): 117-147. Stresses the limitations of subhuman communication.

Schneirla, T.: "The Concept of Levels in the Study of Social Phenomena," in M. Sherif and C. Sherif, *Groups in Harmony and Tension,* Harper, 1953, pp. 54-75. An eloquent and detailed statement of the "levels" position.

———, "Problems in the Biopsychology of Social Organization," *J. Ab. and Soc. Psych.,* 41(1946): 385-402. Includes useful material on the differences between insect and human groups.

Thorndike, E. L., in F. A. Moss (ed.), *Comparative Psychology* (rev. ed.), Prentice-Hall, 1942, Chap. I, "Why Study Animal Psychology?" pp. 1-6. A clear and simply written statement of the assumptions made by psychologists who study lower animals to obtain an understanding of human behavior.

Wheeler, W. M., *Social Life Among the Insects,* Harcourt, Brace, 1923. An authoritative description of the behavior of various insect species.

White, L. A., "On the Use of Tools in Primates," *J. Comp. Psych.,* 34(1942): 369-374. The use of tools by apes and humans is compared and the vast differences are emphasized.

Yerkes, R. M., *Chimpanzees: A Laboratory Colony,* Yale University Press, 1943. An excellent and readable account of the behavior of three generations of chimpanzees in a laboratory colony. Includes results of experimental investigations.

CHAPTER 3 · · ·

Groups,
Language, and
Symbolic
Environments

THE PRECEDING CHAPTER emphasized the significant differences between human and subhuman behavior. The essential difference, as we have tried to show, revolves around communication: man uses language, animals do not. If, then, language is central to an understanding of human conduct, it demands very careful consideration. But language can be, and has been, considered from many different points of view: grammarians have studied its grammar, linguists its forms and mechanics, anthropologists its variations from one habitat to another, sociologists and historians its changes across time; physiologists have noted its anatomical sources, and philosophers have speculated upon its reputed origins and initial development. As social psychologists, we are interested primarily in studying language as a form of human behavior and in considering its relationships to other behavior. In a sense, everything in this text, in one way or another, is germane to that relationship. In this chapter, however, we shall consider only three general aspects of human language: (1) its

45

dependence upon social groups, (2) its nature, and (3) the symbolic environments which it enables man to create.

The Group Bases of Language

THE UNIVERSALITY OF HUMAN LANGUAGE

Anthropologists, who are specialists in this field, assure us that all peoples have a language. Every society of human beings, whether civilized or primitive, possesses some form of language. No tribe has been found, not even among the illiterate, that lacks a system of speech.

Differences among the languages of various countries are very apparent, as any traveler to a foreign land can attest. What is not so apparent, although equally true, is that the language of every human society is complex, intricate, and systematic—the carrier of a great wealth of experience and attitude. "The mechanics of significant understanding between human beings," writes the linguist Edward Sapir, "are as sure and complex and rich in overtones in one society as in another."[1] Every existing language contains at least five thousand words. As examples of primitive language complexity we might note that in the speech of the Abipones, a South American Indian tribe, the verb can take more than 400 endings to indicate mood, person, and tense; and in some Australian aboriginal tongues dual, triple, and even quadruple forms of nouns are in use.[2] Sapir has perhaps overstated the case for the equal complexity of all languages; but no linguist would deny that speech is highly developed the world over. It is for this reason that one writer has referred to language as mankind's "fundamental institution."[3]

LANGUAGE AS PART OF THE SOCIAL HERITAGE

The social heritage of any society consists of its traditional ways of acting, believing, and speaking. This social heritage—often referred to as "culture"—is distinct from the biological heritage. The latter is transmitted from parents to infant by way of parental genes in the chromosomes. The genes determine such physical character- istics as hair color and eye color. A basic difference between biologi- cal and social heritage is that the latter is never passed on biologically from parent to child; the child must acquire the social heritage through some process of learning.

Traditional ways of acting, thinking, believing, and speaking vary widely from country to country and from place to place within the same country. In the United States we thank a hostess for a delicious meal by complimenting her verbally; in another country the compli- ment may take the form of an appreciative belch. In the United States it is assumed that individuals deeply in love with each other will have the happiest marriages; in many other countries love is considered rather irrelevant to the success of a marriage.

The language of a given society is part and parcel of its social heritage. Like other traditional ways, language is passed down from generation to generation nonbiologically. The new-born baby is unable to speak his parents' tongue, nor does he acquire the ability to do so as a result of later bodily maturation. Just as the infant must learn many other customs and traditions of his parents, so he must learn what words go with what objects: he must learn word order, pronunciation, and also—if he learns to write—spelling and punc- tuation.

It is clear that the language learned by the child is not primarily his language so much as it is his society's. Adults have linguistic standards to which the child must conform. Although different indi- viduals may set unique stamps of pronunciation, enunciation, and meaning upon established ways of speaking and writing, neverthe- less there is a common core to all these individual treatments. Webster's dictionary recognizes this when it defines language as "the words forming the means of communication among members of a single nation."

Language is a group product which, like every other part of the social heritage, must be learned.

The child playing in the sand invents a word for the pebbles that fill its hand. The new word is "pocos." Does society adopt this word . . . ? Not at all. Society has an expression of its own for the designation of pebbles, and it does not look with favor on the exercise of further inventive genius. So the child's word "pocos" lingers for a time in the tolerant memory of the immediate family and then passes into oblivion.[4]

Many children invent a baby-talk speech of some complexity, which the parents learn, participating for a while in a bizarre linguistic game. But if the growing child is to be understood by persons outside the family, if he is to become an adjusted member of society, he must eventually employ generally accepted linguistic forms.

Indeed, marked individual deviation from the accepted language meets with disapproval. To be sure, a certain amount of latitude is allowed: Americans do not all pronounce, enunciate, or construct sentences identically. But one must not stray too far from certain linguistic patterns. Generally speaking, a future tense cannot be substituted for a past tense to indicate something that has happened. In the United States, American word order must be used; German word order is scarcely permissible. In France, inflection and intonation must approach a common French standard; they must not be appreciably American or Chinese. Marked deviation from the community's linguistic norm will fall stridently upon the ears of one's friends and associates; they are likely to respond with expressions of displeasure, distaste, snobbery, amusement, or ridicule. Deviants may be even punished: witness how "bad" grammar may deprive a man of vocational opportunities or prevent college students from passing freshman English.

The meanings of correct American speech in the world of the immigrant have been beautifully recaptured by the writer Alfred Kazin:

> A "refined," "correct," "nice" English was required of us at school that we did not naturally speak, and that our teachers could never be quite sure we would keep. This English was peculiarly the ladder of advancement. Every future young lawyer was known by it. . . . It was bright and clear and polished. We were expected to show it off like a new pair of shoes. When the teacher

sharply called a question out, then your name, you were expected to leap up, face the class, and eject those new words fluently off the tongue.[5]

Reactions to the violation of linguistic rules are in no way different from reactions to transgression of other customs and rules. Language is an integral part of a society's social heritage; like other items in this heritage, linguistic ways are public property and must not be grossly violated. And like other items of the social heritage, language may be utilized by individuals and turned to private ends; it may be made to fit the pattern of unique personalities. But individuals must operate within a framework of what is and what is not deemed permissible. Language is essentially a group product, the outcome of the common experiences of members of social groups.

SPECIAL LANGUAGES

The social character of language may be underscored by noting what linguists term "special languages."

By the term "special language" we mean a language which is employed only by groups of individuals placed in special circumstances. The language of the law is a case in point. In the exercise of their profession lawyers employ a language very far removed from that of ordinary speech; it is a special legal language. Another example can be found in ecclesiastical language. A special language is often used in addressing the Deity. . . . All forms of slang are special languages. Students, artisans, and thieves all use a language of their own. . . . They all have this in common . . . when their structure is examined they are found to be the outcome of a common tendency to adapt the language to the functions of a particular group.[6]

Just as each society has a native tongue of its own, each subsection of a given society has some special lingo or slang or specialized word usages of its own. Medical students, for example, have to learn anatomical and medical terms; students of this textbook must know some sociological and psychological terminology; each generation of high-school and college students uses a distinct slang of its own generation; Park Avenue society speaks an English somewhat different from the speech of the tenement districts. Thousands of vocations and businesses each have their special vocabularies, which the newcomer has to acquire and use correctly in order to be "on the inside." This insularity of speech sometimes allows insiders to convey information to one another in the presence of outsiders.

Each special language is based upon and utilizes the framework of the larger society's language. Yet a person who is outside the group which employs a special language is made aware of being a stranger to the ways of that group when he encounters its distinctive vocabulary. Everyone has probably undergone experiences in which he felt a stranger to some group in his own society because he did not possess the key to its language: a civilian among soldiers is a case in point.

Many terms in a special language are of a shorthand variety, designed to save time. Others are coined in order to make more precise references than the ordinary vocabulary permits. Some terms function also in less instrumental senses; they further group solidarity, since, when members use the terms, they are strongly reminded of their membership in the group.

LANGUAGE AND GROUP EXPERIENCES

It has often been said that the history and interests of a people are reflected to an astonishing degree in their language. Many interesting examples of this mirroring of interests can be found. The English, Hiller writes, living near the water as they do, have a language rich in nuances and expressions for the sea; Eskimos, because they are preoccupied with cold weather, make minute distinctions among numerous kinds of snow and snowfall.[7] Klineberg comments on the Arabs' concern with the camel:

> There are said to be about six thousand names connected in some way with "camel," including words derived from the camel and attributes associated with it. These include, for instance, names and classes of camels according to function—milk camels, riding

camels, marriage camels, slaughter camels, etc.; names of breeds of different degrees of nobility of lineage, derivation from different lands, etc.; names of camels in groups, as several, a considerable number, innumerable, and with reference to their objectives —grazing, conveying a caravan, war expedition, etc.; as many as fifty words for pregnant camels, states of pregnancy, stage at which movement of the foetus is first felt, mothers who suckle and those who do not, those near delivery, etc.[8]

To choose an example from our own society, almost any middleclass American woman has a more discriminating color vocabulary than her husband; her vocabulary thus reflects a more direct preoccupation with clothes, styles, and home decoration. Similarly, the special languages of the subgroups in any society provide us with illustrations of this mirroring of interests by language. The idioms and vernacular of sociologists, physicians, soldiers, journalists, bankers, college students, office workers, football players, all reflect their respective dominant interests and concerns.

Language is also the carrier—and the embodiment—of features of the environment which group members feel to be important. Words employed by people designate, refer to, and select aspects of the world relevant to their lives. "For not everything in the world has a name . . . language singles out for specification only those features which are, in a peculiar sense, *common* to the social group."[9] As Lewis says:

Among the Solomon Islanders . . . there are nine distinct names for the cocoanut, signifying stages in its growth, but no word corresponding to our general term "cocoanut." On the other hand, they have only one word which covers all four meals of the day—breakfast, dinner, tea, supper—but no special name for each of these. It is of practical importance to them to distinguish the nine stages of the cocoanut but not to discriminate between "dinner" and "tea." . . . *A concept is a means of preserving distinctions which are of practical importance in the life of a community.*[10]

Examples taken from the argot of the confidence man will illustrate concretely how the members of a group develop concepts that refer to matters of group interest. The confidence man is a criminal who lives by his wits and his tongue; his stock in trade is to relieve people of their money by deceiving them. This is done by persuading the victim to invest money in what is, in reality, a fake enterprise. Here are some terms in the confidence man's vocabulary:

Mark: A victim, or intended victim. Synonyms for mark are apple, Bates, egg, fink, John Bates, Mr. Bates, savage, chump.
To put the mark up: To locate a good prospective mark.
Tow: A bank roll.
To rumble: To excite a mark's suspicion.
The send: The stage in a big con-game at which the mark is sent home for a large amount of money.
To sting: To take a mark's money.
Touch: The money taken from a mark.
To tear off: To cheat one's partner out of his share of a touch.[11]

DEPENDENCE OF GROUP ACTIVITY ON COMMUNICATION

Language is not only a group product and the embodiment of group interests: it is the necessary medium without which most human groups could not exist. Certain small groups, like the family, could conceivably exist without speech; but it is impossible to imagine the rise and development of such groups as the following without the medium of speech: a nation, a senate, the United Nations, the Red Cross, a university, a pressure group, a baseball league, a well-organized factory, a police force, an army.

Sociologists, whose specialty is the study of human groups, point out that, if human beings are to be organized into a group, there must be a certain amount of understanding, agreement, and shared knowledge as to common aims and values—that is, there must be "consensus" among group members. There could scarcely be such consensus in the absence of a medium of communication. Language makes possible the transmission of traditions and skills, the formulation of goals, the discussion of tactics, strategy, rules, and procedures —in short, language makes possible the existence of human group organizations and gives them continuity in time and space.

The Nature of Language

The nature of human communication, as distinct from that of animals, has been touched upon in the preceding chapter. Now it requires a more explicit and detailed treatment.

SIGNS, SYMBOLS, AND LANGUAGE

Classifying and analyzing symbols are exceedingly complex and controversial tasks. Generally acceptable concepts and a stable working vocabulary have not yet been achieved, although various attempts have been made to provide them. Recognizing the difficulty of the problem and the possibilities of confusion, we shall present a greatly simplified account and confine ourselves to making only a few fundamental distinctions.

All living creatures learn to respond to cues in their environment. Inevitably some stimuli come to stand for other stimuli. "The sound of a gong or a whistle, itself entirely unrelated to the process of eating, causes a dog to expect food, if in past experience this sound has always preceded dinner; it is a sign . . . of his food."[12] The dog learns also to respond to visual cues (a stick), to movements (raising of hand), to odors (cat), and so on. Such learning of cues has been called "conditioning" by psychologists, and in the laboratories they have conditioned many animals to respond to "substitute stimuli." The world of any animal (human or subhuman) is full of such cues, and behavior is largely to be accounted for in terms of responses to them. Hereafter we shall refer to learned cues as "signs."

For technical purposes, let us describe a sign as a stimulus which calls for a response that is the same as or similar to the response previously evoked by some other stimulus. We may think of sign-behavior as running a gamut from the very simple to the very complex. It ranges from the most elementary forms of conditioning to the most complex verbal behavior. Between these two poles there exists a wide range of sign situations. A simple sign response may be produced in an animal by repeatedly sounding a buzzer and always feeding him immediately thereafter. This situation may be made more complex in various ways, such as by delaying the reward, by introducing the factor of punishment, by giving the animal multiple-choice problems, or by requiring him to respond to two simultaneous signs. Thus, an animal may be taught to obtain food by pressing a lever; later he may be taught that pressing the lever will yield the usual reward only when a green light is on, and not when a red light is glowing. Experimental psychologists who study the conditioning processes in animals can investigate only the nonverbal sector of the sign range because there is no verbal sign behavior among subhuman animals.

All psychological behavior probably involves sign behavior at some level. Indeed, it might be more correct to say, as some psychologists have, that psychological behavior is sign behavior. To elaborate on this point, let us consider a fairly simple psychological act—the perception of a box. If we ask a physiological psychologist to describe what happens when the box is perceived, he will begin by noting that light reflected from the box reaches the eyes. From that point on, his account will be concerned entirely with descriptions of how the light impinges on the retina of the eye, how the retina is connected with the central nervous system, and how impulses pass through the nerves. The act of seeing, in other words, is described as occurring entirely inside of us. The process of seeing is, in short, a representational or sign process in which the things that occur within us represent, or function as signs of, the real box. When the account is concluded, we are unenlightened as to why we see the box outside of us and as a box, and not as an image on our retina or as something in our heads. As we shall point out in the next chapter, sensory stimulation does not signify external objects until we learn from experience that it does.

Among human beings there is a tremendous range of sign behavior, from the simple thought processes of the illiterate feeble-minded to the complex thinking of the genius. Almost any object, act, occurrence, or quality may function as a sign of something else. The red glow of wood or metal indicates that it is hot; a gesture may reveal anger; a cross is a symbol of religious affiliation or sentiment;

a red light is a warning of danger; a falling barometer forecasts a change of weather; a pointer on a dial tells an aviator how high he is flying; and so on endlessly. Words are, of course, our most versatile signs, for by means of them we can talk of anything to which they refer, whether it is before us or not, whether it is in the past or future, or only imagined.

From such illustrations it will be seen that signs are related to the thing signified in a variety of ways. The relationship of the falling barometer to the impending change of weather is different from that between the cross and the affiliation or sentiment to which it refers, and both of these differ from the relationship between words and their meanings. Signs of the type represented by the cross have been called "icons"; those like the barometer, "indices." One should note that the things signified may be even more varied in nature than signs, for besides referring to all kinds of real acts, events, and objects, signs may also indicate nonexistent things which only can be imagined. Signs may also designate other signs, as when one points (makes a sign) to a notice written on a blackboard (another sign). Signs may also indicate operations to be performed with signs, as when one writes $\times$ between x and y.

Sign behavior is always at least a triadic relationship involving (1) an interpreter, or observer, (2) a sign, and (3) what is signified. If this idea is kept in mind, it will serve to emphasize that nothing functions as a sign until it is interpreted. It also helps to avoid confusing the sign of something with the thing itself.

A further complication must be added by noting that signs may be classified as "conventional" or "natural." A natural sign is a movement, sound, smell, gesture, or any other stimulus which is perceived regularly to precede or be connected with something else. The natural sign and what it indicates occur together in the same space-time framework, and both are thus parts of a concrete situation. For example, the dog that follows the rabbit's trail connects the scent with the actual rabbit because he has learned that the two go together. By contrast, the conventional sign derives its meaning from social consensus and is "movable" or arbitrary, in the sense that different signs (*e.g.*, in different languages) may mean the same thing, and that the sign (*e.g.*, a word) may be used in situations where the object referred to is not present. Conventional signs are relative to social groups or language communities in which the same signs are interpreted in the same ways by a plurality of persons.

Natural signs are not "natural" in the sense that they occur only in nature. They also may be human artifacts, as when the psychologist sets up a sequence of buzz—food in a dog's experience, or when lines in a spectrum are taken as evidence of the presence of certain elements. Similarly, the click of a Geiger counter is a natural sign of the passage of an electron. Symbolic analysis enables humans to notice and respond to much more subtle cues than the natural signs which the lower animals are able to master, and to explain connections between things.

In this book we shall designate all conventional signs by the term "symbols," recognizing that the characteristic forms of human symbolic activity have to do with language or are derived from it. Three important characteristics of language symbols which distinguish them from other kinds of signs may be briefly summarized:

1. They constitute systems, so that the meaning of any single symbol cannot be grasped in isolation, but must be understood within the system. For example: "wife," which is intelligible only in terms of a wider linkage of symbols like "husband," "marriage," and the like.

2. Language symbols, as we shall soon show, are inherently social in character and meaning. They evoke from the person who produces or uses them the same or similar responses as those elicited from the persons to whom they are directed. If communication is faulty, if the speaker talks past the listener, then the words do not function as symbols.

3. They can be produced voluntarily even when the external events or objects to which they refer are absent or non-existent. We may thus say that since people carry their symbolic systems around with them, the fact that one makes assertions about an object does not prove that the object is present or even that it exists.

We should not, however, make the mistake of thinking of language merely as a system of words, as a combination of phonemes, or as the contents of a dictionary. Language is, first of all, a form of behavior. It is not merely a system of symbols, but is the activity of using and interpreting symbols. Speech is often said to be the most primitive and ancient form of language behavior, but speech is meaningless unless it is addressed to an understanding listener. Hence, we may say that conversation is the essential and original form of language, noting not only that language behavior originates in cooperative social action but that it is such action. This is why parrots are not given credit for language behavior, even though they may produce words.

Conceived of in this manner, language becomes at once more significant and more complicated. The act of listening and comprehending, for example, does not itself involve an act of speaking, but only appropriate response to the other's verbalizations. The response evoked by the other's utterances may be a bodily act or it may be a covert or internal response, perhaps leading to a reversal of roles in which the listener becomes the speaker and vice-versa.

SOME NONVERBAL SYMBOLS

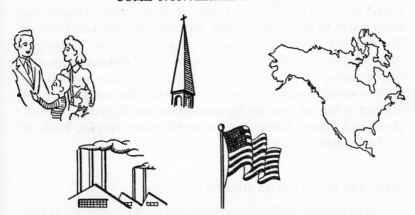

Symbols like these are not language symbols in the narrow sense, although they presuppose linguistic symbols and must be interpreted by means of them.

Conventional signs, or symbols, are not necessarily linguistic, as a brief reference to such cultural items as flags, rings, pins, crosses, uniforms, insignia, art objects, monuments, and music will make clear. However, all nonlinguistic symbols of this sort, as well as all ceremony and ritual, have meanings based on group consensus and are deposits of collective experience; hence they fall into the general category of conventional signs. If we return for a moment to the triadic relationships of observer, sign, and thing signified, the added element that appears in conventional signs is this: instead of a single observer we have a group or a community which interprets the sign in the same way and gives to it its meaning. It is for this reason that conventional signs, unlike natural signs, always involve a group reference and the matter of communicability.

It should not be assumed that human beings operate exclusively on the level of linguistic symbols, although that is their most characteristic mode of behavior, or that this symbolic behavior is itself a single, unified process: it falls into many different types which, in their turn, represent a graded scale from the most simple to the most complex. The use of proper names is an example of a very simple symbolic process, since the person's name refers only to a single object and can be fairly adequately defined by pointing. The use of a class name, such as "human being," is more complex because the name refers to many objects and involves differentiation between "human" and "nonhuman." The use of such terms as "tautology," "contradiction," "truth," "generalization," and "abstraction" is still more complicated because these symbols refer to other symbols and to the manner in which they are interrelated. The manipulations of abstract orders of symbols by mathematicians, logicians, philosophers, and other scholars are among the most complex kinds of symbolic behavior.

SYMBOLIC BEHAVIOR AS SHARED BEHAVIOR

Let us suppose that a dozen dogs have been conditioned so that whenever a buzzer sounds each produces saliva and otherwise behaves as though he anticipated being fed. Then suppose that all twelve dogs are together in one room and that the buzzer is sounded. Presumably, all would respond in the same way to the same stimulus. Can we not say that all of them are responding as a group to a sign which all understand in the same way? To answer this question, let us compare such a situation with that existing in an Eskimo settlement where the food supply is running low. A hunting party sets out to kill seals to replenish the food supply. Can we say that the members of the hunting party, like the dozen dogs described above, are making similar responses to the same stimulus, and that therefore the two types of activity are the same?

A moment's reflection will show that there is a fundamental difference between these two situations. Through intercommunication the Eskimos respond as a group, acting collectively rather than individually. Their behavior is shared; that of the dogs is not. Each member of the Eskimo community grasps the common purpose. In terms of that common purpose, which each understands and knows the others understand, they respond not in the same way but in different ways in order to attain the common goal. Some members of the settlement stay at home and prepare to take care of the kill; others form the hunting party, within which all may play different but coordinated roles.

Perhaps it may be helpful to think of language behavior as analogous to a game of checkers. A game of checkers is not an individual phenomenon; it does not belong to either player. It proceeds according to certain rules which, again, do not belong to any one person; each player must place the formulated rules above his desire to win, or the game ceases. The very existence of the game and the possibility of winning it require that both players understand and abide by the rules. The game of checkers, like language behavior, is a genuinely shared phenomenon.

It is no accident that the Greek word *symbola,* from which our English "symbol" is derived, referred to "the two halves of a broken stick or coin which were kept as tokens of a contract. Thus the word came to mean an item, such as a word, employed as an instrument of communication."[13]

GESTURES AS SHARED SYMBOLS

The shared character of language may be emphasized by noting how conventional gestures are utilized and understood. Gestures—like shaking hands in greeting, showing affection by kissing, and waving good-bye—all seem very "natural" to Americans. Yet these acts do not seem natural at all to the people of some other countries and societies. A Palaung woman in Southeast Asia said, after several Englishmen had heartily shaken her hand: "I suppose that they mean to be kind, but what a strange custom. I am very glad that it is only my hand that they wish to shake and not my head!"[14] Most human gestures are highly conventionalized and stylized, taking on their meaning through cultural definition. The identical gesture may stand for very different meanings in different lands; conversely, different gestures may stand for the same meanings. Only if both persons—the one who makes the gesture and the one who sees the gesture—attach the same significance to it can there be communication between them. An "outsider" will attach the wrong meaning (or no meaning) to the gesture; hence communication will be impaired.

The following cross-cultural mixture of gestures representing "greeting," quoted from Hiller, serves to illustrate the shared and conventional character of human gestures:

> Among the Wanyika, people meet by grasping hands and pressing their thumbs together; dwellers in the region of the Niger join their right hands and separate them with a pull so that a snapping noise is made by thumb and fingers. "The handshake of the Arab seems to be a scuffle in which each tries to raise to his lips the hand of the other." The Ainus draw their hands from the shoulders and down the arms to the fingertips of the person greeted, or they rub their hands together. . . . Polynesians stroke their own faces with the other person's hands. . . . The Fuegians in saluting friends hug "like the grip of a bear." Some peoples greet by placing one arm around the neck of the person saluted and chucking him under the chin, or encircling his neck with their arms. . . . [Among the Ainus a distinction is made] in the manner of greeting appropriate for men and women . . . men rub their hands together, raise them to the forehead (palms up), and then rub the upper lip with the first finger of the right hand. . . . In some Eskimo tribes . . . the courteous way of greeting a stranger is to lick one's own hands, draw them first over one's own face and then over that of the visitor. . . . Among the Polynesians, Malays, Burmese, Mongols, the Lapps, and others—a usual salute is that of smelling each other's cheeks.[15]

Even gestures of assent, dissent, and beckoning—which most

Americans probably feel to be among the most natural and non-conventional gestures—are conventionally defined:

> The natives of New Zealand show assent by elevating the head and chin instead of nodding as we do. The Turk expresses negation by throwing his head back and simultaneously making a clucking noise with his tongue. The inhabitants of the Admiralty Islands indicate a decided, vigorous negative by means of a smart, quick stroke of the nose with an extended finger of the right hand; if the negative is doubtful or hesitant, the finger lingers on the way and is rubbed slowly across the nose. . . . Beckoning is . . . done by motions which are the opposite of those employed in our culture. Some people make this gesture by holding the hand half erect with the palm forward, and moving it toward the person addressed. To beckon approach, the Bahima of eastern Africa reverse the palm in a manner that looks like a sign of repulsion, while the Niam-Niam of central Africa wave their arms in a way which we might take for a withdrawal.[16]

Such gestures would have either no meaning or the wrong meaning to us, as outsiders to these societies: we do not share the gestural symbols of these other peoples.

PSEUDO COMMUNICATION

It often happens that two persons become involved in an argument in which both use the same words, but the words have different meanings for each. When this occurs, a genuine interchange of ideas does not take place, since each individual makes remarks inappropriate to the meanings which the other has in mind. They talk past each other and grow angry at what each feels to be the other's stupidity. If the two parties do not become aware that they are using words in different ways, communication is seriously impeded or made impossible.

If, however, the disputants grow aware of the different meanings possessed by common terms, their discussion often develops into a consideration of proper linguistic usage. Thus, it is apparent that the citizens of the United States and the Soviet Union use the word "democracy" in different senses. Once this fact is appreciated, it becomes necessary to distinguish between "American democracy" and "Soviet democracy," if communication is to take place. Unless there is agreement as to the meanings of terms, persons who believe they are discussing the same things may actually be talking about different things.

EXPRESSIVE VERBAL BEHAVIOR

Up to now, we have been discussing language symbols as if their sole function were to refer to objects or to convey meanings. Thus, if someone says, "We are having lovely weather," we have treated such a statement as an indication by one person to another that the sun is shining, that it is pleasant outside, etc. Obviously, however, this statement may mean something entirely different. The speaker may be in a social situation in which he is expected to talk, whether or not he feels he has anything to say. Since all the people present are at least generally aware of the weather that day, there is really no point in saying anything about it; nevertheless, all are likely to feel more at ease if there is conversation. Here the purpose is not to tell people something they do not already know but rather, by uttering certain sounds, to give evidence of good will and sociability. Hiller has called this kind of conversation "social ritual."[17] Language so used may be termed "expressive" rather than "representative." Another example of purely expressive speech is swearing.

Words used expressively cannot be understood by referring to the dictionary; they can be understood only as conventionalized ways of giving vent to certain feelings. Thus, the nervous woman at a tea talks about the weather; an angry man swears; two persons greet each other by saying, "Hello!" or "How do you do!" In these situations the function of language is not so much communication as expression.

This expressive use of language may seem, at first blush, to be very much the same as the use of sounds made in certain situations by chimpanzees or dogs. But there is a difference. The dog's growl is a biologically natural sound for him to make, but "hello" and other expressive human sounds are conventionalized forms of utterance. No doubt in certain situations all human beings tend toward expressive verbal behavior, but the vocalizations vary immensely from society to society and are socially defined. Thus, we may say that expressive human speech, although on a lower symbolic level than speech designating and describing objects, is nevertheless on a higher level than the expressive utterances of animals. Chimpanzees, for example, can no more be taught to say "hello" appropriately than to use the word "papa" correctly.

In a later chapter we shall discuss aphasia, the loss of power to use language symbols. Studies of aphasia and other speech disorders offer experimental evidence that expressive speech is more primitive than representative speech. Aphasics whose powers of speech are all but gone and who cannot name even the most familiar objects in their everyday environment nevertheless usually retain the ability to swear and exclaim.[18] Most students of aphasia hold that when ability to use language symbols disintegrates, it is logical to expect the most complex forms of language behavior to disappear before the simplest ones do.

Symbolic Environments

THE CATEGORICAL OR LANGUAGE ATTITUDE

We have previously indicated (p. 51) that language symbols implicitly convey attitudes. To state this in another way: we organize or adjust our behavior toward things and persons by means of symbols, and these symbols come to embody a plan of action. "A category . . . constitutes a point of view, a schedule, a program, a heading or caption, an orientation."[19] Thus if one hunter shouts to another, "A duck!" the second hunter immediately looks into the air and makes the appropriate preparations for shooting at a bird on the wing. If the first hunter shouts, "Rabbit!" his partner responds in a different manner. Language symbols do not merely stand for something else. They also indicate the significance of things for human behavior, and they organize behavior toward the thing symbolized.

Some writers have gone beyond this and have pointed to a general attitude toward the world that is implicit in the very use of language and therefore common to all those who use language. They have called this general attitude the "categorical attitude." In its simplest terms it may be described as the realization (1) that things can be named and talked about, (2) that events and objects may be grouped or classified, and (3) that by naming and classifying the features of our environment, new modes of behavior, as well as new possibilities of manipulating that environment, are brought into existence.

The child gives his first evidence of acquiring this attitude when he learns that everything has a name—and soon exasperates his parents by persistent questions: "What's this?" "What's that?" He asks for names and at first is satisfied with mere names, since he identifies the name with the thing named. He has acquired a dim initial appreciation of the importance of language symbols. Later, when he begins to ask, "Why?" the child exhibits a second and more mature phase of the categorical attitude.

We may illustrate the adult categorical attitude by means of an analogy. Let us suppose that a boy who has lived all his life in an isolated rural section of Africa is suddenly placed in the middle of Johannesburg. He sees large numbers of people hurrying past, hears a chaotic jumble of sounds, sees a bewildering array of buildings, billboards, neon signs, trucks, buses, automobiles, and other objects. The people he encounters respond to him in ways which utterly confuse him. He does not know what to do or say or where to go. The city to him is merely an immense buzzing confusion.

We may compare this boy's view of Johannesburg with the view of the world which a man without language would have. As one lives longer in a large city and grows accustomed to it, "things" gradually become classified or categorized. Most of the sounds that assail the ear are disregarded as irrelevant, simply forming part of the roar of the city. The countless motor vehicles are ignored except as hazards that one must consider in crossing a street. The newcomer is astounded by the skyscrapers but soon grows used to them and thereafter may scarcely ever look at them or may use them for various purposes. The attitude of a city resident may be compared to the attitude which man acquires toward the world in general through his use of language symbols. Things have been organized into systems, into categories, in terms of their significance for one's behavior.

CONCEPTS AND CATEGORIES

The terms "concepts" and "categories" will be used almost synonymously here, although they have different connotations that should be borne in mind. "Concept" has a broader meaning which includes "categories" as a special kind of concept. To have a concept of something means to be able to picture it, to describe or represent it to oneself or others, to grasp it intellectually. A concept is a way of thinking about something, which means that it is also usually a way of talking about it. Conceptual thought is communicable thought. Concepts of classes or types may be called "categories." It is through the use of such categories of classification that we are able to group things together and distinguish one type of thing from another and, ultimately, to see the world as orderly. Indeed, without categories one could not think at all in a sophisticated human sense. There is an expression, "categories of thought," which refers to basic concepts, such as those of space, time, substance, and motion, which are regarded as fundamental in human reasoning about the material world.

We have indicated that the categorical attitude impels human beings to group things into classes. By categorizing or conceptualizing our experiences, we are able to analyze them and to respond selectively to some aspects of experience while ignoring others. Through the use of categories and concepts we are able to picture the world as relatively stable, predictable, and orderly and to find unity in its limitless diversity.

An example will indicate the connection between concepts and the language attitude. There is a certain type of animal which we designate as a "cow." When we use the word "cow," we refer to all the cows in the world and also, in a sense, to all the cows that have ever existed or ever will exist. But no two of these animals are ever exactly alike. Cows vary greatly in size, color, disposition, and so on. Nevertheless, we lump them all together, disregarding the differences among them. By so doing, we identify them, thus indicating to ourselves and others their significance for human beings. By means of the concept "cow," we have created unity out of diversity and multiplicity. There are millions of cows, but one single concept may refer to them all.

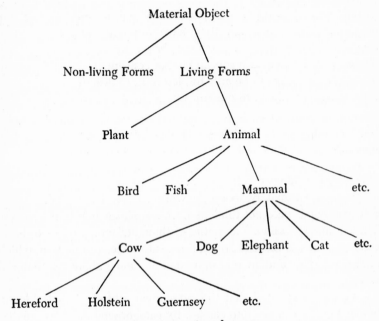

ASCENDING: increasing abstractness.
DESCENDING: increasing concreteness.

Still another implication of the categorical attitude then follows. When we see objects, we see them not only as concrete entities, but also as representatives or signs of the classes to which they belong. Every time we see and recognize an animal as a "cow," we bring into the picture, in an implicit or indirect way, all the other cows in the world which we cannot see and have never seen. It is for these reasons that language concepts are called "universals."

One should not make the mistake of supposing that any given object can be classified in only one way. It may be placed in a number of different categories according to the way in which it is being viewed or used. Thus, it may be classified in a series of classes on an ascending scale of abstractness, so that each class is more inclusive than those preceding it and less inclusive than those that follow. The more abstract the classification, the fewer and more general are the criteria of classification. Conversely, the more concrete the classification, the more numerous and specific are the criteria. For example, a particular cow may be classified on an ascending scale of abstractness as follows: Farmer Jones' cow, cow, mammal, animal, living form, material object. Cows may also be classified as four-legged creatures, objects weighing in excess of one hundred pounds, edible animals, economic assets, sources of milk, livestock, and so on. Each classification carries its own connotation of point of view and potential use. None of them is "natural," or inherent in the nature of the world, although some are obviously more effective for certain purposes than others.

To complicate matters still further, a cow may also be viewed as a composite, not a unitary, object. To a butcher it may be made up of sirloin, porterhouse, T-bone, and other cuts of edible meat. A biochemist, a physiologist, and an anatomist would each describe and classify the cow's components in wholly different ways. Farmer Jones himself might very well think of his cow as something compounded mainly of hay, corn, grass, water, and a little salt.

Dale, discussing the child's growing understanding of the concept of "dog," has made much the same series of points that we have indicated in discussing cows:

> One of the child's earliest learnings is the name for the shaggy thing that barks. It is called *Rover*. Next he learns that *Rover* is like *Sport* and *Shep*, and finally that things that look and act like them are called *dogs*. Once he has the *dog* classification, he may move in either or both of two directions in further classification. He may learn that there are terriers, St. Bernards, shepherds, and poodles; and then subdivide terriers into wire-haired, rat, Boston, etc. He can also go in the direction of more general classification—a dog is a quadruped, an animal, a vertebrate, or a mammal. If he continues, he may arrive at classifications used by the zoologist, involving abstractions that are extensive, precise, and increasingly complex. There are, of course, a variety of other paths that crisscross the two chief directions . . . indicated, in the course of which his concept of *dog* grows richer.[20]

That humans have concepts and categories with which to classify, subclassify, and cross-classify the objects of their environments is thus a fact of great importance. Our concepts and categories give us flexibility of point of view and a multiplicity of perspectives, enabling us to see connections among things in ways which otherwise would be impossible. They also enable us to think of things in terms of their constituent parts rather than as undifferentiated wholes or as total situations. They are therefore indispensable tools in any analytical procedure. All this implies that concepts alter our behavior in the direction of making it more discriminatory, more selective, and flexible: *i.e.*, more intelligent.

ANIMAL CONCEPTUALIZATION

It is sometimes said that animals also have concepts, in the sense that they can be trained, for example, to discriminate between triangles and circles, responding positively to one and negatively to the other. Experimental proof of this is in a sense unnecessary, since

ASCENDING SCALE OF ABSTRACTION AND DESCENDING SCALE
OF CONCRETENESS*

PHYLUM	*Vertebrata*	Vertebrates (including all animals with bony skeletons)
CLASS	*Mammalia*	Mammals (including all hairy vertebrates)
ORDER	*Rodentia*	Rodents (gnawing mammals, like rats, rabbits, squirrels, etc.)
FAMILY	*Sciuridoe*	Squirrels (both true squirrels and flying squirrels)
GENUS	*Sciurus*	True squirrels
SPECIES	*Sciurus carolinensis*	Gray squirrel
VARIETY	*S. carolinensis leucotis*	Northern gray squirrel
INDIVIDUAL		Any particular squirrel of this variety

*From A. C. Kinsey, *An Introduction to Biology,* Lippincott, 1926.

it is perfectly obvious that the lower animals are capable of such discriminations. They make them constantly when reacting differentially to other species, to sex differences, and to food as opposed to what is not edible. One does not ordinarily say, because of this, that animals have conceptions of sexual differentiation or of themselves as members of species. Closer examination of experimental findings invariably reveals that the animal alleged to have the concept of triangularity, for example, or to be able to count to three, actually acts only in a special situation, and then only as a consequence of laborious training and repetition. Rats have been trained to leap against the one of three doors on which there are two marks rather than one or three marks. An unwary observer may conclude from this that the rat had learned to count to three. However, if the sizes and widths of the marks are varied, so that large, heavy marks are mixed with small, light ones, the rat becomes confused and must be retrained in the new situation. The animal which is supposed to possess an idea of triangularity is similarly confused if a minute corner is cut off one of the tips, thereby converting the triangle into a trapezoid, or if one of the sides is slightly curved.

Experiments with concept formation in the lower animals have not been carried to the point where the essential idea of the concept or "connotation" is grasped, free from involvement in a particular concrete situation. When the child learns to understand the number 2, for example, the number becomes a positional point between 1 and 3 in an infinite series and has no necessary reference to anything of a concrete nature. No one who teaches geometry would agree that a student who could sort out only triangles and circles had an intellectual grasp of triangularity and circularity. If this claim were made, one would be unable to explain what happens when the child learns about these matters in the way required to get high grades in his geometry examination.

An essential feature of the full-fledged human concept is that it involves a general formulation and an explicit focal awareness of essentials. This means that concepts are both exact and communicable, the individual being able to specify to himself, and therefore to others, the exact features of the situation to which he is responding. Also, as our earlier discussion has indicated (p. 65), the fact that concepts form parts of a system of communicable ideas means that as abstract ideas they may be moved about, manipulated, applied to new situations, and made to interact with other ideas. Different conceptual systems may also be applied to the same situation as one shifts perspectives. None of these features is noticeable in the so-called concepts formed by animals.

MEANING AND GENERALIZATION

Some students of human behavior do not use the term "meaning" because they object to its implication. For meaning is often thought of as a metaphysical essence which resides in symbols, or in a person's brain, or in objects themselves. We must emphasize that in this book we use "meaning" in a behavioral sense. The meaning of an object or a word is determined by the responses that are made to it: that is, meaning is a relationship, not an essence.

It is easy to slip into the fallacy of locating the meanings of words in the words themselves. But meanings arise, as we have noted previously, out of group activities, and they come to stand for relationships between actors and objects. Our position has been stated precisely and clearly by Lee, who says that language

> . . . is not a system of names for passively sensed objects and relations already existing in the outer world; but neither does it fit experience into predetermined molds. It is a creative process, in which the individual has an agentive function; it is part of a field, which contains, in addition, the world of physical reality, the sensing and thinking individual, and the experienced reality. In this way, each word, each grammatical formation, is not an empty label to be applied; it has meaning, not because meaning has been arbitrarily assigned to it, but because it contains the meaning of the concrete situation in which it participates and has participated, and which it has helped create.[21]

Since a concept implies a unitary mode of action, it enables people to act in the same way toward a variety of objects. There are many types of food, for example, but once a substance has been identified as belonging to the food category, a common mode of behavior toward it is established. Thus every class concept is also a generalization, for it "generalizes" behavior toward everything included within its boundaries. To the invention of generalizations there is no end, for as long as group activity continues and experiences are undergone, new meanings will be discovered and transmitted among members of the group.

Symbols, or conventional signs carrying meanings upon which there is consensus, are from their very nature open to manipulation. Signs operate upon signs, as in algebra, mathematics, or in argument. Concepts breed new concepts as they are manipulated in the handling of problem situations. In group action, differences of opinion and position which are expressed in conversation and debate produce new perspectives and new meanings.

We may imagine that the activities of lower animals make for the appearance of new meanings in their lives also, as when a pet dog is taught a new trick, but these meanings cannot be communicated or shared and hence do not compare with the world of ideas which language opens up. Symbols enable man to escape the narrow confines of the immediate natural world and to participate in the artistic, religious, moral, and scientific worlds created by his contemporaries and his ancestors.

> Without symbolism the life of man would be . . . confined within the limits of his biological needs and his practical interests; it could find no access to the "ideal" world which is opened to him from different sides by religion, art, philosophy, science.[22]

FICTIONS

Language symbols are often used to designate objects and events which are real to those who believe in their existence but whose reality is denied by others. The example which springs most readily to mind is that young children, unlike their elders, may believe in the existence and good works of Santa Claus. The existence of an "Aryan race" was, and still is, a living fact to many Germans, although it was vigorously denied by many other persons both within and without Germany. With the passage of time events and objects which are real to one generation pass into the realm of the disbelieved and the fictional: this has happened to ghosts, witches, and even gods. Yet however unreal all these concepts may be to later generations or to skeptical contemporaries, they do make great differences in the behavior of those who hold and use them.

Race concepts, for example, are largely fictional. Whatever scientists may say about the pitfalls attending the classification of men by biological characteristics, there persist certain socially important classifications of race. Just as men classify objects into categories and act toward them on the basis of class membership, so they classify other men into racial groupings and behave toward

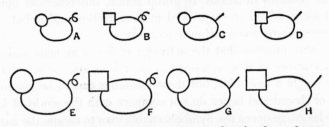

In how many different ways can you classify these fictitious animals? (From S. I. Hayakawa, *Language in Action*, Harcourt, Brace, 1941.)

them on the basis of presumed racial membership. The ways in which one perceives other men as colored or white are as much part of the social heritage as the very words "Negro" and "white." Consequently, classifications of races differ from society to society, as do all other kinds of categorization.

The same individual may be classified differently in different places on the earth's surface, and behavior toward him may vary accordingly. In the United States, any person with the fictional "one drop of Negro blood" is considered a Negro and may suffer indignities if his "true" identity is discovered while he is eating in a Southern white restaurant. In Brazil this same person would not be called a Negro or treated as such. He would be classified as a white even though his colored ancestry were known.

Some racial categories may correspond relatively well with biological fact, although surprisingly few do. Whether they do or not is irrelevant for social action, for people who believe in their validity act according to their belief. We may illustrate this point with a brief discussion of the situation of the Jews. It can easily be shown, both by historical and anthropological evidence, that the Jewish people do not constitute a genuine biological grouping.[23] The earliest Jews of whom we have historical records were of Semitic stock, something like the Arabs of today, but during intervening centuries of migration, intermarriage, miscegenation, and religious conversions, this original stock mixed with a host of other stocks. Hence it is understandable that Polish Jews bear a closer physical resemblance to other Polish citizens than to the Jews of other countries. Similarly, Negro Jews look Negroid, Chinese Jews resemble other Chinese, and so on. Nevertheless, so long as people— Jews and non-Jews alike—look upon the Jewish people as a biological group, human behavior will be affected by this fiction, as events in Nazi Germany have shown all too clearly. Race relations is an area of "as if"; people act as if they and others belonged to genuine races. It is customary in America to regard anyone as a Negro if he has any "Negro blood." Hence mulattoes are described as "Negroes having some white blood," and never as "whites having some colored blood." During World War II, "Negro blood" and "white blood" were sometimes kept in separate blood banks. The idea underlying this practice seems to be that if a white man receives a transfusion of "Negro blood," his skin color may change, or he may be said to have "colored blood" in his veins. It is sometimes supposed that this might effect the individual or his progeny.

To the scientist, these conceptions are nonsense. In the first place, the blood of a pregnant woman does not flow through the vessels of the unborn child. Hence, no one is actually justified in saying that he has his parents' blood in his veins. Moreover, there is no difference between "Negro" and "white" blood, and all blood types are found in both "races." Neither the physical nor the mental traits of the patient or his future offspring can conceivably be affected by blood transfusion.

Popular thinking in this area is based on certain misconceptions about the nature of races, blood, and heredity. It is widely believed that a drop of colored blood makes a man a Negro; that a person with one Negro grandparent has 25 per cent Negro blood and 75 per cent white; that octoroons have one-eighth Negro blood; and so on. These, and similar notions, form an essential part of the repertory of popular American thought and attitude. They have no foundation whatever in biology. Indeed, the evidence points to the essential biological unity of all human types. Not only are all blood types common to all races but the human organism is so uniform throughout the world that for experimental work in physiology and anatomy the race to which the subject belongs is a matter of indifference.

Some students of language phenomena advocate that fictions be eliminated from the language, since they refer to nothing actual. "No other animal produces verbal monsters in his head and projects them upon the world outside his head."[24] Such a proposal demonstrates a misconception of the nature and function of language; for if all the words of our language which have an element of fiction in them were eliminated, we should be poor indeed. Much of our literature, since it deals with fictional characters, would have to be banished. The scientist himself would sometimes be handicapped, for scientific concepts, particularly those on the frontiers of knowledge, are often hypotheses akin to fictions.

Language structures, whether they refer to fictions or to real things, organize behavior with respect to the external world and to things which exist only in a symbolic sense. When there is agreement about things which have no objective existence, these imaginary things, or fictions, assume a quasi-objective character in the sense that, although the words refer to nothing real, the fictions themselves are real, and thus become the basis for social action.

STEREOTYPES

Sociologists have long used the term "stereotype" to refer to certain oversimple, fixed, and usually fallacious conceptions which people hold about other people. Etymologically, the first part of the term derives from the Greek word *stereos,* meaning solid, firm, hard. Historically, it derives—at least in American technical usage—from a book on public opinion by Walter Lippmann, who used it to refer to "the pictures in our heads."[25] Lippmann asserted that because people go to the facts with pre-established classifications, they do not see the facts clearly or in unbiased fashion. "For the most part we do not first see and then define, we define first and then see."[26] There is stereotyped imagery of races, nationalities, national groups, occupational groups, social classes, and the sexes. But it is in the racial area that stereotypes have most often been studied. It has been found, for example, that our movies, radio programs, and popular literature rarely portray Negroes in any role other than that of servant, clown, or low-class person. These are the roles which fit the white stereotypes of Negroes. Common speech is replete with references to colored people as inferior, "uppity," lazy, shiftless, dishonest, and so on.

This imagery is built up by jokes, stories, and other expressions of attitudes and opinions that do not require direct contact or actual perception of Negroes. Most Americans have had no opportunity to meet, or even to see, members of many of the nationality or ethnic groups in the United States. Yet a number of investigators who have tested college students over the last two or three decades have found that the preferential ranking of these groups is consistent and uniform. The following groups are rated in order of diminishing acceptability: (1) Americans, Canadians, and English; (2) French, Norwegians, Germans, Swedes, and other Northern Europeans; (3) Southern European peoples; (4) Jews; and at the bottom are (5) Negroes, Turks, Chinese, and Hindus.

The only persons who did not rank the ethnic and nationality groups in the usual order were either members of minority ethnic groups or radical political groups. The members of ethnic groupings which normally ranked low tended to move their own groups to positions at the top. Politically radical students showed much less ethnic prejudice than the average because their radical political philosophy includes the belief that all ethnic groups are equal.

Once formed, the stereotype tends to persist even in the face of contradictory evidence and experience. A white American can come in contact with clean, intelligent, educated, thrifty, moral, and hard-working Negroes and still stanchly maintain that these people are exceptions to the general rule that Negroes are dirty, unintelligent, uneducated, immoral, and lazy. It is even possible for a white to have had direct contact only with Negroes who violate his stereotyped conceptions of the race—who are "different"—and still continue to hold these conceptions. American Jews are accustomed to being treated as exceptions to the usual stereotype of "Jew." Their gentile friends sometimes tell them: "You are different. I can be friends with you; I am proud to have you as a friend." Hence, the saying sometimes bitterly echoed in Jewish circles: "Some of my best friends are Jews."

Why is it that direct contact with a race does not lead people to see that exceptions are not really exceptions? So long as one classifies certain persons as belonging to a group or race, and attributes certain characteristics to the group in general, those who do not have these characteristics are dismissed as exceptions to or deviations from the norm; and we are told that "exceptions prove the rule." The standard, or rule, as we have already seen, is what the group is supposed to be "by nature." The following table indicates the nature of common stereotyped conceptions of Jews, Negroes, and Turks by listing the adjectives most frequently used in describing them.

The notion of stereotype has been very useful for the social psychologist in investigations of intergroup hostility, but it is not really a special and distinct concept. It provides an effective means of calling attention to erroneous and oversimplified concepts which people have of other people. By their very nature all classifications are selective responses to a complex environment, and thus are necessarily somewhat simplified versions of reality. Stereotypes often are strongly tinged with emotion, but this is also true of many other conceptions. Likewise, since classifications are embedded in systems, many of them resist easy change even when confronted with contradictory evidence. The selective character of perception, as we shall see in the next chapter, helps account for this impermeability to experience.

SYMBOLIC ENVIRONMENTS

Man's symbols are parts of his external environment. We may say, therefore, that man lives in a symbolic environment because (1) he is responding directly to symbols, and (2) his relationships

The Twelve Traits Most Frequently Assigned to Each of Three Groups by 100 Princeton Students[*]

Traits Checked, Rank Order	Number	Percent
NEGROES		
Superstitious	84	84
Lazy	75	75
Happy-go-lucky	38	38
Ignorant	38	38
Musical	26	26
Ostentatious	26	26
Very religious	24	24
Stupid	22	22
Physically dirty	17	17
Naïve	14	14
Slovenly	13	13
Unreliable	12	12
JEWS		
Shrewd	79	79
Mercenary	49	49
Industrious	48	48
Grasping	34	34
Intelligent	29	29
Ambitious	21	21
Sly	20	20
Loyal to family ties	15	15
Persistent	13	13
Talkative	13	13
Aggressive	12	12
Very religious	12	12
TURKS		
Cruel	47	54
Very religious	26	30
Treacherous	21	24
Sensual	20	23
Ignorant	15	17
Physically dirty	15	17
Deceitful	13	15
Sly	12	14
Quarrelsome	12	14
Revengeful	12	14
Conservative	12	14
Superstitious	11	13

[*]From "Verbal Stereotypes and Racial Prejudice" by D. Katz and K. W. Brady, in *Readings in Social Psychology*, edited by T. M. Newcomb and E. L. Hartley, Holt, 1947.

to the external world are mediated through symbols. As Cassirer has aptly noted,

> Man lives in a symbolic universe, . . . [He does not] confront reality immediately; he cannot see it, as it were, face to face. . . . Instead of dealing with things themselves man is in a sense constantly conversing with himself. He has so enveloped himself in linguistic forms . . . that he cannot see or know anything except by the interposition of this artificial medium.[27]

The symbolic environment may be thought of as a substitute environment, but it is important to note that this environment is not a mere reproduction or reflection of the external world. It is rather a reconstruction of the world in terms of the requirements of human conduct. That man is able to invent symbolic structures and be affected by them introduces a new dimension and a new level of interaction into the relations of man to man, of man to the external world, and of man to himself.

We may represent the two types of relationships with the total environment—the direct and the indirect—as follows:

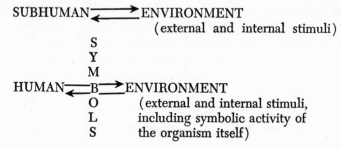

The two types of environment discussed here may be illustrated by contrasting the relations of primitive and civilized man to microbes. Primitive man is generally unaware of the existence of microbes and thus has no symbols with which to designate, describe, and comprehend them. Nevertheless, microbes influence him and he may die because of them. We may therefore say that microbes form a part of the nonsymbolic environment of primitive man but that they do not appear or are not represented in his symbolic environment.

By contrast, civilized man is aware of the existence of microbes and is able to formulate very elaborate statements about them. Microbes today constitute a part of, or are represented in, man's symbolic environment. This fact is undoubtedly of great significance. To have symbols for microbes means to be aware or conscious of them, to comprehend them. It also means that microbes may possibly be controlled and subordinated to human purposes. That civilized man is able to make statements about these forms of life, which are invisible to his naked eye, is thus a matter of the utmost intellectual and practical importance.

Man also turns language upon himself, devising terms and concepts for his own body and its parts and finding various means of describing processes that go on within his own body. Man, in short, becomes an object to himself. He learns not only to make and to be influenced by statements about his physical world; he also learns to formulate verbal propositions about himself and to be influenced by them. Insofar as he is aware of his own responses, they too become part of his environment.

Man's environment, therefore, does not consist merely of natural and external events and processes. It also includes the symbols by means of which man names, classifies, and forms conceptions of things as well as of the world of ideas and values. These symbols are products of group living. They reflect the fact that the members of groups—in the process of intercommunication and adaptation—devise linguistic schemes for classifying, describing, and responding to persons, objects, and events. These schemes form part of the social heritage and are the most significant aspects of the human environment.

Summary

Language is always a group product, and it is both an intrinsic part of the social heritage and the mechanism by means of which this heritage is transmitted from one generation to the next. Language is universal among all human groups, although each separate group tends to develop a special language of its own as an expression of its particular points of view, interests, and way of life. Psychological activity is essentially sign behavior and ranges in complexity from the simple direct responses of lower animals, to the higher thought processes of human beings. Signs are classified as "natural" and "conventional," the latter being called "symbols." The basic type of human symbolic activity is the process of conversing. It is to be stressed that the meanings of symbols arise in interaction and are thus a group contribution. Symbolic behavior, whether language activity or something else, is shared behavior from which common goals and understandings arise. Through the symbolic process, human beings become capable of conceptual thought and come to live in a symbolic environment of their own creation. Because human beings turn language in upon themselves and their own inner lives, they develop self-consciousness as they become objects of thought to themselves.

SUGGESTIONS FOR DISCUSSION AND SPECIAL REPORTS

1. Compile a glossary of terms used by a chosen occupational group and interpret the functioning of the terminology for the group.

2. Compare the views presented in this chapter with those of Charles Morris in *Signs, Language and Behavior*.

3. What is the meaning of "meaning"?

4. Do you think it would be correct to say that human beings have an innate need to communicate?

5. Enumerate as many as possible of what might be called the "diseases" of language.

6. Contrast the positions taken by Stuart Chase in his two books *The Tyranny of Words* and *The Power of Words*.

7. Discuss the pros and cons of whether lower animals should be credited with possessing concepts or some form of language.

8. How would you handle religious ideas in the context of this chapter?

=====

NOTES

[1] E. Sapir, "Communication," *Encyclopedia of the Social Sciences,* Vol. 4, 1942, p. 78.

[2] E. T. Hiller, *Principles of Sociology,* Harper, 1933, pp. 401-415.

[3] C. H. Judd, in *The Psychology of Social Institutions,* Macmillan, 1926, entitled one of his chapters "Language, the Fundamental Institution."

[4] *Ibid.,* p. 195.

[5] A. Kazin, *A Walker in the City,* Harcourt, Brace, 1951, p. 22.

[6] J. Vendryes, *Language,* Knopf, 1925, p. 249.

[7] Hiller, *op. cit.,* p. 115.

[8] O. Klineberg, *Social Psychology* (rev. ed.), Holt, 1954, p. 50.

[9] G. M. de Laguna, *Speech: Its Function and Development,* Yale University Press, 1927, p. 272.

[10] M. M. Lewis, *Infant Speech,* Harcourt, Brace, 1936, p. 224.

[11] Taken from D. Maurer, *The Big Con,* Bobbs-Merrill, 1940, Chap. IX.

[12] S. K. Langer, *Philosophy in a New Key,* Harvard University Press, 1942, p. 23.

[13] F. Lorimer, *The Growth of Reason,* Harcourt, Brace, 1929, p. 83.

[14] Hiller, *op. cit.,* p. 121. (Quoted from L. Milne, *The Home of an Eastern Clan,* Oxford: The Clarendon Press, p. 220.)

[15] *Ibid.,* pp. 101-102, 119.

[16] *Ibid.,* pp. 103-104.

[17] *Ibid.,* p. 111.

[18] H. Head, *Aphasia and Kindred Disorders of Speech,* Macmillan, 1926, and Cambridge University Press.

[19] J. Dewey, *Logic: The Theory of Inquiry,* Holt, 1938, p. 273.

[20] E. Dale, *Audio-Visual Methods in Teaching* (rev. ed.), Dryden, 1954, p. 31.

[21] D. Lee, "Symbolization and Value," in L. Bryson *et al.* (eds.), *Symbols and Values: An Initial Study,* Harper, 1954, p. 74.

[22] E. Cassirer, *An Essay on Man,* Yale University Press, 1944, p. 41.

[23] M. Fishberg, *The Jews,* Scribners, 1911. See esp. pp. 21-178.

[24] S. Chase, *The Tyranny of Words,* Harcourt, Brace, 1938, p. 14.

[25] W. Lippmann, *Public Opinion,* Harcourt, Brace, 1922.

[26] *Ibid.,* p. 81.

[27] E. Cassirer, *op. cit.,* p. 25.

=====

SELECTED BIBLIOGRAPHY

Cassirer, E., *An Essay on Man,* Yale University Press, 1944. A general philosophical treatment of the point of view which your authors share. It is very readable and suggestive.

Cassirer, E., *Philosophy of Symbolic Forms*, Vol. I, Yale University Press, 1953. Difficult reading, but a classic, recently translated.

Dewey, J., *Logic: The Theory of Inquiry*, Holt, 1938. Chap. III, "The Existential Matrix of Inquiry," pp. 42-52. The social bases of language behavior are discussed in moderately difficult prose by a famous American philosopher.

Elkin, F., "The Soldier's Language," *Am. J. Soc.* 51(1946): 414-422. Discusses army lingo as it relates to soldiers' experiences.

Geller, D., "The Lingo of the Shoe Salesman," *Am. Speech* 9(1934): 282-286. An amusing description of an occupational vocabulary.

Hiller, E. T., *Principles of Sociology*, Harper, 1933. Chap. VII, "Language as Consensus"; Chap. VIII, "Communication and Social Participation," pp. 96-127. Discusses in some detail the relations between language, group solidarity, cooperation, and the shared nature of group activity.

Judd, C. H., *The Psychology of Social Institutions*, Macmillan, 1926. Chap. X, "Language, the Fundamental Institution," pp. 187-217. A very general account of the crucial significance of language in human activities and in the rise of civilization.

Laguna, G. M. de, *Speech: Its Function and Development*, Yale University Press, 1927. A general treatment of language behavior, with special emphasis on its social origin and character.

Langer, S. K., *Philosophy in a New Key*, Penguin Books, 1948. The significance of symbolism in art, religion, and myth—and in human behavior generally—is treated in rich, stimulating language by a contemporary philosopher.

Lewis, M. M., *Language in Society*, New York: Social Sciences Publishers, 1948. Discusses in popular style the integrating function of language in industry, politics, and other group activities.

Mead, G. H., *Mind, Self and Society*, University of Chicago Press, 1934. Mead's account of the shared nature of symbols has become a classic, though his style is involved and labored. Not recommended for the beginning student.

Morris, C., *Signs, Language and Behavior*, Prentice Hall, 1946. Concerned with developing an adequate technical vocabulary for the discussion and analysis of sign behavior. The treatment is on a technical and abstract level.

Park, R. E., "Reflections on Communication and Culture," *Am. J. Soc.* 44(1948): 187-205. Suggestive account of the relations among culture, groups, and language.

Riezler, K., *Man: Mutable and Immutable*, Regnery, 1950. A difficult but excellent book by a noted philosopher who stresses language and symbolic worlds.

Vendryes, J., *Language*, Knopf, 1925. Part IV: Chap. I, "Language and Languages"; Chap. II, "Dialects and Specialized Languages," pp. 233-251. An excellent descriptive account of special languages.

White, L., "The Symbol: The Origin and Basis of Human Behavior," *Phil. of Science*, 7(1940): 451-463. This title is self-explanatory.

CHAPTER 4

The Social Aspects of Perception, Memory, and Emotion

WE HAVE SEEN, in the preceding chapters, that the key difference between men and the other animals is that men are able to communicate with one another by using shared symbols. This utilization of language results in a symbolic environment. The highly complex mental processes which characterize man, and which further serve to set him off from other animals, derive from his possession and use of language forms.

Complex psychological and mental activities are learned, not inherited. They depend upon the utilization of internalized language. Human beings carry their symbols about with them and produce them voluntarily in directing and integrating their own responses. However, the individual does not, himself, invent his language cues. He takes them over ready-made from whatever groups contribute to his social heritage.

These groups, in turn, do not invent language out of thin air or in an arbitrary fashion, for language represents the crystallization of collective and cooperative efforts to cope with a real world. Group ways thus carry with them not only the prestige of group sanction but the added assurance that they are tested ways of behaving in actual situations.

The mental processes to be discussed in this chapter as symbolic in nature frequently have been viewed as though they were mechanical. Thus, visual perception has been treated as though it were a process of photographing, and the human visual apparatus has been treated as though it were a camera. What is ignored by this view is that the past experiences of the organism influence its perceptions and that cameras do not have experiences, desires, aspirations, and attitudes. The same mechanical approach has been used in an effort to reduce human emotions to purely physiological functions located in the viscera or in some part of the brain. Research based on this idea has contributed much information concerning the bodily changes which accompany emotional behavior but has not helped to solve the problem of distinguishing between emotions and understanding their nature. Memory has been treated in a similar manner; it has been conceived of as a mechanical record akin to the "memory" attributed by some to electronic calculating machines. But, again, although this has shed light on some aspects of remembering, it has not clarified other important aspects.

What is suggested in this chapter is that the psychological processes are symbolic and social in nature. Perceiving, remembering, and emoting arise in connection with social experience and with involvement in a complex network of communication. They are aspects of human activity and are essential to that activity. Viewed this way, the mental processes are neither mechanical nor separate from the social environment which fosters them.

Perceiving

PERCEIVING AS A SELECTIVE ACTIVITY

The term "perception" refers to the ways in which organisms respond to the stimuli picked up by their sense organs. It used to be thought of as something analogous to such mechanical processes as photographing an object or recording sound on a record. But that analogy to a mechanical sequence is inadequate, ignoring as it does that perception is influenced by interests, needs, and past experiences. The analogy also does not take into account the fact that the total volume of physical stimuli reaching us, both from sources within our body and in the environment, is so great that most of them obviously must be ignored, and so can neither function as cues nor enter significantly into the determination of behavior. Physical illness sometimes reminds us painfully of some of the multitudinous processes that normally go on inside of us without our being aware of them. The hypochondriac is the illustration par excellence of preoccupation with stimuli originating in bodily processes. Ordinary healthful living requires that we be highly selective in the stimuli to which we pay attention and, at the same time, that whole ranges of them be consigned to the background and ignored.

Response to environmental cues constitutes the reality orientation of the organism. The data which are supplied by the sense organs and the receptor nerves are interpreted and acted upon as signs of the nature, location, size, movement, and quality of objects and occurrences. The degree and nature of inner elaboration, or "interpretation," of experience varies among species and among individuals. It reaches its peak in human beings, in whom the elaboration may be very great, and in whom it assumes a symbolic form. The individual's report of what he perceives, and indeed, his idea of what he sees or hears, includes matters of inference, interpretation, and judgement—in short, it does not discriminate between what may be called direct perception, or physical stimulus, and the meaningful elaboration of the perception which occurs when it is classified, named, analyzed, and judged.

> On the face of it, to perceive anything is one of the simplest and most immediate, as it is one of the most fundamental, of all human cognitive reactions. Yet . . . it is exceedingly complex. . . . Inextricably mingled with it are imagining, valuing, and the beginnings of judgment.[1]

It is easy to assume that some simple perceptions are much less complex than they are. Studies of congenitally blind people whose sight has been restored through surgery indicate that considerable learning is required before color and simple geometric figures can be distinguished visually.[2] Senden reports one patient who, after thirteen days of training in discriminating a triangle from a square,

> could not report their form without counting corners one after another . . . and yet it seems the recognition process was beginning already to be automatic so that some day the judgment "square" would be given with simple vision, which would then easily lead to the belief that form was always simultaneously given.[3]

Similar results have been obtained by Riesen[4] with chimpanzees that were reared in darkness. Hebb also reports parallel findings for rats. Data of this kind suggest that learning to perceive involves interpretation of physical stimuli. Meanings are not inherent in the latter, but must grow out of experience.

Stimuli viewed as purely physical events are presented to us by our environment and are not changed in any way by being named, classified, or interpreted. Stimuli become cues, however, when attention is paid to them or when they are responded to. The individual learns to select and interpret the stimuli relevant to his actions and interests and to ignore others or take them for granted. The child at first pays attention only to the grosser aspects of physical stimulation; his perceptions are undifferentiated. For the adult, on the other hand, as Gibson has said,

> The experience aroused by any given array of stimulation is only a small fraction of the potential experiences which might be aroused by it. The number of discriminations which are theoretically possible at any one time is enormous, but only a few are realized. . . . His [the adult's] momentary perception is differentiated, but schematic. What he specifies and distinguishes are only the objects and properties which support his momentary course of action or to which, as we say, he pays attention.[5]

It is easy, but fallacious, to conceive of perception as a single passive act, as if an organism looks out upon an environment and receives impressions of it through the sense organs. This "copy conception" was attacked by Dewey[6] and others who stressed that perceiving is part of a larger organization of activity. Sometimes persons do sit idly and allow stimuli to flow in upon them, but usually they are engaged in some sort of activity. What is noted, and how it is interpreted, in turn affect the course of action. As the action enters new phases, new kinds of cues are sought and evaluated. Lines of activity are typically intermittent and extend over periods of time, as, for example, when an individual is engaged in buying a house, planning for a vacation, or making a garden. When a given line of behavior is temporarily suspended, we have time to ruminate over the past and to anticipate the future. Both past and future may influence our perceptions when we resume the earlier activity. Perceiving as part of the larger pattern of activity is necessarily focused toward the future, even though it occurs in the present. As Ittelson and Cantril, following Dewey's general position, say,

> Perception certainly seems to be of the world as it is right now, or, perhaps, as it was a few minutes ago. Indeed, the definition of perception frequently appears in psychology texts as "the awareness of immediately present objects." . . . [But] While present and past are involved in the perceptual process, the chief time-orientation in perceiving is toward the future. The primary function of perception . . . is prediction of the future.[7]

The facts are that perception is selective, that motivation and needs sensitize one to specific stimuli or sometimes lead to distorted perception, that stimuli are often misinterpreted, and that perceptions of the same situation may vary from individual to individual; but these facts should not cause one to ignore the further fact that reality sets limits to perception. People who persistently see nonexistent objects like pink elephants, or who hear voices when no one is speaking, are out of touch with reality; they are hallucinating. Perception is, therefore, not arbitrary, but is limited by what is actually present in the environment. No one can live in the real world if he sees only what suits him.

Learning to perceive causes behavior to become more discriminating, more flexible, with respect to environmental reality. It does not, however, free behavior from reality. Admittedly the complications introduced into the perceptual processes when they become linked with high-order conceptualizations and symbolic systems, such as one's conceptions of self, increase the probabilities of distortion and error. The perceptions of the lower animal or the child are probably, within their limitations, less subject to error than those of the sophisticated adult.

Selectivity of perception is especially marked in social interaction in which the person's self-esteem is at stake. Psychiatrists and clinical psychologists have long noted the human tendency to ignore or misperceive things which would be damaging to their egos if correctly noted. The psychiatrist H. S. Sullivan coined the expression "selective inattention" for this process in which "we fail to recognize the actual import of a good many things which we see, hear, think, do, and say, not because there is anything the matter with our zones of interaction with others, but because the process of inferential analysis is opposed by the self-system."[8] Some recent experimental studies by psychologists have shown how perceptions are distorted because of the perceiver's needs and motives; and this work supports, if it does not greatly amplify, the observations of psychiatrists and other trained observers.

SOCIAL PATTERNING OF PERCEPTION

It is a fact, observed by psychologists and social scientists, that social influences affect perception in a very marked way. Laymen, of course, have also noticed this phenomenon. The poet Sandburg[9] makes the point effectively in a poem entitled "Elephants Are Different to Different People":

Wilson and Pilcer and Snack stood before the zoo elephant.
Wilson said, "What is its name? Is it from Asia or Africa? Who feeds it? Is it a he or a she? How old is it? Do they have twins? How much does it cost to feed? How much does it weigh? If it dies how much will another one cost? If it dies what will they use the bones, the fat, and the hide for? What use is it besides to look at?"

Pilcer didn't have any questions; he was murmuring to himself, "It's a house by itself, walls and windows, the ears came from tall cornfields, by God; the architect of those legs was a workman, by God; he stands like a bridge out across deep water; the face is sad and the eyes are kind; I know elephants are good to babies."

Snack looked up and down and at last said to himself, "He's a tough son-of-a-gun outside and I'll bet he's got a strong heart. I'll bet he's strong as a copper-riveted boiler inside. . . ."

Three men saw the elephant three ways. . . .

One might object that, after all, each man saw the "same elephant" but "interpreted" it differently. But interpretation is involved in all acts of perception.

A real-estate man looking at a house is not likely to observe the same details as will an artist, a fire-insurance agent, or an architect. When viewing a landscape, artists will perceive details and relationships of line, space, light, and color that escape ordinary "seeing." What is selected and emphasized in perceiving is connected with the observer's perspective, with his value system, interests, needs, and the like. Perception, clearly, is dependent upon previous experience, interests, and concern. These in turn are related to the perceiver's occupation, class, age, and so forth—in short, to his social background.

Perceptual Discriminations Vary from Group to Group · We have noted previously that a middle-class American woman's color discriminations are richer, more extensive, and far more precise than her husband's. In perceiving a dress or a picture, she will not only be more likely to notice color but will notice it more precisely, will classify it more accurately. Differences of interest and point of view may also lead to differences in skin-color discrimination. In our Southern states, people customarily make a very fine distinction between who is "white" and who is "colored"; hence, most Southerners of either "race" are very conscious of skin color. Yet in other parts of the world, such as the Arab countries, where there is a great variety of skin color, people seem to be quite color blind to such differences. The Arab, no doubt, knows such differences exist,

SEX DIFFERENCES IN PERCEPTION

but as these do not have the social significance for him that they have for us, he fails to observe them closely or to see them as we do. Similarly, the authors have noticed that after associating with Negro colleagues they see them as individuals and actually fail to notice skin color—although they may notice each individual's speech or mannerisms or clothes.

To continue this theme of perception and color, an anthropologist[10] has noted, concerning the color perceptions of natives of New Guinea, that "Their color classifications are so different that they see yellow, olive-green, blue-green, gray and lavender as variations of one color." Leaving the field of color, we may again refer to the Solomon Islander's complex and detailed perception of cocoanuts, the Eskimo's fine discriminatory classifications of types of snow, and the Arab's perceptual slant when he observes a camel.

Perceptual Interferences · Preoccupation with a given point of view or perspective often completely prevents a person from perceiving facts or relationships that are relevant to some other problem or point of view. Darwin once remarked that when he was a young man he walked over a plot of ground searching for evidence to prove a geological theory. Many years later, idly retracing his steps, he saw details which had earlier escaped him completely because at that time he had been looking for something else. Darwin commented that the previously unobserved objects were now no less plain to his eye than the ravages of a fire would have been. This sort of experience is frequent in scientific work. Similarly, Mark Twain wrote that after he had become a Mississippi River pilot he rarely perceived the beauties of the river and its banks—he then saw them only in terms of snags, dangerous or favorable currents, proper or improper distances from shore, and the like.

A study making the same point was published by the German psychologist Zillig.[11] She had several popular and several unpopular students perform calisthenic exercises before a class. The popular students had been instructed to make mistakes; and the unpopular ones had been trained so as to make no mistakes. At the end of the exercises the audience was asked to vote on which group had done the exercises correctly. The vote was in favor of the popular pupils. After checking with the children through conversation, the investigator concluded that the voting reflected differences that were actually seen.

Nonvisual Perceptions · Other forms of perceiving—hearing, for example—are also influenced by social factors. Differences in musical taste among groups and among individuals with different social backgrounds are striking. Thus H. Roberts notes:

> My own experience with primitive peoples—Negro, Polynesian, Indian—has shown that it would be extremely unlikely that minute tone differences would . . . be heard, not because of any inherent inability, for in directions in which their interest and welfare lie the hearing of such people is as acute as any, but because their attention has never been directed toward fine distinctions in scale tones, except sporadically in the attempt to copy an admired instrument exactly. They hear delicate nuances of intonation in speech, especially where tone in language has become important to meaning through certain trends of development. They distinguish minute forest sounds where differences convey so much that is vital to them. . . . But these are all in the line of specially developed interests. . . .[12]

However, we do not have to go so far afield: the music of numerous composers, including Mozart and Beethoven, was harshly judged when first played but has been appreciated by later generations who apparently hear very different things in the music.

Differences in food tastes are also instances of social determination of nonvisual perception. The student may be reminded of the cannibal, of Moslem aversion to pork, of American aversion to roasted caterpillars. We may even, with more than facetious intent, suggest that social rather than biological considerations make us regard such combinations as mustard and ice cream, or salami and peppermint candy, as inappropriate.

PERCEPTION AND LANGUAGE

Verbal Symbols Organize Perceptions · We have noted in the preceding chapter that a human being acts toward objects in the light of his classification of them. Categorizing is an integral part of most acts of human—as opposed to animal and infant—perception. An object is perceived characteristically not as an isolated item but as a member of some class. Actually we see class representatives, not bare, unnamed, isolated objects. The reader should glance around the room, making note of what he "sees." Does he not see class representatives: walls, books, pencil, chair, flowers? Linguistic classification is not external or incidental to such perceiving but is an integral part of it. What we term "perceiving" involves linguistic distinctions, for objects cannot be perceived as class members unless the observer's language has already designated these classes or enables him to invent new categories. As Gibson says,

> The factor which makes for the socializing of perception in human organisms, we may suspect, is the process of word-making. Presumably, since only human beings make words, only human beings show the phenomenon of a cultural stereotyping of their percepts. . . . The phenomenal world of a language community is partly determined by its language, i.e., people see what they have words for. A promising explanation of this fact is that the entities of stimulation that get identified, the variables that get discriminated and abstracted, are very much determined by the verbal responses which accompany perceptual and motor activity. Words tend to fix or freeze the objects and qualities which become differentiated out of the stimulus flux; words tend to determine a man's repertory of perceptions. . . . Since people must reach a kind of consensus of mind-reactions in order to communicate, they tend to reach a consensus of individual perceptions.[13]

The linguistic character of even rather simple adult perception is shown in a study by Carmichael.[14] Visual outline drawings were presented to subjects; and as the drawing was shown, a word characterizing it was spoken by the investigator. Thus -⊙- was called either "sun" or "ship's wheel." Reproduction of the outline drawing shortly afterward, from memory, varied according to the word spoken. Carmichael attributed this variation to certain processes, initiated by the word, which affected perception of the drawing.

Bartlett's[15] careful work indicates also how linguistic elements influence perception. Subjects briefly shown the figure ⊠ sometimes thought the square was completely drawn in. In such a figure as naming was of great importance in helping to shape perception. Subjects looking at this figure who saw "picture frames" perceived an object that looked like or The figure was called a pickax by one observer and reproduced with pointed prongs; by another person it was called a turf cutter and drawn with a rounded blade. Several persons called it an anchor and exaggerated the size of the ring on the top. Only one person correctly perceived the pointed blade: he had seen it as a prehistoric battle-ax. Bartlett notes that if a figure seemed odd, disconnected, unfamiliar, it was usually seen in terms of an analogy—that is, in terms of the identity of a known object. He concludes that "a great amount of what is said to be perceived is in fact inferred."

A common-sense maxim holds that, in general, "people see what they are looking for." This is not always true by any means, but the phrase indicates that verbal frames of reference organize perceptual responses. A person's perceiving is likely to follow along the lines of familiarities and expectations. The illustrations taken from the work of Bartlett and Carmichael demonstrate this very well, as does the existence of some types of so-called "suggestion." Thus, when Binet[16] showed subjects "a series of lines of gradually increasing length, but with occasional 'catches' where the lines did not lengthen as expected . . . no one of his forty-five pupils completely escaped the suggestion of increase in length in all lines." This kind of suggestion can be accounted for very simply by supposing that Binet's subjects were "set" to see successively longer lines. Their perceptual responses were organized by their expectations in much the same fashion as those of a prejudiced white person who believes all Negroes to be lazy, dirty, and unambitious.

During the war, American flyers were taught to recognize aircraft. Gibson describes the role of language in this process:

> Before training, the forty novel objects looked more or less alike. Americans did not confuse airplanes with birds as Fiji Islanders might have done, but they confused them with one another; that is, the forty objects looked like only two or three different objects. After training, however, they all looked different. Cor-

respondingly, at the outset the forty objects elicited only a few specific responses and at the end they aroused forty different responses. The responses, of course, were *names*. They were identifying reactions in the sense that there was only one reaction for one object. Similarly, before training a student could make a drawing which represented only a generalized airplane; after training he could make forty different drawings. Presumably he could visualize forty different shapes. Before training only a few properties or qualities of the objects could be observed, but in the end many properties could be seen. The evidence for this is that *adjectives* could be applied, and judgments of more or less could be made with respect to a given adjective. . . . The learning exhibited other interesting phenomena; for instance, the experiments on drawing silhouettes indicated that one kind of constant error was a stereotyping or caricaturing of the shape.[17]

Complex Social Perceptions · If simple perception such as that studied by Carmichael and Bartlett involves naming, analogy, and inference, it may be assumed that more complex acts of perceiving will involve more complex uses of language. By way of illustration, let us consider what is involved when a teacher observes a student "cheating" on a quiz. Does the teacher actually "see" the cheating? In a literal sense this is impossible. All he can see is the student glancing at his neighbor's paper or looking about the room. The actions of the student appear furtive and guilty to the teacher in the examination setting because he attributes to the student certain motives or intentions. He cannot see these motives or intentions, but if they are lacking no cheating has taken place. Concepts of "fairness" and "breaking the rules" are also involved, as well as notions about what acts are taboo during a quiz period. Our most characteristic acts of perceiving occur on this moderately complex level. In order for such phenomena as embarrassment, irony, and humor to be perceived at all, a common background of social experiences among the participants is necessary.

We may illustrate the point further with a cross-cultural example. Among the Murngin, a primitive Australian tribe, respect is expressed by every man to his mother-in-law by strict avoidance, so that if the mother-in-law is seen coming down the path both he and she must avert their eyes and turn aside. By his act the man is indicating his respect for her position. An American observer might perceive this act on at least three increasingly complicated levels. On one level the observer might see only a man and a middle-aged woman walking toward each other, then turning aside and not looking in each other's direction. The second level, assuming the observer knows only how the two persons are related to each other, would involve his seeing son-in-law and mother-in-law avoiding each other and refraining from looking at each other. He would not know what was being expressed—shyness, guilt, hatred, mutual punishment, or fear. The third and most complex level would involve a comparatively thorough knowledge of Murngin family relationships, including recognition of the meaning of "avoidance for respect." In this instance the observer would "see": son-in-law paying respect to mother-in-law by respectfully "avoiding" her.

LIMITATIONS OF CHILDREN'S PERCEPTIONS

Studies of children support the view that perception is a learned way of responding in which verbal elements play a vital role. Because the child has not yet fully internalized the adult's symbols, he does not perceive the world in an adult fashion.

Luria's experiments with children under eight years of age support this view.[18] When presented with a rectangle of four blocks and asked whether they see odd or even, children reply "even." When presented with an incomplete rectangle of five blocks, the number is seen as "odd." But offer the child a complete rectangle consisting of nine blocks, and unlike an adult he will say "even." If then a tenth block is added to make an irregular figure, the child will say "odd." In this and other instances his seeing is not quite equivalent to adult seeing, because his language distinctions are different and fewer. The child sees odd and even in terms of regular and irregular shapes rather than in terms of number.

Because they must learn distinctions made by adults, children must reach a certain age before they can perceive given events, relationships, and objects. Thus infants do not recognize pictures as pictures until they are able to speak: seeing a "picture" involves seeing an object as a member of the category "picture." Similarly, because they lack the appropriate linguistic discriminations, young children are unable to perceive subtle relationships between adults, such as flirtation and irony. As they grow older and acquire additional and subtler linguistic meanings—as their categories become richer and more inclusive—youngsters' perceptions of such events

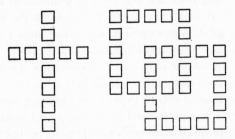

In counting the total number of squares in the figure at the left, young children count the middle square twice. In counting the total number of squares in the figure at the right, they make the same sort of error. (From "The Problem of the Cultural Behavior of the child," by A. Luria, in the *Journal of Genetic Psychology*, 35 [1928].)

become increasingly keen (and frequently embarrassing). There is little doubt that after his second or third year the child's perception, like that of the adult, is fused with and made possible by the utilization of language.

HUMAN AND SUBHUMAN PERCEPTION

We have been maintaining that human perception characteristically depends upon seeing objects as class representatives and therefore depends upon language. A corollary of this is that animals do not perceive objects as members of named classes. Are there any data for this subsidiary contention, apart from the evidence that animals do not possess language systems?

Leaving the great apes aside for the moment, we may accurately say that the lower animals see objects as parts of concrete perceptual situations. As one author[19] notes, "in general [animals] react to a whole situation, and often show a curious incapacity out of such a complex to isolate fragments that must be of great importance to them and are unable to recognize these fragments in other complexes." As an instance of this phenomenon we may note the curious perceptions of the cuttlefish, *Octopus vulgaris*. This animal immediately seizes and eats a crab which it perceives moving across the sandy bottom, but does not recognize a crab dangled on a string before its eyes. It may even attempt to remove the dangling crab by directing a jet of water upon it. When the same crab is allowed to crawl on the bottom, the octopus immediately seizes the prey. The octopus does not see the crab as a crab, does not see it as an object detachable from its normal surroundings.[20]

One of the neatest sets of experiments bearing upon perception in lower animals was performed by Kirkman on black-headed gulls. Russell's description of Kirkman's results is so pertinent to our discussion that it is worth quoting at length.

> If the bird is broody and the egg is in the nest and intact, it will be incubated. Many other objects, very roughly resembling the egg in size and smoothness of contour, but not necessarily in appearance, will, if placed in the nest, be treated as *functionally equivalent* to the egg, i.e., they will be brooded. If a gull returning to its nest finds one of its eggs with a gaping hole in it, made by some marauding gull intent on sucking, it will forthwith complete the sucking of the contents, even though the embryo be far advanced. Generally speaking, for the gull an egg with a conspicuous hole in its side, whether its own egg or another's, whether inside its nest or outside, is "something to be sucked"; it has food valence. An intact egg in another bird's nest has similar food valence.
>
> If an egg, its own or another's, is placed close to the nest of a sitting bird, it will roll it back into the nest—it is "something to be retrieved." Later experiments by Kirkman demonstrate that the gull may also roll into the nest various egg-shaped or other-shaped objects, which are treated as functionally equivalent to the egg.
>
> The egg or egg-equivalent however loses its "retrieving" valence if it is more than a certain distance from the nest. For every black-headed gull there is a maximum distance from the

centre of the nest, be it 1 foot, 1½ feet, or more, beyond which the egg or eggs put outside are completely ignored. They cease to exist for the bird. It may walk over or by them several times in the course of an hour or more and yet be blind to them; they have become "just part of the landscape."

It is clear from these experiments that the valence of an egg changes according to the psychological situation; we may infer also that for the gull there is no such thing as "an egg," but merely something, which according to the circumstances is to be incubated, or retrieved, or eaten. The "egg" may be ignored entirely; it may pass out of the perceptual field, be treated as part of the neutral background. If the gull could form concepts and use words, it would have no concept of "an egg," and no word for it, but would have separate words for the egg-object in different situations. For us "an egg" is recognizable as such in all situations, it is a continuing object, retaining its identity; not so for the bird.[21]

A predominantly situational kind of perception may be characteristic of the lower orders of animals; but what of those animals closest to man in the evolutionary ladder? Some experimentation has been done upon the visual and auditory perceptions of chimpanzees. Their hearing is about like ours except that a higher range of tones is heard over and above the usual human range. It has also been established[22] that chimpanzees can discriminate and respond suitably "to differences in three dimensions of color stimuli: hue, saturation, and intensity; to differences in the shape, size, and surface appearance of solid objects; to distinguish, recognize, and otherwise react appropriately to plane figures and pictorially represented objects." (An ape has been known to extend his arm in greeting to a photograph of himself, thus suggesting recognition of a fellow-ape.)

However, we should note carefully an experiment carried out by Yerkes which suggests that radical differences exist between simian and human perception. In each of four corners of a room Yerkes placed a small wooden box with a hinged lid.[23] The boxes were identical except in color: each was differently painted. An ape was allowed to watch his breakfast being placed "ostentatiously" in one of the boxes. The lid was then closed; the animal was led from the room for five minutes, then again confronted with the four boxes. The boxes may or may not have been shifted about in his absence. Yerkes states that the apes always chose the box that happened to be in the position of the box in which the breakfast had been placed. Such incorrect responses tended to persist, accompanied by "increasing emotional disturbance," when the experiment was repeated. Yerkes reasoned that the animals chose the boxes purely by spatial location; so he varied the boxes according to pronounced differences of shape, size, color, and brightness. The chimpanzees still continued to choose by position instead of by physical characteristics of the boxes. Yerkes' conclusions dovetail neatly with the point we are trying to make:

> The experiment proved conclusively that apes naturally depend upon the general visual configuration of their surroundings instead of on some single aspect such as size, shape, or color.
>
> It may not be amiss to ask how the ape's behavior in this experiment may be translated into human experience. Confronted with the experimental problem which was presented to the animals, we might initially have difficulty because of casual or careless observation. But the chances are that a single error, if we really were highly motivated in the experiment, would stir us to careful examination of the situation and that in our second trial and thereafter we should recognize and identify the food-containing box, not by its location in the room or its surroundings, but instead by its distinguishing characteristic, color. The chances are that we should promptly come to respond in the experiment by depending on the verbal symbol, green for instance, appropriate to the box in which we had seen the food placed, for it is by the use of such symbolic processes that we are able to represent and hold in mind objects no longer present to our senses.
>
> It seems doubtful that our chimpanzee subjects at the outset even noticed the color of the food box. Why should they, since the definite location and spatial relations of the right box to the other features of the room might be expected to serve as cues for correct response? When, quite unbelievably, these customary cues proved to be inadequate or misleading, it obviously

was next to impossible for the ape to discover the single dependable clue . . . and to hold it in mind. Perhaps, after all, the latter
point is the critical one, for unless the significant feature of the
food box is both attended to and held in mind during the inter-
val of delay, correct response can occur only by chance.[24]

Recently apes have been trained to perceive in ways seemingly
comparable to those of humans. When rewards are placed under
red-painted objects, the animal learns eventually to look only under
red objects, regardless of the shape, texture, and material composition of the object and regardless of the particular shade of red, or
how the red is combined with the other colors on the object.

One cannot, however, conclude that apes are able to see as
human beings do. The animals have to be carefully trained, step
by step, before they can discriminate in such a fashion; they do
not ordinarily do so. There is thus no reason to conclude that an
ape can be said to possess the concept of "redness." The possession
of the concept implies the ability to respond selectively to the
quality of redness in new situations and combinations, and to relate
it to the multitude of matters associated with redness—such as wave
lengths, the spectrum, "red Russia," stop lights, warning signals,
blood, and so on.

PREJUDICE, BIAS, AND THEIR BASIS IN "NAMING"

We have already suggested that people often do not perceive
certain food combinations as "belonging together." Their perception
of what belongs together depends, of course, upon processes of
naming and labeling: "condiments" such as mustard and pickles do
not go with "desserts" such as ice cream and cake. The same phenomenon of classifying objects underlies rejections and acceptances,
taboos and preferences, in areas other than that of food taste.

Thus, during the last war, nude or seminude Melanesian women
were often within sight of American fighting men. Yet, for the most
part, the soldiers were not tempted to make sexual advances. As one
veteran stated: "They didn't look attractive to us, they weren't
'white' enough in color or features. Now the Polynesian women—!"

A Southern student expressed much the same view when she refused to believe it possible for a white person actually to fall in love with a Negro.

The field of artistic judgments and art criticism is an especially rich one in which to explore the linguistic categories underlying perceptions. The philosopher John Dewey has complained[25] that many critics approach paintings with prejudgments concerning what is "great" and "poor" art. These prejudgments are based upon standards derived from the study of painters already acknowledged to be "great." Consequently, most of the important artistic innovations are likely to be condemned as outrageous, and their creators as incompetent or even vulgar. The history of every art form is, in fact, replete with the blunders of critics. Dewey terms this kind of criticism "judicial criticism" because the painting is judged not in terms of the given artist's purposes but in terms of the purposes of some other artist or set of artists.

A discerning observer may note that many casual museum-goers judge pictures in precisely this fashion, although their perceptions are less sophisticated than those of professional critics. The naïve person is unable to see much in the painting because his artistic categories are undeveloped. Instead of looking for "plastic values" (such as color, light, space, brushwork, and other technical items), he focuses his attention upon relatively irrelevant aspects of the picture, such as age, price, story, photographic likeness, and reputation of the artist. Consequently, abstract painting may be misconstrued because it does not represent—nor is it intended to represent—anything that is recognizable or real, and medieval painting may be disliked because it "always deals with religious subjects, which don't interest me in the least." We have seen one woman turn away in bewilderment and revulsion after looking in vain for the violin in an abstract Picasso painting labeled "Man with Violin." The major point to be noted about biased perception is the intimate fusion of inference and "raw" vision. We see in biased fashion because we enter the perceptual situation with preformed expectations. To this extent we are all more or less biased, although one may, of course, be aware of his own prejudices.

Remembering

Perceiving involves the response to or interpretation of signs in the form of sensory stimulation resulting from the organism's contacts with the external environment or arising within the organism. Remembering is a response to signs of past experiences, which in some form or other are preserved within the organism. In the one case the sign bridges a spatial gap, in the other a temporal gap. Thus, remembering, like perceiving, is a complex form of sign behavior.

THE SOCIAL BASIS OF MEMORY

Content of Memory · An illustration of how memory is affected by group membership is a story told about a number of Swazi chiefs from South Africa. The chiefs visited England, and after returning home discovered that their most vivid memory was that of a British policeman regulating traffic with uplifted hand. The vividness of this particular memory was related to the Swazi custom of greeting one another with the same gesture.

Bartlett,[26] who has studied remembering among these people, writes that they have the reputation among their neighbors of possessing excellent memories. After testing the memories of several representative Swazi, he concluded that this reputation was unfounded; but he later discovered that Swazi memories connected with cattle and cattle raising were almost phenomenal. As Bartlett explains, cattle raising is a central concern of Swazi society. Mark Twain, writing of Mississippi river steamboat pilots of the early nineteenth century, notes a similar phenomenon. A pilot had to recall thousands of items about the river: its curves, banks, sandbars, currents, snags, and depths. "But if you asked that same man at noon what he had had for breakfast, it would be ten chances to one that he could not tell you."[27]

Similar instances may easily be discerned in our own daily lives.

It is common knowledge that an individual's interests are a good key to what he will remember. If a woman is inclined to gossip she is likely to remember gossip tidbits, although her memory for other items may be far from superlative. People who like poetry may be able to recite dozens of stanzas yet fail to remember algebraic proofs or the names of people whom they have met. Numerous small boys in the United States astound their elders with their ability to remember the batting averages of favorite baseball players. These same boys may be the despair of their teachers because of deficient memory in classroom work.

A series of studies has pointed clearly to the role of social factors in remembering. Zillig[28] presented subjects of both sexes with favorable and unfavorable statements about women. A week later the subjects were tested to see how many statements could be recalled. The women revealed a tendency to remember more of the favorable statements, the men to recall the unfavorable ones. Levine and Murphy[29] studied the memories of pro-Soviet and anti-Soviet subjects for pro-Soviet and anti-Soviet reading materials. They concluded that the forgetting or retention of these materials is affected by the individual's attitude toward communism. Wood[30] asked subjects with favorable and unfavorable attitudes toward Negroes to read an article describing differences between Negroes and whites. The subjects were then asked to write abstracts of the article. They omitted and distorted items in accordance with their attitudes. When similarly biased subjects read and rewrote these abstracts, the omissions and distortions were even greater than in the first abstracting. Watson and Hartmann,[31] in a study of atheistic persons, concluded that the subjects' memories of materials dealing with religious matters were shaped by their beliefs. Edwards[32] concluded that his subjects' political attitudes were linked with their varying degrees of recognition of items covered in a previously presented speech on the New Deal.

Probably most persons could point to instances in their own lives where certain vivid memories were linked with interest and attitude. The studies cited above demonstrate that even run-of-the-mill memories are dependent upon perspective and interest.

MEMORY IN THE LOWER ANIMALS

Acts of remembering are linked with social backgrounds and are intimately related to man's utilization of symbols. Animals of course do remember, but theirs is a relatively primitive level of performance. The deficiencies of their memory, from the human point of view, may be pointed up by a series of experiments.

Suppose that a banana is buried in the ground before the eyes of a chimpanzee, and then the animal is led away to bed. The next morning when he is taken back to the yard he will remember the location of the buried banana. Now let us contrast this successful performance with a less successful one. A chimpanzee is taught to expect food in a box standing to the left of a similar box when a red light is glowing. When a green light is glowing, the food is in the other box. If the red light is turned on and then switched off and the chimpanzee is prevented from going to the box at once, he loses his ability to select the correct one (the one with the food). A delay of very short duration, perhaps a minute or two, has this effect.

We can find a ready explanation for his failure if we remember that the ape responds to natural signs but not to symbols. The ape can remember—we sometimes say "recognize"—the hiding place of the banana because he is in the presence of signs that stand for its burial; that is, he can see the spot in the yard where it was buried. Similarly, the ape can associate the box on the left with a glowing red light. But when the sign is absent, as when the light goes out, he cannot remember. If he could keep repeating to himself "red light, left box, red light, left box," then he could remember correctly in the absence of the light.

Human beings, of course, do this constantly, as anyone who takes the trouble to analyze the experience of following directions will soon realize. Humans do not even have to keep repeating the symbols unless the directions are fairly complicated. They would not, in a delayed-response experiment, have to keep saying to themselves "red light, left box." Comparative psychologists have discovered that the various animal species can remember for varying lengths of time in the absence of signs, but no animal except man can remember for more than a few minutes. Men, of course, can remember for years provided that they have the requisite symbols and are motivated to remember. This is explained by man's possession and use of language forms.

We have already seen, in our earlier discussion of levels of behavior, that even the lowest organisms have memories of a sort. The one-celled animal that becomes conditioned to light or warmth, the bee that finds its way back to the hive, the dog that responds correctly to his master's commands and signals—all these animals are furnishing examples of the operation of "memory." Another memory process of a relatively low order that is found in both man and lower animals is the "kinesthetic," or body, memory involved in remembering a bodily skill long after one has ceased to practice it. It would be as foolish to deny memory to the lower animals as it would be to deny that human memory is immensely superior.

HUMAN REMEMBERING AS A SYMBOLIC PROCESS

Remembering Depends upon Categorization · Man without language would be, like the animals, tied down to concrete situations. He would have no conceptions either of history or of a personal past. Upon reflection, it becomes clear that much of our remembering revolves around memorable events, holidays, and dates. We cast back "in our memories" to last summer; to last Friday; to the week-end before last; to the day we entered college; to our sixteenth birthday. We often recollect by means of such notational devices. If one is asked where he spent last Thanksgiving and what he did, the task of recalling is made relatively easy. If, on the other hand, one is asked what he did last November 6th (unless that is some memorable date, such as a birthday), recollection is likely to be either weak or totally absent.

To hear a melody and recognize vaguely that one has heard it somewhere does not perhaps clearly depend upon language; but to say to oneself, "How does the first movement of Beethoven's

Fifth Symphony go?" and then by an act of "concentration" call up themes from that movement—such remembering is clearly dependent upon a linguistic framework. Music is so closely linked with language that attention could not be kept focused upon that symphony and that movement if the linguistic framework were missing. Similarly, if one asks, "What is the color of my house back home?" it is by virtue of language that one can call up that house and name its color. Without language categories such an act of remembrance would be impossible. Again: we are asked to meet a friend for lunch at twelve o'clock in such and such a restaurant, and at a quarter to twelve we remember our engagement. Could we have remembered without the aid of the appropriate names— time categories—which we verbalize to ourselves, perhaps repeatedly, or which we actually write down on a memo pad? Moreover, how would we remember the past or keep appointments in the future without our systems of time notation?

The psychology of legal testimony supplies an interesting instance of the organization of memory around verbal plans or labels. People may erroneously remember details as having happened, provided that the details fit into a frame of reference. An instance of this is provided by early litigations over patents on the telephone:

> Certain people in a little town . . . gave at a second court-hearing testimony totally different from that which they had given several years earlier at the first hearing. The first testimony was vague and uncertain. In the interval between the two hearings the major subject of discussion in the town had been the apparatus in question. At the second court hearing the people recounted as fully established facts incidents which had apparently been generated by their discussions.[33]

Studies of distortion in the transmission of rumors show the same sort of inaccurate remembering. As it is passed from one person to another, the content of the rumor undergoes alteration, according to how the transmitting person hears and remembers the rumor —both activities depending upon the person's frame of reference.[34]

Not only does society provide the linguistic and other devices used by the individual in registering an event, recalling, identifying, and placing it, but human memory has other important social dimensions as well. French psychologists and sociologists, particularly, have elaborated the idea that the things people remember form interlaced and mutually reinforcing systems organized around group situations. Thus, Halbwachs[35] noted that the student's memory of a given professor, and the course he took from him, is different from the professor's recollection of the student and the course. The student's memory is generally much more precise, he deduces, because his experiences are part of a unique group situation which he shared with others. The professor, on the other hand, experiences each class and the individuals in it primarily as one of a series of similar situations occurring in his professional activity. He has met successive classes in the same room, or in very similar rooms; class follows class, and, as the professor has no special group framework for each of them, he retains only the haziest ideas of what he did, what happened, who was present in any of the classes, or in which buildings and rooms they were held.

Most of our memories, Halbwachs observes, are organized in this way within a framework provided by the group to which we now belong and those to which we have belonged. When we are within a given group, as, for example, our families, over a period of time, the members talk about past experiences and keep them fresh in our minds. Familiar faces and old haunts become linked with memories of past events. When we leave the group for a long time or permanently, the memories fade along with the faces, places, and names until only a bare skeleton or almost nothing remains. If, however, we return after many years to the old group and the old environment, the memories are revived, although they are not the same. As we remember and reconstruct the past, according to Halbwachs, we project ourselves into a group framework and use it to revive and organize past experiences. This argument is used to explain the tendency for memories of experiences in temporary groups—for example, the kind formed on board an ocean liner—to shrink and disappear very quickly. This is especially true if no lasting relationships are established and if one does not again meet any of the persons involved. Human memory, Halbwachs contends, is therefore "collective," or social, in nature. We are able to think of memory as individual only because we overlook or take for granted its group connections.

Some Experimental Evidence · These examples of remembering are, perhaps, quite common-sense ones, although they represent valid evidence. Experimental investigations with both children and adults direct our attention to the linguistic foundation that underlies complicated acts of remembering as well. Bartlett, whose work we have already mentioned, has concluded that remembering is based upon initial acts or perceiving which, in turn, are notably affected by linguistic representations. He observes that memory is dependent upon "schemata," that is, upon a system of labeling.[36] Munn, in a survey of research done upon memory in children,[37] notes that the superiority of two-year-olds over one-year-olds depends at least in part upon linguistic factors: the memory of the older children is aided by their possession of names for colors and knowledge of letters, figures, and words.

A Soviet psychologist, Luria, after conducting a series of ingenious experiments upon children, also states that language is essential for the more complex, adult forms of remembering. His investigations are so conclusive as to warrant including a digest of them here:

A child who can hardly memorize five or six words of the series is asked to commit them to memory, with the aid of the pictures laid out on the table. Not one of the pictures actually reproduces the word in question, and the task can be performed only if the child connects in one structure the word with one of the pictures. Such mastering of association can be acquired, but by no means by all the children. Older children can learn to reproduce by this method, 25-30 words after one reading, while their natural memory could fix 5-6 at most. Moreover, the connecting links were established with extraordinary subtlety. Thus in order to remember the word "spade" the child chose a picture of chickens picking up grain "because they picked it just as the spade digs the earth"; for the word "theater" the child chose the picture of a crab on the seashore "because the crab looks at the pebbles in the sea, and they are just as pretty as a theater."

In the process of play a child was given orally a series of ten figures to memorize; and asked to repeat them in the given order. The child found usually that he could not memorize the series. Then we gave him some material—paper, strings, chips, playing-blocks, pins, hailshot—and asked him to use it for memorizing these ten figures. It was a question of his somehow utilizing the material to invent some system of writing.

The younger and backward children were unable to invent, to memorize with the aid of the material. The functional application of the material is not clear to them; it has nothing to do with the task given. On the other hand, pre-school children, who have attained a higher stage of development, utilize the material for memorizing. The child guesses the possibility of utilizing, say, paper for the purpose and begins to use a method invented by himself. This is usually some system of quantitative marks: a child makes marks on the paper corresponding in number to the figure stated (six times for the figure 6, twice for 2), or else tears off the corresponding number of bits or makes a corresponding number of knots on a piece of string. When the child thus passes from simple, natural memory to artificial means of memorizing, the task of memorizing 10 or even 15 figures became easy. Simple natural memory was replaced by a system of signs and their subsequent reading, and the maximum of work was usually shifted from recollection to a recognition of series.

The invention does not take place at once. At first he guesses he must make marks, but does not guess how to make them distinguishable. Thus he tears off bits of paper and puts them in a heap; or he makes knots but leaves no intervals between them to denote figures. Obviously when he tries to reproduce them he finds himself helpless. Then, after some fruitless efforts, he usually guesses that his notes must assume a different shape; he differentiates his marks in little heaps, in groups.

Set the same problem to a schoolboy of the first or second year of study and you witness something very different. A child who has mastered the writing of letters and figures will not attempt to invent a new system of signs, but will apply the ready-made system of writing. The symbols represented will have the common feature of integral symbols, and not be a mere quantitative inscription representing the number. Thus a pre-school child inscribes by laying aside in heaps the corresponding number of hailshot; a schoolboy, on the other hand, tries to lay them in the shape of a figure. It is extraordinary how the older children always represent figures in that way, in spite of difficulties. Given material such as strings, chips, pins, out of which they attempt to form figures although it would have been easier to adopt the system of knots and scoring-stick marks; it is interesting to note that if your forbid them to represent figures you will make them quite helpless to cope with the task. We have hardly ever seen among children of these school groups any instances of reversion to the method of quantitative counting so characteristic of pre-school children.[38]

Amnesia for Childhood Memories · Why is it that there is such a dearth of recollections of childhood experiences, and a virtually total amnesia for the period of infancy? Some writers have hypothesized that repression of memories takes place. This is an unsatisfactory explanation, since it neither accounts for the forgetting of pleasant happenings nor for the complete absence of memory of the earliest experiences of a fully sentient infant.

Schachtel[39] has argued that the infant or young child lives in a world of feeling and fantasy in which his experiences are such that they quite literally cannot be formulated in words. Hence they cannot be recollected, for the infant lacks symbolic means to retain them and the adult does not have the proper mentality to recapture them later. Schachtel lays great stress upon the stereotyped, abstract, and schematic character of adult language which transforms the growing child in socializing him and renders him in a sense unfit to be a child even in remembrance. We need not adopt Schachtel's nostalgic attitude toward the richness and vitality of childhood imagery, but his emphasis upon the crucial import of symbolic structures for remembrance is important. The infant, lacking these symbolic structures, has nothing to ring his memories upon in order to recapture them later.

A subsidiary but also important point is that the transformations of the child during the course of his socialization makes recollection difficult or impossible. The Luria experiment has suggested this same conclusion. In a study of the development of children's concepts of money, one of the authors[40] found that it was unusual for the children to recollect any of the concepts held at earlier ages. In fact, they rejected notions once firmly believed with no awareness that they had once accepted them—rejected them with ridicule, laughter, and incredulity. This is precisely what one would expect if it is assumed that development implies genuine transformation of behavioral organization. Piaget in his studies of children also has observed that when children are asked where they learned their most recent conceptions, they often remark, "I have always known that."

Halbwachs[41] has suggested that although certain childhood memories can be recaptured, at least in a gross sense, certain others cannot because perspectives have changed. For example, one can often remember the name of a book read as a child, conjuring up the look of the print and some of the imagery of the pictures and possibly even recapturing some of the overtones of the feeling experienced while reading the book. (However, it takes a rare person, like Marcel Proust, the novelist, to recapture feeling.) But, as Halbwachs shrewdly notes, it is literally impossible to divest oneself of the experiences of the intervening years so as to feel exactly as one did when reading the book as a child. He remarks that the effort to recapture feelings poses the same problem as the effort to recapture the spirit of preceding periods in history. We may add that even a Proust, dredging up minute and poignant details of his childhood, gives only the illusion of an accurate recollection. Recollection is active, not passive. Proust's *Remembrance of Things Past* is an artistic and artful reconstruction, a creative act, not the record set down by a passive watcher as his memories file by like a parade. The adult, moving along through the life cycle to new perspectives and abandoning old ones, can be expected to find it difficult to recapture any but the grossest or most static, if poignant, moments of his past.

Emotional Behavior and Social Groups

The nature of emotion has been a controversial question for centuries, and theories concerning it are legion. Students of emotion

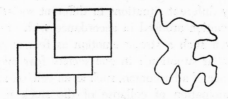

The left-hand figure is easier to remember. Why?

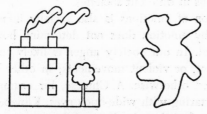

Look at each of these two figures for ten seconds. It is easier to remember the left-hand one, which is much more complicated. Why?

have written about it in terms ranging from the physiological to the cultural. Most of the efforts of psychologists have been concerned with the physiology of emotion: for example, attempts have been made to determine what muscular and glandular patterns of response accompany specific emotions, whether the sources of emotional awareness are in bodily movement or attitude, and what part of the brain is involved in emotional behavior.

Like many other aspects of human behavior, our emotions and feelings are profoundly affected by the fact that we live in complex societies. To the student of human behavior who seeks to take into account the types of feelings and emotions that are found in various societies, the situations which call them forth, and the many-sided conventionalized ways in which they are expressed, it appears that they are to an amazing extent regulated, prescribed, and even defined by groups.

What arouses a given emotion is determined by social situations rather than by physiological processes. Thus, embarrassment is called forth by different situations in different societies. Similarly, shame is an emotion aroused in accordance with prevailing social definitions. Even such a strong emotion as fear is not invariably kindled by similar situations: in one society fear may be aroused by the occurrence of a bad omen, such as an eclipse, and in another society by anticipation of collapse of the stock market. As we shall see below, the emotions connected with even such commonly assumed biological drives as sex and hunger are also aroused by different situations in different societies.

The expression of emotions is also socially influenced, for the physiology of any emotion does not determine how the emotion will be expressed. In our society anger is likely to be shown by sudden, impatient, or violent movements; in other societies anger may be expressed otherwise. A Chinese, for example is likely to show anger by staring with wide-open eyes. Klineberg[42] has noted that "the Chinese find that the faces of Europeans seem constantly to be expressing anger or irritation; this is probably due to the fact that the normally larger and rounder eyes of the Europeans resemble the Chinese eyes in anger."

We do not have to go so far afield as China to see how a society sets patterns for the expression of emotion. In the United States, one may express love in one way in the bedroom and in another way in public. Anger is manifested differently in private and in the presence of company. Expressions of hate are not supposed to be shown before children but may be displayed when children are not present.

Recent anthropological research has pointed to another and more subtle aspect of emotional patterning. Each society provides differential conditions of life for its members, so that certain emotions are aroused more frequently and intensely in one society than in another. The conditions of life among the Dobuans, a Pacific island people, are such that emotions of hostility, suspicion, and envy are frequently and intensely present. The keen competition that characterizes American life is a stimulus to frequent and deep feelings of envy and resentment in the lives of many Americans and of feelings of great elation in others. Zuñi Indians, on the other hand, rarely experience the more passionate and sweeping emotions of romantic love, hostility, ecstasy, or suspicion.[43]

Indeed, we may question whether certain emotions are not peculiar to certain societies and conversely whether certain ones are not altogether absent in other societies. Many emotions are undoubtedly universal, but since the conditions of life vary so widely and the experiences of groups are so diverse, allowance must be made for variation from society to society. In societies in which there is not an elaborate organization of social classes, emotions that have to do with class mobility and the maintenance and change of status can scarcely exist. The very language of such societies lacks a vocabulary for indicating the experiences and the events around which these emotions occur. Americans cannot easily imagine how it would be to experience a medieval sense of religious awe; they cannot appreciate the abasement of self which a caste system implies, or feel the anticipation of the Brahmin as he looks forward to death and reincarnation.

THE LINGUISTIC NATURE OF HUMAN EMOTIONS

The arousal and expression of emotion may be analyzed into three phases, in their order of occurrence:

1. a stimulus or situation which is defined or interpreted in certain ways;
2. an internal response to the defined situation, involving both physiological and symbolic processes;
3. an outward conventionalized expression (by means of words,

gestures, facial expressions, and the like), which serves to indicate the emotion to others.

A given external situation or act does not call forth an emotion until it has been interpreted in a certain way. The emotion is a response not to a raw stimulus as such but to a defined, classified, and interpreted stimulus, to signs with meanings which vary according to situation, as shown in the accompanying tabulation. The physiological aspects of emotional response, such as a rise in blood pressure, a changed heartbeat, and increase activity of the ductless glands, are not learned forms of behavior, but the symbolic processes involved in emotion are learned. The third phase of emotional behavior has sometimes been called the "mimicry" of emotion because persons may voluntarily utilize the conventional means of emotional expression without actually experiencing the genuine emotion. The actor does this constantly, of course, but the same sort of mimicry is commonly used in ordinary life as people strive to conform to the polite usages of social intercourse.

Act	Situation	Definition	Resulting Emotion in the Victim
Slap in the face	Two quarreling people	Insult	Fury and resentment
Slap in the face	In a play	Play-acting	None or simulated
Slap in the face	Father slaps child for lying	Punishment	Shame, etc.
Slap in the face	Twenty-month-old child slaps father	Good spirits	Amusement

The actual learning of emotional behavior, to a considerable extent, reverses the chronology of the arousal and expression of emotion given above. The child is at first encouraged to imitate the outward manifestations of adult emotions, as, for example, at a funeral, even though he may not grasp the significance of the situation at all. Only as the child acquires a greater experience and a better understanding of the significance of death will he be able actually to feel the expected emotions and to conform inwardly as well as outwardly.

An adult who moves into an entirely new social group finds that the modes of emotional expression of the group are at first strange to him. The pressure to conform causes him to adopt the external forms of behavior very quickly, even though at first he is merely play-acting. As he adopts the group's perspectives and begins to see the world as the people around him see it, his play-acting ceases to be play-acting and becomes instead a genuine expression of experienced emotions.

We have been speaking of phase 1 as if the stimulus which aroused the emotional response always comes from outside the organism. Actually, in humans, the stimulus may lie within the symbolic processes. This can be seen plainly enough if one considers the arousal of emotion through daydreaming. A soldier may daydream of going overseas and become fearful at the "thought" of it. This is an event which has not yet taken place. Fantasy may also revolve about past events. A person while fantasying may recall a past insult and undergo emotions similar to those which were aroused by the actual insult; or he may reinterpret the event, perhaps laughing now that he realizes no insult had been really intended. Whether in daydreaming forward or backward in time, the stimulus to emotional arousal is not externally present.

The human being is aware of his own emotional responses, naming, evaluating, and interpreting them in accordance with definitions provided by the groups to which he belongs. Persons not only experience anger but they label their feelings as such; and they are able to tell other people about them. Because of this capacity, human beings have the power of controlling and inhibiting their own feelings to some degree. Thus a devoutly religious person who recognizes that he is becoming angry may check this response and seek a new interpretation of the situation which will allow him to respond, for example, by feeling sorry for the person who has insulted him. An almost uncontrollable impulse to laugh in church at a minister's gesture may be stifled by a quick redefinition—taking the form perhaps of "this is church, laughing would be awful," or of acute fear of embarrassment or shame.

LEARNING EMOTIONS

From the preceding discussion it should be clear that there is no "purely emotional" behavior, but that emotion is a part or a feature of behavior. Because "emotion" is a noun, and because we think of an emotion as finding overt expression, we are inclined to assign causal status to it. When we see someone acting in an angry way, we say that he does so *because* he is angry. This is a figure of speech, not an explanation. What we are actually doing is describing his actions. If we happen also to mention the situation which precipitated the action we are giving a common-sense causal explanation.

Because emotional experiences are conceptual in nature, reflect the individual's background, and are relative to the group's definition of the situation, it would be very strange if physiologists could find a one-to-one correspondence between a given emotion and the characteristic glandular-muscular patterns that accompany it.

> In spite of extensive research it has not been possible to show that each emotion is distinguished by a particular pattern of responses of glands and smooth muscles. Although there are a few characteristic patterns . . . the differences between emotions are often not great and do not follow the usual distinctions. Nor are such responses diagnostic of emotion in general, since they also occur under other circumstances—, for example, after heavy exercise or in a chill wind. . . . In the search for what is happening "in emotion" the scientist has found himself at a peculiar disadvantage. Where the layman identifies and classes emotions not only with ease but with considerable consistency, the scientist in focusing upon responses of glands and smooth muscles and upon excessive behavior has not been sure that he could tell the difference between even such relatively gross emotions as anger and fear. Some means of identification available to the layman appears to have been overlooked.[44]

Children are not born with complex emotions. Various investigators have noted that the infant's emotions, shortly after birth, are generalized and diffuse. As the child grows older his emotions become more numerous and differentiated and are attached to more definite stimuli. In the beginning the emotional reactions are so general and undifferentiated that it is difficult for an adult to label them satisfactorily, beyond noting that the infant is expressing general emotional satisfaction or dissatisfaction or diffuse anxiety or acute fear. The child must learn how to express, in approved fashions, the emotions which he learns, and when and where to express or to inhibit their overt manifestations. In addition, he must acquire both the ability to read the external signs of emotion in his acquaintances and to anticipate how they are going to feel in certain kinds of situations. Finally, he must quite literally learn to react in emotionally complex ways.

As the child learns to remember and to project his activities into the future—as he learns to make the subtle distinction implicit in his language—he becomes capable of complex emotional responses. To illustrate, the learned emotional behavior of a ten-year-old child may be compared with the "natural" responses of an unsocialized child of the same age. This has been done, after a fashion, in a study of a deaf and blind girl by Goodenough.[45] The child, blind and deaf from birth, had been brought up by her parents with very little informal and no formal training. Almost no attempt had been made to teach her even the simplest matters of self-care. The child did not learn any language; and there is considerable doubt whether she even made consistent gestures when "asking" for food, drink, or the toilet. She therefore provides us with interesting data on "natural" rather than "learned" modes of expressing whatever primitive emotions she may have felt. Goodenough observed the child for an hour or more daily for several weeks.

> For the most part the child seems cheerful and docile. She laughs frequently and in response to appropriate stimuli. Her laughter is clear and musical, in no way distinguishable from that of a normal child. Her vocalizations are normally pitched and entirely free from the loud strident tones so often heard

among the deaf. In spite of her usual docility, however, she has at times shown unmistakable signs of anger, which once or twice have amounted to real "temper tantrums." The occasions for these displays have usually been some kind of thwarting of her activities, particularly attempts to overcome certain unpleasant personal habits such as pushing and manipulating her eyeballs, an activity which, it may be inferred from her behavior, yields tactile sensations of particular interest to her. Mild forms of resentment are shown by turning away her head, pouting the lips, or frowning; sometimes by crouching down into a little heap with head on knees, or by thrusting the thumb and index finger into the nostrils. More intense forms are shown by throwing back the head and shaking it from side to side, during which the lips are retracted, exposing the teeth. . . . This is accompanied by whimpering or whining noises, rising at intervals to short high-pitched staccato yelps. In her most violent outbursts the entire body is thrown back and forth; the feet are twisted around each other or beat violently upon the floor; the vocalizations are intensified and as a rule become shriller in pitch; and the head and chest are beaten with sharp flail-like movements of the arms. These blows are usually struck with the open hand, but at times the clenched fist is used. . . . She dances, not in the simple hop, skip, and jump style of normal children but in an elaborate pattern of bows and whirls, bendings and posturings in which the head, arms, and entire body participate. . . . The dance is clearly an expression of pleasure. It is usually accompanied by laughter. . . . It may occur spontaneously when she is in good spirits . . . or it may sometimes be stimulated by giving her a bit of jelly or some other simple treat.[46]

This description serves to bring home the differences between learned and relatively unlearned modes of emotional response. By comparison with the normal ten-year-old child, the responses of this deaf and blind girl are crude and undifferentiated, her gestures bizarre and unsocialized.

HUMAN AND SUBHUMAN EMOTIONS

The emotional responses of animals differ from those of humans in several important ways. Most animals live in groups composed solely of individuals who can see each other. Humans participate in groups as far flung spatially as nations, cities, nationalities, political parties, scientific associations. Around such groups allegiance, loyalty, patriotism, and civic pride develop. It is difficult to imagine how animals could feel patriotism toward something as abstract as "nation," or how they could develop feelings of ethnocentrism. Consider such complex sentiments as those held by many white Americans toward the Negro, or by a premedical student toward his future profession. The complexity of emotional development which characterizes human beings could scarcely exist without such diverse symbols as medicine, "nigger," the British Empire, "Old Glory," sacrament, and so on.

There is another crucial difference between animals and humans: animals are tied down in time to the immediate present, whereas humans can range forward and backward in time. Could many characteristic human emotions exist without the ability to remember? Nostalgia, for example, obviously is dependent on memory of a place, a person, or a period of one's life. Long-suppressed hate could scarcely exist unless a person could turn over "in his mind" past incidents, insults, and injuries.

In animal behavior, linguistic analyses of situation and self are absent, and the modes of expression and the situations which call for emotional behavior are determined by heredity or simple conditioning, not by social conventions or customs. Moreover, the animal cannot verbalize with respect to its own behavior or formulate conceptions of self or of things removed from its sensory world. Consequently, no animal other than man can feel patriotic, reverent, devout, morbid, or embarrassed, for these feelings presuppose, respectively, conceptions—linguistic symbols—of fatherland, divinity, ethics, death, and self. But, one may ask, "Doesn't a dog feel and express such an emotion as anger?" The difference between human anger and canine anger may be expressed by saying that angry dogs do not know they are angry, whereas angry humans are not only angry but know it and can verbalize concerning it, using not only the word "anger" but dozens of other language symbols to indicate the many subtle and intricate ways in which human beings can feel angry.

The Social Character of Human Goals

As befits his position at the top of the evolutionary ladder, man has an almost limitless range of exceedingly complex aims, goals, aspirations, and ambitions. The goal behavior of human beings is conditioned by man's extraordinary ability to project himself into the future. In specific terms, the setting up of goals is an imaginative or symbolic process in which the individual represents to himself a possible future state of affairs which he finds desirable. He then organizes his present behavior in ways which he believes will produce the desired situation. In other words, he selects "means" to attain "ends." The ends or goals of behavior point to the future, but they exist and function in the present.

If, then, human beings characteristically formulate their goals verbally, this implies, in terms of our preceding discussion, that goals are dependent upon self-awareness; that they involve a broad space-time perspective; and that they are conceptualized and socialized.

It is particularly striking, from the point of view of social psychology, that the new-born human infant has few or none of these characteristic human goals. The baby, like any other infant, is limited at birth to purely physiological ends. If we call these ends "goals," we must clearly specify that such goals are linked with the immediate situation, and that they have to do directly with touch, sight, smell, and hearing. It is only gradually that infants come into possession of the human heritage of aims and find their behavior structured around future goals and planned ambitions. The work of sociologists and anthropologists, especially, has made it clear that social influences play a crucial part in determining goals for which men strive.

The nature of the goals one chooses is determined at least in part by the particular subgroups of society in which one participates. Such a complex civilization as ours is composed of many subgroups: social-class, religious, regional, occupational, and age groups, voluntary associations, and so on. Individuals of the same ethnic stock may be members of different social classes; consequently they may pursue widely different goals associated with this class membership. Women living in the same town but participating in different subgroups may aspire variously to become housewives or businesswomen or teachers or mistresses.

Summary

The distinctive qualities of human mental activity are the consequences of man's incorporation and use of language symbols. All mental activity, whether of lower animals or human beings, is sign behavior. Goal behavior involves response to signs representing the future; memory is response to signs representing the past; and perception is response to signs representing the present environment. Skill in interpretation of and response to signs on any level is intelligence. Reason involves the interpretation and use of symbols and is the equivalent of conceptual thought. It is a peculiarly human activity.

Such complex mental functions as perceiving, remembering, and emoting are examples of complex human sign behavior. Individual human beings take over language symbols as part of their repertoire of behavior. This incorporation of group-created conventional signs creates new complexities of response and makes human mental functions something different from, and superior to, those of the lower animals. Mental processes in the lower animals parallel the higher functions in man, but are of a lower order of complexity, being based on simpler forms of sign behavior. Perception, memory, and emotional and goal behavior in the lower animals are more closely tied to biological conditions than they are in man. Unlike the lower animals, human beings are able to assimiliate socially developed symbolic systems which transform their psychic life, add new dimensions to their behavior, and make it possible for them to profit from the experience of past generations in ways unparalleled in the rest of the animal world.

SUGGESTIONS FOR DISCUSSION AND SPECIAL REPORTS

1. Contrast Schachtel's and Freud's views on the loss of childhood memories.

2. Read Ruth Benedict's *Patterns of Culture* and report on the cultural patterning of emotions.

3. Make a study of selective perception in the artistic judgments of art or music critics.

4. Is there "unconscious perception"?

5. How does Communist ideology influence social perceptions?

6. What would happen if people's perceptions were wholly determined by their desires?

7. What does the following statement imply?—"A way of seeing is also a way of not seeing" (K. Burke).

8. Report on the selective perception of some persons to whom you show a series of advertisements or pictures.

NOTES

[1] F. C. Bartlett, *Remembering*, Cambridge (England): Cambridge University Press, 1932, p. 31.

[2] D. O. Hebb, *The Organization of Behavior*, Wiley, 1949, pp. 31-32.

[3] M. Senden, quoted in Hebb, *op. cit.*, p. 32.

[4] A. Riesen, "The Development of Visual Perception in Man and Chimpanzees," *Science*, 106 (1947): 107-108.

[5] J. J. Gibson, "Social Perceptions and Perceptual Learning," in M. Sherif and M. O. Wilson (eds.), *Group Relations at the Crossroads*, Harper, 1953, p. 134.

[6] J. Dewey, *Experience and Nature*, Chicago: Open Court Publishing Co., 1925.

[7] W. Ittelson and H. Cantril, *Perception: A Transactional Approach*, Garden City, N. Y.: Doubleday, 1954, p. 27.

[8] H. S. Sullivan, *The Interpersonal Theory of Psychiatry*, Norton, 1953, p. 374.

[9] C. Sandburg, "Elephants Are Different to Different People," in L. Untermeyer (ed.), *A Critical*

Anthology: Modern American Poetry (1936 ed.), Harcourt, Brace, p. 249.

10 M. Mead, "The Primitive Child," in C. Murchison (ed.), *Handbook of Child Psychology*, Clark University Press, 1933, p. 368.

11 M. Zillig, "Einstellung und Aussage," *Zeitschr. f. Psych.*, 106 (1928): 58-106. See also Klineberg, *Social Psychology*, pp. 206-207.

12 H. Roberts, "Melodic Composition and Scale Foundations in Primitive Music," *Am. Anthro.*, 34(1932): 95.

13 Gibson in Sherif and Wilson, *op. cit.*, p. 136.

14 L. Carmichael, H. P. Hogan, and A. A. Walter, "An Experimental Study of the Effect of Language on the Reproduction of Visually Perceived Form," *J. Ex. Psych.*, 15(1932): 73-86.

15 Bartlett, *op. cit.*, Chap. II. See also M. Sherif, *Psychology of Social Norms*, Harper, 1936.

16 G. Murphy, L. B. Murphy, and T. Newcomb, *Experimental Social Psychology*, Harper, 1937, p. 173.

17 Gibson, in Sherif and Wilson, *op. cit.*, pp. 129-130.

18 A. R. Luria, "The Problem of the Cultural Behavior of the Child," *J. of Gen. Psych.*, 35(1928): 497-498.

19 J. Bierens de Haan, *Animal Psychology for Biologists*, London: Hutchinson's University Library, 1929, p. 38.

20 *Ibid.*, esp. p. 40.

21 E. S. Russell, *The Behavior of Animals* (2d ed.), London: Arnold, 1938, pp. 182-183.

22 R. M. Yerkes, *Chimpanzees: A Laboratory Colony*, Yale University Press, 1943, p. 101.

23 *Ibid.*, pp. 104-106.

24 *Ibid.*, pp. 105-106.

25 J. Dewey, *Art as Experience*, New York: Minton, Balch, 1934, pp. 298-325.

26 Bartlett, *op. cit.*

27 Mark Twain, *Life on the Mississippi*, New York: Bantam Books, 1946, p. 100.

28 Zillig, *op. cit.* See also Klineberg, *Social Psychology* (rev. ed.), p. 219.

29 L. M. Levine and G. Murphy, "The Learning and Forgetting of Controversial Material," *J. Ab. and Soc. Psych.*, 138(1943): 507-517.

30 C. Wood, "An Analysis of Changes Occurring in Successive Stages of Abstracting," master's thesis, State University of Iowa, 1944.

31 W. S. Watson and G. W. Hartmann, "Rigidity of a Basic Attitudinal Frame," *J. Ab. and Soc. Psych.*, 34(1939): 314-351.

32 A. L. Edwards, "Political Frames of Reference as a Factor Influencing Recognition," *J. Ab. and Soc. Psych.*, 36(1941): 34-50.

33 C. H. Judd, *Educational Psychology*, Houghton Mifflin, 1939, p. 354.

34 G. Allport and L. Postman, "The Basic Psychology of Rumor," in T. Newcomb and E. L. Hartley (eds.), *Readings in Social Psychology*, Holt, 1947, pp. 547-558.

35 M. Halbwachs, *La Mémoire collective*, Paris: Presses Universitaires, 1950, esp. pp. 1-34.

[36] Bartlett, *op. cit.*

[37] N. Munn, "Learning in Children," in L. Carmichael (ed.), *Manual of Child Psychology*, Wiley, 1946, pp. 370-449.

[38] A. R. Luria, "The Problem of the Cultural Behavior of the Child," *J. Genet. Psych.*, 35(1928): 497-498.

[39] E. Schachtel, "On Memory and Childhood Amnesia," *Psychiatry*, 10(1947): 1-26.

[40] A. L. Strauss, "The Development and Transformation of Monetary Meanings in the Child," *Am. Soc. Rev.*, 17(1952): 275-286.

[41] M. Halbwachs, *Les Cadres sociaux de la mémoire*, Paris: Alcan, 1935, pp. 113 ff.

[42] O. Klineberg, *Social Psychology* (1940 ed.), Holt, p. 186.

[43] R. Benedict, *Patterns of Culture*, Houghton Mifflin, 1934, Chap. IV.

[44] B. F. Skinner, *Science and Human Behavior*, Macmillan, 1953, pp. 161-162.

[45] F. L. Goodenough, "Expression of the Emotions in a Deaf-Blind Child," *J. Ab. and Soc. Psych.*, 27(1933): 328-333.

[46] *Ibid.*, pp. 300-331.

SELECTED BIBLIOGRAPHY

Bartlett, F. C., *Remembering*, Cambridge (England): Cambridge University Press, 1932. The operation of social factors in remembering is demonstrated in this outstanding book.

Benedict, R., *Patterns of Culture*, Houghton Mifflin, 1934. An anthropologist compares in colorful language the dominant emotions and goals of the peoples of three very different primitive societies.

Blake, R. R., and G. V. Ramsey (eds.), *Perception: An Approach To Personality*, Ronald, 1951. A readable series of papers.

Blondel, C., *Introduction à la psychologie collective*, Paris: Colin, 1928. An excellent systematic treatment of the role of culture in perception, memory, and emotion.

Curti, M. W., *Child Psychology*, Longmans, Green, 1939. Chap. XI, "The Growth of Meanings," pp. 274-305. The character and limitations of children's perceptions are effectively described.

Dashiell, J. F., "Are There Any Native Emotions?" *Psych. Rev.*, 35(1928): 319-327. Indicates that human emotions are learned and that complex emotions cannot be differentiated on other than linguistic and behavioral grounds.

Gibson, J. J., in M. Sherif and O. Wilson (eds.), *Group Relations at the Crossroads*, Harper, 1953, "Social Perceptions and Perceptual Learning," pp. 120-138. An informative paper.

Halbwachs, M., *Les Cadres sociaux de la mémoire*, Paris: Alcan, 1925.

In this important book the social basis of memory is systematically analyzed by a famous French sociologist.

————, *La Mémoire collective,* Paris: Presses Universitaires, 1950.

Katz, D., *Animals and Men,* Longmans, Green, 1937. Chap. IV, "On the Problem of Perception in Animals," pp. 64-93. Investigations of animal perception are reviewed and summarized.

Klineberg, O., *Social Psychology* (rev. ed.), Holt, 1954. Chap. VII, "Emotional Behavior," and Chap. VIII, "Social Factors in Perception and Memory," pp. 170-226. A good textbook survey of social influences on these complex human activities.

Luria, A., "The Problem of the Cultural Behavior of the Child," *J. Genet. Psych.,* 35(1928): 493-504. Description of ingenious experimental investigations of children's memories and perceptions.

Mead, M., *Cooperation and Competition Among Primitive Peoples,* McGraw-Hill, 1937. The several papers which constitute this volume provide valuable comparative data on the goals of a number of different societies.

Russell, E. S., *The Behavior of Animals* (2d ed.), London: Arnold, 1938. Chap. X: "Perceptual Worlds as Functional," pp. 179-191. The differences between animal and human perception are interestingly portrayed by an English biologist.

Schachtel, E., "On Memory and Childhood Amnesia," *Psychiatry,* 10(1947): 1-26. A suggestive paper, interestingly written.

Sherif, M., *The Psychology of Social Norms,* Harper, 1936. A psychologist's report of laboratory experiments on social factors in perception, together with a more general discussion of these factors.

CHAPTER 5 · · ·

Social Isolation

and

Speech Pathology

IN PRECEDING CHAPTERS we have stressed the crucial importance of language for the organization of human behavior. Without language, we have said, we could not be the complex beings that we are. The utilization, interpretation, and creation of high-order signs (which *is* language behavior) distinguish man from the lower animals and give him his characteristically human qualities. The question then arises, what if man did not have language, what if he could not produce and respond to symbols? Of course there is no way of answering this question directly, for all societies, all groups, have always had systems of language. Even men born deaf or dumb become thoroughly human when they learn to communicate symbolically. No adult, once he has learned a language, can be deprived of his knowledge; hence there is no way, even if we wished to do so, to produce a languageless human being in order to see how he would act.

Although it is not possible to rear infants experimentally in a speechless environment or to destroy adults' language functions deliberately, there have been certain unplanned occurrences which have produced conditions very roughly equivalent to those that would be required for such experiments. In this chapter we shall review several of these "natural experiments" for the light they shed, however indirectly, on what happens when language functions are missing or impaired. We shall consider such exceptional individuals as the mentally retarded, children reared in almost complete isolation, feral men, the deaf and dumb, and sufferers from two types of mental impairment called respectively aphasia and schizophrenia. These are very different kinds of unusual human beings, but they all have one handicap in common that matters to us here: their language functioning is minimal or much impaired. Schizophrenic patients are marked by a regression in their use of normal modes of communication. Aphasics are characterized by the loss or disturbance of language responses. Some subnormal persons have never learned to speak, write, or otherwise communicate with facility. Feral children are those reputedly raised by animals in a languageless environment. Children reared by human beings in isolation from society are rare, but a remarkable case has been studied. Finally, the condition of the deaf and dumb is especially relevant to our inquiry. Each of these unfortunate natural occurrences illuminates a different aspect of the relation of language to behavior. Together they provide strong evidence of the importance of language by showing what happens to persons who lack language, who lose it, or whose language ability is seriously impaired.

Isolated and Feral Children

THE CASE OF ISABELLE

A significant case which illustrates the importance of language in the shaping of human behavior was reported upon by K. Davis.[1]

A girl named Isabelle, an illegitimate child, had lived virtually alone with her deaf-mute mother in a single room until she was about six and a half years old. Her behavior was described as being almost "that of a wild animal, manifesting much fear and hostility. In lieu of speech she made only a strange croaking sound. In many ways she acted like an infant." It was said by a psychologist who examined her that "she was apparently utterly unaware of relationships of any kind." At first it was hard to know whether she was able to hear or not, because she was so unresponsive to sound. When tests established that she was not deaf, specialists working with her were inclined to believe that she was feeble-minded and "wholly uneducable," and that it would be futile to attempt to teach her to speak. Her score on tests, even nonverbal ones, was exceedingly low. A Stanford-Binet test gave her a mental age of nineteen months, although her chronological age was more than four times greater, placing her in the low-grade feeble-minded category.

In spite of pessimism regarding the outcome, Isabelle was subjected to systematic training. It was a week before she made her first attempt at vocalization; but in two months she was beginning to put sentences together. Nine months later she could write well, retell a story after hearing it, and recognize words and sentences on the printed page. Seven months later she possessed a vocabulary of between 1,500 and 2,000 words. She had covered in two years the stages of learning that usually require six, and her I.Q. had tripled. When Davis reported on her, she was fourteen years old, had passed the sixth grade in public school, and behaved like a normal child.

It is instructive to note that this child was not actually reared in isolation but had the constant companionship of her deaf-mute mother, who took care of her and from whom she learned gestures. Since later events demonstrated that Isabelle was not mentally defective, it is probable that articulate speech was the crucial environmental factor that had been absent. It is virtually certain that if her mother had not been a deaf mute, Isabelle's retardation would have been relatively slight and would not have attracted any special attention.

The alternative explanation is that her retardation was due

merely to lack of stimulation of a nonverbal sort—that is, from lack of a multiplicity of "contacts"; however, this seems rather improbable. Observers sometimes have stressed the importance of the presence of other people in one's early social environment, without specifically recognizing that the presence of others is not in itself the crucial factor. The person who grows up experiencing extremely restricted contacts with other persons need not be greatly retarded if the few persons with whom he does have contact are intelligent and articulate. On the other hand, a deaf child, if he is given no special training, will be seriously retarded no matter how many adults surround him. Lack of opportunity to learn language behavior is the key to the stunted mental development of isolated and feral children.

FERAL CHILDREN

Numerous reports have been published, most of them of extremely dubious validity, concerning the discovery of "wolf" or "feral" men. One of the more convincing accounts is that of Singh and Zingg,[2] which describes the discovery and capture of two female children by a British missionary in India. The little girls, one about eighteen months, the other eight years old, had allegedly been living in a wolf den. The younger of the two died shortly after capture, but the older one, "Kamala," lived for nine more years in the school operated by the missionary.

When these children were found, they walked about on all fours, lapped up milk from a dish as a dog does, showed a preference for raw meat, and chose the company of dogs in preference to that of human beings, toward whom they showed only hostility. They were, in short, human only in a strictly biological sense.

Before Kamala died, however, she had acquired a considerable number of human accomplishments. She had learned to walk erect and to eat in a "civilized" manner. She preferred wearing a dress to running about nude, and she rejected raw in favor of cooked food. She had also learned to understand simple spoken sentences and to use a speaking vocabulary of about fifty words. In addition, she had come to enjoy playing with other children, and her previously impassive or immobile face had grown capable of emotional expression.

A great many scholars doubt the validity of even this report because its authenticity has not been checked by on-the-spot observation and because many of its details seem fanciful and improbable. We are inclined to believe that the account is genuine, although probably inaccurate in some details.

The Blind Deaf

Persons who are deaf, or deaf and blind, must have special training if they are to learn language. Invaluable in this connection is the report by the noted blind and deaf woman, Helen Keller, who began to learn language at the age of seven. The following is her own story, somewhat abridged, of her discovery of language:

> The most important day I remember in all my life is the one on which my teacher, Anne Mansfield Sullivan, came to me. I am filled with wonder when I consider the immeasurable contrast between the two lives which it connects. It was the third of March, 1887, three months before I was seven years old.
>
> The morning after my teacher came she led me into her room and gave me a doll. The little blind children at the Perkins Institution had sent it and Laura Bridgman had dressed it; but I did not know this until afterward. When I had played with it a little while, Miss Sullivan slowly spelled into my hand the word "d-o-l-l." I was at once interested in this finger play and tried to imitate it. When I finally succeeded in making the letters correctly I was flushed with childish pleasure and pride. Running downstairs to my mother I held up my hand and made the letters for doll. I did not know that I was spelling a word or even that words existed; I was simply making my fingers go in monkey-like imitation. In the days that followed I learned to spell in this uncomprehending way a great many words, among them *pin, hat, cup,* and a few verbs like *sit, stand,* and *walk.*

But my teacher had been with me several weeks before I understood that everything has a name.

One day, while I was playing with my new doll, Miss Sullivan put my big rag doll into my lap also, spelled "d-o-l-l" and tried to make me understand that "d-o-l-l" applied to both. Earlier in the day we had had a tussle over the words "m-u-g" and "w-a-t-e-r." Miss Sullivan had tried to impress it upon me that "m-u-g" is *mug* and that "w-a-t-e-r" is *water,* but I persisted in confounding the two. In despair she had dropped the subject for the time, only to renew it at the first opportunity. I became impatient with her repeated attempts and, seizing the new doll, I dashed it upon the floor. I was keenly delighted when I felt the fragments of the broken doll at my feet. Neither sorrow nor regret followed my passionate outburst. I had not loved the doll. In the still, dark world in which I lived there was no strong sentiment or tenderness. I felt my teacher sweep the fragments to one side of the hearth, and I had a sense of satisfaction that the cause of my discomfort was removed. She brought me my hat, and I knew I was going out into the warm sunshine. This thought, if a wordless sensation may be called a thought, made me hop and skip with pleasure.

We walked down the path to the well-house, attracted by the fragrance of the honeysuckle with which it was covered. Some one was drawing water and my teacher placed my hand under the spout. As the cool stream gushed over one hand she spelled into the other the word *water,* first slowly, then rapidly. I stood still, my whole attention fixed upon the motions of her fingers. Suddenly I felt a misty consciousness as of something forgotten—a thrill of returning thought; and somehow the mystery of language was revealed to me. I knew then that "w-a-t-e-r" meant the wonderful cool something that was flowing over my hand. That living word awakened my soul, gave it light, hope, joy, set it free! There were barriers still, it is true, but barriers that could in time be swept away.

I left the well-house eager to learn. Everything had a name, and each name gave birth to a new thought. As we returned to the house every object I touched seemed to quiver with life. That was because I saw everything with a strange, new sight that had come to me. On entering the door I remembered the doll I had broken. I felt my way to the hearth and picked up the pieces. I tried vainly to put them together. Then my eyes filled with tears; for I realized what I had done, and for the first time I felt repentance and sorrow.

I learned a great many new words that day. I do not remember what they all were; but I do know that *mother, father, sister, teacher,* were among them—words that were to make the world blossom for me, "like Aaron's rod, with flowers." It would have been difficult to find a happier child than I was as I lay in my crib at the close of that eventful day and lived over the joys it had brought me, and for the first time longed for a new day to come.[3]

It is extremely significant that Miss Keller describes the changes which language brought in her life as both an intellectual and emotional revolution. Not only did the acquisition of words give her an intellectual grasp of the world, but it also altered her attitudes toward things and people and toward herself. Indeed, her temperament appears to have been changed. Her memory of her first seven years was vague, and she even hesitates to apply the term "idea" or "thought" to her mental processes during that time. The transformation was, in short, not merely a superficial one attendant upon the acquisition of an additional motor skill; it was a fundamental and pervasive change which altered, and indeed revolutionized, her total personality.

It is interesting to note that a controversy developed over the question of whether Helen Keller had a right to, or could intelligently use, words of sight and sound. Since she was both deaf and blind, how could she talk of colors or sounds? What could such words as "mirror," "reflect," "see," "loud," "flash of light," and innumerable others possibly mean to her? What right did she have to talk about the "azure blue of the sky," the "green grass," the "deep blue pools of water," or the "sound of the human voice"? Influenced by the academic preconceptions of the time, some psychologists contended that she had no "right" to use such terms since they must be meaningless to her.

Helen Keller emphatically maintained that she had to use such words and expressions because there were no substitutes for them if she wished to communicate with her fellows. She maintained, moreover, that she understood these expressions. The idea of the mirror held no difficulties for her because she understood the figurative meaning of "reflect." Such an expression as "I see" was understood and used correctly as in "I see my error," or "I see the point"; and she was able, by means of this sort of analogy, to grasp the meaning of "I see with my eyes." She compared her situation with that of a stranger on an island where a language unknown to him is spoken. This stranger, she says, "must learn to see with their eyes, to hear with their ears, to think their thoughts, to follow their ideals."[4]

Helen Keller also pointed out that ordinary people constantly talk about things that they have never seen, sounds they have never heard, and feelings they have never felt. She might have called attention to the fact that color-blind persons speak of the green grass and the blue sky like the rest of us.

As between the theorist who asserts that words of color and sound can mean nothing to a deaf and blind person, and the deaf and blind person herself who insists that the words do have meaning for her and who uses them correctly, we feel compelled to accept the testimony of the latter. For this is simply another instance of the way in which not only the deaf and blind but all of us are forced to mold our thoughts, feelings, and speech according to the patterns imposed upon us by the societies in which we live. That the deaf and blind person may have conceptions of color—if not actually imagery of color—is no more surprising than that he should have other conceptions.

Such a case as that of Helen Keller shows clearly that the use of symbolism in human life does not depend on any specific sensory datum or exclusively on articulate language. Once a person grasps the principle of symbolic activity, he may use a wide variety of substitute signs or cues in the organization of his behavior. The system of signs which we express in the audible sounds constituting the spoken English language may be translated into written symbols, into finger language, into the system of dots and dashes of the Morse code, or into the intricate secret codes used in modern warfare. All of these external signs, when they are internalized in the thinking process, function in basically the same way as the spoken signs.

The Mentally Retarded

The feeble-minded are retarded in mental ability by reason of injury, disease, or constitutional deficiency. They are conventionally classified into various categories, and range from the vegetable-like idiot to the near-normal moron. In a later chapter we shall say more about these categories. Here we wish to stress the crippling effect on the higher mental processes produced by partial or complete isolation of a person from the life of language communities. Subnormal individuals of the highest types can carry on simple conversation, but on lower levels almost no linguistic communication takes place.

There are thus different levels of sign behavior among the mentally deficient. These differences are revealed in different degrees of socialization, learning, and ability, and in performance on intelligence tests. They are also revealed in different capacities to organize behavior abstractly. An interesting inquiry along these lines has been made by Werner.[5] He studied two groups of mentally retarded children, one group being more retarded than the other. The children were shown a screen in which there were four holes, and they were told that these holes were numbered 1,2,3,4. The investigator then pointed to the holes in a given order—for example, 1,3,2,4, or 4,2,1,3—and the children were asked to repeat the process. The more retarded children succeeded more often on this test than they did on another in which the holes were lighted up in various sequences and the children asked to indicate orally in what order they were lighted. The less retarded children did better on the second test than on the first. Werner explains these results on the grounds that perception in the lower group is more personal and concrete, and that it becomes more abstract and impersonal with increasing mental ability. The gist of Werner's argument is that there are qualitatively different modes of mental organization among the feeble-minded. Furthermore, Strauss and Werner[6] have shown differences of behavioral organization between those who are retarded because of injury to the brain and those whose deficiency is congenital in origin.

The retardation of the mentally deficient in the lowest categories is very much like that of those blind and deaf individuals who have not been specially trained. Neither can enter into the stream of symbols which characterizes the human community. In the mentally retarded a basic biological deficiency prevents the individual from acquiring and manipulating symbols; in the blind deaf, it only prevents him from learning unless he is specially taught.

Behavioral Disorders in Aphasia

We shall use the term "aphasia" to refer in a general way to the loss or disturbance of language responses. Aphasia is often, but not necessarily, brought about by cerebral injury. Aphasic conditions may also be produced under hypnosis or by traumatic experiences. The loss of function may assume various forms such as the inability to read, to write, to name familiar objects, and so on.

The English neurologist Henry Head distinguished four main types of aphasic disorder: verbal, nominal, syntactic, and semantic aphasia.[7] We shall not concern ourselves with such subtypes of aphasic disorders other than to indicate that they exist and that the problem of classifying and naming them is a difficult one. Thus, the four types delineated by Head are not always easily distinguishable or sharply separated. The student should keep three points in mind. (1) The term "aphasia" refers to a variety of disorders which have not yet been satisfactorily classified or uniformly labeled by all writers. (2) Since these disorders vary in severity and in the type of linguistic activity affected, many aphasics are able to make significant statements about their own difficulties and experiences as aphasics. Of course, when the destruction of the language function is relatively complete, this is not possible. (3) The brain injuries which produce aphasia vary greatly in nature and severity, and it is sometimes very difficult and often a matter of controversy to distinguish disabilities which are the consequences of loss of some part of the language function from those which are not.

INTROSPECTIVE REPORTS OF APHASICS

Some of the most significant materials on aphasics are to be found in Head's work. The comments made by some of his patients are interesting and provide a certain amount of insight into their condition. One of them said:

> When I think of anything, everything seems to be rolling along. I can't hold it. . . . I can see what it is. I seem to see it myself, but I can't put it properly into words like you ought to. I can see what it is myself like. My mind won't stop at any one thing. They keep on rolling. Myself, I imagine when you're talking you're only thinking of what you're talking about. When I'm talking to anybody it seems a lot of things keep going by.[8]

Another patient, attempting to explain the difficulty he had in finding his way about London, said, "You see it's like this: with me it's all in bits. I have to jump like this," marking a thick line between two points with a pencil, "like a man who jumps from one thing to the next. I can see them but I can't express. Really it is that I haven't enough names."[9]

A number of interesting comments by these patients indicates that images and the flow of imagery are profoundly affected by the loss of language which occurs in aphasia. Head always asked his patients to draw pictures, both from a model and from memory. One of the patients who had drawn a jug from a model could not do it from memory. He commented as follows:

> I was trying to see the glass bottle; the picture seemed to evade me. I knew it was a bottle, and I could describe the shape of it, and I remember making a drawing of it, and I could describe the drawing. But when it came to seeing it as a picture, I was more or less nonplussed. I often seem to have got the picture, but it seemed to evade me.[10]

When this patient was questioned further it became clear that he experienced images, but that they appeared to be unstable and could not be controlled or evoked at will. He said, "The more I try to make them come the more difficult it is to get in touch with them, as one might say."[11]

Head performed the following test with one of his patients: He rolled bits of paper into wads and had a contest with the patient to see who could toss the improvised balls more accurately into a basket placed some distance away. The aphasic proved more adept than Head. Then a screen was moved in front of the basket so that the basket was not visible, and the contest was repeated. This time Head did far better than the patient; the patient seemed to be at a loss as to what to do. He explained his difficulties:

> When I could see the basket I could follow the line of vision; when it was covered I didn't feel so confident it was in the same place. . . . I'd seen the basket before you put the screen there; I knew you hadn't changed the position, but in some odd way I didn't feel perfectly confident in my own mind that it was in that position.[12]

We noted in an earlier chapter that it is through the internalized use of language that human beings are able to imagine objects and events which are removed in time and space. This point is neatly corroborated in the study of aphasia, for, as the preceding quotations show, the aphasic's flow of imagery is so disturbed that he is unable to visualize objects adequately when they are not immediately within his range of vision.

The inability of some aphasics to deal with objects which they cannot see or touch but must merely imagine is brought out in a curious manner by their inability to strike an imaginary match on an imaginary matchbox, to drive an imaginary nail with a non-existent hammer, or to demonstrate with an empty glass how one drinks water. These same patients are able to strike actual matches, to drive actual nails, and to drink water from a glass when they are thirsty. Goldstein[13] describes these and other inabilities of the aphasic as a regression from (1) an abstract or categorical attitude toward the world to (2) a more concrete attitude.

DISTURBANCES OF VOLUNTARY ACTIVITIES

It is clear from the foregoing reports that aphasics appear to have lost a certain flexibility of orientation so that they no longer seem to be at home in the world. We may put this in descriptive terms by saying that the aphasic is not a self-starter. Since he cannot talk effectively to others or to himself about things or persons that are not actually present, his whole inner life is impoverished and simplified, and his freedom of thought and action is largely lost. He is more or less at the mercy of external stimuli which play upon him.

It is clear from the study of these patients that language provides the instrument par excellence by means of which individuals define situations for themselves and by means of which they initiate and regulate their behavior and adapt it to the responses of others. When his language function is disturbed the aphasic loses his basic means of self-orientation. Because he has no adequate way of formulating his relationships to other persons or to objects, particularly when they are not physically present, the entire field of what we call voluntary behavior becomes simplified and, in terms of normal social requirements, inadequate. The aphasic is often able to function adequately or normally in simple concrete relations. But when he is required to act, as all persons constantly are, on the basis of long-range goals or abstract principles or of merely remembered events, objects, or persons, he tends to fail.

This limitation to the concrete present makes impossible much of the voluntary, or "creative," kind of human behavior—behavior which seems normal because human beings think about things, events, and people and adapt their behavior to these verbal formulations or interpretations. The aphasic is unable to make these verbal formulations; therefore his responses are piecemeal, unintegrated. He responds to each concrete situation as such; and when no immediate demand is made upon him, or when excessive demands are made, he tends to lapse into inactivity or anxiety, realizing that there is something wrong with his inner life.

Goldstein has shown how drastically aphasia affected the intimate social relations of one of his patients. The patient was a husband and father, and prior to his affliction had been devoted to his family. During his stay at the hospital, however, he appeared to show neither concern nor interest in his absent family and became confused when any attempt was made to call his attention to them. A casual observer would have regarded him as callous and indifferent. Yet when he was sent to his home for brief visits he warmly displayed his former interest and devotion.

Goldstein concludes that this patient's "out of sight, out of mind" attitude toward his wife and family grew directly out of his inability to formulate his relationships to his family when it was physically absent. He could not imagine or conceive it adequately, and consequently he could not engage in internalized thinking about it. In short, when his wife and children were not visible to him he was unable to think of them, because he could not produce and manipulate the necessary verbal symbols.

FAILURES OF PROJECTION

In one of the most significant tests he administered to aphasics, Head required the patient, seated opposite and facing him, to imitate his movements. Head placed his left hand to his right ear, his right hand to his right eye, and so on. Then he repeated the tests while the patient observed and imitated these movements as they were reflected in a mirror.

The patients either had great difficulty with the first part of this test or they found it altogether impossible to imitate Head's movements, whereas they were generally able to imitate the movements correctly when they observed them in a mirror. The reason was not difficult to find. When the doctor and patient sat facing each other the patient could not imitate directly, but had to transpose directions (remembering that his left hand corresponded to the investigator's right hand, and so on). When Head's movements were reflected in the mirror, this act of transposition was unnecessary; all that was required was direct mechanical imitation.

In general terms, the significance of this simple but exceedingly effective test may be stated thus: it demonstrates that the person lacking language cannot project himself into the point of view of another person. The patient is unable to guide his actions by imagining himself to be in some other position than the one in which he actually is. We may say that he is enclosed within his own point of view; that his point of view is, to use Piaget's term, "egocentric." Piaget,[18] whom we shall discuss later, has shown that the child's view of the world is originally egocentric in this sense, and that he overcomes this limitation and preoccupation with his own point of view through expanded social interaction accompanied by a growing mastery of language.

In a fundamental sense, normal adult social interaction rests upon the ability of persons to anticipate and appreciate the actual and possible reactions of other people—in short, to assume the role of another person. The loss of this ability in aphasia, in varying degrees dependent upon the severity of the disorder, thus provides powerful experimental and clinical evidence to support the thesis that language is the basic social and socializing institution.

DIRECT AND SYMBOLIC REFERENCE

Head makes a distinction between what he calls "acts of direct reference" and those which require some sort of symbolic formulation between the initiation and the completion of the act. This distinction is roughly equivalent to Goldstein's distinction between the "concrete" and the "abstract" (categorical) attitudes. Acts of symbolic reference imply a complex adaptation involving the recognition of signs, logical symbols, or diagrams. Acts of direct reference are organized on a simpler level.

The aphasic generally functions adequately in acts of direct reference but has trouble with, or is unable to carry out, acts of symbolic reference. The following contrasts provide a few illustrations of the difference between the two classes of acts.

Acts of Direct Reference	*Acts of Symbolic Reference*
Imitating the movements of the investigator as reflected in a mirror.	Imitating the movements of the investigator seated opposite, facing him.

Acts of Direct Reference	*Acts of Symbolic Reference*
Shaving.	Gathering together in advance the necessary articles for shaving.
Selecting from a number of objects before him the duplicate of one placed in his hand out of sight.	Selecting from objects placed before him the duplicates of two or more objects placed in his hand out of sight.
Tossing a ball into a basket which he can see before him.	Tossing a ball into a basket concealed behind a screen.
Exact matching of colored skeins of yarn.	Sorting and arranging colored skeins of yarn in a systematic way.
Pointing to familiar objects in his room.	Drawing a ground plan of his room that shows the location of familiar objects.
Swearing.	Giving the name of the Deity upon command.
Recognizing familiar streets and buildings of a city.	Following directions within a familiar city.
Repeating, fairly correctly, the numbers up to ten and sometimes beyond that, provided he is given a start.	Carrying out arithmetical operations, particularly those involving numbers of several digits.
Piling up the number of nickels equal to a quarter in value.	Stating how many nickels are equivalent in value to a quarter or half-dollar.
Drawing from a model.	Drawing from memory.
Eating at a table.	Setting a table properly.
Finding the letter which follows a given letter of the alphabet by trial and error, when all of the letters are before him on blocks.	Finding the letter which follows another without resort to trial and error.
Using an object in the appropriate manner.	Naming and classifying an object.

Acts of Direct Reference	*Acts of Symbolic Reference*
Striking a billiard ball with the cue so that it collides with a second ball.	Playing a game of billiards.
Copying printed words.	Transcribing printed words into cursive handwriting.

Practically all the activities that are listed above are either completely beyond the reach of subhuman animals or can be taught to them only with great difficulty. The acts listed in the second

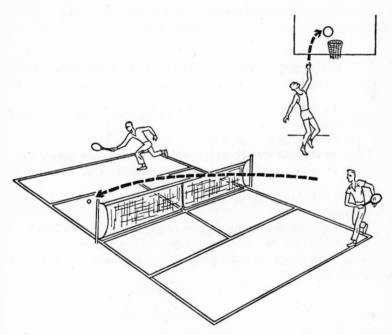

Of these two acts, one is an act of direct reference, the other is
an act of symbolic reference. Which is which, and why?

column are especially difficult for children to execute; they are generally learned later in life than the corresponding acts listed in the first column.

Not all the types of behavior listed in the second column are beyond the capacity of all aphasics. There is considerable variation according to the severity of the disorder and the type of aphasia involved. Moreover, aphasics often learn over a period of time to perform some of the more complex acts listed above, though usually with difficulty, by resorting to more primitive methods than the ones ordinarily used by normal persons. Thus a patient who cannot follow directions in a city may learn a route by sheer repetition and memorization of landmarks. Similarly, he may learn to make change properly by repetition and memorization rather than by calculation.

SUMMARY OF THE APHASIC'S DIFFICULTIES

Goldstein and Scheerer[14] have attempted to summarize in general terms the major difficulties which aphasics encounter. They enumerate the following:

1. To detach the ego from the outer world and from inner experiences.
2. To assume a mental set.
3. To account for acts to oneself and to verbalize the account.
4. To shift reflectively from one aspect of a situation to another.
5. To hold in mind simultaneously various aspects of a situation.
6. To grasp the essential point of a given whole; to break up the whole into its parts; to isolate and synthesize these parts.
7. To abstract common properties reflectively; to form hierarchic concepts.
8. To plan ahead ideationally; to assume an attitude toward the "merely possible" and to think or perform symbolically.

UNRELIABILITY OF INTROSPECTIVE EVIDENCE

The data on aphasia indicate that introspective evidence of the role of language must be interpreted with caution. Just as other functions drop out of consciousness when they become automatic, so language may fade out of the picture when many apparently purely motor and other types of skills of which it is the basis are fully established.

To illustrate our point, one may ask if the game of billiards requires or presupposes language ability. Offhand there would certainly seem to be no possible connection between the propulsion of billiard balls on a green table and the ability to talk. If we ask billiard players about the game, they tell us only that when they aim the cue they make a sort of geometrical calculation and have in their "mind's eye" a kind of geometrical image of the path which they wish the cue ball to take, striking first one and then the second of the two other balls involved. It would appear that language plays no part in this activity.

However, such introspective evidence is contradicted by the facts. The aphasic, even though he may have been skillful at billiards prior to the onset of aphasia, usually loses that skill along with his language ability. He reports that he cannot visualize the three balls simultaneously and that he becomes confused. He does not know at what angle to strike the second ball and may even hit it on the wrong side.

Similarly, one would suppose from introspective evidence that the ability to draw a picture of a cow, let us say, is totally unconnected with language and thus would be unaffected in aphasia. Again, this is not so, as we have reported above. It was Head's standard practice to ask his patients to draw pictures of familiar objects from memory. He requested an English army officer, for example, to sketch an elephant. This officer, prior to his illness, had spent many years in India and had once shown rather good amateur ability at drawing. Nevertheless the drawing he produced was exceptionally poor. It lacked some essential parts, such as the trunk and tusks; some of the parts were in wrong relation to one another; and in general, the whole picture was scarcely recognizable. Later, when the bullet wound which had caused the aphasia had healed and the patient had recovered much of his language ability, he drew upon request a detailed drawing of an elephant. The drawings are reproduced on p. 150.

These are but two of the many illustrations available; they point to the conclusion that language may play a vital role in an activity without the individual's introspective awareness of the fact.

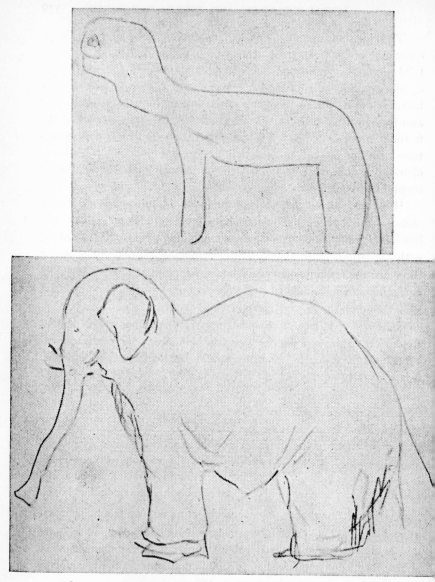

The upper drawing was made by a patient with severe aphasia. The same patient made the lower drawing after he had recovered most of his powers of speech. (From Henry Head, *Aphasia and Kindred Disorders of Speech*. Reproduced by permission of the Cambridge University Press.)

LANGUAGE IMPAIRMENT AND THOUGHT

We shall have a great deal to say about language and thought in subsequent chapters. At this point it suffices to emphasize that language and human thought are so closely interconnected that the latter cannot exist without the former. Thought without language is reduced to the level of the thinking, if we may call it such, that is characteristic of lower animals. The study of aphasia makes it clear that it is erroneous to conceive of thinking and language as two entirely distinct and separate processes. Thinking, speaking to others, and speaking to oneself are inextricably interrelated and interdependent processes. Head has compared the aphasic with a man in solitary confinement whose only contact with the outside world is a defective telephone. While this comparison is picturesque, it is incomplete, for when the aphasic tries to talk to himself, to formulate his own thoughts, he uses the same defective telephone.

The normal human being finds it difficult to imagine how it feels to be an aphasic. There seems to be little in our experience that enables us to project ourselves, as it were, into his position; to see and experience the world as he does and experience the impairment of thought that hinges upon his speech difficulties. We suggest that the student play a verbal game with himself in order to have a better notion of how it might feel to be an aphasic. Suppose one makes believe that he is in a foreign land whose language he knows only moderately well. Conversation with others is necessarily reduced to rather simple and concrete levels, for considerable facility in the language would be required in order to exchange views on complicated, abstract, or philosophical matters. It is easier to talk, with the aid of gestures, about concrete objects that are present, such as the immediate scene and the weather. If an attempt is made to speak of events long past or far in the future, or of objects out of sight, one's vocabulary proves insufficient. However, if one tries to carry on such a normal, slightly involved conversation, the effort is likely to prove exhausting. As an acquaintance of the authors once said:

I went to bed exhausted every night from trying to speak German; particularly when I was with a lot of German people who were engaging in a crossfire of conversation. It was simply exhausting—after a while you felt you wanted to sit down and recuperate. And you felt absolutely frustrated and bottled up; you wonder if you're ever going to think a complex thought again in your life. You can ask for beer and coffee and potatoes, but when you have to discuss a complex feeling or reaction or analyze a political situation, you're simply stalled. You struggle to speak, but you're reduced to the level of your vocabulary.

Suppose that in addition to conversing with others in the foreign language, one also had to converse with oneself (*i.e.*, to think), using only this same restricted vocabulary. How difficult it would be to carry on internalized conversation that had any semblance of complexity!

Apropos of our imaginary verbal game, it is interesting to read the conclusion of an investigator who studied the imperfect English speech of two French children.[15] He noted that certain types of "breakdown" in their speech resembled the defects of aphasics. Breakdowns consisted of tendencies (1) to simplify, (2) to revert to more simple speech reactions, and (3) to avoid speaking of abstract matters. Of course neither this nor our strenuous verbal game faithfully represents the situation of the aphasic; but both should give one an idea of the thinking impairments that arise from aphasic speech disorders.

The Social Isolation of the Schizophrene

SCHIZOPHRENIC THOUGHT

A large percentage of persons in almost any hospital for the mentally deranged is likely to be classified as schizophrenic. Although schizophrenia is a broad category, including a very heterogeneous group within its boundaries, psychiatrists are agreed that schizophrenes suffer impairment of thought processes and disturbances of social relationships.

Generally speaking, the schizophrene has lost contact with society. His speech is often unintelligible, partly because he invents words and partly because he gives many ordinary words a unique signification and combines them in unconventional ways. Since his use of language tends to be individualistic, he cannot carry on sustained normal communication with normal persons. "The schizophrenic becomes so used to his own language that he is no longer able to tell people what he thinks, even when he feels like doing so."[16]

Conversation with a schizophrene leaves one with the feeling that both he and you have been talking past each other. Only those persons who know him intimately or have deep insight into the nature of the disorder can make much sense of his utterances. For the schizophrene, the "demarcation between the outer world and his ego is more or less suspended or modified in comparison with the normal."[17]

These features of schizophrenia are linked with and are indices of the impairment of intellectual processes. This impairment has been conceived of as a deterioration in normal ability to conceptualize and generalize. Goldstein[18] has concluded that schizophrenes give evidence of inability to reason abstractly. (Normal persons, of course, can assume both "concrete" and "abstract" attitudes.) Hanfmann and Kasanin[19] came to substantially the same conclusion from a comparative study of normal and schizophrenic persons. But they note also that schizophrenes differed greatly in the degree of ability to reason abstractly, some showing little or no impairment. This might have been anticipated in view of the heterogeneous character of the group psychiatrically classified as schizophrenics.

A psychologist, Hunt,[20] attacks the view that schizophrenes lack generalizing ability, believing this to be an hypothesis open to debate and lacking validation. A more recent study by Hanfmann and Kasanin[21] has a bearing on this question. They have listed five subcategories of schizophrenes, arranged according to degree of intellectual impairment. Patients in one category suffer no discernible intellectual impairment, whereas patients in the other categories exhibit various degrees of it. This kind of refined classification suggests the direction that future research in this area is likely to take.

A study by Rashkis, Cushman, and Landis[22] throws additional light upon the controversy over the generalizing ability of schizophrenics. These investigators draw distinctions among "abstract," "complex," and "concrete" behavior (these, the reader may note, are in descending order):

> *Abstract behavior* . . . the subject is actively able to grasp the essential aspects of a new situation, to behave in accordance with his attitude, and to account satisfactorily for his behavior. *Complex behavior* . . . the subject selected terms representing aspects of a possible situation without being able to account for his selection. *Concrete behavior* . . . the inability of the subject to grasp essential relationships, to arrange new material in a conceptual scheme, or to relate aspects of a new situation with regard to his own personal experience or sensory preference.[23]

Subjects were given a sorting test. Only normal adults were able to sort on the highest, or abstract, level. Both schizophrenics and normal children (aged thirteen to fifteen years) could sort on the middle, or complex, level. It is interesting to note that paretics (syphilitic psychotics) were unable to attain any complexity or abstractness at all in their sorting: their behavior was entirely on the lowest, or concrete, level.

Few authors have maintained that the schizophrenic actually reverts to earlier modes of thinking as he retraces his development in reverse. Many students of schizophrenia believe that severe schizophrenes operate on a level of reasoning that is lower than the level on which they reasoned before they became severely disordered. However, they maintain that recognizing this is something other than equating adult schizophrenic thought with childhood thought, either of schizophrenic or normal children. As Friedman has noted:

> This functional regression is not total: the schizophrene's perceptual functioning cannot be conceived as of being identical with that of the child; vestiges remain which reveal the efficacy of the individual's past, *i.e.*, the previous functioning on a higher developmental level. This is most clearly observed in the survival of a perceptual discreteness and plasticity of an order not

attained by children, and in the variety of responses which point to a wider acquaintance with environmental stimuli.[24]

Some observers think of schizophrenia as "regression." By this they mean that the patient loses the capacity to reason abstractly and reverts to a lower (pre-adult) level of thought. The more severe the disorder becomes, the more his thinking regresses. This conception of a "peeling-off" or "lamination" process, as it has been termed, is based upon the assumption that the most complex thought processes appear in the developmental career of each person after, and as a result of, the appearance of simpler thought processes.

Cameron has given us an excellent summary description of the schizophrenic's plight, particularly with reference to communication:

> The continual interchange between a given person and those around him not only develops the social character of his language and thought, but also maintains it afterward at an adequate social level. For if this organization falls below the point of intelligibility where others can share it, and if it cannot then be amplified by other words, gestures, signs, or demonstrations, it can no longer function in communication . . . that is just what happens in schizophrenic disorganization. Social communication is gradually crowded out by fantasy; and the fantasy itself, because of its non-participation in and relation to action becomes in turn less and less influenced by social patterns. The result is a progressive loss of organized thinking, and ultimately an incapacity for taking the role of others when this is necessary to enable one to share adequately in their attitudes and perspectives.[25]

Summary

The lack or loss of language, as we have seen, has serious behavioral consequences. Isolated and feral children, and the blind deaf who do not learn a language, fail to become socialized human beings and exhibit the types of behavioral disabilities which the analyses in preceding chapters would lead us to expect. Investigations of aphasia and schizophrenia also seem to confirm the importance of language as the integrative agent in human behavior.

We must, however, make some qualifications and reservations. The data on feral and isolated children are meager and somewhat questionable. The same is true of the material on the blind deaf. Moreover, the phenomena of aphasia and schizophrenia are very complex and subject to controversy. Further research may show some of our interpretations to be wrong: certainly such study will lead to qualifications and refinements. Nevertheless, present knowledge about these several phenomena supports the general thesis that complex mental responses involve complex use of language symbols. Loss or lack of symbols leads to incomplete or inadequate socialization.

SUGGESTIONS FOR DISCUSSION AND SPECIAL REPORTS

1. After an examination of the literature on prisons, report on the effects of solitary confinement.

2. Interview several persons who have lived in a foreign country concerning the difficulties and processes of learning a foreign language overseas.

3. What is your view on the question of whether Helen Keller can really understand the meanings of words of sound and sight?

4. Biological defects may prevent socialization. Does this demonstrate a causal relationship between the body and social behavior?

5. If thinking were radically separate from speech, what difference would this make with respect to aphasia?

6. Can psychoanalytic techniques be used successfully in the treatment of schizophrenia?

NOTES

[1] K. Davis, "Final Note on a Case of Extreme Isolation," *Am. J. Soc.*, 52(1947): 432-437.

[2] J. A. Singh and R. M. Zingg, *Wolf Children and Feral Man*, Harper, 1942.

[3] Helen Keller, *The Story of My Life*, Doubleday Page, 1917, pp. 22-24.

[4] Helen Keller, *The World I Live In*, Appleton-Century, 1938, p. 124.

[5] H. Werner, *The Comparative Psychology of Mental Development*, Harper, 1940, pp. 175-176.

[6] A. A. Strauss and H. Werner, "Experimental Analysis of the Clinical Symptom 'Perseveration' in Mentally Retarded Children," *Am. J. Mental Deficiency*, 47 (1942): 185-188.

[7] H. Head, *Aphasia and Kindred Disorders of Speech*, Macmillan, 1926, Vol. I.

[8] *Ibid.*, p. 256.

[9] *Ibid.*, p. 371.

[10] *Ibid.*, p. 193.

[11] *Ibid.*, p. 195.

[12] K. Goldstein, *Human Nature in the Light of Psychopathology*, Harvard University Press, 1940.

[13] See any of the works of Piaget in bibliographies for Chapters 6 and 12.

[14] K. Goldstein and M. Scheerer, "Abstract and Concrete Behavior: An Experimental Study With Special Tests," *Psychological Monographs*, Vol. 53 (1941), No. 2.

[15] J. Crewdson, "Speech in an Imperfectly Learned Language," *Brit. J. of Psych.*, 32(1941): 82-99, esp. pp. 98-99.

[16] J. Kasanin in J. Kasanin (ed.), *Language and Thought in Schizophrenia*, University of California Press, 1944, p. 130.

[17] K. Goldstein, *ibid.*, p. 23.

[18] *Ibid.*

[19] E. Hanfmann and J. Kasanin, "Conceptual Thinking in Schizophrenia," *Nervous and Mental Disease Monographs*, No. 67, New York, 1942.

[20] J. McV. Hunt in J. McV. Hunt (ed.), *Personality and the Behavior Disorders*, Ronald, 1944, p. 1019.

[21] Hanfmann and Kasanin, *op. cit.*, pp. 46-48.

[22] H. Rashkis, J. Cushman, and C. Landis, "A New Method for Studying Disorders of Conceptual Thinking," *J. Ab. and Soc. Psych.*, 41(1946): 70-74.

[23] *Ibid.*, p. 70.

[24] H. Friedman, "Perceptual Regression in Schizophrenia: An Hypothesis Suggested by the Use of the Rorschach Test," *J. Gen. Psych.*, 81(1952): 96.

[25] N. Cameron in Kasanin (ed.), *op. cit.*, pp. 55-56.

BIBLIOGRAPHY

Cameron, N., "Reasoning, Regression and Communication in Schizophrenics," *Psychological Monographs*, Vol. 50 (1938), No. 1. An important exploratory study of types of reasoning in schizophrenic patients.

Cassirer, E., *An Essay on Man*, Yale University Press, 1944. See pp. 33-38.

A good review of the significance of the data concerning the deaf and blind.

Davis, K., "Final Note on a Case of Extreme Isolation," *Am. J. Soc.*, 52(1947): 432-437. A comparison of two cases of isolated children, with special attention to the case of Isabelle.

Dennis, W., "The Significance of Feral Man," and R. Zingg, "A Reply to Professor Dennis," *Am. J. Psych.*, 54(1941): 425-432 and 432-435. Dennis questions the reliability of the accounts of feral men. Zingg replies.

Goldstein, K., *Human Nature in the Light of Psychopathology*, Harvard University Press, 1940. The first part of this series of lectures is especially interesting for the author's description and interpretation of aphasic disorders.

――――, and M. Scheerer, "Abstract and Concrete Behavior: An Experimental Study with Special Tests," *Psychological Monographs*, 53(1941), No. 2. Tests for the study of aphasic reasoning are described in considerable detail and in fairly technical language.

Head, H., *Aphasia and Kindred Disorders of Speech*, Macmillan, 1926, 2 vols. An English neurologist's famous study of aphasic disorders. Though Head deals with technical and theoretical matters, his style is very readable and the book is filled with abundant illustrative materials.

Kasanin, J. (ed.), *Language and Thought in Schizophrenia*, University of California Press, 1944. A series of papers by students of schizophrenia, organized around the central topics of schizophrenic language and thought. An indispensable reference.

Keller, H., *The Story of My Life*, Doubleday Page, 1917. The autobiography of a well-known blind and deaf woman, written for a popular audience.

Mason, M., "Learning to Speak after Six and One-half Years of Silence," *J. Speech Disorders*, 7(1942): 295-304. A full account of how Isabelle was taught to speak.

Singh, J. A., and R. M. Zingg, *Wolf Children and Feral Man*, Harper, 1942. (Including an introduction by K. Davis.) The first part is a missionary's narrative description of the discovery and development of Kamala. The second part consists of a psychologist's review of the literature on supposed feral men.

CHAPTER 6

The Acquisition of Language and Reason

THE LEARNING OF LANGUAGE is not merely a matter of mastering the mechanics of speech. The symbols which make up a language are concepts and represent ways of acting and thinking. The infant must learn to classify objects and to act appropriately toward them. He must also learn that some words refer to things which do not exist as material objects, but only as ideas, abstractions, or relationships. To teach anyone the conventional meaning of a word is to teach him how to act or think with reference to the object or the concept to which the word refers. The meanings of words are not locked up in dictionaries, but are found in peoples' acts.

The child's learning of language is not merely an intellectual matter: it is also a significant factor in the development of his personality. Language puts the child in touch with his parents and playmates in new and significant ways and initiates his acquisition of broader, more socialized perspectives. It introduces him to new pleasures and satisfactions and also creates a great many new needs and problems. Through learning language he learns of the rules and standards that regulate social relations and develops ideas of morality and religious matters. Language is also the means whereby he is gradually prepared for and later inducted into the roles which he is destined to play and through which he learns to grasp the viewpoints and understand the feelings and sentiments of other persons. By means of language he becomes aware of his own identity as a person and as a member of groups in which he seeks status, security, and self-expression and which in turn make demands upon him. It should be kept in mind, then, that learning the language is much more than the mechanical acquisition of a skill or intellectual tool: it involves a fundamental and significant reorganization of the entire personality.

Since the newborn baby cannot be aware of his elders' symbols, he remains for some time relatively unsocialized. This is what some writers mean when they assert that "children are not born human." Other writers point out that socialization begins even before the child learns language when he begins to learn how to respond to all kinds of stimuli. Learning, they say, does not wait for language to develop. On the other hand, it is clear that until the infant begins to comprehend and use conventional speech, his humanness is only partial. The child becomes socialized when he has acquired the ability to communicate with others and to influence and be influenced by them through use of speech. This implies socially acceptable behavior toward named objects.

However, the learning of concepts one by one in piecemeal fashion is not enough, for concepts are interrelated. That is to say, a language is a system of shared symbols. Such a word as "spoon" refers to more than a piece of shaped metal—although "metal" and "shaped" are themselves complex concepts. The meanings of "spoon" (i.e., modes of response toward it) are linked with and contingent upon a whole system of related meanings: what foods are eaten with spoons, how spoons are handled, what they are made of, where they are placed as part of a table setting, and so on.

The word "money" demonstrates even more clearly that in learning a language, the child is learning to organize his behavior in complex ways. Money, in the United States, is linked with a vast network of important meanings, of which the following are only a few: coins, bank, salary, savings, checks, thrift, getting ahead, success, prestige, failure, security, poverty, riches, luxury, spendthrift, gold standard, income, and profit. To understand the elaborate meanings associated with all these words requires considerable previous learning of somewhat simpler concepts. Thus, the many over-

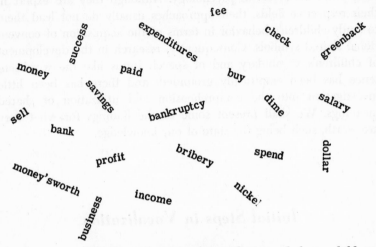

How many different connections among these words has a child
learned by the time he is an adult?

tones of "thrift" cannot be apprehended unless one has some grasp of what "saving," "savings," and other concepts signify. A three-year-old neighbor of the authors', Jimmy, equates money with round, shiny objects. It will be some time before he learns that with money he can "buy" candy, toys, and other items. He has, as yet, no notion that money can be "exchanged," that it must be "earned," that only the government can "mint" it, and that people can be "bought" or "bribed" with it.

Virtually all inquiries into the development of children's language have been carried on by specialists in linguistics and child psychology. Linguists have been preoccupied with the language forms found at successive ages in the child's development. Child psychologists have been concerned with a range of problems, including developmental stages in the child's speech, growth of vocabulary, grammatical forms and their acquisition, functions of language in the child's life, relationships of language with other aspects of development (intelligence, personality), and language and individual differences.

Neither linguists nor child psychologists are primarily concerned with problems of social psychology. Although they are expert in their respective fields, their approaches usually do not lead them to study children's behavior in terms of the acquisition of conventional shared symbols. Consequently, research in the development of children's vocabulary and of speech forms like the word-sentence has been empirically grounded, and there has been little investigation into the comprehension and utilization of shared meanings. We shall present some of the findings for what they are worth, such being the state of our knowledge.

Initial Steps in Vocalization

EARLY VOCALIZATIONS

The human fetus is apparently capable of producing sounds even during the prenatal period. Crying has been heard in prematurely delivered fetuses of five and six months, and clinicians have noted many instances of "fetal crying." The earliest sound uttered by the newborn baby is the well-known "birth cry." Although laymen frequently interpret this cry as an expression of emotion on the part of the baby, physiologists assure us that the sound is physiologically determined, having to do with initiation of respiration and oxygenation of blood.

The infant's earliest cries are reflexes. There is no specificity about them. Except in degree of intensity, all the cries of a one-month-old baby, whether in response to hunger, pain, or cold, are identical in nature.

Although it is difficult to distinguish the exact character of children's early vocalizations, investigators generally agree that vowel sounds of some sort are heard soon after birth. It is not long before some sort of consonant sounds appear in combination with the vowels. The utterance of specific types of vowels and consonants is linked with the infant's physical condition; depending on whether he is in a state of comfort or discomfort, he emits different sounds.

> The back consonants, which appear early and are said to be typical of periods of comfort, are associated with swallowing and belching movements which usually follow feeding, and in the prefeeding period the child typically makes mouthing movements with tongue and lips in anticipation of feeding which are most likely to result in the later *m*, *p*, and *b* sounds.[1]

These early vocalizations continue to increase both in number and variety.

By about the third month, most infants are cooing and babbling. They continue to do so until about the end of their first year. The diversity of sounds emitted by a babbling infant is amazing. During this period children of every race and nationality have the same extensive range of vocalization, many more sounds being produced than are needed for future acquisition of parental speech. Each infant covers a wide range of human sounds, whereas his elders, regardless of their particular language, utilize only a restricted segment of the range. "One cannot fail to hear all the vowels and consonants, diphthongs, aspirates, sub-vocals, nasals, German umlauts and tongue trills, French throaty trills and grunts, and even the Welsh '*l.*'"[2] Hence, babbling has been referred to as the vocal stone-quarry of all human languages.

The period of babbling is marked by playfulness. Sounds are repeated over and over in a spirit of enjoyment, and such vocal play becomes one of the infant's chief interests. The French literary historian, Taine, gave a graphic description of such playful babbling (or "twittering" as he called it):

> At about three and a half months . . . she was put on a carpet in the garden; there lying on her back or stomach, for hours together, she kept moving about her four limbs and uttering a number of cries and different exclamations, but vowels only, no

consonants; this continued for several months. By degrees consonants were added to the vowels and the exclamations became more and more articulate. It all ended in a sort of very distinct twittering, which would last a quarter of an hour at a time and be repeated ten times a day. The sounds (both vowels and consonants), at first very vague and difficult to catch, approached more and more nearly to those that we pronounce, and . . . came almost to resemble a foreign language that we could not seem to understand. She takes delight in her twitter . . . she seems to smile with joy over it, but as yet it is only the twittering of a bird, for she attaches no meaning to the sounds she utters. She has learned only the materials of language.[3]

It is interesting to note that chimpanzee infants, in contrast to even deaf human infants, do not indulge in this sort of vocal play. The Kelloggs, who reared an infant of both species together, observed that while in many respects the two babies were remarkably alike, the human baby continuously vocalized in a playful manner, whereas the chimpanzee did not do this at all.[4]

BABBLING AND IMITATION

Babbling is of key importance because it provides the basis for imitation of other people's speech. In part babbling consists of imitation by the child of sounds uttered by itself. This "self-imitation" accounts for much of the repetitive character of babbling. The infant repeats a sound (such as "dada") over and over, the initial sound acting as a stimulus which sets off a response in imitation of itself, and so on and on (dada . . . dada . . . dada). No sounds are imitated that are not already in the child's repertoire. Whatever new sounds the child acquires emerge spontaneously during vocal play as a result of physical maturation. However, in contrast to new sounds, new sound-combinations may be learned by imitation of people.

When the infant is about nine months old, he is found imitating sounds—and later, the inflections and intonations—of his associates. As time passes, imitation of sounds becomes surer, more exact; intonational imitation grows more certain; word combinations are adopted. The baby acquires the ability to copy adult speech, even though some time may elapse between hearing and responding; no longer must he imitate immediately upon hearing the word. Parents listen to his utterance of certain sounds (such as "ma-ma"), and by repeating these sounds over and over to him, help him to approach adult standards of enunciation.

Through both spontaneous imitation and parental encouragement, the child gradually becomes aware of imitation as an act in itself. He also comes to pay more attention to words and to copy them more exactly. This is because he is beginning to use speech sounds instrumentally, as tools by means of which he can, for example, acquire objects from his parents, or avoid punishment. He learns that satisfying results may be obtained by speaking a given word in given circumstances and by behaving in a given way in response to a given word.

Because of parental reaction to his utterances, the child begins to acquire "meanings" for them. Bare sound, physically produced, takes on a social character. The sound and the social aspects of speech now merge, blend, and shade into one another.

Just how the child passes over to a consistent and conventional use of words is a crucial problem for social psychology. We do not really know the full details of this transformation, from babbling and initial imitation to adult verbal behavior, in which the spoken word is used with a conventional meaning. We shall consider such materials as are available.

Learning to Use and Comprehend Conventional Symbols

INSTRUMENTAL USE OF GESTURES

The child makes expressive bodily movements long before he speaks conventionally. Such gestures may be accompanied by expressive vocalizations. At first these may not be understood by even extremely solicitous parents; but gradually their meanings are discovered so that an approximate interpretation is readily made. As late as his eighteenth month the baby communicates needs largely through gestures and expressive utterances rather than through actual words.

Latif has advanced an hypothesis to explain the development of some of these gestures. He notes that a hungry infant comes to react to the sight of a nursing bottle "by writhing, wriggling and directing its head and eyes toward it."[5] Latif calls this a "whole-body language," since the child's needs and goals are conveyed to parents by the activity of his whole body. At a later period, as soon as he begins to show signs of hunger, the mother quickly presents the bottle.

> Such cooperation on the part of the mother soon reduces the body language of the infant to mere ("conventional") gesture, in which *only a part* and that the earliest part of an action is substituted for the entire action. The responses of the infant thus become merely symptomatic; i.e., symbolic.[6]

Latif is suggesting that the reactions of the infant's associates play an important role in the inauguration of genuine conventional gestures; he implies that without interaction between child and adult there would be no abbreviated gesture (*i.e.*, symbol).

The infant's gestural communication gradually recedes and becomes secondary to his gradually evolving vocal language. Some children are retarded linguistically because they develop an elaborate gesture "language" so well understood by their parents that there is neither incentive nor urgent necessity for learning genuine speech. Parental refusal to respond usually results in the abandonment of such a system of gestures. However, even among adults gestures are not completely abandoned, but continue to be used as subsidiary means of communication. Many people accompany their speech with vigorous gesticulation, and even the most restrained individuals use some expressive movements to supplement and reinforce their words.

The most important point to note about the infant's use of gestures is that it is instrumental. He uses gestures—though he is not aware that he is using them—to reach for something or to avoid something or to call for something. His expressive bodily movements occur within a context of social relations; that is, people react to his gestures and he responds both to people and to their actions with still further gestures. Although at first he makes expressive movements toward a brute physical environment, the responses of his parents soon transform this environment into a thoroughly social one in which his early expressive movements become endowed with a social significance.

USE OF WORDS

Learning Words · The first word spoken by the infant the world over is usually a syllable or repeated syllable such as mama, dada, bebe, nana, wawa, papa. As we have previously noted, the word is expressive of either pleasurable or unpleasurable states. These syllabic phonetic forms become stabilized in the infant's speech by delighted elders, who pick out certain ones and repeat them to the baby until he uses them correctly.

The use of other words soon follows, especially when the infant somehow makes the momentous discovery that things have names. Laguna has an interesting suggestion as to how these names are discovered.[7] The child, she suggests, early tends to point toward objects which he finds interesting. Frequently when pointing he also vocalizes. The pointing is likely to become a "social game" in which his elders join, repeating over and over to the child the names of objects toward which he motions. The child usually delights in this game. Whether or not Laguna's suggestion is correct, when the child has managed to discover that every object has a name he has taken a conspicuous step toward learning parental speech. Some psychologists are convinced that this step is crucial, since it is followed both by awakened curiosity about the names of things and by an increase in vocabulary. Parents are familiar with the curiosity of children who, at this stage of their development, incessantly point to objects asking, "What's that—what's its name?"

Besides discovering that things have names, the child may also be said to discover that names have things, that is to say, that the words which he learns correspond to aspects of the real world. In complex types of learning especially, the progression may be from words to things rather than the reverse. The fact that racial prejudice can be learned before contact with the racial group in question (see p. 75) may be taken as an illustration of this point. The acquisition of a vocabulary sensitizes the individual to certain aspects of the environment which he may encounter later and predisposes him to notice those which correspond with or confirm what he has previously learned through verbal communication alone. It is in this sense that we may say that the world is not made up of ready-made, discrete objects, events, and qualities waiting to be perceived and named, but is rather built up through collective experience and crystallized in linguistic forms. As learning proceeds, this type of movement from words to things tends to become more and more important.

Use of Word-Sentences · Usually the infant's first words are employed as sentences rather than as single words. They do duty as one-word sentences. Analyzed merely as parts of speech, they are characteristically nouns or interjections. The infant, however, uses these words as complete, although—by adult standards—crude sentences. Thus "mama" will have to be interpreted by parents in a variety of ways, depending upon the situation in which the word is spoken as well as the intonation and gesturing that accompany it. "Mama" may mean that the infant "wishes" his mother to come, or that he is hungry, or that he is content, or that he sees his mother enter the room. "Ball" may mean "there is the ball," "where is the ball?," "I want the ball," and so on. These earliest word-sentences cannot be understood out of context, nor without noting associated inflection and gesture.

At this stage of his language development, the child possesses words which have only a partly socialized meaning. That is, he has learned to employ words conventionally (mama, ball, shoe, etc.), with approximately the same meanings that his parents attribute to them. His use of words is close enough to conventional adult usage so that, from the context in which the word is spoken, his parents are able to understand him.

The child is able to use words in an amazing variety of ways because he has not caught on to their full public meaning. As Laguna has written:

> It is precisely because the words of the child are so indefinite in meaning, that they can serve such a variety of uses. . . . A child's word does not . . . designate an object *or* a property *or* an act; rather it signifies loosely and vaguely the object together with its interesting properties and the acts with which it is commonly associated in the life of the child. The emphasis may be now on one, now on another, of these aspects, according to the exigencies of the occasion on which it is used.[8]

Adults, who are much more conscious of the "real" (conventional) meanings of words, cannot employ words so irresponsibly or so variously.

Children use these early words as a way of responding to a situation. A child does not merely name an object with a word (such as naming mama by using the word "mama"). "Mama" means "mama come here" or "I'm glad to see you," etc. As Lewis[9] has noted: ". . . when he speaks the sounds it is his way of dealing with the situation." His words are instruments, they are means of handling his environment. We shall see below how children progress rapidly to the point where words become very effective means for managing the environment and manipulating certain key environmental objects.

BEGINNINGS OF OBJECTIVE REFERENCE

The infant's earliest vocalizations, we have previously noted, are rooted in affective states. But by the time he begins to name objects and speak word-sentences, his vocalizations are more than expressions of affective states. They begin at this stage, or perhaps even sooner, to point toward something in the environment. This may be clearly seen in the instance of childish naming: a name like "shoe" stands roughly for something—whether "shoe," or "tie my shoe," "my shoe is untied," etc. What the word specifies on any given occasion is determined, of course, by that feature of the situation with which the infant is most concerned.

At the same time that the child is using word-sentences, he is also hearing and responding to adult speech. Lewis[10] has reasoned that the hearing and using of words, proceeding simultaneously as they do in the child's development, help to bring about an increasingly definite set of referents for any given word. For example, the word "ball," instead of having variable meanings, begins to get meanings that have increasingly greater correspondence to conventional grown-up meanings. Lewis suggests the process by which this occurs. When the child hears a word spoken the situation in which the word is spoken, along with accompanying intonational qualities of speech, evokes a response in him. Thus "ball" spoken cheerfully by an adult after the child's feeding period will probably call forth a delighted response from the child. Then later, when the child learns to say this word, he will tend to produce the same delighted response in himself, just as if the adult had actually spoken the word. Furthermore, when the adult says "ball" he is apt to be referring to something specific in the situation (the ball itself). So the child, when he comes to utter the word, will not only evoke in himself his previous delight but also his delight over a specific object: ball. The adult, by using the word "ball" (besides probably presenting the ball), calls attention to the object itself. In this way the object is highlighted, lifted out of the total situation. It is linked more specifically with the particular sounds constituting the word.

DECLARATIVE AND MANIPULATIVE FUNCTIONS OF LANGUAGE

We have previously noted the instrumental use of gestures and word-sentences; its implications now call for further analysis. The work of Lewis will be closely followed here since, in our judgment, his is the most careful inquiry into this aspect of our problem.

The child uses his early "conventional" words instrumentally in ways that are either "declarative" or "manipulative." Declarative use involves drawing adult attention to some object. By uttering such words as "chair" or "doll" the child directs adult attention to those objects. Manipulative use of words by the child involves, in addition to drawing attention to some object, a demand that his needs with regard to that object be satisfied by the adult. For example, the word "cookie," when used in manipulative fashion, is equivalent to a demand for aid in reaching the cookie jar and getting a cookie. Or "tick-tock," used manipulatively, might mean "papa show me your wrist watch."

The child's instrumental use of language, whether declarative or manipulative, results in drawing other people within his circle of activity.

> In the declarative use he attracts another's attention and so assures himself of company. If he is delighted, the presence of another person enhances his delight; if he is afraid the presence of another person alleviates his fear. . . . In the manipulative use the child is again using the word as a social instrument; this time as a means of securing the help of others in satisfying his practical wants.[11]

Even before the infant learns any real words, he has used his own vocalizations for declarative and manipulative purposes. But when he learns real words those two instrumental functions become more effective, because they enable him to point more precisely to the objects which attract his attention.

A series of significant points is involved here. (1) The child's instrumental use of sounds has its roots in the child's past; and this instrumental use of sounds merges imperceptibly into his acquisition of conventional speech. (2) The child's learning of conventional speech rests upon his using it as an instrument; that is, upon his calling adult attention to more specific objects and aspects of his environment than was possible with his ambiguous baby vocalizations. (3) Finally, the child's gradual approach to conventional speech presupposes the cooperation of adults. If adults paid no attention whatsoever to him, if he could not use words as social instruments, it is difficult to imagine how the child could ever learn conventional usage.

THE DEVELOPMENT OF COMPREHENSION

Observers generally agree that infants "understand" gestures before they understand speech. A child five months old will observe gestures, and at eight months will display a considerable capacity for understanding them.[12] Such early understanding of gestures is important if one assumes that the child's comprehension of adult gestures is crucial for later comprehension of adult speech. Indeed it is difficult to tell, when the infant is very young, how much of his apparent comprehension of words is due to the words and how much to accompanying facial and bodily gestures. An adult needs to reinforce his words with gestures in order to be certain that an eighteen-month-old child will understand him. Two outstanding students of child behavior, Gesell and Stern, have expressed the view that the child's understanding of adult speech depends more upon the adult's accompanying gestures than upon the words. The assumption underlying this opinion is essentially this: comprehension of speech arises out of gestural comprehension, which precedes and later accompanies the comprehension of speech.

Lewis, whose valuable work on infant speech we have previously utilized, disagrees with Gesell and Stern. He points out that before the age of six months, infants do not respond differentially to coaxing and threatening gestures. They begin to do so at about the eighth month. On the other hand, differential response to intonation of the adult voice appears as early as the third month. Lewis, unlike Gesell and Stern, does not emphasize the significance of gesture for later speech comprehension; but he does emphasize the significance of intonation.

Lewis' views on how the child gradually grasps the meaning of conventional speech may be summarized as follows. The infant at the age of three months starts to discriminate between pleasantly and unpleasantly toned speech. Thus in the beginning of the child's life "the intonational rather than the phonetic form dominates the child's responses":[13] that is, the child responds to intonation more than to the actual meaning of the adult word itself. At first the infant reacts to word intonation largely by expression; then later, chiefly by movements. The intonations which accompany adult words encourage the child to go ahead with or to desist from an act ("don't touch"; "go ahead—drink your milk now, like a good boy").

Opposing and unverified hypotheses are offered to explain the initial development of comprehension. They illustrate and epitomize the inadequacy of scientific accounts of child learning. Considerable effort has been expended upon describing and photographing children and upon collecting factual information about such activities as vocabulary learning. Nevertheless, the facts outrun interpretation. Research aimed at the solution of fundamental theoretical problems is badly needed.

CONVERGENCE OF CHILD AND ADULT MEANINGS

Initial Use of Words Is Inaccurate · When the child first discovers adult words, he does not employ them to specify precisely the same objects that are referred to by adults. Or to put this in common-sense terms: the child does not at first use adult words with their correct adult meanings. To the adult the child's application of words often seems haphazard and frequently amusing.

The infant, in fact, applies sounds and home-made words to objects long before he masters adult words. It is out of these initial vocal references that his ability to use adult words correctly eventually develops. Taine[14] has given us an instructive description of how the child begins to apply vocalizations to the objects of his infantile world:

> She was in the habit of seeing a little black dog belonging to the house, which often barks, and it was to it that she first learnt to apply the word *oua-oua*. Very quickly and with very little help she applied it to dogs of all shapes and kinds that she saw in the streets and then . . . to the bronze dogs near the staircase. Better still, the day before yesterday when she saw a goat a month old that bleated, she said *oua-oua*. . . . *Cola* (chocolate) is one of the first sweetmeats that was given her and it is the one she likes the best. . . . Of herself and without or rather in spite of us she has extended the meaning of the word and applies it now to anything sweet; she says *cola* when sugar, tart, a grape, a peach, or a fig is given her. . . . In the same way the above mentioned little boy of twenty months used the word *teterre* (*pomme de terre*)[15] to designate potatoes, meat, beans, almost everything good to eat except milk, which he called *lolo*. Perhaps to him *teterre* meant everything solid or half-solid that is good to eat. . . . This winter she was carried

every day to her grandmother's who often showed her a painted copy of a picture . . . one of the infant Jesus naked, saying at the same time "There's *bébé*."[16] A week ago in another room when she was asked "Where's *bébé?*" meaning herself, she turned at once to the pictures and engravings that happened to be there . . . little by little she came nearer to the usual meaning. Other children were pointed out to her as *bébés*, and she was herself called by the name and now answers to it. Further, when put down before a very low mirror and shown her face reflected in it, she was told "That's *bébé*" and she now goes along to the mirror and says *bébé*, laughing when she sees herself. Starting from this she has extended the meanings of the word, and calls *bébés* all little figures, for instance some half-size plaster statues which are on the staircase, and the figures of men and women in small pictures and prints. Once more education produced an unexpected effect on her; the general character grasped by the child is not what we intended; we taught her the sound, she has invented the sense.

From this description it is clear that when the child first applies learned words to objects, he does so with different meaning than does the adult. Although Taine thought he had taught his daughter the essential meanings of the word "baby," he had not. Similarly, although the child applied the word "cola" to the correct object, she also applied it to other (incorrect) objects. The child sometimes uses adult words to designate objects outside the adult definition, and sometimes he does not use the word to designate enough objects. "Some words he uses more widely than we do, others more narrowly."[17]

Inaccurate Usage Reflects the Child's Point of View · Why is the child at first unable to grasp the correct adult meanings of a word? For an answer to this question we may refer to our discussion of language in the third chapter. We noted that the vocabulary utilized by any given society or social group necessarily reflects its interests and preoccupations. Or to state this in another way: the distinctions implicit in a society's words are distinctions which members of the society consider important and relevant.

It may be assumed that the infant, before becoming overly

influenced by human association, will make distinctions of importance to him. He will choose features of his world which appear
similar and group them together under an identical word. Where
adults make a distinction between prunes and carrots—as fruit and
vegetable—the infant at first may use the same sound (say "teterre")
to pick out similar features of a solid-something which tastes good.

The child cannot very well group together the same objects as

Which objects in this room are toys to adults? Which objects
are toys to children?

does an adult, for the latter sees the world from points of view
derived from participation in certain social groups. The child has
yet to acquire these standardized categories. Features of his environment that strike him as similar are features that grow out of
his own experiences.

Thus, since chocolate tasted sweet and peaches tasted sweet and
grapes tasted sweet, Taine's daughter called them all by the same
name, "cola." A young acquaintance of ours came to call a small

doll "putzibabe"; he then extended the name to other small objects, including small dogs, and later to his baby sister. Similarly, when an infant touches a rose, his mother may carefully call it "rose"; whereupon he is likely to apply "rose" to all flowers. The child's need to deal declaratively or manipulatively with an object—calling our attention to it, or to his needs with reference to it—often leads him to make naïve and unique use of words.

The child's adoption of adult words is encouraged by the adult's readier response to conventional sounds than to the child's private vocalizations. The conventional sound proves to be a more efficient instrument for calling attention to an interesting object or to one's desires with regard to the object; hence the child has an incentive for appropriating the conventional sound.

Perhaps this is an instance of social pressure. But the child, it should be noted, does not automatically conform to social pressure. His choice and use of words are selective. His experience determines the range and extension of words; the decision does not lie with the adult. For a time the child may stubbornly resist the adult's word, so that even after he is aware of the conventional word, and has imitated it correctly, he may continue to use his own unique word form. Or he may alternate, sometimes using the adult word and sometimes his own. The conventional term has to be accepted by the child as the more efficient instrument of the two before he will adopt it finally.

Contemporaneously with and undoubtedly as a partial result of adult intervention, the child learns to make increasingly adequate distinctions among classes of objects. For instance, he begins to discriminate between a solid-something eaten with a spoon (potato) and a solid-something eaten by hand (bread). The adult encourages the child to make such distinctions and helps to crystallize and fix them by suppling the necessary conventional words. Growing discrimination and adult intervention-cooperation go hand in hand; it is fruitless to inquire which contributes more. Both contributions are crucial to the gradual convergence of child and adult symbols. The child thus stands upon the threshold of mastering his native language; he is becoming capable of employing voluntarily the symbols of the society to which he belongs.

SELF-CONTROL AND LANGUAGE CUES

Rather early in the process of acquiring language symbols the child begins to use them to influence his own behavior. Lorimer[18] has described an amusing instance of this:

> A child of about eighteen months was warned not to put her hand into a certain open chest and not to take out things in the chest. The inhibition was clearly established but the original impulse was strong. For ten enormous minutes I watched with fascination the battle between the impulse and the inhibition, as the little hand reached forward toward the things in the chest and withdrew to the verbal accompaniment "no, no, no!" uttered by the child herself. Then the battle subsided, called to a close by the distraction of other interests.

Such a self-command (the beginnings of what is commonly called "will power") derives from previous adult commands and prohibitions.

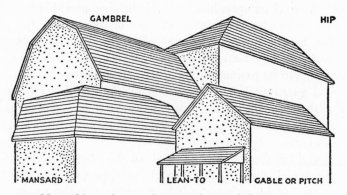

How old would one have to be to understand the concepts: gambrel, mansard, lean-to, and gable? (From Edgar Dale, *Audio-Visual Methods in Teaching*, 1st ed., Dryden Press, 1946.)

The child will eventually internalize his self-directed words so that he will say "no" to himself silently, or will merely think the command. But at an early age, self-directed language is not completely internalized. Let us take another example: ask a young child to say how many pencils are lying on a table. He is likely to touch each pencil, counting aloud "one-two-three" as he touches. If you hold his hands, thereby preventing him from touching the pencils, he either cannot tell you the total number, or he will nod his head in the direction of the pencils and count "one-two-three." Youngsters at play are often overheard giving themselves commands like "put this block there." As the child grows older, language becomes internalized so that counting, commanding, expressing desires, and so on can be carried out silently.

Interesting indirect evidence of the development of voluntary self-control is furnished by Messerschmidt's[19] study of suggestibility in children. This investigator found that suggestibility, as she measured it, increased from the age of four to the age of seven or eight, at which time it reached a maximum. Thereafter it declined steadily with increasing age. Sensitivity to hypnotic suggestion, according to Hull,[20] follows a similar curve over the same years.

Messerschmidt's conclusions may be restated for our purposes. "Suggestibility" is a term which refers to an individual's amenability to control exercised upon him by symbolic cues provided by someone else. Before he has reached the age of four or five the child does not have a sufficient mastery of communication to be suggestible. By the time he is seven or eight he has learned the language well enough to be profoundly influenced by it, but not well enough to be on guard against being misled or victimized by it. In the years that follow, the child's broadened experiences with the many uses and abuses of language give him a more realistic conception of its uses and its limitations.

The child discovers, perhaps at about the time he starts school, that direct and simple acceptance of language cues makes him a ready victim of his classmates, who are not so tender toward him as are his parents. He may discover, for example, that when one of his playmates engages him in an exciting conversation, this may be done merely to lull him into a false sense of security while another playmate sneaks up behind him and perpetrates a practical joke. The verbal "kidding" to which children subject each other is often cruel, but the child quickly learns from it that the remarks of other persons must be discounted, critically interpreted, and guarded against.

Another step in the child's gradual overcoming of his own suggestibility is made when he discovers that his parents are not omniscient or omnipotent. This disillusionment may arrive in a number of ways. He may discover his parents' fallibility by comparing the things they say with what his teachers tell him. Or disillusionment may come as a sequel to the discovery that his parents have deceived him with the myth of Santa Claus or the stork.

When the child ceases to accept the word of his parents as the final law and ultimate truth, he is on the way to making comparative judgments and developing a mind of his own. The suggestions of parents are then no longer accepted automatically but are met with objections and criticisms and compared with "better" ideas emanating from teachers, books, playmates, friends' parents, and so on.

With increasing age, ideas and modes of response become more channelized and fixed. The person builds up increasingly complex systems of belief which he makes the basis of his actions and which he defends against attack. He has become accustomed to the conflicting suggestions which impinge upon him on every hand, and has developed a skepticism and consciousness concerning the motives of other people which partly immunize him against suggestions not in accord with his beliefs.

The Learning of Concepts

Learning language, as we have earlier stressed, requires that the child master systems of interrelated concepts. A number of investigators have studied how children's conceptions of time, space, movement, shape, weight, and numbers progressively become more sophisticated and differentiated. Ames,[21] for example, has traced children's use of terms for time (day, minute, etc.), as these become detached from concrete actions and grow increasingly abstract and inclusive in scope. Studies of children's notions of social relationships, such as those bearing upon social class and race, also show, in a general way, how knowledge of these matters gradually becomes more discriminative and more systematic.

For instance, Stendler,[22] in a study of American small-town children, found that awareness of social class differences develops slowly, passing through four stages: (1) pre-awareness, (2) the beginning of awareness, (3) the acceptance of adult stereotypes of class, and (4) the recognition of individual differences among people regardless of social class. Likewise, it has often been pointed out that young children are not attuned to racial differences, especially to their more subtle aspects. Moreno[23] has reported that when young school children were asked whom they would like to have sit beside them, there was no apparent color discrimination in the first three or four grades. Likewise, E. and R. Horowitz,[24] in a study of a small Tennessee community, noted that Negro and white children attempted to carry on friendships despite parental admonitions and injunctions. One of the chief causes of punishment for the white children was that they kept on being friendly to Negro children.

Let us pursue the matter of children's conceptions of race a little further: the topic is both interesting and of theoretical importance.

Every Negro child in America discovers sooner or later, because of our racial distinctions, that he is a Negro—and is compelled to learn the Negro role as it is roughly delineated in our country. The consequences are momentous, for they apply to the entire range of social relations and to virtually every facet of Negro life.

One would expect that if Negroes must learn to be Negroes, the process could be studied empirically by investigating the skin-color distinctions made by Negro children and the growth of their sense of identity.

A significant recent investigation has been made along these lines. K. and M. Clark,[25] using groups of 119 Northern and 134 Southern Negro children, studied conceptions of self and of race. The children ranged from three to seven years of age. They were given four dolls which were identical, except that two were white with yellow hair and two were brown with black hair. The children were then asked to do the following:

1. give me the doll that you like best
2. give me the doll that is a nice doll
3. give me the doll that looks bad
4. give me the doll that is a nice color
5. give me the doll that looks like a white child
6. give me the doll that looks like a colored child
7. give me the doll that looks like a Negro child
8. give me the doll that looks like you

The responses of Negro children to these requests yielded at least four points of interest (1) There was confusion concerning self-identification. The confusion diminished with age and was greater among the lighter children than among the darker. (2) The children displayed greater facility in identifying skin color than in grasping the significance of the term "Negro." (3) There was consistent preference for the white dolls, which were often characterized as "nice," "of a nice color," and so on. This preference diminished with increasing age. (4) A negative attitude was displayed towards the dark dolls by children of all ages.

These responses demonstrate that racial identification—and all that it implies—must be learned. In learning to label oneself as a member of a racial group, one takes over a large part of the value systems of the larger society in which the learning takes place. It is significant that, although colored children grow up in colored families, they nevertheless learn from their parents and other sources that whiteness is preferable to darkness. A study by Seeman[26] suggests, despite Moreno's study, that many young Negro children show their color biases in their choice of playmates but that they have not yet verbalized their color preference as they will in later years. In his study of upper-class Negro children Frazier noted that parents often try to shield their children from feelings of inferiority and self-abasement.[27] They go to great lengths to conceal from them their racial identity and its significance. But, as Frazier concludes, "upper-class youth cannot escape the effects of the derogation of the Negro by the white world."

The manner in which this learning process is guided and integrated by verbal mechanisms is suggested by the responses of children to the words "Negro" and "colored" in requests 6 and 7 in the Clarks' study. The children showed considerably more confusion with regard to the first term than they did to the second. For example, at the age of five, 30 percent responded incorrectly to "give me the doll that looks like a Negro child," whereas only 7 percent responded incorrectly when asked for the "colored doll." At the age of six, incorrect responses to "Negro" dropped to 17 percent, and at the age of seven, to 7 percent. This decrease with age suggests that learning about the significance of being a Negro may be accelerated by initial experiences at school.

In another study, Yokley[28] presented Negro children with a series of identical diagrammatic faces ranging in color from very dark brown to "white" flesh tones. He found that the very youngest had three classifications: Negro, colored, and white. Negroes were at the darkest end of the series and lived in Africa; American Negroes were not Negro, but "colored." The young children also made inflexible distinctions among these three classes of persons. No one who was of a given skin darkness could be anything but a Negro, and so on. Somewhat older children caught on to the equivalence of "Negro" and "colored," but also made a rigid separation by skin color of white and colored and Negro. Older children grasped the possibility that many white persons could be darker than some Negroes. This confusion about skin color led some children to believe that they and some members of their families were white. The notion of a segregated school—which they all attended—was not grasped at first. This is easy to understand since segregation, as a concept, is complex. Moreover, some children of "white" or light skin color attended the school!

Similar difficulties of identification and conceptualization are experienced by some white children. The point may be illustrated through two examples. R. Horowitz[29] presented pictures of white and Negro children to a group of preschool children of both races. Children were asked to say which child in each picture was like himself. The oldest white girl "who had expressed advanced and well crystallized prejudices against Negroes" chose, in one picture, a

Negro girl "because the latter had curls and she too had curls which were her glory and pride. Although accurately perceiving the racial nature of all the other pictures, she denied that this one was of a Negro child." Illustrative of the same difficulty of conceptualization, though in this case not of self-conceptualization, is the following story related by Sherif:[30]

> A little girl was told by her mother to call older women "ladies." One day the little girl answered the door and then ran to her mother saying that a lady wanted to see her. Her mother went to the door and when she returned she said, "That wasn't a lady, dear, that was a Negro. You mustn't call Negroes 'ladies.'"

In summary, we may note that there are two fundamental aspects, or phases, involved in the process of racial identification. The first is the basic recognition of the criteria of classification which one uses to place oneself and others in given categories. The second aspect follows the first: it involves the acquisition of the roles associated with, and implied by, the classification. The classifications are not universal, either in all societies or in all groups in any one society. The particular racial and ethnic concepts learned in childhood vary with the groups in which the children have membership.[31]

Most studies of children's learning of concepts are of the very general kind described above. Emphasis is upon revealing what children of varying ages know about certain topics, rather than upon the exact tracing of stages and mechanics involved in the development of that knowledge. Our discussion of the nature of symbols and of concepts (see pp. 53 and 65) indicates that change in a given concept is clearly linked with the development of related concepts. As new classifications are found or learned, the child's old concepts are revised, qualified, or assimilated by the new ones. The refinement of concepts waits upon the development of related concepts. Later meanings are built upon and absorb earlier and simpler ones, although the child himself does not usually recollect most of his earlier conceptions. Children at the same stages of conceptual development tend to commit similar types of errors.

These points can be illustrated by a consideration of some steps through which children pass when learning about money and its uses.[32] Concepts of numbers, coins, monetary transactions, and of associated persons like customers and storekeepers are all related in systematic, if immature, ways. At the beginning, children play with money as with other objects, piling it, pushing it. They make no connection between buying and money. Money is a "penny." At around five and half years of age, the American child recognizes also nickels, but cannot consistently match the silver coins put before him to test his discrimination. His preferences for coins are based on their size or upon rote memory of relative significance. Money buys goods, but any coin buys anything. Primitive rules cover exchange; four coins are given for four pieces of candy. As the child sees it, both customer and storekeeper pay each other.

At about six and a half years, all coins are named correctly, and it is recognized that nickels buy more than pennies and less than dimes. But a given coin buys only its exact equivalent, no more and no less; a nickel will not purchase a penny piece of candy. Money now has a more genuine function than formerly; it does not merely accompany each transaction, but in some sense makes it possible, since things are not merely bought, but are worth something.

The child may develop a finer sense of mathematics at this stage. A nickel cannot buy a ten-cent piece of candy, not merely because ten is not exactly five, but because it is more. How much more is yet unknown, for the child's mathematics is simply in terms of "more" or "less." In a vague way, the child is beginning to sense that there is a connection between the amount of money paid by and to the customer. Money now buys services as well as objects, so that the storekeeper's employees—whose existence has now been recognized—can be paid. Storekeepers, who need money to buy things for their families and for their employees, now sell "to make money" rather than merely to service the customer.

Children at this age, about six and a half years, may also reason that customers must pay for the goods because simple taking of them means a loss to the storekeeper. Previously they said one paid "just because," or because "you'd be punished" for taking goods. The owner of a store is still paid directly by a customer, and must actually sell in order to be paid. Something like absentee ownership is not grasped.

At about eight years of age children finally get the arithmetical details straight. Sales transactions are now impersonal, nonwhimsical, and arithmetically ordered. But it is not until almost a year later that certain other relationships become depersonalized. For instance, at the nine-year-old level a customer who is disliked nevertheless receives the same change as one who is well liked. The child also understands now that some of the customer's money goes to the manufacturer, some to the employee, and that the storekeeper gets some of the remainder. (But the contradiction in this notion is that the owner is believed to sell goods for exactly the same price that he paid for them; to do otherwise would not be "fair.") Around the age of nine some children are vaguely aware that goods may, perhaps, be sold for more than cost, but moral considerations plus rigid application of change-making principles confuse the issue. It also occurs to some of the children that the owner pays proportionate amounts to himself and to his employees: "He'd get about fifty dollars; his helpers twenty." Absentee ownership is beginning to appear as a concept. Finally, at about the age of ten, children grasp the concept of profit. They also finally understand that neither the customer nor the storekeeper gets the better of the bargain when the one gets change and the other is paid. It is not until about a year later that the possibility of shortchanging is seen.

The gradual learning and revising of concepts, as the processes have been illustrated above, is not a purely cognitive or intellectual matter, for shifts of conceptualization are correlated with new perceptions, values, and emotions.

Reasoning and Child Development

Sensorimotor Intelligence · It would be incorrect to maintain that babies and very young children do not give evidence of intelligent behavior, for even prior to the acquisition of language they are capable of primitive kinds of "mental" activity. We may term this activity, following Piaget,[33] *sensorimotor*, because through touch, sight, and movement the infant locates and relates objects in space and time. Sensorimotor intelligence has nothing to do with language and develops partly as a result of biological maturation and partly as a result of the child's experiences with objects.

At first the infant does not even realize that objects which have disappeared from his field of vision still exist. They do not have any temporal permanence. Thus, if one covers an object with a cloth while the five-month-old infant is reaching for it, he will cease reaching and lose interest.

> The primitive world is not made up of permanent objects . . . but of moving perceptive pictures which return periodically into non-existence and come back again as a functional result of the proper action.[34]

Nor does the young infant at first have any clear idea of objects in space. Through exploration of objects—rotating and touching them, seeing their various sides—he soon arrives at some elementary notions of space and of the permanence of objects.

The baby's sensorimotor "reasoning" eventually makes him vaguely aware of his body as one among many stable objects. This represents a considerable advance over his initial picture of the world as made up wholly of impermanent objects.

Logic in Children · Many child psychologists believe that "the child's reasoning processes at the age of six are [not] essentially different from his reasoning processes at the age of twelve or eighteen."[35] This belief involves several assumptions. First, children's logic is essentially the same as that of adults. Second, the more frequent errors committed by the child are a consequence of false premises rather than of inferior logic or inability to reason abstractly. Third, these false premises exist because the child has had inadequate experience with the given subject matter. Fourth, adults also, when confronted with unfamiliar subject matter, are likely to commit errors in logic and judgment. This belief in the general equivalence of child and adult reasoning can easily lead to a subtle form of anthropomorphism concerning the child. Our earlier discussion of the evolution of sign behavior implies that children should be expected to acquire mastery of the higher orders of symbolic activity only gradually. This becomes obvious if we consider some of the difficulties with logic which children encounter. Casual observation of the child's speech reveals some of these, but others are not apparent unless the child is trapped into revealing his thought processes through clever questioning and verbal testing. Some of these deficiencies in logic can be illustrated in tabular form.

Difficulties in	*Illustration*
Classifying abstractly (generalizing)	Four trays, each holding a small wooden dog and one other object, are shown to the child. He is asked to name the common element (i.e., the dog). Few children under four or five years of age could name it, could say "all trays have dogs." [Hazlitt]
Realizing that the class name is only a convenience	The young child believes the name is "in" the object, is inseparable from the object. For example, the sun's name is "in" the sun. [Piaget]
Understanding the relativity of relationships	The child maintains that a pebble is light, a boat is heavy. He does not realize that a pebble is light for him and heavy for the water in which it sinks, or that the boat is light for the water, but heavy for him. Another example: the child cannot grasp the following set of abstract relations. "Edith is lighter than Suzanne. Edith is darker than Lily. Which is darkest—Edith, Suzanne, or Lily?" [Piaget]
Imagining the merely possible	Asked to suppose that the sun is really called the moon and vice versa, the child is likely to argue that that is impossible, that it cannot be. [Piaget] Asked "If your brother is a year older than you, how old is he then?" a child with no brother will protest that he has no brother. [Werner]

Difficulties in	*Illustration*
Avoiding logical contradictions and inconsistencies	The child will maintain that big bodies are heavier than small ones, but that a small pebble is heavier than a large cork. He will state that rivers have strength because they flow, and a moment later maintain that rivers have no strength because they can't carry anything. [Piaget]
Understanding logical necessity	If asked why water goes down and smoke goes up, the child answers that heavy bodies fall and light ones rise. His answer is based not on logical necessity but on moral obligation. The object must rise or fall because it is morally obliged to, rather than because it is lighter or heavier than air. [Piaget]
Dealing simultaneously with several logically related matters	The child is asked the following question: "If the animal has long ears, it is a mule or a donkey; if it has a thick tail, it is a mule or a horse. Well, this animal has long ears and a thick tail. What is the animal?" The child cannot answer correctly. Example: "The animal can be a donkey because you say that if it has long ears it is either a donkey or a mule. But it can be a mule, for you say that if the animal has a thick tail it is either a mule or a horse." [Piaget]

The ability to reason abstractly has a lengthy developmental history. The authors recently observed an episode in which a child was unable to describe correctly the kinship relations between his mother and his two maternal aunts, nor could he indicate how many sisters each had. When questioned about the matter in the absence of the women in question, he fell into the confusions and contradictions typical of a five-year-old. However, when all of the adults were seated at the table and he was asked how many sisters each had, he was able to give the correct answers. The effort which this task cost him was unmistakable. He looked fixedly at his mother, then turned and looked at her two sisters one by one, naming each as he did so. Then he repeated the same process for each of his two aunts. The child's behavior clearly represents a phase in learning to understand relationships. At the age of five years the child's comprehension of abstractions tends to be on a relatively low level —his comprehension is concrete rather than abstract, as Goldstein would say. The persons or objects must be physically before him if he is to solve even the simpler kinds of questions concerning their interrelations.

Here is an illustration of how a child may apply what he learned in a relatively concrete situation to one in which a higher degree of abstraction is required. The child has learned, by purchases in stores, that the more pieces of gum were bought the more pennies were needed. He is then shown one stick of gum and asked what it costs. "One penny." Then the stick of gum is broken in halves before his eyes, and the question is repeated. "Two cents." Another half is divided, and the answer is "three cents."

Piaget has analyzed the failures of children on certain tests dealing with concepts of space, number, movement, and the like. His technique is suggested by the following:

> To study the formation of classes we place about twenty beads in a box, the subject acknowledging that they are "all made of wood," so that they constitute a whole, B. Most of these beads are brown and constitute part A, and some are white, forming the complementary part A'. In order to determine whether the child is capable of understanding the operation A plus A' equals B, *i.e.* the uniting of parts in a whole, we may put the following simple question: In this box (all the beads still being visible) which are there more of,—wooden beads or brown beads, *i.e.*, is A < B?
>
> Now, up to about the age of 7 years, the child almost always replies that there are more brown beads "because there are only two or three white ones." We then question further, "Are all

the brown ones made of wood?"—"Yes."—"If I take away all the wooden beads and put them here (a second box) will there be any beads in the (first) box?"—"No, because they are all made of wood."—"If I take away the brown ones will there be any beads left?"—"Yes, the white ones." Then the original question is repeated and the subject continues to state that there are more brown beads than wooden ones in the box because there are only two white ones, etc.

The mechanism of this type of reaction is easy to unravel; the subject finds no difficulty in concentrating his attention on the whole B, or on the parts A and A' if they have been isolated in thought, but the difficulty is that by centering on A he destroys the whole B, so that the part A can no longer be compared with the other part A'.[36]

Piaget has suggested that there are four fairly clear stages in the learning of logical operations. For our purpose there is no need to describe these stages; but the import of his theory is that as children move from stage to stage, the organization of their behavior changes accordingly.

Our discussion of the child's learning of the more complicated forms of language behavior involved in reasoning and the handling of abstract concepts has been based largely upon Piaget's work. It should therefore be noted that Piaget's interpretations have been criticized by other investigators. These critics have contended, for example, that his distinction between children's and adults' logic exaggerate the differences, and that many of the errors which Piaget cites as characteristic of children are also committed by adults. Another criticism is that the development of the child is a gradual process rather than a succession of clear-cut and sharply divided stages. These and other criticisms commonly made of Piaget's work seem to us to be of minor importance. His account of the way in which children think seems to us to be the most valuable one in the literature.

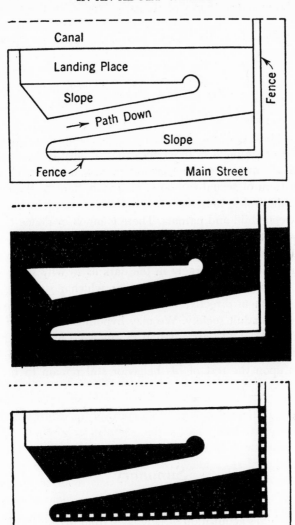

Structure of the Hamburg dock from the points of view of the adult and the child. Black indicates the parts that are significant to the adult (center) and to the child (below). (Diagrams, after Muchow, from Heinze Werner, *Comparative Psychology of Mental Development,* rev. ed., Chicago: Follet Publishing Co., 1948)

Personality and Language Behavior

Studies of the child's acquisition of speech have been largely concerned with speech as a learned skill and have not as yet revealed much about the way in which speech habits and preverbal communication influence the development of personality. Research on the latter problem is beset by extraordinary difficulties. As an example, we may cite the learning of sex behavior. Clearly the child's pattern of sexual response, his conceptions of the masculine and feminine roles, must be profoundly influenced by the interaction between child and parents. There is much evidence to support this view, but the precise nature of this learning and its timing is hardly understood at all. The same is true of many other types of behavior. We are still largely in the dark as to why some children acquire obnoxious patterns of behavior which no one appears to have taught them directly, whereas other children are assimilated smoothly into adult society. We may hypothesize in a general way concerning the child's assimilation of language habits and all that goes with them, but the subtler details concerning the effects of language upon the rest of his behavior still remain to be worked out.

Summary

In the child's acquisition of language, from his earliest babblings and simplest vocalizations to the final convergence with adult speech, the progression is from the instrumental use of words, word-sentences, and gestures to the more complicated forms of speech. Because ways of speaking are intimately connected with ways of thinking, we have emphasized the ways in which the child's assimilation of language is related to self-control, to suggestibility, and to the development of logical thought. The growth of logical comprehension in the child is illustrated by the manner in which Negro children acquire concepts of race and the way in which children's ideas of money and the process of exchange are developed. There is need for much further study of the relationship between language behavior and personality development; on the whole, this has been a neglected research area.

SUGGESTIONS FOR DISCUSSION AND SPECIAL REPORTS

1. Contrast the approaches of Gesell and Piaget to the study of children.

2. Review some of the literature concerning similarities and differences of child and adult thought.

3. Comment on: "A rose by any other name would not be a rose."

4. Question several children of different ages about death and interpret their remarks.

5. Have several children of different ages draw stick pictures of their friends or parents, and interpret the pictures and the accompanying remarks of the children.

6. What hypotheses may be advanced to account for the fact that Negro children often discriminate between white, colored, and black, whereas white children do not?

7. Why does the law declare that it is impossible for a child below a certain age to commit a crime?

NOTES

[1] D. McCarthy in L. Carmichael (ed.), *Manual of Child Psychology*, Wiley, 1946, pp. 491-492.

[2] C. Bean, "An Unusual Opportunity to Investigate the Psychology of Language," *J. Genet. Psych.*, 40(1932): 181-202.

[3] H. Taine, "Note on the Acquisition of Language by Children and in the Human Species," [translated in] *Mind*, 2(1877): 252.

[4] W. N. Kellogg and L. A. Kellogg, *The Ape and the Child,*

McGraw-Hill, 1933, pp. 288-289.

[5] I. Latif, "The Physiological Basis of Linguistic Development and of the Ontogeny of Meaning," *Psych. Rev.*, 41(1934): 76.

[6] *Ibid.*, p. 76.

[7] G. M. de Laguna, *Speech: Its Function and Development*, Yale University Press, 1927, p. 270.

[8] *Ibid.*, p. 91.

[9] M. M. Lewis, *Infant Speech*, Harcourt, Brace, 1936, p. 91.

[10] *Ibid.*, pp. 162-163.

[11] *Ibid.*, pp. 147-149.

[12] C. Bühler, *From Birth to Maturity*, London: Kegan Paul, 1935, p. 56.

[13] Lewis, *op. cit.*, p. 115.

[14] Taine, *op. cit.*, pp. 254-256.

[15] French for "potato."

[16] French for "baby."

[17] Lewis, *op. cit.*, p. 210.

[18] F. Lorimer, *The Growth of Reason*, Harcourt, Brace, 1929, pp. 134-135.

[19] R. Messerschmidt, "Responses of Boys between the Ages of Five and Sixteen Years to Hull's Postural Suggestion Set," *J. Genet. Psych.*, 43(1933): 405-421.

[20] C. L. Hull, *Hypnosis and Suggestibility*, Appleton-Century, 1933.

[21] L. Ames, "The Development of Sense of Time in the Young Child," *J. Genet. Psych.*, 68 (1948): 97-125.

[22] C. Stendler, *Children of Brasstown*, Urbana, Ill.: University of Illinois Press, 1949.

[23] J. Moreno, *Who Shall Survive?* Washington, D.C.: Nervous and Mental Disease Publishing Co., 1934.

[24] E. Horowitz and R. Horowitz, "Development of Social Attiudes in Children," *Sociometry*, 1 (1938): 301-338.

[25] K. B. Clark and M. P. Clark, "Racial Identification and Preference in Negro Children," in G. E. Swanson, T. M. Newcomb, and E. L. Hartley, *Readings in Social Psychology* (rev. ed.), Holt, 1952, pp. 551-560.

[26] M. Seeman, "Skin Color Values in Three All-Negro Classes," *Am. Soc. Rev.*, 11(1946): 315-321.

[27] E. F. Frazier, *Negro Youth at the Crossways*, Washington, D.C.: American Council on Education, 1940. Chap. II, "The Role of the Family," pp. 39-69, esp. p. 69.

[28] R. L. Yokley, *The Development of Racial Concepts in Negro Children*, unpublished doctoral dissertation, Indiana University, 1952.

[29] R. E. Horowitz, "A Pictorial Method for the Study of Self-Identification in Pre-School Children," *J. Genet. Psych.*, 62 (1943): 135-148.

[30] M. Sherif, *An Outline of Social Psychology*, Harper, 1948, pp. 352-353.

[31] See M. Radke, H. Trager, and H. Davis, "Social Perceptions and Attitudes of Children," *Genet. Psych. Monograph*, 40 (1949): 327-447.

[32] This account is adapted from A. L. Strauss, "The Development and Transformation of Monetary Meanings in the Child," *Am. Soc. Rev.*, 17(1952): 275-286.

[33] J. Piaget, "Principal Factors Determining Intellectual Evolution

from Childhood to Adult Life,"
in *Factors Determining Human
Behavior*, Harvard University
Press, 1937, pp. 32-48.
[34] *Ibid.*, p. 37.

[35] A. Jersild, *Child Psychology* (3d
ed.), Prentice-Hall, 1947, p. 380.
[36] J. Piaget, *The Psychology of Intelligence*, London: Routledge
and Kegan Paul, 1950, p. 133.

SELECTED BIBLIOGRAPHY

Ames, L., "The Development of Sense of Time in the Young Child,"
J. Genet. Psych., 68(1948): 97-125. A descriptive study.

Clark, K., and M. Clark, "Racial Identification and Preference in Negro
Children," in G. E. Swanson, T. M. Newcomb, and E. L. Hartley,
Readings in Social Psychology (rev. ed.), Holt, 1952, pp. 551-560. An
important exploratory study of the degree to which Negro children of
various ages identify themselves as Negroes and of their attitudes
toward the role.

Delacroix, H., *L'Enfant et le langage*, Paris: Alcan, 1934. An excellent
detailed compilation of materials on the language behavior of children.

Freidson, E., "Adult Discount: An Aspect of Children's Changing Taste,"
Child Devel., 24(1953): 39-49. An amusing and excellent study of
children's taste for mass-media drama.

Havighurst, R. J., and B. L. Neugarten, *American Indian and White
Children: A Sociopsychological Investigation*, University of Chicago
Press, 1955. Contains interesting comparative materials, gathered
through testing, including some in the moral realm.

Horowitz, E., "The Development of Attitudes toward the Negro," *Arch.
Psych.*, 3, 194(1936). Shows how children in a small Tennesse community learned to be prejudiced against Negroes.

Laguna, G. M. de, *Speech: Its Function and Development*, Yale University Press, 1927. The material on children's speech is scattered but of
high quality.

Latif, I., "The Physiological Basis of Linguistic Development and of the
Ontogeny of Meaning," Part I and Part II, *Psych. Rev.*, 41(1934):
55-85, 153-176. A suggestive technical treatment of the child's acquisition of language.

Lewis, M. M., *Infant Speech*, Harcourt, Brace, 1936. Perhaps the best
discussion of the child's acquisition of symbols from the standpoint
both of concrete details and of general theory.

McCarthy, D., in L. Carmichael (ed.), *Manual of Child Psychology*,
Wiley, 1946. Chap. X, "Language Development in Children," pp. 476-
581. An excellent general survey of research on children's language

development, though not so well-integrated nor so important a contribution as Lewis' volume.

Piaget, J., *The Psychology of Intelligence*, London: Routledge and Kegan Paul, 1950. The most compact statement of Piaget's position.

Radke, M., H. Trager, and H. Davis, "Social Perceptions and Attitudes of Children," *Genet. Psych. Monographs*, 40(1949): 327-447. An interesting study of children's perceptions of race and ethnicity.

Strauss, A., "The Development and Transformation of Monetary Meanings in the Child," *Am. Soc. Rev.*, 17(1952): 275-286. A study of concept development.

Werner, H., *Comparative Psychology of Mental Development*, Harper, 1940. A valuable collection of loosely organized critical comments on numerous studies of various modes of thought. The sections on the thinking of children are especially good.

Werner, H., and E. Kaplan, "The Acquisition of Word Meanings: A Developmental Study," *Monogr. Soc. Res. Child. Develop.*, 15, No. 1 (1952). An excellent study of development, with implications for levels of child thought.

CHAPTER 7 · · ·

Thought

and

Language

THE PRECEDING CHAPTERS have explored the significance of language for human behavior. We have investigated the linguistic and social aspects of perceiving, emoting, and remembering; the drastic consequences of language impairment; and the indissoluble association of language with the child's socialization. Throughout we have emphasized that language is essential to human functioning, *functioning that is exceedingly complex just because men behave symbolically*.

In order to make clear the implications of this position, it will be necessary to introduce further complications into the relatively simple picture of human action that has been drawn. We turn next to a consideration of the lingual, hence social, aspects of "thought." Human thinking processes, as distinct from those of lower animals, depend upon the manipulation of symbols by the thinker; and the problems to which he addresses himself, whether personal or public, arise in the social context, in particular places at particular times.

The terms in which problems are set, and solved, are part and parcel of the whole communicative network in which person and group are involved. We shall put aside until the next chapter the more obviously "social" (or group) facets of thinking. In the present chapter we shall consider subject matter more closely related to our previous discussions of aphasia, schizophrenia, and the acquisition of language and reason in children: we shall be concerned with levels of thought, as evidenced in fantasy and dreaming; with basic language processes as they relate to reasoning; and with the peculiarly flexible character of human thought.

Speech and Thought

BASIC LANGUAGE PROCESSES

As the child gradually acquires mastery of his mother tongue he learns to use it in increasingly complex ways and in a greater variety of situations. Besides learning to understand and speak it, he also learns to read and write it and to think with it. Each of these activities is a part of the symbolic process that is language behavior, but each in some degree develops separately and differently, presenting special problems and adding its own potentialities for the evolution of human personality and human society. Taken together, the various parts of the symbolic process make it possible for organisms to be transformed into self-conscious, self-regulating, social beings.

Speech for Others and Speech for Oneself · For some time after he has begun to speak, the child makes little distinction between words that he addresses to himself and those that he addresses to others. After a time, however, he learns to adapt his remarks to the exigencies of the social situation. He becomes aware of the responses of others to the remarks he makes, and therefore begins to adapt them to the requirements of intelligible communication. The child's development in this respect is usually a fairly continuous one in the direction of increasing clarity and adequacy.

Much of the child's early speech is not directed at others for purposes of communication, but is more in the nature of self-expression or self-stimulation. He not only talks aloud to his parents, but also talks to himself as he plays alone. At this early stage the things he says to himself and those he says to others are very much the same.

As the child becomes an adult he continues to talk to himself, but the things he says to himself become sharply differentiated from what he says to others. If he is alone, where no one can hear him, he may speak aloud, whisper, or mutter to himself. When unexpectedly overheard he is usually embarrassed. Few people will accept a penny for their thoughts because inner speech often deals with matters that are taboo in ordinary conversation.

Listening and Comprehending · Conversation is a very complex activity, for each participant is engaged almost simultaneously in a number of distinct processes. Thus while A speaks to B, B listens to A. But B is also busily engaged in formulating the remarks which he intends to make as soon as A stops speaking. B also may be commenting to himself upon what A is saying to him. Some of these comments may not even be explicitly formulated, and generally they will not be uttered aloud. Thus, B may remark to himself that A is stupid or confused or dishonest; but, when his turn to speak comes, these comments are suppressed in favor of others which meet the conversational requirements of courteous social intercourse. To complicate matters still further, A not only speaks to B; he also listens to what he himself is saying to B: correcting, revising, retracting, and evaluating as he goes along. Both A and B alternate between listening to their own speech and to the speech of the other. The remarks made by each are called forth by and adapted to remarks made by the other.

Comprehension of someone else's speech of course presupposes mastery of the language and is itself the counterpart of speech. The words of the other person act as stimuli which produce in the listener an internal symbolic process that constitutes the act of comprehending. Speech and the comprehension of speech are not different processes: they are different phases of the same process. No one can communicate linguistically with his fellows unless he himself comprehends his own remarks. Conversely, a person does not adequately comprehend the ideas of others until he is able to formulate them for himself. The crucial test of human comprehension of a word is the individual's ability to use the word correctly.

Although it is often held that dogs and other animals "comprehend" things said to them, the standard of comprehension is not the same as that applied to human beings. Parents, for example, do not assume from isolated correct responses that their children understand correctly all the words directed at them. The child is subjected to another and more crucial test; he must himself be able to use the words correctly, not just once or twice, but in a wide variety of situations and in various combinations. If we keep in mind that *the fundamental prototype of language behavior is conversation,* we shall not become confused by the fact that lower animals, such as dogs, seem to be able to comprehend verbal cues. As we have seen, children show a similar subverbal comprehension before they have learned to speak.

Writing · A further elaboration of speech is the development of written symbols. It is almost impossible to exaggerate their importance. The ideas and accomplishments of past generations are preserved in written records, so that each new generation does not begin its career anew, but builds upon what was accomplished before. The significance of writing is suggested by the fact that cultures which have a written language are called "civilizations," whereas those which do not are called "preliterate" or "primitive."

It is true that the existence of tradition, or social heritage, does not depend entirely upon writing. All human societies, including those that are preliterate, have social heritages which include their speech, both as part of the heritage itself and as the mechanism by which the other parts of the heritage are formulated and transmitted from generation to generation. This existence of tradition is a decisive element of control in human behavior, distinguishing it from that of all other animal species.

The development of writing in a society gives a tremendous new impetus to the development and power of tradition. The invention of written records, for example, marks the beginnings of recorded history and of the historical idea, with its manifold intellectual and social implications. Without such recorded history, susceptible to reinterpretation and reformulation by each succeeding generation, rapidly developing social, political, artistic, and philosophical movements could not exist. Entirely new modes of symbolic operation become possible when symbols can be written down as well as spoken—as, for example, numerical and algebraic notation. Without written symbols, most of the achievements that constitute modern civilization would have been impossible.

Although there is a close parallel between writing-reading and speaking-listening, the two processes are not identical. Each has its own characteristics and each adds certain qualities and possibilities of its own to human intelligence.

Writing is in many ways more exacting than speech, for the latter is assisted and supplemented by gestures and intonation, whereas writing stands by itself. Ambiguities, contradictions, possible double meanings, and nuances of meaning, which in conversation could be taken care of by gestures or facial expressions, must be considered as thoughts are translated laboriously into written words, phrases, clauses, and sentences. People often find that their thoughts are clarified and systematized in the attempt to write them. The effort required in writing, the submission to rules governing written language, and the fact that what is written acquires an objective public character all make writing a difficult and exacting art. It is a truism that ideas are changed in the course of formulating them in writing.

INTERNALIZED SPEECH AND THOUGHT

From Egocentric Speech to Thought · From the ages of about three to seven years, the speech which the child directs at himself becomes more and more abbreviated and, to outsiders, less and less intelligible. His self-directed remarks become increasingly truncated. He uses various abbreviating devices. For example, the subject of the sentence tends to be omitted because it is understood implicitly.

It is interesting to ask what happens to the egocentric speech of the child. It does not simply disappear without leaving any trace, but gradually becomes internalized. What begins as external egocentric speaking eventually goes underground. In the process it is transformed. It ceases to be speaking in a literal sense and becomes "thinking."

Ingenious experiments have enabled Vigotsky[1] to discover and describe some features of the gradual transformation. His evidence indicates that the internal speech of adults retains many of the characteristics of childish egocentric speech. It is, for example, very abbreviated, much concerned with self, often highly fragmentary and disjointed, and filled with irrelevancies. The egocentric speech of the child, it should be emphasized, is not mere verbal play; like the adult thought which grows out of it, it serves an adaptive function. Thus, if the child is alone, or in a very noisy room, or if he thinks he is not being understood, his egocentric utterances diminish. However, when he is faced with problems both his references to self and assertions of his own ego increase in number. Speaking aloud apparently helps him solve problems by "thinking them through" aloud.

The process which transforms external language into thought may be nicely illustrated by referring to the manner in which people learn to count. The child at first counts aloud, touches, or points with hands or head to the objects that he is counting. If he is prevented from pointing or saying anything, he is usually unable to count at all. He begins also by counting similar objects, for his counting depends on external features and overt processes which to the adult are not at all essential. As the child grows to adulthood, the external props are discarded one by one. He learns to count dissimilar objects. It becomes unnecessary for him to point, and later it becomes unnecessary for him to count aloud. He may continue to move his lips and count inaudibly to himself, but eventually this external activity also may disappear. The youngster's initial dependence upon external props and upon more primitive activities reappears when he tackles more difficult mathematical problems. For example, the following are instances of how a fourth-grade child adds "by counting":[2]

$$6 \; :: \qquad 5 \; :: \qquad 7 \qquad \quad \because 6 \; \because$$
$$8 \qquad\quad 7 \qquad\quad 3 \; : \qquad\quad 8$$
$$\overline{14} \qquad\quad \overline{12} \qquad\quad \overline{10} \qquad\quad \overline{14}$$

For the person who has some facility at mathematics, the very awareness of number-words may vanish, so that mathematical thought often appears to proceed without any dependence upon language symbols.

A very similar process of internalization is involved in learning to read properly. Here, as in learning to count, the child begins by reading aloud, progresses to reading inaudibly to himself, and ends by following a sequence of ideas with relatively little attention paid to specific words.

The Dualistic Error · There is a strong inclination on the part of many persons to conceive of thinking as independent of the more overt forms of language behavior which precede it and make it possible. Laymen are not the only ones who commit this error. As Vigotsky has written:

> The fundamental error of most investigations in thinking and speech, the fault which was responsible for their futility, consisted in regarding thought and word as two independent and isolated elements.[3]

Language behavior is supposed to have a material or behavioristic basis, whereas thinking is regarded as something separate, distinct, and of a purely "mental" or "spiritual" character—in short, disembodied. The "mental powers" involved in thinking are thought of as seeking external means of expressing themselves, and language becomes merely their external agent or tool. Language is then said to be "a vehicle for the transmission of ideas"—a way of transferring the ideas occurring in the mind of one person to the mind of someone else. Thus the indissoluble unity of language and thought is destroyed—and placed outside the realm of empirical research.

Language and Thought Not Identical · The idea that language and thinking are separate is really nonsensical, since the term "mind" itself refers in a sense to bodily activity—a bodily activity of a very special kind. This does not mean that all thinking involves the use of words or even of symbols, or that speech is to be identified with thought. Obviously, some sort of thinking process goes on, probably fairly continuously, in lower forms of life. Similarly, the infant is capable of simple thought processes without the aid of language, and adults engage in thinking processes which are not dependent upon language or other conventional symbols. We have emphasized this absence of identity between language behavior and thought by calling attention to the fact that when speech becomes internalized it is *transformed* into something else. Although it is demonstrable that language (in the narrow sense) plays a direct role in many thinking processes, it is equally demonstrable that it does not play such a role in all of them.

Consideration of the thought processes employed by the creative artist is instructive at this juncture. Does a painter or a musician need to use language as he paints or composes? Does a sculptor use language as he shapes a stone figure with a live model before him? From the subjective reports of artists and musicians, it is clear that they may manipulate musical and artistic symbols with or without verbally formulating their means and ends to themselves. When artists are asked what a given picture "means," they often reply in what seems to be gibberish or refuse to talk at all, simply saying that the picture should speak for itself. The symbols which they create and use are nondiscursive, nonlinguistic. They cannot very well be translated into verbal symbols. Such nondiscursive thought is naively believed by some to be purely recreational, and easy, as compared to the strenuous thinking of the scientist or mathematician. Dewey, among others, has countered with,

> the idea that the artist does not think as intently and penetratingly as a scientific inquirer is absurd. A painter . . . has to see each particular connection of doing and undergoing in relation to the whole that he desires to produce. To apprehend such relations is to think, and is one of the most exacting modes of thought. . . . Any idea that ignores the necessary role of intelligence in production of works of art is based upon identification of thinking with use of one special kind of material, verbal signs and words. To think effectively in terms of relations of qualities is as severe a demand upon thought as to think in terms of symbols, verbal and mathematical.[4]

Because the artist works primarily with other than language symbols, we should not be misled into thinking that language is irrelevant to his thought processes. Harkening back to our discussion of the aphasic will be helpful at this point, as will a recollection of the linguistic nature of perception.

That thought is neither identical with language nor irrevocably chained to it is suggested by the constant tendency of thinking to run ahead of language and to seek ways of overcoming limitations imposed upon it by language; at other times, and perhaps even more often, language runs far ahead of thought or is used without much thought as it degenerates into mere "verbalism." Creative and pioneering thought often requires the invention of new linguistic, notational, and other representational devices to give it expression. The fact that language is used in the analysis of language behavior and that the latter can be analyzed and criticized, is further evidence of a lack of identity. However, it is easy to carry this line of argument too far and to overemphasize human creativity and originality, or to exaggerate the extent to which thinking can free itself from the limitations imposed upon it by its sources and the instruments it uses.

Fantasying, Dreaming, and Levels of Thought

In discussing aphasics, we noted that these patients could perform acts of direct reference but not acts of symbolic reference—in other words, they characteristically fail to organize their activities on the highest level of abstraction. Such simple dichotomies as "concrete attitude" and "abstract attitude," or "direct reference" and "symbolic reference," do little more than suggest the immense range of sign behavior, from the simplest to the most complex. No man thinks systematically, logically, and on the highest planes of abstraction about all matters, nor do all matters require abstract thought. Some may never learn to think consistently at the highest levels: that is, similar matters may be dealt with on varying levels of abstraction. Young children and schizophrenics can be said to operate for the most part on lower levels than normal adults. Various classifications of sign behavior and thought have been suggested as preliminary to investigation of the full range of thought. Dewey and Bentley,[5] for instance, offer a tentative hierarchy. The idea that thinking covers a range of sign behavior is likely to be a fruitful one. Study of this range is a task for the future. In the meantime, it is worth asking what are its implications for our understanding of such related mental processes as daydreaming and dreaming.

It is common in psychological writing to make a distinction between objective (or rational) thought and autistic (or fantasy) thought. The former is supposed to be more or less impersonal, systematic, objective, and logical; the latter is supposed to occur because it satisfies the subjective wishes and desires of the person and so is, more or less, irrational, illogical, and out of touch with reality. Likewise, dreaming is opposed to daytime adaptive thinking, being either unrelated to reality or relegated to the role of doing what cannot be done by conscious thinking. The conception of a sign series, or range, should lead us to challenge this widely accepted dichotomy of types of mental processes.

FANTASY

The assumption that fantasying, or daydreaming, is a process apart from rational or systematic thinking is associated with the belief that the daydreamer substitutes the satisfactions of the daydream for those denied him, temporarily or permanently, by the exigencies of actual life. Often it is said that he derives three main types of satisfactions: compensation, escape, and release. Compensatory daydreams allow the person imaginatively to attain goals which are otherwise unattainable. The Cinderella legend has its counterpart in the fantasies of anyone who wishes for something he cannot get. The second type, daydreams of escape, occur under conditions of drudgery, anxiety, boredom, hardship, fear, and the like. The fantasies temporarily transport the dreamer into more pleasant surroundings. Daydreams of release function as safety valves by allowing the individual to dissipate his anger, hatred, resentment, irritation, or jealousy in a harmless imaginary form.

Although fantasy is supposed to serve the three functions of escape, compensation, and release, it is not an easy matter to prove that these are its only or its main functions. It is difficult to determine the function of a given daydream merely by examining its content. Even if one knows a great deal about the personality and background of the daydreamer, the fantasy activity may still not fit into any of the three conventional categories.

FANTASY AND REALITY

Reproduced by permission.
Copyright 1955, The New Yorker Magazine, Inc.

The attempt to uncover the function of daydreams is based upon the assumption that fantasying is something special and apart from rational thinking. It is assumed that it must yield special satisfactions or it would not occur. Hence, daydreaming is supposed to occur mainly in connection with situations of stress, anxiety, boredom, and the like. This is underscored further by the vivid and elaborate fantasies of the psychotic and the excessive daydreaming of maladjusted people. However, a closer scrutiny of daydreaming, without previous commitment to a dichotomization of "reality-thinking" and a substitute for it, brings some other relevant matters into focus.

During many of his bouts of daydreaming the normal adult knows perfectly well that he is daydreaming, and furthermore he will sometimes set aside certain times of the day to engage in this often pleasant activity. The young child has difficulty in distinguishing between reality and fancy, sometimes getting them quite confounded in his discourse, to the amusement or exasperation of his elders. The requirements of adult life make it eventually necessary for the child to draw a fairly strict line between fact and imagination. The severe psychoses cause their victims to lose the ability to make this clear separation, at least in their less normal moments. In the psychotic, various types of fantasying seem to constitute "thinking" and "reasoning." These commonplace observations do not lead to a separation of fantasying and reasoning but suggest—not prove—quite the opposite: namely, that fantasying is a type of reasoning. Since fantasying is not a single process, but embraces many types of covert activity, we may, speaking more strictly, say that reasoning of various kinds may occur when anyone fantasies. The fantasy life of the very young child is the dominant, or only, life he knows. He has not yet been sufficiently socialized into correcting his perspectives by checking them against the facts or comparing them with the views of other persons. The severe psychotic does not, for the most part, operate with "consensual validation" (public verification) in mind; the various types of fantasying in which he engages constitute his modes of handling social relationships and responding to the physical world. The maladjusted person gets, we sometimes say, "absorbed in his fantasy life." This is the way he meets the impinging world. The normal adult, although he knows the difference between reality and fancy and between public knowledge and private secret, is not constrained to reason only in socially sanctioned and verifiable modes nor in systematic or rational ways. It is well known that even a scientist presents his findings and checks them for public appraisal in systematic ways, but that his guiding ideas may have occurred to him through processes that are reverie-like. Even the elaboration of ideas that "come as gifts" is not always syllogistic or systematic, although, as we have said, its public elaboration always is.

A "stream of consciousness" or of "associations" is likely to be a peculiarly rich mixture of covert mental processes. Visual and auditory images, subverbal comments, daydreaming dramas, recollections, reseeing of past scenes, self-judgments, internal dialogue, and many more elements jostle each other. Even a daydream that happens to have a fairly tight plot or progression may have intrusions in the form of the daydreamer's comments or judgments. A certain amount of control may be exerted over daydreams by repeating and reviving them. Many daydreams appear to be of short duration and fragmentary and are preceded and followed by conscious and rational thought processes. Like the latter, the fantasying may be absorbing enough to exclude external stimuli which might otherwise impinge upon the awareness of the person—or the stimuli may break the line of reasoning or fantasying. It is easier to daydream when other people are not around to break the reverie, but this is perhaps true for any kind of thinking except that which depends upon immediate reciprocal stimulation and verification.

Some writers, for example R. Faris, have contended that it is "more plausible to consider it [daydreaming] as preparation for hypothetical activity than as consummation."[6] This is certainly one of the functions of all thinking, and there is little reason to deny that it is the function of much fantasying. A point that should be especially noted is that interaction between humans is dramatic in character, and thus a dramatic imagery is required for both actual and imaginary participation in it. For example, a man is preparing for such interaction when he pictures to himself various ways of getting well acquainted with a woman who attracts him. In order to imagine the play of gestures, to judge the effects of conversational lines, he plays out various dramas in his imagination. Out of these a plan, or at least a preparatory act, may emerge.

It is indeed a moot point whether anyone about to enter knowingly upon a new status, or anyone about to embark upon any enterprise involving new interpersonal relationships, can initiate his lines of behavior without daydreaming of himself in his new role.

Cues for actual behavior seem sometimes to derive from this kind of thinking, which is, of course, also intertwined with less pictorial reasoning. Anticipatory fantasying may even occur in an overt or shared form, as when husband and wife plan an exciting trip or anticipate the birth of a child. The preparatory functions of fantasying—rather than the merely wish-fulfilling functions—can be suggested by the experience of immigrants, who imagine what the new land is going to look like and what is going to happen to them there. Visionaries, utopians, and leaders of social movements do not merely plan, organize, and execute. "Dreamer" is a word to be applied to them literally. In order that the symbolism of a movement may recruit members and help retain them, it must be kept vivid and rich.

Like other forms of thinking, fantasying may turn toward the past. It is true that one may help eradicate shame and other unpleasant feelings by refurbishing a past conversation or incident in daydreams. But it is also characteristic of human beings to seek explanations of the past, to "rethink" incidents and discover new meanings in them. Some of this reinterpretation and reconstruction presumably goes on in the form of reverie. Reverie processes abound in times of personal crisis, when the individual is questioning himself about where he is going and must consequently consider where he has been.

These processes are also implicit in any thinking or imagining in which the person seeks to establish relationships with real or imaginary persons. Some people clearly do get pleasure out of imagining meeting movie stars or other celebrities and may daydream long conversations occurring in such improbable situations. This kind of fantasying may not merely be pleasurable; it may transform the individual in his own eyes. Such shifts of self-conception, we are suggesting, may occur even though the dreamer is aware that he is fantasying. Another kind of vision is that sought by the Indian lad who fasts in the desert in order to have an elaborate reverie, or series of reveries, in which sacred animals and gods appear. Here there is social sanction both for the vision and its life-long effects upon the individual—effects which are ultimately important to the life of the tribe as well. This last example suggests also the close connection between ritual and reverie. Ritual, when it is not merely routine, represents a collective acting out of hallowed dramatic sequences; and these, like reverie, may orient one for future conduct. In S. Langer's felicitous phrasing, rituals

> are part of man's ceaseless quest for conception and orientation. They embody his dawning motives of power and will, of death and victory, they give active and impressive form to his demoniac forms and ideals. Ritual is the most primitive reflection of serious thought, a slow deposit, as it were, of people's imaginative insight into life.[7]

Seen in such wider contexts, fantasy processes are multiple in kind and function, and are orienting as well as wish-fulfilling. Most of the literature on autistic thought and fantasying has been produced by psychiatrists and clinical psychologists who are impressed with the great amount and truly fantastic quality of the reveries of their patients. This latter fact, combined with certain witting and unwitting assumptions about the nature of man and his relationship to reality that are made by many psychiatrists and psychologists, leads to an undue stress upon the crippling or merely compensatory effects of fantasy life. Excessive fantasying does not lead to maladjustment, but is a symptom of it.

The assumption that fantasy yields relief and surcease from the trials of an exacting world has pervaded such popular dramatic and literary forms as "soap operas," movies, detective stories, and historical novels. These, it is often said by laymen and scholar alike, allow the audience to lose themselves in the characters with whom they identify themselves and thus escape from harsh reality. It is much more probable that people derive orientation as well as simple pleasure from this entertainment. According to Warner and Henry,[8] soap operas sometimes provide patterns for behavior during marriage crises, and Blumer's[9] study of movie fans, some years ago, made clear that they emulated behavior seen in the movies, turning it to their own uses.

The trouble with the concept of "escape" is that the term so easily becomes an epithet directed against a person of whose activities one does not approve. People thus accuse one another of escaping basic problems. Politically minded writers accuse philosophers and poets of running away from crucial issues and plunging into a miasma of irrelevance. In turn, the former are charged with un-willingness to face squarely the central problem of the meaning of man's existence. The intellectual accuses the common man of indulging in compensatory and "escape" reading instead of reading "good" or "educational" books; and the upper classes are often pic-tured in novels and popular magazines as leading a highly artificial and unrealistic existence. Burke,[10] writing about literary critics, has summarized the difficulties surrounding the concept of escape in the following words:

> Properly used, the idea of escape should present no difficulties. If a situation is unsatisfactory, it is quite normal and natural that people should desire to avoid it and should try any means at their disposal to do so. But the term escape has had a more restricted usage. Whereas it properly applies to *all* men, there was an attempt to restrict its application to *some* men . . . so restricted, it suggested that the people to whom it was applied tended to orient themselves in a totally different way from the people to whom it was not applied, the former always trying to escape from life or avoid realities, while the latter faced realities. . . . There are many critics who avoided telling us precisely what they meant by life, avoidance, and facing reality. In this way . . . they were free to accuse . . . of escape. In the end, the term came to be applied loosely . . . to designate [anyone] . . . whose interest and aims did not closely coincide with those of the critic. While apparently defining a *trait of the person referred to,* the term hardly did more than convey the *attitude of the person making the reference.*

DREAMING

The meaning of dreaming and of particular dreams has long intrigued and sometimes worried men; for books on dreams go back as far as the second century A.D. There is a type of literature called "dream books": these purport to offer guidance in the interpreta-tions of dreams by supplying the meanings of dream sequences and events, usually in terms of predictions for the future of the dreamer. Eating cheese in a dream, for instance, may be said to portend good fortune. The symbols interpreted in dream books are universal, in the sense that anyone eating cheese is in for happy times. These questions of what specific dreams "mean" and whether a universal symbolism exists have had a lively treatment at the hands of scientists during the past century, largely in the fields of psychiatry and psychoanalysis. Social psychologists appear to be much less interested in dreaming, presumably because they do not utilize dreams for obtaining insights into the mental and emotional processes of patients; but dreaming is an interesting, and perhaps important, psychological phenomenon in its own right.

There are many studies of dreaming that deal with physiological correlates, duration, speech, and frequency of occurrence of types of imagery (visual, auditory), with the dream imagery of the blind or the deaf-blind, with sex and age differences, with types of dreams, and the like.[11] The literature of psychiatry is replete with examinations of the meanings of dream symbols and with the roles of certain kinds of dreams in the lives of certain types of neurotics. Despite the considerable bulk of this literature, both empirical and theoretical, the nature and significance of dreaming are areas of dispute.

By far the most influential theory of dreaming is that of Freud. Freud's dream theory is part of a much wider and very elaborate theoretical system concerning the psychological nature of man in general. For our purposes, we need stress here only a few of the chief features of his views on dreams. Various wishes are said to threaten to disturb the sleeper's rest, and dreams perform the function of seeming to fulfill these wishes. Usually the wishes are unacceptable in the sense that the person does not care to admit that he has them. Hence they tend to be excluded from consciousness, or "repressed," during waking hours. In sleep they appear in dreams, but in disguised forms, since even during sleep the person's psychic mechanisms are operating. The obvious, or "manifest," content of the dream is an expression of its "latent," or real, meanings. Freud writes that "we have got to turn the manifest dream into the latent dream, and we have to show how the latter became the former, in the life of the dreamer."[12] Through the technique of evoking the patient's free associations, or nonlogical linkages, the patient and analyst eventually arrive at an interpretation of latent content and a knowledge of the connections between this and the manifest content.

The transformation in the dream of latent content into manifest content is termed the "dream work." Dream work is an example of primitive modes of operation, which are characteristically unconscious. These modes are not rational and objective, and furthermore they do not involve logical connections between propositions. Their hallmark is associations, or nonlogical linkages. This type of mental functioning Freud termed "the primary process"; and the sharply contrasted logical type he considered to be a "secondary process." The primary process of mental functioning manifested in the dream is "regression." The reason that dreams are visual is that there is censorship of undesirable wishes and of "instinctive impulses" which causes these wishes and impulses to emerge in disguised forms. "On account of the . . . process of regression ideas are turned into visual pictures in the dream; the latent dream-thoughts are . . . dramatized and illustrated."[13] Some associations which appear in the dream are not unique to the dreamer but are universal, or at least very common.

Freud pointed out, fairly late in his life, that there were certain possible objections to his wish-fulfillment theory of dreams in the form of contradictory data. Persons who have had serious traumas re-experience these in their dreams: Freud questions what possible satisfaction of impulse can be had by this painful experience. Likewise, the reappearance in dreams of exceedingly unpleasant incidents from early childhood causes pain to the dreamer. Freud tentatively accounts for this partly contradictory evidence by stating that:

> The sleeper has to dream, because the nightly relaxation of repression allows the upward thrust of the traumatic fixation to become active; but sometimes his dream-work, which endeavors to change the memory traces of the traumatic event into a wish-fulfillment, fails to operate.[14]

The Freudian theory of dreams has been considerably amended by Thomas French,[15] an American psychoanalyst. He contends that the mode of mental functioning exemplified in the dream is neither Freud's secondary process nor primary process:

> In fact, it is not associative thinking at all . . . but rather thinking in terms of a practical grasp of real situations: "If I act upon this wish, then I must expect such and such consequences. Shall I

renounce the wish or suffer the consequences? Or is some compromise possible?" The dream's solution may not be very good from the point of view of waking life, but it is always intelligible, once we grasp the nature of the conflict.[16]

French sees dreaming as very like ordinary processes of practical thought, which generally are neither overly logical nor verbally formulated. He rejects the associational psychology which was prevalent in Freud's day, and suggests that the connections between specific latent and manifest meanings are related to the dreamer's attempts to reconcile his conflicting wishes. In French's account we should note particularly that although the notion of wishes is retained, the nature and functioning of dreaming are conceived of very differently.

The psychoanalytic conception of dreaming as wish fulfillment has been attacked repeatedly. Faris, for instance, contends that dreaming is an effort to solve problems, although the nocturnal effort is far less efficient than those of waking life.[17] A more systematic attack has been launched by C. Hall,[18] who argues that dream symbols are not disguised, but are merely representations of ideas: "Dreaming is pictorialized thinking; the conceptual is more perceptual. . . . A dream symbol is an image, usually a visual image, of an object, activity, or scene; the referent for the symbol is a conception." Since different persons may have different conceptions of "woman," for instance, the dream symbols for woman vary accordingly. Hall, who has counted 102 symbols for the male organ in psychoanalytic writing, concludes that "since the referent is not an object, person, or activity but a conception, the 102 different phallic symbols represent 102 ways of conceiving of the male genitals."[19] The dreamer may, of course, hold different conceptions, and hence he may utilize different symbols referring to these conceptions. Dream symbols, consequently, are not universal, although they may be widespread in a given culture. Hall's criticism of Freud seems to stem mainly from two objections: (1) that Freud's "disguise" theory of dream symbolization makes of sleep a more active period than seems likely on the basis of studies and observation; (2) that Freud's associational psychology is *passé*.

H. Sullivan, a thoughtful psychiatrist whose views we shall

encounter again, in his turn would criticize any account of dreaming as cognition on the grounds that the dreamer cannot help distorting his report of what happened during his dream. The point is that there is an impassable barrier between the covert process of dreaming and the verbal formulations of waking life. Even if the dreamer wishes to remember the exact details of his dream, he cannot:

> People who feel that they should analyze . . . a dream . . . into what it stands for, seem to me to be in exactly the state of mind of the person who says to a child of two-and-a-half, "You ought to show more respect for your mother because God on Mt. Sinai said to Moses, 'Honor thy father and thy mother.'" . . . the psychiatrist is dealing with the type of referential operation which is *not* in the syntaxic [verbal] mode, and one merely stultifies himself . . . by trying to make this kind of report syntaxic.[20]

For Sullivan, dreaming is like other mental processes which go on in waking life but outside of awareness, and which have to do with the avoidance of severe anxiety. During sleep the person has less need to defend himself against anxiety-arousing events, so that dreaming functions to guard against anxiety during sleep and (symbolically) to satisfy needs unslaked during the day. No regression is imputed to dreaming by Sullivan and he is chary of interpreting symbols in any but a purely personal context.

These alternative treatments of dreaming suggest something of the controversy surrounding the topic. Is dreaming like logical reasoning—that is, practical everyday thinking—or is it vastly different? Is it problem solving, wish fulfilling? Are the symbols unique to individuals or groups or are many of them universal? We shall not attempt to mediate in this free-for-all. However, because we reject many of the Freudian assumptions about motivation generally (and will make this explicit in Chap. 9), we do reject the views that dreams are disguises for unsanctioned and unconscious instinctual impulses and wishes and that there is unvarying correspondence between a given manifest content and the latent content of a dream. In our view, the living organism, even when asleep or unconscious, is engaged in covert symbolic processes. The processes involved in dreaming are on "lower levels" than those involved in self-conscious rational thought, particularly when the latter is being prepared for public appraisal. It seems unlikely that the modes of sign manipulation employed in dreaming should differ very much, if at all, from those employed in waking hours, particularly when the person is at a very low point of self-awareness.

As for the reporting of dreams, we would agree with Sullivan as to the great difficulty, or even the impossibility, of reporting dreams accurately; and we would add that no one can possibly remember a dream without converting the dream sequence into words and so distorting and probably oversimplifying it. An important aspect of dreaming, for the social psychologist, is that a dream, like any other private experience, can be responded to by the self-conscious person afterward. He may be ashamed of himself for dreaming what he did, or he may be pleased; he may accept his analyst's view or that of some other person, including a fortune teller or the author of a dream book; and, as with all other interpretations, he may change his mind about it at a later time.

Metaphor, Analogy, and Flexibility of Thought

Harking back to earlier discussions of perception and classification (pp. 94-98), we noted that events and objects can be viewed and classified in many different ways. One may make a game of this by trying to see some common object—an apple, for example—from as many different perspectives as possible. Besides thinking of it as an edible fruit, one may imagine it as a ball, a Christmas tree or table decoration, a magical object, a pupil's gift to his teacher, and so on. Each of these ideas leads us to look at the apple from a different perspective and to act "as if" it were what we assume it to be or what we use it for. This ability to switch perspectives, to regard the same event or object in many different contexts, is uniquely human.

When something is treated linguistically as if it were or might possibly be something else, we speak of employing "simile" or "metaphor." So a novelist might describe a helicopter hovering over an airfield as if it were an insect. Metaphorical language is not merely poetic, not simply a colorful embellishment, but is necessary to communication. If it is said that a party was "like a funeral" or that a man's speech was "like the braying of an ass," it is understood that the analogy is to be taken descriptively, not literally.

According to a German linguist, P. Wegener,[21] all discourse involves a context which is well known to speaker and listener, and also a novel element. To express the latter, the speaker will utilize a metaphor or analogy—if precise descriptive terms do not already exist—and the context tells the listener that the analogy is not to be taken at face value. It is impossible to strip explicit or implicit metaphor from speech, for many novel elements cannot easily be handled with extant vocabulary. So the speaker must hint, suggest, evoke. The same is true of speech to oneself. In other words, analogy is at the heart of new perspectives, new orientations, vision, and advance in thought.

However colorful and "concrete" metaphors and similes appear to be, they betray a process of abstraction at work. As Langer[22] has pointed out, a word like "run," when used in connection with rumors, brooks, and so on, has nothing to do with leg action. She suggests that originally all the usages of the verb were probably metaphorical, but now "we take the word itself to mean *that which all its applications have in common, namely, describing a course.*" Wegener has termed such a word a "faded metaphor"; he hypothesizes that "before language had any faded words to denote logical subjects, it could not render a situation by any other means than a demonstrative indication of it in present experience." We need not necessarily agree with Wegener's account of the development of language to see that abstraction rests in some part upon analogy. "The spontaneous similes of language are our first record of *similarities* perceived," Langer writes. But analogical thinking is integral to abstract cogitation of even the most abstract and systematic sort.

We are properly advised against taking an analogy too literally, as in relying upon analogy in order to prove a point in an argument. "The great danger of analogy is that a *similarity* is taken as evidence of an *identity*."[23] However, as the famous economist Keynes once remarked, one must always generalize by analogy from a sample of a class to the entire class, since in many respects each instance is unique and there is no absolute identity of all instances in the class. Despite the great dangers inherent in generalization, generalize we must.

Significantly, new shifts in perspectives are heralded by new analogies or metaphors. When the world was conceived of as round rather than built on the order of a pancake, the new conception led to a restructuring of behavior and social relationships. An extensive new vocabulary is built as a result of acting upon a new abstraction. Those who adhere to old ones will variously greet the new: with ridicule, anger, retaliation, and sometimes with the accusation that the new is in bad taste, as in matters of esthetics. As Burke has remarked, the universe can be sliced like a cheese—"and when one has chosen his own pattern of slicing, he finds that other men's cuts fall at the wrong places."[24] Action based upon new analogies thus challenges loyalties and men's deepest self-involvements.

Keynes' point, as well as our previous discussions of the nature of categories, makes clear that all abstraction, all generalization, is inevitably an oversimplification of reality. Hence all analogies, however fruitful they have been, will be questioned sooner or later. Action based upon a given analogy will not do justice to the claims and rights of some individuals, and eventually the latter will sense this and create their own alternative perspectives. We see this in sectarian splits, in the initiation of social movements, and the formation of new groups designed to meet newly generated demands. The attack on an old metaphor is not always made with slam-bang directness. Since the old can be qualified gradually, it often happens that alterations in social relationships and structures, and even in scientific theory, are made almost imperceptibly—until someone signalizes the really new point of arrival by coining a phrase for it like "manifest destiny" in the nineteenth century, or "the American century" in the twentieth.

The danger and necessity of analogy are the danger and necessity of language itself. No classification covers all qualities of the objects it embraces. Yet without classification and metaphor there would be limited flexibility of behavior, and men's attention would be focused fairly directly upon immediate situations. The danger and fruitfulness of metaphor can be epitomized by a strategy, actually an old and necessary technique often used by the philosopher John Dewey: he would take two sharply opposed philosophical positions and show that from yet another and "transcending" position the opponents were really rivals on the banks of the same local stream. In turn, we can be sure that Dewey's position will be lumped with many that he attacked. From a historical perspective, the positions of even the bitterest opponents often appear to be much closer than the rivals would have thought possible.

Summary

Complex thinking processes, although dependent upon and deriving from a prior use of language, have their own specific attributes which make it impracticable to call them language behavior in a strict sense. The complicated and varied nature of thought processes is exemplified in fantasy and dreaming.

It is to be emphasized particularly that thinking is carried on at many levels, and that these levels are not yet understood very well.

The relations of language to flexibility and thought and belief can be understood through a consideration of the functions of metaphor and multiple perspectives.

SUGGESTIONS FOR DISCUSSION AND SPECIAL REPORTS

1. Analyze some writings about comics or movies in terms of their assumptions about fantasy.

2. Report on some of the literature dealing with "the authoritarian personality" from the standpoint of flexible thought.

3. Read two or three of Piaget's books and describe in detail his views of the relation of language and thought.

4. What are some common-sense notions about the nature of thinking?

5. What are the objections to the dualism which regards mind and body, thought and speech, as radically separate?

6. Review the positions taken in several current psychology texts on the relations between thought and language.

NOTES

[1] L. Vigotsky, "Thought and Speech," *Psychiatry*, 2(1939): 29-52.

[2] C. H. Judd, *Educational Psychology*, Houghton Mifflin, 1939, p. 297.

[3] Vigotsky, *op. cit.*, p. 29.

[4] J. Dewey, *Art as Experience*, Minton, Balch, 1934, pp. 45-46.

[5] J. Dewey and A. F. Bentley, *Knowing and the Known*, Beacon, N. Y.: Beacon House, 1949, p. 16.

[6] R. Faris, *Social Psychology*, Ronald, 1952, p. 100.

[7] S. Langer, *Philosophy in a New Key*, New York: Penguin Books (1942 ed.), p. 128.

[8] W. L. Warner and W. E. Henry, "The Radio Daytime Serial: A Symbolic Analysis," *Gen. Psych. Monograph*, Vol. 37, 1948.

[9] H. Blumer, *Movies and Conduct*, Macmillan, 1933.

[10] K. Burke, *Permanence and Change*, New York: New Republic, 1936, pp. 19-20.

[11] G. Ramsey, "Studies of Dreaming," *Psych. Bull.*, 50(1953): 432-455.

[12] S. Freud, *New Introductory Lectures on Psychoanalysis*, Norton, 1933, p. 19.

[13] *Ibid.*, p. 31.

[14] C. Hall, "A Cognitive Theory of Dream Symbols," *J. Gen. Psych.*, 48(1953): 45.

[15] T. French, "Dreams and Rational Behavior," in F. Alexander and H. Ross (eds.), *Dynamic Psychiatry*, University of Chicago Press, 1952, pp. 35-39.

[16] *Ibid.*, p. 38.

[17] Faris, *op. cit.*, pp. 101-104.

[18] Hall, *op. cit.*, p. 175.

[19] *Ibid.*, p. 170.

[20] H. S. Sullivan, *The Interpersonal Theory of Psychiatry*, Norton, 1953, p. 343.

[21] For an account in English see S. Langer, *Philosophy in a New Key*, New York: Penguin Books, 1942, pp. 111-115.

[22] *Ibid.*, p. 113.

[23] Burke, *op. cit.*, p. 128.

[24] *Ibid.*, p. 136.

SELECTED BIBLIOGRAPHY

Bleuler, E., "Autistic Thinking," *Am. J. Insanity,* 69(1913): 873-886. An old but still useful article which makes distinctions between types of thought.

French, T., in F. Alexander and H. Ross (eds.), *Dynamic Psychiatry,* University of Chicago Press, 1952; "Dreams and Rational Behavior," pp. 35-39. A brief statement of French's position on dreams.

Freud, S., *New Introductory Lectures on Psychoanalysis,* Norton, 1933. The chapter on dreams contains the gist of Freud's influential treatment.

Hall, C. S., "A Cognitive Theory of Dream Symbols," *J. Gen. Psych.,* 48(1953): 169-186. A non-Freudian view of dream symbols.

Rapaport, D., *The Organization and Pathology of Thought,* Columbia University Press, 1951. A very useful book. It is mainly a book of readings taken from such thinkers as Freud, Piaget, Stern, and other Europeans. Pages 689-730 contain the author's own systematic theory.

Sheerer, M., in G. Lindzey (ed.), *Handbook of Social Psychology,* Addison-Wesley, 1954, Vol. I: *Cognitive Theory,* pp. 91-142. Good reading for the advanced student.

Vigotsky, L., "Thought and Speech," *Psychiatry,* 2(1939): 29-52.

———, and A. R. Luria, "The Fate and Function of Egocentric Speech," *Proceedings and Papers,* Ninth International Congress of Psychology, Princeton, 1930, pp. 464-465. This article and the preceding one represent important extensions of Piaget's theories concerning egocentric speech.

Vinacke, W. E., *The Psychology of Thinking,* McGraw-Hill, 1953. A general text which covers a lot of territory.

Wolfenstein, M., and N. Leites, *Movies, a Psychological Study,* Glencoe, Ill.: Free Press, 1950. The themes in movies of three countries are analyzed as recurrent collective daydreams.

CHAPTER 8

The

Social Bases

of

Thought

We have seen that language is a prerequisite for and enters into all but the most primitive kinds of thinking. Since language is a group product, it follows that an individual's modes of thought will be decisively affected by his participation in social groups. In this chapter we shall examine some of the more subtle effects of man's group identifications upon thought structures, logic, bias, and allegiance.

Our general point of view and some of the points to be discussed in detail in this chapter are excellently summarized in the following statement by Mills:

> . . . It is only by utilizing the symbols common to his group that a thinker can think and communicate. . . . By acquiring the categories of a language, we acquire the structured "ways" of a group, and along with the language, the value-implicates of those "ways." Our behavior and perception, our logic and thought, come within the control ambit of a system of language.

A vocabulary is not merely a string of words; imminent within it are societal textures—institutional and political coordinates. Back of a vocabulary lie sets of collective action.[1]

Language and the Structure of Thought

Rather obviously, the content of a person's thought is affected by his social environment. The form or manner of his thinking is similarly influenced. Sapir, making a point akin to that made earlier (Chap. 3) about "symbolic environments," suggests the very great importance that particular languages have for the construction of thought and environments. He says:

> Human beings do not live in an objective world alone . . . but are very much at the mercy of the particular language which has become a medium of expression for their society. It is quite an illusion to imagine that one adjusts to reality essentially without the use of language and that language is merely an incidental means of solving specific problems of communication or reflection . . . the "real world" is to a large extent unconsciously built up on the language habits of the group. No two languages are ever sufficiently similar to be considered as representing the same social reality. The worlds in which different societies live are distinct worlds, not merely the same worlds with different labels attached.[2]

The very structure of a language tends to influence modes of perception and reasoning. This is perhaps less so in the concrete practical realm than on more abstract planes. One of the best illustrations of this point is the manner in which mathematical reasoning is influenced by the nature of the counting system. Think, for example, of the great advantages of Arabic numerals over Roman numerals, even for simple problems in arithmetic, not to mention complicated problems in algebra, geometry, and physics. Many branches of modern mathematics probably could not have been developed by using the Roman system, or without the invention of concepts such as negative numbers, zero, decimal, position, fraction, and the like.

The influences of language structure upon the structure of thought are further illustrated by the difficulties of translators. The translation of other languages into English involves more than merely finding equivalent words, for the translator is faced with the problem of conveying meanings and nuances of meaning which it may be practically impossible to express in English. The Spanish language, for example, has two verbs for "to be": *ser* and *estar*. Their different uses—extremely difficult for a foreigner to master— reflect a mode of thinking resulting from and unique to Spanish culture. The translation of non-European languages into English is even more difficult, since the modes of thought are likely to be still more divergent from ours than are those of peoples living within the general European tradition. Differences between Chinese and American thinking are suggested by the following quotation:

> Chinese poets seldom talk about one thing in terms of another. . . . If a metaphor is used, it is metaphor directly relating to the theme, not something borrowed from the ends of the earth. . . . For our Western taste, used as we are to the operatic in poetry, that is, the spectacular or shocking effect produced by some unusual analogy or metaphor, the substance of Chinese poems seems often mild or trivial.[3]

The following newspaper account suggests some of the difficulties of the conscientious translator when he attempts to interpret English expressions for the Chinese:

> Some of the great difficulties among the diplomats sitting around the international tables here [at the United Nations] arise from the differences in languages, alphabets and, consequently, ways of thinking; and in no tongue is more ingenuity required for accurate, precise translation than Chinese.
>
> The Chinese ideograph script is one of the world's oldest written media, but the talk at Lake Success is so brimful of new ideas, new concepts and new words that, to translate even the basic Charter itself into Chinese, it was necessary to devise almost 2,000 new combinations of characters.
>
> A perfect example of the troubles faced here by Chinese

translators is the word "uranium," which has a persistent way of cropping up in diplomatic reports. The translators went into a huddle and came out with a decision to call the atomic base "U-metal." That, however, only started their headaches.

The symbol for "U" was found in the Chinese word for grapefruit, which in literal translation is the "U-tree." What was just as disturbing, from a purist point of view, was the discovery that the symbol for metal was contained in the first part of the word for "bell," which literally translated, meant "metal boy."

After some cudgeling of brains, however, the calligraphers came up with the proposal to shave off the "tree" part of the "U-tree" character, discard the "boy" part of the "bell" character, and then in the best manner of diplomatic compromise, join the severed remains to form a new symbol: "U-metal" or, as we would say, uranium.[4]

The naïve person tends to regard his native tongue as the "natural language of man," the "best" or "most flexible" one, and in a religious era, as the language of God and His angels. The English-speaking person notes and is tolerant of the peculiarities of French, German, Spanish, and other Indo-European tongues belonging to the same language family as his own. But when he encounters entirely unrelated language structures, such as those of preliterate tongues, he is likely to be nonplussed at first by what appear to him as fundamental deficiencies in intelligibility or as outright departures from common sense, good logic, and good taste.

Although new words may be added to a language with relative ease, the basic structure of a language is highly stable and resists change. Most people who speak a given language are unaware of its structure as something which differs from the structures of other language systems. Consequently, the uniform modes of thought imposed upon them by their native tongue are not recognized or taken into consideration as such, but are accepted as part of the "real nature of the world" or as among the elements of "common sense." Whorf has made the point very clear in the following passage:

> The background linguistic system (in other words, the grammar) of each language is not merely a reproducing instrument for voicing ideas but rather is itself the shaper of ideas, the

program and guide for the individual's mental activity, for his analysis of impressions, for his synthesis of his mental stock in trade. Formulation of ideas is not an independent process, strictly rational in the old sense, but is part of a particular grammar and differs, from slightly to greatly, as between different grammars. We dissect nature along lines laid down by our native languages. The categories and types that we isolate from the world of phenomena we do not find there because they stare every observer in the face. . . . We cut nature up, organize it into concepts, and ascribe significances as we do, largely because we are parties to an agreement to organize it in this way—an agreement that holds throughout our speech community and is codified in the patterns of our language. The agreement is, of course, an implicit and unstated one, *but its terms are absolutely obligatory.*[5]

Since most Americans are acquainted only with the general family of Indo-European languages, they are likely to view skeptically the contention that thinking is not essentially the same the world over. They know that the content of thought varies from group to group; that Russians are concerned with other problems than those that vex Americans; that the impoverished rural tenant farmer thinks about other matters than those engaging the attention of the urban financier; that the day-by-day preoccupations of the natives of the Pacific Islands are vastly different from those of the average American. Nevertheless, one is likely to believe that, although the content of thought varies from group to group, the form of all "correct" thinking is always and everywhere the same. The divergent modes of thought of other peoples—which actually do exist—are thus often regarded merely as varieties of error.

It would be very interesting and revealing to know what effect the English language may have on our thinking processes. It is probably impossible for anyone operating within the framework of our language to become aware of the influences it exerts upon him without first being acquainted with other languages, preferably non-European ones. For this reason, we shall illustrate our point with materials from the ancient Chinese and Navaho Indian languages, both quite different from our own.

The vocabulary of the ancient Chinese[6] was concrete, specific, picturesque, descriptive. Thus almost all words were used to evoke complex and specific images. Where English or French people use the word "mountain" plus adjectives or descriptive phrases, the Chinese used the following words: *K'i,* bare mountain; *Hou,* mountain covered with vegetation; *Ngan,* high mountain near a river; *Tsou,* high mountain; *Ts'ouei,* a high and vast mountain; and so on. Seventeen different words could refer to various kinds of mountains.

Words were never used in a general sense—such as "I climb the mountain"—but with concrete reference, as "I climb *that* mountain." The need of this sort of descriptive precision limited the use of general terms. Thus, instead of "husband," the Chinese word *Kia* evoked a definite, specific, concrete image: that of the household of which he is the master.

A great many redoubled words, such as *Ye-ye,* were used. These have been termed "descriptive auxiliaries." They had a remarkable power of evoking concrete images; they were veritable vocal paintings of noises, movements, feelings, and so on. Thus *Houei-houei* meant the sound of thunder, *Kui-kui* meant solitude; *Kouo-kouo* meant a rapid current. One redoubled word might refer to and evoke three or four or more images. For instance, *Yong-yong* referred to the cry of wild birds, indicating at the same time the response of the female to the call of the male and their characteristic manner of flying in pairs, the female flying a bit behind the male. When used in a different context, such a descriptive auxiliary might refer to an entirely different set of images.

Where the Occidental thinker can express his thoughts exactly and quickly, the Chinese had to do so by a kind of symbolization akin to poetic activity. The writer or speaker used various symbols which together conveyed his ideas by evoking specific concrete aspects of things.

The world thus appeared to the Chinese as a complex of specific aspects and images. Chinese thought, as reflected by the language, was oriented toward particulars, not toward generalizations or abstractions. As Merton has said, "The ancient Chinese language is not equipped to note concepts, analyze ideas, or to present doctrines discursively."[7]

The Navaho language likewise offers an instructive contrast to European languages.

[Navaho language] delights in sharply defined categories. It likes, so to speak, to file things away in neat little packages. It favors always the concrete and particular, with little scope for abstractions. It directs attention to some features of every situation, such as the minute distinctions as to direction and type of activity. It ignores others to which English gives a place. Navaho focuses interest upon doing—upon verbs as opposed to noun or adjectives. . . . The important point is that striking divergences in manner of thinking are crystallized in and perpetuated by the forms of Navaho grammar. Take an example of a commonplace physical event: rain. Whites can and do report their perception of this event in a variety of ways: "It has started to rain"; "It is raining"; "It has stopped raining." The Navaho people can, of course, convey these same ideas—but they cannot convey them without finer specifications. To give only a few instances of the sorts of discrimination the Navaho must make before he reports his experiences; he uses one verb form if he himself is aware of the actual inception of the rain storm, another if he has reason to believe that the rain has been falling for some time in his locality before the occurrence struck his attention. One form must be employed if rain is general round about within the range of vision; another if, though it is raining round about, the storm is plainly on the move. Similarly, the Navaho must invariably distinguish between the ceasing of rainfall (generally) and the stopping of rain in a particular vicinity because the rain clouds have been driven off by the wind. The [Navaho] people take the consistent noticing and reporting of such differences . . . as much for granted as the rising of the sun.

Navaho is an excessively literal language, little given to abstractions and to the fluidity of meaning that is so characteristic of English. The inner classification gives a concreteness, a specificity, to all expression. Most things can be expressed in Navaho with great exactness by manipulating the wide choice of stems in accord with the multitudinous alternatives offered by fusing prefixes and other separable elements in an almost unlimited number of ways. . . . The general nature of the difference between Navaho thought and English thought—both as manifested in the language and also as forced by the very nature of the linguistic forms into such patterns—is that Navaho thought is prevailingly so much more specific, so much more concrete. The ideas expressed by the English verb "to go" provide a nice example. To Germans, the English language seems a little sloppy because the same word is used regardless of whether the one who goes, walks or is transported by a train or other agency, whereas in German these two types of motion are always sharply distinguished in the two verbs *gehen* and *fahren*. But Navaho does much more—for example, when one is talking about travel by horse, the speed of the animal may be expressed by the verb form chosen. The following all mean "I went by horseback":

lii shil niya	(at a walk or at unspecified speed)
lii shil yildloozh	(at a trot)
lii shil neeltaa	(at a gallop)
lii shil yilghod	(at a run)

When a Navaho says that he went somewhere he never fails to specify whether it was afoot, astride, by wagon, auto, train, or airplane. This is done partly by using different verb stems which indicate whether the traveler moved under his own steam or was transported, partly by naming the actual means. Thus, "he went to town," would become:

kintahgoo iiya	He went to town afoot or in a non-specific way.
kintahgoo bil 'i'ii eel	He went to town by boat.
kintahgoo bil o'oor'a	He went to town by wagon.
(etc.)	(etc.)

Moreover, the Navaho language insists upon another type of splitting up of the generic idea of "going," to which German is as indifferent as English. The Navaho always differentiates between starting to go, going alone, arriving at, returning from a point, etc. etc. . . . It is not, of course, that these distinctions *cannot* be made in English but that they *are not* made consistently. They seem of importance to English-speakers only under special circumstances, whereas constant precision is a regular feature of Navaho thought and expression about movement.[8]

The study of non-European languages makes it evident that there are different modes of reasoning. Every human being is introduced, as a child, to a system (or systems) of language embodying certain peculiar and nonuniversal conceptual distinctions. Thus, the child is inducted into traditions of thinking, traditions consisting not only of certain kinds of ideas but of certain ways of thinking.

The point is made particularly clear by a consideration of time divisions. If certain temporal distinctions are not made by one's language, one cannot think in terms of them. Behavior can scarcely be organized, systematized, arranged, defined, regulated, or co-ordinated in terms of temporal categories of which the person is unaware. While our own language:

> . . . always expresses tense with perfect definiteness there are languages . . . which are incapable of doing so . . . in Samoyedic [Siberian] only two temporal forms of the verb are recognized . . . one of these . . . signifying present and future . . . the other indicating the past. . . . The minute temporal distinctions which we recognize as "present," "present perfect," "past," "past perfect," "past future," "future," "future perfect," and "past perfect" are impossible in these languages.
>
> A number of languages clearly reveal the efforts which have been made to render intelligible the elusive and abstract nature of time by interpreting it in terms of space. . . . [In Sudan language for example] the locations in space are crudely expressed by means of body-part words, and these spatial expressions then serve as indicators of time . . . here the fundamental intuition of time is quite different from that to which we are accustomed. . . .
>
> [For] some people future and past fuse linguistically into what might be called a "not-now" . . . in Schambala [African] the same word designates the distant past as well as the distant future. For them there exists only a "today" and a "not today."[9]

Other critical categories—such as those of number, action, and quality—also differ in various languages.

Since the language which people use is largely an inheritance from previous generations, the modes of thought of the present are derived from the past. This has its disadvantages as well as its advantages, for the experiences of past generations are not comparable to those of later ones. The errors of the past are tenacious because they become embedded in the language and popular thought, so much so that they become unquestioned assumptions. Scientific progress often depends upon freeing oneself from the implications of popular speech: note, for example, the sayings that the sun rises in the east and that members of a race are related to each other by blood. Symbolic logicians make analyses of speech, through its logical forms, so that the contradictory and ambiguous qualities of sentence forms can be avoided. Recognizing all this, Sapir reminds us that "Language is at one and the same time helping and retarding us in our exploration of experience."[10]

In setting forth the general hypothesis that language profoundly influences the forms of thought, we are not saying that a given language rigidly determines the form of thought of the society in which it is spoken. But language so thoroughly interpenetrates the modes of experiencing that at the very least it limits the possibilities of perception and of thinking. It may, of course, be argued that language merely reflects the experiences of a people—as its vocabulary reflects the interests and concerns of a people—but to say this is either to confine language to the transfer of ideas or to separate it sharply from culture. The inadequacy of the first alternative was discussed in Chapter 3.

The second alternative is exemplified in a paper by Voegelin,[11] an anthropological linguist. He maintains that the structure of language is the subject matter of linguistics and that "what" human beings "talk about" is culture. He reasons that if language "were merely a part of culture, then linguists should be competent to discuss other parts of culture by virtue of their training in linguistics."[12] He also argues that primates can be taught to learn parts of human culture, but cannot learn any genuine part of human language. As another anthropological linguist, H. Hoijer,[13] has remarked, political scientists and economists and other social scientists are not very competent in each other's specialties; and to say that a primate learns parts of human culture ("culture" in the sense of cultural or common meanings) is highly dubious, to say the least. The sharp separation of culture and language that is suggested by Voegelin and others reflects academic division of labor but, we would argue, little else.

Internalized Audiences and
Canons of Thought

Thinking goes on in the form of a symbolic process, an inner conversation: hence thought, like speech, is formulated in terms of the requirements of communicability. More specifically, this means that the thinker, like the speaker, has in mind an audience to which he adapts the formulations of his thought. This audience may at times assume the form of particular persons whose imagined responses are taken into account, or it may assume the form of a conception of "people in general." At other times, the imagined audience may be represented merely by abstract rules, principles, or standards. These may be considered the equivalent of an audience because they derive their authority from social consensus.

All reasoning involves processes of self-criticism, judgment, appreciation, and control. Socially transmitted traditions of thought determine, among other things, which problems are important, which unimportant; which questions are crucial, which trivial; which solutions are to be rejected out of hand and which ones judged acceptable, and so on.

The fact that thinking is a symbolic process means that a thinker can view and criticize his thought processes only from the standpoint—that is, according to the norms—of particular social groups, because symbols, as we have seen, are group products. To reason "correctly" means to conform to the canons of thought, to the conceptions of right thinking, which prevail within a given circle. To be "right" always means "right" from some point of view. The principles of logic are not absolutes. They are not innate, nor are they immutable rules determined by the nature of the world. They do not exist in a realm of "being" independent of the concrete actions of human beings; they belong to people, to groups, to societies. Their authority is always relative to particular places, particular times, particular groups, and particular types of discourse. Like other conventionalized norms of behavior, the norms of proof, correct reasoning, verification, and scientific method change with the times. They are subject to dispute, criticism, and revision.

Logical classifications and canons are conditioned by the linguistic structures of the society that formulates them. Masson-Oursel,[14] for example, reached the conclusion that ancient Greek, Indian, and Chinese logical formulations were not identical; that problems of logic and their solutions reflected the peculiar emphases and perspectives of each society and the structure of its language. Dewey[15] has suggested that the logical theory formulated by the ancient Greeks reflected their conceptions of the world; and Werkmeister explicitly notes the influence of Greek grammatical structure upon Greek logic:

> The formation of a sentence and its analysis into word units and word classes, as required in Greek language . . . seem to have had their influence upon the development of Aristotle's system of categories . . . the last four categories in particular . . . seem to become fully intelligible only when we relate them to certain basic distinctions which the Greek language recognizes in connection with the verb and verbal action.[16]

The existence of competing logical systems among modern logicians —for example, neo-Thomism (J. Maritain), instrumentalism (J. Dewey), and logical positivism (R. Carnap)—is evidence that even now logical formulations are in a process of change.

C. W. Mills has ably expressed the linkages among thought, audience, and logic which we have suggested above:

> Societal processes enter as determinants into reflection. [There is an] internalized audience with which the thinker converses: a focalized and abstracted organization of attitudes of those implicated in the social field of behavior and experience. . . . The other conditions the thinker and the outcome of their interaction is a function of both interactants. . . . The social and intellectual habits of the audience, as elements in this interaction, condition the statements of the thinker and the fixation of beliefs evolving from that interplay. . . . It is in conversing with this internalized organization of collective attitudes that

ideas are logically, i.e., implicitly, "tested." Here they meet with recalcitrance, and rejection, reformulation and acceptance. The thinker operates logically (applies standardized critiques) upon propositions and arguments (his own included) from the standpoint of the generalized other. . . . It is from this socially constituted viewpoint that one approves or disapproves of given arguments as logical or illogical, valid or invalid.[17]

It is worth noting that no complex society has only one way of reasoning: various types of discourse, representing different modes of thinking and of viewing the world, exist simultaneously. Among the types of discourse which exist within our own society we may mention the poetic, philosophical, scientific, and religious. Each type implies a unique approach to human experience, and each has its own criteria of validity and relevance. The scientist, for example, cultivates systematic doubt and believes only what empirical evidence forces him to believe. By contrast, the poetic approach requires what Coleridge called a "suspension of disbelief." The scientifically minded person who is troubled because the poet does not define his terms as he goes along seeks to apply the standards of one type of discourse to another type to which they bear no relation.

These different types of discourse, corresponding to different frames of reference, imply the utilization of different internalized audiences. For example, the modes of reasoning acceptable in poetic circles are significantly different from those of the scientists, and those of the latter are not deemed appropriate in the area of religious and moral beliefs. As individuals move from one activity to another, say, from the laboratory to the home or the church, they change their frames of reference and their standards of proof, validity, and relevance. For an individual, the importance of any given audience varies according to how relevant he considers its opinion to be; thus, the opinions of the scientist's wife concerning his theories, if she is not a scientist herself, are likely to have less influence upon him than her opinions of his table manners.

Communication Between Social Classes

Social classes are cultural groupings within a society which reflect and perpetuate differences in outlook, education, etiquette and style of speech, vocabulary, and ways of thinking about the world. The social distance between the highest class and the lowest varies from society to society. Primitive societies undergoing Westernization probably exhibit the greatest contrasts in this respect, with the top stratum fully adapted to the ideas, goals, outlook, and techniques of Western civilization, while the lowest stratum remains on a primitive or tribal plane. By comparison, the differences between classes in the United States are relatively small. Nevertheless, there are considerable cultural differences between the classes in our country which are obstacles to free communication and understanding between them.

Much cross-class communication occurs in formalized or routinized situations which restrict the range of communication and direct into more or less standardized patterns. Interactions of maid and mistress, slave and master, employer and employee are instances of such stereotyped situations. However, when unusual situations mix the classes and break up the stereotyped modes of interaction, differences in outlook and ways of seeing the world may become evident and create communication problems.

Riesman and Glaser[18] have pointed out that the polling of public opinion involves the problems of interclass communication when educated, middle-class interviewers deal with persons of other social strata than their own. They say, "It is useful to see the interview situation, and the polling process as a whole, as one form of the continuing conversation between upper and lower levels of our culture."[19]

The people of a community that has been stricken by disaster find themselves in a situation in which established patterns of interaction between the classes are disrupted. The people of a rural

Arkansas town were interviewed after a devastating tornado had destroyed much of the community.[20] Interviewers noticed characteristic differences in the ways in which people of different social strata described the tornado. Middle-class or educated persons were more able to give a detached, impersonal account of what had happened than were members of the lower classes. Accounts by the latter groups tended to be personal and to be based on the individual's own experiences. Perhaps because of limited social experience, they seemed unable to give a clear, general account of what had happened or to take into consideration the experiences of others. Their descriptions were more concrete and personal than those of higher social classes.

From the point of view of the middle-class interviewer trying to determine what actually happened, the descriptions given by middle-class people seemed much more enlightening. They were more systematic and generalized and were easier for the interviewer to obtain. Lower-class persons often seemed to lack a generalized framework around which they might organize their ideas of what had happened.

The difficulties experienced by middle-class interviewers illustrate the point that cultural differences between the classes tend to restrict and impede free communication between them. A person's viewpoint, his modes of speech and thought, are in part shaped by his class affiliations. One's perspective on social relations, the class hierarchy, and community events depends upon one's own position and background of experience within the social structure. Communication is easiest between persons who are roughly alike; it becomes difficult and beset by misunderstanding when it crosses class boundaries.

B. Kaplan,[21] who explored differences in modes of thought in relation to degree of education, noted that the less educated rely more on "concrete symbolism" than the well educated, and that their thought processes are "less differentiated." Since class position is closely correlated with education, this conclusion is relevant to our present concern with interclass communication. The research on social classes carried out by W. L. Warner[22] and his associates also provides some evidence on this point. The psychiatrists Myers and Schaffer have remarked, apropos of therapy with the lower classes, that

> lower class persons do not seem to share with psychiatrists the conception of therapy as a process by which the patient gains insight into his problems . . . it appears possible that lower class patients need to acquire new symbols and values to participate in expressive psychotherapy. . . . Perhaps psychiatrists need to acquire new symbols and values in dealing with lower class patients. . . .[23]

Effective communication between the classes in areas where there are class differences thus poses special problems and requires special skills from an interviewer. One of the first and most obvious requirements is that the vocabulary of the other class be used. A second and more difficult requirement is that the point of view and modes of thought of the other class be understood so that the interviewer can identify himself with the outlook of the person he is interviewing. These precautions and techniques are often not utilized or appreciated in ordinary social intercourse.

Group Identifications

Membership in human groups is not essentially physical but symbolic. This distinction becomes particularly evident when attention is directed toward membership in far-flung secondary groups. Thus, although every American is aware that he is a citizen of the U.S.A., along with about 160,000,000 others, he is personally acquainted with an extremely small percentage of his fellow Americans. He can never see all or even a large percentage of them, to say nothing of seeing them all at once. It is true that the vast majority of Americans live within an area that has boundaries, but this area cannot in the nature of things be directly perceived. Awareness of citizenship is thus made possible through indirect symbolic means.

Such groups as those represented by the terms Christian, Methodist, Negro, politician, middle class, chemist, Air Force, are illustrations of what may be called "abstract collectivities." One can belong to them only in a symbolic sense, although the consequences of membership are often quite concrete. Each of these groups is scattered, composite, and complex. They exercise a unitary influence upon individuals largely because each individual in actual empirical terms is influenced much more directly by his oversimplified stereotyped conceptions of the group, and by his own limited experience within it, than by the group itself as a physical "reality."

Even intimate groups, such as a family living together in one household, depend for their existence on more than the physical proximity of their members. The unity of such a group is not necessarily destroyed when its members are scattered.

Because of the symbolic nature of group membership, questions of affiliation and allegiance must be discussed in terms of identification rather than simple belonging. Objectively speaking, for example, a man may not belong to a given social class, because he lacks either the money, status, possessions, or other social trappings that go with membership in that class. Nevertheless he may think of himself as a member of it. Thus an American bank clerk may, according to economic criteria, belong to the lower middle class but he is likely to identify himself with the upper middle or upper class. To the extent that the clerk identifies himself in this way he will respond to many situations as though he were a member of that class.

The individual's socioeconomic interests may even be in conflict with the interests of a group to whose values and activities he gives allegiance. There are Americans who, in terms of income and status, belong to the lower socioeconomic classes but who think of themselves as belonging to the middle class. They believe in, identify with, and uphold middle- and upper-class values. During the depression some lower-class persons—"scabs" and police—fought for the upper classes against striking members of their own class. As a contemporary American instance of class allegiance we may cite the small businessman's adherence to the values and ideologies of big business. Another striking instance of objectively incorrect affiliation was the support given to the Nazis by persons who in no way benefited from the movement.

Nationalistic modes of thought offer another instance of the way in which men's loyalties may run counter to their interests. Most people still think in terms of a world divided into a number of sepa-

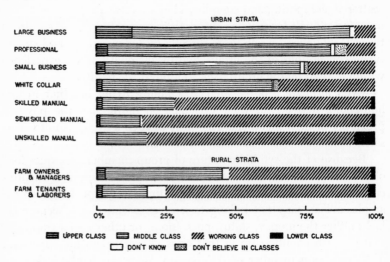

Class identifications of occupational strata in the United States. (From "The American Class Structure: A Psychological Analysis," by R. Centers, in *Readings in Social Psychology*, edited by T. M. Newcomb and E. L. Hartley. Holt, 1947.)

rate, sovereign states, the interests of each of which necessarily conflict with the interests of the others. Modern war is the consequence of this set of loyalties. One of the most critical problems of our day is how to avoid atomic warfare by bringing about a shift of allegiance from nation to world. The United Nations is predicated on the realization—by relatively few persons—that the interests of men in general require solution of many problems on a world-wide non-nationalistic basis.

The individual thinks in terms of the standards and in accordance with the rules of logic and value systems of the groups with which he identifies himself. The vocabularies which he takes over embody the attitudes and values prevalent in these groups. The internalized audiences with which he interacts in the inner forum of reflection represent these groups.

Reference Groups and Frames of Reference

Descriptions of the manner in which individuals are influenced by group norms sometimes employ the term "reference group." This expression refers to the fact that people evaluate themselves and orient their behavior by reference both to (1) the groups in which they hold official membership, and (2) others to which they aspire or to which they hope to belong in the future. A reference group is thus any group with which a person psychologically identifies himself or in relation to which he thinks of himself. It is implicit in this idea that his existing group memberships may be relatively meaningless to the person whose primary "ego anchorages" are established with reference to groups with which he is not formally or objectively linked. This type of anticipatory allegiance is especially noticeable in a mobile society in which the ambition to raise one's status is characteristically encouraged.

Reference groups are thus said to establish the individual's organizing conceptions, or frames of reference, for ordering his experiences, perceptions, and ideas of self. Sherif states the matter as follows:

> The individual's directive attitudes, *viz.*, ego-attitudes, which define and regulate his behavior to other persons, other groups, and to an important extent even to himself, are formed in relation to values and norms of his reference groups. They constitute an important basis of his self-identity, of his sense of belongingness, of the core of his social ties.[24]

Sherif and his collaborators[25] have investigated and described at some length the influence of reference groups on perception and other aspects of behavior. The concept of reference groups has been utilized most extensively by Sherif, who views it as one of the most important integrating ideas in the field.

Merton and Kitt[26] have reinterpreted findings reported in *The American Soldier* in the light of the reference group concept; they showed, for example, how inexperienced troops are influenced by association with soldiers who have had combat experience. Green troops, desiring to affiliate themselves with those who have experience in battle, tend to take over the latter's norms and values and to evaluate themselves by reference to them.

Newcomb[27] applied this concept in a study of the attitudes of Bennington College students. He has suggested that there are positive and negative reference groups: the former being those in which one desires to be accepted and treated as a member; and the latter, those to which one is opposed and in which one does not desire membership.

Hyman,[28] who is credited with the first use of the term "reference group," analyzed the influence of such groups on college students' conceptions of their own status. He found that they compared themselves with others in the following respects, listed in order of frequency: (1) economic, (2) intellectual, (3) social, (4) looks, (5) culture, (6) athletics, (7) prestige, (8) general, (9) character, (10) politics, (11) sexual qualities, (12) religion, and (13) esteem. Among the matters mentioned by students in connection with the ratings they gave themselves were family background, membership in special groups, breeding, people known, money, dates, getting along with the other sex, degrees, achievement, race, formal education, reasoning ability, intelligence, appreciation of the arts, reading, worldly experience, and academic background of the family. Hyman noted that the groups referred to in making comparisons differed among the subjects, and were of crucial importance in self-conception. Thus, one subject whose income was $336 per year gave $900 per year as an amount that would make her "joyous," whereas another subject with an income of $4,000 per year said he would be content with no less than $25,000. Hyman found that, in general, small intimate groups were more important for reference in estimates of oneself than was the general population. Individuals chose the points on which they compared themselves with others so as to achieve the most satisfactory position possible.

Festinger's[29] experiments with voting behavior in relation to religious affiliation also shed light on the way in which reference groups influence behavior. Festinger compared the voting of Catholic and Jewish girls in several types of situations. In one, the girls knew nothing of each other's or the candidates' religious affiliations; in another, they knew the affiliation of the candidates but not each other's; and in the third situation, they knew each other's affiliations as well as the candidates'. These experiments showed that the Catholic girls tended to vote for Catholic candidates when their own affiliation was known to the other voters, and that the Jewish girls voted as Jews mainly when their religious affiliations were not so known. Festinger supposed that Jewish girls felt free to vote as Jews when they were anonymous, whereas Catholic girls felt compelled to vote as Catholics only when they were openly identified as such.

The concept of the reference group serves a useful purpose by stressing two facts: the influences of groups on individual behavior is not determined by sheer physical belonging but by the impact they have on the individual's thinking, and, moreover, groups to which one does not officially belong may be more important than those to which one does belong. The intricacies of such group identifications are frequently portrayed by novelists.

In the book *East Side, West Side*,[30] Marcia Davenport describes certain events in the life of a third-generation Jewish woman living in New York City. The heroine, like many others of her generation, has had little contact with lower-class persons of her ethnic group but moves in wealthy circles. She knows little of Jewish lore and history. Yet in a peculiar way she is identified with her origins, and also, by some sort of transmutation, with all lower-class city people. This identification is linked with her sense of rootlessness but also with her sense of having arrived at a higher class level. We shall quote a few passages from this novel not as proof of anything but to remind the reader that he too can find this complexity of referential processes in his own experience. A companion who is in similar straits remarks to Jessie, the heroine:

We like what we have become, you know that—it would be the phoniest kind of posing to pretend that we didn't. But we don't want the sensation of being chopped off from our roots, either. . . . [Jessie later remarks] To those people a family is scarcely a family without a husband and father, the whole ritual and tradition revolves around him. That's really all I know about the subject and I regret it very much. I would love to know more— but I've never had the opportunity to learn. There must be millions of people like me, who would draw a lot of strength out of their own roots if they had never been cut off from them. . . . You can't go back and do an artificial graft years later, either. . . . [As she is walking through the streets crowded with poor people, she says of them] Probably I'm a sentimental fool because I don't know them and would have nothing in common with them if I did. But I like to be among them and feel the sense of life that I get from them. Do you know . . . sometimes I have a strange idea. I know people who love the country, who say that the sight of trees and meadows and growing things gives them strength, or contentment, or peace . . . that is their contact with Nature and that is real to them. But mine seems to be people like those. . . . You see I can't understand the language they are talking. It could be Sanskrit. But it doesn't matter. I don't need to talk to them. In fact if I had to, there would be very little for us to say. . . . [She stops to shop in a butcher store and engages in lively banter. Her companion asks whether she always does this] Of course, that's why I go there.[31]

The concept of the reference group has been elaborated in an effort to make it square with the complexity of identifications which involve multiple group memberships, positive and negative relationships to the same group, multiple positive and negative group influences in the same situation, and shifting loyalties and relationships. The problem of what constitutes group membership is itself none too easy except when one deals with formal membership, the tokens of which are payment of dues, listing as a member, and the like, and these memberships are often of little or no significance for the person's behavior. Membership in a social class, for example, involves none of these. Does this mean that a person's class membership is to be judged by his way of life and by how he thinks, regardless of occupation and income? If we ask whether the undercover FBI agent in the Communist party is really a member of the Party, some of the problems of determining membership in groups become obvious. Most persons would probably say that in this case, even though the FBI man pays dues to the Communist Party and carries a membership card, he is not really a member because he does not identify himself with the Party, nor does he adopt its position. The Party is, in short, not a reference group for him—or it might be called a negative reference group.

T. Shibutani[32] has recently suggested a redefinition of the reference group concept after considering the salient characteristics of mass societies, in which persons frequently internalize discordant values of different groups. Shibutani feels that "Much of the interest in reference groups arises out of concern with situations in which a person is confronted with the necessity of acting on the basis of alternative definitions, where he must make a choice between two or more organized perspectives." The key problem, then, "in the study of reference groups . . . is that of ascertaining *whose* confirming responses are needed in order to sustain a given point of view." This leads to a consideration of which audiences—actual, imagined, or potential—the person is acting toward and with chief reference to. Defined and used in this way, the concept of the reference group may do more than merely point to audiences otherwise unsuspected by the observer. In its present state the concept is chiefly useful for focusing attention on the more subtle nuances of identification and loyalty.

Experimental Studies in Group Influence

A number of careful experiments dealing with group influence and functioning have been performed. Such experiments are almost necessarily confined to the manipulation of small groups rather than large groups or extensive social structures and organizations. Small-group research focuses on a number of general ideas, including collective problem solving, the conditions of group productivity, pressures on members to conform, interpersonal influence, group settings, and the influence of leaders in group functioning. We shall consider several representative kinds of experiments, each dealing with some facet of group membership as it modifies individual reactions.

In an early type of investigation, called "social facilitation," individual performance on specified tasks was compared with performance in groups. Under certain group conditions the subject improved noticeably, and in others he did not. Moede,[33] for example, found that boys were always able to endure more pain while in the presence of other boys than when alone. Likewise, F. Allport[34] found that simple motor tasks were handled more efficiently when there was an audience. Another of Allport's studies showed that a group situation increased the quantity of arguments presented against excerpts from Marcus Aurelius, but decreased the quality. In an investigation carried out by J. Dashiell,[35] the members of one experimental group worked individually, but each knew he was in competition with the others; and in the second, each worked noncompetitively in the presence of the others. The competitive situation produced superior results. Various experimental studies give information on the ways in which group participants are influenced in making judgments, and others yield comparisons of the average performances of groups and individual members. As an example of a study in the latter class we may cite one by M. Shaw.[36] She presented to both individuals and small groups problems involving a number of logical steps which, in order for a correct solution to be reached, had to be handled in a specific order. (For example, three cannibals and three missionaries come to a river. The problem is to get them across in a boat which will hold only two persons at a time. All the missionaries, and one cannibal, can row. Under no circumstances may the missionaries be outnumbered by cannibals. Thirteen boat trips are required to accomplish the task.) Shaw found that groups performed better than individuals on this test, since as a collective body they were more critical of alternative suggestions.

In another group of studies, the focus is upon establishing the relation between conformity to group norms and the participants' perception of the homogeneity of the group. Thus Festinger and Thibaut[37] used 61 experimental groups of from 6 to 14 members each. Each group, composed of anonymous members, was asked to solve a problem, which was of such a nature that opinions about it could be placed on a seven-point continuum. Each member individually considered the problem, and indicated his opinion privately on a card. Communication among the individuals was restricted to the writing of notes. The nature of the groups was varied to produce different degrees of heterogeneity. The participants' perceptions of group heterogeneity were also manipulated. This elaborate experimentation demonstrated the following, according to the authors:

1. When there is a range of opinion in the group, communications tend to be directed toward those members whose opinions are at the extremes of the range.

2. The greater the pressure toward uniformity and the greater the perception of homogeneous group-composition, the greater is the tendency to communicate to these extreme opinions.

3. The greater the pressure toward uniformity and the greater the perception of homogeneous group-composition, the greater is the actual change toward uniformity which takes place.[38]

Conformity to group norms under conditions of ambiguity was experimentally studied by Sherif[39] in a well-known and often-quoted investigation of the "autokinetic effect." When individuals are confronted with a stationary point of light in the dark, with no stable point of reference to guide them, the light appears to move and the perceivers may even become confused about the stability of their own spatial positions. Sherif studied the influence of such social factors as suggestion and the group situation on the extent and direction of the perceived movement. In brief, he found the following: an individual, in the absence of objectively known information about the light, establishes a standard or a "norm" with which each successive or perceived movement of the light is compared and judged; and he likewise establishes a range within which the light appears to move. The range and central tendency of each individual is different. When the subjects are placed in the autokinetic situation together and compare impressions after having been in it separately, then the norms and ranges tend to converge, but more convergence occurs when individuals have not been previously exposed separately to the situation. Each group eventually establishes its own judgment about the light's movement. When the group member thereafter faces the laboratory situation alone, he carries the group standards with him into his perception.

H. Sperling[40] has rechecked and verified Sherif's findings, and gone on to vary two conditions of the experimental situation. Each of nine subjects was paired with a "planted" subject, and these assistants were instructed to distribute their judgments of the light's movement over a range far beyond that normally reported. Eight of the nine subjects were influenced in the direction of convergence with the judgment of the assistant, but only within certain limits. When confronted with the discrepancy between their initial estimates and those of their partners, they began to watch the light more carefully, and tried to see the other's point of view. Some concluded that their own judgment was more accurate, and all speculated concerning the difference. In a second experimental variation, the subjects were told that any difference between the judgments of partners would be subjective, and that there was no actual movement of the light. They were shown the apparatus to prove the point. Six out of ten subjects were sufficiently impressed so that they then stuck to their own estimates, remaining uninfluenced by their partners' judgments. The other four subjects were influenced toward their partners' estimates; when they were questioned afterward they said either that they had forgotten, or that they had not believed, that the light was really stationary.

Some conditions under which perceptions and reports of perceptions of the objective environment can be swayed by group pressures have been explored by Asch.[41] A group of eight individuals was told to match a given standard line with one of a set of three unequal lines. Each was to announce his judgment. Seven of the group were instructed in advance to give the wrong answer, so that eventually one individual found to his astonishment that he was repeatedly in a minority of one. The errors of the majority in judging the lines were large. The goat of the experiment, who was seated so that he was among the last to report, was naturally affected. "A look of perplexity and bewilderment come[s] over the subject's face at the contradictory judgments of the entire group."[42] The subject often fidgeted, got upset, looked at the lines more attentively, or smiled sheepishly. Each time that it was his turn to make a judgment, he had to stand up and announce it publicly like everyone else. Asch found that about one third of all estimates of misled subjects were identical with, or in the direction of, the distorted estimates of the majority. However, "the effect of the majority is far from complete," since two thirds of the estimates given by the experimental subjects were actually correct. Also there were extreme individual differences among the subjects, some remaining independent throughout the experiment and others following the majority opinion as soon as their minority position became evident.

After varying the experimental conditions Asch[43] was also able to conclude that a disturbance of the unanimity of the majority greatly increased the independence of the critical subject, and that the majority effect on the critical subjects reached its maximum when the latter were outvoted 3 to 1. Further increases in the size of the majority had no effect. When a single instructed subject gave the wrong answers consistently, Asch noted that the majority laughed at him; but respect for the incorrect divergent view increased as the number expressing it increased. When a critical subject found himself in agreement with another person, his independence of judgment was greatly increased; but the withdrawal of the agreeing partner restored the influence of the majority over him.

Asch points out that individuals agreed with majority opinion for different reasons. In only a few subjects were perceptions genuinely altered. Most subjects yielded to the majority because they felt that they must be wrong; that is, they suffered from "primary doubt and lack of confidence." Some of them yielded because they did not wish to appear different, or reasoned that if they reported their defective estimates they would interfere with the experiment. Those who did not yield to majorities were, nevertheless, usually shaken, or, at the very least, sensitive to majority opinion.

Still another experimental approach on small groups that constituted portions of large and more abstract groupings is illustrated by an investigation of Charters and Newcomb.[44] They attempted to show that a temporary arousal or strengthening of group identification would lead to an expression of attitudes that would be closer than usual to the group norm. From a psychology class of 1,300 students all those who had said they were Catholics were divided at random into groups A, B, and C. Group A continued to attend the class with other students at the usual time and in the usual place, whereas Group B met in a small room where the members were told nothing about what was expected of them. These two Catholic groups were used as controls in order to make comparisons with Group C, the experimental one. This group met separately in a small room, where the students were told that they had been called together as Catholics in order to prepare an attitude scale for members of the Roman Catholic Church; discussion of Catholic points of view followed. The members of all three groups and the rest of the psychology class then responded to a series of attitude statements which were so framed that a student might reply to them as a Catholic, as a member of a class in psychology, or from other points of view. Only a small proportion of the items were relevant to membership in the Catholic Church. The investigators wished to test the idea that the Catholic students in Group C would respond as Catholics more often than those in the other two groups and the non-Catholic members of the class. This hypothesis was confirmed, for virtually all relevant answers showed that the handling of Group C tended both to remind the students that they were Catholics and to cause them to respond as Catholics. The responses of the Catholic students of Groups A and B were more like those of the non-Catholics than like those of the experimental group.

The field of small-group research is currently an especially active one, and the number of experimental and field studies is too great to permit any comprehensive review of them here. Some of the work is of only peripheral interest to the social psychologist, either because it focuses on group structure rather than individual responses in the group situation or because findings are of a self-evident nature, with little theoretical significance. In general, however, the research promises to supply a considerable amount of useful information concerning the manner in which individuals are influenced by different types of groups or group situations. Experimental studies in this field are naturally limited by the artificiality and impermanence of small groups in the laboratory, as well as other special features of such groups; and workers in this field have sought to overcome these limitations by making field studies of real-life groups outside the laboratory.

Institutional Influences

Studies such as those described in the preceding section are usually limited, as we have stated, by the fact that they are concerned with small, temporary groups. More difficult to study is the influence of large, complicated groups such as those which constitute the "structure of society" and which are involved in the carrying out of broad institutional functions. Among these institutional complexes are those concerned with religion, science, nationalism, economics, and law.

The following analysis of the function of the religious scholar within the framework of religious institutions illustrates the way in which the behavior and thought of given individuals may be subordinated to institutional requirements.

> The social role of the religious scholar is performed within the sacred school. His social circle is composed of other scholars . . . his status and his function are institutionally regulated by the school. . . .
>
> The scholar's role . . . is strictly determined by the task of the school—the perpetuation of sacred lore. His significance as a person consists in that, within the scholarly group, he is one of the links of the living chain by which transcendent science and divine wisdom, once made accessible to men, remain forever within their reach. He begins as a learner and is gradually admitted under the guidance of teachers to a wider and deeper participation in holy knowledge.
>
> If he leaves the school . . . his function within the school may be terminated; but his spiritual bond with the school is

not broken. If he remains true to his allegiance, he becomes one of the minor links which . . . connect laymen of the outside world with the original, eternal, source of all holy truth. . . . Furthermore, it is presumed that through him . . . youth from the outside world will be attracted to the school and become candidates from among whom a new generation of scholars can be recruited.

If the religious scholar remains in the school . . . he assumes the function of teacher, introducing in turn other learners into sacred knowledge. The latter, especially if stabilized in writing, may in time become so vast that a scholar, even after he becomes a teacher, continues to be a learner, studying under the guidance of either living old masters on higher levels of initiation or the dead who have left their knowledge recorded in books. Thus, the social status of the scholar within the school is at every period of his life determined by the degree of his participation in sacred knowledge, as compared with that of other scholars in the hierarchical order of teachers and learners. . . . It is . . . the first and most essential duty of every scholar to assimilate exactly every truth that is communicated to him by his teachers and in turn to communicate it as exactly to his hearers.

This duty is associated with the great importance which words and other symbols possess in sacred knowledge . . . an exact and faithful reproduction of the symbolic expression of those truths is essential. The same truths cannot be differently expressed, for if they could be they would cease to be themselves. The use of inadequate symbols is not only error; it is also profanation. . . . Not a sound, not a dash or a dot may be changed either by the teacher or the learner. Thence the emphasis on memorizing sacred texts . . . thence also the importance of a perfect writing skill . . . it is obviously impossible for him to introduce any modifications into this knowledge. Nor can he discover personally any new and valid truth that was not known from the very beginning to the first masters, gods, or heroes who revealed the sacred knowledge. . . . And yet it is a fact that the knowledge of the sacred school actually grows in the course of generations. . . .

This growth . . . seems to be mainly a response to demands made by the wider society. New problems of natural technology, reflections about the cultural order roused by social conflicts, new factual observations . . . strange doctrines imported from abroad . . . all these penetrate into the sacred school, which is expected to deal with them.

How can these two functions—conserving tradition intact and recognizing or even introducing innovations—be reconciled? Religious scholars . . . have achieved it by applying always the same guiding principle: Whatever in the domain of knowledge is verily true cannot be new. . . . The total Truth . . . was already known to the spiritual ancestor of the school . . . everything man can ever know truly is already contained in the spiritual heritage of the school. But few, if any, individual men can attain full possession of this heritage. For the sacred text must be *understood*. . . . Only a very few [scholars can] . . . give a better, deeper, more comprehensive interpretation of some of the sacred truths that have not been adequately explained hitherto; but each of them can make only a partial contribution to the understanding of the total Truth as originally revealed. . . .

The growth of the knowledge of sacred schools is thus essentially an accumulation of *commentaries* in which superior scholars interpret . . . either the original holy texts or the writings of earlier commentators. Interpretation consists either in expounding the content of sacred truths or in eliciting their systematic connection or both. By the first method of interpretation, it can be shown that a sacred truth . . . when more fully understood than hitherto, will be found to contain truths which lay scientists or importers of foreign ideas erroneously believe to be newly discovered. . . .

The second method of interpretation permits the religious scholar to rediscover certain holy truths which his immediate predecessors for some reason have failed to transmit or even truths which the spiritual ancestor of the school, knowing that mankind was not yet prepared for them but foreseeing that their disclosure would come in the proper time, intentionally failed to reveal. . . . But there is always a possible doubt as to whether such a discovery really is a rediscovery . . . or merely an uncertain opinion, if not an error. . . . This doubt can be removed only by showing that there is an inner connection between the rediscovered truth and other known truths that are already recognized as dogmatically certain. . . . The religious scholar's commentary is purely impersonal; and he frequently tries to prove by ingenious arguments and references that there is nothing original in what he says, for it is all based on good sacred authority.[45]

The above description offers an interesting contrast to the kinds of activity involved in the perpetuation of scientific institutions. It would take us too far afield to try to indicate in detail the influences upon individuals which proceed from all broad institutional sources in general and from the position of the individual in the social structure in particular. The main point being made here is that these influences exist and need to be taken into consideration, and that they cannot, as a rule, be observed effectively within the relatively narrow framework of laboratory studies.

The Problem of Bias

The preceding discussion has indicated that a person's thought is influenced by his particular position in a social hierarchy and by the positions of the groups with which he identifies himself. The individual may vigorously deny the existence of such influences and sincerely assert that he is "unbiased," "objective," and concerned only with "facts" and their implications. Indeed, influences of the type with which we are concerned usually operate below the level of awareness. It is a rare person who realizes more than a few of his own biases; no one can be conscious of all of them.

The term "bias" refers to the influence exerted upon thinking by conditions other than those that are objectively relevant. Thus, when a statement on economic matters is dismissed on the grounds that its author is a millionaire, a labor leader, a visionary idealist, a conservative, or a radical, it is implied that the author is so obviously biased as to be unqualified to observe or interpret the facts correctly. Since everyone has a position of some kind in society and is identified with certain groups and not with others, one may ask if any one is really qualified to give an unbiased view on any question. The answer involves philosophical considerations outside the scope of this book. We shall simply assume that it is possible to acquire relatively but not absolutely valid knowledge, and then turn our attention to certain features of bias and some methods of neutralizing it.

Since university professors and scientists are generally regarded as relatively objective persons, it will be instructive to point out a number of ways in which they are influenced by matters not inherent in their fields of study and research. Their characteristic biases arise from the nature of their professions, their social relations, the organization of universities, and so on.

A conspicuous bias of the contemporary American scholar is his disposition to think of the external world as being divided neatly into various separate categories that correspond to the contemporary departmental organization of the American university. But the structure of the university is not a reliable guide to the structure of reality, since universities are organized in terms of administrative convenience, pedagogical requirements, faculty policies, and historical traditions both general and local.

Within each academic specialty an individual's standing is determined by what his fellow specialists think of him. A scholar in one field is likely to be indifferent and immune to the critical judgments of outsiders—it is unnecessary for him to read many of the writings of specialists in other areas or to take their theories seriously. Within his own field he is highly sensitive to the opinions of others, particularly those who have high status or are in positions of power. He is likely to deal gently with his own colleagues and to be dealt with gently by them because of the general recognition of mutual vulnerability. The newcomer to the academic hierarchy is especially vulnerable because he cannot afford to risk the enmity of those who are in a position to hire and fire him. Consequently he tends to develop a politely deferent public attitude toward his elders and their theories.

Standards of evidence vary from field to field and from department to department. In some psychology departments today, for example, "experimental" evidence is the only reputable verification of hypotheses. In social science, data must usually be obtained from field research or it must be statistical in nature. In the natural sciences, both the field research and statistics of the social scientist and the experiments of psychologists are likely to be viewed with disdain. Philosophers, mathematicians, linguists, economists, anthropologists, and other scholars all have their own respective standards. The prestige accorded each method is likely to correspond to the status accorded each discipline as well as the acceptance of its "scientific" conclusions by the wider public.

The various "scientific" disciplines constitute a prestige hierarchy, with the physical sciences at the top. The hierarchy itself reflects a societal evaluation of relative social significance. Thus the status of the physical sciences, besides reflecting the high general opinion of the validity of the results in this area, is obviously connected also with the applicability to warfare and industry of these findings. The growing prestige of economics is clearly associated with the increasing complexity of economic structure and the recent emphasis upon governmental planning.

Within the hierarchy, the members of any given field tend to take as models a field currently enjoying higher prestige than their own. They may even seek to amalgamate their field with the next higher one, as for example when psychology is declared to be a biological science. Members of low-ranking disciplines are often troubled by feelings of inferiority, which they seek to assuage by using the vocabularies, concepts, and methods of the higher disciplines. Among sociologists references have been made to relativity theory, Heisenberg's principle of indeterminacy, Bridgman's operationalism, and other subjects which, one would suppose from the terminology, would interest physicists only. In sociology, there is relatively little reference to biology, also a "higher" science. We are not passing judgment on the value of scientists' borrowing from other fields: such interpenetration is often useful and fruitful. But here we are interested merely in noting the possible nonlogical reasons—reasons on the behavioral level—for some of this borrowing.

Academic reputations and salaries often rest more upon research and publication than upon teaching ability. This simple fact has much greater influence upon the activities of professors and students alike than is publicly acknowledged. Candidates for advanced degrees may select research projects in terms of convenience and economy of effort rather than because they hope to contribute to scientific knowledge. Pressure upon professors to publish and do research leads to the publication of much trivial and insignificant material in the learned journals. Research, besides being a means of advancing knowledge, may also be a racket or a means of self-aggrandizement. This is often disguised from the outsider by the use of a specialized technical jargon which has come to be known as "gobbledegook" in government circles. Persons within an academic field who are aware of this do not want to expose their colleagues because of professional loyalty and solidarity, and sometimes because they realize their own vulnerability.

There are also academic fads and fashions. Certain subjects, techniques, or terms become popular for a time and are replaced by others. Textbooks reflect both these fashions and the current schools of thought. This is true particularly in fields outside the natural sciences; yet even these are not immune to such scientific irrelevancies.

This discussion of the pressures that influence scholarly activities is very limited in scope and omits as much as it includes. No mention has been made of a great many other important extraneous influences such as those arising from personal relations, the influence of commercial publishers, the selective recruitment of scholars from various socioeconomic classes, the political-economic power structure of the wider society, "democratic" education, university salary policy, and so on.

If scientists and other "learned men" are not impartial, one may assume that people with fewer pretensions to objectivity are even more biased. And in view of the wide range of extraneous influences that affect the objectivity of the scholar and scientist, one may well ask how it is possible to obtain even approximations of impartiality.

Our previous discussion suggests two answers to this question. (1) By altering the objective conditions bearing upon a person's position, some sources of bias can be reduced or eliminated. It is, for example, easy to think of ways of freeing scholars from many of the pressures that derive from economic sources. But the creation of a new objective situation cannot in itself eliminate all sources of bias, since the new situation leads to the formation of new biases. (2) The influence of bias can be at least partly neutralized by systematically studying it. The person who is unaware of his biases can neither control nor discount them; but when sources of error are brought into the open, named, sorted into classes and analyzed, they can then be dealt with. Discounting one's own biases is very much like discounting the biases of others. If one is able to name the particular perspectives and interests which underlie given views or expressions of opinion, his own or others', he may not be misled by them. The point has been nicely made by Wirth:

> . . . thought . . . becomes fully comprehensible only if it is viewed sociologically. This involves the tracing of the bases of social judgment to their specific interest-bound roots in society, through which the particularity, and hence the limitations, of each view will become apparent. It is not to be assumed that the mere revelation of these divergent angles of vision will automatically cause the antagonists to embrace one another's conceptions or that it will result immediately in universal harmony. But the clarification of the sources of these differences would seem to be a precondition for any sort of awareness on the part of each observer of the limitation of his own view and at least the partial validity of the views of others.[46]

Summary

Perhaps the most fundamental social influence upon human thought is exerted by the very structure of language. Our speech habits lead us, without our realizing it, to conceive of the world along the broad lines and patterns laid down by our mother tongue. Our thoughts come to be controlled to a great extent by the need for communicating them. They are formulated and expressed in relation to imagined audiences and group identifications. Communication across cultural boundaries, as in interclass contacts, is hampered by cultural differences.

The frames of reference and standards of comparison by which we evaluate ourselves and others are derived from groups. Recent laboratory and field studies of small groups, in which group influences have been investigated in a rigorous experimental manner, have furnished further evidence of human sensitivity to the social environment. However, the broad institutional influences within a society, such as those described in the account of the role of the religious scholar in this chapter, cannot, by their very nature, be studied in the laboratory. The central point of this discussion—that human thought is dependent upon a social context—is also related to the problems of detecting and neutralizing bias in thinking.

SUGGESTIONS FOR DISCUSSION AND SPECIAL REPORTS

1. Report on the small-group research movement or on some phase of it which interests you.

2. Look for evidence in recent anthropological literature on the relationship between primitive thought and language.

3. It is sometimes said that the theoretical problems of social scientists reflect the social environment but that the problems of natural scientists do not. Write a report on the way in which the historical development of the natural sciences has been influenced by social conditions.

4. Discuss some possible professional biases of lawyers, physicians, nurses, or engineers. Is there a "professional mentality"?

5. How would you go about writing objectively on a subject concerning which you held strong biases?

6. In what sense, or senses, do animals belong to groups? Do they have reference groups?

7. Is complete objectivity possible on an economic or social question? Is it desirable?

NOTES

[1] C. W. Mills, "Language, Logic, and Culture," *Am. Soc. Rev.*, 4(1939): 677.

[2] E. Sapir, "The Status of Linguistics as a Science," in D. G. Mandelbaum (ed.), *Selected Writings in Language, Culture and Personality*, Berkeley, University of California Press, 1949, p. 162.

[3] W. Bynner, *The Jade Mountain*, Knopf, 1929, p. 27.

[4] The New York *Times*, February 9, 1948.

[5] B. L. Whorf, "Science and Linguistics," in T. Newcomb and E. H. Hartley, *Readings in Social Psychology*, Holt, 1947, p. 214.

[6] This is a paraphrasing of M. Granet's "Quelques particularités du langage et de la pensée chinoise," *Rev. Phil.*, 89-90 (1920): 98-128, 161-195. See also by the same author *La Pensée Chinoise*, Paris: La Renaissance du Livre, 1934.

[7] R. K. Merton, "Sociology of Knowledge," in G. D. Gurvitch and W. E. Moore, *Twentieth-Century Sociology*, Philosophical Library, 1945, p. 387.

[8] C. Kluckhohn and D. Leighton, *The Navaho*, Harvard University Press, 1946, pp. 194, 197-201.

[9] W. H. Werkmeister, *A Philosophy of Science*, Harper, 1940, pp. 126-129.

[10] E. Sapir, "Time Perspective in Aboriginal American Culture; A Study in Method," *op. cit.*, p. 11.

[11] C. Voegelin, "Linguistics Without Meaning and Culture Without Words," *Word*, 5(1949), 36-42; and "Relative Structurability," *ibid.*, pp. 44-45.

[12] *Ibid.*, p. 45.

[13] H. Hoijer, "The Relation of Language to Culture," in A. Kroeber, *Anthropology Today*, University of Chicago Press, 1953, pp. 545-573.

[14] P. Masson-Oursel, *Comparative Philosophy*, Harcourt, Brace, 1926, Part 2, Chap. II, "Comparative Logic," pp. 114-148.

[15] J. Dewey, *Logic: The Theory of Inquiry*, Holt, 1938, pp. 81-98.

[16] Werkmeister, *op. cit.*, pp. 109-110.

[17] Mills, *op. cit.*, pp. 672-673.

[18] D. Riesman and N. Glaser, "The Meaning of Opinion," *Public Opinion Quarterly*, 12(1948): 633-648.

[19] *Ibid.*, p. 633.

[20] The following account is adapted from L. Schatzman and A. L. Strauss, "Social Class and Modes of Communication," *Am. J. Soc.*, 60(1955): 329-338: and "Cross-Class Interviewing: An Analysis of Interaction and Communicative Styles," unpublished manuscript.

[21] Unpublished study by Bernard Kaplan, Clark University, Department of Psychology.

[22] W. L. Warner, *American Life: Dream and Reality*, University of Chicago Press, 1943, pp. 193-194.

[23] J. Myers and L. Schaffer, "Social Stratification and Psychiatric Practice: A Study of an Out-Pa-

tient Clinic," *Am. Soc. Rev.*, 19 (1954): 310.

24 M. Sherif, *Group Relations at the Crossroads*, Harper, 1953, p. 214.

25 M. Sherif, J. O. Harvey, B. J. White, and R. Hood, *Theoretical and Experimental Studies in Interpersonal and Group Relations*, University of Oklahoma, 1954. (Limited pre-publication reports.)

26 R. K. Merton and Alice S. Kitt, "Contributions to the Theory of Reference Group Behavior," in R. K. Merton and P. F. Lazarsfeld (eds.), *Studies in the Scope and Method of "The American Soldier,"* Glencoe, Ill.: Free Press, 1950, pp. 70-105.

27 T. Newcomb, *Social Psychology*, Dryden, 1950, pp. 225-232.

28 H. H. Hyman, "The Psychology of Status," *Arch. Psych.*, 269 (1942).

29 L. Festinger, "The Role of Group Belongingness in a Voting Situation," *Human Relations*, 2(1947): 154-180.

30 Marcia Davenport, *East Side, West Side*, New York, Scribner, 1947.

31 *Ibid.*, pp. 134, 196, and 190-192.

32 T. Shibutani, "Reference Groups as Delimited Perspectives," *Am. J. Soc.*, 60(1955): 562-569.

33 W. Moede, *Experimentelle Massenpsychologie*, Leipzig, 1920, pp. 133-136.

34 F. Allport, *Social Psychology*, Houghton Mifflin, 1924, p. 273.

35 J. F. Dashiell, "An Experimental Analysis of Some Group Ef-

fects," *J. Ab. and Soc. Psych.*, 25(1930): 190-199.

36 M. Shaw, "A Comparison of Individuals and Small Groups in the Rational Solution of Complex Problems," in G. E. Swanson, T. Newcomb, and E. L. Hartley (eds.), *Readings in Social Psychology*, pp. 135-146.

37 L. Festinger and J. Thibaut, "Interpersonal Communication in Small Groups," in Swanson *et al.*, *op. cit.*, pp. 125-134.

38 *Ibid.*, p. 134.

39 M. Sherif, "A Study of Some Social Factors in Perception," *Arch. Psych.*, No. 187, 1935.

40 H. Sperling, "An Experimental Study in Some Psychological Factors in Judgment," master's thesis, New School for Social Research, New York, 1946.

41 S. E. Asch, "Effects of Group Pressure Upon the Modification and Distortion of Judgments," in Swanson *et al.*, *op. cit.*, pp. 2-11.

42 S. E. Asch, *Social Psychology*, Prentice-Hall, 1952, p. 454.

43 *Ibid.*, p. 8.

44 W. W. Charters and T. Newcomb, "Some Attitudinal Effects of Experimentally Increased Salience of a Membership Group," in Swanson *et al.*, *op. cit.*, pp. 415-420.

45 F. Znaniecki, *The Social Role of the Man of Knowledge*, Columbia University Press, 1940, pp. 98-101.

46 L. Wirth, in his preface to K. Mannheim, *Ideology and Utopia*, Harcourt, Brace, 1936, pp. xxvii-xxviii.

SELECTED BIBLIOGRAPHY

Cartwright, D., and A. Zander (eds.), *Group Dynamics: Research and Theory,* Row Peterson, 1953. A collection of research reports, classified under various headings, with an attempt by the editors to present a unifying theory.

Dewey, J., *Logic: The Theory of Inquiry,* Holt, 1938. Chap. V, "The Needed Reform of Logic," pp. 81-98. A comparison of ancient Greek and modern logic as two nonidentical modes of reasoning. Dewey's analysis involves an examination of the social bases of Aristotelian logic.

Durkheim, E., *The Elementary Forms of Religious Life,* New York: Allen and Unwin, 1915. A sociological classic which emphasizes in a general way the social origins of certain basic concepts, such as space and time. A difficult book for beginners.

Hoijer, H. (ed.), *Language in Culture,* University of Chicago Press, 1954. (Also published as Memoir No. 79 of The American Anthropological Association.) Papers and discussions by a number of anthropologists, linguists, philosophers, and psychologists. A provocative book, especially for its handling of language and the structure of thought.

Hoijer, H., in A. Kroeber, *Anthropology Today,* University of Chicago Press, 1954, "The Relation of Language to Culture," pp. 554-573. An excellent review of the point of view presented in this chapter.

Kelley, H., and J. Thibaut, in G. Lindzey, *Handbook of Social Psychology,* Vol. II, Addison-Wesley, 1954, "Experimental Studies of Group Problem Solving and Process," pp. 735-785. A recent survey of research findings with an extensive bibliography.

Mannheim, K., *Ideology and Utopia,* Harcourt, Brace, 1936. Including L. Wirth's preface. A number of highly abstract articles on the sociology of knowledge and the social bases of thought. A very influential book but not suited for the beginning student.

Masson-Oursel, P., *Comparative Philosophy,* Harcourt, Brace, 1926. Part 2, Chap. II, "Comparative Logic," pp. 114-148. Greek, Chinese, and Indian (India) systems of logic are shown to be different and to be conditioned by the social life of their respective users.

Merton, R. K., and A. S. Kitt, "Contributions to the Theory of Reference Group Behavior," in R. K. Merton and P. Lazarsfeld (eds.), *Continuities in Social Research,* Glencoe, Ill.: Free Press, 1950, pp. 40-105. A theoretical and methodological treatment of the concept, with specific reference to data presented in *The American Soldier.*

Mills, C. W., "Language, Logic, and Culture," *Am. Soc. Rev.,* 4(1939): 670-680. A closely reasoned theoretical paper on the relations between groups, language, and thinking. The author makes use of some of Mead's concepts. The treatment is on a high conceptual level.

Riecken, H., and G. Homans, in G. Lindzey, *Handbook of Social Psychology*, Vol. II, Addison-Wesley, 1954, "Psychological Aspects of Social Structure," pp. 786-832. A survey of small-group research emphasizing studies which reveal group influences on individual behavior.

Schatzman, L., and A. Strauss, "Social Class and Modes of Communication," *Am. J. Soc.*, 60(1955): 329-338. The research report discussed in this chapter.

Sherif, M., in M. Sherif and M. O. Wilson (eds.), *Group Relations at the Crossroads*, Harper, 1953. "The Concept of Reference Group in Social Psychology," pp. 203-231. A discussion of the concept of reference group and a survey of some research findings relevant to it.

Shibutani, T., "Reference Groups as Perspectives," *Am. J. Soc.*, 60(1955): 562-569. Presents a strong rationale for utilizing the concept of reference group and attempts to clarify the concept.

Whorf, B. L., "Science and Linguistics," in Newcomb and Hartley, *Readings in Social Psychology*, Holt, 1947, pp. 210-218. An interestingly written paper on the conditioning of reasoning by language structure. Should be read in conjunction with the Hoijer readings.

Wilson, L., *The Academic Man*, New York: Oxford University Press, 1942. The typical behavior of university faculty members is analyzed in terms of roles, status, position, recruitment, pressures, and institutional goals. Eminently readable, although the analysis is oversimple.

Znaniecki, F., *The Social Role of the Man of Knowledge*, Columbia University Press, 1940. The roles and functions of various types of scholars are described in rich and readable detail. Some of the types are technician, prophet, scientist, and sage.

PART 3

MOTIVATION AND
LEARNING

CHAPTER 9 · · ·   **Motivation**

ONE OF THE especially perplexing aspects of the study of human beings arises from the fact that they, unlike any other objects of scientific study, have ideas of their own about why they act as they do. Consideration of what people say in explanation of their behavior inevitably leads to a consideration of motives and motivation. The concept of motivation is especially applicable to human behavior. It is less applicable to the lower animals, and when applied to them is usually translated into biological terms. It is, of course, entirely inapplicable to inorganic matter and plant life. In this chapter we shall be concerned with the concept of motivation as it is applied to human behavior, and we shall see that it poses some of the most difficult and controversial problems in the social sciences.

A Universal Problem

When specific acts are explained in ordinary discourse, the explanations rest upon assumptions about behavior in general. Systems of philosophy also require that assumptions be made concerning the nature of behavior and its motives. In this connection, the problem of motivation is an old one; and it has been handled in many different ways. The various hedonistic philosophies have tended to conceive of the seeking of pleasure and the avoidance of pain as the bases of most action. Another approach has been to think of humans as motivated by certain powerful drives or combinations of drives, such as sex and hunger, love, self-interest, and self-preservation. The sources of the purposes which move men have been found also in supernatural beings or superordinate structures such as God, the state, the community, the economic system, or the class system.

Since human beings have a curiosity about and a deep interest in the "why" and "how" of behavior, every generation makes a fresh attack on the problem of motivation. Nevertheless, one is struck by the tenacity with which certain classical conceptions reappear in new guises. The terminology may be a little new, but the themes are not.

The imputation of motives to others is, of course, an integral aspect of human interaction. It is inconceivable that social life could exist if persons did not make guesses or assumptions about the purposes of others. The mark of human behavior, as opposed to animal behavior, is that it is organized around anticipation of others' responses to one's own actions. (In Chapter 12 we shall discuss this as the process of "taking the role of the other.") Anticipation involves assumptions as to how and why the other will react. It also involves judgments about previous acts of the other, as they have bearing upon his possible future acts. A knowledge of the other's purposes is the most effective basis for understanding what he is doing now and knowing what to expect from him in the future.

Incorrect assessment of such purposes has important consequences, since it may lead to embarrassment, misunderstanding, loss of money and time, or other even more unfortunate effects. When acts are familiar, traditional, routinized, the assessment of motivation is easy and taken for granted. No one raises questions about why people walk erect, build houses, or wear clothes, although the question of motivation is brought into sharp focus when they do not do these things. If the reasons for customary behavior are inquired after, usually by an outsider, the person who is questioned may be at a loss for an answer. In relatively homogeneous societies, the questioning of motives is relatively infrequent, because the bases of customary behavior are infrequently challenged.

> There are societies . . . with little or no group-awareness of group incentives; they have few, or no, formulated ideals of conduct, and they do not attempt to bring their group incentives into the light of day in the guise of accepted motives. Their problems of group behavior are problems of *how* and not *why*. They learn how to behave in this or that contingency; and if ever they ask why—and they rarely ask this unless some [anthropologist] asks them—the answer is, This is how we have always behaved. The society is unified and integrated by the sharp clarity of its techniques coupled with the obscurity of its motives.[1]

In heterogeneous societies, actions more frequently raise questions because the behavior is unfamiliar to some, or because it is performed in contexts which make it unclear. Then some guesswork, and sometimes some sleuthing, is called for on the part of the investigator. The difficulties of correct assessment are further increased by the fact that people very often do not clearly formulate to themselves the purposes of their actions and so can give little help to others who wish to understand them. There may also be several purposes, or levels of purposes, involved in the same act. The importance of clues to future behavior is further underlined by the existence of duplicity in interaction. The concealment of motives and the deliberate misleading of other persons is sometimes cultivated as an art, and appears to be necessary for smoothly functioning social relationships, even relationships among friends, lovers, and kinsmen. "Nothing but the truth" would thoroughly disrupt human relations.

Biologically Rooted Motives

The idea that human behavior has its roots in man's biological nature and can be explained only in biological terms is commonly designated as "biological determinism." The tendency to assume this position is enhanced by the relatively great prestige of, and progress in, the biological sciences as compared with the social sciences. The biological determinist thinks of motives as nothing more than gross bodily conditions. For example, dehydration may be equated with thirst, or contractions of the stomach muscles and low sugar content in the blood may be equated with hunger. There is no question that bodily conditions are connected with motivation and that they condition it in a variety of ways. However, it is an error to regard any gross physical condition as the entire motive for any action. Bodily conditions, such as those ordinarily associated with thirst and hunger, are by themselves inadequate to incite goal-directed behavior until they have been interpreted in certain ways or until the organism has learned what action to take. Before this learning takes place, the gross physical condition of the organism leads, at most, to restless exploratory behavior of an undirected kind.

HUNGER

The case against the view that biological conditions directly motivate particular acts can be made by discussing the phenomenon of hunger. Consider the varied acts associated with eating a meal. Persons with presumably similar physiological states of hunger may act very differently while eating, according to standards of etiquette prescribed by their country and their social class. The foods chosen are not linked directly with the organism's biological structure. Thus, English and American people generally eat different items for breakfast. The Chinese avoid milk and milk products and Americans abhor snake meat, although milk is available in China and snakes in America and both foods are nourishing. As for the duration of meals: the typical American emphasis on speedy break-fasts and lunches seems to be connected mainly with industrial and commercial practices rather than with biological needs, whereas long dinners are related to leisure time and sociability. Nor does the order in which foods are eaten—since it is not identical in all countries—seem to be explainable on biological grounds. Although Americans from long habituation may think sweet food necessary to round off a meal, certain other peoples do not find this so. And scarcely accountable for on biological grounds is the symbolism—social, religious, personal—surrounding the eating of meals. Thus, many whites will not eat with Negroes, and vice versa.

Physical need for food should be clearly distinguished from the verbalized desire for it. It is unwarranted to assume that a newborn infant experiences the physical need for food as anything more than a diffuse, undefined discomfort. The infant simply cries and his parents are likely to assume he needs milk. After repeated feed-ings, he begins to respond in a way which seems to suggest that he has learned to expect milk in a given situation. However, since the infant does not know what milk is and cannot verbalize his need, it is erroneous to equate his attitude toward milk with that of an adult. Only after he has learned to speak and understands the mean-ings of words can he be said to be hungry or to desire food in the same sense that adults do.

The word "hunger" is applied to all three of the following: (1) the sheer fact of biological need; (2) the subverbal appreciation of the connection between the eating of certain substances and re-lief from hunger distress; and (3) the conscious verbal formulation of interpretation of a felt biological need.

The first, or physiological need for food, is obviously unlearned, whereas the third, the interpretation the person makes of his bodily condition, is a learned reaction. The person's interpretations of his needs sometimes do not correspond to biological facts: he may express a verbal desire for food when he does not require it biologically, and vice versa. He may believe he has all the food he requires when actually his body is in a state of malnutrition because he eats inadequate foods. The biological need for food may go unrecognized when the stomach is distended by non-nutritious substances. Through intravenous feedings the stomach may be temporarily by-passed altogether in the feeding process. In other words, physical need for food and verbalized desire for food are distinct and separate phenomena and are sometimes wholly unrelated.

There is, of course, no disputing the existence of a biological need for nourishment in all organisms, including man. But there is a vast difference between acknowledging this need and assuming that specific human ways of satisfying it and thinking about it are simple consequences of biological conditions. As a matter of empirical fact, the average American child spends a great deal of time in learning the proper ways of satisfying his need for food. The necessity is biological—but the social behavior involved in satisfying it is not biological. The same may be said of other similar conditions imposed on us because we are biological organisms.

The learned character of hunger responses may be illustrated by reference to the upbringing of the middle-class American child. He is taught innumerable lessons involving mashed vegetables, baby-food formulas, dessert, eating between meals, using silverware, not playing at the table, and so on. Any parent who spends years teaching his child how and when to be hungry should not believe that hunger-satisfying activities among humans are chiefly biological.

Hunger for food is viewed so persistently as a gross biological matter that it is worthwhile to compare it with the hunger for drugs. This comparison is made in Chapter 11, and brief reference may well be made to it here. In virtually all aspects which are pertinent to the present discussion, opium hunger and food hunger are alike. In both, gross bodily conditions are necessary concomitants. The fallacy of viewing drug addiction as a purely physiological condition is easily perceived, however, primarily because drugs are not necessary to life and because the drug habit is generally acquired when the person is an adult or close to adulthood.

INSTINCTS

Generally speaking, few or no contemporary psychologists and physiologists postulate a direct or automatic connection between biological conditions and complex human action. However, many laymen still do. The offering of general "instincts" as explanations

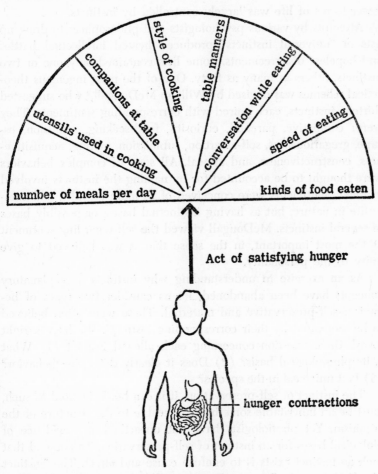

The specific forms of hunger-satisfying behavior are learned.
Necessary conditions for hunger-satisfying behavior are inherited.

of action is a variant of this position. Common speech and popular writing are replete with references to paternal, maternal, gambling, religious and other instincts. During the latter part of the nineteenth century and the early years of the twentieth century, because of the influence of Darwin's work it was standard practice in scholarly works to account for particular acts as expressions of generalized instinctual drives. It was usually also assumed that the behavior of lower forms of life was largely controlled by instincts.

Attempts by various psychologists and philosophers to draw up lists of "universal instincts" produced heated intellectual battles and hopeless disagreements. Some lists contained only one or two instincts, others as many as forty. One of the most ingenious theoretical schemes was devised by William McDougall,[2] who suggested thirteen instincts, each paired with corresponding sentiments. They were: combative, parental, curiosity, food-seeking, repulsion, escape, gregariousness, self-assertion, submission, mating, acquisitiveness, constructiveness, and appeal. All sorts of complex behaviors were thought to be accounted for by naming the instincts involved in them. Sentiments were conceived of as more complex and composite in nature, but as having instinctual bases, or possibly bases in several instincts. McDougall viewed the self-regarding sentiment as the most important, in the sense that it was believed to give unity to the personality.

As an exercise in understanding why instincts as explanatory concepts have been abandoned, let us consider two types of behavior: self-preservative and maternal. These were often believed to be motivated by their corresponding instincts. We have a right to ask three question concerning each alleged instinct (1) What is its physiological basis? (2) Does it clearly determine behavior? (3) Is it universal in the species?

The instinct of self-preservation, if it can be designated as such, must be an inheritable something, traceable to the structure of the organism. Yet physiologists have not unearthed any evidence of biological bases for an instinct of self-preservation. To contend that such an instinct exists is to confuse cause and effect. The "instinct of self-preservation" is not the cause of an organism's activity but merely a shorthand description of the activity. Perhaps, as Klineberg[3] has suggested, self-preservation is a kind of general label standing for a number of physiological drives such at thirst, hunger, and elimination.

We may also note the whimsical operation of an instinct that seems to work all the time for some individuals but sometimes fails to work for others. Japanese statesmen, in accordance with Japanese moral standards, commit suicide to save face; frustrated Americans and Europeans take their own lives; soldiers of all countries defy this supposedly deep-rooted instinct by obeying commands which mean virtually certain death. Unless one presupposes a still stronger instinct or set of instincts which negates that of self-preservation, its vagaries are difficult to account for.

An instinct that is perhaps worthy of more consideration is the "maternal instinct," because a physiological basis for it can possibly be discovered. Investigation of the behavior of rats has disclosed that concern for offspring—as shown by the mother's behavior—begins to decline from twelve to twenty days after parturition, generally disappearing by the twenty-fifth day. It is apparently tied up with gland relief, since maternal concern parallels the development and decline of lactation. Other physiological bases are suggested by the fact that maternal behavior may be induced in male rats by implanting anterior pituitary glands of females.[4]

Assuming, then, that typically maternal behavior in the human mother is rooted in her physiology, can her behavior be adequately explained on physiological (instinctive) grounds? Consider the following eccentricities of the instinct. Psychoanalysts have demonstrated the prevalence of child "rejection" by American and Western European mothers. Apparently these parents do not act in typical maternal fashion: instead of fondling the baby, they ignore or wreak vengeance on it; instead of expending time, energy, and concern upon the growing child, they avoid, tantalize, or hate it.

Maternal behavior is exhibited by women who have never lactated and by little girls before the age of puberty. A mother's love for her children does not disappear when she becomes old and loses the physiological functions alleged to be the basis of mother love. A woman who has her ovaries and uterus removed by surgery does not of course change her attitudes toward her children because of this operation. Further inconsistencies are the practices of abortion and infanticide. How can the instinct permit these acts? Above all, how can it permit female infanticide and discourage male infanticide in one society, and do exactly the reverse in another? Moreover, in many societies it is a common practice to give away children to other families who wish to adopt them; and apparently this is done without outraging motherly impulses.

There is a sense in which behavior of a newborn baby is instinctive. However, the use of the term in this connection is merely descriptive, not explanatory. The older instinct doctrine conceived of instincts as "forces," or causes of whole ranges of human reaction. When we describe the yawning, sneezing, and other similar automatic behavior of a newborn child as instinctive, it is understood that this is only a way of saying that the child does not have to be taught to do these things.

Instinct as an explantory concept has not only been virtually abandoned in the study of human beings, but it has also proved inadequate to account for the behavior of lower forms as well. It is meaningless to label behavior as instinctive if no biological structures or physiological conditions can be shown to be linked with it. Careful investigation of lower species, as we suggested earlier, indicates that their behavior is not nearly as mechanical or automatic as popularly believed, and that even so-called "instinctive patterns of reaction" are always related to and dependent upon the environment in which they occur. It has also been suggested that behavior sometimes believed to be rigidly determined by inherited mechanisms may in fact be the result of early and rapid learning.[5] It is well known that there is no necessary one-to-one correspondence between organs and specific activity. Biological structures should perhaps be thought of as necessary conditions which make certain types of behavior possible but do not determine or explain specific modes of response to the requirements of a changing environment. For instance, it has been observed that

> every bee [worker] in the hive has during its lifetime to pass through all the different jobs. First, in the first ten days of their life, the young bees have the task to attend to the brood, to clean the cells in which the queen will deposit her eggs, to

warm the developing brood by sitting on it, to feed the older larvae with honey and pollen from the store-cells, and, when eventually their own food glands have been developed, to feed the young larvae with the secretion of those glands. Then, in the second period, running from their tenth to twentieth day, they have other occupations, such as to take the food from the returning bees and bring it to the store-cells, to clean the hive, and, further, to build the comb when their wax-glands have fully developed, which happens between the tenth and the seventeenth day. Finally, in the third period, which runs from the twentieth day up to their death, which in summer occurs between the thirtieth and the thirty-fifth day, the bee works as a field-bee, collecting food. . . . There is a clear connection between the execution of the instinctive actions and bodily development. . . . Yet it would be wrong to believe that the appearance of all these instincts is determined by bodily development alone.

This was shown by Roesch . . . he succeeded in dividing a population of bees into two groups of different ages: one younger and one older than eighteen days old. The result of this division was that in the younger population the menace of famine arose, as the foraging bees were wanting. Then, after some days, young bees of 7-15 days old flew out in search of food. At first they were still in possession of food-glands, and so flew out "physiologically precociously." In adaptation to the abnormal circumstances the population was thus split up into two groups of the same age with different occupations. On the other hand, in the group of older bees there arose a menace to the care of the brood, till some older bees took this task upon themselves. Also bees older than the normal builders began to build on the comb, and to that end even developed new wax-glands. . . . Roesch further made the important observation that bees which had been isolated during the first ten days of their life, when brought back to the hive, first went through activities they had missed during their absence.[6]

The outcome of this investigation has been a blurring of the dividing line between instinctive and learned behavior as the necessity of viewing organisms in their environmental situations has received more stress: the concept of instinct as a general unfolding drive or force has given way to a concept of it as a term describing limited segments of behavior in which learning appears to play little or no part.

NEED PSYCHOLOGY

We have said that psychologists do not ordinarily claim that there is a direct connection between physiological states and complex behavior. Nevertheless, they have been reluctant to abandon the conception that social behavior is somehow rooted in biological bases. The concept of need, or drive, may be taken as an illustration. It is a frame of reference which is widely used in some form or other by many psychologists:

> [One] type of need is allied with bodily functions and is variously referred to as biological, biogenic, unlearned, primary, basic. Lists given by various authors do not agree in detail, but Sherif's[7] in *An Outline of Social Psychology* is representative. He lists such motives as hunger, thirst, sex, breathing, and evacuation. Then there are social needs—synonymous as sociogenic, secondary, psychogenic, acquired, and derived, etc.— which are recognized as due to learning. Some of these latter needs are suspected as deriving, often in devious and subtle ways, from the more basic biological needs. But most current writers believe that some if not the majority of social needs originate solely in social interaction. Since needs are learned, and since men learn to want, wish, aspire to, an almost infinite number of things, the numbers of social needs are tremendous, and vary from society to society and group to group. Most writers wisely refuse to enumerate all possible social needs, unlike their careful attempts to list biological needs.

> This kind of motivational scheme grew out of the conviction, or the suspicion, that the basic fact about the human being is his body, and that much of his behavior could be traced to its workings. The more sophisticated treatments eschew the attempt to trace most behavior to the body, but the biological skeleton usually shows through in such statements as: "We have to keep in mind that no matter how real and how absolute acquired motives are felt to be, they constitute the superstructure of human motivation." As the deprivation of biogenic needs (sleep, food, or water) begins to grow intense, the in-

dividual returns or regresses to the level "which is dominated by the biogenic needs, and the superstructure of the acquired motives is subject to collapse in various degrees."[8]

Various criticisms may be made of this position. The concept of primary biological need is itself dubious. To begin with, a person may be unaware of a biological deprivation and so it may not eventuate in behavior: for example, an individual suffering from a vitamin deficiency caused by a poorly balanced diet may not realize that the deficiency exists. People dying of starvation are said not to feel hunger after the first few days. Persons who suffer oxygen deprivation at high altitudes, such as mountain climbers and aviators, do not feel a craving for oxygen, but simply lose their judgment and develop other symptons such as slowness of movement and reaction and poor motor control. They must be taught to expect these effects and how to avoid them through the use of artificially supplied oxygen.[9] As Cole has said: "The only 'needs' which release a stream of energy are those which stimulate us."[10] Physiological needs not based on any innate drive may also be learned, and they may lead to behavior which serves no good biological end. Examples of these "learned needs" are the drug addict's need for morphine and the alcoholic's craving for drink.

No one denies that there are unlearned components in much human activity or that organisms must do certain things to survive. It is also clear that certain physiological lacks or deprivations may lead to attempts to relieve the accompanying distress. Reactions to such deprivation may also be random and ineffective unless the individual is taught to recognize the lack and what to do about it.

Admitting the importance of biological survival and well being does not, however, justify the usual need psychology. Such terms as "primary" and "basic" are rhetorical devices for making human behavior seem to be grounded in a solid biological substratum. The intellectual security thus created is only an illusion which oversimplifies and misrepresents the nature of human goals.

The designation of biological needs as "primary" or "basic" and social needs as "secondary" or "derived" seems to imply two things: (1) that the social are less important, and (2) that they directly or indirectly stem from basic, more fundamental needs. The first point is merely an unproved postulate, and most social psychologists no longer rely upon it.

The idea that human beings are most effectively motivated in terms of their assumed basic biological needs has had some interesting social implications, the shortcomings of which have been demonstrated. It used to be argued, for example, that the workingman's hours could not be shortened or his pay raised because this would leave him unmotivated to do the necessary work of industry. It was felt that laboring men would not know what to do with their spare time. (Needless to say, those who advanced such views did not apply these arguments to themselves.) As *Fortune Magazine* observes:

> . . . Now there is no doubt that, given more time off, some workers might drink too much, or beat their wives, or go insane watching daytime television. Others might work themselves to death in second jobs. But the $30-billion leisure market, the remarkable emergence, almost from nowhere, of a huge, new do-it-yourself market, and even the familiar Sunday-afternoon sight of cars crawling along bumper to bumper, suggest strongly that most American workers have a pretty good idea of what to do with their time off.[11]

Although many social psychologists employ some variant of need psychology in theory and research, most of them today are probably willing to admit that most social needs arise on their own level and are not really expressions, however indirect, of primary needs. Many desires and aspirations associated with eating and sexual behavior, for example, are connected in only the most tenuous ways, if at all, with the primary drives with which they are linguistically connected.

There is an enormous range of behavior which can be accounted for only in terms of social structure. The needs involved are endless in number and are constantly increasing or changing. Each of the unique features of modern, urban, technological civilization has ushered in its appropriate and unique needs. Some cosmopolites feel a need to live in cities of more than a million people; others may have a specific need to live only in New York City or to live in the country even if they must work in the city.

The refinement of symbol manipulation has led to the needs for intelligence, for rationality, for explanations of natural phenomena and of one's own actions. The foreknowledge of old age and death creates the need for orienting oneself to these realities. The unanswerable questions that can be asked about the origin, ultimate meaning, and destiny of man have led to the development of the needs that are satisfied by religious and philosophical doctrines. The formulation of standards and values produces the corresponding desires to be loyal, honest, reliable, and virtuous. Practically every such human ambition, wish, or desire may be called a "need" without furthering the study of behavior at all. As Coutu has noted, people need whatever they think they need.

In the past there have been attempts to classify social needs into a relatively few basic types. One such typology which was famous for many years among sociologists and others was Thomas and Znaniecki's four fundamental wishes: for security, response, new experience, and recognition.[12] However, the classification of human behavior into categories corresponding to assumed needs, wishes, or drives does not at all explain the behavior. Thus, if a husband is said to be unfaithful to his wife because of the "wish for new experience" and another husband is faithful because of "the wish for security," we must still ask why one is unfaithful and the other is not. To label behavior in such terms is quite arbitrarily to impute to the individual abstract and unverifiable motives which are conceived of as the forces or causative agents behind the overt acts. A need as such is not directly perceived; all that can be observed is behavior itself. Hence, the need is first inferred from the act and then used to interpret and explain it. Such explanations are circular or tautological because they do nothing that cannot be accomplished by a simple description of the behavior.

In a striking passage, Allport has brought out both the difficulty of deciding among contending lists of basic motives and the reductionism implicit in them all:

Taking the case of Tolstoy, Adler would find the style of life adopted by Tolstoy to be a consequence of his compensatory striving for power, for health, or for personal integrity.... Freud might decide that the "simplification of life" was a mere ritual evolved to escape feelings of guilt derived from an unhallowed infantile love; or perhaps he would attribute it to a Death Wish. Rank would see it as a desire to return to the peaceful pre-natal life. . . . McDougall might attribute it to the combined effects of the propensities for submission and comfort. H. A. Murray might say that there was a need for submission and inviolacy. . . . Any of these writers, to be sure, would admit that the original motive had become greatly extended both in the range of stimuli which provoke it and in its varieties of expression. But THE COMMON FACTOR IN ALL THESE EXPLANATIONS IS THE REDUCTION OF EVERY MOTIVE, HOWEVER ELABORATE AND INDIVIDUAL, TO A LIMITED NUMBER OF BASIC INTERESTS, SHARED BY ALL MEN, AND PRESUMABLY INNATE. . . . Not four wishes, nor eighteen propensities, not any and all combinations of these, even with their extensions and variations, seem adequate to account for the endless variety of goals sought by an endless variety of mortals.[13]

The concept of need as an explanatory device is hardly distinguishable from the old instinct schemes. However, it may confidently be predicted that this kind of explanation will be with us for many years to come, since the belief in the body's primacy is deeply rooted. Maslow, attempting to resuscitate a frankly instinctivistic theory, affords an instructive example of the varied guises that such explanations can take. In a paper titled "The Instinctoid Nature of Basic Needs," he says:

> . . . Homing pigeons, salmon, cats, etc., each have instincts peculiar to the species. Why could not the human species also have characteristics peculiar to it?
> The commonly accepted theory has been that instincts steadily drop out as we go higher in the phyletic scale, to be replaced by an adaptability based on a vastly improved ability to learn, to think, and to communicate. If we define an instinct in lower animal style, as a complex of innately predetermined urge, readiness to perceive, instrumental behavior and skill, and goal object . . . then this theory seems to be true. . . . Side by side with this evolutionary development there may be found another one, namely for the gradual appearance as we ascend the phyletic scale of new and "higher" urges, instinctoid in nature, i.e., predetermined in greater or lesser degree by the

structure and functioning of the organism. We say "may" because, although we present our hypotheses confidently for
human beings, practically nothing is known about "higher"
urges in subhuman animals. It remains a task for the future to
decide to what degree, and in what sense, rats, dogs, cats, and
monkeys show urges to safety, belongingness, love, respect,
autonomy, self-confidence, curiosity, understanding, or beauty.
(Be it noted again that we speak here of instinctoid *impulses* or
urges and *not* of predetermined instrumental behaviors, abilities,
or mode of gratification, *i.e.*, *not* of instincts.)[14]

Freudian Conceptions

Probably the most influential motivational scheme of this century
is the Freudian. Some variant of it is utilized by most clinical psychologists and psychiatrists. Social workers, child psychologists, and
anthropologists have often found it useful or acceptable. Fragments
of the Freudian terminology and conceptual scheme have also found
their way into popular thought. It is difficult to set forth current
Freudian ideas in a form that would be subscribed to by all
Freudians, because there are considerable differences in viewpoint,
formulation, and emphasis among them. Whatever these differences
may be, there is a fair amount of agreement or a number of basic
points and assumptions.

SOME BASIC POINTS

Among the basic assumptions underlying the Freudian view of
motivation are the ideas that all human behavior is motivated, that
the explanation of any behavior requires that its motives be analyzed, that the energy sources of motives are biological in nature,
that motives range from those which are entirely conscious to those
which are altogether unconscious and that most important ones
are either unconscious or partly so, and that the conflict of motiva-

tional forces plays a dominant role in personality development. The following statement of basic tenets by a noted psychoanalyst would probably elicit fairly general agreement. We are quoting at some length since we are critical of this motivational system and therefore wish one of its proponents to state it for the reader:

Psychoanalysis . . . deals with mental forces acting in the same, divergent, or opposite directions and with their resultants. The forces . . . are subjected to what one could call the "integrative principle," which characterizes biologic processes—the organism and its structural parts form a coherent unity manifesting the tendency to preserve itself and to develop in determined ways. Thus the various needs and urges and impulses of the individual must be co-ordinated so as to lead to integrated conduct, which is necessary for his adaptation to the conditions of reality. Conflicts arise when two or more urges cannot be combined toward such behavior; and so emotional conflicts and their various consequences constitute the most important sources of knowledge of mental phenomena.

To account for the varying degrees of intensity inherent in any mental experience, one must postulate a "charge of energy" which is correlated to nervous excitation. The consciously perceived mental energy corresponds to what one usually calls "interest." It invests every mental process and is discharged in feelings, affects, and emotions as well as in motor activity. . . . Following a general trend of biologic investigation, Freud approached the study of mental phenomena not only from a causal but also from a finalistic point of view. Everyone is directly aware of "aims" which he feels urged to pursue, though the source or the urge is not conscious. He is also aware that he must frequently achieve secondary aims in order to reach his conscious goal. An aim has an object. A simple example is the urge of hunger, the goal of which is to be satisfied and the object of which is food. . . . Freud was concerned with the classification of the basic instincts and drives. This approach led to problematic and controversial formulations and also to a number of uncertainties which have required revision of many corollary concepts. . . . In his first formulation of a dualistic concept of the basic drives, Freud distinguished the self-preservative or *ego drives* from the race-preservative or *sexual drives*. . . . Freud included in the ego drives all self-interest, and he extended the concept of the sexual or erotic drives to comprise all interest in objects which did not serve the self-interest.

The dynamic force of the sexual drives in this broad sense was called "libido." The ego drives were considered to be empowered by a different energy which could not be transformed into libido. . . . [Later] Freud dropped his former dualism, recognizing that the self-preservative and constructive developmental urges were empowered by the same force which characterized sexuality in the broadest sense of the word. But opposite to this kind of energy (libido), which includes all kinds of constructive drives, he postulated a destructive drive tending to dissolution and death. This dualism asserted that in the organism there normally arises not only a kind of energy which is discharged into pleasurable, constructive, and integrated activities but also another kind, the discharge of which determines disintegration and destruction. . . . According to Freud, the two always appear mixed with each other. . . . Some analysts resort to other explanations to account for aggression and destruction. They point out that, since these tendencies are biologically necessary for defense and for achieving security and satisfaction, they need not necessarily be derived from a hypothetical death instinct. . . . The ultimate motive behind every urge and wish which determines human behavior is discharge of tension. But homeostasis alone cannot account for all biologic phenomena with which the mental drives are associated; it is responsible merely for the maintenance and re-establishment of the same conditions—the status quo—in the organism. No growth, no development, no expansion and propagation, can derive from homeostasis alone. . . . [Alexander has] introduced the "principle of surplus energy," and from it he derived certain biologic formulations and theories concerning eroticism, growth, development, and propagation. . . . Through this approach no classification of drives can be formulated; a distinction is made merely between those tendencies which comply with homeostasis alone . . . and those which result from the surplus energy and its discharge in various activities. The latter Alexander calls "erotic drives." According to this theory, the discharge of all surplus energy, by which homeostasis is re-established, is pleasurable. . . .

Repression is the most important psychodynamic phenomenon which Freud discovered in his earliest studies. . . . When a drive or memory . . . undergoes repression, it is . . . subjected to mental processes which are extraneous to the individual's conscious inner experiences, and, so long as it remains unconscious, it is inaccessible to introspection. . . . Repression is one of the dynamic defenses against drives and memories which cannot be controlled by the ego and which thus jeopardize its integration. . . . After undergoing repression, drives and memories . . . become subject to the patterns of mental functioning which characterize the "system unconscious" from which all drives . . . derive. This system is also called the "id." . . . To comprehend the phenomenon of repression and its implications, one must study it from a dynamic as well as from a structural and topographic view. The first considers the forces employed by the ego to maintain the exclusion of a repressed drive from the ego and from consciousness in spite of its pressure from the id . . . the latter concerns the localization of the process in the mental apparatus. It has been said that repression takes place between the system unconscious—the id—and the preconscious—the ego. These mental localities are not anatomically related to different portions of the brain, but are . . . different patterns of mental functioning which maintain a constant reciprocal relationship. . . . It is helpful to repeat that the preconscious and conscious mental phenomena are rooted in the unconscious system. Every drive and interest, every memory and representation of the "inner foreign country," originate in this system.[15]

Thus, according to the Freudian position human behavior is activated either by innate biological needs or by elaborations of them. Human culture is conceived of both as an agency which frustrates and disciplines primitive urges; and as a consequence of such frustration, the basic sources of energy are undirected and goalless and are channelized through cultural forms. Freud says:

> . . . our civilization is built up at the cost of our sexual impulses which are inhibited by society, being partly repressed but partly, on the other hand, made use of for new aims. However proud we may be of our cultural achievements . . . it is by no means easy to satisfy the requirements of this civilization and to feel comfortable in its midst, because the restriction of the instincts which it involves lays a heavy psychological burden on our shoulders.[16]

However complex the social proliferation of instinctual demands may be, these demands are nonetheless a "façade behind which the function of the underlying innate drives are hidden."[17]

Freudian emphasis on unconscious motives involves a corollary skepticism concerning the purposes which people consciously assign to their acts. Psychoanalysts believe that not only is there much duplicity and concealment about motives, but most persons actually know very little about their own motivations. They also point to the difficulty of assessing the motives of others because one's own repressions and motivations get in the way. "The obstacle which one's own repressions constitute against understanding others can be appreciated if one realizes that the uniformity and harmony of the conscious mind are guaranteed by repressions."[18] In the training of psychoanalysts, great stress is placed upon the understanding of one's own motivations so that they will not be allowed to interfere with the effort to understand the patient.

The Freudian scheme of motivation applies to human behavior the "conservation of energy" principle, which holds that energy can neither be created nor destroyed. Repressed wishes carry energy charges and this energy must be discharged in some way or other. It cannot be destroyed. Hence the occurrence of such processes as sublimation, in which forbidden sexual impulses obtain indirect gratification through acceptable modes of behavior such as artistic creation, intellectual pursuits, simple labor, or other not obviously sexual outlets.

Some psychiatrists conceive of their professional task primarily as that of understanding the unique individuality of the patient. Others place a relatively greater stress upon generalizing about classes of individuals and types of behavior and seek to make psychoanalysis a generalizing science. Allport has designated these two ways of approaching behavior as the "idiographic" and the "nomothetic."[19] As to the generalizer's point of view, it is interesting to observe that the various individuals who engage in a given form of behavior (e.g., heavy drinking) usually give a wide variety of contradictory reasons for doing so. For the Freudian who seeks to generalize about the particular form of behavior under scrutiny, the problem thus posed is resolved by searching for the underlying unconscious motives which the individuals themselves do not and cannot give.

The Freudian therapist attempts to give the patient insight into his repressions and unconscious wishes. This is accomplished in the "prolonged interview" in which the patient tells the psychiatrist about himself and the psychiatrist attempts to make the patient conscious of the real (or unconscious) sources of his behavior. Though Freudian theory places a very pronounced emphasis upon the primacy of the unconscious, Freudian therapy emphasizes consciousness as the primary agency through which personality integration is achieved.

EVALUATION

The Freudian system is complex, and as we have stated, it has many variants. We will therefore content ourselves at this point by commenting critically upon those of its aspects which have to do most explicitly with motivation.

The idea that all human behavior and all cultural forms stem directly or indirectly from primal biological sources has already been critically examined in this chapter, and there is no need to repeat our earlier remarks. We may add here that Freudian theory is an especially elaborate form of a modified biological determinism. Despite the ample allowance that contemporary analysts often make for social or cultural factors, the theoretical scheme still presents an extremely oversimplified view of the relationship of men to groups. This is perhaps to be expected from the fact that this body of theory arose from therapeutic practice with individual patients, and that its main focus is still perhaps on therapy.

Because the orthodox Freudian psychoanalyst thinks of society and its functions as growing out of individual biological urges, he is compelled to view the urges which derive from group life as entirely secondary. The sociologist's position is usually that groups by their very interaction generate new "needs"—i.e., wishes, aspirations, ambitions, ideals, values, and goals—and that these needs constantly change and proliferate. This is a pervasive feature of group life and need not, and probably cannot, be explained in terms of primal urges. Individuals are born into or join groups which are already going concerns, often with long histories, and learn the appropriate motives for action in them. As groups change and develop new needs, individuals change with them, dropping old motives and acquiring new ones. The Freudian idea that culture is a dependent variable, that it merely reflects the psychology of the individual, does not square with history and has led to strained and improbable interpretations of many institutions and historic events—war, crime, social movements, marriage, the Nazi revolution, and international affairs, for example. Freud himself set this pattern. The following statement about the origin of religion gives an idea of the flavor of some of these interpretive efforts: "Psychoanalysis ... has traced the origin of religion to the helplessness of childhood, and its content to the persistence of the wishes and needs of childhood into maturity."[20]

One of the features of Freudian psychology which makes it relatively popular today, despite its stress upon instinctive drives, is that it does assign an important role to learning. The instincts that are recognized are only two in number (Life and Death, or Eros and Thanatos), and they are thought of mainly as energy sources having no implicit direction or goals. The direction, form, and content of the resultant pattern of behavior, as well as the objects toward which it is directed, are regarded as a matter of learning. In the actual acquisition of specific behavior, primary stress is placed upon the interaction between a child and his parents and siblings. Although the behavioristic psychologist and social scientist usually do not accept the whole Freudian scheme, they are receptive to the idea that organic drives become harnessed to social motives through a conditioning or learning process.

At the heart of Freudian psychology lies the "energy" postulate, which involves the idea that individuals have fixed quantities of energy at their disposal. What this means is that all socially learned motives are merely transformations of basic urges and do not have autonomous status of their own. The energy postulate leads Freudians to assume further that motives acquired in adult life are merely complex permutations of old ones. As Piaget, criticizing Freud, says: "When there is transfer of feeling from one object to another, we must recognize that in addition to continuity there is construction of a new feeling through the integration schema."[21] Allport makes much the same point when he insists upon what he calls the "functional autonomy of motives."[22] By this he means that a form of behavior, first performed as a means to a given end, may become an end in itself when the original purpose has long since disappeared. The error involved in the Freudian view of motivation is that of confusing historical continuity with functional continuity. The motives of acts being performed now obviously must be operative in the present. The fact that these motives have a history does not mean that they are determined by early childhood antecedents. Some analysts, heeding this type of criticism, qualify Freudian theory, in practice at any rate, to place more stress upon current functioning. Alexander, in an attempt to modify the theory to take account of growth and change, has postulated a "surplus energy in excess of the needs of self-preservation." He writes that

> After the organism has reached the limits of growth, surplus intake in excess over expenditure is discharged in the form of propagation or its sublimated equivalents: in productive and creative activities.[23]

This use of the concept of energy makes no distinctions between types of energy; for example, physical, psychological, moral, and intellectual energy are not distinguished. The inadequacy of this concept becomes obvious if we think for a moment of a person like Gandhi, the great Indian leader. One of his most energetic and influential actions consisted of going on hunger strikes, thus depriving himself of all energy intake. Excess intake of energy often leads not to productive and creative activity, but to the deposit of fat and general torpor. Some notion of the metaphorical character of analysis based on these ideas is provided by Murphy:

> The energies awaiting an outlet break through the barrier at a given spot, are channeled or canalized in the process, and, as the barrier weakens, tend more and more to focus their pressure upon it. . . . Janet's term *canalization* is a good name for this process.[24]

Tempting as it may be to think in this way of human behavior, it should always be kept in mind that when we do so we are making use of an analogy borrowed from the physical world. It invariably turns out that such borrowings do violence to the subtler aspects of human behavior.

One of the major objections to the Freudian system hinges on the conception of "the unconscious" and of unconscious motives, There is no question that people are often unable—or unwilling—to give adequate grounds for their acts or that there is much irrationality in human behavior. Considering the complexity of human interaction and personal life histories, the individual can hardly be expected to be able to account fully and accurately for his behavior and all its antecedents. This fact had been recognized for generations before Freud.

However, the Freudian view of unconscious functioning is open to question on a number of points. First, it exaggerates the extent of unconscious motivation. A great deal of human behavior certainly appears to be routine, standardized, planned, or otherwise rational. The Freudians have been accused, we think altogether rightly, of taking a dim view of the rational processes and of tending to seek for motivational complexities where they do not exist. In the hands of a novice, or as a parlor game, this can be a form of "motive-mongering." At best, such an analytic approach tends either to reduce complex phenomena to terms of individualistic motives or shies away from these phenomena, many of which, like the building of TVA or the establishment of the United Nations, are of a conscious and planned character. When analysts write about a complicated social phenomenon such as crime, they invariably allow their theory to dictate the selection of cases in order that they may stress the irrational and the unconscious. Their case studies of criminals, for example, focus on what might be called individualistic crime or the pathology of crime, such as sadistic murder, rape, and other sex offenses. It is instructive to compare Alexander and Healy's *Roots of Crime*[25] with Sutherland's *The Professional Thief*[26] —one would scarcely believe that they are about the same subject.

Another criticism often made of the Freudian conception of the unconscious is that the term is so loosely used as to confuse issues. It may be used to indicate an experience which an individual has forgotten, or it may be used to designate an innate drive. It may be used to designate an experience that an individual has never had, in the sense that he failed to notice that certain things were happening. It may be used to designate simple ignorance about himself and his acts, or it may refer to his failure to analyze his own behavior. Miller has listed sixteen different usages of the term and pointed out that the writers are not always explicit about how they are using it.[27]

Reactions to Freudian ideas range from complete and enthusiastic acceptance to equally complete and vehement rejection. It was inevitable that the Freudian challenge should have evoked a storm of discussion and criticism. An example of the criticism is supplied by an English psychologist, Eysenck, who states as his view:

> ... psychoanalysis ... is trying to *understand*, rather than to *explain*; ... consequently it is essentially non-scientific and to be judged in terms of belief and faith, rather than in terms of proof and verification; and lastly ... its great popularity among non-scientists derives precisely from its non-scientific nature, which makes it intelligible and immediately applicable to problems of understanding other people. ... Religion and art are two other non-scientific disciplines which in spite of their lack of concern with scientific truths have contributed greatly to human happiness.[28]

Eysenck goes on to make a fairly extended criticism of general psychoanalytic theory viewed as science,[29] making the following main points: (1) Psychoanalytic conclusions are based on unreliable clinical evidence selected from interviews with certain patients. (2) Material presented as evidence is usually an indeterminate mixture of raw data and interpretations. (3) Conclusions are overgeneralized. (4) Principles are applied to general social phenomena such as war and industrial conflict without proof of their applicability. (5) Research guided by Freudian hypotheses is often simply illustrative of preconceptions rather than a crucial test of a theory. (6) Psychoanalytic factual arguments usually beg the question and are based on selected clinical anecdotes.

An examination of any one portion of Freudian theory tends to lead one to a consideration of the whole system. However, we shall confine ourselves here to a few comments on the Freudian theories of repression, memory, and unconscious purposes.

One does not have to deny the existence of repression, or something like it, to quarrel with the Freudian interpretation of it. People certainly do sometimes bury memories so deeply that they are entirely unconscious of their existence; and they are often unaware of impulses and desires which influence them. As used in much of Freudian theory, however, the concept of repression is over-extended, as when it is used to explain why persons do not recall experiences during infancy. The total volume of anyone's experience is so great and behavior is so complex that it seems inevitable that everyone should forget much and that no one should be fully aware of the reasons for his actions. As Cameron and Magaret say: "We all learn to practice selectivity among our own reactions, to accept what fits in with our ideal picture of ourselves and to reject that which seems at variance with it."[30] H. S. Sullivan refers to "selective inattention," which enables us to maintain our self-esteem by not noticing things that may threaten it.[31] The concept of repression calls attention to an important psychological process, but a satisfactory description of the process still remains to be formulated.

Researchers seeking to check the theory that unpleasant experiences are more often forgotten than pleasant ones have found only a relatively slight tendency in this direction. As Faris says: "These studies . . . do not furnish crucial proof of any operation of repression. An efficient repressing mechanism should work better."[32] Since the differences noted are average group differences, it appears that some persons also have an opposite tendency to recall unpleasant experiences.

The Freudian conception of repression rests on a particular view of memory. "For Freud, the whole of the past is preserved in the unconscious . . . another conception of memory has been opposed to it, that of reconstruction-memory."[33] The latter concept, as we have already stated in Chapter 4, interprets memory as a reconstructive act, dependent upon the nature and organization of the material and the linguistic categories available to the person. Forgetting is regarded as a very complex and not necessarily repressive process. A satisfactory theory of repression still remains to be formulated. It is clear that repression is often associated with anxiety and threats to self-esteem, but the precise nature of the connection is not clear.

A final point may be made concerning the Freudian conception of unconscious motivations. By definition they are inaccessible to the individual. This means that evidence concerning their existence cannot be obtained by direct testimony, but their existence must be inferred from what the person says and does. Evidence of this sort is subject to interpretations that differ according to the school of thought followed by the interpreter. The acceptance or rejection by the patient of a specific interpretation in itself proves nothing concerning the correctness of the interpretation. Taken with other evidence, the patient's rejection of an imputed motive is often viewed as proof of its existence, just as is the patient's agreement with the analyst in other circumstances. We may even ask if a wholly unconscious motive can exist at all. As we have already indicated with respect to oxygen deprivation, a person may desperately need oxygen and be entirely unaware of it; as long as this is the case, no appropriate behavior to satisfy the need occurs, and thus the biological need can scarcely be called a motivational force. Vitamin deficiency, withdrawal symptoms connected with drugs, calcium deficiency, and many other similar conditions illustrate the same point. Appropriate behavior is mobilized only through some sort of recognition (consciousness) of the condition, and the corrective behavior may be inappropriate if the condition is misnamed—that is, if it is not recognized for what it is. So-called unconscious motives should probably be called by some other name than "motives" to indicate that they are not like the ordinary conscious ones for which the term might well be reserved.

We have offered such a long and detailed analysis and criticism of the basic Freudian position on motivation because of its great influence upon contemporary thought. There is no doubt that it has provided a needed corrective of rationalistic and static psychologies and suggested new depths and dimensions of behavior. It has fostered a well-warranted skepticism about easy explanations of behavior in terms of its face value. As S. Langer has said: "The great contribution of Freud to the philosophy of mind has been the realization that human behavior . . . is a language; that every *move* is at the same time a *gesture*."[34]

The Marxian View

Another very influential motivational terminology in the contemporary world is that provided by Marxism. Most American social psychologists pay scant attention to it, although in some of the other social sciences—political science, for example—it is more influential. European social scientists give considerable attention to it and, of course, in Communist countries Marxist ideas of motivation are dominant. A brief general consideration of the Marxist view offers an interesting contrast to the Freudian scheme.

The Marxist social scientist conceives of the individual as the product of institutions, whereas the Freudian scheme considers institutions to be the product of individuals. The Marxist locates sources of motives in the social structure rather than the individual. Like the Freudians, Marxists do not take seriously the expressed purposes of people, regarding them as mere surface manifestations or rationalizations of fundamental economic and class interests which may go unrecognized. In Marxist theory these interests have nothing to do with primal biologic urges, but are thought of as arising from the social structure.

The details of Marxist theory are involved. However, the major theme is that the source from which the important motivations flow is the economic system. An individual's position within the economic structure has a pervasive effect upon most of his thought and action. Since individuals share or have similar positions, they form differential social classes and other somewhat less massive and important interest groups. The course of history is conceived of as the struggle for power among these groups.

According to this view, all thoughts, beliefs, philosophies, writings, art, and the like are determined by the basic economic facts of the society and reflect the position in the class structure of those who have formulated or created them. In Marxist terminology, mental products are "super-structure." Marxists have used the term "ideology" to discredit their opponents' arguments and to suggest that these arguments are mere reflections of class interests. The Marxist use of the term "ideology" is not quite identical with the Freudians' use of the term "rationalization," since it refers to a collective or group rationale. Since ideas are thought of as derived from class position, Marxists theoretically disparage as "idealistic" any psychology which attaches much importance to the motivational aspect of ideas, although, as we shall see later, they make practical use of this aspect in the political sphere.

The Marxist position is a radically environmentalistic one, and hence comes into conflict with views stressing hereditary or biological factors in the determination of behavior. In the Soviet Union the anti-heredity bias is so strong that it has been a political issue, and there has been danger in taking the opposite stand. Soviet writers are generally contemptuous of psychologies which place the mainsprings of human behavior in the individual organism, and Freudianism is castigated as "bourgeois" and as evidence of the degeneracy and immorality of capitalist society. The Russian physiologist Pavlov, famous for his studies of conditioning in dogs, is held up as a worthy model in preference to Freud.

The Marxist recognizes a difference between the real interests of a person or class and the perceived interests. Thus in the Marxist view the real interests of white-collar clerks may be identical with those of factory workers because both stand in opposition to an oppressing elite. However, the white-collar worker usually allies himself with his employers and thus, according to the Marxist, betrays his own class interests. He does this because his eyes have not been opened to the way in which society really functions. The Marxist explains white-collar attitudes by reference to the special occupational position of this group of workers. He contends that only through Marxist analysis—that is, analysis in terms of class structure—can the white-collar worker see his true position and recognize his affiliation with the working class. This distinction between "real" interests and perceived interests is paralleled by the

Freudian dichotomy of unconscious and conscious motives. Like the Freudians, Marxists try to help their adherents to bring the real sources of their behavior into the open.

Marxist theory involves some ambiguity, as many critics have pointed out. Although he professes to regard ideas as mere reflections of the basic economic facts of life, the Marxist nevertheless uses and manipulates ideas as powerful tools of action when he tries to get people to acknowledge their real interests. In the practical political arena the Marxist has the greatest respect for the importance of ideas. More consistent with the theory is the belief that the basic economic changes following the seizure of power by a revolutionary elite will bring pervasive ideological changes.

There is a certain amount of significance and truth in the idea that occupation and class position are important sources of motivation. The Marxist theory is much too one-sided, but it has played an important historical role in social science by counteracting individualistic assumptions concerning the motives of men. It has placed a needed emphasis upon institutionally derived loyalties and called attention to economic interests, group allegiances, and intergroup conflicts as determinants of individual action.

A Sociological Conception

RATIONALIZATION AND INTERPRETATION

As we have seen, both Freudians and Marxists regard as suspect the verbal accounts which individuals give of their own purposes. The Marxists often regard such accounts as a cover-up of real economic motives or as evidence of ignorance. Freudians call them "rationalizations" and heavily discount them. Although they admit that some statements of purpose of a rational and conscious sort are in accord with reality, they are mainly concerned with irrational and unconscious motivations.

A technical definition of rationalization is that it "is a common technique by which the ego keeps certain tendencies repressed. . . . Emphasis upon the acceptable motivation allows the ego to keep the unacceptable repressed, since the selected motives can sufficiently explain the act in question."[35] It should be stressed that the psychoanalytic concept of rationalization implies that when acceptable motives are substituted for unacceptable ones, the individual is actually unable to think of the latter: when he denies their existence he is not being dishonest or "kidding" himself. In popular discourse, the term "rationalization" is usually taken to mean "giving socially acceptable but 'phony' reasons instead of the socially unacceptable but 'real' reasons for one's acts." Thus, a woman quarrels with her husband in the morning and throughout the day deals harshly with her daughter on the grounds that she needs discipline. This conception implies that the real reasons for one's acts are usually known, and hence tends to equate rationalization with dishonest or deluded thinking. It is a common belief that honest people do not rationalize or that they do so infrequently.

Strictly speaking, dishonesty has nothing to do with rationalization, for if a person deliberately makes false statements he is not really rationalizing at all but merely lying. A genuine rationalization is a formulation which the individual himself believes to be true even though it may be labeled self-deception by outside observers. The concept is probably used so widely by the layman because it allows him to disregard or discredit the opinions of other people. As Burke has said:

> Much deep sympathy is required to distinguish our reasoning from another's rationalizing. . . . As people tend to round out their orientations verbally, we sometimes show our approval of their verbalizations by the term reasoning and disapproval by the term rationalizing. Thus these words also serve as question begging words.[36]

The central idea of rationalization is that people interpret their behavior and the entire situation in which it occurs either before the act or after the act—or both. Such interpretations sometimes represent distortions, however subtle, of the facts, so that one's face or self-esteem is preserved. Concerning the interpretations that are made after the act, note that they may have to do mainly either with "purpose"—that is, motive—or with "the objective situation" in which the act occurred. For example, suppose that a man shows cowardice when he is attacked or threatened at a party by another man. He may avoid the implications of cowardice, either in his own eyes or those of others, by a rationalization in terms of motives ("I didn't fight because I wanted to wait until a better moment to answer him"); or he may rationalize by interpreting and perhaps distorting the objective situation ("He had a number of friends there and they would have helped him.") Whether the interpretation after the act is chiefly concerned with purpose (of the self or of others) or with the objective situation, distortion or inaccuracy may creep in because of the person's self-involvement. In order to obtain a true or correct interpretation of an event or situation, one thus attempts to rule out all bias stemming from personal involvement and to base interpretation upon genuine evidence, so that if possible all disinterested observers may agree on "the facts." Procedure in courts of law is the classic example of a formalized, if not always successful, attempt to accomplish this. No sharp line can be drawn between a rationalization about a situation and a description of it, for it is difficult to rule out the influence of all personal interest and bias.

In common experience many acts are interpreted more than once. Indeed, if the act is at all important, it may receive several interpretations, sometimes distributed over a number of years. The individual is sometimes aware of this reinterpretation, but more often he is not. This kind of re-seeing of the past we have already discussed as reconstructive memory. It should be apparent that a large proportion of the later interpretation is not at all concerned with the preservation of self-esteem—that is, it is not rationalization in the narrower sense of the word.

Interpretations of an act may also be made before the act takes place. Such preinterpretations include an estimate of the situation in which behavior is called for—including the possible actions, intentions, and expectations held by others—and some judgment of how and why one proposes to act with regard to the situation. The *how* and *why* of the individual's coming act has to do with his purposes; and if he should happen to phrase the matter aloud to someone else and explicitly to himself, he will generally use the word "because" when referring to these purposes. For example, someone is asked what he is going to do next summer and answers "Go to Europe"; when asked "Why?" or "Why next year?," he offers a statement that includes purpose: "Because I am getting to the age where I feel I can spend my savings and because I have never been there." The initial statement of purpose is likely to be somewhat condensed; if he is encouraged the person may present his reasons in more detail. "I have never been there" may be expanded to an explanation that he wants to go to Europe so that he too can talk about Paris when others speak of their experiences there. Purpose, as we are using the term, is synonymous with motive; and Mills[37] has called statements about purpose "motivational statements," whether offered to others or to self, since they are formulated, at least partially, in verbal terms. When others ask us to account for an act, either forthcoming or past, we usually give them a motivational statement so that they may understand the reasons or grounds for our act. The statement that we offer them may be quite false. We may couch it in terms that appear reasonable to them so as to "get by," or we may conceal our real motives for various other reasons.

MOTIVE AND CAUSE

"Motive," as we are using it, should not be confused with "cause." "Motive" has a forward reference in time. It is concerned with purpose and with the anticipated consequences of acts. Causation has a backward reference: it refers to antecedent conditions, *i.e.*, those which immediately precede or accompany an event and which influence it decisively or determine it. Motives are in a sense personal and private, whereas causes are general and public. Causation applies to classes of events, and causal conditions are subject to public verification. The causation of human behavior is poorly understood, but it is known that much more than motives is involved.

Motives appear or are mobilized at the beginning of an act and indeed are a part of the act, since they persist throughout its course.

They may, of course, change during the act by becoming more complicated or more simple, they may be joined by other motives, or they may even be replaced, particularly if the act has considerable duration. Hence, in describing any complicated event in a person's life, reference must be made to the purposes the individual had in mind. But in addition, a whole range of other conditions must be taken into account—namely, the motives of others and the material or objective situation. The individual himself is in a sense the final authority on his own purposes, since he knows better than anyone else what he has in mind, even though the mechanisms of repression or rationalization may have operated to obscure it. With respect to the objective situation, on the other hand, the individual usually cannot be well informed, since it is impossible for anyone to be in possession of all the information concerning his own nervous system, physiological state, and past experiences which might be relevant to an explanation of why he performed a specific act exactly as he did at exactly the time he did.

Before an action is completed the purposes of the behavior are likely to loom large to the person engaged in it. After the action is completed, second thoughts often occur and he may then wonder whether his reasons were as simple as they seemed. When asked to account for past actions, persons often give common-sense, causal explanations rather than motivational ones. For example, a husband may scold his wife at the breakfast table, believing at the time that he is scolding her because she has spoiled the coffee. He may later explain the quarrel by saying that neither he nor his wife had had enough sleep the previous night.

Since motives appear at the beginning of acts or in preparation for action, and since each individual feels his own motives in a direct way, it is easy to understand how they have come to be viewed as causes of the behavior of which they are a part, and indeed as "forces" which "make" the behavior occur. It was a common practice in the earlier years of this century for sociologists to explain institutional and other cultural behavior in terms of the operation of wishes, desires, interests, needs, and other "social forces." However, the idea of causation no longer includes the conception of force in this sense at all. There are many different ideas of causation in the philosophy of science, but on this particular point there is rather general agreement.

The scientific concept of causation is, of course, a general feature of many scientific fields in which no problem of motivation exists. Indeed, in view of the instability and variability of human purposes, and in view of the fact that purposes are really part of behavior rather than mysterious forces lying behind it, motives are not so much explanations of behavior as they are behavioral problems, themselves requiring analysis and explanation. From this viewpoint, the problem of explaining such behavior as stealing, for example, includes the problem of accounting for the fact that people steal from so many different motives.

An example will help to clarify some of the points we have been making. Let us suppose that a company of American soldiers is ordered to advance in the face of strong enemy fire and that the order is obeyed. If we then try to answer the question of why the company advanced in terms of the motives of each soldier we become involved in a bewildering network. Perhaps no two soldiers have advanced for precisely the same reasons, and perhaps they may have advanced for almost opposite reasons. The problem of accounting for the fact that the company actually moves as a unit seems insoluble from this perspective.

From the standpoint of the Army general who issued the order which was passed on till it finally reached the company commander, the individual motives of the men are of little significance in the total picture and are ignored at the moment of action. As the only requirement is that troops obey the orders and fight effectively, it is sufficient for the commander to know that motivations to advance exist in troops. It may be said of a reasonably well-organized and efficient army that it is ultimately the individual soldier's private and personal problem to seek and hold onto whatever rationalization he can find to help him do what he has to do in any case, although indoctrination procedures probably help him. Max Lerner made this point on the group level in a speech at the time of Hitler's rise when he asserted that the Balkan nations would surely have to surrender to the Nazis and that the only problem was what rationalization would be found for the surrender.

These examples point up the truism that people and groups may do the same things for different reasons and different things for the same reason. Since causal generalizations are based upon elements that are common to various instances of a given form of behavior, in problems like the above these generalizations cannot be stated in terms of motive. Psychoanalysts have attempted to meet this difficulty by looking for uniformity and common motivations on the unconscious level. What is suggested here is that the matter may be dealt with in another way, provided that one conceives of motive as something other than a specific determinant of behavior. It may be conceded that most significant human behavior is and must be motivated, but this is a far cry from contending that any given form of behavior must always be motivated in the same way.

The conception developed here may be further clarified by re-emphasizing the fact that gross organic needs ordinarily do not lead to anything but random or restless behavior, and that they merely prepare the organism to respond when an appropriate situation appears and thus to learn rapidly. The ease with which the newly born infant is taught to nurse is a case in point. Organic needs do not automatically trigger behavioral responses which satisfy these needs, as we have seen in connection with oxygen deprivation and vitamin deficiency. K. S. Lashley[38] has made a similar point with respect to rats, noting that hunger does not have a motivational effect upon them in running a maze until they have learned to associate the maze with food. Organic needs become motivational, as a rule, only after the organism has learned to interpret them in certain ways and to associate certain objects or modes of behavior with the satisfaction of the need. In other words, physiological states in human beings give rise to purposes when they are harnessed in conceptual schemes. When this has happened, the drive-satisfying behavior may vary with the intensity of the physiological need (as it does within limits in the case of hunger) and may thus appear to depend directly on it, although this may not be the case. A physiological state of disequilibrium without direction or goals is not a motive—it is merely a biological condition.

UNDERSTANDING AND EXPLANATION

Rejecting motives as an explanatory concept—that is, as causes—does not mean that it is unimportant to know the purposes which people have in mind. Knowledge of the motivation of other people and of ourselves is indeed, as we have said, a constant necessity in all social intercourse. Through such knowledge we are enabled to acquire insight into the actions of others, to identify with them, and to put ourselves in their places imaginatively or to "take their roles," as we shall say in Chapter 12. An individual's motives are part of the way he thinks, and as such cannot be omitted from any adequate description of his behavior. Neither can a fruitful depiction of inter-action between persons be given unless we take into account the purposes of the actors and their assessment of each other's purposes.

The scientific analysis of human conduct should begin by gather-ing information on motives, but it cannot end there. If grasp of motives provided a complete explanation of behavior, artists and creative writers would be the best social scientists: for it is they who teach us most about understanding those who differ greatly from us in conception of the world and in organization of life. "Understanding," in this context, means something other than scien-tific understanding. It refers to what happens when we read a great realistic novel, see an effective play or motion picture, or become intimately acquainted with another person. Through such under-standing we learn to see through another's eyes, to appreciate another's values and motives, and to identify with him. Although we cannot explain the scientific "why" of the other's behavior on such a basis, through our intimate understanding of his background, experiences, knowledge, biases, and rationalizations we are able to anticipate, at least in general, how he will act. This sort of predic-tion of the actions of individuals is more or less intuitive in nature. The person who is asked to explain why he is so sure that his friend will respond to a given situation in a particular way, answers in terms of the intimacy of his acquaintance with him. "Acquaint-ance with," or understanding, and "knowledge about," or explanation, involve two different kinds of knowing, as William James has pointed out.

The explanation formulated on the basis of scientific analysis is of a special character. Ideally, a relationship between events or classes of events is described in some form such as this: If an event of Type A occurs under certain conditions—*a,b,c,d,* etc.—then, and only then, will an event of Type B occur. Thus, if a mosquito of a certain type bites a human being under certain specified conditions, then, and then only, will the bitten person contract malaria. To use an illustration in the field of human behavior: We have argued in Chapter 11 that if a person takes or is given opiates regularly, experiences and recognizes the withdrawal distress that comes when he stops taking the drug, and uses the drug after this recognition, only then does he become a drug addict. Sequences such as this are causal sequences. It will be noted that popular motivational explanations do not take this form. If a hundred thieves are asked to give their motives for stealing, each will give a different account, so that no single statement can be made about the motives of all of them.

Purposes, or motives, as we have said, are formulated. This means that they arise in communication and are either partially or fully stated in words. When thought of in this manner, motives do not exist in a mysterious nonverbal realm such as "the unconscious." As Mills says, "Motives are of no value apart from delimited societal situations for which they are appropriate vocabularies. They must be situated. . . . Motives vary in content and character with historical epochs and societal structures."[39]

Social Sources of Individual Motivation

An individual's motives generally appear to him as peculiarly personal and private, although many of them are in fact learned from others and are in a sense furnished him tailor-made by the society or the groups in which he lives.

When one joins a group of long standing, he finds that the proper codes of conduct, including the ends and means of group activity, have been spelled out in considerable detail. They may even be formalized and embodied in written documents such as the Hippocratic Oath, an oath of allegiance, or in constitutions, contracts, codes, and the like. When persons leave groups and join new ones, they must learn new motivations. As Weber has pointed out in connection with work, for instance, "The motives which induce people to work vary with different social classes. . . . When a man changes rank, he switches from one set of motives to another."[40] Even when persons live rather stable lives, changing their group memberships very little, some of their motives nevertheless change with advancing age according to prevailing social definitions. Although the physical processes of aging are much alike in all cultures, the motivational adaptations to them are endlessly varied.

An individual cannot express purposes or rationalize behavior in terms which he has not learned. One cannot motivate a man to act by using terms outside his comprehension: one must appeal to purposes which he understands and which make sense to him. Conversely, it is incorrect to impute rationalizations to an individual when these involve motivational terms which he does not possess. Nevertheless, such imputation is a common recourse when it is found to be impossible to assess behavior in one's own terms. There is almost always a tendency to explain other people's behavior in terms of one's own vocabulary of motives. This form of incorrect assessment is called "projection" and is seen in a crude form in most romantic historical novels. The characters, supposedly living a century or two ago, are made to rationalize their activities according to the symbols of the twentieth century. Likewise, in American movies, heroes and heroines dress in the clothes of other eras but act as if their incentives were those of twentieth-century Americans. But the projection of motives may take more subtle forms. The disgust we feel with Russians when they interpret a purely "philanthropic" move on our part as "imperialism," or vice versa when we impute motives of "nationalism" to them while they maintain that they are acting in the interests of the working class, are both instances of the projection of motives. The tendency for American radicals to suspect plots behind the acts of upper-class persons, and the attribution of purely selfish economic motives to labor-union leaders by employers, are parallel examples on the local American scene.

The fallacious common-sense imputation of motives has its academic counterpart. For example, psychoanalysts have reinterpreted the private lives of famous persons such as St. Augustine and Leonardo da Vinci in terms of twentieth-century sexual symbols. They thus ignore the fact that these historical characters viewed the conduct of others and themselves in very different terms than do people of our own era. Such scholarly interpretation is equivalent to translating other rationalizations into our own. Since human beings are interested in the lives of past generations, such translating is inevitable. The only corrective to a superficial handling of the past is an adequate understanding of the period under consideration through exhaustive examination of historical sources. The accuracy of the account should rest upon an understanding of the actual symbols available to the historical personages; it should not rest upon the degree to which their motives appear plausible to us in the light of our own motives at the present time.

Morale and Social Structures

The stability and endurance of social groups or structures depends upon getting the members to carry out necessary lines of action. This means that persons must be motivated to perform these actions. When a structure recruits "from the inside," as when persons are born into it, the problem of motivation is handled early through the socialization of the young. But when members are recruited, as in an army or a vocation, the new member must be taught to act in accordance with the essential purposes of the body or group. Since many recruits join voluntarily, some learning of appropriate motivations starts beforehand: for example, the future doctor learns something about the aims and aspirations of the medical profession long before he goes to medical school. Involuntary membership presents the group with the problem of apathy or lack of enthusiasm, since the purposes of the organization may seem irrelevant to the new member, or he may even be antagonistic. These attitudes are exemplified by political apathy among citizens and "going AWOL" among soldiers. Insofar as good citizens and good soldiers decry unmotivated or badly motivated colleagues, they exemplify their own attachment to the long-range functions of the state and the army. Considerable variation in personal motivation may exist among the membership of any group, but in general motivations must be geared in with, or at least not antagonistic to, the group purposes.

Social structures vary tremendously in the amount of latitude permitted to their membership in this regard; and the degree of latitude is related intimately to the nature of the structure. For instance, if an embattled religious sect is to survive it must so arrange matters that group and individual motivations are virtually identical. The very existence of a revolutionary political elite, such as the Communist Party leadership in a capitalist country, also requires that individual and institutional motivations be closely intermeshed. The concept of "party discipline," as the Communists use it, requires that an individual make the party's decisions and policies his own regardless of how they may vary from week to week or how they may appear to him personally. He is required to sacrifice personal comforts and immediate personal desires in the long-run interests of the party, and he is willing to do this because he identifies his own essential interest with that of the party. A group characterized by this attitude is said to have a high morale. This is equivalent to saying that even in the face of setbacks the membership persists in pursuit of group aims, and indeed may thrive upon a certain amount of opposition or suppression, since this adversity supplies additional justification for revolutionary ardor. Self-interest and group interest coalesce so completely in groups of this kind, whether political or otherwise, that the person may sacrifice his own life for the good of the cause and may do so not only willingly but with elation.

Most organizations, of course, allow more latitude between individual and group purposes, and demand lesser degrees of allegiance and sacrifice. For these groups to function effectively it is necessary that there be a certain amount of consensus concerning matters relevant to group survival. Individuals may retain membership for a variety of reasons, some of them quite peripheral: for example, people belong to churches for business and social reasons as well as for religious ones.

In any society some parts of the total structure are generally recognized as more vital than others. There is a corresponding difference in the pressure upon individuals to conform to the controlling norms. Men who "buck the system" because they do not value it or because they will not support the group endeavors are liable to severe punishment. Court martial, imprisonment, and so on are deterrents of deviance; but positive allegiances operate more efficiently.

When a social structure fails to elicit the minimal allegiance necessary for its proper functioning, then we speak of poor morale. Presumably, there are different types of poor morale,[41] depending on the kind of group structure, but essentially, it comes down to a lack of effective coordination because of discrepant individual aims. To take the simplest case first, there may be so little consensus about group values and such diversity of individual purposes that the group cannot act in concert. A more complicated form of poor morale stems from discrepant definitions of group ends on different social levels represented in the group. Whenever the structure is complex, there is a problem of obtaining a working consensus shared by the various echelons. This condition can exist in a political party, an industrial corporation, a religious organization, or a university. Of course, some segments of the organization may have excellent morale, others poor, since they differently evaluate the way matters are progressing.

Summary

Motivation presents an old and thorny problem for the student of human behavior. The manner in which it is handled by the social theorist is likely to determine the way in which he will deal with a great many other problems. A common conception of motives gives them a biological base, as when hunger is identified with the contractions of the walls of the stomach and other bodily conditions. A biological condition by itself has little motivational significance if it is not perceived or interpreted by the individual in whom it exists. The theory of instincts and need psychology are other biologically tinged views with a bearing on motivation. The influential Freudian conception of motivation, which emphasizes unconscious wishes and desires, has serious weaknesses arising mainly from the fact that no theory about the content of the "unconscious" can be proved because the unconscious is, by definition, virtually unknowable. Marxist theory presents an interesting comparison with that of Freud, for in the former the emphasis is placed upon unconscious economic, rather than sexual, motivations. A conception of motives held by some sociologists treats them as essentially verbal in nature, as part of behavior, but as something other than causes of behavior. Knowledge of motives, in this conception, is used primarily to enable a person to project himself into the outlook of another person, *i.e.*, for "understanding," rather than for "explaining," behavior. Motives are learned in social experience, vary from group to group, and are relative to a social context. A consideration of group morale gives some indications of the way in which persons are motivated by their group identifications.

SUGGESTIONS FOR DISCUSSION AND SPECIAL REPORTS

1. Give a Freudian interpretation of a novel or a current motion picture; then try a Marxian interpretation.

2. Analyze a historical novel to determine to what extent contemporary motives are projected into the past.

3. Discuss and criticize the theory of hedonism.

4. Consider various ways of accounting for the fact that considerable numbers of women become nuns.

5. Compare American conceptions of the motives of Soviet citizens with their conceptions of their own motives.

6. Does rejection of "the unconscious" imply that only fully conscious behavior need be taken into account?

7. Why is gambling so widespread? Could it be an instinctive activity?

8. Civilized men, when shipwrecked or starving, have engaged in cannibalism. What does this prove about basic needs?

9. Is it as necessary to rationalize to oneself as it is to others?

====

NOTES

[1] M. M. Lewis, *Language in Society*, New York: Social Science Publishers, 1948, p. 175.

[2] W. McDougall, *Outline of Psychology*, Scribner, 1923.

[3] O. Klineberg, *Social Psychology* (rev. ed.), Holt, 1954, p. 119.

[4] *Ibid.*, p. 80.

[5] D. O. Hebb, *The Organization of Behavior*, Wiley, 1949, pp. 109-120.

[6] J. A. Bierens de Haan, *Animal Psychology*, London: Hutchinson's Univ. Libr., 1946, pp. 43-45.

[7] M. Sherif, *An Outline of Social Psychology*, Harper, 1948.

[8] A. L. Strauss, *Identification* (unpublished monograph). Quotation at end of excerpt is from Sherif, *op. cit.*, p. 38.

[9] N. W. Shock, "Physiological Factors in Behavior," in J. McV. Hunt (ed.), *Personality and the Behavior Disorders*, Ronald, 1944, p. 585.

[10] L. E. Cole, *General Psychology*, McGraw-Hill, 1929, p. 329.

[11] D. Seligman, "The Four Day Week: How Soon?" *Fortune Magazine*, July, 1954, p. 118.

[12] W. I. Thomas and F. Znaniecki, *The Polish Peasant in Europe and America*, Knopf, 1927, Vol. I, pp. 72-73.

[13] G. W. Allport, *Personality, a Psychological Interpretation*, Holt, 1937, p. 193.

[14] A. H. Maslow, "The Instinctoid Nature of Basic Needs," *J. of Personality*, 22(1954): 340-341.

[15] E. Weiss, "History of Metapsychological Concepts," in F. Alexander and H. Ross (eds.), *Dynamic Psychiatry*, University of Chicago Press, 1952, pp. 44-55.

[16] S. Freud, *A New Series of Intro-*

ductory *Lectures on Psychoanalysis*, Norton, 1933, p. 151.

[17] N. E. Miller and J. Dollard, *Social Learning and Imitation*, Yale University Press, 1941, p. 19.

[18] F. Alexander and H. Ross, *Dynamic Psychiatry*, University of Chicago Press, 1952, p. 7.

[19] Allport, *op. cit.*, p. 22.

[20] Freud, *op. cit.*, p. 229.

[21] J. Piaget, *Play, Dreams and Imitation in Childhood*, London: Wm. Heinemann, Ltd., 1951, p. 186.

[22] Allport, *op. cit.*, pp. 190-212.

[23] In F. Alexander and H. Ross (eds.), *Dynamic Psychiatry*, University of Chicago Press, 1952, "Development of the Fundamental Concepts of Psychoanalysis," p. 20.

[24] G. Murphy, *Personality*, Harper, 1947, p. 162.

[25] F. Alexander and W. Healy, *Roots of Crime*, Knopf, 1935.

[26] E. Sutherland, *The Professional Thief*, University of Chicago Press, 1937.

[27] J. C. Miller, *Unconsciousness*, Wiley, 1942.

[28] H. J. Eysenck, *Uses and Abuses of Psychology*, London: Penguin Books, 1953, p. 226.

[29] *Ibid.*, pp. 235-241.

[30] N. Cameron and A. Magaret, *Behavior Pathology*, Houghton Mifflin, 1951, p. 13.

[31] H. S. Sullivan, *The Interpersonal Theory of Psychiatry*, Norton, 1953.

[32] R. E. L. Faris, *Social Psychology*, Ronald, 1952, p. 127.

[33] Piaget, *op. cit.*, p. 187.

[34] S. Langer, *Philosophy in a New Key*, New York: Penguin Books, 1948, p. 41.

[35] Alexander and Ross, *op. cit.*, p. 13.

[36] K. Burke, *Permanence and Change*, New York: New Republic, 1936, pp. 19-20.

[37] C. W. Mills, "Situated Actions and Vocabularies of Motive," *Am. Soc. Rev.*, 5(1940): 904-913.

[38] K. S. Lashley, "Experimental Analysis of Instinctive Behavior," *Psych. Rev.*, 45(1938): 445-471.

[39] Mills, *op. cit.*, p. 913.

[40] M. Weber, paraphrased by K. Mannheim in *Ideology and Utopia*, Harcourt, Brace, 1936, pp. 316-317.

[41] H. Blumer, "Morale," in W. F. Ogburn, *American Society in Wartime*, University of Chicago Press, 1943, pp. 203-231.

SELECTED BIBLIOGRAPHY

Bernard, L. L., *Instinct: A Study in Social Psychology*, Holt, 1924. A good source for materials about an old controversy. An influential book in persuading sociologists to abandon the concept of instinct.

Blumer, H., in W. F. Ogburn, *American Society in Wartime*, University of Chicago Press, 1943, "Morale," pp. 201-231. A clear discussion of different types of morale as related to social structures.

Burke, K., *A Grammar of Motives*, Prentice-Hall, 1945, especially Part I. A difficult but rewarding book along the same lines as the next title, but with a treatment that is more involved and sophisticated.

——, *Permanence and Change*, New York: New Republic, 1936, especially pp. 24-53. A challenging discussion, by a literary critic, of the linguistic nature of motives. Includes excellent critiques of such concepts as escape and rationalization.

Cooley, C. H., *Sociology and Social Research*, Holt, 1930, "The Roots of Social Knowledge," pp. 289-312. A clear statement of the importance of "understanding" in social science. Cooley does not stress the even greater importance of causal explanation.

Ellis, A., "An Introduction to the Principle of Scientific Psychoanalysis," *Genet. Psych. Monographs*, 41(1950): 147-212. A useful critique of various Freudian concepts and assumptions.

Foote, N., "Identification as the Basis for a Theory of Motivation," *Am. Soc. Rev.*, 16(1951): 14-22. A sociological approach to motivation from a viewpoint much like our own.

Lewis, M., *Language in Society*, New York: Social Science Publishers, 1948, Chap. 9, "Language and Integration," pp. 173-198. A lucid exposition of various levels of motivation and the nature of complex motives.

MacIver, R. M., *Social Causation*, Ginn, 1942. A significant discussion of the concepts of causation and motivation applied to the social sciences.

MacKinnon, D. W., in E. G. Boring, H. S. Langfeld, and H. P. Weld (eds.), *Foundations of Psychology*, Wiley, 1948, "Motivation," pp. 112-137. Exemplifies the sort of treatment of motivation, drives, and needs that is fairly generally found in psychology textbooks.

Mills, C. W., "Situated Actions and Vocabularies of Motive," *Am. Soc. Rev.*, 5(1940): 904-913. One of the best discussions of motives, their social determination and linguistic character. Follows K. Burke's *Permanence and Change* fairly closely.

Parsons, T. (ed.), *Max Weber, the Theory of Social and Economic Organization*, Oxford University Press, 1947, pp. 88-107. Remarks on sociological method, including a discussion of understanding, by a famous German sociologist. Style is formidable.

Sherif, M., *An Outline of Social Psychology*, Harper, 1948. A representative discussion of primary and secondary needs can be found here.

Weiss, E., in F. Alexander and H. Ross (eds.), *Dynamic Psychiatry*, University of Chicago Press, 1953, "History of Metapsychological Concepts," pp. 44-55. A good review of Freudian motivational theory.

CHAPTER 10 · · ·

Sexual Behavior

and

Sexual Motivation

As we have seen in the preceding chapter, sexual motivations are often regarded as biological in origin and nature and as central in human life. The fact that erotic activity involves specialized organs and is so obviously linked with biological maturation makes this seem self-evident to many scientists as well as laymen. A closer examination will indicate, however, how inadequate and fallacious this conception is. Sexual activity, like virtually all other complex human behavior, is largely controlled by conceptualization and is often of primarily symbolic rather than biological significance. The symbolic entanglements surrounding human sexual behavior make it extremely hazardous to apply to human beings the findings obtained from the study of lower animals. The present chapter should be instructive in its own right, for we have attempted to show concretely the great complexity of "social needs" and social objects.

The Evolutionary Picture

The general picture of subhuman sex behavior is described in terms appropriate to our purposes by Beach,[1] a psychologist who has surveyed the available literature and himself carried out extensive experimental investigations of the sex behavior of the lower animals. His conclusions may be summarized as follows: (1) Mating behavior in lower animal forms is controlled primarily by inherited mechanisms; specifically, by hormonal secretions and by the strength and aggressiveness of the animal. (2) The central nervous system plays a relatively minor part in the control of sex behavior in the simpler animal forms, its regulatory significance increasing as one ascends the evolutionary scale. (3) Past experience, as opposed to hereditary mechanisms, increases in importance as one proceeds from the simpler forms such as the rat and guinea pig to the more complex apes and humans. A significant part of the sex behavior of male chimpanzees, for example, is learned.

In support of these general statements we may briefly note certain facts. In most lower forms receptivity of the female to sexual advances is determined by hormone balance and by other accompanying physiological changes occurring during the period of heat or estrus. With some exceptions, the female animal is receptive only when she is in heat. This is of course not true of the human female, who may actively desire or entirely reject sexual relations at any time during the menstrual cycle.

Removal or atrophy of the primary sex glands, the testes and the ovaries, produces relatively uniform results in the lower animals, and highly variable, uncertain ones in human beings. Castrated adult men, women who have had ovaries and uterus removed by surgery, and old people whose sex glands have ceased to function all may and do continue to desire and enjoy coitus. Men who find themselves impotent sometimes have their potency restored either (a) by injection of an actual hormone, (b) by the injection of any substance which they believe to be a hormone, or (c) by psychiatric treatment. The student who desires to explore the matter further should consult the extensive experimental literature.[2]

This literature clearly shows that human sex behavior is not controlled in the same way or to the same degree by physiological processes and mechanisms as is that of lower animals. In the sex practices of human beings mental processes play a preponderant role. Past experiences and social influences shape human patterns so pervasively that it is difficult to point to more than a few specific patterns which are determined exclusively by inherited mechanisms or glandular secretions. Moreover, it is a logical fallacy to try to account for the unique features of human sex behavior in terms of the biological conditions which man has in common with other animals.

The point of view we are developing here may be briefly stated as follows: the characteristic and differentiating features of human sex behavior can be traced to the fact that man talks about sex and other animals do not. The possibility of engaging in any sex behavior is of course contained in the biological structure of the individual. The intensity of the sex drive and certain other very general characteristics may be conditioned by biological factors. Isolated elements of the total pattern of sex activity are not learned; they are derived directly from man's biological structure. The orgasm, ejaculation, and nocturnal emission are examples. These relatively mechanical, nonvoluntary parts of sex behavior are natural biological acts.

Although one may designate various individual aspects of sex behavior as natural, unlearned, or inherited, the total organization and over-all functioning of these aspects in given social situations cannot be so designated. The general pattern which an individual adopts cannot be explained biologically; it must be accounted for in terms of the standards or mores which the individual internalizes. Social influences often shape sex behavior along lines that are contrary to what would be called natural in the biological sense. Furthermore, social influences may lead to the complete elimination of some kinds of natural biological behavior, or cause persons to act in a variety of ways which are biologically inappropriate (*e.g.*, to practice exclusive homosexuality).

Hormones, Homosexuality, and Inversion

One of the chief obstacles to a proper understanding of the nature of human sex behavior is the assumption, often made by relatively well-educated persons, that hormones or hormone balance account for the vagaries of sexual behavior. According to this view, heterosexuality is the consequence of a hormone balance, which in the male is weighted on the side of androgens and in the female on the side of the estrogens. (The androgens are the male hormones, the estrogens the female hormones—both being found to some extent in both sexes.) The close connection between these hormones and the secondary sexual body characteristics has been scientifically demonstrated. Hence, many people think that when the female hormones are relatively prevalent in a male or the male hormones relatively prevalent in a female, the result is an effeminate male and a masculine female, respectively—*i.e.*, homosexuals. We shall indicate in the succeeding paragraphs that this conception is incorrect in almost every detail.

Here it is necessary to distinguish among various aspects of sexual behavior and sexual characteristics, and to note the difference between homosexuality and inversion. Inversion refers to the assumption of a female role by a male and conversely of a male role by a female. Inversion is a term descriptive of people and not of the sex act. Indeed, it is quite possible—though improbable—for an inverted male and female to engage in heterosexual relations. Homosexuality, on the other hand, means sexual or love relationships between members of the same sex. Since male and female counter-roles are usually involved in the sex act, even homosexual partners often play opposite sex roles. Hence in homosexual intercourse one partner can be characterized as inverted and the other cannot.

We must also bear in mind the distinctions between male and female secondary sexual characteristics: voice differences, distribution of hair, and so on. Moreover, the presence in a male of relatively feminine secondary physical characteristics does not imply either inversion or homosexuality. The distinction between homosexual and heterosexual behavior is based on the sex of the preferred partner. In short, the terms "homosexual," "heterosexual," and "inversion" refer to behavior, whereas secondary sex traits are structural, biological features of the organism—not forms of behavior.

In the light of these distinctions we may make several observations. (1) Inversion and homosexuality are not identical terms. (2) In experiments on animals, through the injection of hormones of the opposite sex, secondary physical traits of the opposite sex and partial inversion have both been produced. But homosexuality in the human sense of the term has not been brought about. (3) The injection of hormones in humans neither produces nor cures homosexuality, its main effect being to stimulate sex activity without influencing the choice of partners. (4) Homosexuality usually occurs along with heterosexuality in a mixed form. (5) Many male homosexuals are not at all effeminate, and many female homosexuals are not masculine. (6) Probably most effeminate males and masculine women engage in exclusively heterosexual relations. (7) Many deviant forms of human sexual behavior have no parallel among the lower animals. Homosexuality is only one kind of deviation: if we account for it in terms of hormones, then we must ask what possible hormonal basis is involved when humans derive their sexual gratification from intercourse with lower animals, from the collecting of bizarre objects like women's shoes and clothing (fetishism), from injury inflicted by them on others (sadism) or on themselves (masochism), from watching sexual activity in others rather than engaging in it themselves (voyeurism), and so on. If we assume that hormones underly all forms of sex expression, why do not the many deviations in which humans engage occur also among other animals?

The crucial point in connection with the inversion of sex roles in humans is that a male or female identifies with the opposite sex. Thus, a female invert may assert and feel that she is a man, wear masculine clothes, act like a man, assume much of the masculine role in sexual relations, adopt a masculine name, and perhaps even apply the male terminology to her sexual organs, calling the clitoris a penis and the ovaries the testes. This type of inversion is a symbolic process involving the application of language symbols and social definitions to one's own behavior and one's self; but the kind of inversion produced in the laboratory in lower animals can scarcely be equated with the human type. Note too that the inversion of human sex roles cannot be consistently brought about or significantly altered by the injection of hormones. The chief effects of the latter on human behavior appear to be (1) the stimulation

INVERSION?

of sexual activity and the control of various physiological processes, and (2) their influence on secondary physical sex traits.

These factors point to the learned and socially defined nature of sex roles, as we have suggested elsewhere in this book. The child at birth does not identify himself with either sex, for he does not know that sexes exist. He gradually learns this identification and, along with it, acquires the behavior deemed appropriate in his society. For example, the type of partner the male child will learn to prefer—blondes or brunettes, women or men, white or colored women, and so on—is not and probably cannot be ascertained in human biological structure, any more than religious, political, or ethical preferences are so determined. Moreover, various disorders in this learning process may occur. We will cite later simple examples illustrating how this might come about through parental desire that a child be of a given sex, through anatomical peculiarities, and through mistakes in identifying the child's sex at birth.

The newborn child responds positively to pleasant stimuli regardless of source. He does not classify or discriminate among sources. The male child is as likely to have an erection when handled by his father as when handled by his mother. As the child matures and as he learns ways of classifying stimuli and of responding to them, his patterns of sexual expression gradually crystallize and become channelized. The detailed description of this learning process and of the disorders that may occur is still a problem for the combined efforts of social scientists. But that this is the way in which patterns become established seems a highly probable hypothesis—harmonizing with many other things known about the nature of human behavior.

Differentiation of Basic Sex Roles

No society fails to embody in its practices and language the fundamental biological distinction between the sexes. Many societies recognize still further categories, which include men who act like women and women who act like men. These in-between persons are sometimes taken for granted, sometimes looked upon as biological abnormalities. Scientists and sophisticated laymen recognize also another intermediate hermaphroditic class of persons who at birth have some of the genital apparatus, and perhaps physical traits, of both sexes.

Regardless of these intermediate classes, we may take for granted that humans universally recognize the existence of polar biological types: *i.e.*, men and women. It is easy to understand why the incorrect assumption is frequently made that infants "naturally" know to which sex they belong. Every child must not only (1) learn the meanings of "male" and "female" but also (2) classify himself as one or the other. He cannot, at least publicly, identify himself with both or neither.

This poses a problem. How do children learn to identify themselves as members of one or the other sex? The reader who looks for a detailed and exact answer to this question will be disappointed, for pertinent scientific data are rather meager. However, the larger outlines of the process of sex-identification are clear enough.

RECOGNITION OF SEX DIFFERENCES

When young children begin to learn sex distinctions, they employ criteria which betray rudimentary conceptions of the differences between men and women. These criteria vary according to opportunities available to children for observing and conversing about sex behavior. In the United States such experiences vary widely according to social class, conditions of housing, number of siblings in the family, sibling position, moral philosophies of the parents, and other relevant factors.

In an outstanding study, Conn and Kanner[3] have analyzed the criteria which children use to defferentiate the sexes. Although their sampling is deficient—the study covers children ranging from four to twelve years of age, of many social classes—it offers valuable hints about the learning of sex differences.

One of the items which the children mentioned most frequently as a sign of sex membership was clothing. The following table indicates that this sign is learned.[4]

Age at Which Attire Was Noted As Marking Sex Distinction	Percent at Each Age
4	0
5	21
6	83
7	83
8	89
9	82
10	92
11	65
12	67
13	33
14	0

A few children under the age of seven equated sex differences with differences of attire, apparently recognizing no other distinctions. When asked if there would be any difference between undressed boys and girls, these young children were "either puzzled by the questions, or declared categorically that removal of clothes made a distinction impossible."[5] Apropos of this finding is a story involving a five-year-old acquaintance of the authors, who attended a party at which children of both sexes bathed in the nude. When asked how many boys and how many girls were at the party, she answered: "I couldn't tell because they had their clothes off."

Hair was frequently mentioned as a differentiating characteristic of the sexes.[6] Many children thought that differences of hair styles are inherent—though helped along by scissors and the barber. As another young acquaintance of the authors confidently asserted: "Boys have straight hair and girls have curly hair." Differences of urination posture were mentioned spontaneously by 44 children. Although breasts were generally recognized as belonging only to women, they were not spontaneously mentioned by the children as distinguishing features. "There were so many other things closer to the children's interest and immediate awareness."[7] Only nine of the 200 children spontaneously included this distinguishing sign. The method used by the investigators is not open to the charge that children did not mention breasts because of inhibiting taboos.

An interesting finding is that (1) older children spontaneously mention other criteria such as shape of the face, complexion, hands, strength, and gait; but that (2) children below certain ages did not mention these criteria. The investigators conclude that many younger children do not possess the requisite language necessary to see these sex differences. Their summarizing table is below.[8]

That the child has learned to identify persons correctly as male or female does not mean that he has gained an adult conception of sex differences. The meanings of "male" and "female," like those of other symbols, cannot be fully grasped by youngsters. Children have neither the requisite experiences nor, in the case of the youngest of them, the mentality necessary to understand adult concepts of sex contrasts.

Difference	Youngest Age of Naming
Hair	4
Clothes	5
Eyes	5
Hands	5
Face	6
Complexion	7
Hands and feet	8
Figure	8
Strength	8
Gait	9

On the learning of sex differences, Conn and Kanner present helpful data. Older children from urban centers generally recognized and mentioned genital difference between the sexes, but did not always realize that such differences also characterized animals. Consequently, varying conceptions of sex differences were offered. A common notion was that all animals of the same species were of the same sex: for example, all cats are females and all dogs are males. Other criteria for classifying animals were used: for example, some children regarded ribbons as a distinguishing sign and other children regarded names as evidence of sex. Farm children, of course, are likely to be more sophisticated about the sex of animals.

Involved in adult conceptions of sex differences is an awareness of the sex act and its conventional socialized meanings. In some countries and classes, children may be allowed to engage in sex play with others of their own age and have frequent opportunities to witness adult coitus. These conditions prevail among the Trobriand Islanders, a South Sea people. Consequently, this part of the adult symbolization is learned earlier than it is by many American children. The Conn and Kanner figures, which seem relatively trustworthy, indicate that only a small proportion of a total of 200 children under twelve years of age had knowledge of the existence of coitus. There are, however, no grounds for assuming that even these relatively sophisticated children had adult concepts of the act.

LEARNING THE MEANINGS OF SEXUAL BEHAVIOR

The meanings associated with sexual activities must be learned by the child. He does not in any significant degree invent them himself; nor does he acquire them through biological endowment or maturation. He may not understand the full adult significance of many "sexual" words and acts until he is well into adolescence, or later.

Although humans everywhere recognize the existence of sexual excitement, coitus, masturbation, sex organs, and the like, they nevertheless take dissimilar attitudes toward these objects, acts, and events. Words carry or mirror attitudes: *i.e.*, they have meanings. The child—whether American or Japanese or Marquesan, upper or lower class, boy or girl, rural or urban—when he learns words learns also the conventional points of view which they express.

Kinsey[9] has given us some rough but relevant data on differential American class attitudes; we shall summarize a few:

Event or Object	Upper Classes	Lower Classes
"Heavy Petting"	Part of the sex act or a substitute for it.	Not much practiced. As a substitute for the sex act, a perversion.
"Clitoris"	Many recognize its function in sexual foreplay as exciting to female. A function emphasized in widely read marriage manuals.	Word not in common use, nor any equivalent for it, since few know the organ exists. This is true particularly of males, but also to a lesser degree of females.
"Foreplay"	Widely regarded as an important preliminary to coitus.	Generally not considered important.
"Positions"	Some sophistication about possible variations.	Only one position is natural: the American one.

As we might expect, Kinsey found that sexual vocabularies varied tremendously by region, class, race, age, and other groupings. These differences of vocabulary, of course, mirror differences of attitude, and constitute important data for anyone interested in understanding, explaining, and predicting human sex behavior. When the child learns these idiomatic terms he also internalizes the meanings they express. American middle-class parents recognize this fact implicitly, since they teach their children euphemistic expressions for sex organs and sex acts rather than the vulgar terms which the child will pick up later from others of his own age. Public use of technical sex terminology is permissible, whereas the use of corresponding "Anglo-Saxon monosyllables" is tabooed. Although the one-syllable words refer to the same objects and events, they carry very different attitudes. Because words evoke attitudes, such Anglo-Saxon terms would be inappropriate in public discussion.

Anthropologists agree that, although great variations in sexual codes exist, no society sanctions all aspects of all sex behavior and every society frowns upon and forbids certain sex acts. These taboos rest upon basic assumptions concerning the nature of the world, of man, of the sexes and their relations, and so on. As generations succeed one another—at least in our Western world—they develop different philosophies of sex and partly reject the standards of previous generations. Each new generation in turn sets up new standards and taboos which it believes to be improvements on the old ones. This process of substituting one set of mores for another is likely to be called "emancipation" by young people and "immorality" by their elders. It should not be assumed that this process of change over the generations means steady progress toward a sexual Utopia in which everyone will be completely emancipated. Indeed, the very term "emancipated" is meaningless. What is more, sexual codes have a tendency to move back and forth, to change from relative laxity to relative stringency and vice versa, in pendulum-like fashion. Changes in the styles of women's clothing, for example, have often reflected quite clearly some of these changes in sexual attitudes.

MISCONCEPTIONS OF CHILD BEHAVIOR

Laymen and even students of child behavior frequently make the mistake of anthropomorphism: they project adult attitudes and conceptions onto the child, or regard children's ideas and modes of thought and behavior as curious forms of error. This tendency to interpret the behavior of children with concepts derived from and appropriate to adults is also noticeable in the study of the child's sex behavior.

The fallacy is aggravated by the use of the same terms in describing child and adult behavior, or by employing such hazily defined terms as "libido" and "sexual." While the popularization of psychoanalytic theories and concepts has undoubtedly swept away many of the puritanical and mid-Victorian misconceptions about children, it has sometimes opened the way to errors of another kind. Thus, when one states that the infant masturbates, it is usually assumed that infant and adult masturbation are equivalent acts—a very dubious assumption indeed. The rebellion against the reluctance of past generations to face sexual facts has led to an excess of zeal in discovering sexuality in the behavior of children. It must be emphasized that children live in a world of their own; they have their own concepts, their own ways of acting, and their own perspectives. It is just as erroneous to judge children's behavior by adult standards or to read adult motives into it as it is to measure African Bantu behavior by adult American standards.

To describe the behavior of lower animals in human terms leads almost inevitably, as we have seen, to anthropomorphism. Similar strictures apply to descriptions of the behavior of the human child. One has no more right to attribute sophisticated sexual ideas and concepts to the behavior of infants than to attribute them to chimpanzees and dogs.

Here are extreme examples of this type of error. Isaacs[10] writes: "Penelope and Tommy were playing 'mummy and daddy' and Tommy insisted upon being the mummy." The boy's act is interpreted as an attempt to quiet his fear of castration—yet no data are presented regarding the actual state of the child's sexual knowledge or how he may have obtained it. The child-analyst, Klein,[11] provides an even more flagrant example. Her patient was a three-year-old boy. Between the ages of eighteen and twenty months, he slept in the same room with his parents and thus had occasional opportunities to witness coitus, if one can stretch the meaning of the word "witness." The child is therefore, writes Klein, fearfully jealous of his father, feels inferior because of his own lack of physical potency, fears that his mother was hurt by coitus, wishes to smash his father's genitals, wishes to kill his father, and so forth. How can such complex ideas be attributed to young children?

Other child psychologists and psychoanalysts have been much more circumspect in their interpretations. Cognizant of the social origins and learned nature of sexual behavior, many psychoanalysts have pointed out weaknesses in Freud's theory[12] that feminine character may be largely explained in terms of "penis envy" and reactions to it. According to this theory, which Freud reiterated in one of his last books, when the young girl discovers that every boy has a penis she is disappointed and shocked at her own lack of the same organ. Hence she develops a sense of inferiority or penis envy. The traits of character she develops in her childhood and adult years are, according to Freud, the consequences of her attempt to adjust to her sense of inferiority. But the sociologist is inclined to note that reactions of this type are associated with the patriarchal organization of Western European society—that is, a society in which men and masculine values are relatively dominant. This patriarchal situation, however, is by no means universal even in Western society.

Disinterested investigation of girls' reactions to the discovery of genital differences, such as that by Conn and Kanner,[13] shows beyond question that girls do not always respond with penis envy. It is true that some girls exhibit envious feelings but most do not. Instead they accept these differences in a matter-of-fact manner or react with amusement. In the light of the learned character of such behavior, one would not expect all girls to react identically. Freud's overstatement of the case should lead us to be wary of equating children's sexual responses with those of their elders.

By word or act, punishment or reward, and through the various media of communication, the young boy and girl learn the sex behavior associated with their roles; they learn to avoid those acts which will evoke reactions of ridicule, disgust, or anger. The taboos are internalized in the child to the extent that he becomes angry and ashamed if he breaks them.

Sexual Activities and Erotic Imagery

Sexual intercourse requires that the overt behavior of the human male be accompanied and facilitated by an internal symbolic process or flow of thought, which is often called erotic imagery. Such a flow of erotic mental images and ideas is ordinarily necessary before a man can achieve and maintain an erection, and it is certainly a requisite element in the desire to engage in sexual relations. The same is generally true of the human female. To be sure, a woman may engage in sexual relations without having any genuine erotic interest in such relations. However, if we conceive of the sex act as a relationship which is pleasurable and desirable to both parties or which culminates in simultaneous or nearly simultaneous orgasms, then we may say that erotic imagery is equally necessary for both sexes.

The term "erotic imagery" refers to a general process which we have already discussed in other connections as internalized language behavior, though it is not language in the narrow sense of the word. It is through this process that social influences and past experiences exercise their regulatory effects on human behavior in general, including sex behavior. Because they apply some voluntary control over this internal symbolic process, individuals are able in varying degrees to hasten, retard, or entirely inhibit their own sexual responses.

It is impossible in a limited space to point out all the implications when we recognize the symbolic character of human sexual behavior. Indeed, because of the powerful taboos which exist in this field, most of these implications have not been worked out by scientific research. We shall therefore attempt to give illustrations and indications of the significant role played by internal symbolic processes in only a few areas of sexual behavior.

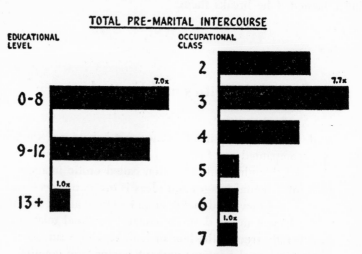

Total pre-marital intercourse, by educational level and occupational class. For the single males of the age group 16-20. The numbers under "occupational class": 2 = day labor; 3 = semi-skilled labor; 4 = skilled labor; 5 = lower white collar group; 6 = upper white collar group; 7 = professional. Relative lengths of bars compare mean frequences for the groups. Note the similarity of data based on educational levels and data based on occupational classes. (From A. C. Kinsey *et al.*, *Sexual Behavior in the Human Male*, Philadelphia: Saunders, 1948.)

ORGASM CONTROL

Most modern American books on sex techniques emphasize the failure of many middle- and upper-class wives to achieve a climax with a sufficient degree of regularity. A great deal of advice is proffered as to techniques which the husband may use to delay his own orgasm while, at the same time, he attempts to hasten his wife's. These procedures represent attempts to teach self-control, nd have to do with a question which apparently never arises in he rest of the animal world.

The problem is related to the operation of our American taboos. There are many formulated rules governing the behavior of boys nd girls during adolescent courtship, and the activities of bride and

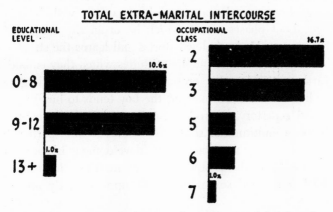

TOTAL EXTRA-MARITAL INTERCOURSE

Total extra-marital intercourse, by educational level and occupational class. For the single males of the age group 16-20. The numbers under "occupational class": 2 = day labor; 3 = semi-skilled labor; 4 = skilled labor; 5 = lower white collar group; 6 = upper white collar group; 7 = professional. Relative lengths of bars compare mean frequences for the groups. Note the similarity of data based on educational levels and data based on occupational classes. (From A. C. Kinsey *et al.*, *Sexual Behavior in the Human Male*, Philadelphia: Saunders, 1948.)

room on the wedding day are prescribed in almost complete detail. By contrast, particularly in bygone generations, sexual behavior was neither specified nor explicitly covered by verbal formulations, but was conceived of as an automatic and biologically natural act which no one needed to learn or to think about in advance.

As a consequence of this lack of appropriate verbalization and of established ways of acting, husbands and wives found that they had to build up their own patterns without much help from past generations. Many young men and women still approach marriage with feelings of apprehension and uncertainty, because they are entering an uncharted world. The usual rules, expectations, and folkways by means of which other significant fields of social behavior are regulated are either nebulous or completely absent in this important area.

The ordinary American boy spends a great deal of time day dreaming about sexual matters and conversing with boys of his own age about phases of sex which he ordinarily cannot discuss with his parents. He hears lewd stories and learns the street vocabulary of sex along with the erotic attitudes which they embody. He may further stimulate his erotic fantasy life by reading pornographic literature. In this manner, the boy tends to build up a rich and varied repertory of erotic imagery and becomes exceedingly sensitive to a multitude of secondary sexual stimuli, particularly if he has few actual sex contacts. This development is made all the more probable by the postponement of marriage for some years after he has reached sexual maturity (approximately around the age of sixteen).

The prevalence of this background in the middle and upper classes probably explains why males of these classes appear to be more responsive to indirect sexual stimuli than are lower-class males.[14] This hypersensitivity may make it difficult for "well-bred" boys and men to control their orgasms during their initial sexual experiences.

Girls of the same social strata have a very different background. They know less about sex, their fantasy life and conversation are less specifically sexual; they masturbate less, and they have a smaller repertory of lewd jokes and vulgar vocabulary. The education and training of girls is more effectively sex-repressive than is that of boys. It is therefore not fortuitous that many women enter upon marriage with what we may call a deficient erotic imagination. The failure of many upper- and middle-class women to achieve orgasms with any regularity may very well be related to the sheer lack of erotic fantasy, quite apart from other inhibiting factors such as prudery, religious scruples, fear, shame, and the entire educative process.

MASTURBATION

A number of interesting human problems about human sexual behavior arise in connection with the practice of masturbation. There are those—like Kinsey, for example—who seek to discuss sexual behavior largely in terms of overt behavior, excluding the accompanying internal symbolic processes. This approach leads to some curious contradictions.

If we defined homosexual behavior in purely overt terms, as a positive sexual response to stimuli proceeding from the same sex, masturbation could be subsumed as a special case of homosexuality. Kinsey, of course, does not do this: he classifies masturbation as either heterosexual, homosexual, or mixed—distinguishing among them in terms of the types of fantasy involved. That is, he distinguishes in terms of criteria which he initially ruled out.

In line with our previous discussion, internal symbolic processes serve as integrative and organizing phenomena in human behavior. That they are cortical in nature and difficult to study in no wise justifies us in disregarding or dismissing them. As we have repeatedly shown, it is through the mediation of such cortical or internal symbolic processes that the mores or ethical codes of a society exert their regulatory influence on human behavior.

The internal symbolic processes, or the erotic imagery usually accompanying the act of masturbation, do not differ in any essential detail from those attending the ordinary heterosexual act. Kinsey[15] notes that before and during masturbation erotic literature and pictures are occasionally used by Americans of the better-educated classes; and he adds that "nearly, but not quite, all males experience sexual fantasies during masturbation. . . . The fantasies are heterosexual when the primary interests of the individual are heterosexual, homosexual when the individual's overt experience or psychic reactions are homosexual." A person's experiences in a social milieu determine which specific excitatory images will accompany and facilitate masturbation. Very much the same excitatory ideas are likely to occur to the same person in the course of the heterosexual act.

It is significant to note the change in attitude toward masturba tion in our country. This practice used to be regarded as the caus of all sorts of harmful physical effects including feeblemindednes and insanity. Research by competent investigators has failed to sub stantiate such a view. Today it is generally conceded that (1) ma turbation is not known to have any necessarily deleterious physica consequences; and (2) the negative effects it does have are chiefl psychological in nature and arise from such feelings as guilt, fea and shame, which are frequently associated with the practice. Th effects of masturbation, in other words, are bound up with the wa in which the act is defined within a given group or society.

INHIBITING AND FACILITATING STIMULI

People sometimes speak of human sexuality in animalistic term implying that human sex urges are aroused, repressed, and eve expressed in ways essentially identical with those of other mammal This view is incorrect, for human sexual responses are channelize in ways which have no parallel in the animal world.

Whole segments of a population may be ruled out as sexual o marital partners for social rather than biological reasons. This i true, for example, of the mutual exclusion of the white and colore sections of the American population, the various castes of Indi and the exogamous clans found among many preliterate people Thus, if a native tribe is divided into four clans or subgroups, a unmarried male in one of them may be required to seek his sexua partners only among the women of one of the three other clans. I such cases, eligible and healthy persons of the opposite sex may no even be perceived as desirable sexual objects if they fall into th forbidden categories. In our own society, such barriers as socia class, age, religion, race, and marital status limit the choice o sexual partners.

Someone else's mother may become an exciting object, particu larly if she is a widow and not too elderly; but sexual response toward one's own mother are not permissible. Although a woma may be sexually attractive, to her own male children she is gener ally a sexual nonentity. This is but one instance of the operatio of incest taboos. Human standards of incest vary considerably from society to society, applying sometimes only to the intimate family group and sometimes to a wide circle of persons many of whom are biologically unrelated.[16] Incest taboos are found only among humans. They are social, not biological, phenomena.

We may cite other instances of classificatory elimination of sexual partners. Many white Americans find it difficult to be aroused by a dark-skinned Negro because of strong race prejudice against colored peoples. Indeed, some who are attracted by white-appearing persons undoubtedly feel repelled when these turn out to be mulatto. Negro men and women have sometimes been repelled by the "washed-out" appearance of whites. Similar barriers may be created by religious, nationality, and age differences and by a host of other matters connected with the individual's standards of beauty, cleanliness, and the like.

The arousal of inappropriate imagery may prevent or interrupt sexual activity. For example: laughter, accidentally caused, has been the ruination of many a love scene. Anger, irritation, disgust, and shock are other deterrents to sexual excitation. Conditions preventing or interrupting sexual activity may have nothing to do with relationships between the partners. Such external factors as too much noise, too much light, lack of privacy, and fear of possible interruption may interfere with intercourse. Internal factors having no direct connection with the over-all relationship between the partners may also prove a hindrance—fear of pregnancy or disease, guilt feelings of any kind. As an example, one newly married couple was physically incapable of carrying out the sex act so long as they lived with the bridegroom's parents. Potency was restored when the couple moved to their own living quarters.

IMPOTENCE AND FRIGIDITY

These two terms are used in a number of ways which are not altogether consistent or logical. Impotence is generally taken to refer to the inability of a male to achieve and maintain an erection sufficient to engage in intercourse, whereas frigidity refers to a general lack of interest or enjoyment of the sex act on the part of a woman. Both terms are highly relative. Every male would be impotent and every woman frigid in some conceivable type of situation. A woman who is exclusively homosexual would probably be frigid with respect to all men, and an exclusively homosexual man might be incapable of performing the sexual act with a woman. This statement needs qualification to allow for the fact that in many sexual relations one of the partners may be activated to positive response primarily by fantasies concerning someone other than the actual sexual partner. It is, perhaps, through the control of the fantasy process that certain individuals have been able to be homosexuals but be happily married and the fathers of children.[17]

Since the anatomical and physiological bases of sex behavior constitute necessary but not determining conditions for the development of sexuality, it follows that impotence and frigidity may be the consequence either of organic or of psychological conditions, the latter being the more common. In terms of the usual conception of frigidity, for example, it appears that American women of the urban middle classes are more likely to be sexually unresponsive than women of the lower classes. No biological explanation of these class differences is available, whereas divergent social backgrounds may sufficiently account for them.

Although a decline in sexual interest and activity during old age is related to organic changes, including atrophy of the sex glands, the connection is not sufficiently close to be called a causal one. Hamilton,[18] for example, notes that many men who came to his office with complaints of impotence were between the ages of thirty-seven and forty. Their ages were, in short, much less than the age at which the cessation of sex activity could be expected on purely biological grounds. Hamilton points out that, as one might anticipate, cases of this type often respond favorably to suggestions that there is nothing wrong with them. Seward,[19] after surveying the research literature, has concluded that "impotence in the aging, to a surprising extent, is the product of psychological attitude."

Thus, impotence and frigidity occur in individuals who are biologically sound. Conversely, sexual activity is engaged in by persons who lack what are often regarded as indispensable biological prerequisites. Women may continue to enjoy intercourse after passing through the menopause, up to and beyond the ages of sixty and seventy years, and Kinsey[20] cites the case of an eighty-eight-year-old man who enjoyed regular sex relations with his ninety-year-old wife. Males who are castrated when mature, as a consequence of war injuries for example, often continue to desire and enjoy sexual relations. Seward[21] cites the case of a fifty-three-year-old man, castrated at the age of twenty-four, whose sexual activities increased markedly after the operation. Prior to it, he had practiced coitus about once a month. Afterward, he had intercourse several times a week with his wife and sometimes with other women as well. His increased potency lasted for thirty years.

Impotence and frigidity, when not organic in origin, may be regarded as the consequences of the ways in which a person thinks about himself and about sexual matters. They are, in other words, learned ways of behaving. The central aspects of this problem have to do with the nature of the internal symbolic processes evoked by sexual stimulation. Thus, if a woman is so affected by her early training that sexual excitation sets up an internal symbolic response in terms of concepts like "evil," "sin," "danger," "fear," "pain," and "immorality," these ideas will prevent or inhibit the flow of a facilitating and stimulating erotic imagery. Moreover, if the individual has been consistently brought up in the manner implied by these concepts, she is not even likely to possess an adequate repertory of sexually stimulating ideas. This means that even if she overcomes the ideas of evil, immorality, nastiness, and the like, she may still not be able to respond fully during sexual intercourse.

Impotence in the male is closely bound up with the individual's conception of self and is often associated with increasing age. The middle-aged man begins to grow aware of his advancing age and sexual decline. Since many American males place a high value on potency as a test and proof of masculinity, many middle-aged and elderly men conceive of diminished potency as a reflection on themselves. Often they seek means of restoring their self-steem by consulting physicians or by taking hormone pills. Some try to reassure themselves by seeking sexual adventures with women other than their wives. A large percentage of the sexual offences committed against young girls are the acts of old men seeking means of bolstering their masculine self-esteem.

CONCEPTIONS OF THE SEX ACT

The symbolic character of coitus is indicated by the different significance attached to it by different people.[22] Some look upon it as sinful under almost any conditions; others consider it sinful only when performed outside wedlock. In this country the act is often thought of as a ritual consummating the emotional union of romantic lovers. There are those who are content to emphasize the sensual or lusty aspects of the act. A commonly held American view is that coitus is a husband's right but a wife's duty.

DIFFERENCES IN SEXUAL ATTITUDES AND PRACTICES IN THE UNITED STATES, BY EDUCATIONAL LEVEL[*]

ITEM	YEARS OF SCHOOLING[**]		
	0-8	9-12	13+
Nudity in sleep	16.1%	34.1%	41.1%
Nudity in coitus, marital	42.8	66.3	89.2
Position in marital coitus:			
female above	17.1	28.3	34.6
standing	7.5	9.1	3.6
Kissing, deep: marital	40.5	56.2	77.3
Breast, oral: marital	33.2	57.5	81.6
Female genitalia, oral: marital	4.1	15.4	45.3
Restraints on pre-marital intercourse:			
moral objections	20.8	25.5	61.4
fear of public opinion	13.5	14.3	22.8

[*] From A. C. Kinsey et al., Sexual Behavior in the Human Male, Philadelphia: Saunders, 1948.
[**] Educational level corresponds roughly to class level.

Like other attitudes, conceptions of sexual intercourse are derived from participation in groups. Kinsey[23] has stressed the importance of some of these groups and especially of social class. He contrasts, for example, the attitudes of upper- and lower-class American males toward coitus and describes the different behavior resulting from these attitudes. The lower-class male spends less time on preliminaries, considers kissing and preparation relatively unimportant, and experiments much less during intercourse. The upper-class male is likely to emphasize foreplay and variation. The sexual training and experiences of the sexes in America are so different that men and women are often likely to have strikingly different views of coitus. Kinsey even suggests that divorces sometimes hinge on the wife's adverse reaction to sexual experimentation by the husband.[24]

Three Sexual Codes

A society as complex as ours inevitably gives rise to differing sexual philosophies and codes. These underlie the divergent sexual behavior of various segments of the population. We may tentatively identify three codes which have some degree of acceptance in the United States: the traditional, the romantic, and the predatory or recreational. These views have to do both with marital relations and with sexual practices in general. Each view has elements in common with each of the other views; yet, as we shall see, each places a somewhat different emphasis upon the meanings of certain acts.

The traditional philosophy defines sexual activity outside marriage as evil, particularly for women. It requires virginity from unmarried women and demands fidelity of both marital partners. The marital relation is looked upon as part of the family system of relations; hence, sexual intercourse is defined mainly as procreative in purpose, although its connection with the affections is recognized. The family as such, however, is considered central; hence, divorce is forbidden except on extreme grounds, regardless of how badly the partners get along with each other personally. Children are desired in order to carry on the family name, the family honor, and in some cases the family business.

This traditional view of sex and marital relations underlies the behavior of a considerable part of the population and especially of the more tradition bound, more "religious," and more "old fashioned." The Catholic and Orthodox Jewish groups emphasize this philosophy more than do most Protestant groups, although all three major religions subscribe to it. Its basic tenets are set forth and glorified in many respectable media of communication, including magazines, newspapers, novels, and radio and television programs.

A philosophy having much in common with the preceding one, but which has additional and opposing elements, is the romantic conception of love and marriage. This view emphasizes the values of being in love. Love is a prerequisite to sexual relations. Love justifies intercourse and intercourse cements the union of lovers. Coitus without love is considered bestial or, at best, meaningless. In its extreme form the romantic view justifies extramarital as well as premarital sexual relations. Fidelity in marriage is regarded as assured if the romance, the mystery, does not fade from the marriage. If love should disappear, however, divorce is desirable unless such factors as poverty or the presence of children must be considered. In the romantic marriage children are undesirable if the bonds of affection would be weakened by their presence. The family is pictured as an affectional companionate unit, and the keynote concept is happiness rather than family name, family honor, or family lineage.

The romantic view is held most prominently by our urban middle classes, especially by young women. The literary diet of middle-class women consists largely of romantic narratives and feature articles about romantic love. Hollywood, while respecting the traditional ideal, also promulgates the romantic view. Indeed, the entire entertainment and advertising industries, recognizing the key importance of the female consumer, exploit the romantic symbols of love and sex that are so popular with their audience. The romantic philosophy is entrenched in the United States, where it rivals the traditional view in prestige. Probably most people who hold the romantic view do not adhere to its most extreme form but either reconcile it with the more traditional familial view or suffer conflicts.

The predatory-recreational philosophy ignores both the institutional implications of sex and the values of romantic love. It is concerned with sex primarily as a pleasurable activity or as a means to personal or selfish ends, and hence often those who hold it seek to avoid the long-term commitments of marriage and rearing a family. This view leads to sexual exploitation when a person is unaware of the limited, predatory orientation of the sexual partner or is too involved to care. The separation of sexual activity from its procreational consequences has been made possible to a large extent by the wide dissemination of contraceptive devices and practices. Since there is always some risk of pregnancy, it is inevitable, perhaps, that men are more inclined than women to hold the predatory view.

The predatory-recreational conception of sex is often temporarily adopted by unmarried persons and by those who must postpone marriage beyond the age of physical maturity. It has a low official status, and is transmitted mainly by word of mouth, through jokes and stories, and through furtive communication. Recently increasing frankness concerning sexual matters has brought this view into the open in novels, magazines, and movies. Kinsey's investigations and other evidence show that there is considerable unofficial and unsanctioned sexual activity that goes on in accordance with this philosophy.

The traditional, romantic, and predatory-recreational philosophies are, of course, not the only sexual codes in existence in America, but they are probably the ones to which most of our people adhere. As we have already noted, the philosophies themselves are not entirely distinct from one another since they possess some elements in common. What is more, because various segments of our population are exposed to all three codes, the views held by specific individuals embody amalgams of them. Young men and women today, for example, commonly act according to a combination of romantic and traditional notions. It is quite common also for a person to behave in one situation according to one code and in another situation according to another code. Thus, a young man may sometimes act predatorily toward unmarried women but romantically toward his fiancée. Since the various sexual codes are also in considerable conflict, the individuals whose actions rests upon them may experience doubt, anxiety, and guilt. Many college girls must reconcile "having a good time" with "being a good girl." Young people of both sexes, faced with choosing a marital partner, often fear that romanticism and domesticity may prove incompatible. Some eligible persons are not handsome but look "steady" and seem to "have a future." Another common conflict—at least among middle-class boys—involves home training versus "being a man": they think according to the unreconciled standards of parents and boys of their own age. The conflict is found in the behavior of college men who vacillate between "saving themselves" and joining their friends on a trip to a house of prostitution; and if they go, they suffer acute remorse and guilt.

Summary

Despite a widespread belief that sexual behavior and motivation are biologically determined, human sexual adjustments are primarily symbolic in nature and the patterning of human sexual responses is learned through social experience in group contexts. A comparison of human and subhuman sexual activities shows that hormonal control declines and is replaced by cortical control and learning mechanisms as one ascends the evolutionary scale from simpler mammalian forms to the great apes and then to man. The influence of symbolic processes and of learning in human beings is predominant; and many forms of deviant behavior, such as homosexuality, fetishism, and inversion, are unique in the human species. There is an absence of evidence indicating that human sex preferences are determined by the sex hormones, and there is positive evidence that the masculine and feminine roles are, like other social roles, learned systems of behavior. The profound influence of symbolic processes on human sex behavior is evident in masturbation, erotic imagery, the control or inhibition of the orgasm, and in different ways of defining or interpreting the significance of sexual activities. Three rival philosophies of love and marriage exert considerable influence on the sexual activities and motivations of contemporary Americans. These have been termed the traditional, the romantic, and the predatory-recreational philosophies.

SUGGESTIONS FOR DISCUSSION AND SPECIAL REPORTS

1. Compare two societies, one monogamous and the other practicing some form of polygamy.

2. Review the Freudian theory of homosexuality.

3. Refer to some of the recent experimental work on the effects of hormones to check statements made in this chapter concerning the irrelevance of hormones to homosexuality.

4. Write a report on the reception of Kinsey's books by the public.

5. What is "natural" sex behavior? How would you determine what natural sex behavior is for any given species?

6. Can lower animals be said to practice polygamy, monogamy, or polyandry?

7. If the mores governing sexual behavior were to be abolished, what would happen? Are mores "natural"?

8. Discuss trends in American sexual mores.

NOTES

[1] F. A. Beach, "Evolutionary Changes in the Physiological Control of Mating Behavior in Mammals," *Psych. Rev.*, 54 (1947): 297-315.

[2] See G. H. Seward, *Sex and the Social Order*, McGraw-Hill, 1946. This book presents an interesting and able review of the whole subject along with extensive bibliographical references.

[3] J. H. Conn and L. Kanner, "Children's Awareness of Sex Differences," *J. Child Psychiatry*, 1 (1947): 3-57.

[4] *Ibid.*, p. 13.

[5] *Ibid.*, p. 13.

[6] *Ibid.*, p. 13.

[7] *Ibid.*, p. 17.

[8] *Ibid.*, p. 16.

[9] A. C. Kinsey et al., *Sexual Behavior in the Human Male*, Philadelphia: W. B. Saunders, 1948.

[10] S. S. Isaacs, *Social Development in Young Children*, London: Routledge, 1933, p. 160.

[11] M. Klein, *The Psychoanalysis of Children*, London: Hogarth, 1932, pp. 42-46.

[12] S. Freud, *New Introductory Lectures on Psychoanalysis*, Norton, 1933. "The Psychology of Women," pp. 153-183.

[13] Conn and Kanner, *op. cit.;* see especially pp. 44-48.

[14] Kinsey, *op. cit.*, p. 363.

[15] *Ibid.*, pp. 510-511.

[16] See W. I. Thomas, *Primitive Behavior*, McGraw-Hill, 1936.

[17] D. Corey, *The Homosexual in America*, New York: Greenberg, 1951.

[18] G. Hamilton, "Changes in Personality and Psychosexuality with Age," in E. V. Cowdry (ed.), *Problems of Aging: Biological and Medical Aspects*, Baltimore: Williams and Wilkins, 1939, pp. 459-482.

[19] Seward, *op. cit.*, p. 222.

[20] Kinsey, *op. cit.*, p. 237.

[21] Seward, *op. cit.*, p. 225.

[22] Thomas, *op. cit.*, pp. 240-272

[23] Kinsey, *op. cit.*, especially Chap. X, "Social Level and Sexual Outlet," pp. 327-393.

[24] Kinsey, *op. cit.*, pp. 545-546.

SELECTED BIBLIOGRAPHY

Beach, F. A., "Evolutionary Changes in the Physiological Control of Mating Behavior in Mammals," *Psych. Rev.*, 54(1947): 297-315. Indicates the increasing importance of the cortex and of learning and past experience in sex behavior as one moves from the simpler animals to the more complex.

Conn, J. H., and L. Kanner, "Children's Awareness of Sex Differences," *J. Child Psychiatry*, 1(1947): 3-57. An important exploratory study of children's ideas of sex behavior.

Dickinson, R., and L. Beam, *A Thousand Marriages*, Baltimore: Williams and Wilkins, 1931. An early pioneering investigation of the sexual behavior of married persons.

Ellis, H., *Studies in the Psychology of Sex*, 4 vols., Random House, 1936. A comprehensive classic study of sexual behavior. Still a valuable work.

Ford, C., and F. Beach, *Patterns of Sexual Behavior*, Harper, 1951. A detailed survey of sexual patterns. The authors give comparative data, both for societies and for species.

Freud, S., *New Introductory Lectures on Psychoanalysis*, Norton, 1933. "The Psychology of Women," pp. 153-187. An application of basic psychoanalytic concepts to the special case of women. Freud's explanation of feminine psychology.

Kinsey, A. C., W. B. Pomeroy, C. E. Martin, *Sexual Behavior in the Human Male*, Philadelphia: W. B. Saunders, 1948. A much-discussed study of the sexual behavior of American men. A valuable book despite the authors' tendency to overgeneralize and despite their neglect of social psychology.

Kinsey, A. C., *et al.*, *Sexual Behavior in the Human Female*, Philadelphia: W. B. Saunders, 1954.

Kuhn, M. H., "Kinsey's View of Human Behavior," *Social Problems*, 4 (1954): 119-125. Examines and criticizes some of Kinsey's basic assumptions.

Malinowski, B., *The Sexual Life of Savages*, Liveright, 1929. A fascinating account of the sexual codes and behavior of a preliterate people. Notable for the way in which it relates sexual behavior to the whole framework of the society.

Seward, G. H., *Sex and the Social Order*, McGraw-Hill, 1946. An excellent summary and evaluation of the research on the sexual behavior of lower animals and man. Stresses the importance of learning and culture in human sex behavior.

Social Problems, 1(April 1954). This issue, entitled "Sexual Behavior in American Society," consists of a number of papers, mainly by sociologists.

Tauber, E. S., "Effects of Castration upon the Sexuality of the Adult Male," *Psychosomatic Med.*, 2(1940): 74-87. Indicates that the removal of the primary sex glands of adult humans has highly variable effects and does not necessarily lead to the cessation of sexual activity.

Terman, L. M., and C. C. Miles, *Sex and Personality: Studies in Masculinity and Femininity*, McGraw-Hill, 1936. An influential study of personality differences between the sexes in the United States.

Thomas, W. I., *Primitive Behavior*, McGraw-Hill, 1936. Chap. X, "Sexual Behavior," pp. 240-272. The wide range of differences in the sexual codes of various peoples is strikingly illustrated.

Zweig, S., *The World of Yesterday*, Viking, 1943. Chap. IV, "Eros Matutinus," pp. 67-91. Describes in an effective literary style the sexual codes and behavior of late nineteenth-century Vienna. An interesting introduction to the social origins of Freud's theories of personality.

CHAPTER 11 • • •

Learning Theory,

Addictions,

and

Habits

THE SOCIOLOGIST and the social psychologist are interested in human behavior which is primarily learned rather than inherited. There exists an extensive literature dealing with the elaborate body of theory on the subject of learning in the field of psychology. Psychological learning theories are based mainly upon experimental work with lower animals and are designed to explain and synthesize experimental findings. Many learning theories purport to be applicable to all learning, both animal and human, and should therefore be of interest to the social psychologist. We wish to focus attention here upon some problems that are raised when the attempt is made to extend existing learning theory to all human behavior. In order to do this we shall first describe some of the characteristic assumptions and concepts underlying learning theory, and then we shall consider the applicability of those assumptions and concepts to some complicated forms of human learning.

Learning Theory

To introduce the main terms in the vocabulary of learning theory we shall use them in describing a simple bit of learned behavior.[1] Three-year-old Johnny is standing on a chair in the kitchen and has just reached into the cupboard for a box of cookies when the bell of the ice-cream truck rings in the street outside. Johnny hesitates, gets down quickly, and runs into the living room, where his mother is sewing. He asks her for a nickel to get some ice cream. His mother looks up from her work, smiles, and says, "Go get a nickel from my purse." Johnny runs to the purse and extracts a nickel, then runs out to the ice-cream truck, hands over the nickel, and, with his mouth watering, gets his ice cream and eats it.

The ringing of the ice-cream truck bell is a *conditioned stimulus* which Johnny has acquired from past experience. Hunger, or the hunger for ice cream, is the *drive* which motivated the sequence; and the eventual satisfaction of this hunger by eating the ice cream could be called *reinforcement,* or *drive,* or *tension reduction.* Johnny's acts between hearing the bell and getting the ice cream would be called *instrumental responses* in *sequence* to a *goal.* His mother's statement to him is another *stimulus* to Johnny, and provides him with a *subgoal,* that of getting a nickel (a *stimulus object*). The watering of Johnny's mouth at the sight of the ice cream is a *conditioned response* because it first occurred only when Johnny was actually eating ice cream. The taste of the ice cream is the *unconditioned stimulus.*

If we go back further we realize that Johnny learned about the bell of the ice-cream truck by hearing it repeatedly and getting ice cream to eat shortly afterward (*repetition, reinforcement*). At first he may very well have become excited by other similar sounds and mistaken them for those of the ice-cream truck (*stimulus generalization*). Eventually, however, he came to recognize the distinctive characteristics of the ice-cream bell (*discrimination*). When the weather became especially hot he learned to anticipate the arrival of the ice-cream man, and would sometimes go outside to listen for the distant sound of the bell (*higher order conditioning*—"hot weather"—"bell"—"ice cream").

If Johnny's mother disapproved of his buying ice cream from the truck she would have the problem of preventing Johnny from going through with the behavior sequence described (*extinction*). No doubt she would go about this by using persuasion and command and by punishing Johnny when he disobeyed (*negative reinforcement*). She might find later that when the ice-cream truck came around again for the first time in the spring that Johnny's impulse to have some ice cream would suddenly reappear in full strength (*spontaneous recovery*), and that the problem of teaching him not to get ice cream from the truck would have to be dealt with again.

CHARACTERISTICS OF LEARNING THEORY

This account of Johnny's getting the ice cream, while representative in most respects, is somewhat unrepresentative of learning theory in that it involves human rather than animal behavior. The charateristic concern of this theory is with stimulus-response linkages. It breaks up complex acts into specific smaller parts and directs attention to overt external behavior. Motivation, or drive, is treated as a biological or quasi-biological "force" or energy source. The S-R (stimulus-response) linkage is often viewed as a causal linkage; and the problem of learning is seen as the problem of discovering the principles or laws which describe the manner in which S-R bonds are established or broken up.

Learning theory is based mainly on experimental studies of lower animals. The use of lower animals for experimental purposes is especially advantageous for various obvious reasons. Some attention is given to experiments on human learning, but these usually deal with the simple, routine types. The use of animal subjects raises the question whether learning is the same in animals and human beings. Theorists of learning disagree sharply on this point. Some maintain that there are different types of learning which have to be examined separately, whereas others argue that learning is a single process, and in time the study of learning in rats will lead to results which will be applicable to the most complex human learning.

The conception of learning in most current theories is a mechanical one based on a hedonistic conception of behavior. Classical hedonism contended that behavior was determined by a balancing of the pleasure and pain anticipated from given lines of action. Learning theory translates hedonism into other terms but follows the same general idea—that organisms do what satisfies them and refrain from doing what does not satisfy them or brings pain rather than pleasure. Mowrer, for example says, "Behavior is reinforced and perpetuated when and only when it is in some way satisfying."[2] The mechanical nature of the theory arises from concentration on external, measurable factors in the work done with lower animals. For example, in working with hungry rats running through mazes, hunger can be measured in terms of the period of time that the animal has been without food. Performance can be measured by the time it takes the rat to reach the food and the speed at which it moves at various points in the maze. The punishment, or pain, may be measured by the strength of the electric current used to shock the rat. The strength of the animal's drives may be determined by the amount of punishment it will accept before refraining from crossing an electrically charged grill on its way to the goal.

Preoccupation with external, measurable aspects of behavior makes for precision of experimental findings. It also leads to the exclusion of such matters as reasoning processes, understanding, insight, and language mechanisms. The absence of language in the lower animals is usually cited as an advantage and a reason for preferring animal to human subjects. When learning theorists devote any attention to language they usually contend that linguistic behavior consists of a system of conditioned responses. Very little research has been done on complicated forms of language behavior; and it is very doubtful if they can properly be regarded as conditioned response behavior.

The amount of experimental research that has been done on problems of learning is very great, and a tremendous range of variations in the learning situation has been explored. The findings of

various investigators are not always consistent, and different interpretations and different types of general theories have been proposed. This means that the social psychologist who expects to find
an accepted theory of learning and established "laws" is doomed to
disappointment. What he finds instead is a multitude of conflicting
theories based on roughly the same mass of data, but emphasizing
different aspects of it. This, of course, for one who wants to apply
learning theory to problems of social psychology, raises the question as to which of the many theories of learning he ought to borrow.

Most researchers in this field concern themselves with the technical and theoretical problems that arise within it and do not attempt to apply their findings to human social life. Some of the
theorists, however, have sought to show that their systems can be
applied to all behavior, including that on a cultural level. Since
much attention is given to rewards and punishments, one might suppose that research findings in this field would be helpful to penolo-
gists, teachers, and parents, who are also concerned with reward
and punishment. Actually, very few such applications have been
made. In the next section we shall present an example of human
learning, drug addiction, as an example of the kind of behavior
which social psychologists wish to account for and to which learning
theory must be applied if it is to be useful in social psychology.

Addictions and Habits

DRUG ADDICTION

An outstanding characteristic of addicting drugs is that their
withdrawal after regular use over a period of a couple of weeks or
more produces an automatic painful physical reaction. Opiate drugs
(those derived from the opium poppy) and their synthetic equiva-
lents are the important drugs of this type. Marihuana and cocaine
do not produce withdrawal distress. The withdrawal distress connected with opiates varies with individuals, and its intensity de-

pends upon duration of use, the amount used, and other factors. The symptoms of withdrawal form a characteristic pattern or syndrome, which in its severe form is unmistakable to those who are acquainted with it. These symptoms begin to appear about four or five hours after the last injection. If no further drugs are taken they increase in intensity for about seventy-two hours and the more noticeable ones disappear only gradually over a period of about two weeks. An injection of drugs during the withdrawal period causes all these symptoms to vanish in a matter of minutes. Withdrawal distress occurs in newborn infants whose mothers are addicts and in various animal species when drugs are regularly administered. This shows that the withdrawal reaction is biological in nature; and it is this fact that has led some students to declare that drug addiction is essentially an organic condition or disease.

It is unnecessary, in view of the publicity given in recent years to teen-age addiction, to describe addiction or withdrawal distress in detail. It should be noted, however, that much of the popular literature is motivated by the purpose of frightening or warning young persons. This has led to inaccurate and exaggerated descriptions of the alleged evil physical effects. The facts are that with the full establishment of addiction after several weeks of regular drug use, a bodily condition of tolerance or "drug balance" is acquired. When this has occurred, the main effect of the drug is to maintain this balance, to prevent withdrawal symptoms, and to cause the addict to feel normal. The user may experience a physical "kick" when he takes his shot, especially if it is a "main liner" (an injection into the vein), but during the several hours between injections it is exceedingly difficult to determine with certainty whether the person is under the influence of a drug or not. Persons who take drugs by other means than hypodermic injection, as for example orally, may never have experienced physical pleasure from taking them. This is especially true when the initial use occurs during an illness.

During the initial period of use there occur several radical changes that amount almost to a reversal of the drug's effects. Thus, the original depressing effect on bodily functions tends to vanish and to be replaced by a stimulating one. Also, the euphoria, or positive pleasure of beginning use vanishes and is replaced by the negative effect of relieving withdrawal distress and achieving approximate normality between shots. Bodily functions originally disturbed by the regular injection of drugs generally return to an approximately normal level when tolerance has been built up. The long-continued use of such drugs as morphine or heroin, contrary to popular belief, does not lead to major tissue destruction or to insanity. Tooth decay, constipation, and sexual impotence, which are relatively frequent among drug addicts, are not invariable or necessary consequences of addiction, and some addicts, especially those who are well-to-do, do not experience them. The principal deleterious effects are psychological in nature and are connected with the tabooed and secret nature of the habit; with the extreme cost of obtaining a supply of drugs at black-market prices; and with resulting changes in self-conception, occupation, and social relationships.

The need for a distinction between habit and addiction may be sharply brought out by noting that most addicts have the "habit" of using drugs before they become addicted. When persons become addicts through medical administration, we have a paradoxical situation in which the patient is addicted and the doctor or the nurse has the habit of administering the drug to patients! A person who made a habit of taking a single injection of morphine every Sunday morning would never become an addict, no matter how long he continued this practice, if he refrained from taking injections at all other times. Hebb,[3] approaching this problem from the point of view of a physiological psychologist and comparing opium hunger with hunger for food, emphasizes the idea that an addiction involves, in addition to habit, the maintenance of a bodily equilibrium. This equilibrium is upset when the addicting substance is unavailable. He notes that biological needs, such as those for food or for drugs, in themselves produce only emotional disturbance, restlessness, and discomfort and become transferred into organized action only after a process of learning has taken place. The existence of physical dependence upon drugs does not necessarily imply psychological dependence. Hospital patients who are given drugs with sufficient regularity to produce tolerance and withdrawal effects nevertheless do not become addicts if they do not recognize the withdrawal symptoms. Conversely, addicts who are imprisoned continue to crave the drug even though they are no longer physically dependent on it. This has led to a distinction in the literature between physical addiction and psychological addiction, and poses the problem of explaining how and when physical dependence is transformed into psychological dependence; that is, into genuine addiction. One of the current conceptions is that this occurs only when the user has some sort of psychological quirk or personality abnormality. We shall see that this idea is not supported by the evidence. Drug users who have regular sources of supply outside the underworld and who are well-to-do can avoid this loss of station in respectable society and may continue to carry on for many years in responsible and legitimate occupations.

Physical dependence upon drugs becomes psychological addiction when the individual understands his withdrawal distress and interprets it as being due to the absence of the drug, and then continues to use it. In using the drug to avoid withdrawal distress, after the latter is experienced and understood, the pattern of addiction, which includes the psychological craving, is gradually acquired. This operates continuously, both when the person has an immediate supply and of course when he does not. It persists in the imprisoned drug user, and predisposes the addict to relapse into the habit when he has ostensibly been cured. A drug user does not realize his addiction until he discovers the difficulty of breaking off the habit, and it is this difficulty which compels him to accept, however unwillingly and painfully, the idea that he has become a "dope fiend." This redefinition of self, coupled with the extreme difficulty of obtaining a regular supply of drugs, tends to compel the ordinary American addict to associate more and more exclusively with other users and with those persons in the underworld or on its fringes who can help him to continue his habit. Maintenance of a regular legal occupation becomes well-nigh impossible, and the user drifts into a hand-to-mouth existence or becomes a criminal.

Experimentation with lower animals has failed to elicit addiction behavior from any of them. Chimpanzees that are given morphine regularly have been trained to connect the injection with relief of

withdrawal distress. When this is done, they show the same eagerness and cooperative attitude with respect to morphine administration that they do to being fed.[4] This justifies, however, only the
conclusion that physical dependence is present, and that the chimpanzee can take *one* of the several steps necessary to becoming
addicted in the human sense. He cannot, of course, understand withdrawal distress as humans do, because such understanding requires
linguistic formulation. The chimpanzee's interest in drugs, moreover,
is associated exclusively with withdrawal distress. When an injection
dissipates the distress, the animal no longer exhibits any craving for
drugs and prefers food to it. Neither does he show any tendency
to relapse into the habit after physical dependence has been broken.
Human hospital patients who have received drugs without knowing
it exhibit the same behavior that the chimpanzees do when unwittingly suffering from morphine deprivation; but they never become addicted if they remain in ignorance of what is transpiring.
Indeed, physicians often pride themselves upon their ability to prevent addiction by keeping the patient in the dark about what he is
being given, using such means as withholding information, switching
drugs and methods of administration, and avoiding the hypodermic
needle which has become a cultural symbol of "dope."

Calling lower animals "drug addicts" in the human sense thus
clearly involves confusion of two types of phenomena—those of
physical dependence and those of psychic dependence. However,
the great majority of experimenters with animals have explicitly
denied that lower animals can become addicted or that they ever
exhibit the craving which is characteristic of human addicts.

If the person's interpretation of his own withdrawal distress is
a crucial event in the initiation of addiction, it is clear that addiction
is a uniquely human phenomenon, made possible by the existence
of language behavior and conceptual thought. The continuousness
of the craving for drugs in human subjects is clearly connected with
human beings' capacity to anticipate the future and hence to obtain
supplies to forestall future distress, and also with the ability to remember and reconstruct the past so as to understand that the withdrawal distress of the present is connected with a long series of

events in the past and with the bodily changes induced by those events. Thus only socialized beings can become psychologically addicted: the insane, the extremely feeble-minded, and young children cannot. This has been noted often in the literature of addiction but without explanation. Apropos of drug use in the very young, addiction is almost never reported in persons under ten years of age, and it has been observed that the custom, widely practiced in India, of feeding opium to children under three years of age has no connection with the possibility of their becoming addicts when adult.

Persons who experience withdrawal distress interpret it in a variety of ways. Many non-addicts who have been given drugs regularly by physicians simply do not notice the distress at all because they assume that it is part of their disease. Others may regard the withdrawal distress itself as a disease and ask the medical man to treat them for it. If the physician in this case falls in with the patient's diagnosis, the type of therapy administered does not matter as long as no opiates are administered, since the patient begins to improve rapidly within about three days. When he has recovered he is none the wiser and none the worse for his experience. Addicts have attributed their first withdrawal experience to such sources as sunburn, stomach trouble, food poisoning, influenza, and post-surgical trauma.

The theory that only abnormal persons become drug addicts is untenable for a number of reasons. A good *prima facie* case could be made for it if some obviously normal person were to take drugs deliberately, with full knowledge of their effects, and demonstrate his immunity to addiction. This has never been done. Even persons who are quite convinced that only neurotics become addicts are generally extremely wary of putting themselves to the acid test. Moreover, all extensive research samplings of addicts reveal that in a substantial percentage of cases no psychological abnormality sufficient to account for the addiction was known to exist prior to addiction. Most of the undesirable personality traits cited as causes of addiction either come after the addiction and as consequences of it, or are widely prevalent in those segments of the population which are exposed to addiction.

OTHER KINDS OF ADDICTION

If we disregard the fact that drug addiction is biologically useless and harmful, we may at once note that there are common forms of addiction that closely parallel the phenomenon of drug addiction. Addiction to food is perhaps the most obvious. The child, shortly after birth, begins to suffer from food deprivation without knowing it. His parents intervene, defining his withdrawal distress as a need for food and imposing their definition on the child so that he learns to make the initial connection between taking food and the relief which follows. Later, as the child masters the language and matures intellectually, he comes to understand the hunger situation, *i.e.*, he comes to conceptualize it. As Hebb says, "Finally, the development of conceptual process controlling eating makes possible an association of eating with other conceptual processes."[5]

When eating becomes a conceptually controlled process people may eat when they are not hungry, may not feel hungry when they need food or even when they are starving, and may be deceived into eating nonnutritious substances in the belief that they are eating food. All of these things also occur in drug addiction. Addicts, for example, characteristically take more than they need to maintain a state of drug balance, the excess being designated by some investigators as the "deluxe dosage." The amount taken reflects what the addict thinks he needs. Drug users may be taken off drugs by gradual reduction, so that after a period of weeks they may be receiving regular injections of salt water which they believe to be drugs. Gradual reduction lessens the severity of withdrawal distress and spreads it out over a longer period. Drug users accustomed to intravenous injections can be given drugs orally without their realizing the nature of the dose.

The dependence of diabetics upon insulin is another example of an addiction which when stopped produces an automatic physical reaction. The main difference between it and opiate addiction probably resides in the fact that insulin addiction is socially tolerated as necessary to the preservation of life. Given a shortage of legal insulin, diabetics set up a clandestine traffic and pay black-market prices, as other drug addicts do. Smoking, alcohol addiction, and coffee addiction are similar instances, although in some of these the physical reaction upon quitting may be slight.

Many other forms of activity may be viewed as addiction in the sense that the discontinuation of the activity may be profoundly disturbing to the person, although the disturbance may not be of a gross physical type. As instances, we may cite the boredom and dissatisfaction experienced by the person who retires from his occupation after a lifetime of hard work. The withdrawal symptoms connected with sexual deprivation, although they have their biological aspects, are primarily psychological. It has been suggested that what is called "homesickness" reflects a form of addiction, and that loneliness arises from one of the most primary addictions of all—the addiction of human beings to society. Persons who have felt the lure of the race track and the gambling casino, or wasted time putting nickels into slot or pinball machines, understand that for some people there is a fatal fascination in gambling and that it may become a powerful compulsion. Persons may also be said to become addicted to political and religious practices and all sorts of other ideological behavior. The test of an addiction in this broad sense may be said to be what happens when the activity is stopped.

The disturbing consequence of abandoning a belief or a practice, when they are not of a gross physical type, evidently arise from the way in which the person conceives of the activity and the satisfaction derived from it. Consequently, compulsive patterns of behavior or belief are more closely connected with personality and with the individual's other conceptions and orientations than is addiction to drugs, where the physical reaction to quitting provides the impetus for continued use.

The use of marihuana involves no problem of physical withdrawal and is said to be "non-habit forming" by addicts as well as by writers on addiction. Nevertheless, there are persons who use marihuana regularly and who go to considerable risk and expense to obtain it, whereas other users are able to take it or leave it. Here again, the decisive factors appear to lie in the personality and in the social environment. Becker[6] has described the use of marihuana, noting that it has become virtually a part of the accepted way of life in some circles. Persons must be taught both how to smoke it and how to enjoy it. Physical symptoms which they had not noticed are pointed out to them and they are literally taught to feel "high" by perceiving the symptoms. The uninitiated may get high when they first try marihuana and not know that they are, or they may regard the new sensations as unpleasant or frightening. However, more sophisticated associates will try to redefine the symptoms as pleasurable, and when they succeed the neophyte comes to view marihuana as a recreational instrument and a source of pleasure.

BREAKING ADDICTIONS

Quitting a habit or an addiction is almost always difficult. The power of those addictions which involve physical withdrawal symptoms appears to be roughly proportional to the severity of the withdrawal reaction. Smoking, for example, is a relatively mild habit and the withdrawal reaction is correspondingly mild. Nevertheless, the magnitude of the black market in cigarettes in European countries after the war showed that persons who are really "hooked" will go to great lengths, pay huge prices, violate laws, and make considerable sacrifices for the sake of tobacco. Quitting such a habit as smoking is further complicated by social factors which lead one's friends and associates to function as tempters and providers of rationalizations for resuming or continuing the habit. In the case of marihuana, most persons who leave the world of jazz or the juvenile circles where it is used probably quit the drug at the same time and with a minimum of difficulty. The reacquisition of all habits, however, tends to be much easier and more rapid than the first learning. This is especially true of alcoholism and drug addiction, in which the only hope of cure seems to lie in giving up drugs or liquor absolutely. It is notorious that the chronic alcoholic and the person who has been "hooked" by drugs can never again in their lives use liquor or drugs casually.

An amusing, but sometimes tragic, aspect of habits and addictions is the elaborate rationalization which the person engages in, sometimes in an almost desperate manner, to excuse himself and to explain his behavior. This process is noteworthy in smokers, especially since the alarm created by the publicity given to the possible connection between lung cancer and cigarette smoking. It is strikingly manifested in alcoholics and drug addicts, who literally overwhelm one with the richness and variety of their interpretations and excuses.

The most favorable situation for breaking old habits and addictions is a new environment, new associations, and satisfying new activities which displace the old preoccupations. Changes which occur with increasing age often automatically lead to the dropping of old activities and the development of new ones, as for example, giving up athletics and playing cards or word games instead. The organization of Alcoholics Anonymous for chronic drunkards has apparently achieved some success in weaning drinkers away from their compulsion. The drinker is required to confess that he is an alcoholic and is powerless to control his craving without help from others and from divine sources. At the meetings of the local branch the former alcoholic is introduced into a society of others who have the same problem that he has and who understand him thoroughly. He confesses his former alcoholic excesses in public meeting, sometimes describing scenes in rich and gory detail. His audience is exceedingly responsive and knows when to laugh, sympathize, or agree. The drinker goes on to tell how he became acquainted with A.A. and what it has done for him, how long he has been sober, how often he has relapsed, and so on. After the formal meeting, refreshments may be served and a social period may follow. Through the organization, new friendships are formed and new activities are urged upon the members, one of the most important being that of actively going to the aid and support of other alcoholics who are in danger of relapse or who are not yet in the organization. Alcoholics Anonymous tends to strip from the drinker his typical excuses and rationalizations, both by the initial confession of powerlessness and by reason of the fact that every member is an expert in detecting them. A similar organization for drug addicts has had relatively little success as yet.

Finally, it should be noted that the moral significance of habits and addictions has not been considered here. Addiction to insulin is clearly on a very different moral plane from addiction to drugs or alcohol, for the latter are generally destructive and degenerative in their effects. The moral aspects of addictions and habits are of the greatest practical importance, but they should not prevent one from seeing and noting the significance of the basic similarities that exist in all of them. Addictions in human beings are characterized by conceptual or ideological elaboration and preoccupation, particularly when the activity is stopped. In those cases in which the cessation of an addiction activity produces an automatic physical withdrawal reaction, the individual's grasp of this event appears to be of crucial significance in stimulating a craving and supporting ideology and style of life. Since ideologies and controlling conceptual mechanisms are peculiarly human, it is not surprising that human beings are subject to many addictions, both good and bad, useful and harmful, of which the lower animals are incapable.

Addiction and Learning Theory

Learning theorists rarely concern themselves with behavior of the complexity and cultural involvement that characterizes drug addiction. One reason for this is that this behavior is not found among the lower animals. Since this is true of most of the behavior with which social psychology concerns itself, learning theory often seems ill adapted to it. Extensions of learning theory to complicated cultural problems seem to lead to oversimplification of the nature of the cultural learning process and to the shaping of facts to fit the theory.

Since learning theorists usually give little attention to language behavior, they are handicapped in considering what the consequences of linguistic activity may be. The problem of explaining why lower animals and infants cannot become addicted to drugs is not readily dealt with by means of S-R concepts. The learning theorist's preoccupation with measurement of overt behavior often causes him to lose sight of the less visible forms of symbolic re-action which are such an important part of human social behavior.

The facts of drug addiction also seem to challenge the validity of hedonistic psychology. According to the theory, the drug addict must use drugs because of the satisfactions he obtains. Yet the drug user is a miserable and harassed person who suffers great humiliation and discomfort for the sake of his habit. He says the drug does not give him pleasure except at the time of injection; except for that it only causes him to feel "normal." Certainly the satisfactions connected with using drugs seem infinitesimal compared with the trouble it causes. On the basis of the theory that negative reinforcement extinguishes behavior, one would think that addicts would quit their habit or, at the very least, would not persist in returning to it after they have been "cured." In order to preserve learning theory, then, it would seem necessary to say that the satisfactions obtained from being a drug addict must be of a very special and unusual nature which causes them to be imperceptible and unintelligible to outsiders.

There are other paradoxical aspects of the behavior of the addict which need to be considered. For example, the casual user of opiates who is not an addict experiences pleasure from the drug with a minimum of bad aftereffects. The same may be said of the casual user of alcohol. In contrast, persons addicted to alcohol and opiates experience a preponderance of evil effects. This makes it appear that these addictions are fixed by the suffering they produce rather than by the pleasure. A drug like marihuana produces considerable euphoria in many persons and there may be few unhappy aftereffects. Nevertheless, marihuana is a "non-habit-forming drug."

Before learning theory can be of much use to social psychology it will have to demonstrate its applicability to learning of the kind represented by drug addiction and other cultural learning. Considerable adaptation will have to be made in the theory, we believe, before such applications will be fruitful. The most far-reaching application is likely to be one that takes the language behavior of man into account. More careful and systematic attempts to extend learning theory to human behavior would be of great benefit to the theory and of great interest to the social psychologist.

Levels of Learning

A current controversy is being carried on as to whether there is only one kind of learning rather than two or more. This controversy has far-reaching implications; for a decision in favor of plural forms of learning would tend to undermine the psychologist's position that the study of learning in lower animals eventually may shed light upon complex human learning. There is already a considerable number of scholars in this field who contend, as Hilgard does, that in order to understand verbal and social learning one has to study it directly. He writes:

> The price paid for over-much experimentation with animals is to neglect the fact that human subjects are brighter, are able to use language—*and probably learn differently because of these advances over lower animals*. It is time that we reinterpret what we mean by comparative psychology. . . . A peculiar twist is sometimes given to psychological thinking which takes the form that a process, in order to be scientifically reputable, must be demonstrated to occur in lower animals. If it occurs only in man, it is excused away because man possesses verbal or related abilities. It would be better to reverse the viewpoint: *only if a process demonstrable in human learning can also be demonstrated in lower animals is the comparative method useful in studying it*.[7]

The view that there are two or more kinds of learning is suggested in another way by Razran,[8] who argues that "The view that learning existing on this planet for hundreds of millions of years has continued in one quantitative continuum without evolving any new qualitatively distinct level seems very unlikely and discouraging." Razran suggests that there are higher and lower levels of learn- ing, and that although the higher levels tend to dominate the lower, the lower persist in the higher. Razran, basing his remarks on ex- periments with human subjects, distinguishes between perceptual and nonperceptual learning, equating the latter with simple con- ditioning. The former, he argues, involves simple conditioning plus perceptual or cognitive factors and is thus qualitatively different. He proposes that the assumption that outside reinforcement is a *sine qua non* of learning is incorrect.

The applicability of work with lower, or nonperceptual, types of learning to some human problems, especially in the therapeutic field, has already been demonstrated. For example, a technique for dealing with nocturnal enuresis (bed-wetting) has been developed. Apparatus was designed so that when the bed of the sleeper is wet the closing of an electrical circuit rings a bell, awakening the sleep- ing person. Repetition of this procedure brings about an effective cure of enuresis in a relatively short time. The technique, based as it is upon simple conditioned-response models, is especially inter- esting in relation to psychoanalytic theories of enuresis, which attribute it to unconscious motivations.

The type of learning involved here is below the perceptual level. In higher types of learning involving cognitive, perceptual, and other processes which are linked with verbal processes, the con- ditioned-response model usually does not work as well. The die-hard behaviorist tends to shy away from this more complex type of learning because it is difficult to control the factors involved and because the consideration of verbal behavior seems to him to lead one back to the "subjective." Probably it is better to face this issue squarely by paying more direct attention to the verbal reports and conceptual processes of the human subject. Verbal behavior is as real as any other behavior, and it is absurd to close one's eyes to it. Learning theory must assuredly take it into account, and this is being increasingly recognized. The ferment of discussion and self- criticism now going on among psychologists suggests that learning theory will expand its horizons to include a more satisfactory ac- count of the complex learning with which social psychologists are directly concerned. When this happens, the solid experimental basis of current learning theory may prove to be of considerable value. An essential feature of a learning theory of the future should be the inclusion of evidence concerning behavior that cannot be studied in the laboratory. The idea that evidence is not evidence unless it is obtained in the laboratory is clearly an illusion not supported by the history of science.

Summary

The body of learning theory exemplified in the field of experimental psychology is based mainly upon experiments with lower animals and to a much lesser extent upon laboratory study of simple types of human learning. Our attention has been focused primarily upon reinforcement theories, which center around the concepts of the conditioned response and the stimulus-response bond. In order to bring out the difficulties of applying or extending this kind of learning theory to complex human behavior, drug addiction and other kinds of addiction were discussed. (Many other examples might have been used.) Finally, it was suggested that there are levels of learning and that the lower are included in the higher. However, since the higher tend to dominate the lower, just as the lower may interfere with or influence the higher, it was contended that a proper understanding of complex social learning requires close consideration of conceptual processes. The highest levels of learning probably involve new principles and require new techniques of investigation. Many of these points are being given increasing emphasis by learning theorists themselves.

SUGGESTIONS FOR DISCUSSION AND SPECIAL REPORTS

1. Review one of the learning theories currently popular among psychologists and consider its applicability to human behavior.

2. Report on B. F. Skinner's utopia—in his book entitled *Walden II*—and indicate how his conception of an ideal society was influenced by his learning theory.

3. Describe the Alcoholics Anonymous movement and explain its apparent success.

4. Report on some of the main theories as to why people become alcoholics. What does each theory assume about learning?

5. Do you agree with the suggestion made in this chapter that human beings become addicted to food very much as drug addicts become addicted to drugs?

6. Interview a number of people to find out if there is a social context to becoming addicted to cigarette smoking; and if so, analyze this context.

NOTES

[1] Adapted from W. W. Lambert, "Stimulus-Response Contiguity and Reinforcement Theory in Social Psychology," in G. Lindzey (ed.), *Handbook of Social Psychology*, Addison Wesley, 1954, pp. 59-60.

[2] O. H. Mowrer, *Learning Theory and Personality Dynamics*, Ronald, 1950, p. 211.

[3] D. O. Hebb, *The Organization of Behavior*, Wiley, 1949, pp. 200-206.

[4] S. D. S. Spragg, "Morphine Addiction in Chimpanzees," *Com Psych. Monograph*, 15(1940).

[5] Hebb, *op. cit.*, p. 199.

[6] H. S. Becker, "Becoming a Marihuana User," *Am. J. Soc.*, 5 (1953): 235-242.

[7] E. R. Hilgard, *Theories of Learning*, Appleton-Century-Crofts 1948, p. 329.

[8] G. Razran, "Conditioning and Perception," *Psych. Rev.*, 6 (1955): 93.

SELECTED BIBLIOGRAPHY

Becker, H. S., "Becoming a Marihuana User," *Am. J. Soc.*, 59(1953) 235-252. A sociological research report from the point of view expressed in this chapter.

Hebb, D. O., *The Organization of Behavior*, Wiley, 1949. In this book there are many astute and original observations on various kinds of learning and on learning theory. The author is a physiological psychologist.

Hilgard, E. R., *Theories of Learning*, Appleton-Century-Crofts, 1948. A comprehensive summary and critical evaluation of various types of learning theory.

Hull, C. L., *Principles of Behavior*, Appleton-Century-Crofts, 1943. Hull presents his theory here in a formal and systematic manner.

Lambert, W. W., in G. Lindzey (ed.), *Handbook of Social Psychology*, Cambridge, Mass.: Addison-Wesley, Vol. 1, "Stimulus-Response Contiguity and Reinforcement Theory in Social Psychology," pp. 57-90. A useful review.

Lindesmith, A. R., *Opiate Addiction*, Evanston, Ill.: Principia Press, 1955, Part I is on the social psychology of the drug habit.

Miller, N. E., and J. Dollard, *Social Learning and Imitation*, Yale University Press, 1941. Learning theory is combined with clinical and experimental concepts.

Mowrer, O. H., *Learning Theory and Personality Dynamics*, Ronald, 1950. Applications of learning theory to human behavior are suggested at the same time that modifications of the theory are proposed to make it more useful.

Skinner, B. F., *Science and Human Behavior*, Macmillan, 1953. The author of one of the most popular reinforcement type learning theories presents his views, and extends them to all human behavior.

Spragg, S. D. S., "Morphine Addiction in Chimpanzees," *Gent. Psych. Monographs*, 15(1940). Compare with A. R. Lindesmith, "Can Chimpanzees Become Morphine Addicts?" *J. Comp. Psych.*, 39(1946): 109-117.

Tolman, E. C., "A Stimulus-Expectancy Need-Cathexis Psychology," *Science*, 101(1945): 160-166. A paper by a leading learning psychologist.

PART 4

SOCIALIZATION

CHAPTER 12 · · ·

Roles

THE DAY IS SUNDAY: a group of people are seated in quiet rows, inside a large cool building, listening to a speaker. The speaker's manner of speech is half entreaty, half condemnation; he is talking of sin, God, and morality. The behavior of the persons involved in this scene is incomprehensible unless one recognizes that this is a church service, and that everybody is acting out a conventional part. In church, members sit quietly in pews and listen or give the appearance of listening. They do not raise their hands to ask questions, to argue with the minister, or to make extemporaneous speeches. There is a fairly definite "churchgoer's" role that is assigned churchgoers in our society, which is played no less rigorously in church than if the scene were enacted upon a stage. Correspondingly, the American Protestant minister acts out a part or role. This entails watching over the morals of his members, admonishing wrongdoers, and entreating parishioners to adhere to traditional standards of conduct. In other situations, the minister may play other roles—lover, husband, parent—but in church on Sunday his behavior is guided and shaped by his ministerial office.

A church service is not the only situation in which human beings

371

play roles; nor is religious behavior the only behavior that is incomprehensible to an observer unless he knows what roles are being enacted. An individual's conduct during the course of a day is largely the performance of a series of roles in a variety of situations. Man is, par excellence, a role-playing organism. This fact has important, even decisive, implications for his life as a human being.

Origins of the Role Concept

The general idea of role is borrowed from the drama. Despite the fact that real-life situations are not worked out according to a script or other rigid prescription, human interaction may be conceived in terms of the dramatic model, with its accompanying notions of actors playing parts, of social situations or scenes, a plot, a script, or a prescription for concerted action, and a certain degree of improvisation that may take place within the parts. In the last twenty years or so this particular model has become highly influential in sociology, anthropology, and social psychology. It has, of course, been used implicitly or casually by historians and other social scientists for many generations.

Two bodies of thought employing the role concept have contributed to theories in social psychology. Each has stressed the role idea in a different context. Anthropologists and sociologists who have been interested in communication and the interrelationships of institutions have needed a term to indicate the relation of individual activities to the larger organization of society. Hence they have linked "role" with institutional terms like "status," "position," and "office." The emphasis here is on systems of interrelated roles, such as those embodied in kinship systems, occupational structures, and age grading. The norms and rules governing these role systems are among the chief matters of concern. One of the most influential contemporary sociological theorists, Parsons, has given the concept of role a central place in his theoretical scheme and has used it in making analyses of such areas of investigation as American kinship, social stratification, age and sex differences, and the nature of professions. He speaks of role as follows:

> Social structure is a patterned system of the social relationships of actors. It is a distinctive feature of the structure of systems of social action, however, that in most relationships the actor does not participate as a total entity, but only by virtue of a given differentiated "sector" of his total action. Such a sector ... has come predominantly to be called a "role." ... Role is the concept which links the sub-system of the actor as a "psychological" behaving entity to the distinctively *social* structure ... institutionalized roles constitute the mechanisms by which extremely varied potentialities of "human nature" become integrated in such a way as to dovetail into a single integrated system capable of meeting the situational exigencies with which the society and its members are faced.[1]

The emphasis in Parsons' work, as in much anthropology and institutional sociology, is on social systems; only secondary attention is given to individuals.

The other route through which role has entered sociological theory has been the attempt to trace the mechanism by which concerted group action takes place without recourse to instinctive mechanisms. Group action used to be accounted for by reference to such outmoded concepts as imitation, gregariousness, herd instinct, and consciousness of kind, or to such mystical or transcendental constructs as group mind, ethos, and *Volkgeist*, or folk spirit. Instinctivist and other individualistic conceptions of group action explained it by reference to forces located solely in individual organisms, whereas the transcendentalists ignored individuals and placed the sources of societal behavior in postulated superorganic realms of one kind or another.

These kinds of explanation were part of a broader philosophic attempt to account for the relationships existing between man and society. Certain philosophers, especially the American pragmatists, attacked this problem by denying any radical separation of organism and environment and of individual and society. This set the task of developing concepts which would be neither individualistic nor supraindividualistic. Through the writing of George Mead, the concept of role was introduced to meet this problem. Unlike the institutionalists, Mead used "role" to describe the processes of cooperative behavior and of communication, not to illuminate the functioning of institutions.

Both of these streams of thought have enriched sociological theory and have helped counteract elementaristic and individualistic theories of social behavior by introducing a situational slant and a social dimension into the consideration of individual behavior. In turn, social psychologists coming from the individualistically oriented traditions of general psychology have adopted the role concept in order to give a greater place to cultural and social influences.

From even this brief sketch of its history, the reader can realize that the concept of role is mainly an orienting, or organizing, one. Its chief function has been to indicate a general approach to behavior. Despite the popularity of the concept there is considerable disagreement as to definitions, however. As Neiman and Hughes[2] have pointed out: "The concept, role, is at present still rather vague, nebulous, and non-definitive."

Close scrutiny of social interaction shows that it is difficult to subsume all acts under role concepts. For example, a role analysis of even a short conversation between an interviewer and a subject would necessarily omit many complexities and nuances of the interaction. In addition, many aspects of the organization of individual behavior cannot be handled in terms of roles, except possibly when other concepts are employed supplementarily. Research based on role theory has not noticeably diminished the ambiguity of the concept. Nevertheless, the role concept has undoubtedly been a useful organizing idea and has led to important insights.

Roles and Social Structure

TRADITIONAL ROLES

In homogeneous and relatively stable societies, most roles are traditional. It is hard for an American to grasp the full extent to which the general outline of life in such a society is prefigured. The child can begin early to see what he is to become, and the old person sees in the young an image of what he once was. In such societies training for roles is effective and rather simple.

Every group has names for some of its more traditional roles. These names indicate offices, jobs, tasks, leadership functions, deviant and other disapproved behavior, privileged positions, status, age, and so on. These traditional roles are often covered by law and formal contract, but always by informal agreement and codes. A distinction is commonly made in the literature between status and role, the former referring to the person's position and the latter to the behavior associated with that position. Statuses, and the associated role-playing, are often evaluated in terms of their importance and the prestige associated with them. Sociological and anthropological analyses are frequently concerned with this evaluation and its bases.

"Situations" become "defined" in the course of group activities. The definitions and the role-responses that they call for become part of the learning patterns of group members; they become, in other words, part of the tradition.[3] They are then passed on to newcomers, such as children who have to be taught the proper responses to make under certain defined conditions: at the table, when going to bed, when playing with other children, and so on. This has prompted the anthropologist Linton to write:

> All societies devote a great deal of time and energy to training their younger members in what they should do under various hypothetical conditions. Children are instructed not only in the behavior which will be adequate in various situations, but also in the cues by which these situations are to be recognized . . . the individual comes to practically all new situations forearmed with a knowledge of the behavior patterns which other members of his society have developed and tested.[4]

Entrance into any group requires that the roles peculiar to that group be learned. For example, newly drafted soldiers are keenly aware, although they may not phrase it in these terms, that they have to learn a whole set of new roles which army life demands of its members. College students will recall that they underwent a similar experience when first entering college. Participation in any new group involves "learning the ropes." These we learn by diverse methods: watching other people act, by imitation, formal instruction, informal chatting, through reading, and so on. ⟩

RIGIDLY AND LOOSELY DEFINED ROLES

Roles differ greatly in the degree of rigorousness or laxity with which they are defined. Thus, such ritualistic roles as those of bride and groom during the wedding ceremony are prescribed in an extremely narrow and inflexible manner. In some social groupings weddings are usually rehearsed beforehand to insure that everyone knows his part. Roles that derive from being "in office" are also rigorously and formally defined. The Queen of England, the President of the United States, army officers, officers of corporations, and others who hold offices find that their behavior, their powers, rights, duties, and obligations, may all be very carefully formulated and even written into constitutions, charters, and other documents. The powers and actions of the ruler of England, for example, are effectively controlled and rigorously circumscribed by an elaborate body of tradition, written and unwritten. When roles are a part of closely articulated institutional structures, they are likely to be specifically and rigidly defined.

At the other end of the scale are roles which are defined only within very broad limits. The behavior associated with these roles is permitted to vary greatly. Thus, the conduct of American parents toward their children is generally expected to meet certain basic requirements; but otherwise wide differences are allowed. The same may be said of American marital roles.

Max Weber has given a clear general statement of the roles characteristically found in bureaucracies. We reproduce part of it because it represents a relatively extreme example of the specific and rigid prescription of behavior.

Modern officialdom functions in the following specific manner:
I. There is the principle of fixed and official jurisdictional areas, which are generally ordered by rules, that is, by laws or administrative regulations.

1. The regular activities required for the purposes of the bureaucratically governed structure are distributed in a fixed way as official duties.

LEARNING TO PLAY ROLES

"Let's play you're a guest, and I'll think of ways of trying to get rid of you." (Copyright 1947 The New Yorker Magazine, Inc. Reproduced by permission.)

2. The authority to give the commands required for the discharge of these duties is distributed in a stable way and is strictly delimited by rules concerning the coercive means, physical, sacerdotal, or otherwise, which may be placed at the disposal of officials.

3. Methodical provision is made for the regular and continuous fulfillment of these duties and for the execution of the corresponding rights; only persons who have the generally regulated qualifications to serve are employed. . . .

II. The principles of office hierarchy and of levels of graded authority mean a firmly ordered system of super- and subordination in which there is a supervision of the lower offices by the higher ones. Such a system offers the governed the possibility of appealing the decision of a lower office to its higher authority, in a definitely regulated manner. . . .

. . . Once established and having fulfilled its task, an office tends to continue in existence and be held by another incumbent.

III. The management of the modern office is based upon written documents ("the files"), which are preserved in their original or draught form. There is, therefore, a staff of subaltern officials and scribes of all sorts. The body of officials actively engaged in a "public" office, along with the respective apparatus of material implements and the files, make up a "bureau." In private enterprise, "the bureau" is often called "the office." . . .

IV. Office management, at least all specialized office management—and such management is distinctly modern—usually presupposes thorough and expert training. . . .

VI. The management of the office follows general rules, which are more or less stable, more or less exhaustive, and which can be learned. Knowledge of these rules represents a special technical learning which the officials possess. It involves jurisprudence, or administrative or business management.

The reduction of modern office management to rules is deeply embedded in its very nature. . . .

The personal position of the official is patterned in the following way:

Whether he is in a private office or a public bureau, the modern official always strives and usually enjoys a distinct *social esteem* as compared with the governed. His social position is guaranteed by the prescriptive rules of rank order and, for the political official, by special definitions of the criminal code against "insults of officials" and "contempt" of state and church authorities. . . .

The pure type of bureaucratic official is *appointed* by a superior authority. An official elected by the governed is not a purely bureaucratic figure. . . .

The official receives the regular *pecuniary* compensation of a normally fixed *salary* and the old age security provided by a pension. The salary is not measured like a wage in terms of work done, but according to "status," that is, according to the kind of function (the "rank") and, in addition, possibly, according to the length of service. . . .

The official is set for a "career" within the hierarchical order of the public service. He moves from the lower, less important, and lower paid to the higher positions. The average official naturally desires a mechanical fixing of the conditions of promotion; if not of the offices, at least of the salary levels. He wants these conditions fixed in terms of "seniority," or possibly according to grades achieved in a developed system of expert examinations. . . .[5]

GENERAL AND SEGMENTAL ROLES

In every society there are certain general behavior systems which broadly define and limit the conduct of the members of that society. Each of these larger systems of behavior may be broken down into a series of more specific subordinate systems.

Thus, there is a general definition and there are certain broad expectations connected with the fact that one is a male or a female. The requirements of the masculine role call for a differentiation of little-boy and little-girl behavior. In adolescence the masculine role is defined in another way, and after marriage in still other ways. In adolescence it involves learning the etiquette of courting, dating, and dancing as well as training for the role of breadwinner. In marriage, the requirements become more exacting. The youth becomes a husband, perhaps a father. He enters, or has entered, an occupation and begins to participate as an adult in community affairs. As his children grow up his role continues to change. Different kinds of behavior are expected from young, middle-aged, and older men. The feminine role is, of course, another such general role which can be divided into a number of parts. We may call these smaller parts "specific" or "segmental" roles.

Another general role which influences the lives of many members of society and colors the entire texture of social relations is that prescribed by the dominant values or ideals of a society. Thus, some societies emphasize philosophic wisdom, others the military virtues; still others place a high value upon scientific or artistic accomplishment. Whatever ideal is accepted compels the individual, if the ideal is to be realized, to follow a certain line of behavior that involves an entire complex of interwoven subsidiary roles.

No role ever stands in isolation, but presupposes and is related to counter-roles with which it is interlocked in more inclusive systems. This can be made clear by a commonplace example of interaction. In a self-service grocery store, the customer brings his selections to the counter; there he is waited on by the store's representative, the cashier. The cashier notes the prices, totals them, and packages the goods; the purchaser then pays in cash, receiving change if entitled to it. The purchaser is then permitted to leave the store with his purchases, and the cashier puts the money away in the cash register. The roles of the two actors in this miniature drama obviously are related to each other; each person has both a conception of the other actor's role and a conception of his own role as he thinks the other sees it. Roles and counter-roles have sometimes been referred to as "ego" and "alter."

Even when only two people are involved in a social episode, there may be more than a single counter-role; that is, one or both of the actors may take absent others into account.

If we were to use the playwright's imagery, we would say that although there are only two main actors on the stage, there are also other actors who are visible only to the audience or to one or the other of the main actors. Thus, one of the actors acting toward a second, may in actuality also be playing toward an invisible third, much as if the latter were actually present. To make the matter more complicated, if actor A is representing a group in an official role with respect to actor B, then in a real sense the entire group should be on the stage: so that when

A makes a commendable statement they could nod in collective approval, and then A would as much respond to them as to B. There are thus also supplementary actors [who] . . . make exits and entrances, fade in and out of the immediate circle of conversation as they become relevant or irrelevant to the action. They may be fictional persons, deities, or persons who have died.[6]

The organization of related roles into wider systems is what is meant by the "structure of society" insofar as one sees social relations in terms of roles. A kinship system is such a system of interlocking roles. Since interaction involves the imaginative taking of others' roles, we may note in passing that counter-roles are to some extent internalized. For example, a policeman may never enact the criminal role, but he knows the criminal's general point of view.

Another example that will indicate the complicated nature of the relationship between role and counter-role is provided by a study of school superintendents.[7] A school superintendent must take into account teachers, principals, pupils, the community at large, PTA's, other superintendents, politicians, community officials, and others. He must take them into account not only as he thinks they impinge upon him, but as they may affect each other.

DISCOVERY OF ROLES

Except for those rigidly prescribed roles that are commonly referred to as "ritualistic," most roles necessarily allow considerable scope for individual initiative and discovery.

There is often a degree of tolerance for, and even appreciation of, individual differences in performance. When the role-player comes to the role as a naïve learner, it is obvious that no one can tell him beforehand of all the potential demands, obligations, and expectations that will be associated with it. But even when he has had experience with a given type of role, he must explore the limitations and possibilities of a new one of the same type, as when an official in one business corporation moves into a similarly or identically named position in another. The fact that the old and new positions are basically alike does not relieve him of the obligation to find out what new kinds of demands will be made upon him by his new associates, or what demands he can make on others. The advice offered him on the basis of his predecessor's experience may be appropriate in general outline but quite inappropriate in particulars, since not only will the new incumbent establish unique relationships with his alters, but he may be stepping into a situation in which the crucial element is that he is succeeding someone. Truman's assumption of the Presidency after Franklin D. Roosevelt's death is a good example of this.

PERSONAL DEFINITIONS

Anthropologists who have studied small, relatively stable societies generally emphasize that definitions are group made. The student who investigates behavior in more complex and changing societies must qualify that view by noting two relevant points: (1) the society or community in which a person lives presents him with a strictly limited set of alternatives, allowing him to choose among them; (2) often the individual is compelled to work out his own conception of a situation when a ready-made, socially prescribed one is not at hand.

These two points may be clarified through illustrations. If an American Protestant husband falls in love with a woman other than his wife, several alternative lines of action are open to him. In order of social acceptability, he may (1) remain faithful to his wife and reject the other woman, (2) divorce his wife and marry the other woman, or (3) make the woman his mistress without divorcing his wife. Other alternatives, such as killing his wife or marrying the second woman while remaining married to the first, are prohibited by law and custom.

As an example of a situation not taken care of by social definition, we may call attention to that created by artificial insemination. What should a child, conceived in this manner, be told when he grows up? How should the husband of the woman who bears the child view the situation, and how should he feel toward the child? These and other personal problems arising in an undefined situation of this kind must clearly be faced, at first, as uniquely individual problems to be worked out by those concerned. If the originally unique problem arises repeatedly, as appears to be happening, law and custom are likely eventually to provide conventional solutions and prescriptions for it.

The manner in which personal definitions of situations are worked out, however, is never wholly original and unique, since the individual necessarily deals with new situations in terms of models derived from previous experience. The concepts which he employs in his analysis and the value system according to which he weighs various alternatives are derived from the groups to which he belongs. Thus, we may say that no definition of a situation can ever be entirely personal, at the same time recognizing that no system of social requirements and taboos ever purports to regulate all behavior.

Role-Playing as Process

VERBAL ORGANIZATION OF RESPONSES

We have up to this point considered roles from a structural standpoint. This in itself does not illuminate the processes of enacting roles. As compared with the amount of attention that has been paid to the former problem, little has been given to the latter. Nevertheless, it is an issue of central significance.

The first chapters of this book have developed the position that language is indispensable to the organization of action. The communication process, therefore, lies at the heart of any discussion of role-playing, since roles involve the complex organization of behavior through verbal means.

Human systems of response, graded in terms of complexity, range from the simple reflex at one end of the scale to the role at the other end. Reflex acts are relatively simple unlearned response systems. They are largely automatic or involuntary, which means that they are subject to little voluntary, or cerebral, control. They can be almost completely described in terms of the organism alone. As we move up the scale in complexity of response systems, it becomes increasingly difficult, and finally impossible, to describe responses by referring to the organism alone. It becomes necessary to view

BEHAVIOR SYSTEMS: SIMPLE TO COMPLEX

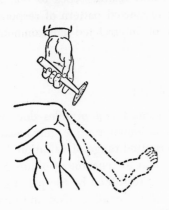

Reflex	*Role*
1. Within organism.	1. Involves interrelationships between organism and other organisms and between organism and environment.
2. Little connection with cortex.	2. Cortex involved and of central importance.
3. Inherited.	3. Learned through verbal communication.
4. Largely nonvoluntary.	4. Largely voluntary.
5. Nonsocial.	5. Socially defined.

them as relationships or as interaction between organism and environment, or between organism and other organisms. Moreover, the more complex the system the higher in general is the degree of cerebral involvement and the greater the part played by learning. The concept of role refers to the most intricately organized patterns of response of which the human organism is capable, *i.e.,* to verbally organized systems of response to an organized, sub-divided, and patterned environment.

All living organisms respond to stimuli or cues, but man's modes of response are organized in terms of the verbal classification of cues. It is for this reason that human beings are forever "defining situations," *i.e.*, naming, classifying, and relating cues to one an-other. The role is an example of an organized pattern of responses made to constellations or clusters of interrelated environmental stimuli.

CHARACTERISTICS OF ROLE BEHAVIOR

It has been emphasized that the enactment of roles does not usually involve a single unvarying continuous routine, but consists of a wide variety of acts within a permitted range of variation. The pattern is discontinuous, in the sense that the enactment of any role is extended in time and is likely to be interrupted by the playing of other roles. This diversity and range of action are unified and given continuity by the individual's controlling conception to which all the phases of the role are referred.

The individual is rather continuously engaged in communication with himself as he enacts his roles. To begin with, he must know or try to figure out what his part in the situation is or should be. This involves making a self-identification, in terms of which par-ticular responses are evoked or suppressed. Every individual has a multiplicity of separate responses at his command. At any given time he could, theoretically, be engaged in any one of them. Role expectations and demands require that he make certain responses at certain times and places and in certain sequences, sometimes whether he wants to or not. (Both teacher and students, for exam-ple, get up for an early-morning class when all of them could easily think of more attractive things to do.) The individual's conception of his role has a controlling function over responses in that it deter-mines which specific responses will be evoked. In the classroom, for example, both teacher and students suppress inappropriate and irrelevant responses which occur to them as possibilities, thus reinforcing each other in appropriate classroom behavior.

Since roles usually have considerable duration in time, responses must be organized in sequences and phases. This requires a continuous reassessment of where the action stands, where it is leading, and its probable consequences. Also required, as George Mead[8] has pointed out in detail, is an indication to one's self of how one's next action will appear to others. In short, an internalized conversation provides an organizing frame for the performance of roles. In the enactment of roles the following are essential:

1. an identification of self;
2. behavior in given situations which is appropriate to this identification;
3. a background of related acts by others (counter-roles) which serve as cues to guide specific performance;
4. an evaluation by the individual, and by others, of the role enactment.

DEFINING THE SITUATION

Implicit in our discussion throughout is the fundamental idea that role-playing occurs in episodes, scenes, or situations. These have to be recognized, named, and catalogued by the individual in order that appropriate action may be taken. No two situations are ever exactly alike, but there is often enough resemblance between the present situation and one formerly encountered to permit it to be recognized and thus to give rise to orderly and regular behavior. Many situations can be immediately "tabbed" because they are routine, or traditional, or familiar. "Sensing the situation" means that one immediately gears himself to it. At the other pole, many situations are problematic and subject to different interpretations. Definition of situations, both familiar and new, is the interpretation of a multitude of cues.

In a problematic situation, action may have to be delayed while one searches for the relevant clues as to its nature, or one may act tentatively without committing oneself in order to elicit further clues. In any case, one never sees the total situation as an omniscient being, or a playwright, might see it. The individual can only perceive what his abilities, categories, and interests lead or enable him to see.

The situation he assesses is one that he has selectively defined, in terms of his experience, his habit of response, his intellectual grasp, and his emotional engrossment in it. The dynamic assessment limits the situation by excluding all the numerous aspects that are not apprehended as relevant to the choice between alternatives. At the same time it includes in the situation various aspects that are not objectively given, that would not be listed in any merely physical inventory . . . it envisages the situation as impregnated with values and susceptible of new potential values.[9]

As MacIver indicates in the quoted passage above, the situation is not a mere physical inventory of external data. It includes, besides one's own values and motives, those which are imputed to others. No hard and fast lines can be drawn between the definition of a situation and the behavior thought to be appropriate to it. Any definition necessarily implies and carries with it a plan of action. One does not usually name the situation and then sequentially decide what to do. Defining the situation and exploring alternative courses of action usually occur simultaneously. These processes are often tied up with a review of preceding events and a reinterpretation of them and of past lines of action.

TAKING OTHERS' ROLES

Imaginatively assuming the position or point of view of another person will be spoken of here as "role-taking" to distinguish it from "role-playing," the larger organization of acts of which role-taking is an integral part. Taking the role of the other, as we have already indicated, is implicit in virtually all intercommunication on the symbolic level. A person, by imagining or actually using the gestures, postures, word, and intonations of someone else and by drawing upon his understanding of that person from past experience, evokes in himself responses which approximate those of the other person. He thus "feels" his way into the other's views, and by so doing makes predictions about the other's behavior. As we pointed out in the chapter on motivation, he is greatly assisted in this process by knowledge of others' motives and of the symbols and values in terms of which they act.

"Empathy" and "identification" are conventional psychological terms which have also been used to refer to role-taking. Sometimes the process is confused with feeling "sympathy." Identification with another person, as for example with a fictitious person on the screen or in a novel, may produce a feeling of sympathy or it may not. Role-taking may be a preliminary step in exploiting the other person or in outwitting him. Opposing generals on war fronts try to project themselves into the enemy's situation and views in order to defeat him, not to sympathize with him. In order to interact effectively and realistically with other persons, even in hostile relations, it is necessary to put oneself into their shoes. However, Coutu has noted that:

> Too efficient role-taking, putting oneself in the place of one's victim, might prevent a policeman from making an arrest, a soldier from bayoneting an enemy, or a surgeon from operating on a patient. . . . professional training is designed to inhibit *role-taking* ability so that the role can be properly played.[10]

What Coutu is pointing to is either a lack of sympathy for the victim or a deliberate suppression of genuine feelings of sympathy and identity.

Another way of describing role-taking is to speak of it as "as if" behavior. A person thinks or acts for a time "as if" he were someone else. This process is close to but not identical with pretense. One who pretends to be something other than what he is, is impersonating; and if his audience is unaware of what he is doing, he is, in a sense, lying. The actor on the stage, however, is known to the audience to be an actor and may win acclaim for his performance of villainous roles. Persons who are skillful at identifying themselves with others are credited with an understanding of people, a shrewd appreciation of human nature, or insight into people. A German philosopher, Hans Vaihinger, erected an entire system of philosophy based on this idea in a book entitled, *The Philosophy of "As If."*[11] He contended that, in a world where knowledge is grossly incomplete, most human behavior, including even the thinking of scientists, must proceed as if this were not the case. We are concerned here with the application to social interaction of this idea of "as if."

The "as if" behavior of taking roles, as Sarbin[12] has pointed out, involves two distinguishable elements: (1) a hypothetical assumption ("Suppose I were John Doe") and (2) a consideration of the consequences of the assumption ("What would I think and do if I were John Doe?"). The first establishes a set, or an idea. This idea must then be held in mind as it is elaborated in specific acts. This process may be illustrated by the way in which military commanders of opposing forces in a war seek to anticipate each other's actions and to "outguess" each other.

The idea of role-taking has found an interesting therapeutic application in the "psychodrama" (and "sociodrama") of Moreno.[13] In psychodrama, an individual who has trouble in his relations with people, as for example one member of a married pair, is encouraged to act out on an actual stage with auxiliary actors (known as "alters" or "alter egos") certain crucial scenes from his married life. This "action therapy," like the prolonged psychoanalytic interview, is said to give the individual new conceptions of his marital situation. It presumably does this by putting the person in the position of an actor and also, in a sense, that of a stage director in charge of a real-life drama in which he himself is deeply involved. The individual is thus compelled to perceive the roles of himself and his marriage partner in new ways, and hence sees his marriage in a new light. The very fact that a family quarrel is moved onto a stage and treated as drama tends to lead the involved persons to view the quarrel, and their parts in it, more objectively. Other devices with similar purposes include playing back tape recordings of interviews or conversations for comment and analysis.

THE CHILD'S EGOCENTRISM

Since taking the roles of others is a skill which must be learned and one which requires some degree of mastery of language, it is not surprising that children do not have this ability at birth and that its gradual development can be traced.

The most extensive and convincing empirical report of the way in which children gradually learn to take into account the points of view of others has been given by Piaget. In a series of books, Piaget[14] has demonstrated and documented what he has called the "egocentric" character of childish thought. The entire intellectual development of the child—from the time at which he can speak with relative adequacy to the point at which he acquires an approximately adult view of himself and the world—is described as a gradual process of overcoming this initial egocentric tendency.

The child is at first enclosed in his own point of view and sees all things from within it. His perceptions and judgments tend to be "absolute," or egocentric, because he is unaware of any other points of view and perceptions. Thus, Piaget points out, most young children of five or so believe quite firmly that the sun and moon follow them as they walk about. At this age the child is not troubled by the logical difficulties which would confront the adult. He does not attempt to account for the many sudden changes in direction of the movement of moon and sun, or to account for the way in which these bodies may appear to other people who are moving in various other directions. His conviction arises from his own perception of movement. Because perspectives other than his own are not taken into account, his own perceptions appear absolute—the only possible ones.

Another illustration is furnished by the child's difficulty in making proper use of such terms as "brother" and "sister." Thus, John and Paul are brothers, aged four and five respectively. If we ask Paul how many brothers he has, he may say "One" or he may say "Two, counting me." If he has decided that he is not his own brother, and is asked how many brothers his brother John has, he usually denies that John has any. By questioning Paul we may sometimes induce him to say that there are either one, two, or three brothers in his family.

Five-year-old Paul's confusion over the significance of the term "brother" arises because the word refers to different persons when he and John use it. Paul is fairly clear about the fact that John is his brother. But because he views the situation absolutely rather than relatively, he becomes confused when required to take any point of view other than his own. He cannot view the family of which he is a part from John's standpoint.

This is another illustration of the young child's egocentricity:

> What will happen when it is a question of imagining distant objects, and of co-ordinating the perspectives of different observers? ... The child is placed opposite a small model of three

mountains, and given a certain number of colored pictures of these mountains; he is then asked which of the pictures show the mountains from the positions occupied successively by a doll on the mountains in the model. The function of age in this development of these reactions is very clear. The little ones do not understand that the observer sees the same mountains quite differently from different points of view, and hence they consider their own perspective absolute. But the older ones discover the relativity necessary to objectivity, after a number of systematic errors due to the difficulty of co-ordinating the relationships in question.[15]

The egocentrism of young children is also reflected in their play activities. Parten[16] notes that "since the young children lack the power of expressing themselves with language, they have difficulty in playing in cooperative groups." Young children playing in the sandpile usually do not really play together, although they are fond of playing in company; older children, however, are likely to play together cooperatively. Another investigator, Bridges,[17] has noted that "two-year-olds usually play or work by themselves with little reference to others except to claim their toys or otherwise interfere with them. . . . Older children engage more often in group play than younger ones and seldom play alone." These and other investigations indicate that as children grow older they learn to play cooperatively; and that in the earlier years, although the child may like to play in the presence of others, he does not in a genuine sense play *with* them. Because the child does not at first grasp the roles of others and because he lacks an adequate time perspective, he tends to act in terms of short-range egocentric goals. His ideas of fair play and of the "rules" are inadequate or absolutistic.

THE DECLINE OF EGOCENTRISM

As a consequence of entering into more extensive and complex social relations, the child eventually becomes aware of the points of view of other persons. He learns that these are often at variance with his own and that they must be taken into account. He learns that though he has a brother, his brother also has a brother (himself); that a pebble is light in weight from one point of view, but heavy from another point of view; that an object may be to the left of one object, but at the same time to the right of another; and so on. His thinking becomes relativistic. He then comes to realize that the sun follows neither him nor anyone else. He learns to conceive of it as the center of a solar system and thinks of the earth as one of several spherical bodies revolving about the sun. When he has achieved this mature point of view, we may say that he has, in a sense, synthesized virtually all conceivable views of the sun as a physical object and can assume the perspective of anyone in any location with respect to it.

Learning to grasp other points of view—learning to become non-egocentric—does not occur overnight. The process is gradual. Piaget places the age of transition at approximately seven, on the average, but some English and American investigators have challenged this. Presumably the age of transition, besides being different in different individuals, also varies from society to society, class to class, and so on. Presumably, too, a child might remain relatively egocentric in some respects and achieve somewhat greater maturity in others. The important point is not the exact age at which egocentricity disappears, but that the disappearance is gradual.

G. H. Mead has described graphically how children playfully imitate the roles of elders or associates and thus gradually develop an ability to see objects, other persons, and themselves from a non-egocentric standpoint. Mead emphasizes what Piaget merely noted in passing, namely, that language is basic in the development of the ability to play roles.

> [There are] countless forms of play in which the child assumes the roles of the adults about him. The very universal habit of playing with dolls indicates how ready for expressing, in the child, is the parental attitude, or perhaps one should say, certain of the parental attitudes. The long period of dependence of the human infant during which his interest centers in his relations to those who care for him gives a remarkable opportunity for the play back and forth of this sort of taking of the roles of others. . . . In the play of young children, even when they play together, there is abundant evidence of the child's taking different roles in the process; and a solitary child will keep up the process of stimulating himself by his vocal gestures [spoken words] to act in different roles almost indefinitely. . . . A child

plays at being a mother, at being a teacher, at being a policeman; that is, it is taking different roles. . . . We have something
that suggests this in what we call the play of animals: a cat
will play with her kittens, and dogs with each other. . . . But we
do not have in such a situation the . . . taking [of] a definite
role in the sense that a child deliberately takes the role of
another. . . . He plays that he is, for instance, offering himself
something, and he buys it; he gives a letter to himself and takes
it away; he addresses himself as a parent, as a teacher; he
arrests himself as a policeman. He has a set of stimuli which
call out in himself the sort of responses they call out in others.
He takes this group of responses and organizes them into a
certain whole. Such is the simplest form of being another to one's
self. It involves a temporal situation. The child says something
in one character and then his responding in another character is
a stimulus to himself in the first character, and so the conversation goes on. . . . In that early stage [of childhood] he passes
from one role to another just as a whim takes him.[18]

The child's playing at being persons other than himself is
paralleled in actual life by the playing of the real roles in which
he is involved with parents and playmates. One of the theories of
play is that it is a preparation for later adult activity wherein the
individual applies the skills that he has acquired. Thus the standards
of fair play and the proper attitude toward defeat in competition
are often said to be learned on the gridiron or on the "playing fields
of Eton." No doubt it is from considerations of this kind that the
widespread absorption of children (and adults) in comic strips
and comic books concerns and alarms some, who feel that constant
identifications with comic-strip characters of doubtful virtue may
lead the children to emulate these fictional "heroes." Without accepting this position one may recognize that this kind of play activity
and fantasying gives the child a repertoire of roles and practice in
switching from one to the other.

The initial role-taking of the young child is simple and limited,
involving only limited and brief fragments of behavior and the imitation of a few specific persons. As the child's circle of acquaintance-
ship is enlarged, as his mastery of communication develops, and as
his real roles multiply in number and become more complex, the
role-taking processes become more complicated, as we shall see.

Perspectives

THE GENERALIZED OTHER AS AN ORGANIZATION OF OTHERS' ROLES

When the child has developed the ability to grasp the role of one other person at a time, he is on the road to becoming a social being. However, before he can participate in organized adult activity, the child must be able to conceive his own role from the standpoint of all other participants. An illustration will help to make this clear.

Suppose that a group of Air Force men is on a bombing mission. Each man has a definite, assigned general role which involves certain duties and obligations. Each man has a clear conception of his general role as he imagines it from the points of view of all the others. He also has a clear picture of how his own role fits in with the roles of each of the other men.

By contrast, the very young child is able to take the role of only one other person at a time. From this simple kind of role-taking the child eventually develops the ability: (1) to take the roles of others in the situation, (2) to organize these roles into an integrated whole, and (3) to view his own behavior from this standpoint. Mead's suggestion of how this learning takes place is as follows:

> If we contrast play with . . . an organized game, we note the essential difference that the child who plays in a game must be ready to take the attitude of everyone else involved in that game, and that these different roles must have a definite relationship to each other. . . . In a game where a number of individuals are involved . . . the child taking one role must be ready to take the role of everyone else. If he gets in a ball nine he must have the responses of each position involved in his own position. He must know what everyone else is going to do in order to carry out his own play. He has to take all of these roles. They do not all have to be present in consciousness at the same time, but at some moments he has to have three or four individuals present in his own attitude, such as the one who is going to throw the ball, the one who is going to catch it, and so on. . . . The atti-

tudes of the other players which the participant assumes organize into a sort of unit, and it is that organization which controls
the response of the individual. . . . Each of his own acts is
determined by his assumption of the action of the others who
are playing the game . . . he has to have an organization of these
roles; otherwise he cannot play the game.[19]

Through his participation in organized games, in play, and in other
activities, the child learns to take the role of the participants and
grasps the fact that the roles of others are intertwined. At the same
time, he comes to see how his own activity within the situation looks
from the standpoint of the others. He sees his own actions as part
of a whole pattern of group activity.

Mead has coined a term for this organization of others' roles; he
calls it the "generalized other." He uses this expression because it
means that one is taking the related roles of all the other participants
rather than the role of just one other person. This concept of the
generalized other applies to the organized roles of participants
within any defined situation.

The term "generalized" other does not refer to an actual group
of people; but rather to a conception or an interpretation which a
person derives from his experiences. He then regulates his behavior
in terms of these supposed opinions and attitudes of others. He
imagines what "people" would say "if they knew" or what they will
say "when they know." The term "people" may not have any specific
reference to actual persons, but may merely represent his conception
of abstract moral standards. These standards widen as role playing
becomes more generalized.

CONCEPT DEVELOPMENT AND THE
ORGANIZATION OF PERSPECTIVES

The child, like the adult, discriminates between persons, acts,
and things in terms of concepts; but the content of his classifications
is different from what it will be as he grows more knowledgeable.
As new classifications are learned and discovered, old ones change,
are revised and qualified. As the child's conceptualizing ability approaches the adult standard his concepts become more numerous

and their interrelationships more complex. His ability to play roles and to understand the actions and motives of others develops in a parallel course.

The earlier role conceptions of children are, from the adults'

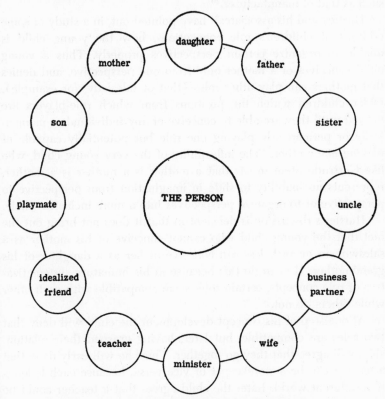

A person learns to look upon his own behavior from the points of view of all these people. He learns their various points of view at different periods in his life, and they have varying importance for the organization of his behavior.

viewpoint, rather curious and often amusing, although in their own way they represent a primitive if incorrect systematization of role. Thus, very young children know there are storekeepers and customers, but they think that the customer buys goods and both he and the storekeeper pay each other. Only the customer buys goods, the storekeeper never does. Monetary activity is confined to buying and selling. Although one storekeeper may help another sell, the distinction between owner and employer is unclear and is not involved in the buying-selling transactions. There are no other roles such as that of manufacturer.[20]

Hartley and his associates[21] have pointed out, in a study of some oddities of children's role conceptions, how the young child is unable to organize certain perspectives properly. Thus a young child conceives of a mother only from one perspective, and denies that mothers can play other roles (that of saleslady, for example). Older children widen the positions from which role-players are viewed until they are able to conceive of any individual as momentarily or permanently playing one role but potentially capable of playing many others. The inflexibility of the very young child, who like Gertrude Stein insists that a mother is a mother is a mother, represents an inability to slide in imagination from perspective to perspective or to organize perspectives into a more inclusive whole.

Hartley's discussion is deficient in that it does not bring out the fact that the young child who cannot conceive of his mother as a saleswoman nevertheless can conceive of her as a daughter of his grandmother. He can do this because in his immature systematization of role concepts, certain roles seem compatible with each other while others do not.

At one step of his concept development the child will deny that two roles are compatible, but later, having grasped their relationship, will agree that they go together. Thus, he will early deny that a teacher can be a storekeeper or vice versa, because each belongs to a different world. Later the child agrees that a teacher could be a storekeeper "after school," but still denies that a storekeeper can be a customer. Still later he sees that a storekeeper can buy in a store and still in a general sense be a storekeeper, but does not yet perceive that the storekeeper must be a customer of manufacturers.

Much of the child's early learning about role relationships occurs in concrete situations where the roles are played out before his eyes. However, most role relationships are rather abstract. Even those relationships that seem most concrete and visible, for example those between a teacher and a pupil, involve much more than is visible on the surface. Greater maturity and breadth of experience are necessary before the child can be expected to understand the subtler aspects of such relationships.

The Generalized Other and Moral Behavior

That generalized others are learned conceptions has two important implications: (1) children do not acquire moral views automatically or mechanically, and (2) even persons belonging to the same groups cannot have identical generalized others. Children are rewarded, punished, and exhorted so that they will conform to adult expectations. However, every parent knows that learning is not a rubber-stamp process and that one cannot mechanically or forcibly inculcate adult ideas into a child.

The concept of the generalized other has been mildly criticized by Mills[22] on the grounds that it implies too great homogeneity and does not take into account the multiplicity and heterogeneity of modern societies. It is argued that the generalized other of a given person is always relative to particular groups and persons, and that not all participants in a given social act have equal influence. A person is said by Mills to build up his moral and intellectual standards only in terms of significant other persons rather than all others in the situation. There is obvious truth in this. The standards of the criminal, for example, do not enter into the generalized other of the law-abiding citizen except to reinforce them by negative example. Even significant others are significant in different ways and to different degrees. A student's intellectual orientation may be described in a gross way by relating it to a specific university, a specific subject, and a specific department. Closer scrutiny may reveal, however, that really decisive influence has been exercised by certain professors, or perhaps only one. The same may be said of moral standards, which are perhaps most usually acquired from parents. The mother's and father's influence upon the child may be very different, and in

some cases, neither of them may exercise the dominant influence—
i.e., the child may acquire moral conceptions from his peers, from a
teacher whom he likes, or from someone else.

The Development of Morality and
Objectivity in the Child

MORAL DEVELOPMENT

In an interesting study, Lerner[23] asked children between the
ages of eight and twelve the following question: "Is it worse to tell
a lie to your father or to your mother?" Typical reasons given for
naming the father were: "because he can punish harder" and
"because you can't get away with it with him." Those who thought
it worse to lie to one's mother reasoned in such terms as: "she is
sweeter" and "she is the best friend you have."

Murphy, Murphy, and Newcomb, in commenting upon Lerner's
study, remark that

> Moral judgments . . . are clearly *not* simply assimilated ready-
> made from the preceding generation, but are reworked in terms
> of the child's needs and degrees of identification with, and re-
> spect for, other individuals . . . many moral judgments of chil-
> dren are in violent conflict with those of their parents and,
> indeed, of the whole social world around them, if a line of con-
> duct close to their own needs is involved. The parent who has
> tried to teach the small child that caterpillars, bugs, spiders, and
> other "pests" must all be exterminated knows that even when the
> whole world backs him up the child may protest that the
> destruction of some tiny animal friend is wrong, and that in
> fairy stories, despite the universal condemnation of the wolf or
> the tiger, the child may alarm the parent by wholeheartedly
> assuming the wolf's point of view. Thus Boeck found a depend-
> able stimulus for protest or tears to lie in the destruction of the
> wolf at the end of the Red Riding Hood story . . . the moral

responses . . . depend not only on the world of culture, but on the individual's own needs.[24]

The needs to which these three authors refer are of course not simply biological ones, but the outgrowths of social experience. It should be self-evident that, just as the needs of any two children are not identical, so their moral experiences cannot be the same.

Studies of the development of children's moral ideas and judgments demonstrate in part that the child moves from egocentric to relativistic moral standards. Piaget[25] has analyzed this aspect of childhood. In his study of lower-class children of Geneva, Switzerland, he discerned a series of transformations in their moral conceptions. (1) The young Genevan up to four or five years of age is characterized by "moral realism." Right is right and wrong is wrong: if a person does wrong he should be punished regardless of his motives. (2) Later the child realizes that moral rules are not objectively real, but reflect group values. This realization is based upon the recognition of multiple perspectives. Geneva children remain at this stage until nine or ten. (3) Then a third level is reached at which the rules are allowed to be altered by considerations of equity; for example, a lame boy may be given a head start in a race. Piaget has demonstrated in general that the child's conception of moral rules changes from the belief that rules are absolute to the knowledge that they are agreed upon. Other studies of American, Swiss, and Belgian children support Piaget's conclusions.[26]

Studies like those made by Macaulay and Watkins[27] also point to the gradual growth of wider moral meanings. Children were asked to make a list of the most wicked things they could think of. Their answers showed that up to nine years of age the child's moral conceptions are rather definite and concrete and are formulated in terms of his own personal relations. After this age moral conceptions appeared to grow more generalized. Stealing and fighting in general were beginning to be regarded as wrong at nine. From the age of eleven years, conceptions began to show the influence of conventional adult notions of sin, although only the children in late adolescence wrote of such sins of the spirit as hypocrisy and selfishness.

As Murphy, Murphy, and Newcomb have noted about the elementary-grade child:[28] "Abstract conceptions of justice and 'fairness' are not yet very clear. 'Ideals' and general rules of the institution have little weight."

Piaget's specific explanation for the direction of moral development is dubious. He hypothesized that the early conceptions of moral rules are absolutistic because of the authoritarian relations that exist between parent and child; and that conceptions grow more relativistic, general, and systematic as cooperative relationships spring up between the child and others, particularly his peers. Neither does it seem adequate to explain the growth of moral conceptions merely as a consequence of reward and punishment, or of learning from specific direct experiences "to recognize a common element in a variety of situations."[29] Conceptions of roles and of rules grow *pari passu*. Built into role conceptions are the justifications and canons appropriate to the roles. When the child is young, his moral standards lack relativity and generality because he cannot grasp the fuller meaning of acts as seen from wider perspectives. It is therefore worthwhile to distinguish between the full and general comprehension of moral values and the learning of a specific rule.

PERSPECTIVES OF THE PHYSICAL WORLD

Just as the actions of people appear in different perspectives, so also do physical events and objects. These different perspectives cannot be called "roles," as this term has been defined, but they are points of view of other persons. If a person were unable to conceive of other, wider perspectives than those provided him by immediate sensory impressions, he would be unable to form any realistic conception of the physical world or to appreciate the accomplishments of science. Thus, no atoms are visible to the naked eye and none have ever been seen, even through microscopes. A person who depended only on direct experience would deny their existence. An objective view of the physical world requires that the various aspects presented by objects in different situations and combinations be synthesized into broader conceptions which will permit various observers to agree on essential, publicly verifiable facts. To achieve such objectivity, one must do something closely akin to what has been called taking the role of the generalized other: one must combine or synthesize divergent and conflicting views into an over-all view which harmonizes them.

The point may be reinforced by recalling a simple illustration which Piaget has provided.[30] He noted, as we have seen, that children often believe that the sun and the moon follow them when they walk. As soon as children are able to communicate such ideas and become concerned with avoiding contradiction, they must necessarily discover that this notion leads to logical absurdities. The moon cannot, after all, follow everyone without moving in different directions at the same time. Discussion and controversy over matters of this kind eventually lead to the realization of apparent (illusory) motion and finally to the idea of relative motion. Advanced general conceptions of motion, as the word "general" indicates, take account of apparent motion.

A simpler illustration of the way in which divergent viewpoints are reconciled is provided by the finish of a close race. Viewed from different angles, different contenders seem to have won. If this were the whole story the question of the winner would always remain a matter of personal opinion and of controversy. By agreement, however, it is recognized that these different perspectives depend on the different positions of the observers; and so the decision is based on how the race looks to those persons who are exactly on the finish line. In horse races the camera which photographs the finish simultaneously from both sides is the final arbiter in case of doubt, and if it fails to indicate a single winner, the race is declared a tie.

The fact that truth appears to be relative to the position of the observer is systematically taken into account in the physical sciences. Ushenko,[31] for example, has discussed what he calls "perspectival" truth. He indicates that what is true in one perspective may be false in another, and that the contradiction is resolved by incorporating limited perspectives into broader and more inclusive ones.

The acceptance by laymen of the scientist's view of the physical world is largely an act of faith. The scientists are the layman's significant others, who probe the mysteries of the physical world, performing complicated experiments and erecting structures of concepts and mathematical symbols far beyond the layman's power of comprehension. The layman's faith is justified, he argues, by the results which everyone can see. A religious person, on the other hand, may take a very different view, rejecting the materialism and one-sidedness of science and seeing the physical world and science itself primarily as evidence of the working out of a divine plan. The significant others in this conception are religious and moral leaders. There are, of course, many different philosophical positions with respect to the nature of the physical world, each claiming priority over all the others.

THE NATURE OF OBJECTIVITY

The ability to take into account the view of other persons, to take their roles, is fundamental to the achievement of objectivity in thinking. Without this ability the individual is tied down to a limited perspective. Since he has no means of making comparisons and of knowing other points of view, his own perceptions necessarily appear as absolutes. The relativity of things is incomprehensible. We have seen an example of this in the child's egocentrism.

Thinking objectively also requires that the individual become aware of the mechanisms of his own thought. In order to discount biases, to make allowance for the uniqueness of one's own views, and to examine critically one's own conclusions, the individual must be able to make comparisons and relative judgments. This is impossible so long as there is no awareness of the existence of other possible views. The transition from childish egocentrism to objectivity is therefore also a transition from individualistic, unrealistic thought to socialized thinking.

In this connection we may note a study by Burks.[32] Forty children ranging in age from four to twelve were given two tasks to perform in situations permitting self-criticism, adult criticism, criticism of a classmate of the same age and sex, and criticism by a classmate. The children were also asked about their feelings toward criticism. Burks formulated her conclusions in terms of stages.

1. The predominantly egocentric stage in which the child is confused about the difference between self and external world; criticisms are offered in terms of the child's own products, "I'll show her how to make one like mine." Criticisms are not genuinely assimilated.

2. The partly socialized stage in which the child attempts genuine social communication but processes of giving and receiving criticism are still subject to egocentric deformation, and criticisms are not really internalized.

3. The completely socialized, reciprocal stage in which there is careful and critical assimilation of criticisms, and criticisms are offered with understanding of the intentions and difficulties of the other child.

Another indispensable requirement for objective thinking is the individual's ability to make a sharp separation between processes that go on only in his own mind and those that are outside and independent of his person. Lacking this ability, he projects his own human sentiments and desires upon the outside world. The complete separation of what comes from inside of us and that which is independent and outside of us is actually exceedingly difficult; perhaps, in a strict sense, it is impossible. Our evidence of the external world is derived from our sense organs, and the symbols and ideas which we use to represent the external world are human creations. The whole broad sweep of intellectual history reveals a persistent tendency to confuse names with things, to ignore things that are not named, to assume that there must be things where there are names, and generally to confuse objects of thought with actual objects and events. This tendency has been progressively reduced, but not by any means eliminated, through research in the natural sciences and in the study of man and through an increasing sophistication of logical and philosophical thought. The child, for example, at first thinks of external objects and events in terms of the necessities and compulsions which he feels in his own life. Clouds, stones, trees, and other objects are endowed with human qualities. The child talks to his toys and to animals as though he might expect them to answer him. This projection of human qualities upon nonhuman objects, as we noted in Chapter 2, is known as anthropomorphism. It is a striking characteristic of childish thought and also occurs in much adult thinking. Geocentrism—the belief that the earth is the center and the hub of the universe—is a similar error: it arises from the inability of people to view the solar system from the standpoint of an outside observer. Another fallacy of the same type is ethnocentrism—the tendency to judge other groups by the standards and customs of one's own group. To understand an alien culture one must, of course, place *oneself* in the role of a member of that culture.

Here again a study of the role-playing deficiencies of (Swiss) children is pertinent. Lerner notes that their

> lack of perspective is clearly indicated in the entirely spontaneous manner in which the child is prone to judge or compare members of other groups (out-groups) in terms of a quite unconscious attitude of superiority or, in general, as a matter of distinctly absolute valuations. The socialization of this sociocentric self is indicated, in turn, in terms of a progressively increasing conscious realization of these centripetal tendencies.[83]

Lerner asked questions designed to uncover familial, school, and communal variants of ethnocentrism (which he calls "sociocentrism"). For example, "A boy here in Geneva told me that boys in X (another town known to the subject) tell more lies, while a boy in X told me just the opposite; who is right, why?" Here are two sets of answers, the first exhibiting sociocentrism, the second exhibiting a more sophisticated relativism.

> 7 years, 0 months: Who is right? *The boy from Geneva because in Geneva they don't tell lies.* And in X? *They do.* Why? *Because they are better brought up.*
>
> 7 years, 7 months: Who is right? *The boy who says that in X they are liars and that in Geneva they are not almost all liars.* Why? *In X they do nothing but tell lies, but not in Geneva.*
>
> 11 years, 1 month: *Both of them wrong because they shouldn't say bad things about other people. Because they also tell lies. . . . I don't know, I've never been there.*
>
> 12 years, 3 months: *But, no, it's the same thing all over: they lie as much as they do here. And we lie as often as they do.*

Any kind of organized group activity presupposes at least a minimum of agreement, or consensus. Objectivity develops from the attempt to resolve conflicting views. Apropos of this point, Murphy and his associates[34] have reviewed studies of how groups of people resolve group problems. They conclude that whenever the thinking of the whole group is better than that of its individual members, this is due in part to:

(a) the larger number of ways of looking at the problem; (b) the larger number of suggestions for a solution; (c) the larger number of effective criticisms of each proposed plan; (d) the patent need to accept social criticism and not be "bullheaded" (as people working alone frequently are).

By progressively freeing themselves from the biases and limitations of their own unique points of view, people are able to assume progressively broader and more detached perspectives. They become capable of agreeing, to a certain extent, upon the "facts" of the case.

The work of the scientist illustrates particularly well the way in which objective knowledge arises from the clash of divergent points of view. Scientific investigation requires the ability to imagine how one's work will appear to the critical eyes of other scientists. Theories, techniques, and findings must all be subjected to examination and rechecking by others before they are accepted. The exact conditions under which experiments and observations are made must be reported so that the same steps can be followed by other investigators. The scientist, in short, must be adept at role-taking. He must be a first-rate critic of his own work. The respect which Charles Darwin commanded as a scientist was due in considerable part to the thorough self-criticism to which he subjected his work. Darwin attempted to anticipate all possible objections and counter-arguments and patiently answered them. Consequently, as each of his books was published, his scientific audience had considerable assurance that its contents were solidly grounded. Of course, even Darwin's findings were not accepted until other biologists had re-checked his observations and experiments; nor were all of his conclusions found to be valid.

Understanding the Roles of Others

Much misunderstanding arises among people when they are unable to appreciate each other's roles. The individual's ability to understand the behavior of others is limited by the range of his acquaintance with forms of behavior like his own or with which he is familiar. The "average" person readily appreciates the motives and views of other people who are like himself. Furthermore, he is likely to have some grasp of the behavior of persons who are somewhat different from himself because he has talked to or read about them. Beyond this, however, there are roles which he may be almost entirely unable to comprehend, such as those of "foreigners" or persons outside the boundaries of Western civilization. Consider, for example, the average American housewife grappling with the fact that a Toda woman of southern India may have as many as three husbands at a time.

In so complex and closely interconnected a world-society as ours, it is vitally important for people to appreciate the existence of many types of roles other than their own. Conflicts among nations, among religious groups, and among subgroups within nations arise from a lack of such understanding. Because of an absence of adequate intercommunication, people do not grasp one another's motives and ways of acting. The chief means of broadening the understanding of people are, of course, indirect ones, such as those involved in learning a foreign language, reading books, and studying anthropology.

Instead of recognizing our failures to understand the acts of others, we usually misinterpret those acts. We assume that the person is playing roles within our own system of values and symbols and interpret his behavior in terms of our symbols instead of his. To choose an example close to the experience of most college students: parents misinterpret many acts of their teen-age children. The real meanings of these acts are not grasped because parents are outsiders to the adolescent age group, to the adolescent world. Conversely, children often misinterpret their parents' acts because of failure to grasp the meanings of adult behavior. An amusing instance of the misinterpretation of roles is the judgment passed upon adult love-making by children in their early teens. The Saturday afternoon movie audience is vociferously critical of any kissing. (Cowboy heroes rarely kiss their heroines.) Misinterpretations are not always harmless and amusing. In a multi-grouped society, misjudgments of roles often have serious results, as both interracial and international relations testify.

Summary

The concept of role is used by sociologists to refer to complex patterns of response which are conceptually organized within a supporting context of other roles called "counter-roles." Social structure may be conceived of as an organization of roles of various types. Individuals discover and adapt themselves to roles, their own and others', in the process of socialization; taking another person's role in one's imagination is an important aspect of role behavior. Through this process the child's single-perspective outlook—his egocentrism —becomes multi-perspectival, or socialized. The development of objectivity, of conscience and morality (and the development of self-awareness, to be considered in the next chapter) have their sources in the person's ability to take the roles of others and to synthesize other's roles in a conception of the generalized other. The role concept emphasizes the situational and dramatic features of human behavior and is an important orienting concept.

SUGGESTIONS FOR DISCUSSION AND SPECIAL REPORTS

1. The leisure-time pursuits of various social groups tell us something about the dreams and hopes of their members; they also

suggest the directions in which self-conceptions are moving. Analyze the recreational behavior of some group in these terms.

2. Analyze a number of awkward social situations in terms of roles that went wrong. Discuss also the social mechanisms that enabled the participants to get through the situation.

3. Report on some of the literature on leaders, including business leaders.

4. Discuss the role requirements of some occupational or professional position, for instance that of the minister or the minister's wife.

5. Compare in detail the requirements of a loosely organized role with that of a rigidly prescribed one.

6. Play is said by some writers to open the door to innovation and creativeness. Discuss this proposition.

7. John Dollard has written that "There is a continual flow of agreement by the [Southern] Negro while a white man is talking such as 'Yes, boss,' 'Sho nuff,' 'Well I declare,' and the like." Discuss the functions of this kind of verbal ritual for the respective roles of a bygone era.

8. People sometimes speak of "meaningless ritual." What does this mean? Can we do without ritual?

NOTES

[1] T. Parsons, "Systematic Theory in Sociology," in *Essays in Sociological Theory*, Glencoe, Ill.: Free Press, 1949, pp. 34-35.

[2] L. Neiman and E. Hughes, "The Problem of the Concept of Role: A Re-Survey of the Literature," *Social Forces*, 30(1951): 149.

[3] See W. I. Thomas, *Primitive Behavior*, McGraw-Hill, 1937, p. 8.

[4] R. Linton, *The Cultural Background of Personality*, Appleton-Century, 1945, pp. 97-98.

[5] Max Weber, "Bureaucracy," in *Outside Readings in Sociology*, ed. E. A. Schuler *et al.*, New York: Thomas Y. Crowell Co., 1952, pp. 402-410.

[6] Adapted from A. L. Strauss, *Identification*, p. 40. (Unpublished manuscript.)

[7] N. Gross and W. S. Mason, "Some Methodological Problems of Eight Hour Interviews," *Am. J. Soc.*, 59(1953): 197-204.

[8] G. Mead, *Mind, Self and Society*, University of Chicago Press, 1934.

9 R. MacIver, *Social Causation,* New York: Ginn and Co., 1942, p. 296.

10 W. Coutu, "Role-Playing vs. Role-Taking: An Appeal for Clarification," *Am. Soc. Rev.,* 16 (1951): 182.

11 H. Vaihinger, *The Philosophy of "As If,"* London: Kegan Paul, Trench, and Trubner, 1924.

12 T. R. Sarbin, in *Handbook of Social Psychology,* ed. G. Lindzey, Cambridge, Mass.: Addison-Wesley, 1954, p. 236.

13 J. Moreno, *Psychodrama,* Beacon, N. Y.: Beacon House, 1946. Vol. I.

14 J. Piaget, *The Language and the Thought of the Child,* Harcourt, Brace, 1926; *Judgment and Reasoning in the Child,* Harcourt, Brace, 1928; *The Child's Conception of Physical Causality,* Harcourt, Brace, 1930; *The Moral Judgment of the Child,* Harcourt, Brace, 1932.

15 J. Piaget, "Principal Factors Determining Intellectual Evolution from Childhood to Adult Life," in *Factors Determining Human Behavior,* Harvard University Press, 1937, pp. 32-48.

16 M. B. Parten, "Social Participation Among Pre-School Children," *J. Ab. and Soc. Psych.,* 27(1932): 263.

17 K. Bridges, *The Social and Emotional Level of the Pre-School Child,* London, Kegan Paul, 1931, p. 82.

18 G. H. Mead, *Mind, Self, and Society,* University of Chicago Press, 1934, pp. 364-365 and 150-151.

19 *Ibid.,* pp. 151-152, 154.

20 A. L. Strauss, "The Development and Transformation of Monetary Meanings in the Child," *Am. Soc. Rev.,* 17 (1952): 278.

21 E. Hartley, M. Rosenbaum, and S. Schwartz, "Children's Perceptions of Ethnic Group Membership," *J. Psych.,* 26(1948): 387-398.

22 C. W. Mills, "Language, Logic, and Culture," *Am. Soc. Rev.,* 4 (1939): 672. Also H. Gerth and C. W. Mills, *Character and Social Structure,* Harcourt, Brace, 1953, pp. 95-98.

23 E. Lerner, unpublished study reported in G. Murphy, L. Murphy, and T. Newcomb, *Experimental Social Psychology,* Harper, 1937, p. 546.

24 *Ibid.,* p. 546.

25 J. Piaget, *The Moral Judgment of the Child,* Harcourt, Brace, 1932.

26 A. L. Strauss, "The Learning of Roles and Concepts as Twin Processes," *J. Genet. Psych.* (forthcoming); M. C. MacCarthy, *Moral Judgments of Children by Age, Sex, and Class,* master's thesis, Indiana University, 1949; E. Lerner, "The Problem of Perspective in Moral Reasoning," *Am. J. Soc.,* 43(1937): 249-269; I. H. Caruso, "La notion de responsabilité et de justice immanente chez l'enfant," *Arch. Psych.,* 29(1942-1943): 114-172.

27 E. Macaulay and S. Watkins, "An Investigation into the Moral Conceptions of Children," *Ed. Forum,* 4(1926): 13-33 and 92-108.

[28] Murphy, Murphy, and Newcomb, *op. cit.*, p. 650.

[29] E. Hurlock, *Child Development*, McGraw-Hill, 1950, p. 438.

[30] J. Piaget, *The Child's Conception of Number*, London: Routledge and Kegan Paul, 1952. Chap. XI.

[31] A. P. Ushenko, "Truth in Science and Philosophy," *Phil. of Science*, 21(1954): 101-117.

[32] B. Burks, summarized in Murphy, Murphy, and Newcomb, *op. cit.*, p. 659.

[33] E. Lerner, "The Problem of Perspective in Moral Reasoning," *Am. J. Soc.*, 43(1937): 260.

[34] Murphy, Murphy, and Newcomb, *op. cit.*, p. 738.

SELECTED BIBLIOGRAPHY

Coutu, W., "Role-playing versus Role-taking: An Appeal for Clarification," *Am. Soc. Rev.*, 16(1951): 182. Criticizes various ways that these concepts have been handled by other writers and offers his own alternative.

Lerner, E., "The Problem of Perspective in Moral Reasoning," *Am. J. Soc.*, 43(1937): 249-269. The results of several experiments upon the moral judgments of Swiss children.

Linton, R., *The Cultural Background of Personality*, Appleton-Century, 1945. Chap. III, "Social Structure and Cultural Participation," pp. 55-82. A well-organized and eminently readable treatment of roles and their general relationship to group structures.

Mead, G. H., *Mind, Self and Society*, University of Chicago Press, 1934. Mead's analysis of the generalized other and of processes of role-playing are included in this important but difficult book.

Newcomb, T. M., *Social Psychology*, Dryden, 1950. The chapters on roles contain useful material.

Parsons, T., *The Social System*, Glencoe, Ill.: Free Press, 1951. An influential but difficult book. In his analysis of social structure, Parsons gives role a central place.

Piaget, J., *Judgment and Reasoning in the Child*, Harcourt, Brace, 1928.

————, *The Moral Judgment of the Child*, Harcourt, Brace, 1932. These two books, along with his *Psychology of Intelligence*, give a good picture of Piaget's views on egocentrism and its disappearance with the development of adult rationality.

Sarbin, T., in Lindzey, G. (ed.), *Handbook of Social Psychology*, Vol. I, Cambridge, Mass.: Addison-Wesley, 1954, "Role Theory," pp. 223-258. Contains a review of some of the literature and a discussion of roles as a psychologist sees them.

Strauss, A. L., "The Development of Conceptions of Rules in Children," *Child Devel.*, 23(1954): 193-208.

————, "The Development and Transformation of Monetary Meanings in the Child," *Am. Soc. Rev.*, 17(1952): 275-286. This and the preceding article are research reports on the learning of roles, concepts, and moral rules.

Znaniecki, F., "Social Groups as Products of Cooperating Individuals," *Am. J. Soc.*, 44(1939): 799-811. Considers the relationships of roles and groups.

CHAPTER 13 · · ·

Self
and
Role

Some such concept as "self" or "ego" is essential to any account of man's social nature or the socialization process. Human beings characteristically act with self-awareness, exercise self-control, exhibit conscience and guilt, and in the great crises of life make decisions with reference to some imagery of what they are, what they have been, and what they hope to be. From the standpoint of the community, and for the sake of common enterprise, it is essential that societal controls be built into persons somehow. These controls are necessary in order that the work may get done with a minimum of force and coercion and in order that a maximum of enthusiasm and indentification of personal interest with the collective interest may be brought about.

It is obviously easier to say that concepts of identity, or "self," are necessary in analyses of group and individual behavior than to write with clarity about the nature and functioning of "self." Philosophic thought has long wrestled with the relationships of subject

413

and object, knower and known, and the general relationships of "self" and the objective world. The literature of these relationships is exceedingly complex and abstract. Psychology, which broke away from philosophy partly as a reaction against such abstruse speculation, also reacted against the very idea of "self" as a scientific concept. It was argued on methodological grounds that the so-called "self" of man was like his soul: it could not be investigated by reliable scientific methods, and therefore had no claim to consideration by scientists. On theoretical grounds, it was banished as a "mentalistic construct" and relegated to the ashcan along with faculties, humors, and other outmoded concepts. It was also argued that stimuli and responses and their relationships could be studied without bothering about whether human beings have selves.

Proponents of the "self" idea have gained the advantage in the controversy in the last few decades. The concept was never entirely rejected in all fields of psychology; it was granted some validity, particularly in child and social psychology. Then, with the increase of the influence of psychoanalytic theory upon studies of personality and in the psychological clinic, there has come a revival of interest in problems of the self; however, as late as 1943 a leading psychologist, Gordon Allport, was attacking selfless psychologies, and in 1949 a president of the American Psychological Association, E. Hilgard, was urging a renaissance of investigations of the self.

The Nature of Self

SELF IS NOT AN ENTITY

The use of such expressions in common speech as "self-consciousness," "I hate myself," "I hurt myself," "I am a problem to myself," and "I will be there myself" are indications of the self in action. However, popular usage of self-words is often inconsistent and confusing particularly because the self is sometimes identified with body and sometimes not. "Self" has both an objective and a subjective reference. The use of the term "self" as a noun seems to imply the existence of a corresponding entity or object. This, however, is an erroneous conception—as erroneous as it would be to think of "speed" in the same manner. Both terms refer to events and relationships, rather than to entities having a definite location in space. It is for reasons of this kind that the self or ego has been described as a "grammatical illusion."

If the self is thought of as a thing, it is reified: that is, it is either conceived of as the body, or is thought of as an entity somewhere within the body. It is common the world over to refer, at least poetically, to some part of the body which is especially favored because it is the seat of selfhood: perhaps particularly the heart, the eyes, the breath, and the brain. Horowitz[1] has reported some amusing answers by subjects to a request that they locate their selves. They named such varied zones as head, face, brain, eyes, heart, chest, lungs, teeth, hands, and genitals. Kluckhohn and Murray's definition of the personality as "the organization of all the integrative (regnant) processes in the brain"[2] is a sophisticated example in technical literature of the tendency to locate the self in a part of the body.

In order to have a self, of course, one must first have a body. Hence some psychologists have spoken of the "physical self" as apart from "the social self." Little is gained by this, since we already have a word to designate the body, namely "body." The self is not in the body as a physical part, neither is it a spiritual or mystical entity located somewhere or everywhere in the organism. Yet the body is implicated in the very notion of self. Without stating what the self is, we may yet note briefly some relationships between body and self.

A person perceives and evaluates his body, its parts and its functioning, much as he perceives and evaluates other objects and events. He also has, as our discussion in later pages will show, conceptions of the inner observation, but which nevertheless enter into his evaluation of himself as a person. He may believe that he has a weak heart and plan his life accordingly. By virtue of private experiences with his physique and the comments of others on it, he comes to have special notions of how much work or how much joy he can get out of his body and what its limitations are: "Oh that this too, too solid flesh would melt . . ." He develops ideas about his appearance and passes judgments upon it. Consequently, he may come to "hate himself" because he believes his body is homely or ugly, despite the fact that his judgment may not be shared by others. Conceptualizations of the body may enter in to self-regard in very oblique and complex ways, as when a man hates himself because he finds he cannot control his actions. We speak then of shame, or sometimes of susceptibility to temptation. The body may be used as an instrument against itself, as when one commits suicide; or it may be mortified as a sign of guilt, submission or holiness. In short, appraisals of the body enter intimately into action and are subtle indicators of self-regard. But this body appraisal is, of course, symbolic in nature. It comes from interaction with others and is thus a social product.

THE SELF AS ORGANIZATION

A Definition · It was pointed out in the preceeding chapter how a person's conception of his role serves to evoke and organize appropriate responses and, as part of the same process, to inhibit other responses. Such role conceptions and role-systems have much greater effect in the control of behavior than a simple verbal command or a single inhibiting response. In the same way, at a higher level of integration, one may think of self as: (1) a set of more or less consistent and stable responses on a conceptual level, which (2) exercises a regulatory function over other responses of the same organism at lower levels.

This definition of self does not imply that the self is a "motivating force." It is not the ultimate vital source of behavior and energy. Neither is it a suprabehavioral court to which all behavior is somehow mysteriously referred. Dualistic notions of this kind often pervade popular thinking about human behavior and are also found in the scientific literature.

The self is rather an organization of integration of behavior imposed upon the individual by societal expectations and demands.

Social requirements and pressures impose limitations upon the degree of inconsistency tolerated in the behavior of individuals and impel the person to eliminate or reconcile such inconsistencies. The organization and integration of lines of activity which appear to the outsider as contradictory or inconsistent are essential parts of what is referred to as the self.

Changes in Self and Self-Involvement · An important aspect of self is that it changes with time throughout the course of one's life.

THE TAXI-DANCE GIRL CHANGES HER NAME*

Real Name	*"Professional Name"*
Christina Stranski	DeLoris Glenn
Agnes Gretin	Lorine Boyle
Marie Boris	Billye Hart
Florence Klepka	Anita Costello
Louise Lorenz	Bobby LeMann
Sophie Zelinski	Gwendolyn Llewellen
Alma Heisla	Helene de Valle
Pearl Babcock	Melba DeMay
Eleanor Hedman	Gloria Garden
Anna Prasenski	Althea LeMar
Mary Bulonowski	LaBelle Shelley
Gertrude Pressley	Betty Lucrece
Alice Borden	Wanda Wang
Mary Maranowski	Jean Jouette

* From Paul G. Cressey, *The Taxi-Dance Hall,* University of Chicago Press, 1932, p. 97.

At the points in his life when old patterns are breaking up under the impact of disjunctive experiences, the person may feel at odds with himself until a new integration, or rationale, is achieved. However, throughout life there runs a thread of continuity contributed by name and constancy of personal identity. The individual assimilates experiences, identifying them as his own and accepting responsibility for the actions identified as his. The symbolism of "keeping a good name" suggests some of this. Persons who try to escape their pasts change their names, give false histories, and try to forget or disown their early experiences. Such disassociation of self from self is, of course, not easy, although it can be in some measure achieved. In certain rare instances, it seems that persons may have two fairly separate identities so that in one of them the person has little or no memory of the other. Such cases are now and then reported in the newspapers, and others have been described in the psychological literature.

The self, as we have defined it, does not enter significantly into all behavior but is differentially involved in various acts; at one extreme involvement is very slight. Psychological experiments dealing with "level of aspiration" have shown that when involvement in a task is increased (*i.e.*, when the individual is appropriately motivated), performance is improved or changed. In many involuntary and automatic activities, little of the self is implicated, although even in these the action may have significance of which the individual is not himself aware. Moreover, an automatic action, like tapping the table with one's fingers, may acquire significance if it is singled out for attention or criticism by other persons so that it takes on meaning for the person himself. Further along in this chapter we shall also discuss some important forms of behavior which are relatively devoid of self-reference, although they are in no sense automatic or routine.

SOCIETY IN THE INDIVIDUAL

Self and Self-Control · Self-control is usually thought of in connection with self-awareness; for example we speak of the person controlling his appetites or curbing his passions. We ought to note, however, that regulatory functioning is not necessarily accompanied by acute self-consciousness. For example a driver may pilot his car quite skillfully for many minutes while engaged in conversation or sunk deep in thought. Any physical skill tends to assume an automatic character, although when it is first acquired it is at the forefront of attention. Some skills, of course, may become the basis of self-esteem, as in persons who use them professionally or competitively, so that they continue to be at the center of attention in a somewhat different way.

The Mechanism of Self-Control · Self-regulation is inseparable from social control. The language mechanisms by which self-control is exerted are derived from social sources, and the regulatory process itself occurs largely in the form of internalized conversation. George H. Mead has paid some attention to this process. He distinguished two phases of internalized conversation. They may be made clear by means of a simple illustration. Let us suppose that a person walks into a bank and finds himself in a position where he can make off, without fear of detection, with a large sum of money. We shall suppose that our hypothetical man is not above temptation in this particular situation. Something like the following (in the form of an inaudible and greatly abbreviated conversation) might take place.

Phase One	*Phase Two*
I could use that money.	But it's stealing.
So what! Everyone steals if they have a chance to.	You know it isn't so.
I could get a new car.	No. Better be honest!
No chance of getting caught.	Dishonest.
Banks make lots of money; they won't feel it.	Isn't right to take it. Isn't theirs either.

If he is above temptation, Phase One does not exist and the conversation does not occur.

The acutal process of conversing internally does not go on in terms of complete sentences or in terms of words alone, but rather as a kind of mental tug-of-war between conflicting impulses, interspersed with visual and auditory images and day dreams and accompanied by corresponding feelings. Such conversations are not necessarily short, nor do they always take place in a single episode. The battle against a particular temptation may be a sporadic and long one that is brought alive periodically by external circumstances.

Much of our thinking, particularly when we are dealing with difficult or problematic situations of a moral or volitional kind, involves these two general phases of conversation. Mead called Phase One the "I" and Phase Two the "Me." The "Me" in his scheme represents internalized group standards; or, said another way, the "Me" is the community in the individual. To Mead, the "I" represented impulses which, in a sense, are supervised by the "Me," either being squashed as they get underway or afterward, or diverted into acceptable channels.

The widespread popular conception that the impulses of the "I" always require supervision and are of a negative and unsocialized character requires considerable qualification. Impulses may be perfectly socialized but nevertheless judged inappropriate to the situation after a brief consideration. Such judgments are continually being made, since life is anything but routine. Control is not necessarily a matter of stemming ignoble temptation or putting the lid on passions: it may be quite the reverse, as when one checks over-generous impulses in favor of other considerations. Furthermore, control may be positive in the sense that a man has to urge himself to do things, the urging representing the regulatory side of his action. A sharp line ought not to be drawn between negative and positive self-control, since lines of action necessarily involve both the eliciting of certain responses and the negation of others. Puritanical traditions emphasize the repressive aspects of control and disregard the fact that the "I" may become socialized and need not be an expression of the brutish side of man's nature.

Social control is not based exclusively, and certainly not primarily, upon coercion. Neither can effective group action be based upon the continuous direct surveillance of individuals. If this were not true, men would revert to sheer brutality and opportunism whenever they were out of sight of earshot of other persons, whenever the chances of detection were slight. Orderly social controls are based on contract, obligation, trust, and responsibility. Even limited alliances involve these.

Theories of human nature that postulate opposition between individual and society picture society as a kind of a policeman watching over the individual. Self-interest is thought of either as being in opposition to collective interest or as utilizing the latter to gain its primary ends. This is a misconception of the nature and function of ethical codes and of the requirements of group life. Compliance with community norms and with contractual obligations is not only a requirement of effective collective action but is a necessity for the creation and fulfillment of individual aspirations. There is no natural opposition of man and society. Asch makes a similar point when he suggests that the accentuation of self is often a response to social failure:

> When the possibilities of entering into appropriate relations with others are barred, the ego turns its pontentialities for care upon itself. Avarice, greed, ruthless ambition often are the answer the ego gives when it fails to find in the surroundings the opportunity for its outgoing needs.[3]

Conscience, Guilt, and Shame · Internal control in moral matters is referred to as *conscience*. What is regarded as right and wrong varies widely among societies, among groups, and even from situation to situation within a homogeneous population. Also, as Cameron and Magaret point out, "The behavior which one man views within an ethical context of 'right' and 'wrong' may be for his neighbor a matter of expediency, taste, or arbitrary cultural control." Naïve judgments are sometimes made about another person's acts because the varied content of consciences is not taken into account. Sometimes, too, conscience is identified with religious precepts. Religion and morality are sometimes so closely intertwined that a coalescence of ethical and religious teaching seems part of the natural order of things. However, in some societies large areas of morality lie outside the religious sphere.

In Western theological writing and in common-sense thinking, transgressions of the dictates of conscience are associated with guilt. One stands alone before his God—or his conscience—and suffers remorse for what he has done or for what he has left undone. The subtleties of guilt and self-judgment and the means of expiation hardly need be dwelt upon. However, some anthropologists, including Benedict and Hsu,[5] have argued that in some countries or societies guilt is not an invariant accompaniment of wrongdoing. It is argued that there are "shame cultures" as well as "guilt cultures," and that in the former remorse is less a controlling mechanism than fear or shame in the face of what other people may think of the wrongdoing. The Japanese, according to Benedict, are said to react with shame in many situations in which we would feel guilt. Margaret Mead has hypothesized that certain modes of childhood training result in the predominance of guilt: such a mode is that in which when parents themselves, rather than governesses and nurses, rear the child, themselves chastise the child rather than calling on gods or bogeymen to do so, and themselves are the models which the child is taught to emulate.[6] Such direct relations of parent and child cause the child to assimilate the standards of his parents early and to feel guilty when he violates them. On the other hand, when not directly reared by his parents, the child views their standards more as externally imposed rules the violation of which causes more shame than guilt.

The differentiation of shame and guilt has been criticized by Honigmann as difficult to put to the test. He notes "the lack of satisfactory, operational criteria by which to verify the existence of either guilt or shame. . . . The identification of guilt or shame remains too much a matter of intuition." He also suggests that within the same society, or even within the same social class, ways of handling children may vary so much that some persons may react primarily with shame and others with guilt.[7] A more basic criticism of the general hypothesis is that although it is valuable, it oversimplifies matters. Shame cultures were first noted because their members appeared to react quite differently than would Westerners in the face of certain moral dilemmas. But the more inclusive point is that in different societies people learn to regulate behavior and atone for failure in different ways. As we have pointed out in earlier chapters, modes of thinking vary from society to society and from group to group. Moral conceptions vary correspondingly. Modes of emotional expression also have social sources, and emotional reactions vary widely. Hence, it is very unlikely that the polar shame-guilt hypothesis takes the entire range into account. It is also possible that an explanation solely or mainly in terms of particular kinds of relations in childhood is too narrow to account for cultural variations in this respect.

Development of Self-Awareness

Human beings have to develop self-control and a sense of self, for the new-born baby has no self-awareness. His actions are determined by bodily needs—by responses to internal and external stimuli—not by any reference to a self. Observers of child behavior have long noted that the child develops a kind of crude self-awareness within two or three years; and that it takes many more years before full adult self-awareness comes into being. The ability to think of oneself as an object, and to have feelings about oneself, apparently evolves throughout the childhood years.

The observation that self-awareness has a gradual development misled many philosophers as well as laymen into thing of this development as a biological process. It was assumed that infants lacked self-awareness because they were physically incapable of experiencing it. Bodily maturation was supposed to provide the capacity to conceive the self. Self-consciousness, in other words, was seen essentially as a natural outgrowth of innate physical endowments. Although this hypothesis was completely disproved by studies made in the nineteenth century,[8] it is easy to see how it could have been formulated. Now, however, there is general agreement that socialization, over and beyond mere biological maturation, is essential to the development of self-consciousness. Deprived of human association, the biologically developing infant could scarcely develop a sense of self.

BODY AWARENESS

The infant at first has no conception of what belongs to his body and what does not.

> At six or eight months he has certainly formed no clear notion of himself. He does not even know the boundaries of his own body. Each hand wandering over the bedspread for things

which can be brought into the mouth discovers the other hand and each triumphantly lifts the other into his mouth; he draws his thumb from his mouth to wave it at a stranger, then cries because the thumb has gone away. He pulls at his toes until they hurt and does not know what is wrong.[9]

He may scratch, claw, bite, and pull parts of his anatomy just as though they were objects external to him.

Slowly the infant learns the boundaries of his own being and learns to make distinctions between what is part of his body and what is part of something else. Shinn has described two incidents in this process:

> The 181st day her hand came into contact with her ear; she became at once very serious, and felt it and pulled it hard; losing it, she felt around her cheek for it, but when her mother put her hand back, she became interested in the cheek and wished to keep on feeling that. . . . To the end of the year, she would . . . feel over her head, neck, hair, and ears; the hair she discovered in the eighth month, 222nd day, while feeling for her ear, and felt it over and pulled it with great curiosity.[10]

This lack of differentiation between body and surrounding environment is merely a specific illustration of the infant's generally blurred perceiving. Piaget[11] has used the term "indissociation" to describe this undifferentiated perception.

CONFUSION OF "SELF" WITH "NON-SELF"

Even after the infant learns to distinguish between body and world, he does not have full self-awareness. The child continues for several years to have difficulty in properly locating processes that go on "within his own mind" and in keeping them separated from external processes. Thus Piaget notes that if the child is asked, "Where is the dream when you dream?" he will say that it is "in the room" or "beside the bed." Asked by Piaget where the name of the sun is located, children usually answered that it was very high in the sky. Conversely, they attributed to words qualities signified by the objects or events. Thus the word "elephant" was declared to be a very "strong" word in comparison to "mouse." The child, of course, also projects human attributes onto various animate and inanimate objects. He may believe, for example, that fish eat three meals a day; that if a pin is poked into a tree, the tree feels it; that it hurts a rock to be broken by a hammer. He assumes that all persons are like himself, that animals are like humans, and that inanimate objects are alive. He may even identify himself with material things:

> The externalization of the ego . . . appears in the child's identification with objects. . . . Identifying himself with the broken doll, with the cut flower, with the eaten animal . . . if a match is burning and becomes smaller and smaller the child may believe that the match feels this painfully and that a corresponding thing might happen to himself.[12]

The young child has a particularly difficult time learning to use personal pronouns correctly. His initial use of "I," "me," "mine," "you" is confused and inaccurate. He hears his mother use the word "you" toward himself, and will address himself as "you" instead of "I." He may speak of himself in the third instead of the first person: for example, "Donnie wants that."

> The two-year-old often confuses quite sadly the first, second, and third persons. He may be overheard to say to himself, "You be careful, William get hurt. No! I won't get hurt." He is first, second, and third person all at the same time.[13]

Cooley has suggested that young children misuse pronouns because they cannot directly imitate them. Ordinary words, such as "apple" or "doll," can be easily imitated, whereas words like "you" or "I" have to be reinterpreted by the child rather than copied directly.[14] Actually, as we have seen, the child at first does not imitate such words as "apple" or "doll" very directly. However, he has his chief difficulties with relationship terms such as "brother," "father," "I," "you," since in his early years he is unaware of perspectives other than his own.

His increasing accuracy in the use of pronouns shows the child's maturing conception of his own existence and individuality. This is reflected also by the acquisition of new pronouns. Before the age of five, first-person pronouns in the plural ("we," "us," "ours,") appear very infrequently in the youngster's vocabulary. They increase as the child grows older and becomes more conscious of his participation in groups.

THE LOOKING-GLASS SELF

There is a close connection between self-awareness and imagining how one looks to other persons. As an illustration, we may consider what is popularly termed "self-consciousness." Almost everyone has been placed in a situation in which he felt an acutely heightened sense of self, that is, he was extremely conscious of his existence and appearance. Consider, for example, a student making his first speech in a public-speaking class: he perspires, fidgets, feels tense, may even have "butterflies in his stomach." Although he may be on good terms with everyone in his audience, he concentrates on such thoughts as "What are they thinking of me?" "How do I look?" "What kind of an impression am I making?" Nor does our imaginary fright-stricken student have to face an audience to feel acutely self-conscious: he need only think of facing the audience to experience some of the same symptoms. "Mike-fright" has been known to occur to radio speakers before a "dead" microphone. "Self-consciousness" is an extreme example of being self-conscious; it illustrates very well the connection between self-awareness and imagining what one looks like to others.

Cooley, when he coined the phrase "the looking-glass self," had this connection in mind. His analysis is worth quoting:

> As we see . . . our face, figure, and dress in the glass, and are interested in them because they are ours, and pleased or otherwise with them according as they do or do not answer to what we should like them to be; so in imagination we perceive in another's mind some thought of our appearance, manners, aims, deeds, character, friends, and so on, and are variously affected by it.
>
> A self-idea of this sort seems to have three principal elements: the imagination of our appearance to the other person; the imagination of his judgment of that appearance; and some sort of self-feeling, such as pride or mortification. The comparison

with a looking-glass hardly suggests the second element, the imagined judgment, which is quite essential.[15]

As we have noted, the newborn infant lacks the ability to visualize himself through the eyes of others. He is not born with this ability: he must acquire it through learning.

LEARNING TO TAKE THE ROLE OF THE OTHER

Language is necessary to the development of self-awareness. Many writers have recognized this relationship and expressed it in various ways. Some have suggested the importance of linguistic anchorages like address, salutations, and property. Others have regarded parental use of the child's name as an important factor. Still others have assumed that the use of pronouns by both the child and his elders helps fix the youngster's ideas of self-reference. But none of these views is as concrete or as convincing as G. H. Mead's.

Mead notes that among the most significant adult vocalizations, from the standpoint of the child, are those which have to do with himself. These are picked up, imitated, and gradually incorporated in the evolving system of signals or cues which the child uses to stimulate himself. He hears his name repeated over and over by others who accompany it with appropriate gestures and activities to indicate what it means. The remarks which he is able to remember and to repeat to himself gradually increase in complexity: at first he can use only simple words, then groups of words, and later simple sentences. Finally he becomes capable of rehearsing in his imagination entire conversations in which he has been involved. He learns to ascribe motives to his actions, he becomes concerned over the reactions of others to his behavior.

Through this process of self-stimulation, he learns to think of himself as a person, with personal points of view, feelings, ambitions, and goals. Such recognition of himself as a person necessarily means that he recognizes or conceives of himself along lines similar to the conceptions that others have of him. In this inner forum, this personal rehearsal and dramatization of roles, the young individual learns to apply symbols to himself and to his own behavior. As Mead has pointed out, young children are characteristically deficient on the "Me" side. They respond directly to stimuli (Phase One of the internalized conversation), but do not have the means, or have inadequate means, of controlling their responses (Phase Two).

In the course of responding to himself, the child (1) develops an awareness of his own responses, (2) learns something of their consequences, and (3) achieves a certain objectivity about them. Fundamental in the process is the medium of language. Individuals become aware of objects, as we have noted before, when they are able to name and classify them. Similarly, they become aware of themselves when they learn to apply symbols to themselves and to their acts.

To the necessity of symbolization for the realization of selfhood, there ought to be added an emphasis upon the turmoil which may accompany this development of self-symbolizing. This was succinctly noted by Baldwin,[16] writing around the turn of the century. He pointed to the fact that self-conceptions depend upon assessments of others' perspectives toward one, and since wrong assessments as well as correct ones are made, the child cannot learn about himself without some turmoil. In the writings of Freud and other psychoanalysts this point is raised to a central theme. The child identifies closely with one of his parents, takes over some of his moral perspectives, and applies these to his own behavior. But the identification is fraught with peril and the internalization of parental views may result in a harsh control over basic impulses. In a later chapter, we shall deal in some detail with the Freudian view; here we wish only to note the emphasis, undoubtedly a proper one, upon the shocking and painful nature of the experience of acquiring a self.

Individuality and the Social Character of the Self

The preceding discussion indicates that the self is a social product, since it is a consequence of the individual's incorporation within his own personality structure of a social process—conversation. Indeed, in a sense, the self is just this process of intraindividual communication. Selves do not exist except in a field, or social environment, from which they cannot be separated. Intraindividual communication is only a part of the total communication network, which extends also to relations between individuals and between the individual and groups. The very idea of an isolated self as an atomistic unit is an error. Symbolic behavior, as we have shown in earlier chapters, is shared behavior. "Self" therefore implies "others" and is inseparable from them. The meanings of the symbols by which selves are organized are contributed by the responses of others. The fact that a self always seems to belong to an autonomous biological organism should not cause one to neglect the fact that it is built upon a social foundation and that it continues to draw its sustenance from its roots in social relations. As G. H. Mead has said: "No hard-and-fast-line can be drawn between our own selves and the selves of others, since our own selves exist only insofar as the selves of others exist."[17]

However, a common-sense idea of individuality runs counter to this. It is thought that because persons have unique bodies and somewhat unique experiences, they are quite autonomous products. There is no need to deny individuality in affirming the basic social nature of self. As Cooley has said, the use of the word "I"—which of course expresses individuality—would be inconceivable in the absence of an audience to address or to exert power over.[18] But in an even more subtle sense, the social nature of the self necessarily implies, rather than denies, individuality. The generalized other, the organized community, the "Me," is not a mere importation into the person; it is an assimilation attended, as remarked before, with anguish, anxiety, concern, and care—to use an old-fashioned but very meaningful term. In a report of a series of observations of his young daughter, Cooley contended that a sense of appropriation was crucial to the development of a sense of self. He pointed to the early and passionate use of pronouns like "mine" and "my." In a limited way, Cooley was getting at a much larger point, namely that people are not compliant automatons. Psychiatrists base tedious methods of psychotherapy on the knowledge that you cannot just tell the patient about himself—he must learn it for himself and pretty much at his own rate of speed. The conceptions which people have of their bodies, their actions, and their pasts are not mere reflections of the perspectives of others. They are amalgams of these perspectives—many of them originally discordant and some of them discovered by the person, rather than taught him directly. In a later chapter dealing with personality change we shall have much more to say about individuality. Here we are stressing mainly that the perspectives on self derived from significant others are like any other perspectives in that they are not adopted *in toto* or retained entirely on faith. All perspectives are tested and tried out in action. They are appropriated and possessed.

This set of assertions is in direct opposition to a view, fairly prevalent among social scientists, that the individual adapts himself to and is at the mercy of existing external conditions, including social ones. A variant of this view is the idea that children somewhat mechanically absorb perspectives of adults, particularly of parents, so that character gets passed along in a fairly regular manner despite wars, depressions, conquests, or other social change. This is something of an oversimplification, even for a homogeneous and slowly changing society. It is even less valid for a world in which change is rapid and in which each generation faces new problems.

Defense of Self

It is commonly remarked how extraordinarily obtuse all of us are in situations in which our self-esteem is involved. People often embark upon and continue in relationships with other persons without much insight into the character of the relationship. Such blindness, it is generally understood, is explicable in terms of one's self-conceptions. Psychiatrists who deal with gross and persistent errors of this kind speak of them in such terms as "defense mechanisms," "security operations," and the like, the central idea being that the person meets supposed threats to self-regard with characteristic modes of defense. Defense modes include, among others, selective inattention, anxiety reduction, evasion of responsibility, rationalization, pretense, and the disowning of undesirable qualities in oneself.

COMMON DEFENSE MECHANISMS

The theoretical treatment of anxiety by the psychiatrist H. S. Sullivan points up some of these conceptions. Even in the earliest months, according to Sullivan's theory, the child encounters situations which arouse his anxiety, and he learns to grade them in terms of the anxiety they provoke and to stay away from the most severe. Unavoidable anxiety situations come to be handled by a variety of means designed to minimize anxiety and to maximize satisfaction. Sullivan states that "the self-system comes into being, because of, and can be said to have as its goal, the securing of necessary satisfaction without incurring much anxiety."[21]

A fundamental conceptual device which children utilize, according to Sullivan, is to classify experiences as pertaining to the "good me," the "bad me," and the "not me." The first category is for acts which are approved; the second, for acts that are disapproved, and hence induce some anxiety; and the third, for acts which are so anxiety-provoking that they are more or less disavowed or "dissociated." Sullivan notes that the "not me" is tied up with emotions of dread, horror, and loathing, and is expressed obliquely with a lack of awareness—as, for example, in nightmares.

The "self-system" arises from the child's attempt to avoid anxieties arising in interpersonal relations with significant others, and especially with his mother. This system is not equivalent to an incorporation of the mother's perspective, but

> is an organization of experience for avoiding increasing degrees of anxiety which are connected with the educative process. But these degrees of anxiety cannot conceivably . . . mean . . . what the mothering one, the socializing person, believes she means, or what she actually represents, from the standpoint of the culture being inculcated.[22]

Sullivan maintains that protection against the paralyzing affects of severe anxiety is a necessity and that learning to protect oneself is part of one's educational experience.

The self-system tends to become stabilized in a generalized defense against anxiety. The person then, according to Sullivan, becomes "selectively inattentive" to happenings which could change him, since change itself leads to anxiety. Hence, awareness of one's own acts is greatly restricted, as is the understanding of others' acts. One need not assume with Sullivan that anxiety avoidance is the central feature of behavioral organization, but certainly ideas of self do interfere with what is noticed and what is learned. People do strive to maintain self-esteem and raise defenses against threats to it.

A person with insight into his own deficiencies and weaknesses and the situations in which they become manifest to others may consciously maneuver to avoid competitive games, for example, and may choose as companions persons who will not shame him by their superior skills or attainments. Thus, the need to maintain self-regard often produces a vicious cycle; those very situations wherein a weakness could be overcome are avoided. A good part of social relations is unconsciously devoted to the search for companions and activities which allow weaknesses to remain hidden or relatively unnoticed while one's stronger points are exploited.

Characteristic defenses of self may occur without realization of their nature by the individual. Some of these have been given names. For instance, a person who has failed to reach certain goals may substitute less ambitious ones in a general lowering of his level of aspiration. Another well-known device is "rationalizing," which we use in this context to mean explaining away or excusing one's failure. Another method characteristically used by some people is the shifting of one's own fault onto another: this is called "scapegoating" or "displacement." Persons aware of undesirable qualities in themselves may bolster their self-esteem by "projecting" the same qualities onto others, as when a selfish person says that it is a selfish world, *i.e.*, that everyone else is selfish too. In handling personal relations it is common for attack to be met by counterattack, whether verbal or physical. Among the more complex forms of defense is identification with an aggressor, which permits a vicarious sharing of some of his strength.

The cultural patterning of defense mechanisms is reflected in the existence of the conventions of politeness which function, at least in part, to shield sensitive egos and to allow delicate relationships to exist. As with other forms of behavior, different defense mechanisms are stressed in different groups, and the standards of politeness and rudeness vary accordingly.

There are also conventionally sanctioned tactics for defending the self which are constantly used in a quite conscious manner. These include such homely devices as physical withdrawal, changing the subject, doing favors for one's opponent or flattering him, creating diversions, sparring for time, and exploiting the vulnerable points of the attacker. Human interaction is such that one's status is often challenged, feelings hurt, and reputation impugned by the acts, whether intentional or not, of others. Anyone who does not learn to cope with these occurrences is in a peculiarly helpless and vulnerable position. Orrin Klapp[23] has illustrated this point very vividly in his discussion of fool-making situations. As he says,

> Fool-making situations are so constantly presented to the average person that he may be unable to avoid occasionally falling into the role. Life is a continual process of fool making . . . humor, derision, and belittlement are constantly assigning this role . . . social relations are continually rendered unstable by fool-making. . . . Among the major routes of escape from the fool role are the following: . . . Avoidance of the imputation by "taking" a joke and "laughing it off" implies that there has been no injury, that the jibe is ineffectual or inapplicable. . . . A counter-joke or effective repartee "turns the tables" and makes the other a fool; "having the last word" or getting the best of a contest of wits has, in fact, the effect of defining the winner as a clever hero. . . . A similar strategy involves acceptance of the fool role and its use as a "ruse" or "trap" for a clever victory. . . . [And] by suffering or showing "human" traits which arouse sympathy, a person can escape from the fool role. Excessive persecution, e.g., "carrying a joke too far," tends to make a martyr out of the fool.[24]

Psychiatrists have worked out elaborate terminologies and explanations of individual—and unconsciously used—defense mechanisms, for neurotic and psychotic patients are notable for lack of insight into their own behavior. We may accept many of the psychiatric descriptions of normal devices for self-defense without necessarily agreeing with the explanations of them. Psychiatrists tend to overstress the unconscious nature of these defense processes both because of the importance of the unconscious in their theoretical systems and because of their concern with patients in whom this aspect of behavior is exaggerated. The relatively stable and secure person may discover these processes or recognize them when they are pointed out to him. One need not be altogether skeptical about the role of rationality at this point. Normal persons are able to assimilate a fair amount of criticism, direct or implied, without serious injury to self-esteem and without reversion to self-delusion. Retrospective analysis of one's past actions cannot help but give one new perspectives and further insight into one's characteristic ways of handling personal reactions. Techniques used by the young child do not necessarily survive the maturing effects of broader experience.

DEFENSE BY DETACHMENT

Transcendence of self is made possible by the fact that through using symbols and taking the roles of others one may take the view of an outsider (observer) of one's self and one's own actions. This may lead either to concern over self and reputation or to detachment. Probably relatively few persons achieve any large measure of disinterestedness in their view of themselves, but those who do are recognized and appreciated for it. It is thus one of the most effective ways of maintaining self-esteem.

One of the outstanding signs of the achievement of this detachment is a sense of humor, especially about one's own foibles, mistakes, and weaknesses. The man who can joke when the going is rough, or in the face of failure, danger, or death, exhibits this detachment. The American officer in World War II who, in a critical phase of combat, asked his men, "What's the matter, do you want to live forever?" offered an example of it. "Gallows humor," like that of the conquered peoples of Europe who made bitter jokes at their own expense, is the expression of more than mere irony and resentment, since it indicates a realistic appreciation of an actual predicament.

PRIVACY AND THE SELF

Privacy is also related to defense of self, as the expression "invasion of privacy" makes clear. Societies everywhere have unwritten rules that allow persons to withdraw from interaction in certain situations. The retreat to privacy may be used to escape from interaction which is troubling, embarrassing, or deflating. Some people who cannot successfully cope with certain kinds of social relations make a virtual fetish of privacy.

Privacy has positive values as well. It is perhaps an absolute necessity to withdraw to repair one's energies, to ruminate over the significance of past events, and to plan. It is only in moments in which one is not reacting to other people that communication with self can be at its best. Periods of privacy designed for this very purpose are institutionalized in all societies. An obvious example is the prescription by various religions of periods of meditation, fasting, and prayer.

When others try to get at secret thoughts and intimate biographical details which the individual wishes to reveal to no one, or only to very special persons, barriers are erected. Inopportune revelation of self leaves one at the mercy of others. Privacy may be conceptualized as a series of concentric circles. The inner circle is forbidden to all trespassers. One's trusted intimates may enter into the second circle, and so on, as one moves to the outer circles which are accessible to all. This spatial symbolism is actually embodied in the architecture of dwellings, houses of worship, and public buildings and in the rules permitting or forbidding entry into various rooms.

Allowing another person to enter into the ego's central core of privacy is a delicate process fraught with peril to both parties. It is attended by misgivings and release, by hesitations and abrupt moments of confiding. Betrayal of this degree of confidence is destructive and corrosive. It has an effect like that of being turned over to the enemy after seeking refuge in the house of a blood brother. The recipient of confidence is also in a delicate position, since he may unwittingly betray the confidence or it may put him in a moral dilemma. Impersonal, institutionalized places of confessional, such as the church and the doctor's office, are designed to protect both parties.

Summary

The concept of self is an indispensable one in the description and analysis of human interaction. The self is not an entity which can be exactly located in space or as a part of the body, nor is it identical with the body. It is rather an organization or integration of an individual's reactions to (conceptions of) his own behavior. It arises from the taking of roles and the incorporation of conversation into the personality. Self-awareness is not inborn; it develops gradually in the child as he undergoes socialization. The consequences of self-awareness include the development of self-control and conscience and the learning of devices to maintain or enhance one's self-esteem. Among the latter the assumption of a detached view of one's self is peculiarly effective. The need for privacy is associated with the existence of self-conceptions in human beings, for it is in privacy that one looks over and refurbishes one's ideas of self. In the next chapter we shall turn our attention to the interrelation of self-control and social control.

SUGGESTIONS FOR DISCUSSION AND SPECIAL REPORTS

1. Trace the reaction of psychologists away from, and their return to, "metaphysical" concepts such as "self."

2. Write a paper based upon interviews with several persons about their childhood nicknames and their possible effects upon self-conception.

3. Interview nurses, or members of some other occupational group, and interpret the occupational self-conceptions that you find.

4. Trace the rise of a public hero and his fall from public favor.

5. Compare the humor of two magazines that appeal to different social strata, and interpret your results.

6. Homogeneous and heterogeneous societies must develop somewhat different methods of inducing individuals to control themselves. Discuss this point.

7. Discuss the culturally patterned aspects of privacy: for instance, bodily parts, spatial sites, gestures that permit or forbid the invasion of privacy, times of the day, and so on.

8. Compare Mead's concept of the "I" with Freud's concept of the "id."

NOTES

[1] E. Horowitz, "Spatial Localization of the Self," *J. Soc. Psych.*, 6 (1936): 379-387.

[2] C. Kluckhohn and H. A. Murray (eds.), *Personality in Nature, Society and Culture* (1st ed.), Knopf, 1948, p. 9.

[3] S. E. Asch, *Social Psychology*, Prentice-Hall, 1952, pp. 320-321.

[4] N. Cameron and A. Magaret, *Behavior Pathology*, Houghton Mifflin, 1951, p. 285.

[5] R. Benedict, *The Chrysanthemum and the Sword*, Houghton Mifflin, 1946; F. L. Hsu, "Suppression vs. Repression," *Psychiatry*, 12(1949): 223-242.

[6] M. Mead, *And Keep Your Powder Dry*, New York: Morrow and Co., 1942, pp. 128-129.

[7] J. J. Honigmann, *Culture and Personality*, Harper, 1954, pp. 291-294.

[8] See M. Sherif and H. Cantril, *The Psychology of Ego-Involvement*, Wiley, 1947, pp. 156-178.

[9] G. Murphy, L. Murphy, and T. Newcomb, *Experimental Social Psychology*, Harper, 1937, p. 207.

[10] M. W. Shinn, "Notes on the Development of a Child," *Education*, 1(1891): University of California publications, p. 143.

[11] See discussion by G. Murphy, *Personality*, Harper, 1947, pp. 336-337.

[12] W. Wolff, *The Personality of the Pre-School Child*, New York: Grune and Stratton, pp. 8-9.

[13] G. W. Allport, *Personality*, Holt, 1937, p. 161.

[14] C. H. Cooley, "A Study of the Early Use of Self-Words by a Child," in *Sociological Theory and Social Research*, Holt, 1930, p. 230; originally published in *Psych. Rev.*, 15(1908): 339-357.

[15] C. H. Cooley, *Human Nature and the Social Order*, Scribner, 1902, p. 184.

[16] J. M. Baldwin, *Social and Ethical Interpretations in Mental Development*, Macmillan, 1897.

[17] G. Mead, *Mind, Self and Society*, University of Chicago Press, 1934, p. 164.

[18] C. H. Cooley, "A Study of the Early Use of Self-Words by a Child," in *Sociological Theory and Social Research*, Holt, 1930.

[19] B. Bettelheim, *Symbolic Wounds*, Glencoe, Ill.: Free Press, 1954.

[20] From a lecture by Herbert Blumer.

[21] H. S. Sullivan, *The Interpersonal Theory of Psychiatry*, Norton, 1953, p. 169.

[22] *Ibid.*, pp. 166-167.

[23] O. E. Klapp, "The Fool as a Social Type," *Am. J. Soc.*, 55 (1949): 157-162.

[24] *Ibid.*, pp. 159-161.

SELECTED BIBLIOGRAPHY

Bain, R., "Self-and-Other Words of a Child," *Am. J. Soc.*, 41(1936): 767-775. An observational study of the child's initial use of personal pronouns. A re-check of an earlier observational study by C. H. Cooley.

Freud, A., *The Ego and the Mechanisms of Defense*, New York: International Universities Press, 1946. Descriptions of individual defense mechanisms and psychoanalytic explanations of them.

Goodenough, F., "The Use of Pronouns by Young Children: A Note on the Development of Self-Awareness," *J. Genet. Psych.*, 52(1938): 333-346. Along the same line as the Cooley and Bain studies, but more extensive and systematic.

Horowitz, E., "Spatial Localization of the Self," *J. Soc. Psych.*, 6(1936): 379-387. Response of people to questions concerning the bodily location of their selves.

Kuhn, M. H., and T. S. McPartland, "An Empirical Investigation of Self-Attitudes," *Am. Soc. Rev.*, 19(1954): 68-78. A recent study which attempts to quantify an elusive subject matter.

Mead, G. H., *Mind, Self and Society*, University of Chicago Press, 1934. Especially the section on "self." This is an invaluable reference for certain aspects of the materials covered in this chapter.

Murphy, G., *Personality*, Harper, 1947. A good discussion of the literature on self and self-awareness. Emphasizes the importance of the concept for the psychologist.

Schilder, P., *The Image and Appearance of the Human Body*, New York: International Universities Press, 1950. A provocative book by a well-known psychoanalyst.

Sherif, M., and H. Cantril, *The Psychology of Ego-Involvement*, Wiley, 1947. Especially Chap. V, "The Problem and a General Characterization of Ego-Involvements," pp. 92-116; Chap. VII, "The Genetic Formation of the Ego," pp. 156-198. The same remarks apply to this and to the Murphy reference above.

Sullivan, H. S., *The Interpersonal Theory of Psychiatry*, Norton, 1953. This is an extremely important and influential book. Sullivan's views of self and its development are well worth studying. The book is not difficult.

Turner, R. H., "Self and Other in Moral Judgment," *Am. Soc. Rev.*, 19 (1954): 249-259. A research report.

CHAPTER 14 · · ·

Self-Control
and
Social Control

IN THIS CHAPTER we shall deal with the more general aspects of the control of human behavior by the manipulation of symbols, looking at it first in relation to the individual and then in relation to the group or society. Just as the individual is capable of voluntary self-control, so also, in a sense, is society. This chapter is concerned with the nature and interrelationships of self-control and social control and with the implications for the freedom of the individual that are inherent in current techniques of manipulating public opinion effectively.

In his provocative novel, *Nineteen Eighty-four,* which describes a utopia in reverse, George Orwell touches upon some crucial relations between social control and individual autonomy. Orwell has the government controlling the actions and thoughts of citizens through propaganda, suggestion, and the most subtle kinds of education—the manipulation of history and language. Not only does the government rewrite history; it also develops a new language, "Newspeak," the purpose of which

> was not only to provide a medium of expression for the world-view and mental habits proper [to the people of the country], but to make all other modes of thought impossible. Its vocabulary was so constructed as to give exact and often subtle expression to every meaning that a . . . member could express, while excluding all other meanings and also the possibility of arriving at them by indirect methods. This was done by the invention of new words, but chiefly by eliminating undesirable words by stripping such words as remained of unorthodox meanings, and, so far as possible, of all secondary meanings whatever. To give a single example, the word "free" still existed in Newspeak, but it could only be used in such statements as "The dog is free from lice." It could not be used in its old sense of "politically free," or "intellectually free," since political and intellectual freedom no longer existed, even as concepts. . . . Countless other words, such as *honor, justice, morality, internationalism, democracy, science,* and *religion* had simply ceased to exist. A few blanket words covered them, and in covering them, abolished them. All words grouping themselves around the concepts of liberty and equality, for instance, were contained in the single word crimethink.

Of course no government can ever prevent the rise of special languages or entirely control the kinds of experiences which give rise to deviant and diverse behavior. Nevertheless Orwell's novel suggests some of the problems of retaining a measure of autonomy and freedom of action in a world in which the manipulation of attitudes and opinions has become a fine art. Our discussion of this problem of the interrelationships of social control, self-control, and individual autonomy leads us into a consideration of the nature of voluntary behavior and the phenomena of hypnosis and suggestion. Crowd behavior will be discussed as an example of behavior in a social situation in which individuals appear to lose their autonomy and become puppet-like in their responses to deep irrational impulses. The concept of attitude will be briefly discussed, and propaganda and education are considered as different and opposing ways of influencing and shaping attitudes.

Voluntary Behavior

The popular conception of voluntary behavior is that it involves control of behavior by an internal psychological force called "will" or "will power." This force is not thought of as being dependent upon any specific biological or neurological structure and is usually believed to be "free" and therefore essentially unpredictable. Its most typical manifestation is in choosing among alternatives.

The discerning student will recognize in this commonly held, but naïve, view the same dualistic distinction that is generally made between thinking and language. Just as language supposedly expresses thinking and is its vehicle, so voluntary behavior is supposed to be merely an expression of the person's will.

A sounder, more scientific view is the conception of voluntary behavior as a type of activity which depends upon the internalization of language. We have noted that as one ascends the evolutionary scale from the simplest forms of life to man, the central nervous system assumes greater and greater dominance. Internal cortical processes are not solely determined by stimuli from outside the nervous system, but depend also upon stimuli which originate within the system. Voluntary behavior, from this point of view, depends upon the ability of people to initiate responses within themselves which in turn inhibit or facilitate other responses. These controlling responses are verbal in nature or are derived from verbal behavior.

As a simple example, we may note that although persons ordinarily drop hot objects automatically, they can be prevented from doing so if they are warned in advance and thus conditioned not to drop them. If a person is told that a painfully but not dangerously hot object will be placed in his hand for two seconds and that he will be given fifty dollars if he does not let go, he is likely to inhibit his ordinary reflexes.

Views of volitional behavior that are remarkably alike in some of their basic outlines have been developed by Clark Hull, from the study of hypnosis and suggestibility; Luria, through the experimental study of child psychology and of hypnotism; Head and Goldstein, from the study of aphasia; and Hudgins from experiments on voluntary control of the pupillary reflex.

Hull[2] finds that there are two fairly distinct levels of human behavior: "an upper or symbolic level, and a lower non-symbolic or instrumental level." Symbolic acts are described as "pure stimulus acts, acts which function purely as stimuli to evoke other acts." The most common form of symbolic behavior is speech. Hull applied this scheme to hypnotism and voluntary behavior. He indicated that in the hypnotic situation the symbolic stimulation is (1) produced by one individual, and (2) carried out on the instrumental level by another. In voluntary behavior, however, the same person performs both the symbolic act and its instrumental sequel. To illustrate: the hypnotized person drinks a glass of water because he is told to do so by the hypnotist, whereas in ordinary life one drinks a glass of water because he tells himself to do so. The "will" is thus conceived by Hull as a symbolic process, as control of one's own behavior through self-stimulation (or what he calls "pure stimulus acts").

Hudgins[3] has demonstrated experimentally that the individual's control of his own responses by verbal mechanisms can be extended even to some reflex activities which are ordinarily beyond voluntary control—for example, the pupillary reflex. The way in which the result was accomplished throws a great deal of light on what is sometimes called the "will." The subject was first conditioned to produce the pupillary reflex when a bell was sounded through the simultaneous flashing of a light into his eyes. An electric circuit was then arranged so that when the subject closed his hand at the vocal command of the investigator, the light and bell circuits were closed, thereby causing the bell to ring and the light to go on. Finally, all other stimuli except the verbal command were eliminated and the subject's pupils were observed to contract when the experimenter gave the command. The next step in developing voluntary control of this conditioned response was to require the subject himself to repeat the verbal cue. The commands were first repeated aloud, then in a whisper, and last subvocally. The subjects were finally able to cause the pupils of their own eyes to contract merely by thinking of the verbal command.

Luria,[4] approaching the study of voluntary behavior from another perspective, also emphasizes that it involves the use by the individual of auxiliary verbal cues. He notes that people do not control their behavior directly by the exertion of "will power," but can do so only indirectly through the mediation of verbal self-stimulation. For example, if a despondent person is urged to "buck up and be cheerful" he cannot do so merely by wishing it. However, if his attention can be directed to more cheerful subjects by talking with him or by inducing him to engage in some recreational activity such as a game of tennis, the desired result may be accomplished. Similarly, as Hudgins' experiment indicates, no one can cause the pupils of his eyes to contract merely by concentrating or exerting "will power." Intermediate steps, such as those used by Hudgins, must be included.

The views of Hull and Luria, and the experimental results obtained by Hudgins and others, all point toward the same conclusion. Further corroborating evidence is found in the study of the aphasic who loses a large part of his voluntary self-control and initiative when, because of the impairment of his language abilities, he is no longer able to stimulate himself by means of verbal cues. (See Chap. 5, pp. 140-152.) That people stimulate themselves by their own verbal activities complicates the problem of controlled experiments with human subjects, as many psychologists have noted.[5]

Like the notion of will itself, the idea of "freedom of will" is based upon a false view of symbolic behavior. As a corrective we may note several points. To begin with, "free will" is not entirely free, for it is bounded, restricted, and limited by the culture of the actor. Thus, it does not occur to the readers of this book to make choices involving the values of the Bantu, Japanese, or Balinese, nor to act like these people. This may appear to be a trite observation, but its truth is often ignored. It is, for example, commonplace to blame persons who, from an objective point of view, ought not to be blamed. Thus, children are often held responsible for stealing before they know what stealing really means. Our blaming rests upon the assumption that these persons know better and have a genuine choice of attitude and act. This assumption is often false. Whatever "will" may be, it cannot operate outside the confining limits of the actor's system of symbols.

Human social behavior is not mechanically determined by immediately given external events and situations. It is organized symbolically. Human freedom is thus a relative matter. Man is not entirely bound by the physical conditions of space and time, but he is enclosed within symbolic systems. The thoughts of the prisoner in solitary confinement cannot be controlled by his jailers, but they are controlled and limited by the social groups which have imposed their standards, their moral codes, their symbols, upon the prisoner.

One of the authors once listened to a passionate plea for individual freedom addressed to a class of several hundred students by one of its members. The speaker argued that "the individual" should free himself from all "herd" influences, from all groups and institutions; that he should think and act as a free individual. This view represents a logical consequence of the popular misconceptions of "freedom," "free will," and "individuality." Its essential absurdity will be clear to anyone who reflects upon it for a moment. In the first place, if this student desired to be free of all institutions, he obviously should not have learned English or any other language. He should not have attended a university, or spoken to a class as he did. The obvious implication of his view is that man can be free only if he avoids all human contact and civilization.

Many years ago the French sociologist Durkheim[6] opposed individualistic notions of freedom and autonomy by pointing to the body of moral and social rules which are chronologically antecedent to the birth of every individual. These group rules Durkheim saw as largely controlling the behavior of individual members, duty and voluntary behavior being closely linked. Durkheim stressed that concepts and categories are supraindividual, the product of collective activities, and that since individual thinking necessarily utilizes concepts, the idea of individual volition apart from group norms is an illusory one. Blondel[7] has modified this position by arguing that it is not necessary to deny genuine individual autonomy merely because a person must always make his choice within a framework provided by his society. Freedom of the individual, he contends, is itself a social product. Man, in contrast to lower animals, is free precisely because he is a social animal living primarily in a symbolic world. To this should be added a point which we have already made in another context, namely, that no two situations are ever completely identical; hence all behavior possesses some degree of novelty, and some of it requires genuine decisions. The discovery of values and the consequent organization of behavior along new lines free men from slavish obedience to tradition; at the same time, tradition enters into the organization of new as well as customary behavior.

Hypnosis

The phenomenon of hypnosis provides striking examples of symbolic control over a wide range of human behavior. The hypnotized subject may be viewed as one who, in a peculiar sense, is relatively lacking in self, because behavior, ordinarily evoked by the person himself, is evoked by another person—the hypnotist. A whole range of behavior may be elicited from a subject by simply ordering him to act and feel in certain ways.

HYPNOTIC PHENOMENA

The behavior elicited in hypnosis is in many respects unusual and puzzling. We shall therefore begin our discussion by describing some of it, turning then to the theories that have been proposed to account for it, and finally considering its implications in relation to less extreme behavior of somewhat similar nature.

What is called the "hypnotic trance" is induced in a subject primarily by talking to him. A variety of specific devices may be used. The person may be placed in a relaxed position and told that his eyelids are heavy, that he is becoming sleepy, and that, as the hypnotist slowly counts to fifty, his sleepiness will increase until, on the count of fifty, he will be in a deep sleep. The subject may be asked initially to fix his eyes on a bright, rhythmically moving object to facilitate the process. Whatever the specific devices used, the essential factor is communication—usually verbal communication. Hypnosis may be induced over the radio or by a voice recording. The hypnotist cannot, however, induce the trance in anyone with whom he cannot communicate verbally. Lower animals, for example, cannot be hypnotized. Neither can feeble-minded persons, the insane, or very young children.

Susceptibility · Susceptibility to hypnosis, contrary to popular belief, is not correlated with lack of intelligence or lack of "will power." The person who follows the commands of the hypnotist and who succeeds in focusing on them to the exclusion of anything else may be hypnotized, even though he does not wish to be and even though he believes that hypnotic phenomena do not exist or are merely "faked." Persons who are overcome by amusement, who think of other matters, or who react in opposition to the commands, naturally do not make good subjects.

Distortion of Perceptions · When the subject has been hypnotized he can be induced to do, say, and apparently believe many things that are contrary to his ordinary behavior and beliefs. He can be made to report seeing and hearing things which the hypnotist tells him he will see and hear, such as thirteen strokes of a nonexistent clock. He will squirm uncomfortably when told he is sitting on a warm radiator, and will reach out happily to gather in coins supposedly raining from the skies. He will eat make-believe fruit, carefully peeling a ficticious banana. Told that a lemon is an apple he may agree that it tastes like one. Lewis and Sarbin[8] have shown that when a subject eats a make-believe meal under deep hypnosis, his gastric hunger contractions are apt to be inhibited as though he were eating real food. Actual perceptions can be "wiped out." Thus, the subject is told he cannot see a pack of cigarettes lying before him, and so will not reach for them when ordered to smoke. He can be told that some person in the room is absent, and when asked to count the people present will omit this person, although he will not collide with him if he walks about.

One of the most impressive features of hypnosis, in popular thought, is the inhibition of pain reactions. As is well known, the subject under hypnosis who has been told that he will feel no pain neither reports pain nor flinches when a pin is stuck into his hand or a flame is applied to his finger tips. Although rarely used since the development of anesthetics, hypnosis has been used in surgical operations, dentistry, and childbirth. For purposes of entertainment hypnotists often demonstrate that hypnosis affects the memory. Some subjects can recite poetry once learned but apparently forgotten, or recall events of early childhood. The subject may also be asked to re-enact his first day at school, or his tenth birthday, and may do so with seeming fidelity.

Posthypnotic Suggestion · Posthypnotic action can be suggested during the actual trance. When the subject is being taken out of the trance, it is standard practice to suggest that he will remember nothing that occurred during the session, and he will report that he does not remember even when later urged to try. The subject may be told that five minutes after waking he will feel intense thirst, but will not know why. Five minutes later he will get himself a glass of water. It was reported that one subject was told that when reading the even-numbered pages of a book he would breathe twice as fast as usual, and half as fast as usual when reading the odd-numbered pages. Several weeks later he was still doing this. Some persons have tried to break habits, such as smoking, by means of hypnosis, but this technique is not particularly successful, since the effects of hypnotic suggestion fade out unless they are renewed.

Moral Behavior Under Hypnosis · A controversial question is whether the hypnotic subject can be made to do anything which will harm him or which is counter to his moral ideas. Affirmative evidence is provided in a report of an investigation by Rowland.[9] He asked, and eventually persuaded, some of his subjects to reach out to touch a rubber rope (actually a coiled rattlesnake under glass). Some subjects, after hesitating, followed his command that they throw acid at him (he was protected by an invisible sheet of glass). It has argued that the subjects knew they were in an experiment and that therefore the proof is inconclusive. However, of 42 unhypnotized subjects, 41 refused to follow instructions about reaching for the snake, and the one person who complied did so because she thought it was an artificial snake and became frightened when told it was not. Experimentation to determine the limits of this kind of suggestion is beset by obvious difficulties.

Conceptual Control in Hypnosis · Some writers have characterized hypnosis as a kind of enthusiastic faking. The argument is that the subject, although he appears not to experience pain or various sensations or to see objects manifestly present, actually is merely reporting what he thinks he is supposed to. This point has been explored in experiments by Pattee.[10] He designed a box with two openings, one on the left covered with red glass, the one on the right with green glass. Inside the box were prisms which actually reversed the lines of vision. The hypnotized subject was told that he could not see with his left eye and then was told to look through the box with both eyes open and report the color that he saw. The subject thought that he saw green and denied seeing the red, because he thought that it was his right eye which perceived the green; actually, because of the prisms, it was his left or "blind" eye. Other experiments along similar lines indicate the same sort of results for hearing. Other investigations on the capacity of hypnotized subjects to regress to childhood show conclusively that they do not actually regress, but merely re-enact the gestures, or simulate the performances, which they believe to be appropriate. The performances on this kind of test, including writing, drawing, and IQ test performances, are about the same as those of nonhypnotized persons who are asked to play-act.[11]

Skepticism about the actual perceptions of the hypnotized subject is warranted in the light of the aura of mysticism which surrounds the topic in everyday discourse; but in a sense, this skepticism misses the point. Since hypnotism involves control by the central nervous system, *i.e.*, through concepts, it is to be expected that the subject acts in terms of his own conceptions. An old demonstration will illustrate the point nicely. When he is told that his hand is numb up to the wrist, the subject reports that this line of numbness is there and responds accordingly. He reacts, in other words, according to the conceptions of neurology suggested by the hypnotist and not in accordance with actual neural structure.

The central problem of hypnosis has to do not with whether the subject's conceptions or reports are accurate, but why he acts as though they were.

Hypnotic compliance with outside commands, requests, or "suggestions" carries an aura of the fantastic or mysterious. Yet conformance with commands, requests, or suggestions under normal waking conditions seems, to most people, an ordinary fact of life. This is so even when the suggestions and demands are fairly extreme. Even the phenomena of hypnosis find their parallels in normal behavior. To illustrate this to himself, the reader might stretch out his arms before him parallel to the ground; and then imagine that an iron bar runs through his right arm from shoulder to hand. His right arm is likely to become, as it does in many people, rigid and heavy. Some people, if asked to clasp their hands tightly and imagine them to be stuck together, have momentary difficulty in wrenching them apart. Everyone recognizes that he can deliberately and imaginatively transport himself into certain social situations and so temporarily lose contact with reality. Much behavior, as everyone knows, is determined by what one believes, fantasies, or imagines to be true. The mysteriousness of hypnosis arises largely from the fact that the source of control in hypnosis is another person.

THEORIES OF HYPNOSIS

Theories of hypnosis center around explaining how the outsider gets control. Ordinarily, an individual who receives commands or suggestions makes some evaluation of them before translating them into commands which he gives himself. Of course, if one is crossing the street and someone shouts "Look out!," he reacts without thinking it over; but usually self-stimulation is requisite to action, and involves the regulatory self system described earlier.

The Conditioned-Response View · Among the theoretical explanations of hypnosis is that it is a form of conditioned response. This theory is embodied, for example, in the writing of Hull, who was mentioned earlier. The central idea is that words become linked with acts and tend to call forth these acts. Hence, "the withdrawal of the subject's symbolic activities would naturally leave his muscles relatively susceptible to the symbolic stimulation emanating continuously from the experimenter."[12] Viewed as conditioned response, the response to hypnotic suggestion, or indeed to any suggestion, involves no new principles. Pavlov makes this point when he says, "We can . . . regard 'suggestion' as the most simple form of the typical conditioned reflex in man."[13] The verbal suggestion of the other person is but an external stimulus acting to arouse a conditioned response or a set of such responses. Asch[14] has pointed out that the older speculations on the nature of hypnosis were often very much like contemporary conditioning theory.

The stimulus-response conception of hypnosis, like general conditioning theory, is subject to criticism for avoiding the issue of how self-control operates or fails to operate. It assumes that language behavior and all intellectual processes are reducible to stimulus-response mechanisms. By regarding hypnosis as merely another instance of conditioning, this view in effect denies that the phenomenon of hypnosis raises any special problems or that it in itself requires any explanation at all.

Freudian Interpretation · Although Freud used hypnosis in therapy in the early part of his career, he later abandoned it in favor of free association and other psychoanalytic techniques. However, hypnosis is still used in therapy to some extent. Freud viewed the hypnotic relation in terms of dominance and subjection. Other analysts, like Jones and Schilder, conceive of it as a kind of sexual response. Analysts generally do not pay much attention to hypnosis or advance specific theories to account for it.

A variant of the Freudian approach is represented by the view of Guze.[15] He notes that different hypnotic subjects respond differently to the same command. He interprets this as due to "their typical manner of dealing with their desires and drives." Hence, Guze hypothesizes that "all hypnotic commands become 'wishes,' (*i.e.*, desires and drives) in the subject's thinking." The subject handles them as he handles his other wishes: he may accept the wish enthusiastically, resist it but carry it out, reject it, carry it out and feel remorse, and so on. The point that individuals behave differently in response to the same stimulus, whether under hypnosis or not, is well taken. But Guze's account does not particularly advance our knowledge of what hypnotism itself is. Neither is his description of hypnosis as a heightened state of emotion illuminating.

A *Role Theory* · Another attempt to explain hypnosis is that it is goal-directed behavior, the object of which is to behave like a hypnotized person, "as this is continuously defined by the operator and as this is understood by the subject."[16] This conception implies complementary roles of hypnotizer and hypnotized, and T. Sarbin[17] has made this view more explicit. The subject, he says, attempts to enact the role of a hypnotized person, and the success of the attempt is a function of three factors: favorable motivation, role perception, and aptitude for role taking. The subject is likened to an actor on the stage, who also strives to act a fictional or "as if" role. The hypnotizer is analogous to the stage director. Both actor and hypnotized subject may lose themselves in the excitement of the role in the sense that they focus full attention on it and fail to notice many events that occur concurrently. Sarbin's account is designed to explain the differential ease with which persons can be hypnotized. Correlation of role-taking ability with susceptibility to hypnosis is not an easy matter to test, since the former ability is a fairly vague one. Sarbin's formulation, however, has the virtue of making the subject an active participant in the hypnotic process rather than a puppet, and it does point to an over-all organization of behavior. On the other hand, calling hypnosis "role-playing" does not explain it. Such a definition merely says that the behavior is organized much like other behavior and involves a process of interaction. In a sense, hypnosis is explained away by first noting how subjects act and then suggesting that they act this way because they think they should.

Thus, despite many years of close scrutiny, the nature of hypnotic behavior is still largely unknown. Yet any social-psychological scheme must take it into account. The fact that the hypnotizer gives verbal commands or suggestions that are more or less obeyed by the subject implies that the study of hypnosis must be approached through the study of language behavior and the communication processes. This, in turn, means that the study of hypnosis will profit directly from studies of two kinds, neither having to do exclusively with hypnosis: (1) the study of other forms of suggestion, command, request, and persuasion, and ways of influencing others in general; (2) the investigation of the nature of self-control.

Virtually all investigators refer to the narrowing of the focus of attention or consciousness of the hypnotized subject. He does not notice many sounds and sights, and conflicting or distracting suggestions from bystanders are ignored and possibly not heard. Likewise, the commands of the hypnotizer do not arouse, to the extent that commands ordinarily do, consideration of alternative courses of action. This is what loss of self-control under hypnosis means. This is not to say that the subject always obeys without some conflict or indecision. Indecision or consideration of alternatives necessarily involves seeing one's actions, imaginatively, ahead of time from various viewpoints. This awareness of alternative perspectives vanishes or is greatly reduced under hypnosis.

Suggestion

William McDougall defined suggestion as the acceptance of a proposition in the absence of logically adequate grounds. This squares with common-sense expressions like "He is gullible" and "He will swallow anything." The basis of this usage is the recognition that an irrational process is at work. During the nineteenth century considerable stress came to be placed upon the illogicality of human behavior. LeBon, for example, placed irrationality and suggestion at the center of his thinking about crowd behavior. Tarde, a French judge, wrote extensively on imitation and suggestion, and his notion that these processes underlie much social life attracted attention in many countries. The instinct doctrine emphasized the nonrational aspects of human nature and give support to the trend, as did the Freudian conception of the unconscious. The development of mass media of communication and of self-conscious advertising and propagandizing, along with the rise of the Nazis and other anti-intellectual movements, have provided more evidence of man's irrationality.

The term "suggestion" has sometimes been applied to situations in which the suggestion may be said to emanate from behavior or from the situation rather than from persons. Thus, if a subject is shown a series of lines, each one longer than the one before, he will come to expect the next one to be still longer and may judge it to be so even if it is not (the Binet illusion). This involves an anticipation on the basis of previous experience and is not necessarily irrational.

The most usual technical usage of the concept of suggestion is something like McDougall's, and the source of suggestion is usually thought to be other persons. Numerous experiments show that people's judgments are affected by the statements and opinions of others, especially persons with prestige. Thus a quotation by Thomas Jefferson about the occasional necessity of rebellion was given to subjects for evaluation. Later they were told that the author of the statement was Lenin. Re-evaluation downward was made by subjects who thought less well of Lenin than Jefferson.[18] Many similar experiments, turning upon the misnaming of writers and artists, gave similar results. Suggestibility such as this is perfectly well known in a common-sense way. Courts of law, for example, recognize it and seek to guard against it. Logicians have a term for a fallacious argument called the argument *ad hominem*, which seeks to discredit an opinion or line of reasoning by attacking the man who presents it. Much of the experimentation with suggestion has been devoted to proving that it occurs and showing the extent of its occurrence. Little work has been done toward determining the conditions under which it operates or fails to operate, or what mechanisms are involved.

The line between suggestion and rational advice is sometimes very difficult to determine. When the man of prestige gives an opinion or a suggestion, particularly when he is a specialist with a formalized status, such as a physician, the opinion is not to be lightly disregarded by an intelligent person, regardless of whether he has any real grasp of the reasons for the suggestion. In an era of specialization much must be taken as a matter of faith. Persons who are unable to see their way through difficult problems of any kind are, perhaps, particularly open to suggestion. This is because they hope to have new alternatives presented (*i.e.*, suggested) to them, or, being desperate, they are willing to try any proffered solution. An experiment by T. Coffin[19] produced this same conclusion. He notes that "there is a tendency for suggestibility to increase with the difficulty of the problems" presented to subjects, and that suggestibility tends to decrease when subjects are given more information and understand the problems better. Response to suggestion certainly has its irrational and unrealistic aspects, but much of what is called suggestibility actually involves judgment and reasoning and may represent a quite realistic adaptation. The very term "suggestion" is vague. In its broadest sense it encompasses virtually all social interaction and learning. When we speak of a "suggestible person," we often mean merely that we do not understand the basis of his choices and decisions.

IMITATION

The concept of imitation has had a history much like that of suggestion. For a time in the late nineteenth and early twentieth centuries it was elevated to the rank of a universal explanatory principle, or instinct. After this period of popularity it again became a common-sense descriptive term rather than a technical explanatory one. Like "suggestion," "imitation" covers a whole gamut of behaviors, ranging from rational copying to unwitting and irrational mimicry. As an example of the latter behavior one may cite the way in which speech and gestural mannerisms are unwittingly adopted by one sojourning in a foreign country. E. Faris[20] gives an amusing instance of this. He lived for a while with a preliterate people who used

> a rather inelegant gesture, which consisted of pointing with the lips instead of with the hand. The lips were protruded in an exaggerated fashion toward the object indicated. One could hardly imagine oneself wishing to acquire this gesture, and when a friend one day told me I was doing it, I denied the statement, but a little later, when caught in the act, had to confess.

Taking over the mannerisms of others is tied up with adopting something of their perspectives. This may be done with or without awareness. When we imitate others deliberately the imitation is not a blind activity, but implies choice and some degree of reasoned decision. In the latter sense, imitation is little more than learning from direct observation. A person taking up a new occupation doesn't wait to be told everything, but watches what others do and follows their lead. Instead of taking over another person's behavior, however, one may reject it or act in an opposite manner. Thus, E. Faris has pointed out that a person who is trying to develop a more erect and soldierly carriage may be reminded of his resolve by the sight of a slouching person. The variety of mechanisms involved in imitation, and the diversity of the acts to which it refers, has caused the concept, like that of suggestion, to drop out of extensive use except as a rough descriptive term.

Crowds and Loss of Self-Control

There is a long tradition, running back especially to the French sociologist LeBon, which views crowd behavior as something akin to hypnotic behavior. LeBon thought that in the crowd

> the disappearance of the conscious personality, the predominance of the unconscious personality, the turning by means of suggestion and contagion of feelings and ideas in an identical direction, the tendency to immediately transform the suggested ideas into acts; these, we see, are the principal characteristics of the individual forming part of a crowd. He is no longer himself, but has become an automaton who has ceased to be guided by his will.[21]

Mechanisms of imitation and suggestion have been put forward in the past in explanation of the impulsive and sometimes incredibly destructive actions of crowds. A principal feature of crowd behavior is the striking manner in which persons appear to lose much of their ordinary self-control and sense of responsibility so that they engage in "uninhibited" acts which later appear strange even to them. Crowds have been classified in many different ways. We shall discuss three types in order to illustrate the influence which crowds have on their members.

THE ACTING CROWD

The acting crowd starts out as a mere aggregate of individuals, most of whom do not know each other. When the crowd is large this atmosphere of anonymity is enhanced. The gathering may be the result of a series of exciting rumors and events, like the Yugoslavian street mob which shortly after the outbreak of hostilities in World War II stoned a local German travel agency. The participants of an acting crowd occasionally may be brought together without such an elaborate build-up: they may gather out of curiosity, for example, and may end up by acting en masse. Nevertheless their action must arise from some sort of common background of experience. Generally, however, the gatherings and behavior of an acting crowd can be traced to some background of shared tension and unrest; this is true of lynch mobs, revolutionary crowds, and food rioters. Although there may be considerable diversity in its membership, the behavior of the crowd is based upon common backgrounds of experience.

The actual formation of the gathering is dependent upon an event which people see as interesting or intriguing. Attention is focused upon that event, and thus responses to competing stimuli are momentarily inhibited. A concrete example will make this clear:

> [Shortly after the outbreak of the Russian revolution, a mass of lower-class people was looting up and down the streets of the town.] Irina came from her room and, heedless of everything, sat down at the piano and began playing chromatic scales. We all rushed at her in horror. But it was too late. They'd heard the scales. . . . Groups began gathering in front of the windows and we heard a drunken voice shout: "We spill our blood at the front and the bourgeois play here on pianos!"[22]

When people are in close physical proximity and are all focusing upon the same object, they may talk, jabber, shout, and gesticulate about it. The attention of members of the crowd may shift from the initially exciting object. But this does not mean that the crowd will disperse, for the members may continue to interstimulate one another by shouting, gesturing, and talking and through sheer physical proximity. Consequently, excitement is cumulative and shared —the crowd is constantly restimulated. Hangers-on and latecomers often get drawn into the crowd against their wills by the rising excitement and tension.

The effect of milling, shouting, and gesturing is to produce a temporary common mood, very much as an exciting party will cancel out initially different moods and produce similar ones in all or most of the guests. The members of the crowd become set to respond in very similar ways to the same stimuli, whereas previously their potential responses may have differed considerably. For example, if the police order a gathering crowd to disperse, uncoordinated variable reactions are probable, whereas after the crowd has formed it is likely to react to such an order as a unit.

The crowd may mill about and shout for some time, as though it were on the verge of acting en masse; but eventually participants may begin to drift away until the group disappears. At other times the crowd members may become more and more excited and eventually act as a massive unit, as a mob. When this happens they set out toward something or after someone.

Although the mob in action may be terrifying, there is always a gradual build-up and a background of prior events which makes its actions intelligible. The intensely exciting interaction has the effect of inhibiting divergent responses and facilitating similar ones. Perceptual and emotional responses are narrowed down; they become focused on a relatively narrow range of stimuli. In common-sense terminology, people at this time are interested only in seeing, hearing about, thinking about, and remembering certain things; their attention is concentrated and channelized by the shouts and excitement that emanate from the crowd. To return to the looting Russian mob:

Groups began gathering in front of the windows and we heard a drunken voice shout: "We spill out blood at the front and the bourgeois play on pianos!" "To the devil with the bourgeois!" cried another. "Bash in their fat faces for them!" "Get them out from behind their curtains!" "Out with them!" "Hang them!" "Shoot them!" And like a hundred-headed monster, the frenzied crowd made a dash for our door.[23]

Such slogans are spontaneous expressions of intensive direction of interest, and their effect is to organize further the immediate responses of most hearers, preparing them to respond to the same stimuli in similar or identical ways. When collective excitement has reached this pitch of intensity it does not take very much to get crowd members to act as a unit. The unity may be partial; for example, a section of a crowd may beat up an inquiring latecomer, while the attention of the rest of the crowd is directed elsewhere. When the crowd does constitute a genuine unit, a phrase, a word, or even a gesture may be sufficient to precipitate the entire mass into action.

It is conventional to note that the crowd is fickle and changeable; that it may shout its approval of a slogan at one time, only to ignore or to be angered by it immediately after. Some members of the crowd may even attack the person who uttered it. Reactions are spontaneous and may be successively contradictory, but only because the crowd is set to respond as a unit without possessing stable conventional definitions to guide it. To be sure, the members of a crowd are not so fickle that they may do anything and everything. A group of white Southern lynchers does not kill white people or destroy the property of white people, except by mistake or to get a Negro. A revolutionary mob never decides to go to the movies or ride bicycles. There are limits to what a mob will do.

A crowd is not always destructive; its action may be noble or sacrificial. Sometimes the perceptions of crowd participants are so focused on certain objects that they are indifferent to the more sordid temptations of everyday life—as in this instance: "The howling, swarming, ragged crowd which invaded the Tuileries [palaces] during the revolution of 1848 did not lay hands on any of the objects which excited its astonishment, any one of which would have meant bread for many days."[24]

Under conditions of normal living, people suppress, inhibit, and control their responses by means of an internalized symbolic process. Some actions, however, occur unwittingly and without conscious control. The number of responses that are made without awareness is increased in crowd situations because crowd members become increasingly focused on the responses of other people and on external events, and grow steadily less attentive to themselves. One may observe this reduction of self-awareness at a basketball or football game. As the crowd becomes absorbed in the game, people make gestures and utter sounds and statements of which they are scarcely aware and which they would ordinarily inhibit or suppress. In the intense interaction of the acting crowd, this loss of inhibition—of self-control—is more evident. There is some evidence that memory for events occurring in the crowd is blurred. A "condition that makes recall difficult is the lack of clear-cut action that would help participants reconstruct events."[25]

Because the acting crowd acts spontaneously and unself-consciously, it may be an important instrument for social change. Of course it may simply dissolve after letting off collective steam, but it may also prove to be the historical spark that sets larger events into motion, as did the Petrograd street crowds of 1917. In the crowd situation, as Sherif notes, "formulas or slogans arise or become standards . . . which [also] on later occasions may move the individual to action."[26] The symbols temporarily shared by the crowd members may be carried over, later becoming part of the response systems of persons who were not members of the crowd. A series of crowd incidents or even a single incident may have the effect of rousing people to talk and act with respect to far more important matters than the crowd activity itself. The acting crowd may, in short, become a symptom of shifting loyalties and new orientations.

THE EXPRESSIVE (OR DANCING) CROWD

The description of the acting crowd holds also for the expressive crowd up to a certain point. It sometimes happens that a crowd reaches an intense pitch of excitement without either dispersing or going into action toward a goal. Participants jostle, mill, shout, but for some reason do not respond collectively to any proposed plan or inciting slogan. The members continue to jostle, mill, and shout—only more intensely. "The crowd has to act, but it has nothing toward which it can act, and so it merely engages in excited movements."[27] In their excitement participants may laugh, weep, grunt, growl, bark, leap, dance, jerk, twitch. This they tend to do rhythmically and in unison, until large segments of the formation are engaged in making the same responses over and over. Some revival meetings take this form. The following description of a huge nineteenth-century Kentucky revival composed of many crowds will serve to show to what extent people may lose control of themselves—though the writer has probably embroidered a bit on reality.

> A great number were seized with an impulse to leap or jump. . . . Some became cataleptic and remained in that condition from a few minutes to several days. Many were affected with the "jerks," a spasmodic contraction of the muscles which sometimes caused the head to turn from side to side with such rapidity that the features were indistinguishable; sometimes the whole body was affected and the head was jerked backward and forward so violently that the head almost touched the floor behind and before, and the reversal of the motion was so sudden that the hair, if it was long, would crack and snap like a lash. . . . Others, drawn double, with head and feet together, rolled round and round like a wheel, and still others were dashed to the ground and bounced from place to place like a football. . . . Others hopped about like live frogs. . . . Many others fell suddenly to the earth as in an epileptic fit; this was called "the falling exercise." One person's falling seemed to be the signal for others . . . it was very contagious. Where these vast crowds were assembled, the number of those affected ran into the hundreds. . . . There was another class known as the "barkers" . . . people would get down on all fours and bark and growl like dogs . . . would get down in front of the preacher and bark as long as he preached. At first those who had the barks felt very much humiliated at being compelled to do a thing that seemed so degrading, but later they were regarded as possessing a larger measure of the Holy Spirit. . . . The "holy laugh" was

another peculiar feature. . . . Sometimes while the sermon was in progress half the congregation would be laughing aloud in the most serious way . . . for they regarded it as a part of the worship.[28]

The sober and sophisticated twentieth-century churchgoer may well ask what all this vulgar and irresponsible behavior has to do with religion without recognizing that his own religion or denomination may have sprung from just such a source. The members of an expressive crowd, meeting for the first time, have a background of individual restlessness, discontent, and tension.

This kind of behavior is not necessarily induced by a single meeting or a single inflammatory speech by a revivalist. Historical evidence indicates that despite the background of personal and social unrest, revivalists sometimes had to work on a community for several days before a cumulative effect was reached.[29] Following Blumer,[30] we may note that the intense and rhythmical movements of the expressive crowd provide a temporary but powerful organic release. The person feels immensely exhilarated, and fulfilled. The probability that the source of this catharsis will be recognized by the person as purely physiological is small: it is but a short step for him to assume that the miraculous release has come from a divine source. It is particularly easy to make this assumption because the ecstasy is shared with others.

The collective ecstasy may end in nothing more significant than a temporary sense of well-being; or it may encourage people to strive for a repetition of the experience. It may even result in a decision to meet again at regular intervals for more of the same miraculous, inspired activity. In this case the original expressive acts, such as "quaking" or "shaking," may be defined as sacred, as may the meeting place and the utterances of leaders. The end product may be the establishment of a new religious sect or movement.

THE AUDIENCE CROWD

An audience may be described as an "institutionalized crowd."[31] It meets at a predetermined time and place for a specific and announced purpose, and its behavior is strictly conventional. The "speaker crowd," on the other hand, may be thought of as an audience which becomes so aroused and excited as to break through the ordinary conventional rules which govern, let us say, the behavior of an ordinary citizen attending a concert or a public lecture.

One who addresses an audience in order to arouse it to crowd-like action must transform it from a subdued, self-controlled aggregation of persons into an excited or activated unitary mass of people. As excitement increases in pitch, the crowd becomes more and more subject to the control of the skillful demagogue who knows how to manipulate it.

Various techniques of arousing collective excitement have received wide publicity in connection with their use by the Nazis and the Italian Fascists. To provoke excitement it is better to have your audience standing, close together if possible, rather than seated in standardized, fixed seats. The singing of songs helps to break down "social distance," makes people feel more akin, and calls up common memories, pleasant or unpleasant. Singing also sets up rhythmic movements in the crowd, which help to break down barriers of individual reserve and to increase general feelings of excitement. Singing takes their attention off their own individual responses, as do colorful flags, striking uniforms, stirring music, torches, and other dramatic stage effects. Night meetings are probably more effective than daytime gatherings. The Nazis were past masters in planning and setting the stage for meetings of this kind. The speaker himself must strive for drama, excitement, rhythm, and tension. He may plead, accuse, command, cajole by turns. Whatever he says must fit into his listeners' categories of experience, must be couched in their language. To arouse them he must utilize their own stereotypes, slogans, emotions, and memories, but he must subtly shape these for his own ends. Hitler in his speeches, for example, drew on German middle-class hatred of the English, the French, the Communists, the Jews, the big business corporations, war reparations, and the Versailles Treaty.

The responses of the audience indicate to the skilled demagogue whether or not it is being carried along. If untouched, the audience remains a stolid and unresponsive aggregation of individuals;

but if it catches his excitement and tenseness it responds in kind. People may yell, clap, stamp, whistle, gesticulate, or hurl imprecations at their absent enemies. As the barriers break down, persons become less self-conscious, speaking and shouting to each other spontaneously.

The speaker may be content merely to arouse a common set of responses from his audience or to channelize their thinking along certain desirable paths. Usually, however, he seeks also to influence overt behavior. He may ask his listeners for monetary contributions, for their time and their services, or he may ask them to join an organization or to resign from another. In some instances the primary goal of the speaker may be to urge his audience into mob action—demonstrating, hanging, burning, stoning, smashing, and the like. Although he himself may lead them into doing these things, the speaker may be content to let anyone else lead them so long as they move toward the goal he has set up. A famous illustration is Antony's "Brutus is an honorable man" speech in Shakespeare's *Julius Caesar*:

> For I have neither wit, nor words, nor worth,
> Action, nor utterance, nor the power of speech,
> To stir men's blood: I only speak right on;
> I tell you that which you yourselves do know,
> Show you sweet Caesar's wounds, poor poor dumb mouths,
> And bid them speak for me: but were I Brutus,
> And Brutus Antony, there were an Antony
> Would ruffle up your spirits, and put a tongue
> In every wound of Caesar that should move
> The stones of Rome to rise and mutiny.
> *(Julius Caesar*, Act III, Scene ii)

Speakers to audience crowds sometimes arrive at positions of considerable power. Their listeners come to attribute to them infallibility and wisdom and a touch of the supernatural. Some social scientists have called this type of speaker a "charismatic" leader. It is particularly in the early stages of social movements that charismatic individuals reach prominence. In our time, Lenin, Gandhi, Hitler, Father Divine, and Dr. Townsend, among others, have been thus idealized and worshiped.

In the modern world, the crowd–speaker situation is one of the commonest and most important means of influencing public opinion. Politicians know the value of personal face-to-face contacts—they still find it necessary to make campaign tours. It is probable that no significant movement has ever originated except through face-to-face contacts between leader and followers; although when a movement has once gained momentum it may be organized, directed, supported, and given an added impetus by press, radio, and other indirect media. More will be said of this in the section on propaganda and persuasion.

Persuasion and Propaganda

Propagandists and advertisers are often described as persons who manipulate others by symbolic means. Propaganda and advertising are special instances of control by suggestion as MacDougall defined it, and differ primarily in degree from the extreme represented by behavior under hypnosis. They differ also in being mass phenomena brought about by special organizations and agencies set up to influence large numbers of persons. Some persuasion of this sort is on a face-to-face basis, but most of it is necessarily indirect through the mass media of communication.

With the rapid and extensive evolution of the mass media and a growing appreciation of the power they confer, the question of the individual's freedom to make up his own mind on public issues becomes acute, and there has been no dearth of critics to point this out. The ability of the citizen to reach intelligent conclusions depends upon the accessibility of undoctored evidence and facts. The question is: How can the citizen separate the wheat of truth from the chaff of propaganda and advertising? As we shall see, posing this question by no means implies that propaganda and advertising should be abolished or that people would suddenly become rational if they were.

EDUCATION AND PROPAGANDA

In the study of propaganda, investigators have wrestled with the problem of differentiating it from education. A common argument is that the propagandist, for ulterior motives, seeks an uncritical and unreasoned response. A counterargument has been that the same may be said of many educators; and that, in any case, the psychological processes involved in propagandizing are of the same general nature as those involved in education or any persuasive process. "The term *propaganda* does not refer to a process generally different from other processes of cognitive reorganization, but is an *epithet* applied by some people to certain persuasive techniques."[32]

At the one extreme, it is held that anyone who tries to convince another person on any subject at all is engaged in propagating an idea or point of view hence that we are all propagandists much of the time, especially whenever we try to make someone else see things as we see them. At the other extreme, it is maintained that propagandists deliberately withhold part of the truth in their efforts to persuade.

What, then, shall we call the reformer who is absolutely convinced of the nobility of his mission and who scrupulously tells the truth as he sees it? Is he propagandizing or teaching? What shall we call a professor of science who in his lectures implicitly advocates the scientific point of view while teaching the subject matter of his course? Some people would characterize the reformer as a propagandist and the scientist as a teacher; others would describe both as teachers; and still others would view the reformer as a teacher and the scientist as a propagandist.

It may be conceded that some educators regularly inculcate propaganda, and that all may, at some moment or other, do so. It is also true that propaganda campaigns may serve to enlighten and teach some people. This does not mean that we shall deny that there is a basic and useful distinction between educative and propagandistic processes. To argue that both are instances of influencing or persuading, and are therefore the same, reveals some disregard of gross differences and some lack of logic.

The very institutional forms through which propaganda and education are administered are immensely different in intent, means, and effect. In contrast to the characteristics of propaganda (or advertising) agencies, let us consider briefly some of the usual features of a university or a school. Discussion, which involves the expression of contesting viewpoints, is encouraged; and if it is not, as in the lecture system, then the listeners will probably hear differing views from different teachers. Too, students are free to discuss the lecture among themselves and to go to the library to check its accuracy and study opposing views. Ideally, the teacher himself presents more than a single viewpoint and suggests or assigns reading that covers considerable ground. Even when exercises are utilized, as in mathematics, the aim is to make the student so skillful that he can use for his own purposes the techniques he learns. Ideally, also, no ulterior motives are served in education. Independence and originality are valued and encouraged, and the uncovering of new facts and perspectives is welcomed.

Cynics who are interested in disparaging or debunking particular educational institutions tend to blur the lines between education and propaganda by calling such educative processes "idealistic" and "rare." The comparative rarity of educational systems like that described does not detract from the point, which is that education aims at increasing individual autonomy, although not at the expense of the general community. When we speak of an individual as having "had an educative experience," we get at the heart of education: namely, that his eyes have been opened to new knowledge and new perspectives, and that he is therefore in a certain sense free to move in new directions. Those who differ most bitterly over educational philosophies agree, at least, on this general aim of educational institutions. Even totalitarian regimes, with their strictly controlled educational systems, carefully distinguish between propagandistic teachings and education for responsible posts which require initiative, intelligence, and creative thought rather than rote skill or political enthusiasm. Sheer propaganda, for instance, would certainly not suffice to maintain the pace of a nation's scientific progress. The elite in totalitarian regimes recognize the necessity of guarding against being taken in by their own propaganda. The same problem exists wherever state-sponsored propaganda is disseminated. Each governmental agency must, in order to operate effectively, base its plan upon a realistic appraisal of the actual facts. This means that various agencies must be informed concerning each other's facts and propagandas.

The differences between educative and propagandistic processes are also made evident by comparing the products. From educational institutions there comes a stream of persons among whom are the future scientists, judges, statesmen, physicians, educators, technicians, and intellectual leaders. Education produces dissent and diversity of opinion. The typical products of a monolithic state-controlled propaganda system differ greatly from this group. The Communist Party member who unswervingly follows the Moscow line, changing his opinions from week to week, is a familiar example of the latter.

It is a travesty of fact to argue that the "cognitive processes" developed in the educative process and reflected, let us say, in the typical publications of university professors, do not differ in kind from those that enter into the speech of a party hack or demagogue or the advertisement urging us to smoke a certain brand of cigarette or to use a certain kind of toothpaste. When educational institutions go to seed and become doctrinaire, or when they are taken over by a government to be used mainly as propaganda mills, their characteristic features are drastically changed. This change is immediately reflected in methods of instruction and in the nature of the product. Those who can see no genuine differences between education and propaganda sometimes commit the error of affirming that learning is, in its own way, just as tinged with emotion, irrational appeals, selectivity of facts, and other persuasive devices as is propaganda. The fallacy in this is the assumption that rational thinking ought to take place in an emotional vacuum. At one time the Institute for Propaganda Analysis, established to provide defense against propagandistic tactics, tended to assume that all propositions were statements of fact and therefore true, or not statements of fact and therefore propaganda.[33] Hence, the expression of any opinion, belief, evaluation, or point of view was made suspect and a subject for propaganda analysis. What is not taken into account in this conception is the reasoning process by which inferences are drawn from facts. The scientist who formulates a new theory is thus neither stating facts nor propagandizing.

Perhaps the basic omission in the idea that education and propaganda are examples of the same process is the failure to consider the relationships that exist between ideas and the objective world. If ideas are viewed only as ideas, and if all truth is regarded as relative and a mere function of agreement, without reference to fact, propaganda and education are indeed indistinguishable, and any viewpoint becomes interchangeable with any other. We recognize this type of cynicism in opportunistic thinking which regards the intellectual life as a racket and ideas as mere instruments for the furtherance of career and self-interest.

If a valid separation of educational instruction and propagandistic suasion can be made, it is profitable to make inquiry into the presumably different institutional origins and functions of each. Conceiving propaganda merely as a technique of influencing people's opinions and actions and concentrating on its psychological aspects minimizes or obscures these differences. Students of social organization cannot afford to accept the amalgamation of all forms of persuasion. It is often necessary in mass societies, in order to get quick action, that the slower processes of ratiocination and public discussion be short-circuited. The facts that propaganda appeals are irrational and that public discussion is curtailed should not blind us to the further fact that both education and propaganda have significant, although different, functions.

The fear of propaganda is not justified solely on the grounds that it may appeal to the emotions or abbreviate the realistic appraisal of issues. The chief danger arises from seizure and monopolistic control of the channels of information and propaganda, as in dictatorships. When this happens competing propagandas and channels of information with no propaganda intent are not permitted to exist, and the citizens thus perceive few or no alternatives. In this sort of regime the individual loses virtually all autonomy in those areas over which propaganda rules. Insofar as there are competing points of view presented in the public forum, even in the form of campaigns, to that extent there is freedom to balance and choose. In a mass society in which so many group interests are in conflict, promotional campaigns are a necessity if interests are to be served—including the interests of those at whom the campaigns are directed. The point can be driven home by reference to advertising. It is true that much advertising is false or slanted and is designed only to increase profits. This advertising is nevertheless not without usefulness to the buyer, since advertising keeps him informed, gives him alternatives, and suggests new styles and products.

Aside from its political and community uses, propaganda appears to be a necessary ingredient in the formation and spread of social movements of all kinds. Such movements thrive when many people simultaneously face the same baffling, frustrating, undefined, or anxiety-producing circumstances. Our age is rich in such situations. Even a partial list would be staggering. For illustrative purposes we will content ourselves by referring to wars, revolutions, depressions, inflations, invasions, and shortages of housing, food, and fuel. Sherif has termed such circumstances "critical situations."[34] Less spectacular but equally critical are those undefined issues for which we have no precise labels—such as the specter of old age faced by active but aging people. Confronted by inflation or depression or any other situation of stress, masses of people grow anxious and tense; they talk about the problematic situation, listen to proposed solutions, and become targets for both propaganda and sources of new propaganda.

Nations which emphasize reason and individual autonomy are concerned with the preservation of civil liberties, including the right to free public exposition of false and even potentially destructive ideas.

The underlying assumption in a democratic society is that free competition in the market place of ideas leads to what we might call "the survival of the fit." Ideas which stand up well in free public debate survive and come to be accepted, and others are discredited. The opportunity to examine ideas and debate them publicly without restriction is believed to be an important educative experience which promotes rationality and strengthens a democratic society.

PROPAGANDA ANALYSIS

Investigators of propaganda generally have contributed little of theoretical importance to social psychology and have noted mainly the rather obvious techniques used by propagandists. They have drawn heavily on the observations made by propagandists themselves. The principles and techniques enunciated in propagandistic writing and by advertisers have been translated into a technical idiom. For example, the effectiveness of repetition may be explained by the investigator in stimulus-response terminology. The literature is full of reference to selection of facts, slanting, cardstacking, the bias induced by name-calling, stereotypes, the big lie, and many other devices and techniques. Elaborate studies have been made of the slanting of war news, of political speeches, and of reporting and editorializing in various newspapers and magazines. All of this has served to make Americans aware of propaganda, has debunked particular campaigns, and has revealed the structure and workings of propaganda agencies. It has added little to the knowledge of the communication process, which is the essential part of being propagandized.

PROPAGANDA AS COMMUNICATION

In free discussion, for example in a parliamentary debate, an issue is attacked from as many different perspectives as can be conceived of by the participants. As the debate progresses and final solutions are approached, most of the early proposals are dropped for one reason or another. In informal argument the discussion is not formally structured, but the procedure is essentially the same. In contrast, the aim of the propagandist is to win the argument come what may, and he will use whatever devices appear effective. The aim of all these propagandistic techniques and tactics is to narrow the range of argument and simplify the issues. The aim is not to get at truth or the nature of reality, but to convert.

The propagandist's need to minimize the number of alternative views of any issue often leads him to array all views in two opposing camps, the right and the wrong, the expedient and the inexpedient, the good and the evil, the sacred and the vile. The common tactic of fusing all opposing positions into one is illustrated by the attempt to influence Americans' voting in national elections by picturing the issue as one of choosing between "creeping socialism" and "the American way of life," or between "the welfare state" and "liberty." When opponents protest that dissimilar views are being lumped together, this is either denied or the differences are minimized as essentially unimportant. The propagandist seeks to prevent the listener from grasping the perspectives of multiple others by discrediting them in advance or blocking them from view. The narrowing of perspective falsifies the real situation.

The propagandist thrives on crisis situations in which the need for action is urgent. Where no real crisis exists, it is to his advantage to make it appear that there is one, and thus cut off deliberation and lengthy discussion. He seeks to create a sense of urgency and present danger. Issues and events are pictured as historical turning points, or as portents of doom: "The crisis must be faced"; "Inaction is suicide"; "My plan is the only one"; "All good people are on our side." Much propaganda does not, of course, go to such lengths to simplify issues and situations, and, in the nature of the case, cannot. The balance of contending parties is too even and the fluidity of alliances too great.

There is a tendency in our generation to overrate the effectiveness of propaganda devices and of propaganda in general. This may possibly be explained, as some students have suggested, by the seemingly miraculous propaganda triumphs scored in the twentieth century. Two outstanding examples may be noted: the success of the English and American governmental propaganda campaigns in getting the United States into World War I, and the general success of the Nazi propaganda machine, particularly within Germany, in doing what it set out to do. Nevertheless, we should recognize that propaganda, immensely influential as it is, has definite limitations.

THE LIMITATIONS OF PROPAGANDA

The propagandist must play upon the response systems of people, and sometimes he will find his human subjects very recalcitrant. Whereas he may be able to elicit certain responses, he may be unable to elicit others. He may, for example, be able to make his audience listen to his propaganda but may find it impossible to make them act on it because of other and stronger opposing tendencies—as in the case of many Europeans who agreed with Allied underground propaganda but were too afraid of the Nazis to engage in sabotage. Two excellent examples of the direction of propaganda at relatively unresponsive audiences were the Republican political campaigns for the presidency conducted by Landon (1936) and Dewey (1944, 1948). In all three campaigns the propaganda media were largely on the side of the defeated candidates. The propagandist, even if he is very well aware of the symbol systems of his audience, may evoke conflicting responses, including some that are antithetical to his ends.

To continue with this list of propaganda limitations: the propagandist who misjudges his audience may easily elicit responses which are irrelevant or even negative to his purposes. A story was circulated during the French-German *Sitzkrieg* or "phony war" to the effect that troops from the south of France, shortly after they had been stationed opposite the Siegfried line, were addressed by the Germans over a loudspeaker. They were told that their English allies had landed in northern France and were already making love to and seducing French women. The targets of this propaganda barrage laughed heartily, since their own wives and girls were safe in the south of France. The German propagandists, so the story goes, had been unaware of the very pronounced regional biases of Frenchmen.

Another limitation is implicit in the extensive use of propaganda over long periods of time. The limitation is illustrated by the Nazi use of anti-Soviet propaganda. For years the Nazis inveighed against Soviet Russia as their greatest enemy. In 1939, when the

Germans and Russians signed a mutual nonaggression pact, German propaganda did a turnabout. Later, when the Germans invaded Russia, Nazi propagandists labored to convince their countrymen that the Russians again were villains. The propagandist, although he generally has long-range purposes in mind, works largely in terms of practicable short-range goals. Consequently, his propaganda is likely to suffer over a long period from inconsistency and contradiction. These may in time work against him as people become generally suspicious and skeptical. Hence, propagandists use the truth when it suits their purposes.

Worst of all, the propagandist may face an audience that is hostile to the ideas which he wishes them to accept. The revolutionist, in the early stages of a revolutionary movement, has to contend with such a problem. All that he can accomplish with most listeners is to catch their attention and make them aware of the existence of a new perspective. The revolutionists may labor over a period of years to build up a receptive frame of mind, or what Doob[35] calls "pre-action responses." The building up of such responses, according to Doob, can be called "a sub-propaganda campaign."[36] Most propagandists, in fact, prepare the ground in just this way before embarking on an all-out campaign.

The propagandist who is hampered by the prevailing system of beliefs may have to wait for "events to take their course" before his campaign becomes effective. In an open-class system, for instance, it does little good to talk about the cruel and heartless upper classes. But when the class structure begins to grow rigid, so that a great many people meet with frustration in their efforts to climb, revolutionary propaganda falls on more receptive ears. We can find non-revolutionary examples of this same phenomenon. In the early days of World War II, Germans were relatively immune to Allied propaganda that they would lose the war. After the setbacks in North Africa and Russia and the bombings of their cities, the Germans began to believe the Allied propaganda which had predicted these events.

A further limitation upon the propagandist is imposed by the central roles and loyalties of his audience. If the revolutionary propagandist, for example, tries to arouse antagonistic reactions toward basic institutions like the family, the church, or the government, he runs up against the peoples' conceptions of themselves as fathers, churchgoers, and loyal citizens. Nazi attacks on religious institutions backfired for this reason. The propagandist may prudently have to change his tactics and make partial compromises with the loyalties of his audience. He may have to wait until some of these fundamental loyalties are weakened by the pressure of events before his propaganda becomes effective. Ordinarily, the astute propagandist avoids a head-on clash with any deep-seated values of his audience and plays for smaller stakes. Communist propaganda in India, for example, does not inveigh against the sacred cow, nor indeed does the government of India itself dare to do this, despite the cost of maintaining countless unproductive animals. In the long run the people of India may acquire a more practical, less sacred conception of the cow; meanwhile, this whole subject remains relatively closed and must be handled gingerly.

The fundamental limitations of propaganda are strikingly demonstrated by its close association with force and other means of direct coercion. The aim of propaganda is, after all, to bring about action. If propaganda fails, other methods may be used. In totalitarian countries, police coercion and propaganda are so closely intermeshed that it is hard to separate them. It is often said that violence is resorted to when propaganda fails, but the arrest, imprisonment, and execution of recalcitrant persons are themselves consciously used so as to maximize their psychological, or propagandistic, effects. The use of force, by arousing fear, masks what is going on below the surface and thus makes it difficult for the leaders to know the extent to which propaganda is accepted. Outward conformity may disguise complete skepticism and concealed hostility. Among the best indices of the rejection of the official line, aside from overt opposition, are various forms of indirect criticism, such as stories, jokes, and rumors, and the development of the "grapevine." The very resort to violence tends to produce skepticism concerning propaganda at the same time that it inhibits the expression of this skepticism.

Summary

The loss of self-control under hypnosis indicates the extensive role of language mechanisms in voluntary behavior and suggests that the will should be conceived, not as a psychic force or entity, but as self-regulation by means of language cues. Behavior under hypnosis is a more extreme form of the type of influence constantly exerted by people over each other in ordinary social intercourse and designated by such terms as "suggestion" and "imitation." Since social control also implies control of behavior by symbol manipulation, it is closely related to self-control. The behavior of the individual in the crowd situation illustrates the manner in which persons seem to lose self-control under the influence of social pressures. The techniques of propaganda and education offer contrasting means of influencing mass opinion. The prevalence of propaganda in the modern world is a threat to individual autonomy which is dealt with in democratic societies by permitting a maximum of free discussion and by keeping channels of information open. The power of propaganda is limited in various ways; and it inevitably carries with it the danger of self-delusion.

SUGGESTIONS FOR DISCUSSION AND SPECIAL REPORTS

1. Write a report on magic and social control.

2. Trace the advertising industry's changing notions about the public's suggestibility and how to manipulate it.

3. Interview the members of some relatively homogeneous group concerning their notions of responsibility and self-control; then interpret their notions in the light of the kind of group it is.

4. Discuss the recent furor over "communists on the campus" in terms of education, propaganda, and considerations of "free will."

5. Discuss some of the relations of authority, submission, personal autonomy, and responsibility.

6. Discuss the conceptions of "will" in two different religious traditions.

7. "Free will is a semantic illusion." Is this so?

8. Contrast the loss of self-control in an acting crowd and the loss of self-control in persons who yield to a great personal desire.

NOTES

[1] George Orwell, *Nineteen Eighty-four*, Harcourt, Brace, 1949, pp. 303-304, 308.

[2] C. L. Hull, *Hypnosis and Suggestibility*, Appleton-Century, 1933.

[3] C. V. Hudgins, "Conditioning and the Voluntary Control of the Pupillary Light Reflex," *J. of Gen. Psych.*, 8(1933): 3-51.

[4] A. R. Luria, *The Nature of Human Conflicts*, New York: Liveright, 1932.

[5] See H. Cason, "The Role of Verbal Activities in Conditioning Human Subjects," *Psych. Rev.*, 41(1934): 563-571.

[6] E. Durkheim, *The Elementary Forms of Religious Life*, New York: Macmillan, 1915.

[7] C. Blondel, "Les Volitions," in Dumas, G., *Nouveau Traité de psychológie*, Paris: Alcan, 1939, Vol. VI, pp. 317-397.

[8] J. N. Lewis and T. R. Sarbin, "Studies in Psychosomatics: The Influence of Hypnotic Stimulation on Gastric Hunger Contractions," *Psycho. Med.*, 5(1943): 125-131.

[9] L. W. Rowland, "Will Hypnotized Subjects Try to Harm Themselves or Others?" *J. Ab. and Soc. Psych.*, 34(1939): 114-117.

[10] F. Pattee, "The Genuineness of Unilateral Deafness Produced by Hypnosis," *Am. J. Psych.*, 63 (1940): 84-86. Also "A Report of Attempts to Produce Uniocular Blindness by Hypnotic Suggestion," *Brit. J. of Med. Psych.*, 15(1935): 230-241.

[11] P. C. Young, "Hypnotic Regression: Fact or Artifact?" *J. Ab. and Soc. Psych.*, 35(1940): 273-278; J. Keir, "An Experiment in Mental Testing Under Hypnosis," *J. Men. Sci.*, 91(1945): 346-352; T. R. Sarbin, "Mental Changes in Experimental Regression," *J. Personality*, 19 (1950): 221-228.

[12] Hull, *op. cit.*, p. 397.

[13] I. Pavlov, *Conditioned Reflexes*, New York: Oxford University Press, 1927, p. 407.

[14] S. E. Asch, *Social Psychology*, Prentice-Hall, 1952, p. 402.

[15] H. Guze, "Hypnosis as Emotional Response: A Theoretical Approach," *J. Psych.*, 35(1953): 313-328. Also "Hypnosis as

Wish Fulfillment: A Projective Approach," *Brit. J. of Med. Hypnotism,* 2(1951): 6-10.

[16] R. W. White, "A Preface to the Theory of Hypnosis," *J. Ab. and Soc. Psych.,* 36(1941): 503.

[17] T. R. Sarbin, "Contributions to Role-Taking Theory, I: Hypnotic Behavior," *Psych. Rev.,* 57 (1950): 255-270.

[18] I. Lorge, "Prestige, Suggestion, and Attitudes," *J. Soc. Psych.,* 17(1936): 386-402.

[19] T. E. Coffin, "Suggestibility and Levels of Difficulty," in G. E. Swanson, T. M. Newcomb, and E. L. Hartley, *Readings in Social Psychology* (2d ed.), Holt, 1952, pp. 11-18.

[20] E. Faris, *The Nature of Human Nature,* McGraw-Hill, 1937, p. 78.

[21] G. LeBon, *The Crowd,* London: Unwin, 1916, pp. 35-36.

[22] A. Rachmanova, *Flight from Terror,* John Day, 1933, p. 173.

[23] *Ibid.,* p. 173.

[24] LeBon, *op. cit.,* p. 65.

[25] G. E. Swanson, in R. Freedman *et al., Principles of Sociology,*

[26] Holt, 1952, p. 568.

[26] M. Sherif, *An Outline of Social Psychology,* Harper, 1948, p. 109.

[27] H. Blumer, "Collective Behavior," in R. E. Park, *Outlines of the Principles of Sociology,* Barnes and Noble, 1939, p. 238.

[28] C. C. Cleveland, *The Great Revival in the West,* University of Chicago Press, 1916, pp. 101-102.

[29] From an unpublished study by R. R. Wohl.

[30] Blumer, *op. cit.,* pp. 238-240.

[31] K. Young, *Social Psychology* (rev. ed.), Crofts, 1944, p. 399.

[32] D. Krech and R. Crutchfield, *Theory and Problems of Social Psychology,* McGraw-Hill, 1948, p. 330.

[33] See issues of *Propaganda Analysis,* published by the Institute for Propaganda Analysis, New York.

[34] Sherif, *op. cit.,* pp. 401 ff.

[35] L. W. Doob, *Public Opinion and Propaganda,* Holt, 1948, p. 354.

[36] *Ibid.,* p. 350.

SELECTED BIBLIOGRAPHY

Blumer, H., in A. M. Lee (ed.), *New Outline of the Principles of Sociology,* Barnes and Noble, 1946, "Collective Behavior." Contains a good treatment of crowd behavior of various kinds.

Coffin, T. E., in G. E. Swanson, T. M. Newcomb, and E. L. Hartley (eds.), *Readings in Social Psychology* (rev. ed.), Holt, 1952, "Suggestibility and Levels of Difficulty," pp. 11-18. A research report.

Doob, L. W., *Public Opinion and Propaganda,* Holt, 1948. Especially pp. 231-422. A competent, readable book covering many aspects of propaganda.

Krech, D., and R. Crutchfield, *Theory and Problems of Social Psychology,*

McGraw-Hill, 1948. Contains a good review of propaganda studies down to year of publication; also considers attitude studies.

Newcomb, T. M., *Social Psychology*, Dryden, 1950. Chapters 4, 5, 6, and 7, especially, deal with the concept of attitude, and with studies of attitudes.

Sarbin, T. R., "Contributions to Role-Taking Theory, I: Hypnotic Behavior," *Psych. Rev.*, 57(1950): 255-270. Presents a theory of hypnosis in role-taking terms.

Swanson, G. E., in R. Freedman, *et al.* (eds.), *Principles of Sociology*, Holt, 1952, "Social Change in the Urban Society," pp. 554-584. A discussion of crowds and other mass phenomena.

White, R. W., "A Preface to the Theory of Hypnosis," *J. Ab. and Soc. Psych.*, 37(1942): 309-328. Another theory of hypnosis in terms of goal-directed behavior.

PART 5

PERSONALITY STRUCTURE AND CHANGE

CHAPTER 15 · · ·

Conceptions of

Personal

Organization

STUDENTS OF HUMAN BEHAVIOR usually agree that behavior does not consist of unrelated fragments and processes. Separate acts are parts of response systems which become integrated in such a fashion that the organism exhibits continuity of behavior and develops a unique pattern of individuality. It is to this continuity and organization that the term "personality" refers. In common-sense discourse, the term is often used in a way that implies that personality is a somewhat mysterious quality separate from a person's behavior, a kind of unique individuality, soul, spirit, or quality that lies behind and is expressed by behavior. This is an illusion arising from the observed fact that persons undoubtedly do act in repetitive and highly charac-teristic ways. But personality, as a social psychologist must conceive it, can only refer to some kind of organization or integration of be-havior. In a sense, all parts of this book discuss the patterning and organization of behavior, but our special concern in this chapter and the next is the more inclusive perspective implied by "personality" or "personal organization" and with the general features of that organization, particularly as these are viewed by sociologists.

General Definitions of Personality

First, a word may be said about the long—and stormy—tradition of deciphering, explaining, and describing personalities and personality types. The term "personality" itself derives from the Latin *persona*, which referred to the theatrical mask used in Greek drama by Roman actors. However, "personality," and the related words "character" and "character structure," have long since come to refer to inner aspects of the person as well as his expedient actions or outward expressions. Depictions of personality types have come down to us from ancient literature through writings known as "literary characterology." Some of the portrayals are lively and acute and remind us strongly of currently recognized types. The themes which run through these characterologies are still highly relevant to theories of personality. MacKinnon points to some of these:

> One finds in the writings of the literary characterologists two implicit theories concerning the structure of personality. One . . . has emphasized the importance of some dominant trait as a dynamic and directive force in giving stability and consistency to the personality. The other . . . has stressed the existence of a unique style of life coloring the various traits of a person and revealing itself in all that he does.[1]

We have said that there is agreement that behavior is organized, or structured. This is not to say that there is, or ever has been, anything like a general agreement as to the nature of that organization. Allport,[2] in a historical survey of writings about personality, has listed fifty different definitions of personality which he has grouped in various categories—sociological, theological, biosocial, psychological, and juridical. Here are a few examples. A sociological definition by E. Faris: "Personality is the subjective aspect of culture." An "intricately synthetic" definition (Allport's term) by E. W. Burgess: "Personality is the integration of all the traits which determine the role and status of the person in society. Personality might, therefore, be defined as social effectiveness." Prince defined personality in an omnibus and fence-straddling fashion as "the sum-total of all the biological innate dispositions, impulses, tendencies, appetites, and instincts of the individual, and the acquired dispositions and tendencies—acquired by experience." Gesell suggested that personality is "the pervasive superpattern which expresses the integrity and the characteristic behavioral individuality of the organism." Allport gives a psychologist's view, stressing adjustment: "Personality is the dynamic organization within the individual of those psychophysical systems that determine his unique adjustments to his environment."

Some idea of the diversity of emphasis in such definitions can be obtained from the following list of points stressed in them: (1) external appearance and superficial attractiveness, (2) the bodily self, (3) self-conceptions, (4) memory, (5) self-control, (6) reason and rationality, (7) traits determining status, (8) individual uniqueness, (9) reputation, (10) sum total of all innate and acquired traits, impulses, dispositions, etc., (11) style of life, (12) character, (13) temperament, (14) adjustment to environment, (15) hierarchic organization, (16) subjective aspect of culture.

Since the concept of personality, in a sense, encompasses all of behavior and is thus a concern of theorists in many different areas, this diversity should not come as a surprise. There is no possibility of synthesizing all of these definitions, or of formulating a "correct" one. Our problem in this chapter will be to point to some of the abiding issues in order to indicate what contributions sociologically oriented investigators may be able to make. To do this, we shall first consider alternative approaches. These include the biological, Freudian, and elementaristic approaches as well as that of the "ego psychologies."

Biological Conceptions

One of the most venerable and persistent conceptions of behavioral organization has been that behavior is a correlate of, or is determined by, biological factors. Two variants of this are the humoral and the skeletal explanations, each having roots in Greek thought but having modern champions who have produced new variations on the basic themes.

Endocrine Glands · The oldest known humoral conceptions stem from Empedocles and Hippocrates, who lived about the fifth century B.C. Temperament was thought to correspond to proportions of the various humors in the body. The humors were blood, black bile, yellow bile, and phlegm, and the corresponding temperaments were called sanguine, melancholic, choleric, and phlegmatic. This classification of temperaments (but not the theory of humors) is still given in almost its original form by some social scientists and psychologists—something of a commentary on either the rate of progress in studies of temperament or on the wisdom of the ancient Greeks. The naïve conception of humors has long since been superseded by advanced physiological notions of glandular balance, homeostasis, and the like. The basic idea remains unchanged, however: this is that some basic features of behavior are determined by physiological functioning or organization. Periodically, as new physiological or biochemical discoveries are made, new champions of the biological view emerge and enjoy brief periods of popularity. In the 1920's, stimulated by the development of endocrinology, a number of glandular theories of personality appeared. Schlapp and Smith[3] proposed a glandular theory of criminology which they hopefully called "the new criminology." It was never taken up seriously. Likewise Berman,[4] more interested in general traits, suggested that there are types of personality the temperamental or social characteristics of which correspond to the particular gland that is dominant in the person. The thymocentric personality—that of persons with a very active thymus gland—for example, was supposed to be characterized by moral irresponsibility, criminality, lack of inhibitory capacity, and general incapacity.

Anatomical Emphases: Gall and Lombroso · The skeletal, or anatomical, view of temperament has also had a long history. Its modern-day proponents have been drawn mainly, and understandably, from medicine and physical anthropology. One variant of the conception, which had a popular vogue in the early nineteenth century, was phrenology, first promulgated by Franz Gall. He proposed that the mind was composed of distinct faculties, each corresponding to an "organ" of the brain. Gall attempted to discover clues concerning the development of these organs and their relative importance through the study of the skull. The title of Gall's chief work accurately reflects his approach to what is now called personality. Translated, it is: *Anatomy and Physiology of the Nervous System in General, and of the Head in Particular, with Observations on the Possibility of Recognizing Many Intellectual and Moral Dispositions of Man and of Animals from the Shape of Their Heads.* Gall's system was enormously popular on the Continent, in England, and in America. The possibility of finding reliable physical indices to personality remains an appealing one to many persons and is periodically explored in popular and scientific writings.

Later in the nineteenth century, an Italian criminologist, Lombroso,[5] popularized an anatomical explanation of criminality. There was, he thought, a born criminal type, different in bodily form from the normal population. Capitalizing on Darwinian theory, Lombroso called the criminal type an "atavism" and described it in terms of certain physical stigmata, such as the shape and proportions of the skull. This theory is still with us in modified form in the work of the physical anthropologist, Hooton,[6] who has made studies purporting to demonstrate anatomical differences between the criminal and noncriminal populations and among different types of criminals. Hooton further assumes that the anatomical differences somehow account for criminality. Although Hooton's methods represent a considerable refinement of Lombroso's, they have been subjected to severe, if not devastating, criticism, and few criminologists accept his conclusions.

Somatotypes: Sheldon · A somewhat more sophisticated, elaborate, and general theory of anatomical determinism, and one that commands considerable respect among certain psychologists, is that of Sheldon and his associates.[7] They claim to have found a set of three basic body types: endomorphic, mesomorphic, and ectomorphic. They have also found seventy-six combinations of these three basic types, which they call "somatotypes." Roughly speaking, extreme endomorphy is characterized by a massive and highly developed digestive system and by relatively undeveloped somatic structures (bone, muscle, connective tissue). The hallmark of endomorphy is softness and rotundity. Extreme mesomorphy is characterized by strong somatic structures, and its hallmark is uprightness and sturdiness of structure. Extreme ectomorphy is characterized by relatively slight development of both visceral and somatic structures, and by the relatively inadequate protection given the nervous system and sensory tissue by poor musculature and by body linearity. The hallmark of ectomorphy is stooped posture and hesitant movement.

Sheldon has reported high correlations between each of these three body types and three corresponding types of temperament, and these temperamental types are believed to be derived from or caused by the bodily structures. For example, the temperament associated with extreme endomorphy is called visceratonia. Visceratonia is characterized by, for example, relaxation of posture and movement, slowness of reactions, love of eating, pleasure in digestion, love of polite ceremony, liking for people, indiscriminate amiability, greed for affection and approval, even flow of emotions, tolerance, complacency, and love of comfort. Sheldon holds that, despite any and all changes in style of living, even to the point of famine, the person's body type remains quite constant. He argues further that the physique is to physiological processes what a conductor is to the players in a symphony orchestra: it organizes the basic bodily processes. Temperament is conceived as a layer between the levels represented by bodily structures and processes on the one hand and culturally acquired behavior on the other. Hence, it seems logical to Sheldon to attempt to prove the existence of lines of connection between somatotypes and types of temperament. He compiled a list of the traits which he regarded as "temperament" by combing the literature on traits, then boiled down all synonymous trait names until he was left with fifty basic ones. He then used a technique which enabled him to isolate clusters of associated traits. He ended up with three clusters of twenty traits each.

His procedure is open to serious question on various grounds; but the principal weakness is his inclusion in the concept of temperament of behavior which ranges from that which is conceivably to some degree inherited (deep sleep), through what is probably a product of interpersonal learning (greed for affection and approval), to that which would appear to be culturally acquired (love of polite ceremony). No attempt is made to explain how temperamental traits are derived from bodily build. Other aspects of behavior, such as the strength and speed of emotional reactions, which, according to Sheldon's conception, might well be biologically determined, are not included, although Sheldon has claimed wide-reaching implications for his theory that extend even to such matters as national character and juvenile delinquency.

On the positive side, Sheldon's scheme has the virtue of making distinctions among levels of behavior, some of which may be more closely related to physiological bases than others. It is conceivable that certain reactions—such as intensity of emotion—may be closely correlated with biological variables, although this has not been demonstrated. What is usually loosely called "temperament" is a grab-bag of those reactions and traits which have not been satisfactorily traced to either biological or social sources. It may be that further refinement of biological and sociological research eventually will eliminate the need for such a concept as temperament, but constitutional theories will probably always appeal to some scholars, as will the typologies implied in these theories.

The Elementaristic Approach

Elements · The basic idea of what is sometimes called elementarism, or the atomistic conception of behavior, is that of isolating simple indivisible units or elements. More complex patterns of response are thought of as consisting of combinations of these elements or fragments of behavior. Ordinarily inherent in this system is the conception that a whole can be analyzed properly only by subdividing it as far as possible into its constituent elements and subjecting them to minute analysis. The properties of the whole, it is assumed, reflect the properties of the parts. As suggested by the term "atomistic," this conception lies behind centuries of physical research into the nature of matter.

The atomistic conception which proved very powerful in the natural sciences has naturally been imported into the behavioral sciences as well. Applied to the analysis of human personality, it leads, as indicated, to the search for and analysis of elements. Various conceptions of the elements of behavior exist. One of these conceptions, which we will examine in more detail, thinks of behavior fragments called "traits" as the basic units. Others emphasize reflexes (conditioned and unconditioned), stimulus-response bonds, conditioned responses, habits, and the like. The postulated elements may be bits of behavior or they may be "mental" or "dynamic," as are attitude, motive, sentiment, impulse, idea, wish, desire, interest, urge, drive, or need. Historically, other unit concepts have been used, like idea, sensation, urge, and faculty.

The Stimulus-Response Conception · The stimulus-response view, for example, is based on what may be called a telephonic model, with the brain corresponding to the central telephone exchange and the nervous system to the network of telephone wires. Theories which stress drives and emotions ordinarily use hydraulic analogies, picturing tension mounting behind barriers of inhibition like water behind a dam.

Elementaristic conceptions may, of course, be combined with other theoretical systems. By themselves they tend to neglect or oversimplify the broader organizational or structural aspects of personality which emerge in social interaction. The atomistically oriented researcher often feels that the concepts designed by social psychologists and sociologists to handle such matters are too vague and broad to be useful in a scientific enterprise. Elementarists in this stimulus-response tradition therefore do not usually study or theorize about the whole personality and its organization. Definitions of personality offered by them are likely to stress the idea that the ultimate concrete elements of which personality is compounded are specific stimulus-response linkages. It is deemed futile to study the whole personality before its smaller parts are understood.

The stimulus-response approach (learning theory) to human behavior has been discussed and commented upon in Chapter 11. With respect to theories of personality organization, it is clear that the orientation of this school of thought is such that it cannot be expected at present to produce specific theories on the organization and development of the total human personality.

Trait Psychology · One of the most common psychological approaches to personality is through the study of traits. Trait psychology has received an impetus both from a reaction against specificity and from the applicability of statistical methods to discovery and correlation of traits. Trait theory assumes general traits: It "postulates broad, generalized, complex, overlapping, but relatively stable and enduring dispositions to action as the important and genuine components of personality."[8] Let one of its chief proponents state the view in common-sense terms:

> If someone asks, "What sort of a person is Jones?" I may reply that he is averagely social, rather lacking in conscientiousness, and unduly vain; or I may say that he is a fop. In the first case I describe him by traits and in the second by pigeonholing him in a type. Initially these alternatives correspond to adjectives and nouns. All writers employ both devices. . . . Convenience, such as the availability of suitable types or traits, will generally dictate which we use. In modern psychology the normal personality has more frequently been described by traits and the abnormal by types.[9]

Trait names are purely descriptive of behavior and so, of course, every-day language has an enormous number of them. Allport and Odbert[10] have listed over 17,000 of them. Cattell[11] points out that some of these are very crude, since "manual dexterity," for example, can refer to many different kinds of dexterity. In an attempt to formulate trait clusters and typologies, psychologists utilize methods of correlation which reveal the statistical interrelationships among traits. This leads to such distinctions as that between surface and source traits. The latter are more basic ones, from which the former are derived. Another distinction is between common and unique traits. The common trait is something like selfishness, which many persons possess to some degree; the unique trait is one that is peculiar to the individual like "a powerful interest in Korean butterflies or a strong attitude in favor of reducing the tax on tricycles, which extremely few people would share to any scorable degree."[12] Until recently it could be said with some justification that trait psychology had done little more "than to imply that a person is a simple sum-total of his departures from the average" and that "individual distinctiveness arising from the arrangement and organization of factors remains completely untouched."[13] This criticism is less true today, for trait psychology has attacked the problem of personality structure in close affinity with learning theory and clinical psychology. Thus,

> In general, a structure is what is inferred to account for a function, i.e., for a repeated pattern of behavior. A dynamic structure is thus something that accounts for the stability of dynamic functions, namely, a repeated pattern of responsiveness to a stimulus, of striving in a particular fashion, and of recurrently seeking a particular goal. An especially important aspect of structure is that which deals not only with single dynamic traits, but also with the interrelation and organization of dynamic traits.[14]

Regardless of recent attempts to utilize various clinical concepts like superego and repression, the basic conception of the unit trait remains. Consequently, the major stresses appear to be on such matters as the measurement of traits, the devising and validation of tests, the statistical interrelationship of traits, and the manner in which traits are distributed in individuals and in populations.

The difficulties which trait theory encounters in attempting to handle the structure of personality are indicated by Gordon Allport. He discusses or mentions various unifying factors, or principles, such as self-consciousness, memory, imagination, intention, striving, and the biological conditions of unity. None of these, he argues, account for the consistency of successive acts. "To make good this lack, there must be an account of *structural* consistency."[15] This is provided, he thinks, by a theory of interdependent and overlapping traits.

This really says very little beyond arguing, as Allport does elsewhere as well, against "separate and independent elements" (or traits). It tells us nothing about how traits come to be interdependent, how they are established, and how they remain interdependent during periods of change; nor does it account for the conflict and discordance of traits either in two discrepant social situations or in times of head-on collision of values. In short, the concept of trait carries too great an explanatory burden in Allport's system, and in common with other elementaristic psychologies, does not handle particularly well the relation of personality structure to social structure.

As an illustration of the strengths and weaknesses of this kind of an approach in a specialized field, one may point to intelligence tests, into which immense effort has been put. These represent a very valuable practical instrument; but despite considerable theoretical concern over intelligence, one can learn little from the literature on intelligence testing about the nature and functioning of intelligent behavior in either individual or group life.

Attitudes as Elements · A few decades ago, when the concept of attitude became popular, it was widely thought of as a revolutionary new concept and as "the keystone in the edifice of American social psychology."[16] Many sociologists and social psychologists felt that with this concept they had discovered something basic in the study of human social behavior. Attitudes were called the basic units of personality. Many studies of attitudes were made and all sorts of attitude tests and measuring devices were invented.

On theoretical grounds social psychologists became interested in attitudes because they had come to realize and stress that the organism was not a passive responding agent at the mercy of external stimuli. This realization had earlier underlain the use of such terms as "pre-disposition," "set" (or "mental set"), and "apperceptive mass." "Attitude" gradually came to be used as an overall term referring to all kinds of predisposing tendencies which the reacting person brings to a situation. Various writers were thus enabled to define attitude to suit the needs of their theoretical positions. As the term was used more widely, its meanings multiplied proportionately. A common thread running through the definitions and discussions is that individuals have "states of readiness" with which they meet their environments, so that behavior possesses a certain stability and predictability. The notion of a state of readiness implies that attitudes lie dormant or latent when not being expressed. This agrees with common-sense observation, since an individual is credited with an attitude toward something—let us say, toward the Republican Party—even when he is engaged in activities having nothing whatever to do with politics.

Out of this kind of consideration the idea developed that attitudes are separate from behavior and are more general than their specific overt expressions. Hence a distinction came to be made between attitudes and opinions, the latter being taken to mean verbal reports from which attitudes can be inferred. It was noted that opinion is not an altogether reliable index of attitude, because the person expressing it can be concealing true attitudes, or may honestly say one thing but do another when the time comes to act.

It cannot be denied that the concept of attitude represented an important change in the theory of social psychology of a few decades ago. From a preoccupation with instinct theory and the heredity-environment controversy, social psychologists in the 1920's turned with enthusiasm to the new concept of attitude and its exciting implications. The latter included the idea that the most important knowledge one can have of a person is a grasp of his point of view, his personal outlook on the world. The attitude concept stressed the fact that human beings do not respond automatically in stereotyped ways to external situations, but that their responses are always relative to ideas, perceptions, and dispositions carried over from past experience.

The concept of attitude still carries these meanings today, and social scientists have pretty generally accepted them. However, the use of the concept in various ways has tended to reduce its clarity. Too, attitudes are no longer thought of as the elements of personality. Having served its function in ushering new ideas into social psychology, "attitude" seems to have again become a common-sense term. Because of its varied meanings, it is usually necessary to use more precise substitutes if one wishes to avoid misunderstanding on specific issues. As a general term, it is indispensable and still widely used and will be found on many pages of this book.

Ego as Ordering Principle

The Total Personality · Elementaristic, or unit, theories in psychology are staunchly opposed by theories which stress the organism's unity and wholeness. Field or holistic conceptions, receiving particular impetus from writings in biology and physics in the last half-century, rest upon an assumption that is diametrically opposed to the atomistic one. The whole is seen as something different from the sum of its parts. The unity of the organism is not reducible to its parts nor to the relationships among them. In the area of personality, the holistic emphasis is reflected in phrases like "the total personality," "personalistic psychology," and "striving for unity." Segmental or atomistic studies of complex mental functions are criticized because functioning cannot be understood aside from the functioning of the whole organism. "Everything mental is a totality or a part of totality."[17] Holistic theories do not by any means abandon the empirical study of persons nor abjure quantitative methods, but since the total personality is the central focus, they are more receptive to nonquantitative and nonexperimental techniques which try to assess this totality and its functioning. The holistic conception is best represented in general psychology by a school of thought known as Gestalt psychology, which directly influenced thought in social psychology through such theories as the topological psychology of Kurt Lewin and the personalistic views of William Stern.

The general reaction against atomistic conceptions has been part of the climate of the last twenty years, and in social psychology has produced various bodies of theory which emphasized ego, self, and other organizing concepts. One general idea is that "In every whole there is a leading principle according to which it is organized."[18] The problem is to describe the nature and functioning of this ordering principle and to relate overt behavior to it. These theories attempt to account for the development and maintenance of personality structure in a social milieu, but nevertheless retain many individualistic assumptions.

Some Variants · One specific conception which is fairly widespread and influential is that the organism strives to maintain a consistency of unity. Thus Rogers maintains that: "Most of the ways of behavior which are adopted by the organism are those which are consistent with the concept of self."[19] The view is expressed by the use of such terms as the striving for self-realization, for self-consistency, for the maintenance of self-esteem, and in popular speech in terms of needs for harmony and peace of mind.

Lecky provides a clear formulation of the basic view. He rejects mechanistic or atomistic conceptions in favor of the notion that: "One source of motivation only, the necessity to maintain the unity of the system, must serve as the universal dynamic principle."[20] He also rejects the Freudian stress upon conflict: "Not conflict but unity must be the fundamental postulate."[21] Translated into psychological terms, this means that the person strives for self-consistency in his values. His values "are organized into a single system, the preservation of whose integrity is essential. The nucleus of the system . . . is the individual's valuation of himself."[22] When the person encounters any value which is in opposition to his self-valuation, he resists it and is likely to reject it. Conflict in the person's life is not due to the person himself, but to environmental changes which set the problem of choosing between rejection and the disturbance associated with assimilation.

A variant of the view of the ego as the ordering principle is that offered by Sherif and Cantril, which stresses "ego-attitudes." This represents the combination of holistic and elementaristic views. The basic idea is that the person's ego is involved in all kinds of actions important to himself: he "inevitably uses himself as a central point of reference."[23] The ego is conceived of as composed of a constellation of ego-attitudes. Like any other attitudes, these are learned and are not immutable, but may change through the social experiences of the person. This means, according to Sherif and Cantril, that the ego is not "an entity" and it is not fixed and changeless. However, many attitudes, including the ones that have reference to self, are relatively enduring so long as the individual possesses fixed points of reference. These authors state: "It is these ego-involved attitudes that, to a large extent under usual circumstances, determine and direct the particular way in which the individual goes about releasing his instinctual tendencies and drives."[24]

Criticism · The position of the ego psychologists is an attempt to introduce into the framework of elementaristic psychology the concept of ego with its broad sociological connotations. But as Asch has said, "As long as one views the individual as a sum of elementaristic items, there is no authentic place for the self."[25] This attempted synthesis of psychological and sociological views has satisfied neither psychologists nor sociologists. The latter usually feel that ego psychology deals inadequately with the social factors influencing personal development and organization and does not do full justice to the ego's inherently social nature. Also, the attempt to fit the concept into the motivational schemes of individualistic psychology has not seemed convincing.

The Freudian Conception of Personality

The View · Freudian theorists have made a very direct and elaborate attack upon the problem of personality organization. However one may view the fundamental assumptions of Freudian theory, it must be granted that Freud faced the problem squarely and much of the influence of his works rests upon this fact. His scheme bears upon central issues such as the matter of types, symbolization, and the nature of conflict and personality disintegration and offers explanations of development and change. Although clinical and experimental psychologists have borrowed from Freud, psychoanalysis is not elementaristic, or atomistic, in its tradition and basic position.

It represents a radical break with conventional psychology. It is often called "dynamic" to point up the stress which it places on conflict, process, and development. It is based on clinical sources rather than on experimentation, animal psychology, testing, or the study of physiology and neural mechanisms.

From the study of repressed or unconscious material, Freud turned his attention to the repressing forces and eventually developed the tripartite scheme of the "mental apparatus" involving the id, ego, and superego.

> The *id* is the original powerhouse of the mental apparatus; it contains the inherited instinctive forces which at birth are not yet organized into a coordinated system. The *ego* is conceived as a product of development which consists in the adaptation of the inherited instinctive drives to one another and to the environment. The *superego* . . . represents the incorporation of parental attitudes which are determined by the existing cultural standards. After maturation the ego becomes the dynamic center of behavior. . . . The ego's function . . . is to carry out . . . coordinated rational behavior and is aimed at maintaining a constant condition . . . within the organism. . . . In satisfying biological needs and in defending the organism against excessive external stimulation, the ego performs its homeostatic tasks with the help of four basic faculties: (1) internal perception of instinctive needs, (2) external perception of existing conditions upon which the gratification of subjective needs depends, (3) the integrative faculty by which the ego coordinates instinctive urges with one another and with the requirements of the superego and adapts them to the environmental conditions, and (4) the executive faculty by which it controls voluntary behavior.[26]

When the ego is threatened by impulses in disharmony with reality or social standards, conflicts and anxiety result. The ego reacts by erecting defenses against the threatening impulses. These are

> partly bulwarks which favor repression, such as over-compensation or rationalization, and partly vents by which the repudiated tendencies can find an outlet, such as projection, substitution,

displacement, or turning impulses directed against external objects against the self.[27]

The concept of superego is worthy of special note because here Freud makes a place for the internalization of cultural standards. The superego is described as the product of identification with the parents, whose traits and orientations are introjected or internalized.

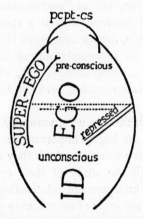

FREUD'S DIAGRAM OF ID, EGO, AND SUPEREGO
"the [object of] therapeutic efforts of psycho-analysis . . . is to strengthen the ego, to make it more independent of the superego, to widen its field of vision, and so to extend its organization that it can take over new portions of the id. Where id was, there shall ego be. It is reclamation work, like the draining of the Zuyder Zee." (From Freud's *New Introductory Lectures on Psychoanalysis*, New York: Norton, 1933, pp. 111-112.)

The origin of the conflicts which give rise to the superego is placed in the Oedipus situation, in which the child's sexual impulses are directed toward one of the parents. The repression of these impulses and a successful resolution of the Oedipus complex develops a strong superego, which continues to develop through the influence of further identification with other persons who become parent substitutes. The superego is also the vehicle of the ego-ideal, by which the ego measures itself, toward which it strives, and whose demands for ever-increasing perfection it is always striving to fulfill.[28] Large portions of the ego and superego remain unconscious; the id is wholly so, and entirely unsocialized: "it knows no values, no good and evil, no morality. . . . Instinctive cathexes seeking discharge . . . is all that the id contains."[29]

The Freudian view of unconscious impulses in socialized disguises involves the idea of symbolization. Acts and statements are taken, not at face value, but as "unconscious representatives" of concealed desires and motives. This is a special use of the term "symbol." As an example, dream images, or the manifest content of dreams, are regarded as representations of the latent content, or real significance. Thus, feces, money, gift, child, and penis "are taken as having the same meaning, and can be represented by the same symbols."[30]

The defenses which the ego uses, variously referred to as mechanisms or dynamisms, are highly important processes in the system. Aside from the defensive function which they are said to serve, we may note that through the study of their operation, the analyst handles the matter of interpersonal relationships. Viewed from one angle, these processes are ways of maintaining personality structure; from another angle, they appear as modes of interaction with other persons.

Typologies of personality proceed logically from the Freudian conceptualization of personality organization. The theory of psychosexual development, which assumes that all children go through successive phases or stages of development, implies that at any stage certain reactions and tendencies are dominant and characteristic. Personality types represent various possible adult outcomes of psychosexual development—that is, differences in content and interrelationship of ego, superego, and id.

Abraham,[31] in building upon the observations of Freud, has suggested oral, anal, and genital types of personality. The oral type, for example, is produced as follows: the forced interruption of nursing leads to substitute satisfactions, since the sucking impulses are unsatisfied. Some of these, like thumbsucking, may themselves be tabooed, only to result in other oral expressions such as excessive babbling, excessive talking, sucking and chewing of sticks. The mouth-centered child grows up into the oral-type adult who is "hungry for the reinstatement of the full mothering experience. The child becomes a nutrient type; he craves to receive, not to give; he needs protection, warmth, sympathy, support."[32] The other two types are similarly produced by substitute reactions to parental tabooing of anal and genital activities. The extreme anal type is "parsimonious, meticulous, punctual, tied down with petty self-restraints. Everything that is free, uncontrolled, spontaneous is dangerous. . . . The genital type, correspondingly, is centered in eros, finds goodness and pleasure compatible."[33] Such types are the products of early familial experience, closely linked with the ways in which parents handle the basic bodily needs of the child. The characteristic modes of behavior of these types can be observed in interpersonal relations among adults. Since they are universal, these types cut across cultural, occupational, social-class, and all other groups. However, as the more culturally minded Freudians have emphasized, cultures and subcultures differ in the predominant types that they produce, since child-raising methods differ from one culture to another and since methods are more or less homogeneous within a given milieu.

Evaluation · Evidence to corroborate most of this theorizing is not at hand and is difficult to obtain. One reason for this is that the evidence is mainly presented in clinical and anecdotal form which allows interpretation to be presented in the guise of data. Whatever evidence exists is not sufficient to convince anyone who is not relatively sold on many of the basic assumptions of the Freudian approach.

To sociologists, as we have indicated elsewhere, the Freudian motivational scheme usually seems inadequate to handle the social dimensions of behavior. The fundamental concepts for explaining behavioral organization grow organically out of this motivational scheme. The ego, id, and superego are not merely names for functioning or for behaving, but become "little men" to use Coutu's expression, endowed with purposes and personalities of their own, able to initiate and block and channelize action. They are entities within the person whose domestic quarrels, compromises, and courtships, behind the iron curtain of the unconscious, determine the action of the person.

As we have already remarked apropos of motives, sociologists usually feel that the influence of social structures upon personality structure is inevitably slighted or over simplified by most orthodox Freudians. This is reflected most clearly in the simplistic treatment of the superego. The superego, representing the cultural side of behavior, is too exclusively linked with sexual development and identification with parental figures. This is regarded by most sociologists as a too limited conception of how culture gets inside of a person.

The attempt of Freudians to find universal typologies is noteworthy, but it suffers from some of the same limitations as other aspects of the Freudian scheme. The alleged types are too exclusively linked with the presumed details of psychosexual development and identification with parental figures. Although typologies grounded on basic interpersonal patterns of childhood, even if not universal in applicability, can be of great usefulness, in this case, as in others, Freudians claim too much. Since there are important dimensions of behavior other than those which psychoanalysts stress, other typologies based on social roles, institutional functioning, and the like, are also useful and important.

Summary

In a wide range of general conceptions of personality, or personal organization, it is agreed that behavior is organized; however, the nature and bases of the organization are variously conceived. Biological factors, such as hormones and bodily build, are given great weight by some writers, whereas others place the stress elsewhere. Different assumptions underlie elementaristic and holistic views, and these effect the ways in which personality is conceived and studied.

A systematic and influential treatment of personality organization was offered by Freud and has since been revised and elaborated by the analysts. Many psychologists and some psychiatrists remain unconvinced of the validity and fruitfulness of this scheme. We turn now to a consideration of the ways in which sociologists and anthropologists are inclined to approach this problem.

SUGGESTIONS FOR DISCUSSION AND SPECIAL REPORTS

1. Read Freud concerning the id, ego, and superego. Discuss his scheme in terms of how it handles the relation of individual to culture.

2. Report on the concept of homeostasis in psychological writing.

3. Compare several theories of criminal behavior, showing their derivation from theories of behavior-in-general.

4. Outline in detail a recent system of trait psychology.

5. "Self-realization" sometimes is said to be the chief end of civilized man. Discuss this either pro or con.

6. Criticize the shortcomings of the distinction between derived and basic needs.

7. Discuss elementarism as an approach to personality.

8. How does Sheldon, and others with similar views, derive personality from biological bases when personality apparently is a psychological phenomenon?

NOTES

[1] D. MacKinnon in J. McV. Hunt, *Personality and the Behavioral Disorders*, Ronald, 1944, Vol. 1, p. 14.

[2] G. W. Allport, *Personality, a Psychological Interpretation*, Holt, 1937, pp. 24-54.

[3] M. G. Schlapp and E. H. Smith, *The New Criminology*, Liveright, 1928.

[4] L. Berman, *The Glands Regulating Personality*, Macmillan, 1928.

[5] C. Lombroso, *Crime, Its Causes and Remedies*, Little, Brown, 1911. His first book, *Criminal Man*, was published in 1876.

[6] E. A. Hooton, *Crime and the Man*, Harvard University Press, 1939.

[7] W. H. Sheldon, S. S. Stevens,

and W. P. Tucker, *The Varieties of Human Physique,* Harper, 1940; and, by the first two authors, *The Varieties of Temperament,* Harper, 1942.

[8] MacKinnon, *op. cit.,* pp. 40-41.

[9] R. Cattell, *Personality,* McGraw-Hill, 1950, p. 5.

[10] G. W. Allport and H. S. Odbert, "Trait-Names: A Psycho-lexical Study," *Psychological Monographs,* Vol. 47 (1936), No. 211, pp. 1-171.

[11] Cattell, *op. cit.,* p. 21.

[12] *Ibid.,* p. 32.

[13] Allport, *op. cit.,* pp. 9, 10.

[14] Cattell, *op. cit.,* p. 153.

[15] Allport, *op. cit.,* p. 347.

[16] G. W. Allport, "Attitudes," in C. Murchison (ed.), *Handbook of Social Psychology,* Worcester, Mass.: Clark University Press, 1935, p. 798.

[17] Allport, *Personality, a Psychological Interpretation,* quotation from W. Stern, p. 551.

[18] A. A. Angyal, *Foundations for a Science of Personality,* New York: The Commonwealth Fund, 1941, p. 21.

[19] C. Rogers, *Client-Centered Therapy: Its Current Practice, Implications, and Theory,* Houghton Mifflin, 1951, p. 507.

[20] P. Lecky, *Self Consistency; A Theory of Personality,* New York: Island Press, 1945, p. 81.

[21] *Ibid.,* p. 81.

[22] *Ibid.,* p. 82.

[23] M. Sherif and H. Cantril, *The Psychology of Ego-Involvements,* Wiley, 1947, p. 93.

[24] *Ibid.,* p. 96.

[25] S. Asch, *Social Psychology,* Prentice-Hall, 1952, p. 279.

[26] F. Alexander and H. Ross (eds.), *Dynamic Psychiatry,* University of Chicago Press, 1952, pp. 9-10.

[27] *Ibid.,* p. 2.

[28] S. Freud, *New Introductory Lectures on Psychoanalysis,* Norton, 1933, pp. 92-93.

[29] *Ibid.,* p. 105.

[30] *Ibid.,* p. 139.

[31] K. Abraham, *Selected Papers* (ed. E. Jones), cited in G. Murphy, *Personality,* Harper, 1947.

[32] Murphy, *op. cit.,* p. 746.

[33] *Ibid.,* p. 747.

SELECTED BIBLIOGRAPHY

Allport, G., *Becoming: Basic Considerations for a Psychology of Personality,* Yale University Press, 1955. A theoretical essay.

———, *Personality: A Psychological Interpretation,* Holt, 1937. The opening chapter contains a good historical review, and the remainder of the book is organized around the concept of traits.

Angyal, A. A., *Foundations for a Science of Personality,* New York: The Commonwealth Fund, 1941. A psychiatrist formulates an approach to personality.

Asch, S. E., *Social Psychology,* Prentice-Hall, 1952. Chap. 2, "Structured

Properties of Experience and Action," pp. 43-71, and Chap. 3, "Psychological Invariance and Change," pp. 72-114. A well-known Gestalt psychologist criticizes elementaristic conceptions.

Cattell, R., *Personality*, McGraw-Hill, 1950. A text by one of the best-known trait psychologists.

Freud, S., *New Introductory Lectures on Psychoanalysis*, Norton, 1933. A late series of papers.

Kluckhohn, C., and H. A. Murray (eds.), *Personality in Nature, Society and Culture* (rev. ed.), Knopf, 1953. A collection of papers. The first one by Kluckhohn and Murray, presents one approach to personality.

Lecky, P., *Self Consistency*, New York: Island Press, 1945. A brief and easily read view of personality that stresses the non-atomistic nature of personality.

Murphy, G., *Personality*, Harper, 1948. A discursive and eclectic book by a social psychologist who has been influenced by many currents.

Rogers, C., *Client-Centered Therapy*, Houghton Mifflin, 1951. Chap. 11, "A Theory of Personality and Behavior," pp. 481-533. A clinical psychologist stresses self and self-realization in his theory of personality.

Sheldon, W., in J. McV. Hunt (ed.), *Personality and the Behavior Disorders*, Vol. 1, Ronald, 1944, pp. 526-549. Sheldon outlines his somatotypes and relates them to temperament and gives some historical background to the body-type approach.

Sherif, M., and H. Cantril, *The Psychology of Ego-Involvements*, Wiley, 1947. The authors stress ego-attitudes as the heart of personality.

CHAPTER 16 · · ·

| Social Structure |
| and |
| Personal |
| Organization |

SOCIOLOGISTS AND ANTHROPOLOGISTS have developed their own special perspectives concerning personality in the course of their study of men and institutions. Although there are the usual differences of opinion and emphasis, there are certain common points of view in these fields. Since sociology has traditionally been concerned with groups and institutions and anthropology with cultures, these disciplines have generally adopted a strongly environmental position and developed cultural and institutional theories of personality: that is, they approach the study of personality largely in terms of how individuals participate in groups and how they are influenced in the process. The priority of society is taken for granted, both chronologically and causally. E. Faris' definition of personality as "the subjective side of culture,"[1] although formulated some years ago, nevertheless indicates where the weight is placed. Emphasis is less on personality *per se* than upon persons as members of functioning social units.

Some History

The modern sociological position began to be developed in the works of such social theorists as Marx, Sumner, and Durkheim. We have already discussed the Marxian conception of the individual and the Marxian theory of motives as being derived from the person's position in the class structure. Durkheim, writing around the turn of the century and in the early decades of the twentieth century, opposed the dominant individualistic psychology of his day with the conception that individual motives and psychological processes are dependent upon and derived from society, rather than the reverse. Sumner, in a famous book on the folkways and mores of societies which left a lasting imprint upon American sociology, emphasized the relativity and variability of customs and their constraining influence upon individual behavior, and so led sociological thought down the same path as did Durkheim and Marx. Anthropological thinking followed somewhat similar lines.

CULTURAL DETERMINISM

Sociologists and anthropologists have sometimes argued that the study of individuals is irrelevant for the understanding of broad institutional and cultural patterns. Cultures and societies are conceived of as having their own lives and laws and so to be studied on their own level. As White says:

> Culture is not determined by man, by his wishes, will, hopes, fears, etc. Man is of course prerequisite to culture; he is, so to speak, the catalyst that makes the interactive process possible. But the cultural process is *culturally* determined, not biologically or psychologically.[2]

Conversely, it has been argued that individual behavior is culturally determined, and that therefore explanations of behavior must not be sought in forces within the individual, but rather in forces in the social environment. This view of the individual as something of an automaton and of culture as something that "somehow hovers above the members of the society and pushes them around"[3] is commonly called "cultural determinism." It obviously leaves little place for social psychology, and is open to question on other grounds as well. Two of the most serious criticisms are that it retains the dubious dichotomy of individual and society and repeats in reverse the error of individualistic psychology, which derives society from individual sources.

A cultural heritage does not become an individual's possession through a mysterious absorption of the "intellectual climate," nor are his attitudes and thought processes a simple reflex of that heritage. Cultural patterns do not exercise a direct, mechanical, unmediated influence but an indirect and symbolically mediated one. Patterns are shaped and transformed as they are assimilated into the person's own individually defined view of himself and of the world.

The development of social psychology, both by sociologists and psychologists, is itself an indication of dissatisfaction in those fields with the implications and consequences of the "individual-versus-society" dichotomy. The rise of social psychology in the sociological field was stimulated in part by antagonism to individualistic psychological theory and in part by a realization that naïve cultural determinism did not provide adequate answers. Many introductory textbooks in social psychology even today include a section on the person or the individual in which they borrow heavily from individual psychology and sometimes from psychiatry, and often also refer matters of individual behavior to such large abstractions as "society," "nation," "social class," and "the group." Probably few sociologists and anthropologists subscribe to extreme cultural determinism. With an increasing concern for individual behavior, there has been greater interest among them in developing theoretical schemes concerning it which will embody characteristic sociological and anthropological perspectives.

MEAD AND BEHAVIORISM

There is a line of thought in sociology which is traditionally opposed to individualistic psychology and cultural determinism on the grounds that the eighteenth-century dichotomy (individual versus society) on which both are based is sterile. Instead of separating individual and society and then trying to bring them together again, sociologists of this group deny the original separation: individual personality itself is conceived as inherently social. A brief glance at G. H. Mead's attempt to avoid the dichotomy will serve as an illustration.[4]

At the time that Mead wrote, mentalism was under attack from behaviorists. Mentalism included the ideas that the individual, through introspection, had access to his own mental processes and that the forces which determine behavior are to be found in subjective mental states or states of consciousness. Behaviorists, led by John Watson, slashed at these notions of inner forces, insisting that the only observable and verifiable data of psychology were to be found in overt behavior. "Consciousness" and other concepts referring to subjective states and forces were either banned entirely or translated into the behavioral terms of stimulus and response, conditioned and unconditioned.

One of the results was to set the stage for a heavy environmentalist emphasis in psychology. Watson himself was a radical environmentalist who claimed unlimited possibilities for the control of behavior through conditioning. Mead accepted many ideas of the behaviorists, but attempted to transcend them. He agreed on the profound importance of the environment and on the primacy of behavior, but he did not wish to throw the baby out with the bath by discarding all the concepts of mentalistic psychology and ignoring the "subjective." He regarded subjective states as behavior that required study quite as much as any other behavior. On the other hand, he viewed Watson's concept of "environment" as too limited, since it did not give adequate consideration to social relationships, especially communication processes. In Mead's treatment of the self and the generalized other, he sought to deal with mental processes in behavioral and cultural terms, and thus to by-pass the dilemma posed by the concept of the individual versus society, and as well as by the related dichotomy of organism and environment.

Organism and Environment

The general sociological emphasis on environment offers the possibility of avoiding the difficulties attending an explanation of behavior in terms of inferential forces inside of individuals. Sociologists also formerly talked of "social forces," which they sometimes located inside the individual in the form of socially derived interests, attitudes, wishes, and the like. The structure of personality need not be handled in these terms, and many sociologists no longer do so.

It is a truism that all organisms differ in biological makeup, and that these differences condition behavior. The sociological orientation does not require a denial of this elementary fact. However, the comparative study of cultures has made it clear that biological differentiation does not go very far in accounting for either differences or similarities of personality structure. Even in biology it has come to be recognized that the concepts of organism and environment are not separate and sharply opposed, and hence that even in lower organisms the milieu is decisively involved both in the organism's behavior and in its biological development. As a matter of fact, it is often difficult to determine clearly what belongs to an environment and what belongs to the organism. This may sound surprising, for after all does not everything within the skin form part of the individual and everything outside the skin part of the environment? The matter is not so simple. Consider the following points:

Taking literally the statement that the organism is within the body surface and the environment outside it, one has to consider . . . that one should accordingly call the food before ingestion a part of the environment and after ingestion a part of the organism. It would be a very strange logic, however, to regard an object at one time as environment and at another time as part of the organism merely because it is located in some internal cavity of the body, such as the stomach. Thus the criterion for being part of the environment or of the organism would merely concern the location of an object in space. . . . Is it not more logical to regard the content of the gastro-intestinal tract as environment rather than as part of the organism, that is, as an insinuation of the environment into the body? . . . To take another example, should we regard urine, when it is in the bladder, as part of the organism and after it passes the urethral orifice as part of the environment? . . . What is the difference between a phagocyte and another monocellular being, for example, a bacterium occasionally contained in the blood stream? One could say that the phagocyte belongs to the organism because it exerts a useful function in the organism. Usefulness, however, is not a sufficient criterion to decide whether something belongs to the organism or to the environment. Utilitarian relations exist also in the case of symbiosis, but we would not regard the symbiotic animal or plant as a part of its symbiont. If we take the convergence of functions to mutual usefulness as a criterion of "belongingness" to the organism, then we should be compelled to consider . . . the *bacteria coli* in the intestines as part of the individual, since these organisms probably have a useful function in the digestion of cellulose. In that case one could state perhaps that the phagocytes belong to the organism because they originate from the organism itself, while the bacteria do not derive from the organism. But the genetic derivation itself is not an adequate criterion either. We would certainly hesitate to call the sputum a part of the organism or the egg a part of the hen.[5]

From such a statement it is clear that however distinct environment and organism are in common-sense usage, for biological purposes they are not entirely distinct and separate. Social scientists could ask with equal justification where in certain instances are the dividing lines between individuals and their social environments. For example, are the ideas which language embodies part of the individual who holds them, or do they belong to the society to which the individual in turn belongs?

The argument—whether environment or organism is more important—is based on the incorrect view that the two are quite separate from each other. It is often reasoned, in a common-sense fashion, that: "Here is a person and here is his environment." Or that the individual is "in" the environment: if the city is "environment," the city-dweller is immersed in it. Actually, the individual and environment are not distinct nor is one immersed in the other. They are relative and reciprocal to each other.

This can be illustrated both on biological and on social levels. Thus to a cow, the cow's digestive system being what it is, grass is a nutritious object. Trees, as environmental objects to cows, are things which yield protection from sun and rain. Grass and trees can be seen to be related in certain ways to cows because of the cow's nature. The same objects are related in totally different ways to birds: grass is something that houses insects, or can be used in making nests; trees are landing places, shelters, and supports for nests. Along these general lines, biologists note that the "same" environment is different to the same animal at different times according to whether it is hungry, tired, in heat, and so forth. This same general position is thoroughly implicit in all that we have already said about the selective nature of human perception.

The relationships of an organism to its surroundings are continuous, reciprocal, and indissoluble. Environments do not simply exist; they exist only in relation to the given organism. Conversely, the existence and functioning of the organism presuppose and require the appropriate environment. It is fruitless and inconsequential to ask whether heredity or environment is the more important. The question itself does not make sense. Both are important and necessary. But to say that both are necessary is not to say that both determine behavior in the same way. Biologists point out that in the activities of the simplest organisms the connection between behavior and structure is relatively direct and stable, although even here a relatively constant environment is always necessarily presupposed. As organisms become more complex and specialized, the relationship between biological structures and forms of behavior become less direct, less stable, more variable. Moreover, as organisms grow more complex they have a tendency to be increasingly influenced by that part of their environment which is constituted by the presence and actions of other organisms. The human organism is so complex and the possible range of its behavior so great that human behavior cannot be accounted for in terms of structural variations.

Continuity and Consistency

One of the central problems in the study of personality is to account for the continuation and repetition of certain behavior. "Every study of personality evokes assumptions about continuity: Short range continuity, as in predicting, from yesterday's performance, how father will respond to junior's temper tantrums tonight; long range continuity, as in predicting that the girl of today will make a good wife and mother over the years."[6]

Various answers have been proposed for the solution of this problem, as we have seen. In biologically oriented views the grounds of stability are found primarily in the organism itself, and in Freudian psychoanalytic theory they are located in the genetic momentum of early childhood experiences. Typically, the sociologist traces stability of personality to stability of social environment rather than to factors within the individual himself.

Every society must fulfill certain minimum requirements in order to maintain its existence and continuity. These have been said to include the following:

A. There must be an economic and social division of labor.

B. There must be ways of evaluating people's activities. This evaluation results in relative ranking of persons according to status.

C. There must be ways of recruiting and selecting people for various positions and roles.

D. There must be formal and informal means of social control to maintain order, obedience, co-operation, and general co-ordination of activities.[7]

RECRUITMENT AND TRAINING

In order for a society to function, its members must possess or develop appropriate motivations, traits, and consistent modes of action relevant to the execution of social activities. Complex social structures such as military establishments, religious orders, and occupational groups must either develop or recruit members who meet their particular requirements in these respects. This does not mean that the individuals selected and shaped by these structures are uniform products. Quite the reverse, for a complex group needs and attracts different types of personnel to carry out its diverse organizational functions. Even groups that maintain their membership through reproduction rather than recruitment give differential training to the young to fit them for different social positions.

Although there is always much individual diversity within large organizations, the initial selection and rejection of members sets some limits to the range of diversity. Closely knit specialized groups may severely limit diversity, as may also simple groups with relatively little complexity of role differentiation. Individuals, too, select and reject roles by voluntarily joining and dropping out of organizations. In an individualistically oriented society there is a tendency to assume that the individual does all the selecting, so that the roles he plays reflect, or merely reinforce, existing personality traits. An individual is thought of as choosing his occupation, religion, club, place of residence, and so on in terms of the needs of his personality. It is perfectly clear, however, that this is not the whole story and that groups have mechanisms for attracting desirable personnel and rejecting the undesirable.

Organizations have formal and informal codes according to which vacancies are filled and recruits are judged. The formal codes are most obvious, involving as they do requirements as to age, skills, and specialized experience as well as competitive examinations, certifications, and so on. The informal codes are less apparent. For every status there are likely to be requirements which the members know but the recruit does not. Sometimes it is necessary that such requirements be kept secret or disguised, as when racial limitations are placed on a job. The candidate may find to his chagrin that the unspoken requirements are the real ones. The full extent of the personal and social qualities that are demanded for a position or membership may not even be fully appreciated by the members themselves. E. C. Hughes[8] has pointed out the status dilemmas faced by both newcomer and old members when the former, having obtained posts, are found to lack certain qualities not included in the explicitly formulated criteria. The older members may refer to the newcomer as lacking in tact, poise, *savoir-faire*, gentlemanly behavior, the proper personality, and other intangible qualities. Hughes points out that it is precisely these qualities which makes for unself-conscious and efficient group relations. Matters of power and self-interest as well as simple congeniality are also involved.

Methods of canceling out errors in recruitment are likewise varied, running from simple ejection to subtle pressure. Errors in recruitment in a large organization are often handled by methods less drastic than ejection or ostracism. The misfits may be assigned to posts where they will do no harm ("kicked upstairs") or transferred to parts of the organization to which they may be better suited. Homogeneity within various segments of a structure may be the result.

Behavior of group members is also given consistency and coherence by the fact that once a person is accepted into an institutional structure its very functioning requires that he learn to act, think, talk, and feel in certain new ways. Institutions, in addition to formal methods, always have informal ways of inculcating the proper modes of reaction in their members.

Formal educational systems constitute means by which institutional ends are served. Gerth and Mills have said that the key sociological questions about education include: "(1) Who gets educated? (2) By whom are they educated? (3) How are they educated? (4) For what roles are they educated? (5) When are they educated? (6) Where are they educated?"[9]

Training may be provided by special educational units within specific parts of the social structure, as when in-service training is given in an occupational group, or when a religious body sets up a parochial school system. On the other hand, the official educational system consisting of public and private schools provides some of the requisite preliminary training for certain occupations and professions. The educational system is closely linked with the class structure, and also plays an important part in inculcating common national values. Training varies according to the positions for which the students are headed, and candidates for given kinds of jobs, posts, ranks, and offices undergo much the same kind of training.

For jobs requiring certain mechanical skills only, the teaching process may be a direct one involving learning through example and demonstration. At the opposite extreme, one may consider the training of the psychoanalyst, who must himself be analyzed in a prolonged and delicate process to qualify himself for his profession. In general, the modes of interaction between teacher and learner are set by the nature and requirements of the position and usually involve much more than the simple transmission of skills. Even the transmission of skills is often not as simple as it sounds and may involve matters having to do with evaluating and handling social relations.

Fortune magazine recently reported on a new trend in the training of young men for managerial positions in large corporations. General Electric, for instance, needs to fill 1,500 executive jobs in the next decade, and must train men for them in a wholesale manner.

To build up the pressure in the pipeline, G.E. each year stocks its central training pool with over 1,000 fresh college men. For at least fifteen months . . . these trainees are essentially students, and though they try their hand at a succession of job situations, the basic program is that of a teaching institution. There is a faculty of 250 full-time G.E. people and their basic apparatus includes . . . catalogues, textbooks, examinations, grades, and an alumni publication. . . . G.E.'s curriculum teaches specific job skills . . . it also conveys a heavy indoctrination in the managerial view. Trainees take courses in such subjects as labor, personnel, law, better business management. . . . The very diversity of their training . . . underscores the jack-of-all-trades nature of the professional manager—and his superiority. G.E. officially encourages a man to be a specialist if he wants. The phraseology G.E. uses in describing the choice, however, is illuminating. It asks the trainee to ask himself "Will I specialize in a particular field?" or "Will I become broad gauge, capable of effort in many fields?" Trainees don't have to read too strenuously between the lines.

No aspect of the management curriculum so interests the trainees as the "human relation" teaching that pervades the entire program. If the task of the manager is not to work so much as the managing of other people's work, it follows that getting along with people is far and away the most important skill of all. One of the most popular subjects is a four-month course on "effective presentation" . . . the trainee is exposed to psychological insights and communication techniques ("Never say anything controversial") that G.E. believes worth-while guides to good interpersonal relations. . . . One must sell himself, to be sure, and trainees think a lot about this; they also see it, however, as a means to the end of a well-adjusted, stable work group. Thanks to this schooling, trainees prophesy, when they reach positions of authority they will not drive their subordinates. They will motivate them.

The critical importance of getting along with people is driven home to the trainee by the sheer mechanics of the program. He learns human relations by doing as well as by precept, for the social life built into the program makes rubbing fellow trainees the right way mandatory. . . . the trainee enjoys what is essentially a continuation of fraternity life, and when he goes out to the branches he will find that . . . his social needs can be filled within the company orbit.

Getting along with one's peers is as important in class as in after-hours camaraderie. A trainee takes his schooling as a member of a group, not as a lone individual, and the give-and-take in the "case study" group discussions is itself a practical lesson in group dynamics. . . . premium [is] put on skilled communication with one's superiors. Somewhere along the line trainees must get themselves hired into a regular job; deliberately the company program has been so set up that this rests in great measure on the way in which trainees take advantage of the many contacts that rotation from place to place affords. First-name informality is encouraged on both sides, and the trainees quickly learn not to be inhibited in taking the initiative.[10]

For positions deemed to be of great importance, such as those of leadership in a society or an organization, training may be prolonged, vigorous, and many sided. It may require that the individual pass through various phases of training and apprenticeship, though these may not be the terms used to describe the process. Movement through these phases is often correlated with mobility in space, as when a person being groomed for a high executive position in a corporation starts his career in outlying branches or is initially assigned an office far from the centers of policy and decision making.

The informal aspects of institutional teaching are at least as important as the formal. There are a number of points which help to account for the way in which persons in the same positions come to share the same modes of response. The newcomer to a group, association, or institutional structure finds, after all the formal requirements have been met and formal induction has occurred, that he still has much to learn. This learning occurs through ordinary casual conversation and social interaction, both with other newcomers who are meeting up with the same problems and with older members who have some of the answers. The newcomer always finds that actual procedures and requirements are far different from the way they are officially described. He may have to learn this through bitter experience. Special vocabularies are passed on to the recruit largely through ordinary conversation, through the discussion of daily incidents, giving advice, and gossiping. The classifications thus learned may be entirely new to the novitiate, running counter to his old ways and calling for some transformation of character. Remarque has caught this latter aspect in his graphic description of his own entry into the German army in World War I.

Once it was different. When we went to the District Commandant to enlist, we were a class of twenty young men, many of whom proudly shaved for the first time before going to the barracks. We had no definite plans for our future. Our thoughts of a career and occupation were as yet of too unpractical a character to furnish any scheme of life. We were still crammed full of vague ideas which gave to life, and to the war also, an ideal and almost romantic character. We were trained in the army for ten weeks and in this time were more profoundly influenced than by ten years at school. We learned that a bright button is weightier than four volumes of Schopenhauer. At first astonished, then embittered, and finally indifferent, we recognized that what matters is not the mind but the boot brush, not intelligence but the system, not freedom but drill. We became soldiers with eagerness and enthusiasm, but they have done everything to knock that out of us. After three weeks it was no longer incomprehensible to us that a braided postman should have more authority over us than had formerly our parents, our teachers, and the whole gamut of culture from Plato to Goethe. With our young, awakened eyes, we saw that the classical conception of the Fatherland held by our teachers resolved itself here into a renunciation of personality such as one would not ask of the meanest servant—salutes, springing to attention, parade-marches, presenting arms, right wheel, left wheel, clicking the heels, insults, and a thousand pettifogging details. We had fancied our task would be different, only to find we were to be trained for heroism as though we were circus-ponies.[11]

COMMON PROBLEMS AND SOLUTIONS

An important influence upon the molding of the newcomer's thought and action along institutional lines is his encountering of certain standard dilemmas, conflicts, and otherwise difficult experiences. The older members stand ready in the roles of informal teachers to supply the proper explanations and rationales and generally to point the moral of new experiences. Their interpretations are all the more impressive because old-timers often indicate in advance what is going to happen with almost clairvoyant accuracy. They themselves become models to be emulated, since they know the ropes. How the newcomer to the job learns to loaf, for example, is shown in the table below.

QUOTA HOURS LOAFED, BY PERCENTAGES OF TOTAL QUOTA HOURS
AND AVERAGE HOURS PER QUOTA DAY OF LOAFING*
(By Months, March through August, 1945)

Month	Total Quoted Hours	Quoted Hours Loafed	Per Cent Hours Loafed	Hours Loafed per Quota Day
March	69.3	7.6	11.0	0.88
April	76.3	10.35	13.6	1.09
May	69.8	5.15	7.4	0.59
June	83.5	15.2	18.2	1.46
July	84.8	21.4	25.2	2.02
August	85.9	22.2	25.8	2.06
Total	469.6	81.9	17.4	1.39

* From Donald Roy, "Quota Restriction and Goldbricking in a Machine Shop," *American Journal of Sociology*, 57 (1952), 435.

The fact that people share certain statuses or positions within social structures means that they are subject to a great many common experiences. The sheer fact of long-continued association with others of the same rank and position leads to common ways of perceiving and thinking about the social relationships involved. Segments of the larger organization create over a period of time their own mythologies, rituals, and peculiarities of perspective. Insofar as the person becomes identified with his branch, his unit, his rank, he internalizes its values as well as the more general values of the entire organization. Since members of an organization also meet dangerous, embarrassing, and humiliating situations as groups rather than merely as persons, the segments of an organization develop common anxieties and such common ways of dealing with them as, joking, gossiping, jumping on subordinates, and performing other "symbolic acts."

THE INDIVIDUAL AND HIS COMMITMENTS

The institutional order, it can thus be said, provides at least a general framework for the organization of individual behavior. It is clear that the connections between social organization and personality structure are complex and often bafflingly indirect, and that personalities also influence social organization. Persons are not merely the reflections or mirror images of their social statuses, but themselves have a part in choosing positions and through their sagacity and blunders help to change facets of their organizations.

The sociologist and anthropologist are understandably wary of any theory of personality which fails to take into account its institutional and organizational aspects. But merely to trace the complexities of social organization and then to infer personality correlates leaves open the problem of how the person himself manages to organize and internalize the social perspectives to which he is heir. This is a legitimate inquiry.

It is common experience that when any new role is played, one feels that he is play-acting. The part feels foreign. The façade or masklike features of performance take precedence—whether the person feels ill at ease or self-conscious or whether he feels that he is playing a clever or hilarious game. C. W. Mills has written that "The long acting out of a role . . . will often induce a man to become what at first he merely sought to appear."[12] But it sometimes happens that a person may occupy a status and act appropriately in it without ever becoming committed to its values and goals. Many servicemen in the last war appear to have gone through the external motions of being soldiers, assuming peculiar and "unnatural" poses, ways of speaking, and modes of dealing with their fellows. Many felt these gestures were a pretense, an outward show, and that behind the formal military façade they were essentially only dressed-up, coached, and trained civilians. In relation to these individuals it is appropriate to refer to military values as peripheral rather than central to their ways of life, even though they were soldiers *pro tem.*

As a person ceases to feel strange and "out of step" in a new role, the feeling of pretense and make-believe fades. In addition, we may note that the person comes to feel pride in acquiring the skills and meeting the problems of his new situation. By repeatedly taking a gun apart, the rookie soldier develops new attitudes toward the gun which may include such new sentiments as pride, affection, or active dislike. Even the latter, of course, is evidence of involvement.

In order for a job, rank, office, or any other status to exert a pervasive and decisive influence upon a person, it must in some way become linked with his self-conception. At the heart of this linking of self-regard and social position is a fateful commitment to doing well as "that kind of person." A civilian soldier is not insulted by being told that he is not a soldier, but a professional military man is. The latter's behavior is largely oriented around his being a soldier. It is, therefore, a matter of some importance to him to believe that he is a good one, in a good army, preferably one of the "best soldiers in the best damned army in the world."

We say that a person's commitment to central statuses, or those roles which are important to him as a person, is fateful because failure to uphold the standards will be read by the individual himself as failure and will cause him to feel guilty or ashamed, to lose self-respect, and to make efforts to redeem himself. When conception of self is based on a simple central status all other statuses tend to become subordinate to this one, and to be judged by reference to it. To continue with the example of the professional military man:

he will tend to judge many nonmilitary phases of his life in terms of the bearing they have or are likely to have upon his military career. The higher his status, the greater will be the demands of his profession on him for more total commitment and the greater will be the probability that this commitment will eclipse or take precedence over any others. In discussing morale, we have already seen that certain social organizations demand almost total devotion and allegiance of members, even to the exclusion of familial and other roles which may cut athwart the group purposes. Even family roles may become impossible to maintain or may become subordinate to and subtly colored by more essential loyalties.

TRAITS: CONSISTENT AND INCONSISTENT

When a person is dedicated to the pursuit of certain ends, whether organizational or individual, we speak of him as having relatively enduring traits. This is only another way of saying that he repeatedly acts in characteristic ways: that although on occasion he may act out of character, his behavior can generally be expected to run true to form.

It would be a gross oversimplification of human character to suppose that even the most single-minded and "driven" person displays only a single set of traits or that his behavior is consistently organized around a single identity. Perfectly pure, perfectly selfish, and perfectly consistent characters are found only in fiction, and not very good fiction at that, because such single-dimensioned characters are easily recognized as unreal and unconvincing.

Mr. Smith as a Businessman Is	*Mr. Smith as a Father and Husband Is*
shrewd, cagey	gentle
business-like	affectionate
tough-minded	considerate
hard-hearted	understanding
competitive	friendly
mercenary	generous

The traits listed in these two columns are somewhat contradictory. Which are Mr. Smith's "real" traits: those at the right? at the left? neither? or both?

The fact that most persons occupy different statuses simultaneously and that each of these calls forth typical behavior means that they show different sides of their nature to different persons. To a single observer the behavior may appear inconsistent, and the person himself may even be aware of his own incongruent behavior. The following description of the feelings of a married man after a "night out" illustrates this:

> The next morning, he hated himself. His soul was in revolt, disgust rode him, he could not bring his mind to anything, he kept thinking of the sordid, degraded hours of the night. He felt besmirched, befouled, as though he had fallen down in the mud and had come back to his home with daubed and dirty clothing. Paula, his children, his old father-in-law, the servants, looked at him; he wondered if at a glance, by the remotest possibility, they could guess where he had been. . . .[13]

Inconsistencies and even contradictions in behavior patterns of individuals are inevitable. Statuses and roles are usually so organized and rationalized that people find it relatively easy to explain or even deny the inconsistency. "When in Rome do as the Romans do" is a motto of wide applicability. Inconsistent traits may even be called for in the performance of a single role, even a simple one:

> It is an instructive sight to see a waiter going into a hotel dining-room. As he passes the door a sudden change comes over him. The set of his shoulders alters; all the dirt and hurry and irritation have dropped off in an instant. He glides over the carpet, with a solemn, priest-like air. I remember our assistant *maître d'hôtel,* a fiery Italian, pausing at the dining room door to address an apprentice who had broken a bottle of wine. Shaking his fist above his head he yelled (luckily the door was more or less soundproof):
>
> *"Tu me fais*—Do you call yourself a waiter, you young bastard? You a waiter! You're not fit to scrub floors in the brothel your mother came from. *Maquereau!"*
>
> Words failing him, he turned to the door; and as he opened it he delivered a final insult. . . .
>
> Then he entered the dining-room and sailed across it, dish in hand, graceful as a swan. Ten seconds later he was bowing

reverently to a customer. And you could not help thinking, as you saw him bow and smile, with that benign smile of the trained waiter, that the customer was put to shame by having such an aristocrat to serve him.[14]

Many different situations may call for rather similar kinds of behavior, thus encouraging the development of what may be called general traits.

Where a majority of the institutional roles making up a society follow a similar principle, the character traits formed in one context have a chance to operate in another. To this extent the opportunity for general traits to develop in persons is maximized.[15]

An individual who develops a strong commitment to certain ends and ways of achieving them will also tend to display certain general traits as he defines situations in terms of his central purposes. Thus it is said that teachers tend to carry the teacher-pupil relationship with them out of the schoolroom. Cressey, in a study made some years ago, showed that taxi-dance girls carry certain responses to clients over into relationships outside the dance hall. The taxi dancer became sophisticated, tough-minded, money-minded, and exploitative.[16]

ROLE AND TRAIT

It is generally recognized that inconsistencies in behavior are produced by variations in situations. The trait conception of personality does not handle this fact adequately, because it implies the existence of opposed or polar traits in the same person. Thus, the domineering businessman who is also a henpecked husband would be credited with both submissiveness and dominance. The sociological conception of role handles this situation more simply and effectively by noting that the two opposing forms of behavior occur in different contexts.

Instead of attributing a pair of opposing traits to the same person, one need only say that a person is submissive in one of his roles and dominant in another. Or again, instead of characterizing a person as honest or dishonest, the problem is rather one of indicating that in certain roles or situations he can be trusted and not in others.

The role approach to the problem of consistency of behavior emphasizes that behavior patterns, or traits, whether consistently followed or not, are always relative to the situations in which they occur. Even a general trait or response pattern consistently followed by a person in all his roles presupposes some constancy in the roles. This is indicated by the fact that persons whom we think we know very well often change in surprising ways, for example, when they become rich or famous, are elected to high office, are drafted into the service in wartime, change their occupations or their wives, or suffer great misfortune. As Gerth and Mills, say, there are no universal traits "irrespective of specific contexts."[17]

Sex, Class, and Personality

Common speech and custom give evidence of the importance attached to membership in certain broad social categories. This may be made concrete by asking oneself: "What and who am I?" or by noting what one wishes to know about a stranger. Among the items which occur to one at once are sex, age, social class, race, religion, nationality, and occupation. These help to establish the main features of identity and help to predict probable behavior and the general form of the interaction that may be expected to take place.

SEX ROLES

The pervasive manner in which the individual's responses become integrated through the playing of general roles such as those indicated above can be illustrated by noting some consequences of the confusion of sex roles. Imagine what it would be like to discover in one's teens that one had been mistaken about his sex. There is actually no need to speculate what it would be like to experience a reversal of sex roles, for there are authentic accounts of boys who were mistakenly reared as girls and of girls who were mistakenly reared as boys. Seward in her book *Sex and the Social Order* cites three interesting cases which illustrate the impact of this sort of experience.

1. A seventeen-year-old individual who had always regarded herself as a girl complained of failure to menstruate. Examination revealed a large clitoris, but an absence of uterus, tubes, ovaries, vagina or mammary tissue. There was neither prostate nor seminal vesicles, but the patient did have undescended testes and predominantly male secondary sex characters including a deep voice which is an important diagnostic sign of masculinity. From early childhood, S.M. had assumed the feminine role. "Her" earliest memory concerned an episode representing herself in this role at the age of four in doll play. During adolescence, like normal girls, "she" became interested in boys and dances, and later, in sewing, cooking, and housework. Moreover, she experienced typical feminine phantasies of being married and having a family.

2. The case of James is of special interest because of a follow-up after fourteen years. James spent his first fourteen years as "Margaret." [His parents believed him to be a girl because of his anatomical peculiarities.] He was never comfortable as a girl. He suspected that he was not a girl at five years of age when he noticed that his genitals were like his brother's rather than his sister's. At eleven his voice changed and at twelve he rejected the feminine role. Although he had been accepted by girls it was as a tomboy. On his fourteenth birthday he was officially transformed into a boy by change of clothing and residence. Although at first he had the reputation of being a sissy among the boys, he over-compensated and became a tough boy. Later his adjustment seemed more normal. Even after fourteen years [later] in the masculine role, however, James' masculinity structure was still weak and his heterosexual adjustment uncertain.

3. "Martin Murgey," also reared as a girl. . . . A testis was found to coexist with female genital organs. Although he had been rather a tomboy, while still in skirts, he said he would be

content to belong to either sex. The appearance of a beard and the deepening of the voice, however, proved so embarrassing that he welcomed the suggestion of his essential maleness. Psychological study following surgical readjustment revealed a trend of interest toward certain typically masculine occupations, a taste for outdoor activities and for social-athletic pursuits. His M-F [masculinity-femininity trait test] scores averaged more masculine than those of unselected male groups of his age and education. The test also revealed the effects of social conditioning; on those parts which depend on habit and experience, his ratings were more feminine than the male norms while on those in which the wish to be masculine determined the score, he made a more masculine showing on the test.[18]

A former nurse has described, in an unpublished document available to the authors, some interesting reactions to a forced changing of sex roles.[19] "Frankie" was brought to the hospital for examination at the age of five, and "he" was there diagnosed as a genuine female whose clitoris had been previously mistaken for a small penis. In the children's ward, before the examination, Frankie showed a decided preference for the company of little boys and a certain amount of disdain both for girls and for activities which she termed "sissy." After the child's real sex had been determined, the nurses were instructed to treat Frankie as a little girl:

> This didn't sound too difficult—until we tried it. Frankie simply didn't give the right cues. It is amazing how much your response to a child depends on that child's behavior toward you. It was extremely difficult to keep from responding to Frankie's typically little boy behavior in the same way that I responded to other boys in the ward. And to treat Frankie as a girl was jarringly out of key. It was something we all had to continually remind ourselves to do. Yet the doing of it left all of us feeling vaguely uneasy as if we had committed an error. Even remembering to say "her" instead of "him" was difficult. One of the internes just flatly stated that he couldn't do it and referred to Frankie either by name or as "it." After the surgical examination Frankie was in bed and for a few days was satisfied with the more peaceful entertainment which we furnished and in which we vainly hoped she would become interested. But after a few days she began to demand trains, wagons and guns. About the same

time Frankie became increasingly aware of the change in our attitude toward her. She seemed to realize that behavior which had always before brought forth approval was no longer approved. It must have been far more confusing to her than it was to us and certainly it was bad enough for us. Her reaction was strong and violent. She became extremely belligerent and even less willing to accept crayons, color books and games which she simply called "sissy" and threw on the floor. She talked constantly of the wagon she had been promised for Christmas and what she and the other little boys with whom she played would do when she was well and home again. She also objected strenuously to the hospital gown she wore insisting that it was too "sissy" and that she would wear pajamas or nothing. Her departure from the hospital created a disturbance: her mother had brought a dress and Frankie took one look and set up a howl. Her mother finally got her dressed, stepped out of the room to the nurses' station and went back to find a completely nude Frankie. Frankie went home in a pair of hospital coveralls.

These cases of mistaken sexual identity strikingly document the decisive organizing function of sex roles. It is unnecessary to seek for explanations of behavioral and personality differences between the sexes exclusively in the biological or anatomical realm. Social definitions connected with the different bodily structures and function of the sexes, of course, enter decisively into the conceptions that persons have of themselves. However, definitions of femininity and masculinity vary wide from society to society and are closely linked with other broad social categories such as those which we have mentioned—class, age, race, nationality, occupation, and so on.

SOME NAMES OF WOMEN'S PERFUMES. FACETS OF THE FEMALE ROLE?

Tweed	Vol de Nuit
Blue Mist	Danger
Appleblossom	Shocking
Desert Flower	Tabu
Quelques Fleurs	Aphrodisia
Lotus	Moment Supreme
New Horizons	Ecstasy
Anticipation	My Sin
Shanghai	Menace
Intoxication	Goddess

SOCIAL CLASS AND BEHAVIORAL ORGANIZATION

A person's general style of life is profoundly influenced by his position in the class hierarchy and his evaluation of the chances of improving that position. Popular recognition of this fact is evidenced by the interest in what a man's occupation is and in noting cues and outward symbols of his probable financial status. The symbols and actualities of wealth also indicate power and position and are buttresses of self-confidence. We have seen that Marxian theory maintains that an individual's motives and ideas, and indeed his whole personality, are determined by influences of this type. Without subscribing to this doctrine, we may note that its widespread influence testifies to the general appreciation of the significance of class.

Men everywhere classify one another in terms of relative status, prestige, and power; and in complex societies they recognize that persons belong to one of several social classes which possess these attributes in varying degrees. The number and kinds of classes in any given country are closely related to its economic and occupational structure. To demonstrate this in detail would take us far beyond the limits of our text; but one may easily grasp the point by visualizing how markedly different would be the number, kinds, and rank of classes in the United States if ours were an agricultural and pastoral land.

To appreciate the effects of class membership on the organization of behavior, we need merely note that within the same country the members of different classes have somewhat different social heritages. Situated as they are on different rungs of the social ladder, the members of the various class strata view the world differently, classifying experiences differently and attributing diverse significances to the same activities and objects. Note, for example, the dissimilar ways in which money and the pursuit of money are viewed by the investing classes and the laboring classes in the United States. A large library could be filled with books and articles describing the different values and standards of European classes in such matters as child rearing, marital relations, family relations in gen-

The Social Perspectives of the Social Classes*

UPPER-UPPER CLASS   LOWER-UPPER CLASS

UPPER-UPPER CLASS	Code	LOWER-UPPER CLASS
"Old aristocracy"	UU	"Old aristocracy"
"Aristocracy," but not "old"	LU	"Aristocracy," but not "old"
"Nice, respectable people"	UM	"Nice, respectable people"
"Good people, but 'nobody'"	LM	"Good people, but 'nobody'"
	UL	
"Po' whites"	LL	"Po' whites"

UPPER-MIDDLE CLASS   LOWER-MIDDLE CLASS

UPPER-MIDDLE CLASS	Code	LOWER-MIDDLE CLASS	
"Society" { "Old families"	UU	"Old aristocracy" (older)	"Broken-down aristocracy" (younger)
"Society" but not "old families"	LU		
"People who should be upper class"	UM	"People who think they are somebody"	
"People who don't have much money"	LM	"We poor folk"	
	UL	"People poorer than us"	
"No 'count lot"	LL	"No 'count lot"	

UPPER-LOWER CLASS   LOWER-LOWER CLASS

UPPER-LOWER CLASS	Code	LOWER-LOWER CLASS
	UU	
	LU	
"Society" or the "folks with money"	UM	"Society" or the "folks with money"
"People who are up because they have a little money"	LM	"Way-high-ups," but not "Society"
"Poor but honest folk"	UL	"Snobs trying to push up"
"Shiftless people"	LL	"People just as good as anybody"

* From A. Davis, B. Gardner, and M. Gardner, *Deep South*, University of Chicago Press, 1941, p. 65.

eral, occupational pursuits, recreation, religious beliefs and practices, and politics.

To turn to a more specific aspect of the problem, different types
of class structures affect their members' personalities differently.
We may illustrate this by comparing, in order, four general types
of class stratification: (1) a relatively closed class system, (2) the
same system, becoming less closed, (3) a relatively open class system, and (4) the same, becoming less open.

In a relatively closed system, the classes are rigidly stratified
from top to bottom in decreasing orders of rank, prestige, privilege,
and power. The classes themselves are virtually frozen, as are the
positions of individual members. By this we mean that the classes
themselves do not change relative positions except very slowly; and
also, that one who is born into a given class remains there for his
entire lifetime. This type of class structure is known as a caste system. Generally speaking, the lives of caste members are tightly
organized around their general caste role, so that one may readily
see how immense areas of their behavior are related to their relatively fixed social position. Unlike a person in present-day America,
a member of a caste does not focus upon the hopes of rising or the
fears of falling in the class heirarchy, for he can do neither. In the
traditional caste system of India, the caste position into which a
person was born determined not only occupation, but also dress;
access to religious shrines and temples and the water supply; birth,
marriage, and death customs; ways of behaving toward or avoiding members of other subcastes; legal status; and food customs and
taboos. Criminal occupations and marginal ones, such as begging
and prostitution, became matters of caste monopoly and were handed
on from parents to children. Caste status was even conceived as a
decisive influence in the individual's fate after death and in possible
future existences. The societies of medieval Europe and the South
in the pre-Civil War United States are other examples of relatively
closed class systems.

When a relatively closed system of stratification grows more
fluid, the behavior and personal organization of many of its members
are affected. As one example, we may note the era in European

history when feudalism was gradually coming to an end. A new group emerged on the historical scene, growing increasingly prominent and powerful: the merchant or business class. It gradually acquired economic and political power; but not until later did it gain social prestige. When the new business class finally gained social ascendancy and merged with the old feudal nobility at the top of the social ladder, it found itself in turn beset by clamoring classes from below.

The relatively open, or mobile, class system may be exemplified by that prevalent in most of the United States prior to the present century. In general, Americans who had ability, luck, and connections, or appropriate combinations thereof, rose with a fair degree of regularity from the classes into which they had been born. Other Americans fell correspondingly in their relative positions. However, the example of the United States is somewhat complicated because as each immigrant group came to this country, it was usually relegated to the position at the bottom of the class ladder. In a relatively open system in which one characteristically rises or falls as an individual, hopes and expectations focus on rising in the social scale. People are thought of in terms of "have risen," "will rise," "shows promise of rising," "failure—didn't rise," "has been up and down several times," and the like.

When this type of class system begins to grow more rigid, there develop correspondingly different types of experience and conceptions of self. Many peoples' hopes and expectations are still focused upon rising; and for failing to achieve their aspirations they often blame themselves instead of the objective difficulties which block their rise. Considerable discontent is engendered because opportunities for class climbing have actually lessened. As the opportunities diminish, people begin to grow more realistic. They may hope, but not really expect, to rise, so they become resigned or content themselves with consolidating the position into which they were born. When members of the lower or middle classes believe they have no chance to rise as individuals, they may adopt the idea of changing position through organized group action designed to improve the status of their whole class. There has been much discussion and debate over whether the trend in the United States is toward a closed class system. Whatever the trend may be, there is no question that it, and men's conceptions of it, will profoundly affect the personalities of Americans.

Even in a society like that of the United States, where the class structure is relatively fluid and class lines are not always sharply drawn, the influence of class position upon personal behavior is still potent. We have noted how the class into which one is born makes him heir to speech habits, moral standards, conceptions of family, and a great many other beliefs and attitudes. Inherited class position also affects longevity, the nature and duration of education, probable future income, and other "life chances." The individual's participation in other social structures, and his position in them, are profoundly conditioned by his initial class position.

Class position leaves an individual a legacy of purposes for which to strive, and prescribes a range of means for reaching these ends. Upwardly mobile persons who conceive of upper-class position exclusively in terms of wealth, and what Veblen called "conspicuous consumption," often retain their driving ambition after it has served its purpose of making them wealthy. For full acceptance into elite circles they must learn new esthetic, intellectual, and recreational standards. Motives having to do with raising one's status or maintaining it may become such an absorbing preoccupation that virtually all activities and energies are bent to this end. The American ideology of success in open competition emphasizes the rewards and virtues of this sort of striving, and leads to the evaluation of self and of others in terms of it. For those who fail and thus are affected adversely, some consolation is offered by other facets of popular ideology—such as that the rich lead artificial, tense, immoral, and irreligious lives; that wealth doesn't bring happiness; and that leaving home to "make good" isn't worth the sacrifice. The connectives between class and self-conceptions are sometimes fairly direct and easily discernible, but sometimes they are indirect and very subtle. Sociologists are inclined to look askance at any personality theory which does not explore these connections to the full.

Sociological and Anthropological Approaches to Personality Typing

Typologies of personality are always relative to the basic assumptions and aims of the one who does the classifying. Theorists who are biologically oriented construct typologies with anatomical and physiological dimensions and correlate them with temperamental or behavioral traits. Psychological theories of personality tend to formulate typologies in terms of stable traits, habits, conditioned responses, or whatever the basic unit is thought to be. The focus is on the individual and how he interacts in personal relations. Psychiatric and psychoanalytic typing is concerned primarily with behavior syndromes associated with maladjustment, or with patterns derived from early childhood and carried over into adult interpersonal relations.

SOCIAL TYPING: IMPLICIT AND EXPLICIT

Sociological and anthropological typologies are of varying kinds, but they are generally related not so much to personal relationships as to social roles in the matrix of group and institutional functions. This kind of typing is closely akin to popular classification when the latter is based on a sense of group membership and social position. Common speech is liberally interlarded with implicit and explicit typing which often reflects very acute perception of the origins and consequences of group life. In fact, the special vocabulary of a group that has any history whatever will contain terms referring to types of persons, both within its own ranks and in groups with which it is in close and important contact.

The terms for these types carry heavy loads of admiration, appreciation, envy, opprobrium, and other attitudes and sentiments. The argot of thieves offers the following picturesque examples: "sucker," a noncriminal; "burglar cop," a police officer who accepts bribes from thieves; "square cop," a police officer who does not accept bribes; "slave," laboring man; and "rapist" any prison inmate who is not a thief. Many social scientists are inclined to reject such typologies out of hand, marshaling a series of objections against them. They are said to be mere conventional labels; they are said to do violence to the richness of the facts since they focus on one or a few aspects of personality and ignore many others; they are based on insufficient experience and observation, not to say poor sampling; they betray the biases and preconceptions of the person who does the typing. Last, and most serious, the scientist notes that popular typing is rigid in the sense that once one uses such a classification he hangs on to it tenaciously in the face of contradictions and exceptions. In short, these are stereotypes. But to see in terms of stereotypes is to see objects as class members. If the scientist's classifying is different it is because he does something in addition. We shall consider scientific typology in a moment. First let us consider, with particular reference to personality, whether common-sense stereotyping of personality is not useful for everyday purposes.

This process of naming "kinds" of persons enables one to act appropriately, thus: "He's a stuffed shirt—stay away from him." Like any other act of categorizing, it saves time and effort: one does not have to find out for himself that the man is a bore. On the other hand, the speedy and facile stereotyping of people on the basis of immediately recognizable mannerisms often leads to errors of judgment. The mistakes that we make in sizing up people when we meet them for the first time illustrate the dangers of stereotyping.

One may decry the tenaciousness with which stereotypes are adhered to even in the face of objective evidence, but one can scarcely deny their functional usefulness in the lives of individuals and groups. Nor for that matter can one deny the partial empirical validity of some stereotypes of persons propelled into recognition by common parlance and by the illuminating descriptions of various novelists.

In an effort to facilitate investigation and construct general theories, social scientists have often used popular typologies as points of departure. In the study of a community, for instance, a great deal of initial insight into both institutions and persons is afforded by discovering what classifications are made by the people themselves. This procedure has become part of the working method of the social scientist. Sociologists have called these common-sense classifications "social types." In the Chicago Negro world, such racial types as the following are recognized: "the white man's nigger," "the barfly," "the striver," "the jive cat," "the uppity."[20] These terms are meaningful, of course, only if one has an acquaintance with the values and perspectives of the categorizing group. Sometimes terms for types are lifted out of context and used by other groups in quite different ways, frequently to the amusement or indignation of the inventors. An example of this is the different meanings the term "H(h)oosier" has in the underworld and in polite society. In the latter it means a resident of the state of Indiana; in the former it refers to a "rube," a yokel, or unsophisticated person. Many persons who use it in the one sense do not know of its other usage. However useful popular typologies may be for initial orientation and exploratory study, they do not lead automatically to the construction of fruitful social theory.

In the analysis of social structures, sociologists find it useful to construct typologies of many sorts: of the structures themselves, of groups, statuses, social relationships—and of the persons who enact the roles. Any of the socially produced uniformities which we have hitherto been discussing can become the basis of a type. "The discernment of such types . . . is a major part of the social psychology of institutions."[21] The specific typology with which the investigator works will vary greatly, depending upon the kind of social relationships under consideration. Most such types, because they are institutional or historical, are not universal in scope; and they cover only segments of the individual's behavior, albeit often very important ones.

NATIONAL CHARACTER

There is another kind of typing which has engaged the efforts of some investigators, mostly anthropologists, in recent years. This is the characterization of whole peoples and nations, whether preliterate or civilized. Such characterization is not a totally new enterprise. Writers and scholars for centuries have attempted descriptions of what was called the *genius* or *ethos* of peoples. Impetus for this kind of inquiry was provided by ethnological investigations of a large number of preliterate cultures, and, since the last war, by some practical interest in the psychological backgrounds of other nations, enemies and allies alike.

Contemporary anthropologists may attempt to depict societies in psychological terms as functioning wholes or configurations. The observer seeks to characterize what may be called the "essence" of the culture in psychological terms, *i.e.*, in terms of the people's view of the world and of human relations. As Gorer has written, this leads to the discovery of key "themes" which predominate in the society.

> The principle of *congruence* is a convenient label for the fact . . . that the goals of the various institutions . . . are coherently related to one another; that if the end results of institutional activities are inspected, they will be seen to fall into patterns in which a small number of themes are dominant; that if the results of the activities of the personnel are inspected, they will be seen to gratify a relatively small number of wishes besides those biologically necessary for survival and reproduction.[22]

Following logically from this emphasis upon cultural themes and configurations is the idea that configurations have their counterparts in the individuals of each society. Given cultures produce one or more types of personality designated by such terms as "national character," "character structure," "model personality," and "basic personality structure." The assumption is that societies continue, although their personnel changes. This implies that the characters and predispositions of the new recruits to the society do not differ in any marked or consistent degree from those whose ranks they join or whose places they fill.[23]

In arriving at their characterization of cultures and personality types, anthropologists of the culture-personality orientation have relied upon conventional ethnological techniques and data, but have paid particular attention to life histories and observation and interviewing of persons and have focused sharply upon child training as the main determinant of personality.[24] In their explanations some writers have leaned particularly upon concepts drawn from learning theory and psychoanalysis. In some recent anthropological work, interviewing and observation of persons has been supplemented by psychological analysis of secondary data—films, novels, laws, and proceedings of meetings, for example. "These segments of material are chosen in such a way that the regularities found in one segment can be checked against those found in another segment."[25]

Anthropologists have themselves questioned the validity of many of the characterizations of societies as being oversimple and in some degree biased. No one questions the existence of gross differences in psychological makeup between societies. The question is whether even small nonliterate societies are as homogeneous as is sometimes assumed; and whether, therefore, the number of personality types produced in such a society is not larger than is assumed. More recently, there has been a wider formulation to include

> the study of the *range* of personalities in a society. Characteristic personality sub-types may develop from the differing situations of the life of persons who play different roles in a given group.[26]

Linton, who had a deep interest in the idea of basic personality type, made the following judgment concerning it: "The existence of different personality norms for modern nations as wholes has not been established."[27]

Few have gone to the length that Kardiner has in suggesting a supernational character type. Kardiner's scheme represents a combination of anthropological, psychoanalytic, and historical approaches. He believed the chief influences in character formation to stem from family structure and basic child-rearing practices. Religion, marital practices, sexual practices, ways of handling societal crises, and the like, are thought of as derived from or intimately connected with the basic personality of the society. Kardiner raises the question whether the whole Western world does not have a more or less basic characterology, although it has changed with time, and varies from nation to nation. He concludes that "In geeral . . . 'human nature' as we find it in Western man has not change much insofar as his character structure, or rather the range characters, is concerned."[28] He suggests as a note of caution th his studies are exploratory and that there may be great differenc between nations within the common Western psychological fram work.

The dangers inherent in general descriptions of societies an in the postulation of common national characters are great. Ar social scientist whe seeks to characterize a modern nation has t handle a host of detailed problems and meet a number of exactin requirements. These have to do with sampling, regional difference migration, ethnic differences, social classes, diverse group affiliatior and standards, cultural conflicts, and enormous bodies of literatur and historical materials. Margaret Mead has attempted to mee criticisms of attempts to formulate national descriptions by agreein that great differences may exist among subgroups in a nation an that knowledge of the national pattern is not sufficient to perm prediction about the distinctive regional, class, or other subpattern However, she maintains that "the version of the wider cultura pattern manifested by the members of any sub-group in a cultur may be expected to be systematically related to the wider cultura pattern."[29] It follows that any member of a group, "provided h position within that group is properly specified," will exemplif some aspect of the national character. One may agree in principl that each subgroup, particularly if it has not migrated to the cour try recently, reveals something to us about the nation at large, bu it is unwarranted in advance of actual study of the subgroups t say much about them. Most modern countries probably have mor heterogeneity than we sometimes give them credit for. It also seem questionable to place too great weight upon child-rearing practice and early experiences as the determinants of national character.

The characterizations of peoples have also been criticized on th grounds that the investigator's own biases and perceptions inevitabl color his account. This is perhaps especially true when the peopl described are non-Western and unable to reply and thus correc the interpretation, but it is also true of characterizations of Western societies. When the people characterized are able to read the books written about them, they often find the descriptions amusing or in some part quite incorrect. An interpretation of Americans by an English scholar (Gorer) was vigorously criticized; so were many of the points made by an American (Mead)[30] of fellow Americans. Japanese scholars do not put much faith in the interpretations of Japanese personality made by Benedict[31] and LeBarre, two American anthropologists.

The terms used in depicting a society are inevitably taken from one's own psychological vocabulary. The description, consequently, turns out to be not an objective description on which all observers will agree, but simply an account of how society appears to the observer. Thus Kroeber has been able to say about DuBois' characterization of the Alorese that it

> . . . seems one-sidedly repellent. . . . The appraising observer comes from a culture which values internalization, conscience, reliance, scruple, courage, consistency of feeling and relations, dignity, and achievement, qualities that are underdeveloped in Alor. Hence the picture is black.[32]

We have Englishmen's characterizations of Englishmen, Americans, Russians, and Germans; and we have American portrayals of Americans, Germans, Japanese, Englishmen, and Russians; and presumably Russian social scientists are busily characterizing themselves, Americans, Englishmen, and other peoples. Probably little agreement could be found among the various assessments of the same nation by scholars of different nationalities. Although these characterizations undoubtedly give us important information about how the people of one country think about those of another and of themselves, there remain two questions: Which of the various accounts comes closest to the truth? Is any one of them more than a partial and distorted portrayal of the great variety of personalities found in any nation? Despite all criticism—ours included—these studies are valuable as correctives to too-easy generalization about personality and as a contribution to our understanding of the comparative learning situations in which persons are formed.

Summary

Sociologists and anthropologists, influenced by their ideological tradition, generally emphasize the influence of the social environment as the broad determinant of personality development. The existence and perpetuation of a society imposes requirements which restrict diversity and variability and tend to shape the personalities of its members by giving them common experiences within the social structure. The existence of cultural inconsistencies poses problems for the individual and is reflected in personal organization. Broad social categories, like those of sex and class, constitute a framework for the organization of large areas of individual behavior. Attempts to distinguish social and personality types and to describe national character suggest the manner in which common social experiences create uniformities among persons. The analysis of the social structure provides a picture of the general setting and the broad influences which condition and limit personality growth and differentiation. As such it is a prelude to a more direct examination of the ways in which individuals make their personal and specific adaptations. Before going on to a consideration of how sociologists and anthropologists deal with adult personality organization and change we will first present two developmental theories of early personality growth—those of Freud and Sullivan.

SUGGESTIONS FOR DISCUSSION AND SPECIAL REPORTS

1. There are many novels and autobiographies concerning upper class Bostonians. Write a report on social class and the Bostonian personality.

2. Trace the efflorescence and decline of the heredity-environment controversy.

3. Compare legal and medical education, paying attention particularly to the social psychology of occupational training.

4. Contrast prewar training in the United States army with that more typical of the war years.

5. Write a report on the training of high school teachers and its possible effects on "teacher mentality."

6. Interview actors and trace the subjective processes of mastering a new role.

7. Compare: (1) British conceptions of American character, (2) British conceptions of British character, (3) American conceptions of American character, and (4) American conceptions of British character.

8. How great a difference is there in character according to region in America?

9. Work out a glossary of social types as designated by some group, and interpret the functions of the terminology for the group.

NOTES

[1] E. Faris, "The Concept of Social Attitudes," *J. Applied Soc.*, 9(1925): 404-409.

[2] L. White, in R. W. Sellars, V. J. McGill, and M. Farber, *Philosophy for the Future*, Macmillan, 1949, p. 374.

[3] M. E. Spiro, "Culture and Personality; The History of a False Dichotomy," *Psychiatry*, 14 (1951): 31.

[4] G. H. Mead, *Mind, Self and Society*, University of Chicago Press, 1934.

[5] A. A. Angyal, *Foundations for a Science of Personality*, New York: The Commonwealth Fund, 1941, pp. 89-92.

[6] G. Murphy, *Personality*, Harper, 1947, p. 714.

[7] Paraphrased from A. K. Cohen, "On the Place of 'Themes' and Kindred Concepts in Social Theory," *Am. Anthro.*, 50 (1948): 436-443.

[8] E. C. Hughes, "Dilemmas and Contradictions of Status," *Am. J. Soc.*, 50(1945): 253-259.

[9] H. Gerth and C. W. Mills, *Character and Social Structure*, Harcourt, Brace, 1953, p. 251.

[10] "The Crown Princes of Business," *Fortune*, 48(1953): 152-153.

[11] E. M. Remarque, *All Quiet on the Western Front*, Little, Brown, 1929, pp. 20-21.

[12] C. W. Mills, "Situated Actions and Vocabularies of Motive," *Am. Soc. Rev.*, 5(1940): 908.

[13] Charles Norris, *Pig Iron*, Dutton, 1925, p. 392.

[14] George Orwell, *Down and Out in Paris and London*, Garden City, N. Y.: Permabooks, 1954, pp. 78-79.

[15] Gerth and Mills, *op. cit.*, pp. 178-179.

[16] P. G. Cressey, *The Taxi-Dance Hall*, University of Chicago Press, 1932, p. 40.

[17] Gerth and Mills, *op. cit.*, p. 178.

[18] G. H. Seward, *Sex and the Social Order*, McGraw-Hill, 1946, pp. 177-178.

[19] We are indebted to Elizabeth Bornholdt for this document.

[20] See S. M. Strong, "Social Types in a Minority Group," *Am. J. Soc.*, 48(1943): 563-573.

[21] Gerth and Mills, *op. cit.*, p. 110.

[22] G. Gorer in M. Mead and R. Métraux, *The Study of Culture at a Distance*, University of Chicago Press, 1953, p. 63.

[23] *Ibid.*, p. 62.

[24] For example, G. Gorer and J. Rickman place great emphasis upon the swaddling of infants in the explanation of Russian character in *The People of Great Russia*, New York: Chanticleer Press, 1949. Gorer and LeBarre stress early and severe toilet training as a key to Japanese personality. (G. Gorer, "Themes in Japanese Culture," *Transactions of the New York Academy of Sciences*, Vol. V, 1943, pp. 106-124: W. LeBarre, "Some Observations on Character Structure in the Orient: the Japanese," *Psychiatry*, 8(1945): 319-345.)

[25] M. Mead in A. Kroeber, *Anthropology Today*, University of Chicago Press, 1953, pp. 652-653.

[26] M. Herskovitz, *Man and His Works*, Knopf, 1948, p. 50.

[27] R. Linton in A. H. Stanton and S. E. Perry (eds.), *Personality and Political Crisis*, Glencoe, Ill.: The Free Press, 1951, p. 144.

[28] A. Kardiner, *Psychological Frontiers of Society*, Columbia University Press, 1945, p. 433.

[29] M. Mead, *op. cit.*, p. 647.

[30] G. Gorer, *The American People*, Norton, 1948: M. Mead, *And Keep Your Powder Dry*, Morrow, 1942.

[31] R. Benedict, *The Chrysanthemum and the Sword*, Houghton Mifflin, 1946.

[32] A. Kroeber, *Anthropology*, Harcourt, Brace, 1948, pp. 588-589.

SELECTED BIBLIOGRAPHY

Bendix, R., and M. Lipset, *Class, Status and Power*, Glencoe, Ill.: Free Press, 1953. A book of readings on social stratification, many of them pertinent to the effect of class on person.

Gerth, H., and C. W. Mills, *Character and Social Structure*, Harcourt Brace, 1953. A systematic attempt to relate social structure and personality.

Hiller, E., "The Social Structure in Relation to the Person," *Soc. Forces,* 16(1937): 34-44. Deals with some relationships between personality and participation in status groups.

Hughes, E. C., "Institutional Office and the Person," *Am. J. Soc.,* 33 (1937): 404-413. The nature of office or position, and patterned movement through positions.

Kardiner, A., *The Psychological Frontiers of Society,* Columbia University Press, 1945. Written by a psychoanalyst in collaboration with anthropologists. The data is drawn mainly from primitive societies.

Kroeber, A. L., "The Superorganic," *Am. Anthro.* (new ser.), 19(1917): 163-213. The argument of cultural determinism is set forth in this early article by an eminent anthropologist.

Lindesmith, A. R., and A. L. Strauss, "A Critique of Culture-Personality Writings," *Am. Soc. Rev.,* 15(1950): 587-600. A critical review of writings in this field.

Mead, M., in A. L. Kroeber (ed.), *Anthropology Today,* University of Chicago Press, 1954. "National Character," pp. 642-667. A comprehensive review of literature on this subject by an acknowledged leader in this area.

Merton, R. K., "Bureaucratic Structure and Personality," *Soc. Forces,* 18(1940): 560-568. An attempt to outline the kind of personnel produced by bureaucracies.

Parsons, T., "A Revised Analytical Approach to the Theory of Social Stratification," in R. Bendix and M. Lipset, *Class, Status and Power,* Glencoe, Ill.: Free Press, 1953, pp. 92-128. A difficult but rewarding paper which deals, especially in the latter pages, with the American class system.

Spiro, M. E., "Culture and Personality: The History of a False Dichotomy," *Psychiatry,* 14(1951): 19-46. A thoughtful review and criticism of various types of cultural determinism.

Strong, S. M., "Social Types in a Minority Group," *Am. J. Soc.,* 48(1943): 563-573. A description of social types in a Negro community, following the community's own terminology.

CHAPTER 17

Two Theories

of Early

Personality

Development

THE AREA OF DEVELOPMENTAL THEORY is one of the most hotly contested in the whole field of social psychology and one that includes some of its most important and difficult problems. Although no one denies the importance of early childhood learning, some writers are partisans of the crucial effect upon personality of prelingual experiences occurring in the first year or two of life, and a few stress the birth experience itself or even the prenatal period. The so-called "childhood disciplines," *i.e.*, nursing, weaning, swaddling, bladder and sphincter control, are given great prominence by some writers, who are in turn criticized and sometimes jeered at by others who call them "chamber-pot determinists." The latter critics place the critical age for personality development further along, or simply argue that the first years of childhood are not necessarily crucial. Some of the bitterest issues are avoided by empirically minded child psychologists who content themselves with amassing concrete data without doing much theorizing. Textbooks in child psychology are usually catalogues of miscellaneous information. A French critic, in a review of an American handbook in this field, remarked that despite the hundreds of studies reported upon there was hardly a breath of humanity in the text. There are not many theories which plot out personality growth in phases or stages, but there are many variants of the Freudian position. This theory sketches fairly definite stages of personality development in relation to the stages leading to sexual maturity. Some of these variants are highly influential in popular thought, into which they have entered through nursery schools, women's magazines, and child-rearing manuals. Women nowadays are warned against the dictates of the "maternal instinct" and against the promptings of common sense. Fads and fashions in child rearing come and go, as Stendler noted in her historical survey, "Sixty Years of Child Training Practices."[1] The Freudian conception of development is debatable, but little has been offered to take its place, and so it is the dominant general theory in this field. We shall turn first to some aspects and variations of this theory.

Early Experience as Crucial

THE BIRTH PROCESS

Psychoanalytically oriented writers usually pay some attention to the "birth trauma" as a possible determinant of later development, even when they do not ascribe the great importance to it that Rank did.[2] Rank was impressed by the abrupt transition which birth appears to be and made this "trauma" central in his system. This position is rejected by virtually everyone as purely speculative. The more moderate position is exemplified in a paper by Wile and Davis.[3] They suggest that the mode of birth—slow, fast, spontaneous, or with instruments—may have an effect on such reactions as aggressiveness and hyperactivity. Other writers, including Greenacre,[4] contend that birth establishes an anxiety pattern and that situations similar to the birth experience later arouse this anxiety and play a role in individual differences in reaction to anxiety. The maternal attitude of anxiousness toward the premature child is also thought to affect the child's relations with the mother. Bernfeld[5] has classified societies as "foetusphile" or "foetusphobic," depending upon whether they extend the foetal period (warm baths, protective covering, cradle) or terminate it at birth (cold baths, few wrappings, few clothes). According to Benedek,[6] the era of rigid feeding schedules in America (roughly from 1910 to 1930) was a "foetusphobic" reaction which expressed the new status of women. Bernfeld argued that foetusphobic treatment might produce a low anxiety threshold and possibly even lead to the beginning of adult fatalism.

DEPRIVATION

In all these writings which speculate on the psychological import of birth, the traumatic, anxiety–producing nature of the experience is emphasized to some degree. But, according to some writers, the months immediately after birth are especially crucial for the general direction which the child is to take. The logic of this position is well brought out by Ribble, who has written that:

> . . . it is reasonable enough to suppose that the sensitive organism of the human infant would register the effects of experiences related to body security and well-being or to insecurity and lack of personal care. Once registered, these experiences . . . would be expected to foster responses of positive grouping on the one hand, or of negative resistance or withdrawal on the other. These early mechanisms of reaction might then readily gain momentum so as to alter or even to distort the succeeding phases of personality development.[7]

Chief among the agencies which lead to the well-being of the helpless infant in the first months is, of course, the mother. It is hypothesized that the fondling of the infant and the satisfaction of its bodily needs facilitate physiological integration and contribute to its feeling of security and confidence. When such maternal attention is minimal or lacking, the baby is said to suffer a traumatic experience that results in lack of confidence and, in extreme cases, in psychological disorders and even physical deterioration. The chief evidence for these extreme results is of two sorts: a study of "hospitalism" by R. Spitz[8] and studies of infants unduly deprived of maternal care.

Spitz contrasted the results of the handling of infants in an excellent foundling home with those in a penal institution for women. The two institutions, located in Latin America, differed only in one major respect: in the foundling home the children were taken care of by nurses (seven or more to a nurse), whereas in the prison each child was reared by its own mother. The prison children turned out to be markedly superior. All survived the first year, whereas in the foundling home the mortality rate was 30 percent. After the second year, 75 percent of the foundling survivors were below normal in weight, 83 percent were below normal in height, 76 percent could not walk alone, and 90 percent had fewer than six words in their vocabulary. The prison children were normal or above average in these respects. On the basis of this evidence Spitz has assigned an especially critical role to the mothering process wherein the child learns to distinguish objects, to imitate, to play, to feed himself, to walk, and to develop "emotional relations." These kinds of observations have been repeated nowhere else, but if validated with a surer methodology they would establish a problem: What is there about the mother-child interaction that produces such dramatic consequences? Spitz himself cautions that further investigation is required to isolate the causes of the deterioration observed in institutionalized infants.

Less extreme effects of maternal deprivation have been noted in other studies. This evidence is subject to differing interpretations and to methodological criticism. Nevertheless, agencies in charge of children who are available for adoption are being advised that it is better for a young child to live with his own mother, even if home conditions are not very good, than to be placed in an institution or in a foster home. The argument is that the transfer to even a good foster mother constitutes a radical and potentially disruptive experience.[9] Two psychologists, Hutt and Miller,[10] who are sympathetic to the deprivation theory, state that it is "tempting to infer that all degrees of deprivation leave permanent traces. . . .

[But] even if a relationship is postulated between infant deprivation and adult insecurity, we should not expect to be able to predict
the latter directly from the former." They note what is well known:
the effect of what happens during the first year can be greatly
altered by later experience. In some societies parental handling of
children changes tremendously after the first few years, and the
children show the results of this topsy-turvy treatment.

THE INFANT DISCIPLINES

Among the most obvious learning of the infant is that which has
to do with the management of his own body and its functions. He
must be taught to handle them in prescribed ways, and this teaching
starts in almost the first hour. The experiences which are associated
with this training are sometimes said to be crucial for personality
development. The differential personality types produced by each
society or subsociety are related to the infant disciplines, since:
"Societies differ in the intensity of demands, modes of disciplines,
timing, and rewards and punishment. This variety of regulatory
standards may determine in great part how the child learns to relate to others."[11] Among the disciplines frequently studied and cited
as important are bowel and bladder training, nursing, weaning, re-
straint of motion, eating, and control of thumbsucking and masturbation. Writers who adhere to the idea that personality is established by the infant disciplines have attributed Japanese character,
for example, to the rigid bowel training which Japanese children
are said to be subjected to, whereas they consider Russian character
to be the consequence of the swaddling of infants in that country.
Too precipitous training of the child in weaning, cleanliness, sex
taboos, and the control of aggression is said to lay the foundation
for obsessive ambition and extreme competitiveness in adults. G.
Gorer, a British anthropologist, has sought to account for many
aspects of American character and American culture in terms of the
way in which babies are fed in the United States.

H. Orlansky[12] has made a critical evaluation of the data and
assertions bearing on the influence of infant care on personality
development. He has shown that there is no body of evidence to

demonstrate connections between infant experiences and adult personality patterns. Some of his main points may be summarized as follows: (1) Various writers attribute different and contradictory effects to the same or similar childhood experiences. (2) The alleged influences of given infant disciplines or types of experience on personality have not been proven within our own society, to say nothing of others. (3) The method of "proving" that early infancy is of primary importance is shot through with anthropomorphism and unsupported assumptions. (4) Postinfantile childhood experiences are probably of more vital importance in shaping personality than the prelingual ones.

Defenders of the infant-discipline doctrine have sought to meet criticism of their position by qualifying it. Thus it is commonly asserted (1) that if postinfantile experiences tend to reinforce the personality trends established in infancy, the resulting adult traits will conform to the infantile pattern; however, (2) if later experiences run counter to earlier ones, the resulting adult character may not be predictable from infantile experiences alone. Others have said that the same adult personality trait may be caused by different patterns of childhood experience, that a given infant discipline may result in several quite different personality trends, and that individual biological differences and cultural differences have to be considered in predicting what the consequences of given infantile experiences will be. Still others have admitted that, although certain attitudes may be established in the child by his early sex experiences, these attitudes may subsequently disappear if they are not reinforced by later experiences.

Few if any would dispute that there is a special significance attached to first or early learning. The training of the body and its functions assuredly plays a part in the adult's conception of himself —who he is, and what he can do with his body. Furthermore, it probably does help lay some of the groundwork of relationships with significant others. But the exact nature of the psychological traces left by such early experiences, especially the prelingual ones, is very difficult to specify and no one has yet done it in a way that seems convincing to recalcitrant critics. Whatever the traces are, they do not appear explicitly in communication, since persons do not readily recall their earliest experiences and are almost totally unaware of their effects. Scholars who tend toward an emphasis upon unconscious processes are drawn rather naturally to an interest in early childhood learning, whereas those who lean toward a stress upon verbal communication and direct learning are more disposed to emphasize the importance of later experience.

Psychosexual Development: Freudian Theory

The general Freudian thesis of personality development has been concisely stated by Benedek:

> The integration of the *sexual drive* from its pre-genital sources to the *genital primacy* and to functional maturity is the axis around which the organization of the personality takes place. From the point of view of personality development, the process of interaction is the same in both sexes. Men and women alike reach their psychosexual maturity through the reconciliation of the sexual drive with the superego and through the adjustment of sexuality to all other functions of the personality. . . . *The sexual drive is organized differently in men and women, in order to serve specific functions in procreation.*[13]

In our presentation of Freudian developmental theory we shall rely mainly on Benedek's summarization. It should be remembered that there is some divergence of opinion among Freudian psychoanalysts and others who subscribe to the general outline as Benedek gives it. She herself indicates some of the points of divergence.

THE STAGES

The early developmental history of the child is described in terms of the dominance of certain sensitive, or "erotogenic," zones, such as the oral, anal, and genital regions. The infant's earliest libidinal pleasures are connected mainly with his mouth. He sucks at his mother's breast and his own fingers, and he also uses his mouth to explore and test the objects he encounters in the external world. The oral phase of development occupies approximately the first year. Abraham distinguishes two phases of this stage: the passive-receptive, in which the child merely has things done to him, and the active-incorporative, in which the child is able to reach actively for objects. During the oral period, if the infant's instinctual needs are not adequately met, insecurity, anxiety, and conflict develop. Throughout this period the child is "narcissistic," deriving most of his gratification from himself and his own body, with little reference to external objects. However, the child is learning what causes him pain and which of his actions bring disapproval and withdrawal of love. The differentiation of id and ego has begun as the child begins to establish relationships with his mother and with objects.

In the second phase the anus becomes the dominant erotogenic zone. "Its double function—retention and elimination—becomes the center of interest and the source of pleasure."[14] Toilet training then becomes critical. Parents, in a fashion that depends on their cultural and personal backgrounds, attempt to teach the child sphincter control. By this time the child understands adults well enough so that he can cooperate with or resist them, depending upon the kinds of relationships that have been established. "Toilet training," Benedek says, "is the ego's first conscious struggle for mastery over an id impulse."[15] The mother's approval is balanced against the instinctual pleasure of soiling. When the mastery of the impulse becomes a goal in itself, a new phase begins. The ego, even in the absence of the mother, resists the id impulse. This represents a big forward step in building personality structure. One of its immediate results is that the child is now vulnerable to threats from id impulses which may break through against the controlling ego. This conflict also represents a clash between the pleasure principle and the reality principle. The former, in the service of the id, strives for immediate gratification; the latter postpones immediate gratification for later ones through a mastery of the reality situation.

The particular method of toilet training employed is important, since it causes the child to react in certain ways. Thus, oversevere training seems punitive to the child and may lead him to rebel and become hostile toward the mother. This creates a vicious circle as the mother reacts to his rebellion. When sphincter control is secure, the conflict situation diminishes and the child is ready for the next step. During the anal period differences in learning between the sexes begin to appear. Benedek remarks that mothers generally recognize that girls are more easily trained than boys. This is because the girl identifies with the mother more readily, whereas in boys a good relationship with the mother is merely preliminary to self-assertion and eventual identification with the father. The roots of competitive behavior are said to lie in the achievement of sphincter control. A British analyst, Jones, even stated that the model for competitive behavior among men derived from boyish competition in urinating.

The third general stage is called oedipal or phallic, because the child's sexual urges, originally directed toward his own body, now become intensified and directed toward the parent of the opposite sex. For obvious reasons, boys become aware of genital gratifications earlier than girls. The mother is the object of the boy's first heterosexual interest. The girl's development is slower and more complex. Her sexuality remains more diffusely located in sensations of the skin and in motor coordination rather than focusing on the genitals. As we have noted in a preceding chapter, Freud postulated that the sight of the male genitals arouses "penis envy" in the girl, and that this is instrumental in breaking the girl's attachment to her mother and directing her erotic impulses toward the father and eventually to other males. Freud believed penis envy to be the key to feminine psychology. (This is one of the points at which some analysts disagreed with Freud.) In any case, the girl is said to turn toward the father, thus arousing an instinctual conflict between attraction to the father and the potential loss of gratification of needs by the mother. However, sometimes after lengthy conflict and vacillation, the girl develops her own kind of oedipus complex—the electra complex. The boy's oedipal development is more direct, yet there is a crucial conflict associated with it. The boy is in competition with his father for the mother, but cannot win. Although he cannot actually consummate his urges, he feels guilty and "expects retaliation to be directed toward the organ from which he receives pleasure. The fear of castration—mutilation—develops, in varying intensity, even if a threat of physical punishment was never uttered."[16] Fear of castration brings about ambivalence toward the father. The boy tries to please him by identification with him in nonsexual areas of behavior and tends also to idealize him. Identification with the father leads to internalization of the father's moral code, although the working out of the oedipus complex, and the associated development of a mature superego, takes many years. In the meantime, genital urges may find expression in masturbation or other substitute activities and attachments. Benedek also lists various ego defenses against sexual tendencies which help to repress and resolve the oedipus complex. These include the intellectualizing of curiosity about sex, development of infantile sexual theories, denial of sexuality in the parents, and identification with the opposite sex. The latter is a defense against the dangerous heterosexual urge. This is known as a "negative oedipus complex" and is usually temporary, since it is not a feasible solution of the sexual problem. The various phases of the resolution of the oedipus complex do not occur in a fixed time sequence but may occur more or less simultaneously.

During the oedipal period, the structure of the personality becomes much more complex and differentiated. The superego is developing and is in conflict with the id. The ego is now undertaking the function of mediating between (1) the id and the superego, and (2) the id and reality. At this stage, the ego represses the sexual tendencies, thus initiating the latency period.

The beginning of the latency period coincides in our society more or less with the beginning of school. "The desexualization of the child's interest enables him to comply with environmental requirements and thus to expand in mental and social growth."[17] The basic biological tendencies of giving and taking, retaining and eliminating, and other tendencies from the anal and oral stages continue to develop into more complex forms. Oral receptive pleasure continues in the form of pleasure in the reception of material and spiritual gifts. During latency, children learn how to share. Aggressive incorporation appears in the form of envy, jealousy, and maliciousness. Passion for collecting betrays the retentive tendency. Boys characteristically collect masculine objects (*e.g.*, stones, strings, keys) and girls accumulate feminine objects (*e.g.*, beads and dolls). If either sex evinces much interest in the wrong kind of objects, this is an index of bisexuality. The existence of the latency period as a biologically determined stage is another point upon which all Freudians do not agree.

The next phase is brought about by the onset of puberty and is coterminus with adolescence. The physical maturation which occurs in this period reawakens latent conflicts and the ego must again master them. Girls, for example, become sensitive to the changes in their bodies and may become ashamed or shy. In both sexes, attempts are made to master sexuality through repression, a technique which was successful in the earlier oedipal stage. As the sexual drive becomes more urgent, "all the available resources of sublimation are mobilized, and expansion of interests and achievements is generated."[18] Safe ego gratification is afforded by these interests. Yet "the ego . . . cannot withstand for long the pressure of the instinctual impulses; the defenses yield and the instinctual tension is released."[19] During adolescence, also, the child discovers new values and ideals and appraises those of his parents, thus reactivating his old conflict with them: the boy quarrels more with his father, the girl with her mother. As the child becomes more independent of the parents, the superego becomes less rigid and a new and more complex level of personality integration is reached. Sexual maturity requires a personality which accepts both the sexual drives and the social regulation of them.

The systematic account of development offered by Freudians ends at about this point. Later events tend to be interpreted as a working out, in relation to an adult environment and advancing age, of earlier genetic occurrences. This account of development must be viewed as an ideal, or average normal, picture. Children, it is said, vary in the rates at which they pass through some or all of the phases; some experience one or more phases only in dreams or fantasies. Sometimes part of a phase may be repeated as a consequence of regression, which is in turn a consequence of disappointments. Adolescence is such an especially tortuous process that some analysts refer to the "normal psychopathology" of the period. It is also noted that some individuals do not go through adolescence to the final stage but remain fixated at earlier points, and that if the process goes awry libidinal urges may find expression in a wide variety of curious or abnormal ways.

CRITICISM AND APPRECIATION

By way of criticism of this account, we can do no better than to quote Benedek herself to show what is left out of it. In discussing the anal stage, she comments briefly on the development of speech during the second and third years:

> It is in another area of maturation that the child learns to speak. . . . This complex process is considered to be the result of the progressing maturation of the speech apparatus and of intellectual accomplishments and is, therefore, not usually discussed in connection with the psychodynamic aspects of personality development.[20]

She touches briefly upon initial learning of words and sentences and notes how the child "has stored in his mind symbols related to . . . experiences" that occur before the development of language and that these experiences and symbols may never reach the level of verbalization, but may form the content of the unconscious.[21] This is virtually all that is said of language behavior. The separation of "emotional experience" from cognition which is implied in the above quotation from Benedek is characteristic of psychoanalytic thinking. It stems from the classical tripartite distinction between cognition, conation, and affect (intelligence, will, and emotion). Those who make this distinction neglect the fact that emotional experiences do not exist as pure states but are shot through with cognitive elements. The fiction of the separation of intellectual development and personality development can be maintained only if one disregards or vastly underrates the role of language in the organization of behavior, including emotional behavior.

A second major criticism is that a "genetic fallacy" is persistently maintained when the last event in a chronological series is identified with the first. Benedek's frequent use of the term "model" (as in the suggestion that urinary competition provides the model for all later male competition) is an illustration. The attribution of sexuality to both newborn infants and adults is another. Some analysts have themselves made note of the resulting confusion, and have differed with Freud on this point. The same type of fallacious genetic reasoning is evident in the conception of the biologically rooted drive as the theme which unites all processes throughout the developmental sequence. Although learning is given an important place, its primary function is seen as the harnessing of the id drives in socially acceptable ways. The genetic approach of the Freudian analyst gives his explanations a narrative character. If it is asked why two persons whose childhood experiences appear to be substantially the same turn out very differently as adults, the analyst's answer will frequently consist of two biographical narratives.

A third difficulty arises from the general character of analytic theory itself which makes it difficult or impossible to subject it to empirical tests at crucial points. In a recent review of psychological studies of children, Koch has pointed out that there is virtually no evidence of a nonclinical sort on which to base an evaluation of psychosexual stages.[22] With respect to some minor points, it has been possible to check the implications of the analytic account. Through checking, for example, the existence of the latency period, the validity of the concepts of sublimation and repression, and the oedipus complex itself, as described by Freud, have been made questionable. Anthropologists, through the use of comparative data, have raised serious doubts of the alleged universality of some of the central factors in the developmental process, such as Freud's concepts of the superego and oedipal attachments. The assumption that development is virtually over, except for minor variations, when adulthood is reached, appears questionable to sociologists.

On the other hand, despite the many objections that have been raised concerning it, Freudian developmental theory has some clear-cut virtues. The very fact that it is a general theory concerning areas of human behavior which are vital to self-esteem makes it significant and challenging. It at least proposes explanations for many forms of behavior which are ordinarily passed over in silence by other psychological systems. Analytic theory has also performed the function of calling attention to the subtlety of human inter-action and to the existence of concealed factors which the subject himself is unable to report. It has sought to isolate and analyze critical experiences in the life of the child and has described, with much clinical detail, various significant processes, such as identifi-cation with parents, and other mechanisms of interaction and ego defense. Close contact with patients provides the analyst with a continuous flow of clinical data which is of great value to anyone interested in childhood development, regardless of how it may be interpreted.

The Developmental Theories of Sullivan

Theorists who do not subscribe to the central tenets of the Freud-ian position are disposed to locate the critical junctures in de-velopment at other points and to ascribe somewhat different significances to them. This is true even of formulations that focus exclusively on children. One of the most systematic and thoughtful accounts of personality development, and one which differs in im-portant ways from the Freudian position, is that of H. S. Sullivan. Like Freud, Sullivan developed his position mainly out of his experience with psychiatric patients. Through his close association with anthropologists and other social scientists, he came to place more emphasis on the social environment than Freud had. He re-pudiated much of the Freudian vocabulary and developed one of his own. The "interpersonal theory" of psychiatry which he formu-lated has found expression in an influential journal and has also been disseminated through the work of his students. Perhaps be-cause of the great difficulty of communicating with schizophrenes, he early became concerned with the nature of communication. Sapir, who markedly influenced his thinking on communication, was a pioneer anthropological linguist. The roles in development which Sullivan ascribes to communicative processes and the cultural milieu gives his work special significance for the social scientist. Our discussion of his position will be based primarily on Sullivan's posthumously published lectures.[23]

SOME CENTRAL CONCEPTS

Several of Sullivan's basic ideas were sketched previously in our chapter on the self (pp. 431-432). It will be recalled that for Sullivan the avoidance of severe anxiety is central to human behavior, and that a "self-system" starts to develop in infancy as a protection against overmuch anxiety. The process of selective inattention was mentioned in this connection. Sullivan formulated several other concepts that require elaboration before an account of his developmental stages will make much sense to the reader.

From the first moments of life, the infant is in interaction with adults, mainly of course with his mother, who is concerned particularly with satisfying his initial bodily needs. The mother, too, has needs, which in turn are met by her general activity in caring for the child. Sullivan thus says that the situation is "integrated" insofar as it is meaningful for both organisms. In adults, a mutually satisfying friendly conversation would be an illustration of an integrated situation. Situations may be "resolved" when the needs are met. There is then no longer any reason for continuing the immediate interaction unless new bases immediately arise. Situations "disintegrate" when they are terminated before they are resolved. Anxiety may play a large role here: it arises, for example, when one makes friendly overtures to a desirable person and is rebuffed.

There are, according to Sullivan, three modes or types of experience: the prototaxic, parataxic, and syntaxic. These terms refer to the manner in which experience is registered and to the nature and degree of inner elaboration which it is accorded. In the prototaxic mode there is an absolute minimum of inner elaboration, and experience consists mainly of discrete series of momentary states which can neither be recalled nor discussed. The syntaxic mode, in contrast, involves a maximum of inner organization and elaboration, and because it is fully encompassed by symbolic formulation and is logically ordered it can be discussed and completely communicated to others. The parataxic mode of experience lies between the other two. In it, experience is partially organized or organized in a quasi-logical manner, but there are also elements of which the individual is unaware. Parataxic experience can be discussed by the adult human subject, but Sullivan states:

> The mode which is easiest to discuss is relatively uncommon . . . experience in the syntaxic mode; the one about which something can be known, but which is somewhat harder to discuss, is experience in the parataxic mode; and the one which is ordinarily incapable of any discussion is experience in the prototaxic or primitive mode.[24]

The child's earliest experiences are in the prototaxic mode, but he quickly progresses to the parataxic as soon as he begins to make sense out of his environment and notes certain interconnections and simple sequences. Lower animals also are capable of reaching the parataxic level, according to Sullivan. The syntaxic mode begins to appear with the learning of language and is hence confined to human beings, although Sullivan takes pains to emphasize that it is rarely possible for us to express all aspects of an experience in words. Roughly, one may say that the three modes represent the incommunicable or ineffable (prototaxic), the partially communicable (parataxic), and the wholly communicable (syntaxic). This scheme allows a considerable place for unconscious behavior without positing an "unconscious mind" or instinctual urges as the mainsprings of behavior.

Sullivan's treatment of needs, as we shall see, is a fluid one. The infant quickly develops new needs in addition to the initial bodily ones, both through experience and maturation. Needs appear chronologically, some not until several years have passed. Thus the sexual drive, or, as he terms it, the "lust dynamism," does not arise until puberty. (Here Sullivan explicitly departs from Freud, who views the sexual drives as present from birth.) The various needs are given sophisticated treatment and are not regarded as inner forces. Apart from elementary biological needs of the infant, most of the needs with which Sullivan is concerned arise in interpersonal interaction and do not have to do with biological matters. Needs come to be satisfied in highly complex ways through interaction. Much satisfaction, Sullivan holds, must take place through sublimation—that is, by indirect means. This is because the initial means adopted are met with reactions by significant others which arouse anxiety in the person.

STAGES

Sullivan's designation of stages is itself a clue to important differences between his position and that of orthodox Freudian psychoanalysts. His own brief summary of these stages brings out these differences and focuses attention immediately on the communicative process.

> *Infancy* extends from a few minutes after birth to the appearance of articulate speech, however uncommunicative or meaningless. *Childhood* extends from the appearance of the ability to utter articulate sounds of or pertaining to speech, to the appearance of the need for playmates—that is, companions, co-operative beings of approximately one's own status in all sorts of respects. This ushers in the *juvenile era,* which extends through most of the grammar-school years to the eruption, due to maturation, of a need for an intimate relation with another person of comparable status. This, in turn, ushers in the era that we call *preadolescence,* an exceedingly important but chronologically rather brief period that ordinarily ends with the eruption of genital sexuality and puberty, but psychologically or psychiatrically ends with the movement of strong interest from a person of one's own sex to a person of the other sex. These phenomena mark the beginning of *adolescence,* which in this culture (it varies, however, from culture to culture) continues until one has patterned some type of performance which satisfies one's lust, one's genital drives. Such patterning ushers in *late adolescence,* which in turn continues as an era of personality until any partially developed aspects of personality fall into their proper relationship to their time partition; and one is able, at *adulthood,* to establish relationships of love for some other person, in which relationship the other person is as significant, or nearly as significant, as one's self.[25]

Sullivan's account of infancy and childhood covers much of the same ground that has been covered in those chapters of this text that deal with the development of language, thought, and self. He emphasizes the role of anxiety in the origin of the self-system. The Freudian concepts of the ego, id, and superego are not included, and there is no discussion of instinctual drives or of the oedipus complex. In childhood, along with the gradual learning of the syntaxic use of language, the child may also use language as an anxiety-reducing instrument, as when he verbally disowns certain of his actions—"I didn't do that, it was my hand," or "I did it. I am sorry." Parents' demands for apologies and explanations further this use. During childhood the need for tenderness, which appeared during infancy, is manifested and elaborated in the desire for play and physical contact with others, particularly the mother. If the mother is consistently unable to respond with tenderness, a child may be compelled to sublimate the need or he may give it up. Like other observers, Sullivan remarks upon the fact that children learn to deceive adults and so escape rebuff and anxiety. Sullivan is constantly concerned with inadequate means of handling issues that may be taken by the child, and at this point notes a number of inappropriate modes of concealment which may lead to trouble later. One of them is the use of verbalisms or rationalizations to ward off punishment.

Vicious cycles of malevolent development may start through interaction of the sort that occurs when the mother continually disparages the father and explains the child's misbehavior by saying he is like his father. This may establish the conviction in the child that he is detestable and unworthy and must expect always to be treated badly. Such an unfortunate turn of events may "very easily prevent a great deal of profit from subsequent developmental experiences. . . . There is literally a slowing down of healthy socialization."[26] Important in Sullivan's thought is the idea that any developmental mishap may prevent and slow up the learning process. The arrest of development is not a static thing, for the person continues to change and develop; however, "the freedom and velocity of the constructive change are very markedly reduced."[27]

In late childhood the child becomes more aware of his identity as a male or female and begins to adopt appropriate behavior. His knowledge of other cultural perspectives also broadens. Like Piaget, Sullivan emphasizes the necessity, imposed by the requirements of others, for the child to begin to distinguish between reality and fantasy (autism, or autistic thought). Toward the end of this period, the child has learned to sort out that which he must conceal from that which he can talk about because it will make sense to adults.

Even when malevolent or other inappropriate personality organization has developed, the transition to the next stage introduces a real possibility for correction. Sullivan is impressed by the amount of change that can occur "as one passes over one of these more-or-less determinable thresholds of a developmental era."[28] This means that the child is, to some extent, given the choice of a fresh start, although the older he grows the more he becomes the heir of his own past.

The juvenile era begins at about the time the child starts to school. School plays a key role in various ways. Many more "authority figures" appear on the child's horizon—teachers, playground bullies, traffic policemen, and other parents—and he has to learn to live with all of them. By the end of this era, authority figures, including the parents, are being compared with one another as persons. The parents are no longer regarded as the most perfect people on earth, nor are they any longer endowed with omniscience. At the beginning of the era, children typically begin to desire contact and play with other children; this sociability is in contrast to the greater egocentricity of younger children. Hence, the school child is open to tremendous influence from his peers. He learns that they have points of view and discovers how many perspectives there are. Through his interaction with them, some of it brutal and antagonistic, he learns a great deal about how to handle himself without suffering unduly from anxiety. He must face the possibility of ostracism. Toward the end of the period, especially, he begins to be sensitive to his reputation, i.e., his general self-conception deriving from juvenile groups. Sullivan notes that mobility of the parents may be disastrous by causing the child to continue to be a stranger as he goes from one school to another.

The juvenile era is given tremendous weight by Sullivan as a determinant of future development. It is "the time when the world begins to be really complicated by the presence of other people."[29] Through rough-and-ready interaction with all these new people, the child's misconceptions of self are corrected and he acquires a wider grasp of selfhood and his place in the community. If he is fortunate in his development he emerges with an "orientation in living," that is, an idea of how to satisfy his needs without arousing too much anxiety.

> To the extent that the juvenile knows . . . what needs motivate his relations with others, and under what circumstances these needs . . . are appropriate and relatively apt to get by without damage to self-respect, to this extent the person has gotten a great deal out of his first big plunge into socialization.[30]

If he has not learned this, he is in for trouble. He may, for example, use the technique of disparaging others as a protective device: this is equivalent to saying "I am not as bad as the other swine." This does not give a secure base to a sense of personal worth.

Preadolescence is ushered in by an interest in a new type of personal relationship: friendship with a person of the same sex. This is quite different from previous relationships, for it turns upon intimacy and collaboration in satisfying each other's expressed needs.

> Because one draws so close to another, because one is newly capable of seeing oneself through the other's eyes, the preadolescent phase . . . is especially significant in correcting autistic, fantastic ideas about oneself or others.[31]

Participation in preadolescent gangs has a similar desirable effect. The need for chums arises both as a result of interpersonal development and of maturation. Sullivan emphasizes the great therapeutic effects of these preadolescent intimacies in saving persons from previous unfortunate courses.

However, the preadolescent period is also an era of danger because of differences in rates of development among friends. Children reach puberty at different ages: the variation within the same sex may be as much as three or four years. Hence, some preadolescents lag behind the others. Some still require intimate chumship when the others no longer do, or one child may not yet need these intimate relationships when most of his peers do and so later may have to establish such relations with a much younger or much older person.

The early stage of adolescence is defined "as extending from the eruption of true genital interest, felt as lust, to the patterning of sexual behavior which is the beginning of the last phase of adolescence."[32] Sullivan thinks of lust as the last of the masturation needs and draws a sharp line between it and the need for intimacy. The need for intimacy starts much earlier and has an independent development. At the onset of adolescence there is a significant change in the object of intimacy. If there has been no very serious warp in development, the child begins to seek increasing intimacy with a member of the other sex, the pattern of intimacy being much like that of preadolescence. In America the fulfillment of this need faces serious obstacles, since it runs into the sex taboos. The obstacle which prevents access to intimacy leads to reverie and fantasy, and in the gang children may engage in discussion pertaining to it. The discussion of "who's who and what's what" in the heterosexual world is of great profit for those of the gang who are already in the adolescent stage.

In adolescence, life becomes tremendously complicated by the elaboration of potentially conflicting needs. The appearance of lust, a very powerful need, adds greatly to the problems of the era. There may be collision between the requirements of lust and the maintenance of self-esteem. Genital urges may create acute self-doubts, puzzlement, embarrassment, and other unpleasant reactions. Because of the way sex is viewed in Western society, the desire for sexual activity often clashes with a sense of security in interpersonal relations. This is true in adolescence and in later life as well. Intimacy and lust requirements may also conflict with each other. A common manifestation of this conflict is the separation of persons into two mutually exclusive classes: those who can only satisfy one's lust, and those who can only satisfy the need for intimacy and friendship. The distinction between "good women" and "bad women," "sexy" girls and "good girls," conveys this idea.

Thus satisfying one's lust must be at considerable expense to one's self-esteem, since the bad girls are unworthy and not really people in the sense that good girls are. . . . The trouble . . . is that lust is a part of personality, and no one can get very far at completing his personality development in this way.[33]

The shift in the sex of the desired object of intimacy may also clash with security needs. For instance, the parents may disparage and ridicule the adolescent's interest in the opposite sex. The parents may be jealous, may not wish the child to grow up too fast, or may fear sexual accidents. The various collisions of needs may lead in this stage to homosexual play, but more usually produce autosexual behavior, i.e., masturbation.

Sullivan points out that the "number of wretched experiences connected with adolescents' first heterosexual attempts is legion, and the experiences are sometimes very expensive to further maturation of personality."[34] They may be destructive to self-esteem and may erect permanent barriers to satisfactory heterosexual consummations.

Several unhappy long-term outcomes include the following: there are people who feel pursued by the opposite sex and expend a great deal of energy trying to avoid them. Lust may be disassociated from consciousness and may be expressed only in fantasies. Lack of potency may be connected with failure to resolve the lust-intimacy problem. In some persons, the appearance of lust may be accompanied by the continuation of intimacy needs on the preadolescent level, leading to transient or persisting homosexual tendencies, with the genital drive handled in a variety of ways—homosexual reverie, homosexual relations, autoeroticism. In some persons, lust may mature, although they remain chronically juvenile. The Don Juan type or lady's man, and on the feminine side the persistent "tease," are often chronic juveniles, according to Sullivan. These people have a need to be envied by others of their sex, and hence often boast of their conquests.

Sullivan indicates the extreme diversity of alternatives which face the adolescent. He has to discover "what he likes in the way of genital behavior and how to fit it into the rest of life. That is an achievement of no mean magnitude."[35] The range of alternatives is demonstrated by showing that there are about forty-five patterns of behavior that are "reasonably probable." Sullivan reaches this figure by setting up classifications of intimacy, kinds of objects of lust, and types of sexual activity.

Late adolescence is for Sullivan the period when the mode of sexual activity is decided upon. In addition he lays stress upon the great growth of experience in the syntaxic mode of communication. Through formal education and work experience, persons acquire greater insight into their own and others' behavior and may develop enormously in knowledge and maturity. Many adults, because of their developmental heritage, are greatly restricted in what they can learn from a potentially enlightening environment: "Large aspects of living are, as it were, taboo—one avoids them."[36] As to the truly mature person, Sullivan confesses that psychiatrists have very little to say, since they do not meet them in their offices as patients. With the progress of the patient toward maturity, the psychiatrist loses sight of him.

> But one can guess a few things. I would guess that each of the outstanding achievements of the developmental eras . . . will be outstandingly manifest in the mature personality. The last of these great developments is the appearance and growth of the need for intimacy—for collaboration with at least one other, preferably more others; and in this collaboration there is the very striking feature of a very lively sensitivity to the needs of the other and to the interpersonal security or absence of anxiety in the other. Thus we can certainly extrapolate from what we know that the mature, insofar as nothing of great importance collides, will be quite sympathetically understanding of the limitations, interests, possibilities, anxieties, and so on of those among whom they move or with whom they deal. Another thing which can quite certainly be extrapolated is that, whether it be by externally widening interests or by deepening interests or both, the life of the mature—far from becoming monotonous and a bore—is always increasing in, shall I say, importance.[37]

EVALUATION

Sullivan's view has much in common with the Freudian conception. In both there is considerable attention given to unconscious features of behavior, and both focus attention on the dynamic interplay of personal relations. Both have a place for bodily maturation and posit a close relationship between this maturation and the development of personality. They are also alike in that they are mainly derived from clinical experience with adults rather than first-hand, intensive study of children. One further point of similarity is that both more or less terminate their systematic accounts of development at the threshold of adult life. The differences between the two conceptions will become apparent as we review some of the main general features of Sullivan's scheme.

Sullivan's account provides an important place for needs which arise sequentially. Sex appears late, rather than early, as in Freud's account, and is not given supreme priority. Many of the important needs arise from interpersonal relations rather than biological bases.

Those needs that are of biological origin, such as the infant's need for "tenderness," quickly become transformed as they are felt and interpreted and as they enter into progressively more complex interpersonal patterns. Even what Sullivan calls "lust," with its obvious biological concomitants, is of this nature. The needs which arise in interpersonal relations, although associated with biological maturation, are essentially consequences of the developing complexity of the communicative processes and the self-system. Instinct is not inevitably in conflict with society—indeed, Sullivan explicitly rejects the instinct theory and the id concept which makes man an essentially evil being held in check by social proscriptions. The "unconscious mind" in which Freud located the instinctual impulses does not appear as such in Sullivan's theory, although he makes ample provision for the unwitting aspects of behavior.

The crucial experiences of each era are specified pretty clearly by Sullivan and in such a form that empirical testing of his views is possible. He presented his position as a tentative one, recognizing the need for empirical validation. He acknowledged that a great many of these critical experiences, and even the stages themselves, might vary from culture to culture. The role of various adults as representatives of culture, rather than as unique personalities, is always recognized and often specified. Like other writers, Sullivan has emphasized the important fact that the differential rates of biological and experiential development of children may crucially affect personality development. His treatment of some of these consequences, as in his discussion of the transition to adolescence, shows great insight. Following a line of thought which has generally taken hold in recent years, he also emphasizes the uselessness and possible danger in training the child before he can assimilate the training experience.

The scheme is genuinely developmental in the sense that no genetic fallacy is introduced. No stage is in any way a repetition of a preceding one, and in each stage genuinely new behavior emerges. A tremendous possibility of change is acknowledged by Sullivan, particularly during transitions into new stages. Concerning preadolescence, he says, somewhat satirically:

> It is self-evident, I suppose, that I am conspicuously taking exception to the all-too-prevalent idea that things are pretty well fixed in the Jesuitical first seven years. This idea has constituted one of the greatest problems for some anthropologists who have tried to translate psychiatric thought into anthropologically useful ideas. The anthropologists have noised at them from all sides the enormous importance of infantile experience—meaning experience certainly under the age of eight. Yet one of the most conspicuous observations of an anthropologist working anywhere is that children of the privileged, who are raised by servants, do not grow up to be like the servants. This is a little bit difficult for an anthropologist to reconcile with the tremendous emphasis on very early experience. My work has shown me very clearly that, while early experience does a great many things . . . the development of capacity for interpersonal relations is by no means a matter which is completed at some point, say, in the juvenile era. Very far from it. And even preadolescence, which is a very, very important phase of personality development, is not the last phase.[38]

So-called "arrests of development" are not viewed by Sullivan as "fixations" or "regressions." The capacity to learn from experience is greatly reduced by such arrests, but change and development go on. This change is not conceived of as merely a new form of an old personality organization, but as a genuine, if unfortunate, innovation.

A central concept in Sullivan's system is that of "consensual validation," by which he means the manner in which the meanings of symbols and the validity of ideas, including ideas of self, are confirmed in the process of communicating with others. (This is the same idea that has been discussed in numerous other places in this text.) Sullivan notes that symbols do not carry meaning but evoke it in user and listener, and that consensual validation makes symbols precise and powerful instruments in handling both people and ideas. Through his emphasis on the effects of the communication process upon the developing personality, Sullivan introduces a social dimension into the very center of individuality. This is in line with his explicitly stated idea that the scientific analysis of interpersonal relations requires a "field theory" rather than an elementaristic or atomistic approach. Sullivan's main contribution has not been in the analysis of what he called the syntaxic mode, or public communication, but in his more discriminating treatment of the "unconscious." He has reinterpreted the unconscious as a distortion of the communication process through such mechanisms as: (1) selective inattention, (2) dissociation, (3) misinterpretation, and (4) masking processes. Cottrell has said of Sullivan:

> Sullivan attempts to show the influences within a given culture which channellize awareness. . . . If we accept [G.] Mead's analysis of the way in which meaning emerges from an incorporated verbal structure of rights and duties, Sullivan's work suggests an important amendment. The meaning that is borne by verbal interchange in interpersonal relations can be completely distorted by the dissociated elements which are at work to set the tone and color of the situation.[39]

Our criticism of Sullivan's developmental scheme is based mainly on what it leaves out rather than what is included. The omissions can be attributed in part to Sullivan's explicit psychiatric interests and in part, possibly, to the scantiness of his actual writings. The gravest omission is the lack of consideration of personality change after the initiation of adulthood. By implication, the importance of such change is suggested, but it is not discussed. The consequence of this is that such influences as the following are left out: the influence of occupational status and other adult statuses, the shifting of age memberships, including the effect of children on parents; adaptations to the approach of death; the handling of slow or abrupt changes of statuses of many kinds. The sociologists Cottrell and Foote, who are admirers of Sullivan, have also commented upon Sullivan's tendency to emphasize early patterns to the exclusion of later experiences. They remark that, according to the logic of his own position, this should not be done.

> If the maintenance of certain characteristic patterns of inter-personal behavior depend for their support on significant others, then to alter the composition of any person's community of significant others is the most direct and drastic way of altering his "personality."[40]

The developmental account itself, insofar as it deals with children, must be amplified, as Sullivan himself recognized. It can be extended, of course, by actual investigation of children. Cultural variation as well as variation by sex, and the general influence of social structures, must be more extensively taken into account. A wider range of psychological processes also needs to be included.

One major reservation about the account itself is justified. Sullivan makes anxiety virtually central to—actually the basic motive of—human behavior. No one should, of course, deny its great importance. Despite his great sophistication about the ramifications of anxiety and the associated needs for security and intimacy, Sullivan's treatment of this central concept is very like that of the older motivational theories. In his defense it should be said that he was very tentative about the centrality of anxiety:

> In discussing the concept of anxiety, I am not attempting to give you the last word; it may, within ten years, be demonstrated that this concept is quite inadequate, and a better one will take its place.[41]

The research on children that has been done in the last two decades by anthropologists and sociologists considerably amplifies our knowledge of cultural variations in child rearing and child development. However, this research does not—except as it accepts and details the psychoanalytic developmental account—provide an over-all systematic developmental theory. Sullivan does.

Summary

Experiences of childhood and youth are interpreted differently by two important theories. Freudian theory emphasizes events in the first months and years, such as the birth process and the disciplines imposed upon the infant. Freud's theory has the advantage of covering much ground and providing an inclusive general theory, but it is open to serious criticism. Sullivan's account, although derived from an originally Freudian outlook, places a very different interpretation upon early personality development, and one which avoids most of the weaknesses of the Freudian view. Both theories, however, carry the individual only to the threshold of adulthood. Our next chapters will deal with adult personality, personality change, and disorganization.

SUGGESTIONS FOR DISCUSSION AND SPECIAL REPORTS

1. Suggest some amendments that need to be made to Sullivan's account of development.

2. Compare the developmental sequence for children in two or three primitive societies, paying attention also to sex differences.

3. Interview a number of mothers to see if, and how, they utilize books and magazines and other products of the mass media for ideas on child rearing.

4. Analyze the kinds of information and advice about child-parent relations that newspaper columnists give their readers.

5. Contrast methods of child rearing and training in contem-

porary and colonial America. Or, for some decade of our history, do this for farm and city.

6. Compare the treatment of symbols by Freud and Sullivan.

NOTES

[1] C. B. Stendler, "Sixty Years of Child Training Practices," *Pediatrics*, 36(1950): 122-134.

[2] O. Rank, *The Birth Trauma*, London: Kegan Paul, Trench, Trubner and Co., 1929.

[3] I. Wile and R. Davis, "The Relation of Birth to Behavior," in C. Kluckhohn and H. Murray, *Personality in Nature, Society and Culture*, Knopf, 1948, pp. 297-314.

[4] F. Greenacre, "The Biologic Economy of Birth," in *The Psychoanalytic Study of the Child*, Vol. I, International Universities Press, 1945, pp. 31-51.

[5] S. Bernfeld, *The Psychology of the Infant*, Brentano's, 1929.

[6] T. Benedek, "Adaptation to Reality in Early Infancy," *Psychoanalytic Quarterly*, 7(1938): 200-215.

[7] M. Ribble, "Infantile Experience in Relation to Personality Development," in J. McV. Hunt (ed.), *Personality and the Behavior Disorders*, Vol. II, Ronald, 1944, p. 261.

[8] R. A. Spitz, "An Inquiry into the Genesis of Psychiatric Conditions in Early Childhood," *The Psychoanalytic Study of the Child*, Vol. I, International Universities Press, 1945, pp. 53-74; also, "Hospitalism: a Follow-up Report," *Ibid.*, Vol. II, 1946, pp. 113-117.

[9] J. Bowlby, *Maternal Care and Mental Health*, Geneva: World Health Organization, 1951.

[10] M. Hutt and D. R. Miller, "Value Interiorization and Personality Development," *J. of Social Issues*, 5(1949): 9.

[11] *Ibid.*, p. 13.

[12] H. Orlansky, "Infant Care and Personality," *Psychol. Bull.*, 46 (1949): 1-48. See also A. R. Lindesmith and A. L. Strauss, "A Critique of Culture-Personality Writings," *Am. Soc. Rev.*, 15 (1950): 596-597.

[13] T. Benedek, "Personality Development," in F. Alexander and H. Ross (eds.), *Dynamic Psychiatry*, University of Chicago Press, 1952, p. 100.

[14] *Ibid.*, p. 71.

[15] *Ibid.*, p. 72.

[16] *Ibid.*, p. 82.

[17] *Ibid.*, p. 88.

[18] *Ibid.*, p. 97.

[19] *Ibid.*, p. 97.

[20] *Ibid.*, p. 74.

[21] *Ibid.*, p. 76.

[22] H. L. Koch, "Child Psychology," *Ann. Rev. of Psych.*, 5(1954): 1-26.

[23] H. S. Sullivan, *The Interpersonal Theory of Psychiatry*, ed. H. Perry and M. Gamal, Norton, 1953.

[24] *Ibid.*, p. 29.

[25] *Ibid.*, pp. 33-34.

[26] *Ibid.*, p. 217.

[27] *Ibid.*, p. 218.
[28] *Ibid.*, p. 227.
[29] *Ibid.*, p. 232.
[30] *Ibid.*, p. 244.
[31] *Ibid.*, p. 248.
[32] *Ibid.*, p. 263.
[33] *Ibid.*, pp. 269-270.
[34] *Ibid.*, pp. 271-272.
[35] *Ibid.*, p. 297.
[36] *Ibid.*, p. 306.
[37] *Ibid.*, p. 310.

[38] *Ibid.*, pp. 248-249.
[39] L. Cottrell and R. Gallagher, "Developments in Social Psychology, 1930-1940," *Sociometry Monogr.*, No. 1, New York: Beacon House, 1941, pp. 23-24.
[40] P. Mullahy (ed.), *The Contributions of H. S. Sullivan: A Symposium,* Hermitage House, 1952, p. 193.
[41] Sullivan, *op. cit.*, p. 8.

SELECTED BIBLIOGRAPHY

Benedek, T., in F. Alexander and H. Ross (eds.), *Dynamic Psychiatry,* University of Chicago Press, 1952, "Personality Development," pp. 63-113. A useful summary of the psychoanalytic account of psychosexual development.

Blum, G. S., and D. R. Miller, "Exploring the Psychoanalytic Theory of the 'Oral Character,' " *J. Personality,* 3(1952): 287-304. An attempt by two psychologists to check, by means of experiments, one aspect of psychosexual development theory.

Erikson, E., *Childhood and Society,* Norton, 1950. Contains a treatment of the author's well-known developmental stages. His position is a modified Freudian one.

Hilgard, E. R., in E. Pompian-Mindlin (ed.), *Psychoanalysis as Science,* Stanford University Press, 1952, "Experimental Approaches to Psychoanalysis." A review of some of the experimental checking-up on psychoanalytic theory, including some studies on psychosexual development.

Miller, D. R., and M. L. Hutt, "Value Interiorization and Personality Development," *J. Soc. Issues,* 5(1949): 2-30. A useful survey of literature down to the year of publication. Covers comparative materials by anthropologists also.

Mullahy, P. (ed.), *The Contributions of H. S. Sullivan: A Symposium on Interpersonal Theory in Psychiatry and Social Science,* New York: Hermitage House, 1952. Evaluations of Sullivan's work. See especially the interesting paper on Sullivan's methods of interviewing and a judgment of his contribution to social psychology by two sociologists, L. S. Cottrell and N. N. Foote.

Orlansky, H., "Infant Care and Personality," *Psychological Bulletin,* 46 (1949): 1-48. Reviews the literature and passes severe judgment on the infant-discipline school.

Sewell, W. H., "Infant Training and the Personality of the Child," *Am. J. Soc.*, 58(1952): 150-159. An attempt to check some Freudian hypotheses. Findings are negative.

Spitz, R. A., "Hospitalism: An Inquiry into the Genesis of Psychiatric Conditions in Early Childhood," *Psychoanalytic Study of the Child*, 1(1945): 53-74; also "Hospitalism: A Follow-up Report," same journal, 2(1946): 113-117. Studies of deprivation in infants.

Sullivan, H. S., *The Interpersonal Theory of Psychiatry*, Norton, 1953. Contains the fullest account of Sullivan's theory of development.

CHAPTER 18 · · ·

Personality

Change

WE HAVE POINTED OUT in the preceding chapter that theories of personality development usually deal with the effects of experience on the person before he reaches maturity or adulthood. Although the assumption implicit in this approach—that these early experiences are of an especially critical nature—is undoubtedly sound, it is far from correct to assume that important personality changes do not occur in adults or that they occur in some adults but not in most. We shall now concern ourselves with some of the major types of personality change in adults and the social influences that bring them about.

The Inevitability of Change

The real problem concerning personality change is not so much that of accounting for the fact that change occurs as of explaining why it is sometimes so slight. Experience is cumulative and non-repetitive. As a person matures and advances in years he constantly faces new problems and new situations. In childhood and youth, the demands of socialization and the rapid maturation of the body require a long and often arduous process of adaptation. In later years, bodily changes of another sort intrude themselves with advancing age. Marriage, rearing children, and pursuing an occupation are not simply events in a person's life; rather, they are processes requiring continuous learning and constant change over long periods of years. It is characteristic of personal relations that they do not remain fixed but are always evolving and becoming different.

Allowance must also be made for the unforeseen, unscheduled events which sometimes jolt people out of their accustomed ways or project them into new and unfamiliar roles. Wars and invasions, divorce, economic depressions, disease or sudden disaster, the acquisition or the loss of wealth, change of occupation, growing or sudden fame are events of this unscheduled type which may lead to profound changes in personal outlook and organization.

The dynamic character of human relationships carries with it both threat and opportunity. New situations, new problems, and unforeseen events keep the way open for the acquisition of new knowledge and broader appreciations. As Sullivan has indicated, a characteristic feature of true maturity is that one continues to learn from new experience, from failure as well as from success. It is when people fail to sense the potentials in themselves and in situations and are blind to the excitement of events that they become problems to themselves.

In this chapter, we shall seek to supplement the account of the developmental stages discussed in the preceding chapter, noting other sources of personality change and considering aspects of social life and social organization which come especially into the purview of the sociologist.

The Life Cycle

The developmental theories that we have discussed break off more or less at the entrance into adulthood. Any full account of personality development and change must take into account the complete life cycle. The conceptualizations of the stages of life— what they are, when they begin and end, which behaviors are appropriate at each stage—are, of course, linked closely with social structure. There is no universal series of developmental stages, although there are certain life problems which recur in virtually all societies in about the same sequence. R. Havighurst[1] has referred to the "developmental tasks" that have to be handled at different ages in childhood. The same notion holds, in a general way, for the entire personal career.

CAREER SCHEDULES: OCCUPATION AND MARRIAGE

Among these tasks for the young adult is the undertaking of adult work, or acquiring an occupation. This point may or may not coincide with the stabilization of sexual relations in the marital union. There is great variation from culture to culture in the spacing of these two events. In the old caste system in India, occupation was determined at birth, and the future marriage and sexual partner was often selected by the parents, with appropriate ceremony, before adolescence. In Western society these matters are handled later and a much greater range of individual choice is permitted. An advantage of the caste system, and indeed of many relatively closed class systems, is that the individual possesses a sense of security and an assured position in the community. The broad outlines of the life pattern are determined once and for all by collective decree, as it were, with the lack of choice compensated for by greater individual security and the sense that one faces life's problems as the member of a large family group, and beyond that a subcaste. During the colonial period in America (and to some extent in the farm population today) the child's induction into the community work pattern began very early, long before marriage. This apprenticeship was an integral part of the preparation for the roles of later life.

In America today, embarkation on a career or beginning paid employment generally precedes marriage by a few years. Some occupations require such extensive preliminary training that marriage is often postponed, sometimes with consequent effects on personality development. In some countries marriage may be unduly postponed for various economic reasons, as in Ireland and Sweden. This greatly affects the relationships between work and marriage and between marriage and premarital sex relations. Myrdal[2] points to the high rate of illegitimacy and premarital intercourse in Sweden and the general attitudes of toleration of these consequences of a tradition of late marriage.

In rural Ireland the farmer's son who is to inherit the land upon his father's retirement or death is expected to postpone his marriage until this occurs.[3] Compensatory provisions are made for the other sons at this time also, and their marriages are thus likewise postponed. Because of this situation the inheriting son's marriage is often delayed until middle age. The unmarried son who works for his father is spoken of as "boy," even though he may be close to fifty years old. Control of farm policies and finance is exercised by the father, who also controls his son's life and arranges for his marriage. When the son finally marries and takes over the parental farm, his parents, if still alive, continue to live there and may continue to exercise considerable control. The son's bride, for example, may not achieve full domestic responsibility until after the birth of her first child.

In 1926, in some sections of rural Ireland, as many as 88 percent or even 90 percent of the males between the ages of twenty-five and thirty were unmarried, as compared to 39 percent unmarried in the same age group in the United States. This pattern of late marriage, or no marriage at all, is also found in Irish towns and cities, but to a lesser extent. The inordinate delay in assuming adult marital and work roles imposed by this system means that strong, energetic, healthy young men are obliged to mark time waiting for the opportunity to assume the full adult role. This has been linked by Bales with certain patterns of alcoholism in Ireland.[4]

In the United States also there is a hiatus between arrival at physical maturity and entrance into the adult occupational status. Reuter[5] and others have suggested that middle and late adolescence is in some respects a period of enforced leisure because there is little place in the world of work for persons of this age, and that some of the peculiarities and problems of adolescence rise from this fact. In the urban middle classes, Parsons notes the existence of an adolescent or "youth culture" which grows up as a result of this delay in reaching adult status.

> Perhaps the best single point of reference for characterizing the youth culture lies in its contrast with the dominant pattern of the adult male role. By contrast with the emphasis on responsibility in this role, the orientation of youth culture is more or less specifically irresponsible. One of its dominant roles is "having a good time" in relation to which there is a particularly strong emphasis on social activities in company with the opposite sex. . . . Negatively, there is a strong tendency to repudiate interest in adult things and to feel at least a certain recalcitrance to the pressure of adult expectations and discipline. . . . Youth culture has a strong tendency to develop in directions which are either on the borderline of parental approval, or beyond the pale, in such matters as sex behavior, drinking, and various forms of frivolous and irresponsible behavior. . . . Thus the youth culture is not only . . . a matter of age status as such, but also shows strong signs of being a product of tensions in the relationship of younger people and adults.[6]

Without subscribing to all of these rather general, if suggestive, statements, one can agree that some of the stress marking the adolescent years comes from the delay in assuming adult status, especially for the male.

Marked deviations in time of arrival at occupational maturity play havoc with social relations for both the precocious young person and the laggard. The precocious often become involved in bitter familial or even legal conflicts, particularly perhaps with the father, whose self-esteem depends so much upon being a provider for his family. Howard S. Becker[7] has pointed out that jazz musicians often begin their careers in the mid-teens and invariably run into opposition from their parents because playing in a band greatly diminishes parental control. The money earned contributes greatly to the increase of independence, of course. A dramatic instance of parental opposition to too-rapid growing up was reported a few years ago in the press. The parents of a very successful twelve-year-old evangelist, who claimed to have been in heaven and seen God, sought a court order to make him cease his activities and to regain legal control of him from his manager. A reverse twist of occupational precocity occurs when the parents, sensing fame and fortune, push a child into becoming a prodigy. This is probably most obvious in the careers of child movie stars and precocious pianists and violinists.

Marriage almost universally marks a point of transition in the life cycle the world over and is accordingly celebrated in elaborate ceremonies that express the importance of this milestone to individual and group. As is true of the beginning of any stage, marriage may precipitate important crises in the person's life. Relatively stable societies recognize this and have worked out established means of minimizing difficulties and handling them when they arise. The high divorce rates in some societies indicate both a more tolerant view of mismarriage and less solid instruments for maintaining marriage regardless of personal cost. Without passing judgment on the values and evils of divorce, it is perfectly clear that even in groups where divorce is accepted there is much trauma associated with it, especially when children are involved.

It is trite to observe that people make momentous discoveries about themselves during the early years of marriage and often change in unanticipated ways. The rearing of children marks a new phase. It has often been remarked in technical and popular literature that this calls for considerable realignments in marital relations, particularly perhaps at the beginning of the phase.

Farther along in the life cycle, every society makes provision for the relaxation or severing of parental control as the child moves into adult status. All societies provide, too, for gradual or abrupt relinquishment of work responsibilities by the parents. American society differs from many others in that the conjugal family, which is set up as a well-nigh separate and independent social and pro-creational unit, is the typical family group. When the offspring leave home to establish their own households, this leaves the parents with the task of continuing to maintain the original one—ideally without help from anyone, even their children. The result of this is that the mother retains domestic responsibility until in-capacitated, and the father continues to work long after the last child leaves home. This sets the stage for many of the crises and tragedies of advanced age. Among the problems are: the mother's adjustment to an empty house; the father's loss of self-esteem if he is prematurely incapacitated for work; and the unhappy conse-quences which follow when parents and married children must live under the same roof when neither expected nor wanted to. In extended family systems in which several generations live together, parental control over the married children in the household may not be completely removed until enfeeblement or death of the "old man." This system is often linked with the older man's pre-eminent occupational status and with the control of property and wealth. Different systems of this general kind create their own special problems of security and anxiety. Personality is still in the making, even at advanced ages.

Only a very few of the many relevant aspects of the life cycle that are pertinent to personality change have been mentioned in this brief account. Perhaps enough has been said to make it clear that the later periods of life must not be ignored nor explained away in any account of personality change. Theory tends to be too exclu-sively based upon the study of children and abnormal individuals. The manner in which the mature, normal adult is shaped and pro-foundly affected by later events and by his participation in group life is thus largely ignored. These later changes cannot be dis-missed as superficial or as external changes rung upon an old theme, especially in the absence of investigation.

Status Changes

The life cycle, as we have been discussing it, is a sequential passage from one rather general status to another. In heterogeneous societies, it is evident that there is a large degree of choice in the assumption of many statuses. The anthropologist R. Linton has made a well-known set of distinctions among ascribed, assumed, and achieved statuses. Ascribed statuses are those to which individuals are assigned without having much to say in the matter and "without reference to innate differences or abilities."[8] There is no recruitment for this type of status. Assumed statuses are chosen by the individual himself: occupational statuses are examples. Achieved statuses involve rivalry and special aptitudes: an aspirant must demonstrate superiority against other claimants for the position.

Preparation for a change of status or assumption of status often begins far ahead of time. Impetus for the training often comes not from the candidate but from others. As we have said, the training for roles and the development of the fantasy life of the individual are integral parts of getting the individual ready for the change. In relatively static societies there are fewer choices of status, and the paths one may follow are well traveled.

At any point in life [in a homogeneous community] the adult can consolidate previous experience in the light of current roles. A youngster sees his probable future career in the activities that others of his sex perform in the village. They are going through sequences that he too will go through when he is older. In this way the present constitutes a dependable training situation for the future. Past experience can always be consolidated as growing children or even adults understand their contemporary roles and prospects in the light of what they have already experienced. "The trembling hand of old age, as it strokes a child's feverish skin, contains in it a promise not only of the bearableness of illness, but also of the bearableness of death itself, or of the unbearableness of both."[9]

This prepared passage from status to status has been termed "scheduling" by Foote. It "is like the game of musical chairs, except that people know in advance when the next change is coming, and as a rule no one gets left out."[10]

As men and women make the passage to new statuses in such a community, they slough off old motivations and acquire new ones. Moreover, movement into new positions is supported by communal rationales which explain the move and give justification for it. The rationales are heavily charged with feeling and value and are embodied in contracts, ceremonies, rituals, myths, and other institutional forms. They provide the individual with clues to what he can expect, how he is to comport himself, and the meaning of his new experiences. This last point is especially important, for experiences, as we have seen, require interpretation. Even in a mobile society like ours there are plenty of such public rationales, mythologies, and ceremonies which help candidates of all ages through their *rites du passage*. Pregnancy and childbirth are periods of which this is true. When some people speak of the "old wives' tales" about childbirth they are simply preparing to substitute for them another rationale, sometimes a scientific one. Every social structure, every society, generates mythologies; and these provide individuals with generalized rationales as well as cues for appropriate behavior in times of stress. The truth or falsity of a myth is irrelevant: as long as people believe it true, it can be a touchstone in their lives. The purely fictional Horatio Alger legend—part of the general mythology of success stories—seems to have played such a role in the careers of many American businessmen.[11] Mythologies are transmitted through stories, drama, poetry, art, and songs which recount the exploits of heroes and portray the facing of ordeals, the resisting of temptations, and the overcoming of enemies. Mythologies provide models: the martyr (John Brown, Sacco and Vanzetti), the avenging hero (MacArthur), the conquering hero (Jack Dempsey) are extolled and may be emulated.[12] Upon his entrance into new groups and new statuses, the novitiate always is introduced to the appropriate mythologies and may derive orientation from them.

The passage from one status to another or the assumption of

additional statuses makes it necessary for the person to reconcile, amalgamate, and synthesize their requirements. When passage is institutionally well prepared, statuses flow into one another, are "continuous," to use a term of Benedict's.[13] When the way is not so prepared, and the new statuses call for at least a partial yielding of allegiance to old ones, which is accompanied by a sense of conflict, then we may speak of "discontinuity."

WORK CAREERS

Some of the complexity of status changes and their potential effects upon personality may be indicated in a brief discussion of occupations. The hundreds of occupations in our society are roughly graded in a prestige hierarchy, and within each business or profession there is also a similar grading. In our type of society social position or class standing is intimately linked with the work in which one is engaged and with one's ranking within that occupation. Family status in terms of class depends primarily on the occupation of the husband; the wife and children try to live up to what they believe the family status to be, but ordinarily they can do little or nothing to change it. The husband's work, his income, the rate at which he is promoted, his hours of work, the distance he must travel every day—all these influence the structure of the family, the nature of the husband-wife relationship, and the personalities of all the members of the family. Needless to say, there is tremendous ego involvement in income and occupation on the part of the whole family, but this is especially true of the man.

Selecting One's Work · In adolescence, according to Sullivan, a primary preoccupation is with what stance to take *vis-à-vis* the opposite sex and indeed toward sex in general. Side by side with this, or sometimes a little later in America, comes the question of occupational choice. Among males there are, at first, tentative ventures into the working world in summer jobs or other temporary employment. It is a rare person who settles down in the first kind of occupation that he tries.[14] Having established a stable sex relation, particularly after marriage, a man tends to assign increasing significance to his occupation, since the entire family has some interest in economic well-being and he himself has an interest in personal advancement and becomes involved in personal relations on the job. Inevitably, the meanings of work and occupation shift with changed relations at home and in the occupation.

At the time that a young man either chooses or falls into his vocation, his conception of it tends to be stereotyped, romanticized, schematized, and often over optimistic. In apprenticeship training, such as that undergone in plumbing, carpentry, and other skilled trades, the neophyte is apt to have a truer picture, for very often relatives or friends of the family are in the trade. The same is true, of course, of family businesses. The recruit can scarcely know much about his future if he chooses one of the new occupations and specialties that are emerging constantly. The implication of this is that during the course of an occupational career many men will occupy statuses the existence of which they did not dream of, and encounter new social relationships. In transit, therefore, their motivations, aspirations, and self-conceptions may be profoundly altered. This is so despite the fact that occupation selection also operates to sort out people who are not suited to given jobs and lines of work.

Power · Work relationships engender power motivations because they involve dominance and subordination. From the very first job, men are in a position to be ordered and commanded, and every step upward in the hierarchy gives the individual progressively greater authority to give orders to others. The authority may include matters as final as sending a man to his death, and as trivial as expecting and receiving deference. Power is not just a matter of manipulating people for selfish ends: it is a necessary factor in societal action. It is for this reason that men are judged and accorded prestige on the basis of their efficiency in the exercise of power and leadership. There are power-hungry persons who utilize work relationships to satisfy their ambition, but others acquire a taste for power after entering the occupational world. The earlier motivations of adolescence and early adulthood are often displaced and even abandoned as people become absorbed in the satisfactions of receiving public acclaim, making a name, receiving deference, and generally wielding influence over others. The exercise of power is a seductive experience, as is reflected in the well-known saying:

"Power corrupts, and absolute power corrupts absolutely." Those who become absorbed in acquiring power face the problems of where to stop and what to do about other matters that may interfere. Previous commitments to wife, family, and friends have to be reconciled with the new goals or sacrificed to them. The person who devotes himself to the acquisition of power necessarily does so at considerable expense to interpersonal relationships. This is so whether he is a businessman, priest, or musician: all occupational positions have power implications.

Alfred Adler,[15] who early took his departure from the Freudian camp, built a system of "individual psychology" in which the striving for dominance, rather than sexuality, is considered to be central in human personality. He was impressed by the tremendous significance of the desire for power. He saw the beginnings of this drive in the child's perception of his helplessness and general physical inferiority to adults. The later search for power seemed to him largely an unconscious compensation for this fundamental "inferiority complex." But taste for and discovery of power may arrive much later and as the outcome of experience. It is not necessarily a universal attitude.

A large number of the significant problems of the male in middle life, and of women who work, are associated with their jobs. Some of these have been touched upon in Chapter 16. Here we particularly wish to note that the kinds of critical junctures which a man faces, when they occur in the life cycle, and how they are handled are closely associated with occupational statuses.

Security and Promotion · In some occupations there is considerable promise of eminence and personal security, at least after the novitiate has made a beginning or is "in." These occupations may be recognized generally by their clear-cut ranks, fairly automatic promotion, and steady increments of salary and tenure. Military and civil service and academic careers often fall into this group. The crises in these occupations tend to occur early, before a man is assured of tenure or before he has committed himself to that career, but they often occur at the points where for some reason promotion is delayed or blocked.

Even relatively stable occupational structures such as these may lose stability through contraction or rapid expansion, however. When rapid expansion occurs, new kinds of recruits flood in, competition may become more severe, and the old hierarchies of payment, seniority, and promotion are upset. Some individuals may have organized their lives around the expectation of slow movement and of assuming only limited responsibility and authority. Rapid expansion often promotes these individuals to higher positions and may cause them distress and turmoil. Severe personality problems engendered or precipitated by quick growth of the army are described in a study by Maas, Prince, and Davie.[16] A point which brings out particularly well the connectives between social class, work, and personality is discussed by the authors: those who suffer most from unexpected upgrading are typically of low educational level and come from low-income families.

The Status Game · In contrast to relatively stable occupations, others are hazardous and continuously competitive in the sense that one's position cannot usually be consolidated merely by length of service. The worker in such occupations may be subject to demotion or discharge. Unskilled labor, of course, insofar as the unions do not hedge the right to fire at short notice, is of this nature. Higher executive positions also often fall into the "hazardous" category. However, the extra hazard in executive jobs is compensated for by the higher pay and sometimes by the existence of a fairly extensive market for executive talent. Some positions require competitive striving all through the career, sometimes for very high stakes. The recent popular literature about salesmen and executives portrays some of the effects of this competition. Where there is severe competition, virtually all social relationships, in and out of the office, may be drawn into the occupational orbit. William Whyte has commented on how the wife of the junior executive is used as a pawn in the status game:

> It is still . . . a man's world. So, at least, it is to the executive's wife. Resolutely anti-feminist, she conceives her role to be that of a "stabilizer"—the keeper of the retreat, the one who rests and rejuvenates the man for the next day's battle. . . . [She] must also be a social operator—and when husbands and wives sketch out the personal characteristics of the ideal wife it is

the equipment for this role that comes first to their minds. What they ask for, more than any other quality, is gregariousness—or a reasonable facsimile. . . . she must be a highly adaptable "mixer." . . . Second nature to the seasoned wife . . . are the following:

Don't talk shop gossip with the Girls, particularly those who have husbands in the same department. . . .

Don't turn up at the office unless you absolutely have to.

Don't get too chummy with the wives of associates your husband might soon pass on the way up.

Don't be disagreeable to any company people you meet. You never know. . . .

Be attractive. There is a strong correlation between executive success and the wife's appearance—particularly so in the case of the sales wife.

Be a phone pal of your husband's secretary.

Never—repeat, never—get tight at a company party (it may go down in a dossier).[17]

What makes severe competition especially poignant and invidious is that the individual necessarily competes with others like himself. Hence his friends are also his rivals and, in very subtle ways, he is thus thrown into treacherous social situations. At best, personal friendships between the competitors are restricted in degree of intimacy and mutual trust.

As one young executive puts it, "If I go ahead as I hope, and some of our friends progress as little as I think they will, there's going to be friction. My wife can't see this." . . . Laments one wife now in midpassage, "I love people and I've made many intimate friends in the company, but since Charlie got his new job it's just been hell on us. He has so much control over their lives, and it's gotten so complicated."[18]

The relative weights of severe competition and institutional security are currently being debated in the business world. The old-style business leader came up the hard way, winning his way to the top through competitive qualities of one kind or another. The newer strategy is to take well-trained, bright, young graduates of top-flight schools and give them virtual assurance of future executive positions within the company.

Frustrations, Satisfactions, and Identifications · In a complex economic order, technological changes increase and decrease the relative prestige of occupations and specialties within occupations. Some technical skills may be made obsolete, as when machines decrease the need for certain kinds of skilled craftsmanship. It does not always happen that a man then becomes unemployed, but he faces a loss of self-esteem. Anyone who depends upon a single skill for his livelihood is open to this kind of occupational hazard. Some occupations place such a premium on skillful performance that loss of ability to function at this level leads to dismissal or taking a back seat. This may occur at any time in an individual's working years, but is a special danger in the later years. Hence the industry may, with foresight, provide safer or less specialized jobs for workers who cannot "keep up"; otherwise the person himself must make provision for this possibility. Even if he does so his self-involvement with the old skill may be so great that considerable trauma or sorrow may follow when he relinquishes it. The skilled machinist, the airplane pilot, and the baseball player alike must anticipate the decrease of skill; the movie actress who is approaching middle age must recapture her audiences by taking roles more suitable to her age, if she does not wish to retire.

Certain occupational statuses involve dealing with clients. In learning to cope with them, strategies are evolved and certain styles of speaking and gesturing are learned. Self-esteem is bound up in subtle ways with having clients of a certain kind, and persons in service occupations often come to identify in curious ways with their clients. Edna Ferber has caught this in her fictional characterization of a man of lowly social origins who is the proprietor of a food store in an exclusive urban area:

> When they wanted something special, something rare, something precious in the food line, then Aye Wun Stores, Emanuel Sweilbach, Prop., could supply it. . . . No dainty too exquisite, no source too remote, for his providing.[19]

We are not so much interested in sketching the nature of these identifications as in noting that if the clientele should shift, usually through physical mobility, a personal crisis may occur. An example is that of the school teacher whose school neighborhood deteriorates and who has to "readjust" to succeeding waves of immigrant, and successively poorer, children. Critical decisions must be made in some careers when a portion of one's clientele is moving to other neighborhoods: the dilemma is whether to remain in the old locale and shift customers or take a chance and follow the old.

Although the consequences of occupational position have barely been touched upon, enough has been said to suggest how crucial these consequences may be for the development of personality and of personal relations. In a less differentiated society than ours, occupation may not be of such great significance in shaping a man's destiny and character; but, where the division of labor is complex, the way one makes one's living is of the utmost importance. Although the therapeutic value of work is recognized, the full significance of work for personality theory has not yet been fully grasped. We would concur with E. C. Hughes, who states the view forcefully:

> In our particular society, work organization looms so large as a separate and specialized system of things, and work experience is so fateful a part of every man's life, that we cannot make much headway as students of society and of social psychology without using work as one of our main laboratories.[20]

Contrast, Marginality, and Identity

CONTRAST AND IDENTITY

The ideas that one has of oneself depend upon contrast and identification with others. The significance of one's relations with other people does not depend upon whether the relationship is friendly or not, for hostile relationships may be quite as meaningful as any others. The idea of unity or of integration does not exclude the possibility of conflict and of contrast. Thus one should think of the unity of personality as one that embraces a certain amount of conflict or ambivalence. Persons build up conceptions of themselves by comparing and contrasting themselves with others and by pitting the groups to which they belong against those to which others belong. Contrasts as well as similarities, hostility as well as approval, are involved.

A sociologist, Copeland,[21] some years ago made an analysis of what he termed "the contrast conception" held by whites and Negroes in the ante-bellum South. Black was a symbol of evil and lowness; white, of purity. Whites held their superior status by virtue of a natural order of being. Without their ever thinking about it, their conceptions of themselves, their self-esteem, depended to a substantial degree on the solid fact that they were not Negroes. The Negro's view of himself was dominated even more completely by the inescapable fact of race and color.

Insofar as significant others label the individual in certain ways, he finds himself reacting, willy-nilly, in terms of that assignment of status. From this flow some of the most complex actions and reactions. The contact of ethnic groups generally embroils people in interaction in which such preordained categories play a part. Europeans and Americans in Asiatic countries become "sahibs" and "memsahibs" whether they wish to or not. With the best intentions in the world, the outsider who has firmly resolved to draw no color and class lines finds himself fitting more and more into the pattern laid out for him. Innumerable stories and accounts have described the transformation of self that occurs in this meeting of peoples. It has been said, and is doubtless true, that no Negro in the United States can escape the effects of his affiliation, even though he be surrounded by sympathetic whites. By indirect and often unwitting gestures he is constantly reminded that he is a Negro—even though the gestures indicate acceptance, respect, friendliness, and admiration.

Those who do the categorizing of minorities are also affected, sometimes in even more complex ways than those who must submit to the dominant categorization. James Baldwin,[22] a white American liberal, has written some passionate lines which reveal the impact of race relations on some whites. He agrees that the position of the Negro in America has improved greatly but notes that the gulf between the races is essentially unchanged.

We do not know what to do with him . . . if he breaks our . . . sentimental image of him we are panic-stricken and we feel ourselves betrayed. When he violates this image, therefore, he stands in the greatest danger (sensing which, we uneasily suspect that he is very often playing a part for our benefit); and, what is not always so apparent but is equally true, we are then in some danger ourselves—hence our retreat or our blind and immediate retaliation. Our dehumanization of the Negro then is indivisible from our dehumanization of ourselves: the loss of our own identity is the price we pay for our annulment of his . . . in our estrangement from him is the depth of our estrangement from ourselves. We cannot ask: what do we *really* feel about him?—such a question merely opens the gates on chaos. What we really feel about him is involved with all that we feel about everything, about everyone, about ourselves.[23]

Relationships of this sort between somewhat hostile groups standing in different status positions may be described as polarizations. To some extent, each group becomes dependent in attitude and orientation upon the other. The influences on the subordinate group are perhaps the more powerful and pervasive, since its members cannot escape the necessity of taking a position of agreement or opposition, of conformity or rebellion. Whichever position they assume, the norms of the dominant group set the pattern. The member of the subordinate group cannot simply be himself, but must adapt himself to or react against the stereotypes which the dominant group imposes. The polarization of social relationships thus leads to corresponding polarization of personality.

Persons may organize their lives around status contrasts and conflicts so that these become assets to them. The old-style labor union leader who throve on injunctions and strikes has passed from the scene, but his modern successor still capitalizes on the opposition of interests. A man who has concentrated on a battle for many years needs his opponent, in a very real sense; it is disconcerting, and sometimes disorganizing, to find that the antagonist has disappeared. To use a domestic example, people are frequently astonished to see a widow go to pieces after the death of her husband, although when he was alive they may have quarreled bitterly and constantly. Riesman[24] has remarked that social scientists have placed too much stress upon the punishing aspects of alienation, conflict, and marginality to the neglect of the gratifications proceeding from them. The existence of inequity, unfairness, dishonesty, and betrayal makes it possible for some persons to obtain the satisfaction of knowing themselves to be "right," or of becoming reformers, champions of truth and justice, or martyrs.

MARGINALITY AND IDENTITY

Persons who stand in an ambiguous position between contrasting ethnic groups have been called "marginal men."[25] The idea of marginality has much wider applicability: it may be used to describe any transit from one allegiance to another. Since in the course of time all of us become reconciled with or forget about old foes, acquire new ones, encounter new rivalries and enmities, and can scarcely retain all our old loyalties, we all experience marginality.

Personality "integration" implies a sort of loose-jointed flexibility, as one continuously moves out of his established orbit and then catches up with himself. Too great rigidity of circumstances or life pattern is stultifying. Riesman, criticizing the concept of personality integration, tells of an experience of R. E. Park:

> The old man [an old ex-slave] was poor, and undoubtedly worse off in all material respects than under slavery. In fact, he used to boast about what a good life he had had under his old master. Park asked him whether he was not sorry about having been emancipated, and the old man replied that, no, he liked freedom —for, he said, "There's a kind of looseness about this here freedom." . . . I myself feel that a certain looseness and disorderliness and ambiguity of attitude are a part of the good life. One might ask, why do I have to take my stand on every issue? Why need I be all of a piece? Why need I be so integrated as to lack the looseness of joint which would enable me to move easily into new positions?[26]

Then Riesman adds that "terms such as 'integration' are traps of ambiguity—I would not quarrel with someone who defined my kind of unintegrated, loosely ordered life as a form of integration on a higher level!"

Turning Points and New Directions

The fact that human beings make objects of themselves—appraising, evaluating, judging themselves—is of crucial importance to the whole process of personality change. The undergoing of new experiences and the acquisition of new facts necessarily lead to the reassessment of past actions and commitments. Self-conceptions undergo progressive reorganization as past experiences are weighed and future contingencies considered. Just as one discovers new facets in the personalities of others from their unanticipated and unpredicted acts, so also does one keep on discovering new things about oneself. Self-discovery is a continuous process; but one may note that it has its dramatic moments in sudden crises of redefinition which start people off along new lines.

Self-appraisal involves new directions, new decisions; it is surrounded by a "halo of 'can' and 'cannot,' 'will' and 'will not,' 'should' and 'should not.' "[27] "The I, as subject, in reviewing the Me's, as objects, continually moves into a partially uncharted future."[28]

Human interaction brings about continual realignment of relationships. Acts performed toward or in the presence of others are on the record and cannot be taken back with an "I didn't really mean it." Relationships evolve, progress, and cannot be frozen—even when the participants, as when they are lovers or friends, decide to keep the relationship eternally fixed at its current moment.

The Episode · The sequence of phases of developing relationships has been pointed to by many writers. Thus Blumer has described the "variable career" and "developing character" of interaction,[29] and Foote has called attention to the importance of the episode: "At the conclusion of any episode of interaction, the position of the participants vis-à-vis each other is always and necessarily different from what it was at the commencement of the episode."[30]

Those who participate in the episode may not be alert to its results. It often happens that we discover the meaning of a conversational exchange some time after it has occurred. We may then look back upon it as the point at which things began to go down-hill or to improve: we see it as the significant juncture at which we began to draw closer to or draw away from a friend or colleague. Episodes frequently prove to be cumulative in effect. This is recognized only gradually by the participants, who may not be able to put their fingers on which precise moments or interchanges were crucial. But the very recognition of cumulative change in relationships itself is a turning point, for it calls forth reappraisal. This is the sort of thing that happens constantly among married couples who may drift for months without recognizing the gradual, minute, but significant changes in the domestic relationship. Recognition of the shift may result in discussion, decision, and an attempt "to do something about it" if it is bad and to further it consciously if it is good. Of course, people may be more or less alert to change in relationships without consciously taking stock of what is occurring. It is not unusual to become alive quite suddenly, through a gesture or an act, to the "true meaning" of recent developments. People fall in love and out of love this way. Men who grow friendly with women often discover that the grounds of the relationship have shifted under them. Since there are in all episodes at least two actors, and since the meanings of the interaction are assessed differently and at different rates by them, it follows that the courses of relationships are highly variable and somewhat indeterminate. It is easy to see also why the involvement of the self with another —whether the involvement is one of friendship, or enmity, or of any other nature—proceeds by jumps and spurts as one or the other (or both) of the participants makes appraisals of what is happening.

Turning Points · The critical junctures at which there is major, rather than minor, stock-taking of self may be termed "turning points." It is at these points that the person finishes off phases or eras in his life course and moves on to others. We see this perhaps most clearly in the aging process. Transition from one age grade to another is not necessarily attended by uncertainty or trauma; sometimes it even arouses excitement. In a society oriented toward youth, as in America, the passage into middle and old age often is made with reluctance or may be a traumatic experience. The day that a man reaches fifty, the point at which he feels that he is no longer fit for tennis, the time when a woman recognizes that her skin is no longer firm, or when lines appear around the neck: these are poignant moments in the lives of persons who do not look forward to old age.

Turning points are of an infinite variety. Some are institutionalized, at least in part, so that people are enabled to prepare for them and carry on through them; the death of a spouse and the attainment of high political office are instances of this. But many contingencies are unforeseen and are not handled in socially prescribed ceremonies. This does not mean that they are unique, are not experienced under similar conditions by others. Social organization, after all, determines the patterns of personal careers so that many persons experience challenge, humiliation, and betrayal under very similar circumstances. To these crises people may respond quite differently, although we may be sure that when enough people undergo the same sort of crises, rationales for explaining and handling them will spring up, spread, and become common property. A very striking instance of this was the public concern in America, during the Korean war, over soldiers who were captured by the enemy and "brain-washed" to the point of giving vital information, signing false statements, or becoming Communists. This betrayal constituted a very special kind of traitorous act. Definitions and explanations of it and ways of dealing with it must therefore be worked out in public debate as well as in legal proceedings.

Such debates lead to the discovery of new positions and the emergence of new values. In turn, new directions in behavior are based on these newly evolved positions and values. Consequently, any effort to account for human development in terms of fixed stages is foredoomed. In a limited sense, one can discuss the universal aging process and the more or less world-wide developmental tasks of the individual and note how various social structures provide frameworks for ordered and typical steps in personality development or change. But, as we remarked in the beginning of this chapter, change is a constant feature of human life. The problem is to account for its directions. In some measure this account must always be *post hoc* rather than predictive or proscriptive.

The Inducement and Guidance of Change

Everyone knows how difficult it is to persuade others that they ought to change in desired directions. We are all, from others' points of view, obstinate sinners. The mechanisms for the maintenance of one's self-conception, and hence of position, are numerous, and among them we may briefly note selective inattention, defense of ego, and commitments to others. The latter are especially noteworthy. People incur obligations and develop loyalties, and wittingly or unwittingly are afraid to move out of the orbit containing the significant others to whom they are so committed. Time or such catastrophic events as death, war, and depressions help to free persons from such alliances, but anyone who wishes to induce someone else to adopt a radically different religious or political stand, or to break sharply with a current style of life, can find small solace in this.

Techniques of Persuasion · Quick change requires that the adult person undergo turmoil. If he is to change his prevailing conception of self, that conception must be thrown into doubt. If his loyalties to colleagues, friends, and parents are to be loosened, these latter must be impugned, attacked, shaken from pedestals, questioned. A certain amount of self-doubt and doubt of others can be induced by verbal means, but it is also essential that crucial situations be established wherein the person sees himself and the others, if possible, acting in ways that run counter to his cherished conceptions. Religious conversion, which is followed by a radical change in style of life, illustrates these processes. Preaching, accusation, and rhetoric in general are important in bringing about conversion; but it is essential that the person to be put into situations in which he will feel guilt, will feel and see his usual actions as strange, and in which he will be forced to review his past history and find himself wanting. R. Wohl[31] has observed that the mass religious conversions so prevalent in nineteenth-century America were not the easy products of a little preaching. A minister worked hard, frequently over a period of some days, to establish all the requisite conditions for the transformation of self. Elsewhere, in discussing "dancing crowds" (p. 461), we have noted how the elation and other, less familiar feelings aroused in the crowd receive a collective interpretation and may lead to the formation of a religious group and a sharp break with former modes of living.

Creation of a crisis provides the condition for changing the direction of the personal career, but in itself it is not enough. Crisis calls for self-appraisal and self-examination, but does not automatically indicate direction. Some converts not only drop out or backslide, but move off in other directions—to alcohol, to other social movements, or to cynical manipulation of others. If the reformer is to make use of a crisis, he must help plot the course from there on in order to prepare the convert for difficulties and to help the rationale of the course become part of his thinking. This is done in religious conversions by various devices, such as predicting the harshness of parents and relations when the convert attempts to tell them about his revelations, and predicting that friends will abandon him because of the new beliefs.

Brain-washing · In a very suggestive, although necessarily very incomplete book, Hunter[32] has described the so-called "brain-washing" technique used by the Chinese Communist Party on students in the years following their accession to power. Brain-washing was essentially an attempt to break old loyalties, principally to family and social class, and to develop new loyalties to country and to party. To do this, the person had to be convinced that his parents were evil, or at least misguided because of their way of life; and he had to develop a self-conception organized around participation in the Communist movement. The tactics of conversion varied with school and circumstance, but a fairly standard set of procedures seems to have been utilized.

To begin with, propaganda and lectures unveiled a new terminology—that of the Communists—which ran counter to familiar concepts in a great many ways. The meaning of the new terms could not be fully grasped at first, but they provided an initial vocabulary for the reinterpretation of events, persons, and groups. Students were sent to work in the fields so as to feel like the common people. They were sent to see village justice wreaked upon former landlords —often a harrowing experience for the onlooker whose parents might also be landlords. Any who could not bear to watch were accused of sentimentality—a characteristic of the ruling class. A detailed biographical essay (called a "thought seduction essay") had to be written and turned in to the teacher who, having read it, criticized it as revealing "deep set contradictions" in their lives. The point of this criticism was to force the student to reveal publicly his former beliefs and actions, especially when he himself wanted to forget them because they were not in harmony with Party teachings. Students were then induced or compelled to confess their sins in class, admitting that they had helped the Japanese, and so on. Criticism of each student by every other was encouraged, and those who held back were prodded by name-calling ("lagging-behind particle") and other punishments.

Presumably, some persons were relieved by making their avowals and were supported by others' commentaries; but in general, public avowal and criticism are very destructive processes. Ordinarily one is protected from certain kinds of adverse comment by the conspiracy of silence that governs polite intercourse. Selective inattention does not get much chance to operate effectively in such procedures as those we have described, because the individual's illusions about himself are challenged directly. This challenge was increased by the mutual hostility engendered during these sessions. The right to privacy was invaded: not only did current acts and thoughts come under scrutiny, but the intimate details of past history were examined. The student was asked to explain the "why" of his acts, and then alternative motivations were pressed upon him.

The turning point in the brain-washing process appears to have been the genuine public confession, when the student got down to rock bottom and accused himself of having been a wastrel, an exploiter, a coward, and so on. This amounted to a genuine public relinquishing of past identity. The anguish attending this process is suggested by the cutting off of contacts with parents, the renaming of one's family as "exploiters," and the sundering of relations with wives. It was at this point that the more serious consequences of the new perspective began to come home to the convert. The parable of Lot and the pillar of salt is applicable here: there was no turning back.

One of the final steps in the process was the writing of a "thought conclusion essay" consisting of an autobiography written to show how far one has come, in the desired direction, and in what ways, and including a ruthless renunciation of the past. This essay had to be read aloud to the class and was subjected to public criticism. When the candidate was finished with this ordeal, he was compelled to rewrite his essay along more acceptable lines. Not everyone, of course, went through to the final steps in the process. Some committed suicide, some ran away, and others were not deemed to require the full treatment.

It would be an error to regard brain-washing as a process as superficial as its name implies. There can be no doubt that it is a technique of what one might call "forced conversion," and that it sometimes brings about fundamental and permanent changes in outlook. In the testimony of Americans who have been temporarily subjected to the treatment there is often a note of profound respect for its potency. Ardent anti-Communists, who remain so after a period of Communist indoctrination, often unwittingly use the Communist vocabulary or accept some of its assumptions.

Summary

Although the main features of personality organization are determined in the first decades of life, personality is never fixed. It continues to change throughout adult life. Conceptions of self arise from social interaction, and since social interaction changes continuously, so does self-conception. Among the important social influences upon adults are those associated with marriage, family, and occupation. These aspects of adult life are handled differently in different societies, with significant consequences for personal development.

Some status changes are handled and facilitated by socially prescribed scheduling, by ceremonials, and by supporting public rationalizations. Other status changes are of a personal nature. The
influence of occupation on personality is an especially important
one, particularly for the adult male. Personality change becomes
evident in critical episodes which may be considered turning points.
The dramatic effects of certain types of persuasion, such as "brain-
washing," illustrate the manner in which adult personality change
may sometimes be brought about deliberately.

SUGGESTIONS FOR DISCUSSION AND SPECIAL REPORTS

1. Compare the "typical" life cycles of men and women in
America.

2. Do the same for men (or women) in two different societies.

3. Trace the career line of a prominent government official and
interpret this career sociologically.

4. Discuss the dating and courting process in terms of crisis,
ritual, stages, and turning points.

5. Write a report on an occupation, tracing its possible influence
upon its members as they rise in status within it.

6. Interview persons who have vacationed abroad and interpret
how they have changed as a result of travel, and why—or why not.

7. What do novels or magazine stories suggest about the personality problems of "class-mobile" men and women?

8. Discuss freedom and marginality versus conformity and security.

9. Does fashion, as in clothes, promote freedom, autonomy, and
choice, or does it regiment and confine taste and choice?

NOTES

[1] R. J. Havighurst, *Developmental
Tasks and Education* (new ed.),
Longmans, Green, 1952.

[2] A. Myrdal, *Nation and Family,*
Harper, 1941.

[3] C. M. Arensburg, *The Family*

and Community in Ireland, Harvard University Press, 1940.

⁴ R. F. Bales, "The Fixation Factor in Alcohol Addiction: An Hypothesis Derived from a Comparative Study of Irish and Jewish Social Norms," unpublished Ph.D. thesis, Harvard University, 1944.

⁵ E. B. Reuter, "The Sociology of Adolescence," *Am. J. Soc.,* 43 (1937): 414-427.

⁶ T. Parsons, "Age and Sex in the Social Structure of the United States," *Am. Soc. Rev.,* 7(1942): 607.

⁷ H. S. Becker, *The Professional Dance Musician in Chicago,* master's thesis, University of Chicago, 1949.

⁸ R. Linton, *The Study of Man,* Appleton-Century-Crofts, 1936, p. 115.

⁹ J. J. Honigman, *Culture and Personality,* Harper, 1954, pp. 346-347.

¹⁰ N. Foote, "Concept and Method in the Study of Human Development" (mimeographed manuscript), p. 28.

¹¹ R. Wohl, "The 'Rags to Riches' Story: An Episode of Secular Idealism," in *Class, Status and Power,* ed. R. Bendix and S. M. Lipset, Glencoe, Ill.: Free Press, 1953, pp. 388-395.

¹² O. E. Klapp, "The Creation of Popular Heroes," *Am. J. Soc.,* 54(1948): 135-141; "Hero Worship in America," *Am. Soc. Rev.,* 14(1949): 53-62.

¹³ R. Benedict, "Continuities and Discontinuities in Cultural Conditioning," *Psychiatry,* 1(1938): 161-167.

¹⁴ D. C. Miller and H. Form, *Industrial Sociology,* Harper, 1951, pp. 535-538.

¹⁵ A. Adler, *Understanding Human Nature,* Garden City, N. Y.: Garden City Publishing Co., 1927.

¹⁶ H. S. Maas, C. H. Prince, and G. E. Davie, "Personal-Social Disequilibria in a Bureaucratic System," *Psychiatry,* 19(1953): 129-137.

¹⁷ W. H. Whyte, *Is Anybody Listening?* Simon and Schuster, 1952, pp. 150-156.

¹⁸ *Ibid.,* pp. 159-160.

¹⁹ E. Ferber, *Nobody's in Town,* Doubleday, Doran, 1938, pp. 90-91.

²⁰ E. C. Hughes, "The Sociological Study of Work," *Am. J. Soc.,* 58(1952): 426.

²¹ L. N. Copeland, in *Race Relations and the Race Problem,* ed. E. T. Thompson, Duke University Press, 1939.

²² James Baldwin, "Many Thousands Gone," *Partisan Review,* 8 (1951): 665-680.

²³ *Ibid.,* pp. 665-666.

²⁴ D. Riesman, "Some Observations Concerning Marginality," *Phylon: Atlanta University Review of Race and Culture,* 12(1951): 119-120.

²⁵ E. V. Stonequist, *The Marginal Man,* Scribners, 1937; R. E. Park, *Race and Culture,* Glencoe, Ill.: Free Press, 1949.

²⁶ Riesman, *op. cit.,* p. 126.

²⁷ K. Riezler, *Man, Mutable and Immutable,* Henry Regnery and Co., 1950, p. 78.

²⁸ A. Strauss, "Identification," unpublished manuscript.

[29] H. Blumer, "Psychological Import of the Human Group," in M. Sherif and M. Wilson (eds.), *Group Relations at the Crossroads,* Harper, 1953, pp. 185-202.

[30] Foote, *op. cit.,* p. 8.

[31] In an unpublished paper.

[32] E. Hunter, *Brain-Washing in Red China: The Calculated Destruction of Men's Minds,* Vanguard, 1951.

SELECTED BIBLIOGRAPHY

American Journal of Sociology, 57(March 1952). This whole issue is devoted to the sociology of work and includes several papers bearing directly upon the subject matter of this chapter.

Becker, H. S., "Some Contingencies of the Professional Dance Musician's Career," *Human Organization,* 12(1953): 22-26. An informative research report.

Erikson, E. H., "Identity and Totality: Psychoanalytic Observations on the Problems of Youth," *Human Development Bulletin, Fifth Annual Symposium,* University of Chicago Press, 1954, pp. 50-71. A psychiatrist makes many acute remarks about the transition from adolescence to adulthood.

Goffman, E., "On Cooling the Mark Out: Some Aspects of Adaptation to Failure," *Psychiatry,* 15(1952): 451-463. Treats of various institutionalized and patterned ways of handling failure and people who fail.

Hall, O., "Types of Medical Careers," *Am. J. Soc.,* 55(1949): 243-253. A sociological study of kinds of medical careers in relation to differential social structures.

Hughes, E. C., "Social Change and Status Protest," *Phylon: Atlanta University Review of Race and Culture,* 10(1949): 58-65. A thoughtful essay dealing with marginality, changing self conceptions, and social change.

Hunter, E., *Brain-Washing in Red China: The Calculated Destruction of Men's Minds,* Vanguard, 1951. Contains such useful materials, admittedly incomplete, as those utilized in this chapter.

Maas, H. S., C. H. Prince, and G. E. Davie, "Personal-Social Disequilibria in a Bureaucratic System," *Psychiatry,* 19(1953): 129-137. Problems and solutions of regular army personnel in a changing army.

Parsons, T., "Age and Sex in the Social Structure of the United States," *Am. Soc. Rev.,* 7(1942): 604-616. An attempt to generalize about the adolescent years in terms of age, class, family, and other social positions.

Radin, P., *The World of Primitive Man,* Schuman, 1953. Chap. 7, "The Crises of Life and Their Rituals," pp. 151-180. Contains a good discussion of status transitions.

CHAPTER 19

Conflict
and
Disorganization

IN THE LAST SEVERAL CHAPTERS we have dealt with the way in which complex response systems are built up and how they depend upon intercommunication and group life. We now turn our attention to the corollary problem already touched upon, namely, how response systems may be blocked, broken down with consequent trauma to the person, or thrown into confusion by influences of a cultural nature. Our discussion of status changes has set the stage.

The Nature of Disorganized Behavior

INTEGRATED AND DISORGANIZED BEHAVIOR

Behavior is integrated when specific responses have become organized into systems. This means that a given specific response may at different times be a part of different patterns of response. For example, some of the same muscle contractions are involved in playing golf, taking a walk, going hunting, and marching. As Angyal[1] has aptly remarked, the same act may have "multiple functions." When a response is induced in a system it functions in definite ways within that system. Thus, in learning to clean a gun a person makes new combinations of responses, arranging them in an appropriate sequence to accomplish the desired result.

Under certain circumstances the smooth operation of response systems becomes disturbed and loses its integrated character. Behavior becomes fragmented and chaotic. During fires, people are reported to have done such things as throwing furniture out of upper-story windows and carefully lowering mattresses on a rope. Under combat conditions unseasoned troops may fire wildly into the air, urinate involuntarily, and perform other equally inappropriate actions, at the same time forgetting many of the responses laboriously drilled into them during their training period. This disorganization may be temporary or it may crystallize into permanent forms. Symptoms of disorganization include such behavior as rage, crying, irrelevant acts and remarks, tension, rudeness, preoccupation, apathy, erractic action, loss of self-control, unrestrained laughter or sobbing, headaches, exhaustion, and trembling. Disorganization may arise from many sources, including such various physical or biological conditions as alcoholic intoxication, physical deterioration or disease, and brain injury. Temporary disorganization is probably experienced by everyone when the unexpected happens, as when one's car is stolen or involved in a traffic accident, or when one breaks or loses a familiar and necessary object. Our concern in this chapter will be with culturally induced disorganization of relatively serious types.

Disorganized behavior is often described as a consequence of conflicting of impulses, blocking of drives, frustration, delay of gratification, situational complexity, and disruption of habit or routine. The mechanics involved in the disorganization of behavior are complex and not very well understood. A contrast of the disorganized behavior of lower animals with that of humans is a useful preliminary to a discussion of the phenomenon, perhaps not so much because of the similarities between human and animal disorganization as because of the differences that the discussion will bring out.

Disorganized behavior has been experimentally produced in animals by giving them problems of discrimination which are just beyond their powers. Thus, in Pavlov's laboratory,[2] dogs were fed when shown circles but were not fed when shown ellipses. The ellipses were then made more and more like circles until the dogs were unable to discriminate among the figures. They squealed, barked, wriggled, tore off the experimental apparatus, and generally "went to pieces."

Disorganized behavior has been produced in animals by various other methods including simultaneous feeding and punishing. The resulting behavior shows many general similarities to that of human neurotics. Thus in Masserman's experiment,[3] cats displayed "anxiety" by restlessness, trembling, crouching, hiding, and by disturbances of pulse and respiration. Other symptoms included attempting to escape and hiding their heads in the food box without touching the food. Some of the animals starved themselves for long periods of time or took only very small quantities of food. Masserman characterized the behavior of "neurotic" cats as deviant, vacillating, ambivalent, and biologically inefficient.

The experimentally induced disorganization of animals has customarily been referred to as "experimental neurosis." Nevertheless, as Liddell[4] says: "It is regrettable that this designation has become embedded in the literature." Masserman entitled his book on cats *Behavior and Neurosis,* but warned against equating animal neuroses with human neuroses.

> . . . Although the patterns of these phenomena are highly suggestive of their more complex symbolic and persistent counterparts in the human, nevertheless, no cat that I have observed thus far has had the imagery to solve its anxiety by, let us say, strutting, growling, or dressing like Mussolini in overreaction to feline feelings of frustration and inferiority. Similarly, a cat will show experimental behavior abnormalities only if a relatively elemental drive, such as hunger, be frustrated or made internally conflictful.[5]

INTEGRATIVE FUNCTION OF THE CORTEX

Certain similarities of disorganized behavior exist among the various mammals. These are undoubtedly linked with the cortex, which all mammals possess; for disorganization on a cortical level is directly reflected on the motor level. This can be seen in an experiment like the following,[6] in which a general breakdown of ordinary response systems can be brought about in animals and humans alike.

The subject is placed in a room having several exits, all of which are locked except one. While the subject is learning the correct way of escape, he is mildly punished. In this situation the subject quickly learns the correct exit. On a subsequent trial, when punishment is made severe, he frequently becomes upset, excited, and acts blindly. He returns again and again to doors which have already been tried and found to be locked. Disorganization in this experiment results from what Murphy[7] terms "high tension." "The tension level has become so high that the decision process itself is seriously impeded." The simultaneous disruption of many motor-response patterns produced in this experiment is related to disorganization on a cortical level. It is similar to the motor breakdown that ensues when any organism is thrown into a state of panic. In panic there is

a ghastly sensation from within, from all over within . . . nothing remotely like reasoning or the elaboration of sentience . . . a tendency to random activity, but practically no movement of the skeletal system because it is inhibited by diffusion of stimulus and contradictory motor impulses.[8]

Even mass panic, as in an outbreak of fire in a crowded theater, is always preceded by this instant of immobilization or shock.

Despite many similarities between human and animal panic reactions, there are also important differences which must be considered. Human beings usually become panicked in situations which have previously been linguistically defined as fearful or terrifying. There is often a preliminary build-up of anticipation and tension involving rumor, discussion, and the like, as in the situation of the soldier going into combat for the first time.

As one ascends the evolutionary scale, the cortex plays an increasingly important integrative role. The disorganization of behavior changes correspondingly in character. In the lower forms the situations which precipitate confused or disorganized responses involve simple sign situations and elementary biological drives. They have nothing to do with verbal mechanisms or linguistic distinctions. Human conflicts and the disorganization of social responses characteristically occur on a symbolic level, which implies that they involve social situations.

Anyone may easily find in his own experience examples of the disruption of behavior in social situations. The first reaction of a student as he looks at a difficult examination is a case in point. The following are experimentally induced instances of the same reaction. Lewin[9] found differential performances on intellectual tasks in noncompetitive and competitive situations. Under competitive conditions, inefficiencies of behavior were evident. "One rushes ahead to do the immediately necessary thing, instead of holding the action in suspense while getting the over-all picture of what is required."[10] A similar set of reactions was produced in an experiment by Goldworth,[11] who set a time limit for the performance of an intellectual task. In itself this time limitation did not result in disorganized behavior. It did so only when the subject's self-conceptions were disturbed by the possibility and fear of failure in a competitive situation.

The importance of verbal behavior in producing, preventing, and eliminating disorganization on a motor level has been convincingly demonstrated in experiments performed by Luria.[12] Subjects were required to respond to a word stimulus by simultaneously speaking a word and pressing a bulb with the right hand. Movements of the left hand were also recorded without the subjects' knowledge. The responses of subjects ranged from extremely disorganized to well organized. Well-organized people were characterized by synchronization of speech and motor responses, regularity, and so on. Disorganized persons exhibited general lack of coordination. "Every excitation . . . at once passes over without any obstruction to the motor sphere." Luria believes that in the individuals who produced the organized responses, the various requirements of the task are kept at the cortical level until the appropriate motor responses are integrated.

He found, as one would expect, that this regulatory activity works least effectively in children and in the feeble-minded and in normal adults who are fatigued or who are required to perform an extremely difficult task.

INTERFERING BEHAVIOR SYSTEMS

The disintegration of response systems is sometimes connected with the fact that systems may interfere with one another. To take a very simple illustration on the motor level, let the reader attempt to move one hand in a circle parallel to the ground at the same time that he moves the other up and down in a vertical line. A more complex example on another level is that of a woman who loves to eat rich pastry and who also wishes to keep a slim figure.

Behavior systems may interfere with one another in a number of ways. A single dominant system may, for example, simply inhibit all other activity. The reaction of extreme fear is an example of this. Another type of interference may occur when two response patterns are of about equal intensity. In this case, each may intrude upon and interfere with the other. Or the interference may be between two systems of unequal dominance, with the minor one exercising a sort of harassing or heckling effect upon the dominant pattern. The dominant activity may be carried out only with an effort and is likely to produce fatigue. Anyone who has had to force himself to do something will recognize that the task cost him special effort.

Social Bases of Disorganization

We have noted that human behavior is symbolically integrated; hence disturbances on the symbolic level create disturbances on the motor level. Since the possession of given language symbols is dependent upon one's participation in specific social groups, it follows that the genesis and development of disorganization is connected with participation in groups. The structure of personality arises within a social matrix and its maintenance depends in part upon the existence of favorable external conditions. The way people organize or fail to organize their lives reflects to a considerable degree conditions within the social order that includes them. The conflict and competition, the heterogeneous groups and value systems, the inconsistency of the mores, all may be reflected within the person. Troubles which may appear to be purely personal turn out to be social in origin. Personality disorganization is to a considerable extent the consequence of social disorganization.

Psychiatrically oriented investigators tend to equate disorganized behavior with neurotic behavior without realizing that neuroticism is only one type of disorganization. The sources of disorganization are usually traced to childhood experiences within the family group, with little emphasis upon later experiences and upon groups other than the family. The social scientist emphasizes that disorganized behavior includes more than neuroticism, that it may have its sources in a great many types of social situations, including the family group. He notes, too, that disorganization may develop at any time in the individual's life.

Conflicting behavioral patterns or roles, when they are taken over and incorporated within the individual, become focal sources of trouble. This is particularly so when the roles involved are central to the person's integration. Luria's experiments[13] with hypnosis provide excellent examples of how disorganized behavior may be induced in a subject by asking him to play a role that is in sharp conflict with his conception of himself. In one experiment Luria suggested the following to a hypnotized subject:

> You are in great need of money. You go to a friend in order to borrow from him; he is not at home. You decide to wait in his room and suddenly notice on his bureau a wallet fat with money. You open it and find many five-ruble notes. You make a decision; you quickly take the wallet and conceal it on your person. You cautiously go outside and look around to see if you

are detected. You have stolen money and now you are afraid that there will be a search of your home and that they will discover you.

When the hypnotized subject was awakened, he had forgotten what had happened during the hypnotic trance, but various motor and psychological tests showed that his responses were disturbed and disorganized.

CONFLICTING ROLES

That our society is not homogeneous means that persons are often called upon to play incompatible roles or are compelled to choose between two roles, both of which they would like to play. The student can, no doubt, give his own illustrations of conflicting

CONFLICTING STUDENT ROLES

ROLE 1	ROLE 2
Expectations of one's college friends: good joe, parties, campus politics, fraternity affairs, dating, athletics, out with the boys, etc.	Parental expectations: good grades, conscientious study, writing home regularly, spending money carefully, preparing for future occupation, etc.

requirements and choices which are imposed upon him. An instance which has been documented in sociological literature is the conflict between the roles of housewife and career woman. Many women would like to be both but choose one, with a consequent residue of doubt and conflict. Other women combine the roles and often suffer the consequences of trying to reconcile behavior systems which are not entirely compatible with each other.[14]

Gouldner[15] has pointed out that a "progressive" labor leader often has difficulty in reconciling the demands made upon him by his occupational duties with those made upon him by his wife. His role demands long hours, identification with the workers, and working for ideals rather than for personal advancement. In his role as husband the labor leader is expected to provide a comfortable middle-class living for his family and to devote a reasonable proportion of his time to his family. If his wife is a union member herself and continues to take an active interest in union affairs, the conflicts in her husband's roles will be lessened. As Gouldner states:

> For the most part, however, intermarriage among union members, merely retards the wife's propensity to function as a "transmission belt" for the dominant [middle-class] social values.[16]

Conflicting roles on a wider scale may be illustrated by Lynd's summary[17] of major alternative goals in American life:

> . . . [between] saving and spending; between playing safe and "nothing ventured, nothing gained"; between "you've got to look like money in order to make money" and spending your money for things you really want; between (if you are a woman) having "brains" and having "charm"; between things that are "right in theory" and "wrong in practice"; between change and stability; between being loyal and "looking out for Number One"; between being efficient and being human; between being democratic and "getting to know the right people."

UNCOORDINATED ROLES

Roles are always played within a framework or setting which includes the expected responses of others. Because of this interdependence of roles and counter-roles, behavior is thrown into confusion when the responses of others fail to conform to expectations. Social disorganization is said to exist when this lack of coordination of roles becomes general throughout society. Expectations concerning the probable responses to one's behavior constitute the links that bind roles together to form social structures.

Confusion or lack of coordination among the roles that make up a social structure inevitably results in considerable individual confusion. Thus, marital friction in America often reflects the conflicting expectations of husbands and wives owing to the changed functions of the family, new methods of training children, changes in sex mores, the shifting status of women, and so on. A patriarchal husband requires a wife who will play the appropriate counter-role of submissive homemaker and will be mismated with a wife who has equalitarian ideas. Conversely, a submissive woman who likes to feel protected, guided, and dominated will be mismatched with a husband who expects her to be an equal partner in marriage. The poor articulation of roles in these examples illustrates the kinds of uncoordination that are common in complex societies.

LOSS OF FUNCTION

In complex societies many persons are prevented from engaging in activities which seem meaningful for them. The resulting disorganization is manifested in restlessness, bafflement, depression, boredom, irritability, resentment, and in active though erratic attempts to regain a sense of belonging.

The loss of functions of the aged in our society is a striking example. In old and even middle age, persons often find themselves stripped of practically all their important roles. This loss of function sometimes produces profound apathy and melancholy and may even have harmful effects upon the person's health. In some societies elderly people continue to play vital roles, as heads and advisers of large families, as ruling elders, and as repositories of accumulated wisdom. In modern urban America, old people do not ordinarily fulfill any of these functions. Since the American male attaches great importance to his occupation, voluntary or involuntary retirement from active remunerative employment often deprives him of vital props to his self-esteem. The recent popular interest in the problems of the aged has given us a new field of study called gerontology:

it reflects both the increasing average age of our American population and growing recognition of the generally unenviable position of elderly people in our society.

Another instance of significant loss of function is the loss of the parental role in the case of persons who derive fundamental satisfactions from it. This is particularly apparent in the behavior of many middle-aged urban middle-class mothers. Their children, usually few in number, are grown up and relatively independent. The drudgery and satisfaction of child-bearing and child-rearing are largely over. Their husbands are away at work most of the time. There is either relatively little housework to be done, or there are servants available to do it. As a consequence of this situation, many well-educated, capable women exhibit signs of restlessness, irritability, and boredom.

Loss of function may also ensue when persons move from one society to another, provided there is little or no prestige given to accustomed roles in the new milieu. White Russian *emigrés* who are unable to forget their former high status or their consuming hatred of the Soviet Government are interesting instances of this. So too are many refugees and emigrants who previously enjoyed high status, but no longer enjoy it. Thus, a recurring aspect of the unadapted immigrant's behavior is that he talks a great deal about past roles and past status. He escapes into the past because he has lost his function and status in the present.

BARRIERS TO CLASS MOBILITY

In an open class system many people aim for higher rungs on the ladder of success. In America, at least, the way is supposed to be open to all, regardless of race, color, or creed. Hence, there is bound to be a considerable disparity between aspiration and achievement. The competitive, open class system of the United States promotes ambition and thereby intensifies frustrations and discontent on the part of those who do not make the grade. A closed class system, which circumscribes the ambitions of its members, does not produce the same failures and frustrations.

The mythology of American life holds that anyone who works

hard and applies his energies will ultimately be recognized and rewarded in proportion to ability and merit. Despite the fact that only a few reach the pinnacle of success, and in disregard of the almost insuperable barriers to upward mobility faced by some sections of the population because of race, color, or creed, the American credo still insists that any one can get to the top if he "has the right stuff."

All sorts of propaganda and advertising devices operate to raise the level of aspiration and to multiply the probabilities of frustration. We are constantly urged to buy more and better goods, to drive new automobiles rather than old, to buy life insurance, to invest, to save, to spend. The motion pictures daily present alluring pictures of happy, adventurous, well-dressed, opulent, and successful people to millions of aspiring lower- and middle-class Americans. The propaganda and advertising media aid in intensifying our efforts to improve ourselves, to elevate ourselves, to increase our incomes, and to expand our standards of living. The higher a person's ambitions, the greater the probability of discrepancy between hope and accomplishments.

Experimental work on levels of aspiration indicates that people change their aspirations in accordance with their accomplishments. The individual's goals may be differentiated into (1) those he wishes he could attain, (2) those he realistically expects to attain, and (3) the more modest ones to which he can easily reconcile himself. In concrete terms, these points may be illustrated by showing that a B student in college dreams of making straight A's, expects to make B's, but is able to reconcile himself to an occasional C. If he drops below this level he is likely to protest and to be disturbed. He may assert that he has been the victim of injustice or unfair treatment. If a student's grades drop sharply when he goes from high school to college, for example, he is likely to change his aspirations accordingly. Conversely, if they rise, as frequently occurred with veterans who resumed their studies after several years in the army, he may quickly redefine his goals upward. The C minus, which may formerly have been quite satisfactory, now becomes an unexpected failure.

Upward adjustment to income level and social status is easier and pleasanter than downward adjustment. Persons on the lowest income levels aspire to the next higher brackets, and imagine that if they earned $5,000 a year most of their troubles would end, whereas persons on the highest economic levels look upon a reduction to $5,000 a year as a great personal disaster. It is often necessary to scale one's goals downward. Many young men had to do this when they left the army. During periods of deflation and depression, large segments of the population are required to make drastic and painful adjustments of this kind.

In a society like ours, dominated by pecuniary values, the individual's ideas of his personal worth are profoundly affected by the level of his income and the prestige of his occupation. His conception of the social order is strongly colored by his position in it. If it is high, if he has wealth and possessions, and if he is moving upward on the scale or at least maintaining a high position, he is likely to feel contented with the social-economic system and to believe that it distributes rewards in a just manner in accordance with individual merit. Criticisms or expressions of discontent by persons not so well situated as himself may strike him as threats to his security, as dangerous and subversive doctrines.

Personal disorganization may follow as a consequence of not doing so well as one had hoped, or of having to scale one's social and economic aspirations downward in connection with loss or reduction of income. When a broad section of the population is thus affected by loss of confidence in the societal *status quo,* criticisms of the established order and demands for social change may lead to the growth of reform or revolutionary movements.

THE COLLAPSE OF SOCIAL WORLDS

Much demoralization and disorganization occur when the social structure of a country changes rapidly and extensively. The recent war provides many illustrations of such wholesale disorganization. Countless Europeans lost their stable anchorage points. Families were broken up or destroyed. Homes, schools, museums, and libraries disappeared. Persons displaced by the war returned to their communities to find that the people, occupations, institutions, and even the physical landmarks around which their former ambitions and purposes had centered, were gone. In such cases, one may very appropriately speak of the collapse of social worlds.

The shock of these experiences produced different effects in different persons. For some, the tragedy was overwhelming and irretrievable, producing apathy, indifference, or despair. Some sought new occupations and renewed faiths. Others no doubt will live the remainder of their lives in nostalgic memory of the past. Still others have sought refuge in foreign countries.

The Nazi occupation of European countries drove many people to despair and suicide. To some Austrians the Nazi occupation represented an irrevocable doom. The wave of suicides was a symptom of their despair. The journalist Gedye[18] wrote from Austria at the time:

> It is quite impossible to convey to anyone outside Austria in how matter-of-fact a way the Jews of Austria to-day refer to this way out of their agony. . . . Jewish friends spoke to one of their intention to commit suicide with no more emotion than they had formerly talked of making an hour's journey by train . . . it is impossible . . . to imagine what it means for one-sixth of the population of Vienna to be made pariahs over-night, deprived of all civil rights, including the right to retain property large or small, the right to be employed or to give employment, to exercise a profession, to enter restaurants, cafés, bathing beaches, baths or public parks, to be faced daily and hourly, without hope of relief, with the foulest insults which ingenious and vicious minds can devise, to be liable always to be turned over-night out of house and home, and at any hour of every day and every night to arrest without the pretense of a charge or hope of a definite sentence, however heavy—and with all this to find every country in the world selfishly closing its frontiers to you when, after being plundered of your last farthing, you seek to escape. For most of the non-Jewish victims of the Nazis, many of whom are now sharing the punishment of the Jews, there is a hope that one day the nightmare may pass. For the Jews there is none while the Nazis rule.

At the close of the war the counterpart of this phenomenon occurred as the Nazi leaders, in their turn, saw their world falling about them. Durkheim[19] has described this type of suicide as "anomic suicide." He contrasted it with another type of suicide which he called "altruistic." Rather than representing despair and reflecting group disorganization, this "altruistic" kind of self-destruction indicates a high degree of social integration. The Japanese practice of hara-kiri is an example, as is the Indian custom of suttee and the former European military tradition which led defeated generals to "fall upon their swords."

There are, of course, catastrophes other than those attending war that result in widespread feelings that the moral and social bases of existence have collapsed. Severe depressions and inflations deprive entire populations of stable economic and moral reference points and are accompanied by the usual signs of disorganized behavior. Personal disasters of various kinds may produce similar effects.

DEPRIVATION SITUATIONS

Human responses to deprivation of fundamental needs such as those for food, shelter, warmth, and sexual expression furnish excellent examples of ways in which the exaggeration of one set of responses may interfere with or lead to the disintegration of others. The individual who becomes preoccupied with securing something he is deprived of tends to subordinate other activities to this end. If the deprivation is severe and prolonged, pathological forms of behavior and substitute satisfactions may appear, and the person may even lose or violate his moral, esthetic, and ethical standards. As Sherif[20] has said of the person in a deprivation situation: "His perceptions, memories, imagination, and, if circumstances permit, his actions are colored accordingly."

A recent experimental study of the starvation of human subjects has documented these effects.[21] Thirty-six men who volunteered for the experiment were placed on an inadequate diet for six months and carefully observed. All of the subjects were in good health, between the ages of twenty and thirty-three, and of more than average intelligence. During the course of the experiment the subjects lost interest in music, recreation, intellectual matters, and in anything not connected with food. All of them knew in advance the purposes of the experiment, but in spite of this some resorted to theft to increase their supplies of food. Day dreaming about food tended to interfere with every other activity. The subjects lost interest in sex. In some instances, former attachments completely collapsed.

Information concerning other deprivation situations, such as sexual frustration, imprisonment, and confinement in concentration and detention camps, confirms this general picture. In the case of hunger the assessment of effects is complicated by the physical deterioration brought about by semistarvation. However, somewhat similar effects often occur among prisoners in penitentiaries who are deprived of their freedom although given adequate quantities of food. The prisoner's perspectives often become narrowed down and focused upon certain limited matters in much the same exclusive way that the hungry man concentrates on food. Thus, the prisoner may spend his time devising schemes for getting himself released; he may brood over real or fancied injustices; or he may nourish bitter hatreds. The effects of sexual deprivation follow the same general pattern, to the extent that prisoners' heterosexual patterns of behavior sometimes break down and change to homosexual patterns.

FAILURE IN BASIC ROLES

Severe disorganization of behavior is brought about when a person conceives that he has failed in a basic role. This is equivalent to saying that he assumes certain activities to be so important that if he fails in performing them, he believes himself a failure as a human being.

Among the more important types of failure are those which cast fundamental doubt upon one's worth as a man or woman. The point may be illustrated by the behavior of an American soldier who believed his genitals had been shot away, although actually they were only slightly and temporarily injured. The man "went to pieces." While he was unconscious, the doctors treated and bandaged him. When he regained consciousness he looked down at his bandaged pelvic region and, still assuming that his manhood was irrevocably lost, went "berserk" again. The bandages had to be temporarily removed before the patient could be calmed down again. Commoner and milder illustrations of masculinity failure are the reactions of men when they realize that they are sterile. If a man defines his inability to have children merely as a medical matter, his status is not much involved. But if he conceives of this inability as a reflection upon his prowess as a male, upon his essential masculinity, he is likely to exhibit many signs of what has been loosely termed "ego breakdown."

In the Western world, conceptions of masculinity are also organized around occupational status. Hence, the loss of employment represents a severe blow to men who are not accustomed to being unemployed. The following case history, taken from Angell's study[22] of American families during the 1929-1933 depression, describes the responses of a male to his continued unemployment:

> He has completely lost his *role*. He is unable to face what he considers exposure. He considers himself a failure. His inadequacy stands revealed to himself. . . . Without his shield of a good job he cannot face the rest of the world. . . . Very often he talks deprecatingly of himself. Sometimes he will sit for hours and do nothing but stare. He lacks initiative of any sort. He hates activity of any kind, hates to look for work. . . . One feels a tension, a conflict, a strain when he is about. Sometimes when this strain is too great he "goes to pieces" in a most pitiable, horrible way. All his inhibitions, his restraints, are lifted and he reveals all his hurts, his disappointments, frustrations—till it is more than others can bear. . . . He is now incapable of making the least decision for himself—for instance, to wear or not to wear a coat is a source of conflict.

Lazarsfeld and Zeisl[23] have described how an entire village can become apathetic, resigned, and vegetative when unemployment is general and chronic.

Failure in a basic role almost necessarily spreads to other associated roles. Under certain conditions virtually all of an individual's central roles may be involved. The experience of concentration-camp victims is a case in point. The Nazis developed a series of techniques designed to humiliate, defile, and degrade their prisoners and to break down self-respect. Prisoners were required to do such things as to strike each other, to curse God, to declare their wives to be prostitutes, and to accuse themselves of vile actions. One of the Nazis' victims, Bettelheim,[24] kept a careful account of the progressive deterioration that resulted. He himself managed to escape the more extreme effects by virtue of focusing upon his study, thus maintaining, as he notes, his self-respect and his conception of himself as a scientist.

Reactions to the initial shock of seizure by the Gestapo seemed to depend upon previous group memberships and associated self-conceptions. Politically educated prisoners were proud that they were important or dangerous enough to attract the Gestapo's attention. Nonpolitical, middle-class prisoners were confused; they were convinced that their seizure was a mistake. They resented being treated like ordinary criminals. After some time, when they realized the actual situation, "they disintegrated." Suicides characterized this group. They lost their middle-class sense of propriety and self-respect. Upper-class people were generally unable to accept the the realities of the situation and assumed that they would soon be released because of their importance or prominence.

The first major reaction to Nazi brutalities within the camps consisted of a kind of "dissociation." Prisoners experienced a sense of detachment as though these things were not real or could not be happening to them. "It was as if what happened did not 'really' happen to oneself. There was . . . the split between the 'me' to whom it happened, and the 'me' who really did not care and was a detached observer."[25]

The most general long-run effect of concentration-camp treatment, as described by Bettelheim, was to break down "adult frames of reference." The prisoner's conception of himself as an adult was gradually destroyed as he was cursed, slapped, and pushed around like a child. Inmates were compelled to do such things as to soil themselves, to obtain permission to eliminate, and to say "thou" to one another, which in German is used indiscriminately only among small children. They also felt debased by the performance of childish and senseless tasks, such as carrying heavy rocks from one place to another and back again. As a final consequence, many inmates internalized the values of the Gestapo. They began to use the vocabulary of the guards, and later they applied some of the guards' brutal techniques to one another. Prisoners imitated the dress of the Nazis, prided themselves on being as tough, and copied their recreations. "One of the games played by the guards was to find out who could stand to be hit longest without uttering a complaint. This game was copied by old prisoners."[26]

Adjustments to Conflict

There are relatively patterned ways of minimizing friction and conflict and of dealing with it when it occurs. Toby,[27] for instance, has noted the following specific means of dealing with conflicting role requirements: (1) repudiating one of the roles, (2) playing off one group against another by explaining to each the conflicting demands made by the other, thus mitigating their demands, (3) stalling for time and allowing pressure to subside, (4) redefining the situation, (5) leading a double life, playing the appropriate role in each situation but keeping them separate so that the conflict is not obvious to others, (6) escaping from the situation by changing environments, and (7) becoming ill under the pressure and thus acquiring a socially acceptable excuse for failing to do what would otherwise be expected.

All of these, except the tactic of changing one's environment or escaping, may be thought of as involving the attainment of some degree of integration by renaming and regrouping the elements of the situation. We have already discussed this type of adjustment under the title of "rationalization" and in the chapter on personality change (pp. 297-300 and 587-588). That is what happens when psychiatrists succeed in getting their patients "to see things differently." It also happens in the course of everyday life as friends confide in each other, give each other advice, and, in general, change each other's perspectives concerning their own acts and roles. In this way they help one another over rough spots. Catharsis, or the talking out of one's problems, often involves just such reconstructing or rationalizing. Conversion as it takes place in a religious revival is another instance of the some process.

Disorganization of a temporary character, such as that produced by having an automobile accident, usually signalizes the beginning of a new sequence of organized behavior after the initial shock has been assimilated. The occupants of the car, if relatively uninjured, may at first feel at a loss and be upset by the turn of events, but quickly become involved in reporting the accident, doing something about the car, and informing their friends of the enforced changes in their plans. A certain amount of disorganization is an inevitable accompaniment of any change or reorganization of behavior. Taken in small doses, it is a stimulus to learning and growth.

The phenomenon of dissociation is a special type of restructuring. It consists of the carrying out of potentially conflicting lines of conduct without permitting them to come into actual conflict. This is achieved, it is sometimes said, by keeping them apart in "logic-tight compartments"—which means either (1) that the incompatible elements of the systems are not perceived by the person, or (2) that a satisfactory rationalization of some kind is created to account for the incompatibility. A standard example of the first situation is provided by the devout businessman who does not see any elements of conflict between business and Christian ethics. An example of the second kind of adjustment is that made by the orthodox Jewish people who live in predominantly Gentile communities where it is difficult for them to keep up the practices of their faith. At first, they experience some feelings of guilt and emotional disturbance, but eventually they solve their problems by such rationalizations as: "To be successful I have to live like other people"; or "It is hard to be orthodox in a Gentile community and I am no martyr."

A common kind of dissociation occurred during the recent war: married soldiers engaged in illicit sex affairs while remaining "subjectively" loyal to their wives. Departures from strict marital fidelity were rationalized in terms of a dichotomy between sex and marriage. As one observer has phrased it:[28]

. . . They would talk to me for hours about their wives, their families if they had any, and their plans for the future of their family. Frequently, however, the morning after one of these talks, they would tell me in jocose fashion about some gal they had slept with the night before. There was no embarrassment about such confessions and probably a few hours later they would be telling me again how much they loved their wives. The explanation, I am sure, lies in the complete dissociation in the minds of these particular soldiers between their wives and families, on the one hand, and the necessity of relieving their glandular pressures on the other. In their eyes, there is no connection between these two things.

Summary

Complex human response patterns develop within and depend upon the social environment. Consequently, they may become disorganized through the operation of pressures, external to the individual, which originate within group life. Disorganized behavior may take a number of forms—of which neuroticism is only one. Conflicting and uncoordinated roles, the collapse of social worlds, deprivation, and failure in basic roles are illustrations of the manner in which individual disorganization may reflect external social conditions. Individuals may successfully adapt themselves to disharmonius features of their social environment by various devices which eliminate or mitigate the effects of the conflicting demands. Dissociation permits a person to engage in inconsistent or contradictory behavior patterns without being aware of the potential conflict. We turn next to forms of behavior that are easily confused with those discussed in this chapter, but which are of a fundamentally different character.

SUGGESTIONS FOR DISCUSSION AND SPECIAL REPORTS

1. Contrast different explanations of suicide, especially those offered by psychiatry and sociology.

2. Under conditions of great stress, such as starvation, it is said that the veneer of culture is stripped off and that men regress to animal-like behavior. To what extent do you agree?

3. What happens to persons during a community disaster, such as an earthquake, an air raid, or a tornado? Be sure and distinguish panic behavior from disaster behavior.

4. Analyze some of the role conflicts of American women as revealed in magazine stories.

5. Edmund Burke once said that "A very great part of the mischiefs that vex this world arises from words." Discuss the implications of this statement.

6. Report on some of the psychological consequences of unemployment during depressions; for instance, are men or women more greatly affected?

7. Are "work" and "play" supplementary or opposing activities? Trace the relations of work and play in two or more different societies or social classes.

8. Report on some "crises of conscience" and role dilemmas which appear in different types of motion pictures.

NOTES

[1] A. A. Angyal, *Foundations for a Science of Personality,* New York: The Commonwealth Fund, 1941, p. 303.

[2] I. P. Pavlov, *Conditioned Reflexes,* London: Oxford University Press, 1927, pp. 290-292.

[3] J. H. Masserman, *Behavior and Neurosis,* University of Chicago Press, 1943.

[4] H. S. Liddell, in J. McV. Hunt (ed.), *Personality and the Behavior Disorders,* Vol. I, Ronald, 1944, "Conditioned Reflex Method and Experimental Neurosis," p. 404.

[5] J. H. Masserman, "Psychobiologic Dynamisms in Behavior," *Psychiatry,* 5(1942): 346.

[6] G. V. Hamilton, "A Study of Trial and Error Reactions in Mammals," *J. Animal Beh.,* 1 (1911): 33-66.

[7] G. Murphy, *Personality,* Harper, 1947, p. 312.

[8] H. S. Sullivan, "Psychiatric Aspects of Morale," *Am. J. Soc.,* 47(1941): 279.

9 K. Lewin, "Intelligence and Motivation," *Yearbk. Nat. Soc. Stud. Educ.*, 39(1940): 297-305.

10 Murphy, *op. cit.*, p. 308.

11 Unpublished study cited in Murphy, *op. cit.*, p. 308.

12 A. R. Luria, *The Nature of Human Conflicts*, Liveright, 1932.

13 *Ibid.*, p. 140.

14 See M. Komarovsky, "Cultural Contradictions and Sex Roles," *Am. J. Soc.*, 52(1946): 184-189.

15 A. Gouldner, "Attitudes of 'Progressive' Trade-Union Leaders," *Am. J. Soc.*, 52(1947): 389-392.

16 *Ibid.*, p. 391.

17 R. S. Lynd, *Knowledge for What?* Princeton University Press, 1939, p. 103.

18 G. E. Gedye, *Fallen Bastions*, London: Victor Gollancz, 1939, p. 305.

19 E. Durkheim, *Le Suicide*, Paris: Alcan, 1897.

20 M. Sherif, *An Outline of Social Psychology*, Harper, 1948, p. 408.

21 A. Keys, J. Broyels, A. Henschel, O. Mickelsen, and H. L. Taylor, *Experimental Starvation in Men*, Lab. of Physiological Hygiene, University of Minnesota, 1945.

22 R. C. Angell, *The Family Encounters the Depression*, Scribner, 1936, p. 201.

23 M. Lazarsfeld and H. Zeisl, "Die Arbeitslosen von Marienthal," *Psych. Monographen*, 4(1935).

24 B. Bettelheim, "Individual and Mass Behavior in Extreme Situations," in T. M. Newcomb and E. L. Hartley (eds.), *Readings in Social Psychology*, Holt, 1947, pp. 628-638. For the original and fuller account, see also an article of the same title in the *J. Ab. and Soc. Psych.*, 38 (1943): 417-452.

25 *Ibid.*, pp. 632-633.

26 *Ibid.*, p. 637.

27 J. Toby, "Variables in Role Conflict Analysis," *Soc. Forces*, 30 (1952): 323-327.

28 From document quoted in M. Sherif and H. Cantril, *The Psychology of Ego Involvements*, Wiley, 1947, p. 390.

SELECTED BIBLIOGRAPHY

Angell, R. C., *The Family Encounters the Depression*, Scribner, 1936. A study of personal and marital problems resulting from the impact of the depression.

Angyal, A. A., *Foundations for a Science of Personality*, New York: The Commonwealth Fund, 1941. Chap. IX, "Disturbances of Integration," pp. 303-342. Suggestive and systematic treatment of personal disorganization by a psychiatrist.

Benedict, R., "Continuities and Discontinuities in Cultural Conditioning," *Psychiatry*, 1(1938): 161-167. Individual problems arising as a result of movement from one age group to another.

Bloch, H. A., "The Personality of Inmates of Concentration Camps,"

Am. J. Soc., 52(1947): 335-341. Description of the effects of concentration camp experiences.

Blumer, H., "Social and Individual Disorganization," *Am. J. Soc.*, 42 (1939): 871-877. A theoretical treatment of the relations between individual and social disorganization.

Gouldner, A., "Attitudes of 'Progressive' Trade Union Leaders," *Am. J. Soc.*, 52(1947): 389-392. Analyzes the clash of loyalties associated with the office of progressive trade union leader.

Hughes, E. C., "Dilemmas and Contradictions of Status," *Am. J. Soc.*, 50(1945): 353-359. This paper is concerned with the incompatible requirements which almost any role entails.

Hulett, T. E. J., "Social Role and Personal Security in Mormon Polygamy," *Am. J. Soc.*, 45(1940): 542-554. The unstable position of the Mormon male under a system of polygamy.

Komarovsky, M., "Cultural Contradictions and Sex Roles," *Am. J. Soc.*, 52(1946): 184-189. Descriptive study of some dilemmas of American college women.

Liddell, H. S., "Conditioned Reflex Method and Experimental Neurosis," in J. McV. Hunt (ed.), *Personality and the Behavior Disorders*, Vol. I, Ronald, 1944, pp. 389-412. Useful as a source of information on the literature of animal neuroses.

Luria, A., *The Nature of Human Conflict*, Liveright, 1932. A brilliant experimental study packed with information about the mechanics of disorganized behavior. Not easy reading.

Lynd, R. S., and H. M. Lynd, *Middletown in Transition*, Harcourt, Brace, 1937. Replete with illustrative materials on the contradictory values in American life.

Thomas, W. I., and F. Znaniecki, *The Polish Peasant in Europe and America*, Knopf, 1927 (4th printing). Especially Vol. II. Illustrates with a wealth of materials the disorganization connected with movement from one culture to another.

Toby, J., "Variables in Role Conflict Analysis," *Soc. Forces*, 30(1952): 323-327. A sociological approach to the study of personality disorganization.

Turner, R., "The Navy Disbursing Officer as a Bureaucrat," *Am. Soc. Rev.*, 12(1947): 342-348. The role conflicts of this office, and the solutions taken by the officer.

PART 6

DEVIATION

CHAPTER 20 · · ·

Individual

Deviation

By the term "individual deviation" we refer to behavior labeled as "deviant" or "abnormal" which does not have a cultural base: that is, it is not prescribed as customary by a group. Some of these forms of deviation arise from biological causes and others from what may be called personal, or personal-social, causes. Many do not constitute clearly defined behavioral entities, and many are incompletely understood. Some are not the primary concern of social psychologists, but preoccupy rather the biologist, the psychiatrist, and the clinical psychologist. However, there are aspects of individual deviation which bear directly upon the problems of social psychology, particularly the deficient socialization of the subnormal person, the desocialization of the psychotic, and the social patterning of deviancy. In the next chapter, by way of contrast, we shall discuss groups which are deviant.

The Subnormal

In a preceding chapter, "Social Isolation and Speech Pathology," we discussed mentally retarded persons with regard to levels of behavioral organization. The point stressed there was that because of biological defect—or, as some psychiatrists argue, possibly also because of early learning experiences[1]—complex mental processes are retarded or absent, and behavior is organized on lower levels than are normal. Here we wish to emphasize that the behavior of such subnormal persons is generally considered as peripheral or deviant to that of the rest of the community. Except for the most intellectually competent of them, they are often placed in custodial institutions or are, at best, cared for by their families, who label them as "different" and sometimes "mentally deficient" or "feeble-minded." Hence the retarded have sometimes been referred to as "unsocialized," insofar as they are wholly unable or only partially able to participate in normal social relations.

Subnormal persons are generally classified into three groups according to ascending intelligence and social sufficiency: idiot, imbecile, and moron. There are, however, no sharp dividing lines; the terms are simply convenient labels for indicating approximate degrees of social and intellectual deficiencies.

The lowest type, idiots, do not learn even the simplest occupational tasks. They cannot take care of their own ordinary physical needs or protect themselves from ordinary dangers. Their mental insufficiency is so marked that they are incapable of the simplest forms of speech.[2] They may be viewed as "isolated men" who, though surrounded by socialized humans, are unsocialized. Lacking the biological equipment necessary to grasp language, they are consequently outside the working framework of society, except in the sense that they are fed, clothed, housed, and otherwise cared for. Idiots have been appropriately described as vegetative.

Imbeciles can be trained with difficulty to care for themselves, to protect themselves from danger, and, under supervision, to handle simple tasks. They may learn simple forms of speech but show a marked poverty of ideas. That they must be institutionalized or carefully supervised suggests that they fail to grasp the more complex meanings implicit in ordinary social situations. The imbecile, for example, cannot be expected to understand such intricacies of role-playing as are involved in marital relations.

Morons, who are the highest type among the subnormal, are only relatively mildly retarded and can sometimes live reasonably normal lives provided their jobs are simple and demands upon them are not complicated. This relative normalcy may include marriage and raising a family. In many matters, however, the moron "resembles persons of a much younger age than his own."[3]

Most mentally retarded persons are harmless and are tolerated or taken care of outside of institutions; the lower grades, of course, are institutionalized more frequently than the higher. The retarded adolescent, because of his general inability to internalize social norms, may fall into antisocial behavior, including especially sexual delinquency. When this happens he is likely to be considered "morally depraved" or "degenerate" and treated accordingly. Hence the term "sex moron." Specialists interested in the training and care of these persons argue that such definitions are wrong and therefore seek to substitute other definitions for the deviant behavior. Generally, they wish to view these problems as medical or clinical rather than moral or criminal.

The social definitions applied to the mentally retarded vary tremendously by era and place, being related not merely to the state of knowledge but also to the period's religious and social philosophies. The retarded are, for example, no longer regarded as "possessed," although they are still often punished for legal transgressions, particularly if these are sex offences or violent crimes.

The current concern with euthanasia, or "mercy killing," of the mentally deficient reflects the decline of powerful religious sanctions against the taking of human life, even when that life is one of hopeless vegetative idiocy. Recent cases widely reported in the newspapers indicate that sometimes physicians deliberately allow grossly defective infants to die, if indeed they do not actually kill them. Sometimes, as in a case known to the authors, a defective child is allowed to die with the prior consent of the parents.

The Psychotic

Like the mentally retarded, psychotic persons are found the world over. All psychotics engage in some form of bizarre, peculiar, unusual, or annoying behavior. Most of them exhibit traits which are detrimental or dangerous to themselves or others, involving disorientation, confusion, suicidal or homicidal tendencies, and other gross inabilities at self-management. Disturbance of emotion, thought, and social relations are usual; and speech subnormalities, memory defects, and motor disorders are common. Other prominent symptoms are delusions, mental confusion, depression, disorientation, hallucinations, destructiveness, apathy, elation, and stupor.

From the standpoint of the social psychologist, the chief characteristic of psychoses is that they involve serious impairment or complete breakdown of the basic mechanisms of communication. Because of this disorder, the psychotic individual is generally isolated from the society of his fellows. He is not only unable to communicate effectively or to form social groups with other psychotics, but he is also largely beyond the reach of normal persons who seek to establish verbal contact with him. In contrast to feeble-minded persons, who are unsocialized or incompletely socialized, psychotics may be described as desocialized. They are people who were once relatively normal and who no longer are.

Social criteria are crucial in defining mental retardation and psychoses, for psychoses presuppose prior normality and infants are rarely called psychotics. The infant born with a serious cerebral defect is appropriately designated as defective or feeble-minded rather than psychotic, if the defect prevents him from learning a language and from developing the complex mental abilities that are taken for granted in normal persons. If a similar structural defect of the brain appears later in life, after the individual has learned a language and becomes socialized, it is likely to produce an organic psychosis. The defect in this case leads to behavioral symptoms, such as language disorders and delusions, which do not appear in individuals who are feeble-minded from birth. A cerebral defect in later life brings about a breakdown of mental functions and communication; in the infant, it simply prevents mental functions and communication from developing.

The psychotic individual has learned the fundamental symbolic devices in use in his society, and for a time has used them in the standard manner. The onset of the psychotic condition is marked by eccentric use of words and by other overt behavior of a disorganized kind. These symptoms indicate that the internal symbolic processes by means of which ordinary adults control their behavior are not functioning smoothly. If severe deterioration occurs, virtually all communication ceases and the higher mental functions disintegrate.

In most cases, however, the psychotic continues to use language. He talks, but he does not talk like other people. The meanings which he seems to attach to words are private and unshared rather than public and shared. His talk has the characteristics of "double talk." The listener who is unaware of the psychotic condition may for a time struggle to follow the apparent trend of the person's remarks, but as absurdities multiply he realizes that there is something wrong. No longer able to regard the psychotic's words as symbols, he responds to them as mere signs or symptoms of a mental disorder.

THE ORGANIC PSYCHOSES

Psychoses with definite and known organic bases are termed "organic," in contrast to the "functional" psychoses, which have no definite organic bases that have yet been discovered. In organic psychoses the varied psychological manifestations are symptoms rather than underlying causative factors. The disorders may therefore be described as fundamentally organic with symbolic symptoms as secondary features. Therapy must necessarily be primarily medical, although, as doctors know, there is a sense in which psychotherapy is involved in all medical treatment.

Organic psychoses are produced by a wide variety of conditions. Infection and intoxication are common sources. Thus, when syphilis invades the central nervous system, as it does in perhaps five percent of the cases, paresis sets in. The symptoms of paresis may take various forms, some of which resemble those of other types of mental disease. If the disease is not checked, the deterioration of all mental functions continues until it is complete and ends in death. Alcoholic psychoses, derived from intoxication, are of two principal types: temporary and permanent. Delirium tremens is the temporary type; if the patient successfully passes through the immediate period of alcohol withdrawal, he recovers normality. The permanent psychosis resulting from the destruction of tissue through long-continued abuse of alcohol is called Korsakow's psychosis. Psychotic conditions may also be brought about, either temporarily or permanently, by sleeping sickness, the use of drugs, or by disturbances in the cerebral circulatory system due to cerebral embolism (blood clot) or hardening of the arteries (cerebral arteriosclerosis). Other types of organic psychoses may follow from injury or accident, from disturbances of metabolism, nutrition, or endocrine function, and from brain tumors.

The types we have mentioned by no means cover the entire field; they have been presented primarily as illustrations. From the point of view of the social psychologist, the organic psychoses are of interest mainly as illustrations of desocialization through disorders, diseases, and injuries of the central nervous system.

THE FUNCTIONAL PSYCHOSES

The existing categories of the functional psychoses do not represent a genuine classification of separate diseases, but merely of symptom complexes, or syndromes. This may be explained, in part, by the complexity and overlapping of symptoms. The specific category in which a given individual is placed often depends not on the presence or absence of certain symptoms but on their relative prominence in the total clinical picture. It is therefore quite common for experts to diagnose the disorder of the same patient differently without having any definitive way of settling the disagreement. The three major types of functional psychoses are manic-depressive psychosis, paranoia, and schizophrenia.

The dominant feature of manic-depressive psychosis is its pattern of violent emotional changes or cycles. In the manic phase the psychological processes speed along in high gear. The patient is overactive, overexhilarated, overtalkative, and seems almost immune to fatigue. In the depressed stage, the situation is reversed. The patient is slow or depressed in all his reactions and deeply melancholic.

The chief features of paranoia are systematic delusions of grandeur or of persecution and misinterpretations of actual events to fit in with and support the delusion. The patient broods and fantasies about the intentions and goals of other persons, consistently misconstruing them in accordance with his own ideas of grandeur or persecution. As the paranoiac becomes more and more involved in his delusions he tends to become increasingly isolated socially, withdrawing into his own inner world. There is considerable overlapping of symptoms between this type of psychosis and the paranoid type of schizophrenia.

Schizophrenia, as previously noted (pp. 152-155), is characterized by withdrawal from and loss of contact with the outside world. The schizophrene, typically, is almost exclusively wrapped up in his own inner world. As Page says:[4] "They are solitary individuals who rarely associate or converse with others. A group of patients may share the same ward for years and never exchange a word with one another or learn the identity of their wardmates. Each is exclusively preoccupied with his own private world." A striking illustration of the schizophrene's isolation from the world of reality is the manner in which the heavy bombings of London during World War II failed to make any impression upon patients of this type in the wards of the London hospitals. Amid all the uproar and confusion they continued to be almost completely engrossed in their own private ideas and delusions.

Schizophrenes often find highly fanciful meanings in the actions of other people. As their thought becomes disorganized, they may become certain that hypnotism is being practiced upon them, that the atmosphere is being poisoned, that their minds are being read, and that they are being controlled by sinister outside agencies. The patient sometimes believes that diabolical machines are being used upon him or that peculiar changes are occurring within his body. Preoccupation with sexual and religious matters is common. Hallucinations are very frequent. There may be unaccountable shifts in affection and hate, and other incongruous emotional reactions. The patient is often, but not always, indifferent and apathetic.

It is often assumed that the functional psychoses are psychological in nature and origin. This point of view is by no means established, even though there is some evidence to support it. Many competent observers are convinced that the functional psychoses are fundamentally organic in character, but that the organic basis is of such a nature as to be undemonstrable by existing techniques. Some notion of the disagreement that exists concerning the etiology of the functional psychoses may be obtained from Cameron's brief summary of the theories of schizophrenia. He notes:

> Some writers have regarded schizophrenia as a form of regression. Piaget puts schizophrenic thought at a point somewhere between the ego-centric thought of the child and that of a normal intelligent adult. Freud described it as regression to infantile narcissism, and others have compared schizophrenic thought with that of primitive man. It has also been described as reduction in association tension, loss of thought initiative, intra-psychic ataxia, reduction in the range of attention and in central control, agnosia and apraxia of thought, overdevelopment of inner inhibitions, regression to concrete and perceptual thought from an abstract conceptual level, and as social disarticulation. Some writers believe that there is essential psychological continuity from the normal to the clearly schizophrenic, while others believe that there is a definite chasm or break between them which can only be accounted for in terms of some organic disorder.[5]

Although this controversy has not been settled, the burden of proof seems to rest with the "functionalists." There has been a great deal of research on the physiological, structural, and biochemical conditions associated with the functional psychoses. Although decisive results have not been attained, differences of glandular function, reduced physiological responsiveness to stimulants, and other physiological or biochemical differences between these psychotics and normal persons have frequently been noted. The results have strengthened the conviction of some scientists that a definite organic basis of the functional psychoses will ultimately be discovered. It has led other scientists, however, to draw exactly the opposite conclusion. Recent successes in treating functional psychoses by brain surgery and shock therapy tend also to support the structural or organic view, though they by no means validate it completely. The whole position of the functionalists is weakened by the circumstance that some mental disorders which were once believed to be psychogenic in origin are now known to be organic, as for example, paresis.

It is curious today to note that Boyle in 1826 attributed the high incidence of paresis among men to mental shock and excessive drinking. He also stated that its higher incidence among soldiers than among civilians was due to even more excessive drinking, to privations, and to the French soldiers great disappointment at the defeat of Napoleon. T. Kellogg in 1897 asserted that "civilization favors general paresis through the demands which it makes on physical and mental powers, competition, reckless and feverish pursuit of wealth and social position, overstudy, overwork, unhygienic modes of life, the massing of people in large cities."

In an interesting recent article an anonymous psychiatrist[6] expresses skepticism concerning the psychogenic nature of neuroses and psychoses and the effectiveness of psychotherapy. He states that in 1954 "only one mental disease was really being cured,"[7] namely syphilis of the brain, and adds that "It is certain that many other major types of mental disorder will eventually be found to have a physical basis." He expresses his doubts concerning the effectiveness of psychotherapy in reducing the prevalence of mental disorder. His doubts on this score are shared by others. Eysenck[8] for example, notes that if present evidence is taken at face value it appears that approximately two out of three cases of mental disorder recover under psychotherapy, and that the proportion of recoveries for those who do not receive psychotherapy is also two out of three.

According to the "structuralists," social and psychological manifestations of a psychosis are merely symptoms. The functionalists, on the other hand, formulate theories of the origin of the functional psychoses which take these symptoms into account as causative factors. Thus, Cameron[9] has proposed that paranoia is due essentially to deficiency in role-playing. The individual develops persecutory ideas which grow into elaborate systems because he cannot adequately communicate with others. He is unable to rid himself of his delusions or to correct them on the basis of experience because the ideas are of such a nature as to preclude the possibility of self-correction. Every experience of the paranoiac, as he himself perceives it, reinforces his beliefs. The more elaborate the system becomes, the more difficult it is to change it. The paranoiac eventually, according to Cameron, comes to live in an unreal world or "pseudo-community" of persecuting persons. Cameron's statement may be regarded either as a theory of the causes of paranoia or as a mere description of the typical course of its symptoms.

The structuralist and functionalist views generally rest upon a mind-body dualism. The functionalists think in terms of a disembodied "psyche" influencing the "body." The structuralists view the body as the only substantial reality and dismiss the "mind" as something spiritual and intangible. A nondualistic vocabulary for the discussion of these problems is not available.

However, an interesting nondualistic approach to the problem of the functional psychoses has been presented by the French psychiatrist Blondel.[10] Although his theory is unverified, it presents an interesting compromise between the extremes of the dualistic position. According to Blondel, the ordinary responses of an individual presuppose a background of internal stimuli arising from the various parts of the body and from normal physiological reactions. He calls these internal stimuli the "kinesthetic mass." In the nonpsychotic person these processes are the setting within which the higher functions occur. The socialized individual responds to these internal stimuli in terms of the categories provided by the society of which he is a member. Thus, people respond to certain types of internal stimulation by reporting: "I am hungry" or "My foot is asleep."

Blondel believes that in the psychotic this kinesthetic mass is disturbed so that he becomes aware of internal stimuli which cannot be taken care of with the usual labels. He develops the notion that curious and fantastic things are happening within him. When he attempts to describe his experiences to other people he finds that they do not understand him and hence regard his remarks as queer or crazy. Their response leads him to withdraw, and this in turn accentuates the break in communication.

Finding himself rebuffed by others, the psychotic withdraws into his own private world but continues to attempt to adapt himself verbally to his strange sensations. In his struggle to assimilate his essentially unique and unassimilable experiences, he builds up ideas which seem fantastic and senseless to others. The curious speech and distorted reasoning of the psychotic, as conceived of by Blondel, is an attempted symbolic adaptation to an organic disturbance. The origin and nature of this organic disturbance are not accounted for by Blondel. Presumably, however, the disorder would be in the central nervous system, whatever its causes might be.

Blondel's theory, whether or not it will stand the test of verification, has interesting implications because it avoids the usual mind-body fallacy. Even if all the psychoses should turn out to have organic causes, the study of psychological symptoms would not be irrelevant to the study and understanding of psychotics.

H. S. Sullivan's conception of schizophrenia is something like Blondel's, for he too stresses the crucial role of the uncanny and of the inability to communicate and designate it. But he does not make physiological stimuli the cornerstone of his analysis.

> In the schizophrenia state, very early types of referential process occur within clear awareness, to the profound mystification of the person concerned. And since many of these referential processes are literally historically identical with the composition of the not-me components in personality, their presence is attended by uncanny emotions. . . . [These] schizophrenic processes which we encounter represent attempts on the sufferer's part to

communicate types of processes that most of us ceased to have within awareness by the time that we were two-and-a-half.[11]

SOCIAL STRUCTURE AND PSYCHIATRIC DISORDERS

As already indicated, the psychiatric disorders are not fixed disease entities but are vaguely defined, overlapping collections of symptoms the etiology of which is not understood. These symptoms appear to vary by class, region, and society. This apparent variation suggests that the social structure plays a complex role in influencing the symptomatology of mental disease.

Ethnic Variations · Certain symptom complexes characteristically appear only, or primarily, among certain peoples. Anthropologists have noted instances of this sort: *e.g.*, an obsession with cannibalism or a compulsive craving for human flesh has been reported to exist in certain Eskimo and Indian tribes and in the Marquesas Islands. The classical area of this obsession, known as the "Witiko psychosis," lies between Lake Winnipeg and Labrador, that is, in the territory of the Cree and Ojibwa Indians. Another symptom complex which is similarly limited to certain areas is "running amok," which is fairly frequent among such groups as the Malayans, Balinese, Fuegians, Melanesians, and Siberians and in India. Arctic hysteria, involving the mechanical repetition of words and phrases addressed to the victim, is said to be another example of such a localized disorder.

Carothers,[12] in a study of mental illness among Africans in mental hospitals, reports that there is a relative absence of cerebral arteriosclerosis, obsessional neurosis, ideas of guilt, and involutional melancholia in the African hospitals. In India, schizophrenia is reported to be infrequent, and there is a much higher incidence of manic-depressive psychosis than of other types of psychosis.

Urban Patterns of Distribution · In the United States, several studies have shown wide discrepancies in symptomatology by areas within cities and by social classes. Faris and Dunham[13] and other investigators have shown that the known incidence of most types of psychotic disorders is highest near the center of the city and declines in all directions outward. Different types of psychosis exhibit different patterns of distribution within a city but there is little agreement on the precise character of these patterns or on how they may be explained.

Since these studies necessarily deal with known cases, it has been argued that the differences in the rates for various areas merely reflect the differences in detection, recording, and perhaps diagnosis of cases rather than the actual incidence. It is also possible that higher rates in the center of a city are the results of statistical error, stemming from differential rates of transience.

Mental Disorder and Social Classes · Another theory, called the "drift hypothesis," is that the mentally abnormal tend to migrate to slum areas as a result of social failure. This idea has recently been tested in a careful study made by Hollingshead and Redlich[14] in New Haven, Connecticut. They point out that with respect to schizophrenics, the drift hypothesis assumes two things: (1) that schizophrenia occurs randomly in the population, and (2) that because of social incompetence, schizophrenic persons tend to drift downward in the class structure and into corresponding geographical areas. The data of their study shows that neither of these assumptions appears to be valid. They found, for example, that

> 91% of the patients . . . were in same class as their families of orientation (parents) . . . that only 1.3% of the patients were in a lower class than their families, whereas 4.4% were in a higher class.[15]

The drift hypothesis was also invalidated by these findings: (1) patients who had migrated to New Haven in the course of their lifetimes were not concentrated in the lower classes, where the incidence of schizophrenia was highest; (2) the lowest class (Class V) patients who were native to New Haven did not drift to the slums, but had always lived there; and patients of the two top classes (I, II) had always lived in upper-class areas. Patients of the middle classes (III and IV) had histories of more residential movement, but did not seem to have a tendency to drift to the slums.

Hollingshead and Redlich have also corroborated a point made in earlier studies (for example, that by Faris and Dunham) that the incidence of mental disorders varies by class status and geographic area. Rates for psychosis in general were found to be much higher in the lower classes than in the higher, whereas the reverse was the case with neuroticism, for which the upper classes had much the highest rate.

DISTRIBUTION OF NEUROSES AND PSYCHOSES BY SOCIAL CLASS[*]

Social Class	NEUROSES		PSYCHOSES	
	Number	Percent	Number	Percent
I	10	52.6	9	47.4
II	88	67.2	43	32.8
III	115	44.2	145	55.8
IV	175	23.1	583	76.9
V	61	8.4	662	91.6
Total	449		1,442	

Chi square = 296.45. P < .001.

[*] From A. B. Hollingshead and F. C. Redlich, "Social Stratification and Schizophrenia," *American Sociological Review*, 19(1954): 167.

It must be taken into account that it is impossible to get complete figures on mental disorders for any sizable community. The New Haven study was based on a psychiatric census of patients undergoing treatment, diagnostic study, or care. Taking the figures at face value, the differential class rates are striking, but their meaning, as the authors themselves suggest, is subject to various possible interpretations. We may suggest, for example, that psychiatrists more readily diagnose lower-class persons as psychotics than they do upper-class persons. Concealment of mental disorder may also vary by class. Methods of treating mental cases are also known to vary by class, and this may affect the rates. Even if the differential incidence of psychoses by class is taken as a fact, the significance of this from the point of view of causation remains problematic.

The Social Psychology of Therapy · Treatment of mental disorders by psychotherapy is a process of social interaction between doctor and patient. Therefore, we need not be surprised to learn that psychiatrists prescribe different treatments by class; or that fewer lower-class persons go voluntarily for treatment to psychiatrists; or that the neurotic patients of psychoanalysts come infrequently from lower socioeconomic and less educated groups, and indeed, as Spiegel[16] has noted, hardly seem to understand what psychiatric therapy is all about when they do come to clinics. As Meyer and Schaffer[17] suggest, some of the effectiveness of psychiatric treatment by middle-class practitioners of lower-class patients may be impeded by the difficulties of cross-class communication. In this connection we may recall our previous discussion of differential modes of communication and thought in social classes (Chap. 8).

The complexities and implications of treatment viewed as social interaction have been brought out by the studies of Schwartz and Stanton[18] and by Ruesch and his associates.[19] The former investigators, by closely watching interaction in mental-patient wards, have shown how the appearance and disappearance of symptoms are related to the ideologies and interpersonal relations of the hospital staff itself. The Ruesch study revealed that certain types of delayed recovery from physical illness, clearly psychiatric in character, seem to be heavily concentrated in the lower middle class (75 per cent). The investigators suggest that this concentration is related to middle-class orientations toward status, authority, and the medical profession itself and is also related to other psychological characteristics of the middle classes that stem from taboos against direct and exaggerated expression of tension and anxiety. Hence delayed recovery and its treatment must be regarded in terms of the social relations existing between prestiged physicians and hospital staff on the one hand and patients of certain social backgrounds on the other hand.

Social Influences on the Content of Psychoses · Not only do the specific symptoms which patients exhibit bear some relationship to a milieu in which they live; the symptoms are also related to and grow out of the individual's prepsychotic, or socialized, behavior patterns. This is true regardless of what the primary causation of the various mental diseases may be. The fact that in severe psychosis there is a radical break with reality and with normal social living does not mean that all previous behavioral organization is sloughed off. Thus Carothers[20] explains the absence of guilt among African psychotics as due to the relative absence of guilt in normal social life there.

Apropos of the same point, Miller and Swanson[21] have established that defenses against conflict vary by social class and that the same class differences occur among schizophrenics. In persons of the lower classes there is a relatively frequent resort to direct physical aggression and dependence upon gross bodily movement. "In pathologies . . . found in the lower class . . . the patient uses his voluntary neuro-musculature for expressing his conflict." On the other hand, middle-class patients, like their normal counterparts, tend to cope with their problems by rumination and conceptualization.

Differing Cultural Definitions · In recent years, certain anthropologists have tried to trace a connection between social and individual psychiatric disorder. They equate normal behavior with average behavior. Hence, they see the abnormal as equivalent to any marked deviation from the average. This statistical approach implies that abnormality is relative to a given culture. Since normality is the average for a group, it will differ from group to group depending upon cultural definition. Consequently, behavior that is considered abnormal in one society may be considered quite normal in another; and vice versa. As Benedict has claimed:[22]

> One of the most striking facts that emerge from a study of widely varying cultures is the ease with which our abnormals function in other cultures. It does not matter what kind of "abnormality" we choose for illustration, those which indicate extreme instability, or those which are more in the nature of character traits like sadism or delusions of grandeur or of persecution, there are well-described cultures in which these abnormals function at ease and with honor, and apparently without danger or difficulty to the society.

One should not assume, from a statement like that above, that psychotics can be made normal or nonpsychotic by transplanting them into another society. The psychotics of each society get their own special kinds of delusions from their cultural environments; but there is an immense difference between the delusions of the psychotic and those which are, for example, inculcated in a whole population by the mass media of communication. As Wegrocki says:

The delusions of the psychotic and the delusions of the Northwest Coast Indians cannot by any means be equated. Mechanisms like the conviction of grandeur are abnormal not by virtue of [being] unique ... but by virtue of their *function in the total economy of the personality*. The true paranoic reaction represents a *choice of the abnormal:* the reaction of the Haida chief represents no such choice. ... When the Plains Indians by a rigid physical regimen of exhaustion and fatigue plus a liberal dose of suggestion achieves a vision, that achievement is not an abnormal reaction in the same sense that the usual hallucination of the psychotic is.[23]

The Sick Society · Another view of psychiatric disorder conceives of society as the culprit. Mental disorder is thought of as a consequence of the disharmony of social organization and social values. This is not unlike the view of the French philosopher Rousseau, who thought that man was essentially good but had been corrupted by social institutions. Thus Fromm[24] characterizes the predominant personality of the twentieth-century Western world as gravely maladjusted. He points to the importance of the impersonal money market, where things are judged not by their intrinsic value but by what they bring in the market. He notes also that the impersonal market has resulted in an impersonal evaluation of persons and personalities. One must have the kind of personality that "sells" if one is to succeed, get ahead, climb, and win esteem. But, says Fromm, this kind of "marketing orientation" leads to a self-conception based precariously upon the fickleness of the market: one may go out of style, one may meet with a superior rival, and so on. Fromm conceives of societies as ranged upon a continuum, some producing mainly healthy individuals, some producing mainly maladjusted individuals, and other societies ranging in between. Some societies allow human potentialities to flower, blossom, and find creative expression, while others stifle inherent human potentialities.

It is, of course, impossible to test the validity of a position like Fromm's. His outlook contains an element of romantic nostalgia for the simple life of past eras. Since statistical data on mental disorders are extremely unreliable and incomplete, it is impossible at present to compare societies in this respect. Broad generalizations like those which Fromm and others make must accordingly be regarded with cautious skepticism.

The Neurotic

Another deviant type that has received an immense amount of attention is the neurotic. Neuroses are usually distinguished from psychoses as being of relatively minor gravity and not involving the radical break with reality or the extreme social incapacity that characterize psychoses. Neurotics, although they generally conform to cultural requirements, are afflicted with various types of symptoms which may be quite painful or awkward for them.

Types of Neuroses · As with psychoses, the classification of neuroses is not a definite and clear-cut one and is primarily a matter of convenience and of agreement concerning predominant symptoms. The following classification by Malamud,[25] one that has been fairly widely used, will give some idea concerning neurotic symptoms.

1. *Hysterias or conversion neuroses.* Emotional conflicts are expressed in the form of physical or mental symptoms. For example, a soldier may develop hysterical paralysis under combat conditions and be unable to move his legs, even though no organic grounds for paralysis exist. He may recover the use of his limbs if he is told that he has been discharged from the army, that the war is over, that the hospital is on fire, or the like. Four types of conversion are generally recognized: (*a*) the creation of physical symptoms where no signs of organic pathology can be found, as in the example above; (*b*) the exaggeration of organic symptoms or their persistence when the cause no longer exists; (*c*) the creation of organic pathology, as for example, indigestion and stomach cramps; (*d*) the creation of mental symptoms that resemble those of the psychotic, as for example

those of the soldier who has been withdrawn from combat and has hallucinations of exploding bombs and shells or re-enacts a combat experience.

2. *Psychasthenias or anankastic reactions.* The individual engages in behavior or has ideas which appear to him to be beyond his control. These include (*a*) obsessions, (*b*) phobias or fears, and (*c*) compulsive acts. A simple illustration of an obsession is a melody, a phrase, or a remark which keeps running through the individual's head to such an extent that he is unable to turn his attention undividedly to other matters. An instance of a phobia or morbid fear is provided by an acquaintance of the authors, who worried constantly throughout many of his adolescent years that he would become insane. Compulsive acts may take many forms, such as constant washing of the hands or stepping on cracks in the sidewalk.

3. *Faulty control of emergency reactions.* Anxiety, fatigue, instability, and sense of guilt or of inadequacy appear in situations which do not warrant their occurrence. This may be contrasted with their appearance in those situations which actually call for their arousal.

Neurosis, Psychosis, and Normality · Lay persons often confuse the meanings of the terms "neurotic" and "psychotic" and use them interchangeably. This popular confusion had to be taken into account by army medical authorities in their treatment of neurotic soldiers during World War II. In order to secure cooperation and to reassure them that they were not "crazy," persons with neurotic symptoms were told:

> Your condition is not like that of the insane. For them, of course, nothing can be done, except custodial care or surgery or electric shock treatments; but we can do a great deal for you who are neurotic by helping you understand your neurotic reactions and helping you overcome them.[26]

Many, if not most, psychiatrists conceive of psychoses and neuroses as of such different degrees of gravity and so different in symptomatology that they prescribe radically different methods of treatment. Thus, although psychotherapeutic methods have virtually captured the field of treatment of neurotics, they are used much less or not at all with psychotics. The use of such therapy with psychotics has been advocated to a limited degree, on the assumption that no absolute gulf exists between psychoses and neuroses. Some psychiatrists and psychologists regard neuroses and psychoses as different segments of an unbroken continuum. Cameron and Magaret, for instance, say:

> In popular thinking, and in the discourse upon which it depends, there is a chasm between pathological behavior and the normal reactions from which it must always derive. To span this chasm between normal and deviant behavior is one of the chief goals of behavior pathology.[27]

Most psychiatrists and psychologists, while admitting the existence of marginal cases and the limited usefulness of psychotherapy for psychotics, nevertheless regard neuroses and psychoses as qualitatively different. Advocates of this view stress that neuroses do not ordinarily turn into psychoses or vice versa, as should occur if the difference was merely a matter of degree. They also point out that the breakdown of the mechanisms of communication is so complete in such a large proportion of psychotics that it seems contentious to argue that differences between them and normal individuals or neurotics involve only a continuum. The effectiveness of psychotherapy with some psychotics by no means proves the case for the continuum theory, but may be interpreted as due to more than ordinarily skillful communication with desocialized persons.

Neurotic persons are like normal people in many crucial ways. They join groups, hold positions of responsibility, and otherwise participate in ordinary social activities. Their neuroticism may indeed be completely unknown to many of their associates. This fact supports the argument for the existence of a continuum between the neurotic and the normal. The extreme neurotic may be relatively incapacitated in his social relations, but most neurotics are not. The continuum view is further supported by the fact that anybody may display neurotic symptoms in certain situations involving stress and anxiety. Many war neuroses were of this character; when the soldier was no longer in physical danger, his neurotic symptoms often disappeared. Treatment techniques derived from the study of neurotics have been widely employed by clinical and child psychologists, social workers, and others who deal with normal persons who find themselves in situations of unusual stress and insecurity.

The view emphasizing continuity between neurotic behavior and ordinary behavior seems reasonably plausible but should be taken as postulate rather than as fact. Clear-cut cases of neuroticism exhibit elaborately organized systems of response which may be regarded as qualitatively different from those of ordinary persons. It is doubtful that such neurotic response systems can be adequately characterized as exaggerations of normal response.

Etiology · Turning to the question of etiology: although psychoanalytic explanations of neurosis virtually dominate the field, there are psychiatrists who claim that constitutional factors may be of primary importance. Environmental explanations vary according to the general position and training of the psychiatrist. Psychiatrists have been criticized for being culture-bound and for taking people of their own society and class as prototypes of people in general. Thus, some psychiatrists consider that lack of parental affection or harsh parental authoritarianism are the primary sources of neuroticism in children, without taking into account that such generalizations may be inapplicable to children in other societies or classes. Thus Green[28] has pointed out that although Polish-American children of the lower socioeconomic classes do not have close ties of affection with their parents and endure harsh discipline, they do not develop the neurotic symptoms that one might expect. As the influence of social science increases, psychiatrists are becoming considerably more aware of the dangers of this sort of ethnocentrism. Nevertheless, a general overview of the literature in this field indicates that, with relatively few exceptions, specialists in this field pay little attention to cross-cultural comparisons. Sociologists tend to be critical of the primary emphasis upon family relationships, as they are perhaps more sensitized to wider group memberships than are the psychiatrists.

The Eccentric

In spite of the influence of custom and group norms, the behavior of no one is entirely that of a rubber stamp for his society. Most of the differences between individuals are taken for granted or pass unnoticed; however, some deviations may be singled out for attention, since some persons may appear to exhibit such an unusual number of deviant patterns that they become labeled as "eccentric," "different," or "independent." These deviations are not of the type that warrant psychiatric attention, nor is there any reason to believe that they are all of a neurotic nature. They express tastes and personal inclinations or represent specific modes of action, often routinized, to which individuals somehow become attached. It would be well not to confuse personal eccentricities with cultural differences. For example, an old lady who wears old-fashioned hats, or an Indian woman who wears a sari in the United States, should not be called eccentric. A Westernized native who returns to his tribal home in Africa in European clothes should also not be included in this group. However, although the logical distinction involved here is clear, it is often easier to make in theory than in practice.

Eccentricity is probably a universal phenomenon, although it appears to be more prevalent in some societies than in others. Anthropologists have found such deviants in preliterate societies. The universality of idiosyncratic behavior points up the fact that the norms of society cannot regulate every aspect of life and are not meant to. A considerable but varying latitude of individual variation is permitted. Even in the most strictly regulated community there is always a live-and-let-live attitude toward certain behavior. If the behavior is conceived of as harmful or dangerous either to the community or the person, it is usually defined by such terms as "criminal," "subversive," "degenerate," or "immoral," and appropriate controls are applied. Any society sets limits within which deviation is tolerated and beyond which it is not. The precise points at which these limits are drawn furnish significant clues concerning the society's functioning.

On the other hand, eccentric behavior within limits of allowability may also be valued positively by a society: it may, for example, be regarded as colorful, humorous, enterprising, interesting, or exciting. Apart from furnishing entertainment and interest, eccentrics serve as innovators, producing new modes of behavior which may be taken up as fads or as permanent parts of the social heritage. In countries, including the United States, in which change and innovation are valued and in which individuality and independence are stressed, idiosyncratic behavior often attracts favorable publicity and attention. As is often observed, a broad tolerance of variability promotes a sense of freedom and facilitates social change.

The innovative function of eccentricity, and its potential for arousing hostility or antagonism, have been well brought out in an interesting study of a small Guatemalan community made by Tumin.[29] He describes two of the principal deviants in the village. One was a hero and a successful curer of disease in a community where there is much anxiety over sickness. To his fellow Indian youth, who are being alienated from traditional ways, his behavior represents "one of the few imaginable future alternatives."[30] On the other hand, the second eccentric was wholly negativistic; he offered no alternatives for the norms which he too violated. He was a scapegoat, disliked intensely and viewed as a threat. Tumin notes that "in each case the deviant behavior appears to have its genesis in relatively unique and idiosyncratic facts of the individual life histories. Their deviations . . . are not understandable as *products* of the culture pattern in any determinate sense."[31]

There have been some efforts to explain eccentricity in terms of the biological differences between persons. Benedict, for example, has advanced the idea that deviant persons are deviant because their inherited "congenial responses" do not quite fit into the ongoing culture into which they are born.[32] There is no evidence to support this theory, although it is clear that biological conditions are in some instances clearly associated with the development of unusual behaviors, as with the crippled, the blind, spastics, and other persons who are physically defective.

Summary

The deviant forms of behavior, although they are affected in various ways by cultural influences, are basically individual rather than group ways of acting. Feeble-minded persons are largely incapable of socialization by reason of their low intelligence. The psychotic is an individual in whom the communication process has broken down and who becomes incapable of acting as a member of a group by reason of this fact. Some psychoses are clearly the consequences of organic defect, injury, or deterioration, but the causes of others are not understood and are the subjects of theoretical controversy. The latter types—the functional psychoses—appear to be distributed in characteristic patterns related to such sociological variables as nationality, race, and social class. Psychotic symptoms differ in content in different cultures and are also evaluated in different ways. Neuroses are quantitatively different from psychoses in the sense that they do not involve the breakdown of communication and do not isolate the person. The category of eccentric behavior takes into account other unusual deviations from accepted norms. Our next concern will be with group ways of behavior which are regarded with concern or disapproval as deviations from "normal" or "proper" ways.

SUGGESTIONS FOR DISCUSSION AND SPECIAL REPORTS

1. Review the conceptions of the differences between psychoses and neuroses that are found in the psychiatric literature.

2. What is proved about the etiology of psychosis by the fact that psychoses appear to be more frequent in some societies or classes than in others?

3. What sorts of people become psychiatrists or consult psychiatrists?

4. What, besides consulting a doctor or a psychiatrist, do people do about their troubles? Are there class differences in this respect?

5. Do lower animals ever become psychotic or neurotic?

6. Interview a number of people on the subject of mental disease and try to determine the various types of conceptions which they hold. What difference might these conceptions make in their behavior?

7. Interview several doctors who practice different medical specialties on the place of psychiatry in medicine. Interpret your results.

NOTES

[1] N. Cameron and A. Magaret, *Behavior Pathology*, Houghton Mifflin, 1951, p. 183.

[2] E. P. Doll, "Notes on the Concept of Mental Deficiency," *Am. J. Psych.*, 54(1941): 119.

[3] Cameron and Magaret, *op. cit.*, p. 159.

[4] J. D. Page, *Abnormal Psychology*, McGraw-Hill, 1947, p. 737.

[5] N. Cameron, in J. McV. Hunt (ed.), *Personality and the Behavior Disorders*, Vol. II, Ronald, 1944, pp. 891-892.

[6] "A Psychiatrist's Choice," *Atlantic Monthly*, 194(1954): 44-46.

[7] *Ibid.*, p. 44.

[8] H. J. Eysenck, *Uses and Abuses of Psychology*, New York: Penguin Books, 1953, pp. 193-208.

[9] N. Cameron, "The Paranoid Pseudo-Community," *Am. J. Soc.*, 49(1943): 32-38.

[10] C. Blondel, *The Troubled Conscience*, London: Kegan Paul, 1928.

[11] H. S. Sullivan, *The Interpersonal Theory of Psychiatry*, Norton, 1953, p. 327.

[12] J. E. Carothers, "A Study of Mental Derangement in Africans," *Psychiatry*, 11(1948): 47-86.

[13] R. E. Faris and W. Dunham, *Mental Disorders in Urban Areas*, University of Chicago Press, 1939.

[14] A. B. Hollingshead and F. C. Redlich, "Social Stratification and Schizophrenia," *Am. Soc. Rev.*, 19(1954): 302-306.

[15] *Ibid.*, p. 304.

[16] J. Spiegel, in a speech delivered to the Chicago Psychoanalytic Society, 1953.

[17] J. K. Meyer and L. Schaffer, "Social Stratification and Psychiatric Practice: A Study of an Out-Patient Clinic," *Am. Soc. Rev.*, 19(1954): 310.

[18] M. S. Schwartz and A. H. Stanton, "A Social Psychological Study of Incontinence," *Psychiatry*, 13(1950): 399-416; and A. H. Stanton and M. S. Schwartz,

"The Management of a Type of Institutional Participation in Mental Illness," *Psychiatry*, 12 (1949): 13-26.

[19] J. Ruesch, *Chronic Disease and Psychological Invalidism*, University of California Press, 1951.

[20] Carothers, *op. cit.*, pp. 82-83.

[21] D. R. Miller and G. E. Swanson, "Defense Against Conflict and Social Background," unpublished manuscript.

[22] R. Benedict, "Anthropology and the Abnormal," *J. Genet. Psych.*, 10(1934): 60.

[23] H. J. Wegrocki, "Critique of Cultural and Statistical Concepts of Abnormality," *J. Ab. and Soc. Psych.*, 34(1939): 170-171.

[24] E. Fromm, *Man for Himself*, Rinehart, 1947.

[25] J. McV. Hunt (ed.), *Personality and the Behavior Disorders*, Vol. II, Ronald, 1944, pp. 838-839, 848-854.

[26] J. C. Whitehorn, in F. Alexander and H. Ross, *Dynamic Psychiatry*, University of Chicago Press, 1952, "Psychodynamic Approach to the Study of Psychoses," p. 256.

[27] Cameron and Magaret, *op. cit.*, p. 3.

[28] A. W. Green, "The Middle-Class Male Child and Neurosis," *Am. Soc. Rev.*, 11(1946): 31-41.

[29] M. M. Tumin, "The Hero and the Scapegoat in a Peasant Community," *J. Personality*, 10 (1950): 197-211.

[30] *Ibid.*, p. 206.

[31] *Ibid.*, p. 210.

[32] R. Benedict, *Patterns of Culture*, New York: Penguin Books, 1946.

SELECTED BIBLIOGRAPHY

Cameron, N., and A. Magaret, *Behavior Pathology*, Houghton Mifflin, 1951. A good basic text on individual deviancy.

Doll, E., "The Feeble-Minded Child," in L. Carmichael (ed.), *Manual of Child Psychology*, Wiley, 1946, pp. 845-885. A useful review of the literature on the feeble-minded.

Dunham, H. W., "The Social Personality of the Catatonic-Schizophrene," *Am. J. Soc.*, 49(1944): 508-518. A personality profile of a psychotic type, from the standpoint of a sociologist.

Faris, R. E., "Reflections of Social Disorganization in the Behavior of a Schizophrenic Patient," *Am. J. Soc.*, 49(1944): 134-141. Case study consisting largely of the patient's own remarks. The interpretation is sociological.

Faris, R. E., and H. W. Dunham, *Mental Disorders in Urban Areas*, University of Chicago Press, 1939. A pioneering study on the relation of social environment to mental disorders.

Green, A. W., "The Middle-Class Male Child and Neurosis," *Am. Soc. Rev.*, 11(1946): 31-41. An acute criticism of any explanation of neurosis that leaves class factors out of account.

Grinker, R. R., and J. P. Spiegel, *War Neuroses*, Philadelphia: Blakiston, 1945. Report by two psychiatrists of investigations of war neuroses.

Hollingshead, A. B., R. Ellis, and E. Kirby, "Social Mobility and Mental Illness," *Am. Soc. Rev.*, 19(1954): 577-584.

Hollingshead, A. B., and F. C. Redlich, "Social Stratification and Psychiatric Disorders," *Am. Soc. Rev.*, 18(1953): 163-169. This and the paper above represent a combined sociological and psychiatric attack on certain of the mental disorders.

Honigman, J. J., *Culture and Personality*, Harper, 1954, Part V, "Psychiatric Problems," pp. 369-423. A good review of anthropological writing as it bears on psychiatric problems.

Malamud, W., "The Psychoneuroses," in J. McV. Hunt (ed.), *Personality and the Behavior Disorders*, Ronald, 1944, pp. 833-860. This is a helpful survey of the types of neuroses and the literature bearing on them down to date of publication.

Riesman, D., *Individualism Reconsidered*, Glencoe, Ill.: Free Press, 1954, "Some Observations Concerning Marginality." A thoughtful essay, with the author careful to point out some of the advantages of being marginal.

Ruesch, J., *et al.*, *Chronic Disease and Psychological Invalidism*, New York: American Society for Research in Psychosomatic Problems, 1946. Monograph reported on (in part) in this chapter.

Stanton, A. H., and M. S. Schwartz, *The Mental Hospital*, New York: Basic Books, 1954. A psychiatrist and a sociologist write about the mental hospital as a network of social relations.

Stonequist, E. V., *The Marginal Man*, Scribner, 1937. Contains some good illustrative materials on racial and ethnic marginality.

Tumin, M. M., "The Hero and the Scapegoat in a Peasant Community," *J. Personality*, 10(1950): 197-211. Two deviant types in a simple community.

CHAPTER 21

Deviant

Subsocieties

ONLY THOSE GROUPS which are generally perceived to be outside the framework of respectable and responsible society, and to some extent at odds with its values, are properly called "deviant subsocieties." Such groups are regarded by outsiders as queer, perverted, abnormal, or dangerous, but they cultivate their own philosophies and rationales to explain, justify, and excuse their behavior. The deviant social world is organized on the basis of its deviation—that is, the deviant behavior is a matter of group custom—but in many other respects it shares the values of the wider society which condemns it.

ABNORMALITY VERSUS GROUP ORGANIZATION

There is a tendency to think of criminals, drug addicts, homosexuals, hoboes, prostitutes, religious extremists, and other such social deviants as personally maladjusted or abnormal. Psychiatrists, for example, sometimes automatically classify such individuals according to psychiatric categories and seek to account for their behavior in the same way that they deal with neurotic behavior, which is not group prescribed.

This procedure is unsound and leads to confusion. Undoubtedly some addicts, some criminals, and some prostitutes are unequivocally neurotic or abnormal. However, there are others who appear to be well adjusted and psychologically normal. If the homosexual behavior itself is not used as a basis for judgment, some homosexuals show no other evidence of abnormality. The same reasoning applies to other individuals whose deviant behavior has a group basis. It has not been conclusively demonstrated, even with respect to the criminal population, that there exists a significantly higher percentage of psychological abnormality than in the general population.

Within criminal groups there are found more or less the same individual psychological variations as in other occupational groups. Criminals themselves distinguish between neurotics and non-neurotics within their own ranks, and with some justification are amused and somewhat contemptuous of "bug doctors" (psychiatrists or psychologists) who think all criminals are abnormal and consistently seek evidence to substantiate this idea. Indeed, criminals often are inclined to think of themselves as normal and to regard the psychiatrists as "queer."

One of the defining characteristics of deviant societies is that they develop philosophies in support of their way of life and of their customs, which are attacked and threatened by outsiders. The philosophy of a deviant group is expressed in its special language, or argot.

The World of the Taxi-Dance Hall as Reflected in Its Special Language[1]

Africa. The Black Belt, especially the colored cabarets. *Playing Africa,* clandestine prostitution in the Black Belt.

Black and tan. A colored and white cabaret.

Buying the groceries. Living in clandestine relationship.

Fish. A man whom the girls can easily exploit for personal gain.

Fruit. An easy mark.

Line-up, the. Immorality engaged in by several men and a girl.

Make, "to make." To secure a date with.

Monkey-chaser. A man interested in a taxi-dancer or chorus girl.

Monkeys. Dancing girls, either chorus girls or taxi-dancers.

Nickel-hopper. A taxi-dancer.

Nigger. Term for Filipino.

Nigger lover. A girl who "dates" Filipinos.

On the ebony. A taxi-dance hall or taxi-dancer countenancing social contacts with men of races other than white.

Paying the rent. Living in clandestine relationship.

Picking up. Securing an after-dance engagement with a taxi-dancer.

Playing. Successfully exploiting one of the opposite sex.

Professional. An investigator.

Punk. A novitiate; an uninitiated youth or young girl, usually referring to an unsophisticated taxi-dancer.

Staying white. Accepting dates from white men only.

When members of the group are labeled in ways which displease them they argue back and counterattack. Outsiders who criticize them are accused of misunderstanding, misinterpretation, or discrimination. All of this adds to the difficulty of applying the concepts of normality and abnormality to members of such groups. These concepts are much more conveniently applied to persons who cannot talk back or who agree with the appellations. The question of normality is relative to the particular perspective from which these groups are viewed, and is thus a matter of opinion. The fact that they are often called abnormal, or have other epithets applied to them, simply signifies disapproval.

A sharp differentiation must therefore be made between divergent behavior which stems from group sources and the type of behavior with which practicing psychiatrists are ordinarily concerned. The person who believes that he is being injured by the magical practices of his associates may well be diagnosed as a psychotic and a paranoiac if he lives in a university community. If, however, he is a member of a group which generally believes in magical practices, the diagnosis would be different, for the belief in magic would be entirely expected and normal. If he did not share the general belief in the efficacy of magic, he might well be thought peculiar by his associates.

SOCIAL DEFINITIONS OF DEVIANCY

There is nothing about many specific kinds of activity which automatically causes them to be regarded in the wider community as dangerous, queer, or perverted. Certain acts are sanctioned in some communities and negatively evaluated in others; and over a period of time definitions inevitably change as public orientation shifts. Addiction to opiates, for example, is regarded as a medical problem in most Western countries, and was so regarded in the United States until recent decades. Homosexuals are one of the groups discriminated against in Western countries, but this particular bias is not universally shared even there. Indeed, when people meet homosexuals under predominantly normal conditions, as in some occupations, homosexuality is taken for granted and homosexuals are assumed to be pretty much like other human beings.

Historical changes in definitions of deviancy are striking and many illustrations could be cited. Thus, the treatment of religious sects is a highly variable matter and in a given period depends upon whether the sect espouses practices that seem shocking or dangerous to its neighbors. During one period of its history a sect may be viewed as a menace to public morals, and at another merely odd or peculiar. When politics get mixed into sectarianism, then the sect may come to be regarded—at least for a time—as unpatriotic or even downright subversive. Of course a sect, or any other group, may engage in practices running counter to general moral standards and yet escape widespread attention. But if through some combination of circumstances the glare of publicity falls upon the group, influential groups of good citizens may demand that something be done about its degenerate or dangerous practices. When public furor dies down, the group may continue its traditional practices more or less unmolested; but it remains vulnerable as long as the practices themselves fall within the definition of deviancy that is generally current.

It is a historic fact, too, that when members of influential groups meet outsiders whose behavior is shocking and strange, they may not merely think the outsiders different, but may believe them to be degenerate and inhuman. This has happened repeatedly when white Europeans spilled over into strange areas of the globe over the last five centuries. With domination comes a kind of tolerance: the superordinate group believes that it knows the people that it dominates and develops a rationale, in racial terms or otherwise, to explain the different behavior of the Asian or the African. It may, in fact, be hazarded that whenever peoples meet initially, whenever they discover each other's existence for the first time, strangeness and mutual ethnocentrism are likely to be accompanied by imputations of deviancy. Since conquering or superordinate groups generally have an advantage in making their definitions stick, only their definitions of deviancy may survive. Within a single country, social classes may discover each other too. Historians have pointed to the discovery of the lower-class Englishman by the middle classes during the nineteenth century and to the parallel discovery by good Americans of the astonishingly depressed conditions of living among low-class immigrants in their cities.

Definitions of what constitutes deviant behavior, and what is done about it, no doubt usually reflect the opinions of politically dominant groups. Thus "bookies" are law violators in the United States, but operate legally in the United Kingdom; and on another level, gambling is legal in Nevada and illegal in the other forty-seven states. Some groups find it to their advantage to make certain definitions prevail, and over a period of years may be influential in shaping public opinion. There seems to be little doubt that American policemen have had a hand in defining drug addiction as a criminal rather than a medical matter. The main opposition to legalized bookmaking in the United States is said to come from church groups (on moral grounds) and from race-track associations and the gambling syndicates (on mercenary grounds).

Social Structure Includes Deviant Groups

SOME SOCIAL FUNCTIONS

Although all deviant subsocieties are, by definition, beyond the pale, they are related to and arise from the structure of the wider society. Some quite clearly perform functions for accepted groups. There often exists, for example, a double standard of talk and action with regard to various of the vices. Respectable men of all social classes take advantage of the availability of prostitutes, and quasi-criminal or quasi-underworld organizations capitalize on this patronage. It is not these organizations but the persistent market for prostitution which makes it difficult to suppress. The market for the prostitute's services presumably reflects the inadequacies of those legitimate institutions which regulate sexual and affectional behavior. Occasionally, zealous advocates of vice suppression may succeed in outlawing a particular form of activity, such as gambling, which happens to be an integral part of the way of life of some people. Illegal organization then flourishes around the otherwise unfulfilled demand for the banished activity or commodity.

Some scholars have even suggested that the very existence of vice and of criminal groups serves to buoy up the self-conceptions and uneasy consciences of respectable citizens. The efforts of the latter to suppress the evils and to control the deviants are supportive in that they make for self-righteousness. It is tacitly understood that attempts at suppression usually fail in the long run: and if they were to succeed too completely there would be some disappointment even among the respectable citizens, either because of hypocrisy, or because esteem is derived from a public stand against vice. Too complete a "cleaning up," it is also recognized, makes for a dull community; "open towns" are interesting! They attract tourists and stimulate legitimate business as well as shady enterprises.

DEVIANT GROUPS AND THE WIDER SOCIETY

Various deviant activities stem from the fact that deviants adhere to many of the same values that good citizens do, but find it easier or more feasible to implement these values through illegal means. It is perfectly plain that "con men" enjoy making a killing for its own sake, and, much like businessmen, gain status from big deals. They use the profits of the game to buy standard American goods. It is well known that much automobile theft is committed by young men who use the automobiles for dating their girl friends—

or to stage holdups to obtain money for spending upon status symbols and pleasure. Religious sects also reflect the wider social context from which they arise. The Bible is still the chief source of dissident doctrine, and the more esoteric American cults which utilize yoga and other non-Christian systems are remarkable for their stress upon individuality and personal striving. Presumably the existence and functioning of various sects has consequences for the wider community in that dissident groups bring innovation and siphon off discontent from the more established groups.

Deviant Groups: Criminals, Drug Addicts, and Homosexuals

It is obviously impossible to describe all the deviant groups which exist. We shall discuss three by way of illustration and in order to make additional theoretical points.

THE CRIMINAL

As we have remarked, American emphasis upon success, money, and competition, as well as the great proliferation of occupations and division of labor, have resulted in the development of illegal occupations that are integral parts of our commercial and occupational world. Students of criminology have classified crime and criminals in a great variety of ways. The criminal underworld is itself a complicated social structure with occupational diversity and status systems. For our purposes, we may classify criminals into three categories: (1) conventional criminals (2) white-collar criminals and (3) racketeers.

The Criminal Occupations · The conventional criminals may be either professionals or amateurs: "occupational" and "nonoccupational" would be equivalent terms. Most murder, rape, and arson, for example, is not committed as an occupational activity, and a great many persons from respectable society commit an occasional theft, murder, or other offense. The conventional criminal occupations probably number in the hundreds. An immense number of specific devices and skills may be employed, and as in any occupation new ones are constantly being invented and old ones improved. These skills may be roughly classified as: those involving violence or threats; those involving manual or mechanical dexterity and skill, such as picking of pockets, shoplifting, safe cracking, and automobile stealing and stripping; those involving verbal dexterity and histrionic ability, frequently called swindling, fraud, and confidence games. In the last type, some mechanical or manual skill may be called for, as in the shell game or in three-card monte. The specific types of fraud are legion.

Each of the various criminal occupations has its own specific rules and norms which guide and control the behavior of its practitioners. Each has a hierarchy of status positions and possesses prestige relative to others, this prestige reflecting underworld public opinion. There are codes regulating standard performances, as for any legitimate job: a "fingering job" ordinarily yields a regular 10 percent; "the nut" (expenses) is always subtracted from the money gained "at the top" (before dividing).

White-collar crime consists of offenses committed in legitimate occupations or businesses, as, for example, by corporations in the course of their regular business operation.[2] A businessman may break the law knowingly either for mercenary reasons or because he feels that he must because his competitors do likewise. Sometimes he may break a law because the law itself is vague and the boundaries of legality are not clear. Sometimes corporations challenge the legality of a statute by deliberately flouting it to see if the court decision will uphold their action. There is no world of white-collar crime as such.

The third general type of crime is racketeering. We are here using the term to designate underworld business activities. This means the provision of contraband goods or services for a market which usually includes clientele from the respectable world. Gambling, prostitution, and the bootlegging of liquor and drugs are examples. These businesses are organized like any other, with certain special features such as the prominence of bribery—involving collusion of public officials—and the inability of underworld businessmen to enforce contracts and settle disputes in the courts. As a substitute for court decision, racketeers have their own methods for settling disputes and enforcing the fulfillment of contractual obligations. Racketeers, like conventional criminals, are part of the general criminal milieu.

The Criminal World · Criminals of the first and third types have identifications with a somewhat vague but nonetheless real criminal world, a world that is somewhat wider than particular occupations or rackets. This world, much like that of the artist or the professional athlete, is not sharply set off from other worlds, but does command a certain loyalty and allegiance from its members. Criminal argot reflects something of the unity of the world when it designates all outsiders as "squares" and all insiders as "right." Marginal persons, such as lawyers who engage in dubious or dishonest practices, are called "kinky" to designate their separate status.

> The professional thief . . . has semi-legitimate acquaintances among lawyers, fences, fixers, bondsmen, and politicians. These . . . are making money from the thief but are supposed to be members of legitimate society. He may call upon them, also, for assistance for the less legitimate purposes. . . . The thief is somewhat suspicious of all individuals in legitimate society other than those mentioned. He believes that whoever is not with him is against him. Any non-criminal individual not personally known . . . is a possible danger and, as an individual, is somewhat disliked on that account. This feeling is reinforced by occasional trouble which results from perfectly proper acquaintances. . . . [There is considerable] danger that the thief may run into if he tries to make legitimate contacts with strangers. Because of this, the professional thief lives largely in a world of his own and is rather completely isolated from general society. The majority of them do not care to contact society except professionally.[3]

The fact that all insiders are on the shady side of the law lends symbolic cohesion. The intense hatred felt for informers or stool pigeons is an index of this cohesion and of the need for secrecy in the face of the outside world. Of course all groups, occupational or otherwise, require for their very functioning that certain secrets be withheld from nonmembers. This is of special importance for criminal groups, for obvious reasons. An important ingredient in the ideologies of the underworld is the preservation of trade secrets and the maintenance of a close mouth before outsiders. Even the ex-criminal who writes a book about his experiences may feel uneasy about revealing current techniques, and may therefore write mainly of past history and of well-known crimes. The lines drawn between underworld and general society necessarily involve a certain suspicion and wariness:

> One of the personal characteristics of the thief is extreme suspicion. This may be accounted for by the fact that he exists in a suspicious world. . . . The first thing in his mind in every touch is whether he is under suspicion. . . . He must decide whether there is an ulterior motive in any word or act of a prospect. He must often be courteous, kindly, and solicitous, and, because he has to play this role, he is naturally very sensitive to these characteristics in anyone else. Therefore, if someone would do or offer to do something for him which is unusually kindly, he immediately becomes suspicious.[4]

Life Styles of Criminals · Although criminals of any country resemble the citizens of that country in many ways, cherishing and striving for many of the same ends, they also develop their own style of life. A professional thief cheerfully says that "the professional thief rejoices in the welfare of the public. He would like to see society enjoy continuous prosperity, for then his own touches will naturally be greater."[5]

Somewhat different styles within the criminal world arise from the different occupations; but existence within the criminal milieu lends certain general features to them. The professional criminal usually operates in terms of short-range goals. He becomes a liberal and unconcerned spender of money and worries only about the immediate future. Probably this is true even for the racketeer groups, whose conspicuous consumption is a matter of public comment. In recent years, racketeers have tended to move into middle-class suburban areas and to take over some middle-class manners and standards. High living, with an emphasis on drinking, horseracing, and gambling, is a feature of most criminal circles. In fact, in an economic sense, many criminals partly live off other criminals: the holdup man may spend his gains with a bookie or lose his money at gambling. There is a famous apocryphal story told about a criminal who found himself in a strange town and who asked an associate where they could gamble. He was told that there was only one joint but that it was crooked. This information only led him to exclaim, as he prepared to be fleeced, "What are we going to do, there isn't any other." Criminals often do not marry (but may use the term "wife" to refer to the woman with whom they are currently living). They associate with women of easy virtue who are part of, or marginal to, the criminal milieu.

The professional criminal is aware of his somewhat different style of life and of the attitudes which respectable citizens have toward him. He knows and often partly accepts the values of respectable society toward crime, and hence shows symptoms of uneasy conscience. He protects himself against his conscience by means of rationalizations which are extremely varied and often ingenious. If he steals from someone who is rich he argues that the rich are themselves usually dishonest. If he steals from the poor, he argues that they spend it on drink anyway. The confidence man likes to point out that the victim has to be willing to cheat someone else before he himself can be fleeced. (Incidentally, the criminal invariably objects to calling the victim a victim; he much prefers to call him "mark" or "sucker." As one thief said: "That makes it sound bad to call them 'victims.'") The criminal also likes to point out that many persons, such as the police, lawyers, prison staffs, and others from respectable society, make money from him or have jobs which depend upon the existence of crime. He may point to the stimulating influence he has on the insurance business and the manufacture of safes, locks, keys, and burglar alarms.

The professional criminal often thinks of his activities as an occupation or a business and may not consider himself an enemy of society. He does not usually hate the police, lawyers, judges, and others who play a role in sending him to prison, unless they violate what seem to him to be the rules of the game and the standards of sportsmanship. As a famous "madam" complained:

I didn't resent the honest cop and I was able to stay in business because of the dishonest variety. But the members of the gendarmerie who really started my adrenalin flowing like wine were the boys who believed in playing it both ways, and who wouldn't have turned a hair if their own mother happened to be the one caught in the middle.[6]

Recruitment · Many criminals talk about "packing the racket" or going "legit." That they consider leaving the criminal life indicates its tensions and hazards. Criminals often feel a certain envy for those of their number who have managed to go straight. There is indeed a kind of folklore among them concerning instances of this kind. Nevertheless it is not easy to leave the underworld once a person has become rooted in it and has an investment and involvement in it. His friends are in the underworld, and he is accustomed to its routines, satisfactions, and excitements. His loyalties tie him to it. When he tries to abandon it, he is not only drawn back but is also pushed back because he is tagged by respectable society and cannot escape his past. When he tries the good life, he often finds it dull and frustrating, and may discover that he does not have the requisite skills and knowledge to give him the standard of living he is used to. Not much is known about the drift out of the criminal world, but there is some evidence of a shift with increasing age to marginal, semilegitimate occupations. Individuals who make this change often do not altogether renounce underworld associations but do manage to avoid the worst risks.

There is an extensive literature on the causation of criminal behavior, and all sorts of theories from biological determinism to the strictly environmental have been proposed and defended. These theories closely parallel and grow out of general theories of human behavior such as those which are briefly outlined in Chapter 15, "Conceptions of Personal Organization." However, two broad problems exist in this area. One is to account for the origin of criminal groups. This is a historical and sociological problem and does not deal with the behavior of individuals. The other is to explain how a given individual comes to join a criminal group and to accept its way of life. This is of interest to the social psychologist.

The criminal underworld does not maintain itself biologically, for reproduction rates are low and criminals who do have children often try to keep them from following a life of crime. (This statement does not necessarily apply to other countries. In India, for example, criminal occupations, as well as prostitution and begging, have been matters of caste heritage and have been passed on from parents to children.) As a consequence, the criminal population is maintained by a process of recruitment concerning which relatively little is known. It is commonly assumed that adult criminals are recruited from juvenile delinquents, but this is only partly true and varies by types of crime. A substantial portion of adult offenders have no records of juvenile delinquency and evidently embark on criminal careers relatively late in life. A recent autobiographical account by a convict doing a life term in the Iowa State Penitentiary indicates that this man's first venture into crime was as a bank robber during the depression when he was in his early twenties.[7]

Most juvenile delinquents come from the slums of large cities and are brought up in homes characterized by poverty and ignorance. Such juvenile criminals, tough as they may sometimes be, are automatically disqualified for certain types of criminal occupations, such as the confidence game, which require the manners, dress, and speech of the better-educated classes. The tough urban juvenile delinquent, if he becomes an adult criminal, is thus likely to become a gunman or to enter some part of the occupational hierarchy of crime which makes demands that his slum training enables him to meet. In the higher branches of villainy and the more refined types of fraud, superior intelligence, command of language, histrionic ability, stable nerves, and other such qualities are required. Neuroticism, feeble-mindedness, psychosis, and other abnormalities of character and personality are just as much obstacles to success in crime as elsewhere. This is why criminologists are, or ought to be, exceedingly cautious about drawing conclusions about criminals from the study of persons in prison. The more capable and successful criminals are probably not sent to prison as often as the defectives, the abnormal, and the unintelligent.

Virtually all criminal occupations that offer reasonable returns without unreasonable risks require a certain amount of training or tutelage. Safecrackers, it is said, are recruited from persons in the mechanical trades. Receivers of stolen goods often come from the business world. For some years the top American racketeers have had "heist" (holdup) backgrounds, and have usually been of Italian origin. Confidence men, according to one criminal, usually come from small towns or the country.

Perhaps no other institution contributes so much to criminal recruitment as the prison. In it persons of all degrees of sophistication are thrown together for long periods of time. The stigma of the prison sentence prevents the ex-convict from getting into noncriminal occupations, and imprisonment has provided him with information concerning a wide variety of illegal ways of making a living. His prison associates become contacts which the amateur may use if he wishes to turn professional.

DRUG ADDICTION AND THE ADDICT'S WORLD

In Chapter 11 we discussed addiction as a learning process and an aspect of personality development. We shall now look at addicts as constituting a deviant social group.

The Social World of the Addict · It is well known from newspaper publicity that drug addicts constitute a submerged social group, albeit a loosely organized one, in the United States. This is a far from universal phenomenon. Before the attempt at suppression of the drug trade which began in 1915, American drug addicts, for the most part, were scattered throughout respectable society and did not form a deviant subsociety. When addicts are treated as medical cases, as they are in England and in most European countries, they are deviants only in the same way as are people who take sleeping pills or insulin shots. The social world of the drug addict is not called into being by the direct effects of the drug habit, but rather by the attitudes and actions of nonaddicts. For example, it was reported that during World War II the Japanese failed to make provision for supplying a number of diabetics in Hong Kong with insulin. Consequently, a flourishing black market arose and the diabetics joined together in exchanging information and generally helping each other to maintain their supplies. If the situation had become permanent there is no doubt that a diabetic subsociety would have been formed.

Similarly, American opiate addicts joined together in a loose group organization only when they were compelled to by the effects of antinarcotic legislation. When police enforcement of this legislation threatened to deprive addicts of their supplies, an informal organization arose to cope with the situation by furnishing smuggled drugs to the users. Marked as criminals and outcasts, addicts gravitated together for mutual protection, aid, and consolation. Addicts exchange information concerning matters vital to getting a steady drug supply; they discuss techniques of drug use and of avoiding the police, and generally talk about their common experiences.

No doubt some drug users in the United States are outside the addict's special world and have little or no contact with other users. Most addicts in this category of outsiders are probably either members of the medical or allied professions, or are well-to-do persons with steady and relatively unthreatened sources of drug supply. Some of these persons are not known to be addicts by any but a few intimate associates; and others may be known as addicts in their local communities, yet participate fully in community life.

The Addict's Argot · Out of the interaction within this subculture a special language, or argot, has arisen which reflects the special concerns of the addict: for example, the peddler from whom he buys is a "connection"; a doctor who prescribes drugs is a "right croaker"; a disruption of distribution channels by arrests is a "panic"; a person who is experimenting casually is a "joy popper" with an "ice cream habit"; a full-fledged addict has a "Chinaman" or "monkey on his back"; a person who goes off drugs suddenly without medication "kicks his habit cold turkey"; one who sniffs the drug is a "snorter"; one who uses it hypodermically "shoots it," and is either a "skin shooter" or a "main liner." It is a significant sociological fact that the American drug user has developed a rich and varied argot, whereas European addicts apparently have not. This, of course, is because there is what we may call an "addict culture" in the United States—a subculture that, like other subcultures, has a tradition, a philosophy, norms and codes, and means of renewing itself through the recruitment of new members as the habit spreads.

The Underworld Addict · The underworld addict is set apart by public definition and develops a way of life that is centered upon drugs as his dominant concern. His life is organized around the endeavor to keep himself adequately supplied. Unlike the addict with a legitimate supply, the underworld user must depend upon the illegal peddler and must pay fantastic black-market prices. Patronage of the black market requires much time and effort and also usually leads to arrest and acquisition of a criminal record, making it difficult to hold a legitimate job. In any case, most legitimate jobs do not pay well enough to support a drug habit at black-market prices. All of this means that the American drug user must seek other quicker means of making money. Theft, prostitution, and drug peddling are the most common means employed. The fact that addicts often act as peddlers or "pushers" is of considerable significance in the recruitment of new users, since this means that the tremendous drive of the habit is harnessed to the perpetuation of the drug problem.

The underworld addict is unable to focus on long-range goals because he is constantly preoccupied with today's and tomorrow's supply. A pervasive feature of the life of this type of addict is the frantic need to keep one step ahead of a dwindling and constantly threatened supply—hence the argot term, "frantic junkie." The addict's time is broken up according to the demands of his habit and his days center on the times when he customarily "scores" with his "connection," or when he takes his shots. For the poorer addict these "connections" are erratic and irregular, due either to difficulties in raising the necessary money or in locating the elusive and suspicious peddler. In addition to these hazards, the addict must constantly be on the alert to avoid the police and the addicted "stool pigeons" who work for them. He must be ready to move at any moment, he must travel light, and if he is picked up he must be careful to have no incriminating evidence on his person. Addicts become exceedingly ingenious in all of these respects, so much so that even relatively unintelligent persons seem to have their dull wits sharpened by the need for dope. The drug user spends a good deal of his life inventing new devices and tricks, scheming and maneuvering to raise money, to keep his underworld connections, and to evade detection.

Addicts become addicted not only to drugs but to a way of life. When they try to leave this way of life and renounce their habits they find themselves drawn back to their old haunts and associates. They also find it difficult to adjust themselves to the normal routines and values of the ordinary world and to escape the stigma of their past. The failure of addicts to "kick the habit" permanently is doubtless tied up with their reluctance to abandon old associates and a familiar environment. The use of drugs thus is much more than a biological matter or a mere question of pharmacology.

Public Attitudes Toward Addiction · Addiction to drugs is generally regarded as either a medical problem or as a moral and criminal problem. In the United States prior to 1915, it was regarded mainly as a medical matter. After the drug-suppression program began it came to be viewed and treated as a criminal matter. Special-interest groups played a part in developing this definition. This was accomplished relatively easily, since there existed a general public disapproval of addiction and a sense of mystery concerning the strange power of the habit and the transformation of character that it brought about. This negative imagery has now been elaborated and become more lurid. Lurid paper-bound books tell of "gripping true adventures of a T-man's war against the dope menace" and portray heavy-lidded young women toying with hypodermic needles with the masculine hands of the law hovering in the background.

The prohibition method of dealing with vice is itself a peculiarly American method. Critics of the use of police suppression regard it as a manifestation of a Protestant "uplift" fervor. Whatever the explanation may be, in terms of its consequences police suppression has succeeded no better with addiction than it has with other forms of vice, such as alcoholism, gambling, and prostitution.

The recruitment of new addicts seems to be closely tied up with the existence of illegal supply lines and with the underworld culture of the addict, which are direct consequences of prohibition methods of control. The effects produced by prohibition set up a vicious cycle leading to enhanced demands for more prohibitory legislation. Such legislation gets increasing support as public imagery of the addict assumes even more lurid and melodramatic aspects. An interesting peripheral question that is raised here is as to the limits of legal control of deviant behavior.

European observers have often commented upon what seems to be a peculiarly American legal philosophy. This philosophy places special emphasis upon the idea that the law should express the highest ideals and make no compromise with evil. European legal philosophy, in contrast, places relatively greater emphasis upon adapting laws to existing practices in order to avoid the consequences of driving underground certain types of behavior.

To maintain the illusion that vice is being eliminated and that virtue is protected, it is necessary that various myths and stereotypes be maintained. Ceremonial gestures are made from time to time to reassure the public. Among these are publicized "drives" against vice, exposés, stories of "ring busting," the glorification of the police, and reports of police accomplishments.

Complete cynicism concerning the motives of policemen and newspaper publishers, and other interested parties who stage clean-up campaigns, is not warranted. Such drives do achieve temporary results and they are demanded and appreciated by the public. Basic reforms, however, usually come more slowly and in less spectacular ways. Most persons "in the know" recognize the ceremonial and strictly short-run significance of these spectacular battles with evil.

THE HOMOSEXUAL

Many different theories exist concerning the origin of homosexual behavior in the individual. The older theorists argued about whether it was an inherited or learned form of sexual expression and often compromised by concluding that it might be either. The outstanding competing views on the subject today are (1) that it is a matter of the glands and (2) that it is learned. In Chapter 10 we have sketched some of these conflicting general theories and have indicated that the current consensus of opinion is that homosexual behavior is probably always a learned form of behavior.

Authorities do not agree, however, on just how homosexuality is learned. Presumably the basis for it is laid at a very early age when the child forms conceptions and attitudes on sexual matters from his experiences in the family group and from experiences with his own body. We are interested here in the place accorded the homosexual in society.

Public Opinion of Homosexuals · Like drug addicts, homosexuals may be so scattered as to have relatively little contact with others like themselves. Public censure, however, tends to cause them to congregate in places, especially cosmopolitan centers, where heterogeneity and size of the population makes for more anonymity and tolerance. In all of our forty-eight states there are laws which make homosexual behavior illegal and criminal, but the police of big cities make little effort to enforce these laws.

As with other forms of vice (if homosexuality is a vice) there is a divided or ambiguous public opinion. In general, homosexuality is recognized and tolerated with amusement, sympathy, compassion, and only mild disapproval. It is often accepted as a matter of fact in many segments of our society, particularly among people who have had close contact with it. The ambiguity of public opinion is reflected by the tendency of people to maintain a conspiracy of silence about known homosexuality until it comes to public attention. When this happens all parties are embarrassed, but agree that something must be done to assuage that portion of the public which thinks of homosexuality as a dire evil to be sternly suppressed by police action. The police of large cities ordinarily tolerate or ignore homosexual activity as such, and only become concerned when it involves open scandal or is associated with other illegal activities.

Known male homosexuals are not allowed to hold certain types of positions (*e.g.*, in the State Department), but may be tolerated or even expected in others, such as hairdressing, designing women's clothes, some artistic pursuits, or ballet dancing. It is an interesting question as to why concentration should occur in certain professions and occupations. This may possibly be partly accounted for by a tendency of male inverts (effeminate males) to seek and prefer employment in activities generally regarded as somewhat feminine and not quite appropriate for males. Concentration in an occupation also may be accounted for by the opportunities it provides for contacts of the desired kind with other males.

There are many misapprehensions about the homosexual and the life he leads. It is sometimes thought that homosexuals are always effeminate, detached, suicidal, or inclined to antisocial conduct stemming from their sexual deficiency. Actually, like other social deviants the homosexual shares most values dominant in his country, his social class, and his occupation. What homogeneity there is among these persons, apart from their sexual behavior, is largely brought about by the negative public evaluation of them.

> If there is any characteristic of homosexual life that has been instrumental in the development of homogeneous group traits, it is probably the pretense and the mask. Millions of people could not possibly live through each day of the year, concealing, pretending, deliberately lying, without reacting in similar manner.[8]

Apart from the constant threat of blackmail and public disgrace, it may be embarrassing to the homosexual in relations with ordinary persons to have them know of his peculiarity. Hence he may become skillful at concealing his homosexual identity and at manipulating interaction to discover whether or not he may safely reveal his identity to a given individual. Many homosexuals become sensitized to the detection of homosexuality in others and develop techniques of communicating with each other. Occasionally the signals are misread (as is also true, of course, in heterosexual relations) and so the homosexual leaves himself open to unpleasantness or even danger. Like the criminal, they are wary of associations with outsiders unless they know what to expect. As with other "minority groups," outsiders sometimes form friendships with insiders and so function as connecting links between respectable and nonrespectable worlds.

The Homosexual Subculture · There is a loosely organized homosexual subculture and typical forms of association exist within it. D. Corey has described the world of the homosexual in terms which, in a general way, fit the world of the criminal or the prostitute:

> One writer describes it as a *submerged world,* while another speaks of *a society on the fringe of society.* Both are correct, accurate, yet incomplete, for there is not one submerged world, one society on the fringe of society, but several, almost countless, different and disparate and dissimilar and almost disconnected, yet all having some relationship to one another, sometimes through an individual or two who travel in several of these submerged-island societies at once, or related on the other hand merely by the similarity of pursuits and personalities, or perhaps related primarily by the association that exists only in the imagination of the hostile world.[9]

In this world homosexuals court, make love, have friends and acquaintances, engage in ordinary business with each other, and develop a common argot and a group philosophy. Since they are under censure, they develop protective and operational rationales. One rationale is that homosexuality is a biological disorder, and hence other people should adopt a live-and-let-live attitude and not cast blame. Another is that homosexuals are superior to others in intelligence and sensitivity—artistic and other accomplishments by homosexuals are pointed to in evidence. Some will even argue that their forms of lovemaking are superior, and note with pride the complex domestic relations that grow up among them. Celebrations of homosexual romance in literature are used as support. Further powerful ideological support is gained by denigrating the general public which misunderstands or discriminates, and by exaggerating the prevalence of homosexual practices. Kinsey's claim that some forty percent of all males have had some homosexual experience was probably greeted with considerable satisfaction by many exclusively homosexual individuals.

In a study of male homosexuals in Montreal, a sociologist, Maurice Leznoff,[10] has indicated that the core of homosexual society consists of those homosexuals who are relatively unsecretive in their activities and inclinations. The danger of being exposed as deviants either is disregarded or does not exist for them. These overt homosexuals are the mainstay of the homosexual world. They are easily recognizable by outsiders, and since they do not fear detection, they congregate in fairly public places: certain bars, restaurants, and the like. More numerous are those who practice homosexuality secretly or covertly. These, known in the lingo as "butches," are usually indistinguishable from ordinary heterosexual males because concealment is deemed vital. They hesitate to risk exposure by being seen in the company of known homosexuals or by appearing at homosexual parties and hangouts. However, as the homosexual's friendships, even among overt homosexuals, are not necessarily or even generally sexual in nature, the covert homosexual often has to seek a sexual partner. This often brings him into direct, and even public, contact with the overt homosexual at well-known hangouts. He thus risks discovery. Apparently there is some antagonism between overt and covert homosexuals, at least in Montreal: the covert homosexual, who generally is better educated and of higher occupational status, looks down on the other, and is perhaps even hostile toward him because his very visibility calls public attention to the fact of homosexuality.

Other homosexual types include those who go further in their attempts to maintain secrecy and concealment. They confine their expressions of sexual interest to a single other person and never mingle in groups of their own kind. Undoubtedly, also, there are others who, although they recognize their own homosexual impulses, do not reveal them overtly to anyone else.

Recruitment · The process of recruitment into the homosexual world is tied up with the public sanction against homosexuality and with the discovery by individual deviants that such a world exists. People may even reach middle age without recognizing their homosexual tendencies for what they are. Discovery of identity may come in various ways, including contact with other homosexuals, who may also introduce them to the ways of "the gay society." The uninitiated may be inducted by chance contact or by being picked up. It is sometimes averred that hardened homosexuals pervert or seduce other persons. This is extremely doubtful. Whatever the causality of homosexuality may be, it is not as simple as this. An individual may ordinarily be seduced only if he cooperates and finds the experience to his taste.

The discovery by the homosexual isolate of a preformed world is an event of great psychological importance. It shows him that he is not alone and provides him with a supporting milieu. Probably most pronounced or exclusive homosexuals recognize their deviance during adolescence, so that most movement into the homosexual world takes place during adolescence or early maturity. As he enters into homosexual associations, the novitiate acquires the knowledge essential to his participation in the deviant world. This includes knowledge of social skills, the signs of recognition and communication, and the more subtle modes of interacting with both homosexuals and normal people. The Montreal study suggests that initial sexual contacts often are accompanied by confusion and guilt, since the new activities run counter to general public sanction against such activities, a sanction previously internalized by the person himself. The initial affair with an experienced homosexual not only inducts the neophyte into the strange new world, but affords him the rationales necessary for making the transition from the outside to the inside.

Homosexual experience of some of the trauma of aging is apparently similar to the experience of heterosexuals in our society. The Montreal homosexual world values youth. The aging homosexual seeks to avoid loneliness and isolation by means of a permanent union, or homosexual marriage. But these unions, lacking the institutional supports given the heterosexual variety, are usually unstable and temporary. As a consequence, loneliness is a common fate for the aging homosexual who finds himself unable to compete with younger persons.

Although we have hitherto been discussing homosexuality as something sharply set off from heterosexuality, the dividing line is actually not a clear one. Persons who are exclusively homosexual are far outnumbered by those who are in varying degrees capable of both kinds of attachments. Such persons sometimes move in and out of homosexual circles, but do not form groups of their own organized around their own catholicity of response. The subsociety of the exclusive homosexual is loosely organized and is thus able to absorb part-time homosexuals, homosexual isolates, and covert homosexuals, as well as those whose tastes and attachments are exclusively and overtly homosexual.

Summary

A great deal of behavior that is ordinarily thought of as evidence of psychological abnormality or perversity is, in fact, governed by group norms and values and is hence cultural in nature. Behavior of this kind is qualitatively different from the forms of individual deviance discussed in the preceding chapter. Members of deviant subsocieties are subject to many of the same types of pressures toward social conformity as are other persons; and the deviant subsociety is itself an integral part of the social structure. Criminals who make crime an occupation or means of livelihood form a criminal subculture called the "underworld," whereas other criminal types—*e.g.*, "white-collar" criminals—remain members of respectable society and do not form social groups. The way of life of the underworld criminal reflects both the fact that the criminal shares many of the values of the wider society and that he is at the same time in conflict with some of these values. Drug addicts form underworld subcultures in some countries and not in others, depending upon the manner in which drug use is defined by law and custom. Homosexuals also form distinct social groups within our society, but, as in the case of criminals and addicts, they do not always or necessarily do so. The matter of accounting for the continued existence of a deviant subsociety involves the study of recruitment to it; and this problem is separate and different from that of explaining how given persons come to be homosexuals, criminals, or addicts.

SUGGESTIONS FOR DISCUSSION AND SPECIAL REPORTS

1. Describe a deviant subsociety.
2. Discuss conceptions of normality and abnormality.
3. Present the point of view of a deviant group, such as a criminal one, trying to make it as plausible and attractive as you can.
4. Are there normal homosexuals?
5. Under what circumstances are deviant groups tolerated or suppressed?
6. Describe some "functions" which criminals may be said to perform.
7. What attitudes would you expect American criminals to take toward the problem of combating communism? Why?
8. Describe the status system of the underworld.
9. Is there honor among thieves?
10. What kinds of social or legal controls do you believe should be applied to homosexuality?
11. Under what circumstances should an attempt be made to suppress deviant groups by police action? What makes behavior criminal?

NOTES

[1] P. G. Cressey, *The Taxi-Dance Hall,* University of Chicago Press, 1932, pp. 35-36.
[2] E. H. Sutherland, *White-Collar Crime,* Dryden, 1949.
[3] E. H. Sutherland, *The Professional Thief,* University of Chicago Press, 1937, pp. 164-166.
[4] *Ibid.,* pp. 168-169.
[5] *Ibid.,* p. 172.

[6] Polly Adler, *A House Is Not a Home,* Rinehart, 1953, p. 144.
[7] Thomas Runyon, *In for Life,* Norton, 1953.
[8] D. W. Corey, *The Homosexual in America,* Greenberg, 1951, p. 97.
[9] *Ibid.,* pp. 114-115.
[10] M. Leznoff, *The Homosexual in Urban Society,* master's thesis, McGill University, 1953.

SELECTED BIBLIOGRAPHY

Adler, Polly, *A House Is Not a Home,* Rinehart, 1953. A revealing discussion of prostitution by a former madam.

Becker, H. S., "Becoming a Marihuana User," *Am. J. Soc.*, 59(1953): 235-242. This analysis is very helpful in understanding how persons are recruited into and trained by deviant groups.

Clemmer, D., *The Prison Community*, Christopher, 1940. Life inside prison walls described and analyzed by a sociologist.

Corey, D. W., *The Homosexual in America*, Greenberg, 1951. The author, himself a homosexual, describes the life and makes a strong plea for a more tolerant and enlightened public attitude.

Davis, K., "The Sociology of Prostitution," *Am. Soc. Rev.*, 2(1937): 744-755. The author views prostitution as a part of the social structure and as a consequence of the operation of the social norms governing sex and marriage.

Faris, E., *The Nature of Human Nature*, McGraw-Hill, 1937. In the chapter entitled "The Sect and the Sectarian" there is an especially good general statement of the significance of subsocieties for personality development. (See also *Am. J. Soc.*, 60(1955): II, 75-89.)

Masters, John, *The Deceivers*, Viking, 1951. A novel which portrays the techniques and the extraordinary philosophy of the criminal subcaste of India from which our word "thug" is derived.

Mayhew, H., *London Labour and the London Poor*, 4 vols., London, 1862. Lively descriptions of street and underworld types and of their ways of making a living.

Runyon, T., *In for Life*, Norton, 1953. A lifer's story of how he became involved in crime, went to prison and made good there.

Street, L., and D. Loth, *I Was a Drug Addict*, Pyramid Books, Random House, 1954. A drug addict's story, but not necessarily a representative one.

Stroup, H., *The Jehovah's Witnesses*, Columbia University Press, 1945. A significant study of a well-known sect.

Sutherland, E. H., *The Professional Thief*, University of Chicago Press, 1937. A thief's discussion of stealing as an occupation, with comments and analysis by a noted criminologist.

Index

Index